William W.
Hagen

Germans, Poles, and Jews

The
Nationality
Conflict
in the
Prussian
East,
1772-
1914

CO-AKQ-805

The University
of Chicago
Press
Chicago and London

WILLIAM W. HAGEN is associate professor
of history at the University of
California, Davis

The University of Chicago Press, Chicago 60637
The University of Chicago Press, Ltd., London

Hagen, William W
     Germans, Poles, and Jews.

     Bibliography: p.
     Includes index.
     1. Poland--Relations (general)--with Prussia.
2. Prussia--Relations (general) with Poland.
3. Poland--Ethnic relations. 4. Prussia--Ethnic
relations. 5. Jews in Poland--History. 6. Jews
in Prussia--History. I. Title.
DK4185.P85H33   305.8'00943   80-10557
ISBN 0-226-31242-9

CONTENTS

LIST OF MAPS

LIST OF TABLES

Poland in the eighteenth century was an exotic, aristocratic
empire. War and diplomacy since the fourteenth century had carried the frontiers of the state far beyond the medieval Polish
heartland. Danzig and the Baltic coast, Wilno in Lithuania,
Belorussia to the outskirts of Smolensk, the Ukraine to the gates
of Kiev and south to Turkish Moldavia: these conquests of their
forefathers the eighteenth-century nobility regarded with proud
but ill-founded complacency.

The Polish Commonwealth (<u>Rzeczpospolita Polska</u>) was the
granary of Europe. During the fifteenth and sixteenth centuries,
the Polish nobility--the <u>szlachta</u>--staged an agrarian revolution,
expanding their seigneurial lands into large estates and depress-
ing the tributary medieval peasantry into hereditary serfdom. The
landlords monopolized the surplus of the rich Polish plains. Each
year their agents guided the harvests down the rivers to the Commonwealth's great port at Danzig, where they were sold and shipped
westward, chiefly to Amsterdam. The volume of grain exported
through Danzig rose rapidly in the sixteenth century, reaching a
peak in 1618 never again to be attained. But even in the late
eighteenth century, Poland's exports to the west were still vital.
Often the Polish lords were on hand to seal their transactions in
Danzig. By the time they had returned to their country seats,
they had exchanged a large part of their earnings on their crops
for luxury goods imported from Western Europe.

Poland's towns withered under this regime. The merchants
and craftsmen lost the better part of the nobility's patronage.
Everyday goods and tools were manufactured on the landlord's
estates, rather than purchased in town workshops. At the village
inn, the gentry's underlings siphoned off the peasantry's meager
earnings, while the estates usurped the brewing rights of the
towns. After three centuries under the yoke of the gentry, the
Polish cities had lost their Renaissance dynamism. Many were

nothing more than sleepy, ramshackle country market towns. Others
were mere villages.[1]

Until 1572 Poland was ruled by hereditary kings, who had
centralized the state and led it in its successful expansion to
the east. But already in the fifteenth century the nobility
had begun to wrest fatal concessions from the financially pressed
monarchs. These transformed the szlachta into sovereign masters
checking the Crown's legislative, fiscal, and diplomatic powers
through the gentry-dominated parliament. From 1572 until the collapse of the state at the end of the eighteen century, Poland's
kings were elected one after the other by the whole body of the
nobility. Upon their election, they swore to uphold szlachta
privilege, to abjure the principle of heredity, and to entrust the
high offices of state to the great aristocrats. Concentration of
land and wealth in the hands of a few dozen families subjected the
Commonwealth in the seventeenth and eighteenth centuries to the
magnates' ambitions, interests, and antagonisms. The middle gentry
and impoverished nobles were the great families' pawns. Stalemates
among the magnates opened the way to foreign interference in
Polish politics: the courts of Versailles, Petersburg, Vienna,
Potsdam, and Dresden discovered that royal elections in Warsaw
could be manipulated, just as factions in the Polish parliament
could be bought. Fatally weakened by the wars, rebellions, and invasions of the years 1648-1721, the last century of the Commonwealth's existence (1697-1795) presented the sorry spectacle of
self-serving or impotent rulers, shortsighted magnates quarreling
for the spoils of high office, and continuous foreign interference,
especially by the future partitioning powers, to uphold "Polish
liberty" against the revival of a strong monarchy. The eighteenth
century Enlightenment inspired a movement for reform of the state,
but it crashed on the shoals of aristocratic self-interest and
foreign opposition.[2]

The serf-estate economy and the szlachta's monopoly of
political power were two of the pillars of the Polish Commonwealth.
The third was Catholicism. In the sixteenth century many of the
Polish nobility embraced the Protestant cause. But after securing their control of the state at the monarchy's expense, the
gentry returned to the Catholic fold. The culture of seventeenth
and eighteenth-century Poland radiated from the Jesuit schools.
It was both Latinate and Polish, baroque and classical, legalistic
and orthodox. As social tensions and political failures mounted,
the church and the gentry grew insular and intolerant, insisting
on the identity of Polish and Catholic interests.[3]

The Polish Commonwealth was a multiethnic and multireligious society. On its eastern and southern borders, Lithuanian, Belorussian, and Ukrainian were the languages of the masses. Only the Lithuanians had been fully assimilated into Polish Catholicism; the others clung to their Orthodox or Uniate faiths. Settled throughout the Commonwealth was the largest population of Jews in Europe, cultivating a Hebrew literary tradition and speaking Yiddish in their everyday lives. In the north and the west, settlements of German Catholics and Protestants, burghers and peasants, spanned the Commonwealth's borders.

None of these religious and national minorities possessed a landed gentry of its own. The old Lithuanian, East Slavic, and German noble families had been admitted to the privileged sphere of the Catholic gentry and Polonized. Like the Polish serfs and burghers, the Commonwealth's minorities lived on the szlachta's sufferance.[4] But the partitions of Poland (1772-95) stripped the Polish nobility of their sovereignty. Until the restoration of Polish independence after World War I, the fortunes of the peoples of the vanished Commonwealth were tied to the Russia, Austrian, and Prussian states under whose rule they suddenly found themselves.

This book is a history of nationality conflict in the lands seized by Prussia in the Polish partitions. It is a study of the Prussian government's labors first to Prussianize and later to Germanize its Polish subjects, particularly in the province of Poznań, the heartland of Prussian Poland. It focuses sharply on Polish resistance to Prussian rule, organized in the course of the nineteenth century into a formidable nationalist movement. It is, therefore, a history both of Polish society in the Prussian east and Prussian eastern nationality policy, or Polenpolitik. But it does not neglect the Germans and Jews in the Poles' midst. The monarchy's struggle with the Poles drew the Germans and Jews into a three-cornered conflict in their eastern homeland which grew more bitter as Polish resistance to Berlin stiffened.

The book's argument, briefly put, is that failure to disarm the Polish nationalist movement drove the Prussian-German ruling classes to embrace a radical, racially defined eastern imperialism aimed at the forcible uprooting of the Prussian Poles and the systematic Germanization of their lands. Bismarck and his successors championed an anti-Polish "Prussian mission in the east" as part of their bitter struggle to shield the oligarchical and semiabsolute German Empire from its domestic opponents. The

Poles, who in 1910 mustered every tenth subject of the King of
Prussia, not only stood accused in German conservative-nationalist
eyes as irreconcilable national foes, threatening to engulf the
Prussian east in a "Slavic flood"; they also figured among Bismarck's "enemies of the Reich," together with the autocratic
empire's socialist and liberal antagonists. Defeat of the Polish
nationalist movement in the eastern borderlands was scarcely less
vital to the Imperial regime than holding the German left at bay.
The connection reemerged starkly under the National Socialist
dictatorship: the invasion and devastation of Poland and Eastern
Europe followed upon the liquidation of Weimar democracy and the
violent repression of the workers' parties.

In a work such as this, place names become problematical. I
have used English names for Polish and German towns and regions
wherever possible. Lacking English equivalents, I have employed
German or Polish names according to the national composition
during the period 1772-1914 of the town or region in question,
adding the Polish or German alternative in parentheses. It is
unfortunate that no English version of "Poznań" or "Posen" exists.
Although the population of the province centering on the city of
this name was predominantly Polish, both under the old Commonwealth and during the period of Prussian rule, the Polish place
name obscures its nationally mixed character. But for the sake of
simplicity and consistency, I have used "Poznań" throughout, except in translations from the German, where "Posen" is natural.
The terms wielkie księstwo poznańskie (Grossherzogtum Posen) and
Provinz Posen (prowincja poznańska) appear here as "the Grand
Duchy of Poznań" and "the province of Poznań." "Poznania" refers
to the same region.

The Foreign Area Fellowship Program supported my research in
its first stages. Grants from the University of California helped
to conclude it. I received expert assistance from the archivists
and librarians of the Wojewódzkie Archiwum Państwowe, the Biblioteka
Uniwersytetu im. Adama Mickiewicza, and the Biblioteka Raczyńskich
in Poznań; the Bundesarchiv in Koblenz; the Geheimes Preussisches
Staatsarchiv in West Berlin; and the Staats-, Haus- und Hofarchiv
in Vienna. Professors Dr. Jerzy Topolski and Dr. Lech Trzeciakowski very kindly assisted my research in Poznań. Professor Dr.
Stefan Kieniewicz and Professors Anna Cienciala, Eugene Lunn, and
James Sheehan patiently read this work at one or another of its
stages. Their thoughtful responses helped me greatly. To Profes-

sor Witold Jakóbczyk I wish to express my special appreciation for his unsparing aid and counsel. Professor William H. McNeill followed this work through all its phases. His advice and encouragement were unfailing and invaluable. To him, as to all those friends and colleagues who helped in this work, I offer my thanks.

The Origins of the Nationality Frontier

In the western and northern provinces of the Polish Commonwealth bordering on eighteenth century Brandenburg-Prussia, Poles,
Germans, and Jews lived intermingled like villagers' plots in a
medieval field. In the tenth century, when Poland entered the
orbit of western Christendom, no Polish-German frontier existed.
Jewish trading posts east of the Rhine ended at Magdeburg on the
Elbe.[1] Not until the end of the thirteenth century did the westward expansion of the Polish state and the eastward advance of
German marcher-lords engulf the independent Slavic settlements on
the Baltic plains.

The Germans' conquests were the more extensive. By the early
fourteenth century they dominated, both politically and culturally,
not only the lands between the Elbe and Oder rivers, but also
Silesia, East Prussia, and Pomerania west of Danzig. In the year
1308, the Teutonic Knights, conquerors and colonizers of East
Prussia, seized Danzig-Pomerania, blocking the Polish monarchy off
from the sea. Not until 1466, after long wars, did Poland recover
this strategic territory from the Knights, incorporating it into
the Polish Crown as Royal Prussia until in 1772 Brandenburg-
Prussia detached it in the first partition.

After the Polish conquest of Royal Prussia the German-Polish
political frontier was for more than 300 years one of Europe's
stablest. During these centuries, the only major disturbance on
this border was the brief war of Brandenburg's Frederick William,
the Great Elector, waged alongside Sweden against Poland in 1656-
57. Frederick William switched sides, however, in exchange for his
release from vassalage to the Polish Crown as Duke of East Prussia,
a title the Hohenzollerns had inherited in the year 1618. This was
a blow to the Polish state, but a minor one in comparison with its
difficulties then and thereafter with the Swedes, Russians, Cos-
sacks, and Turks.

The expansion of medieval Germany to the east of the Elbe was

not merely a process of political conquest. More importantly, it
was a massive colonization movement which, at its twelfth- and
thirteenth-century peak, planted hundreds of thousands of western
German peasants on the soil of the Baltic plains eastward to, and
beyond, the Oder. The Slavic settlements east of the Elbe, like
the Balts in East Prussia, were engulfed by a sea of Germans and,
with some bloody exceptions, gradually assimilated into the
German linguistic and cultural world. But medieval German colonization went farther. From the twelfth to the fourteenth
century, Polish kings and dukes, bishops and abbots, eager to
develop their thinly populated lands, encouraged the settlement
of Germans in towns and villages alike. In these centuries
German influences fundamentally reshaped Poland's economy and
social structure. Tens of thousands of Germans came to live in
Poland as peasant farmers, village mayors, artisan masters,
merchants, and clerics. At the same time Poland's rulers encouraged the settlement of Jews, who fled the heightening
religious persecutions of late medieval Germany and western
Europe to become state minters and financiers, moneylenders,
merchants, and artisans in Poland's burgeoning towns. Relatively
free from Christian reprisals, their numbers increased steadily
into the seventeeth century.[2]

In the fourteenth century, population contraction in Germany
and a feudal reaction against foreign influence in Poland brought
German colonization slowly to a halt. In the course of the
following two centuries, most of the Germans in Poland succumbed
to linguistic and cultural Polonization. As the Catholic Church
in Poland broke away from western, and especially German tutelage,
the rural German settlers, most of whom had struck roots in Great
Poland without having created massive German ethnic islands,
imperceptibly faded under Church influence into the Polish-speaking population. In these years inability to maintain a German-
speaking priesthood in the countryside was enough to undermine
German identity.[3]

In the towns of the fifteenth and sixteenth century, Polonization of the Germans involved open conflict. Wealthy German
burghers and merchant-patricians had already, by the fourteenth
century, attracted the political and social hostility of the
poorer town population, largely Polish but including also Germans.
This antagonism deepened after the conversion of most of the
German burghers in Poland to Lutheran Protestantism in the sixteenth century. After the political triumph of the Counter-
Reformation in Poland, the Catholic church allied itself with the

Polish urban poor and petite bourgeoisie, who had remained faithful to the old religion, and launched a campaign of repression
against the town-dwelling Protestants. In the early seventeenth
century, anti-Protestant riots, often led by Jesuits, destroyed
Protestant churches in such cities as Poznań, Cracow, and Lublin.
Protestant property was plundered and laws were proclaimed severely
limiting, if not altogether prohibiting, the practice and propagation of the Protestant faith. Thus a decree of 1620, never fully
applied in practice, banned Protestant worship in Poznań.[4] Under
such pressure, urban Protestantism, primarily a German religion,
suffered a massive loss of adherents. Catholicism, an increasingly
self-consciously Polish faith, became the dominant religion in
most of Poland's towns. German Catholics found it increasingly difficult to maintain a German-speaking clergy. A decree of 1632
confined church services in the German language to but one of
Poznań's numerous Catholic churches.[5]

By these means most of the descendents of the medieval German
settlers in Great Poland lost their linguistic and psychological
ties with German culture. But Royal or West Prussia presents a
different picture. In the thirteenth and fourteenth century,
German peasant colonization went hand in hand with the assimilation of the local Slavic nobility into the ranks of the German lay
and clerical leadership. Especially during the rule of the
Teutonic Knights (1308-1466), the land came under the domination of
a thoroughly German nobility, precisely the social class lacking
among the German settlers in Great Poland. Under Polish domination
after 1466, however, a large majority of these German nobles succumbed to Polonization. It was the policy of the Polish Crown,
stalwartly resisted by the Royal Prussians for a century, to
incorporate the province fully into the legal, legislative, and
fiscal structure of the monarchy. In 1569, the royal Decree of
Lublin accomplished this, extending crown appointments in Royal
Prussia to Polish nobles, introducing the Polish language alongside
Latin and German for official use, opening the Polish parliament
to Royal Prussian representation, and, in general, assimilating the
status of the Royal Prussian nobility to that of the rest of the
Polish szlachta. Although many West Prussian German nobles had
embraced Lutheranism and Calvinism in the earlier stages of the
Reformation, they gradually returned to Catholicism at the end
of the sixteenth and in the course of the seventeenth century,
since the Counter-Reformation succeeded in disqualifying dissident
nobles from public office and leases of crown lands. Eager to
enjoy the full panoply of aristocratic Polish privileges, the West

Prussian German nobility joined the _szlachta_ in language, religion,
and mentality until, by 1772, "German noble surnames were great
exceptions."[6] This in turn produced widespread Polonization of
the German peasant population in Royal Prussia, particularly where
Polish peasant immigration introduced the harsher forms of Polish
serfdom, as in the southern parts of the province. In the greater
part of the Bishopric of Ermland (Warmia), however, where intensive medieval colonization had effectively Germanized the villages
and towns and where a lay aristocracy was lacking, the church conceded the maintenance of a German priesthood and thus ensured the
preservation of the ethnic character of the peasants and burghers
down to the first partition.[7] Conversely, in the Bishopric of
Chełmno (Kulm), the church forbade the practice of Protestantism
and employed a strictly Polish priesthood, which resulted in the
Polonization of the medieval German colonists in that area.[8]

West Prussia's three principal cities--Danzig, Elbing, and
Thorn--had thriven as German-dominated centers of the Vistula
grain trade from the late Middle Ages. They converted early and
with conviction to Lutheranism. Thanks to their financial indis-
pensability to the Polish kings, in 1557-58 they obtained royal
guarantees of religious freedom within their walls, a freedom
they preserved almost wholly intact, together with their German
ethnic character, down to the partitions. Danzig (Gdańsk) was
virtually a free city within the Polish Commonwealth, which granted
it self-government, its own legal jurisdiction, freedom from royal
taxation in return for grants paid the Polish kings on their accession, and the right to conduct an independent commercial policy
with foreign nations.[9] But the Protestants of Thorn (Toruń)
found themselves increasingly obliged to admit Catholics to public
office and merchant and artisan guilds, particularly after what
came to be known among Germans as the "Thorn Bloodbath of 1724."
In the wake of tumults attending a Jesuit ceremony in Thorn, twelve
German magistrates were sentenced to death by a Catholic tribunal.
Ten were finally beheaded in the most celebrated instance of the
religious intolerance of the Polish ruling class in its years of
political decline and advancing xenophobia.[10]

Thus, in contrast to Great Poland, a sizable proportion of the
medieval German colonists' descendents preserved their German
ethnic character in Royal Prussia through the long period of
Polish sovereignty. In both Great Poland and West Prussia, however, it was not the medieval wave of German and Jewish migrations
alone which determined the character of the eighteenth century
nationality frontier. From the second half of the sixteenth cen-

tury to the time of the partitions, a second wave of settlers from
Germany swept over western and northern Poland.

The pioneers of this movement were not Germans but rather
large numbers of Dutch Mennonites who, menaced in their religion
at home, accepted the offers of the Protestant West Prussian
nobility to settle as free peasants in the Vistula delta. In
return, the immigrants built dykes to control the river channels
and paid money rents to the noble lords owning the once-swampy
wastes which they had converted into rich farmland. This was the
beginning of a movement, running parallel to the rise of the serf-
estate export economy on the already cultivated soil of Poland,
in which the szlachta encouraged peasant immigration from the west
in order to bring the vast stretches of Poland's still virgin
forest and swampland under the plow. Unwilling to commit their
own serf labor to this task, they offered attractive terms and
religious toleration, at first to the Mennonites but thereafter
mainly to German Protestants who fled, in the seventeenth century,
religious persecution in Germany and, in the eighteenth century,
military conscription and regions of land hunger to try their luck
in Poland. They and their descendents constituted a privileged
class of peasants among the masses of Polish serfs. They would not
undertake their arduous new lives without guarantees of full personal freedom, ample fields in the wastes they had cleared, and a
hereditary contractual claim to their lands in exchange for money
rents. These terms of tenure were almost precisely what most
Polish and Polonized serfs lacked but hungered to have. Yet, just
as it was in the szlachta's interest to subject the native peasantry to serfdom and thus to create a supply of "free" labor
producing for the export market, so too, if foreign colonists
could make a profit from previously unused land, by settling them
on their estates the nobility could skim the top from these
profits and fatten their wallets.[11]

This form of peasant colonization spread down the Vistula
Valley, into the Netze (Noteć) region, and beyond to Great Poland
proper, where in the seventeenth and eighteenth century it was
vigorously pursued not only along the western fringes of the province adjacent to Silesia and Brandenburg, but in the heart of the
land as well. After the partitions, the Polish nobility in Russian
Poland began settling German farmers on their land, so that this
second wave of German colonization, following upon the medieval
movement, lasted into the early twentieth century. In Royal
Prussia and Great Poland such German colonists came to be called
Hauländer, a corruption of the word Hollander recalling the Men-
nonite pioneers; the Poles accepted the term in the form of olędrzy.

There was an urban counterpart, beginning in the second half of the seventeenth and lasting through the eighteenth century, to the second wave of German peasant settlement in western and northern Poland. The devastation wrought in these regions by the Swedish invasion (1655-60) and particularly by the second Northern War (1700-21), whose impact on Great Poland can be compared with that of the Thirty Years War on Germany, depopulated the towns as well as the villages. Since the nobility had succeeded in imposing their seigneurial authority on many of the towns, urban economic collapse meant a loss of aristocratic revenue. Thus in the seventeenth and eighteenth centuries the Catholic gentry opened many town gates to Protestant German refugees, especially from Silesia, and to German Catholic immigrants as well. In eighteenth-century Great Poland, immigrant burghers rebuilt fifteen devastated towns and founded ten wholly new cities. In these and other towns throughout Great Poland, the Netze district, and Royal Prussia, a flourishing woolen and linen textile industry arose in the eighteenth century. This was the work primarily of German artisan workshops. It was organized commercially by the Jews and profitably taxed by the nobility.[12]

Unlike their medieval forerunners, most of the settlers in the second wave of migration to Poland retained their German language and cultural character. The guarantees of religious liberty the German Protestants received from the Polish nobility, though sometimes violated, ensured the maintenance of a German-speaking clergy, German Protestant village schools, and a few secondary-level German academies. As in the past, German Catholics were more exposed to Polonization, but they were a minority among the immigrants. They maintained their ethnic identity best in the towns of a predominantly German Protestant character along the Silesian-Brandenburg border, where the Polish Catholic church's influence was limited. One may speculate, in the light of later historical experience, that, outside those towns where church practice neglected German-language services and thus wittingly or unwittingly promoted Polonization, German Catholics assimilated into Polish culture chiefly by means of intermarriage, which was common both before and after the partitions.[13]

In the wake of the two long waves of German eastward settlement and medieval Jewish migration to Poland, reinforced by Jewish refugees from Germany during the Reformation, the eighteenth-century nationality frontier cut deep into the Polish Commonwealth. On the Silesian-Brandenburg border of Great Poland, second-wave Germans had reinforced first-wave survivors in Germanizing a

broad frontier strip. Settlements of <u>Hauländer</u> were scattered about
the Poznanian villages, while Germans and Jews were numerous in all
western and northern Polish towns. The Polonization of Royal Prussia after the fifteenth century had been balanced by second-wave
German peasant colonization in the Vistula delta and the rise of
the German-dominated textile industry in Royal Prussia, the Netze
district, and Great Poland.

But the nationality frontier also crossed the political borders of Brandenburg-Prussia. In Upper Silesia, conquered together
with the rest of that province by Frederick the Great, a large
population of Polish-speaking peasant-serfs tilled the lands of
German or Germanized Slavic noblemen and magnates. Polish was
spoken among the common people in the towns as well. In central
Silesia to the east of the Oder, Polish villagers and urban workers
also survived in a largely Germanized setting, but most of Silesia
had been lost to the Poles in the first wave of German eastward
expansion. In 1348, Casimir the Great had recognized Bohemia's
suzerainty over the Silesian duchies and, despite Polish strategies
to regain the province in subsequent centuries, it was progres-
sively integrated into the German political and cultural sphere as
it passed from Bohemian to Habsburg to Hohenzollern rule. The
Polish population in Silesia stood on an economically and culturally depressed level, speaking only a Polish dialect, out of contact with formal Polish culture and dominated by a Catholic clergy
which, while it communicated to its parishioners in their own
tongue, bowed to the German Bishopric of Breslau.

The Polish-speaking peasantry of the southern and eastern
areas of East Prussia, numerically weak in comparison with the
Upper Silesians, were divided from the culture and society of the
Polish Commonwealth by their Lutheran faith, to which their immigrant forefathers, who had been settled by the Teutonic Knights
in the Middle Ages, had turned along with the German East
Prussians in the sixteenth century. Social ascent for these Polish
speakers, as for the Silesian Poles, meant Germanization in the
schools or in urban occupations, a process which occurred rapidly
in nineteenth-century East Prussia.

Along the Baltic coast, to the west and northwest of Danzig,
lived yet another Slavic population, Catholic peasants, workers, and
fishermen heavily influenced by the German rural and urban upper
classes. These were the Kashubians, descendents of the Slavic
Pomeranians, speaking a tongue closely related to Polish. They
were separated from the Polish heartland by the mixed-nationality
zone in the Vistula delta and led an insular, traditional life untouched by politics before the late nineteenth century.

8

MAP 1.--The Polish-German nationality frontier in 1771
(approximation).

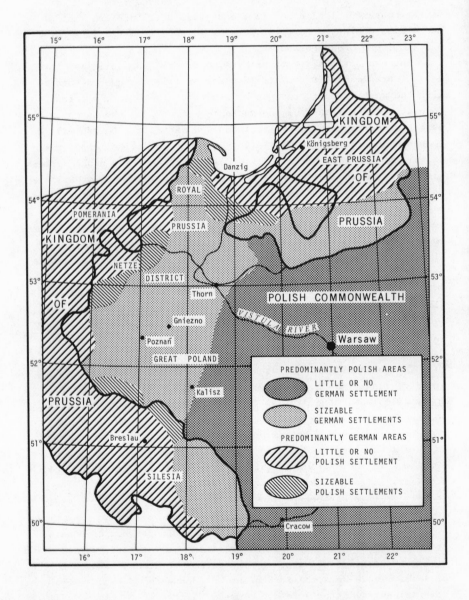

The Polish settlements in East Prussia and Silesia and the Kashubian lands on the Baltic represented passive zones of the nationality frontier in the eighteenth and most of the nineteenth century as well. The vital center lay in West Prussia and Great Poland.[14]

The Economy of Great Poland
and Royal Prussia in the Eighteenth Century

Polish society, in the last years of Polish political independence, was riven by serious tensions. These arose, on the one hand, from the displacement of power and wealth within the ranks of the nobility away from the lower and middle szlachta into the hands of the magnate latifundists. Clearly visible from the mid-seventeenth century, this process revealed itself above all in the magnates' engrossing of the lesser szlachta's estates and in the political and financial dependence into which they drew many squires who managed to retain their lands intact. On the other hand, the productivity of the export-based Polish serf-estate economy was declining in the seventeenth and eighteenth centuries, as was proven by falling seed-yield ratios and total exports from Danzig. Rather than making innovative investments to overcome falling output or introducing changes in the status of their serfs which would encourage greater labor productivity, the szlachta remained captives of the notion that their welfare was solely a function of the total commercializable surplus of grain which maximum exploitation of their serf labor force could produce. Fixed upon domination of the labor of the Polish peasantry and upon competition with the towns through the establishment of serf-operated rural industries, the gentry blocked the way towards the emergence of a productive market-oriented peasantry and prevented the development of a populous urban sector which could have functioned, had the peasantry been freer to supply it with agricultural products, as a basis for the material enrichment of the Polish common people, both urban and rural, and as a supplement to the Western European grain market. Moreover, the nobility's drive to maximize their estate domain lands and to minimize the total area of peasant farm plots, together with their antiurban orientation, held the size of the Polish population to a relatively very low level. Before the partitions, Poland, excluding the Duchy of Courland, covered an area of 283,000 square miles, but counted only about 11.5 million inhabitants.   Its average of 39 persons to the square mile contrasted starkly with that of late-eighteenth-century France, a country of peasant farmers, which stood at 128, as well as with Prussia's average of 75.[15] Prussia too was largely a land of serfs and noble estates, but the Hohenzollerns set some

limits to the landlords' exploitation of the peasantry and upheld the towns for the sake of royal revenues. In Poland, because serf labor was scarce, vast areas of the Commonwealth went
uncultivated, to the szlachta's loss. Hence the steady influx
of German colonists and the relative security of the Polish Jews,
without whom many towns, cut off from in-migration from the
enserfed Polish villages, would have collapsed.

The result of the szlachta's economic policy--generalizing
about the whole of the eighteenth-century Polish Commonwealth--
was peasant poverty and backwardness, a threadbare and numerically
weak bourgeoisie, and a nobility which, despite declassing in its
lower ranks, lived in homespun abundance if not aristocratic
opulence. But the Polish landlords faced a critical challenge to
their way of life in the advancing internal crisis of the serf-
estate economy itself.[16]

Royal Prussia and Great Poland were enmeshed in these social
and economic patterns, yet they exhibited certain distinctive
features setting them apart from the central, eastern, and southern
Polish provinces. Above all, their economies were stimulated by
a greater variety of markets and by a more abundant circulation
of money than elsewhere in Poland. Although both regions were
fundamentally agrarian, their town economies were, if not robust,
at least relatively vital--in Great Poland thanks to the textile
industry, whose principal market was the vast Polish hinterland,
and in Royal Prussia thanks to textiles and the export grain
trade. The gentry in both provinces benefited both from their
very proximity to the Baltic port, sparing them the costs of
lengthy grain shipments, and from the buying power of the local
towns, based on the earnings of commerce and manufactures. The
result was that both regions earned more from exports abroad
and to other provinces of the Commonwealth than they spent on
imports, thus accumulating capital for local investment and
economic growth. It can be argued that during the eighteenth
century Great Poland and Royal Prussia were entering upon paths
leading away from the traditional Polish serf-estate system and
towards the first stages of a capitalist economy; but for the
partitions, these lands might have pulled the rest of the Commonwealth in the same direction.

The population of Great Poland (that is, of the voivodeships
of Poznań and Kalisz) rose from 560,000 in 1720 to 800,000 in 1793,
an increase of 43 percent. The arable land expanded in the same
degree. Over 800 villages were founded or refounded during the
eighteenth century, almost half of them as German Hauländer
villages.   Total grain output rose between 1720 and 1793 by almost

25 percent, bringing Great Poland's harvest to within ten percent of its peak figure at the end of the sixteenth century, before soil exhaustion, labor inefficiency, and war had inaugurated the decline of the serf-estate economy.

Perhaps most important was the trend among the nobility towards converting peasant labor dues into money payments. This freed many peasant-serfs with medium and large holdings to supply the local urban markets while the estate-owners employed part of their money rents to hire wage workers as a supplement to the labor of the remaining serfs, who continued to cultivate the domain lands in return for their plots. In 1793 roughly 30 percent of the peasants in Great Poland owed money rents instead of labor services, while for Poland as a whole the comparable figure was 10 percent. It was not only German colonists who were free of servile labor dues; in the second half of the eighteenth century Polish serfs had their dues converted until they outnumbered the colonists two to one. This process (oczynszowanie) was a major step towards the abolition of serfdom, which was the indispensable precondition of capitalist development in Poland. Meanwhile, thanks to the influx of German textile artisans, Great Poland's woolen industry was producing 2 million meters of cloth annually by 1793--70 percent of the Commonwealth's total output and two-thirds of neighboring Prussian Silesia's.[17]

Similarly, Royal Prussia possessed a more advanced social and economic structure than the rest of the eighteenth century Commonwealth. Here too were numerous villages of legally free, rent-paying farmers and many busy textile towns. On the large estates, intensified production doubled the province's grain exports through Danzig between 1720 and 1769.[18]

Polish Society on the Eighteenth-Century Frontier

The national diversity of the frontier was transcended by the homogeneity of the class which dominated it overwhelmingly. The settlements of Germans and Jews interspersed among the masses of the Polish common people gave the Polish nobility no reason to regard Great Poland and Royal Prussia as anything but integrally Polish lands. Great Poland had been the cradle of the tenth century Polish state, and Royal Prussia, though contested in the middle ages by the Poles, had been secure in their political grasp since the fifteenth century. The Commonwealth was self-evidently a multiethnic state. What counted was the monopoly of political power and the social preeminence of the Polish Catholic nobility. These were as secure in western and northern Poland as they were in Lithuania and the Ukraine.

About 3,000 estates spanned the countryside of Great Poland, while Royal Prussia counted some 2,000. In Great Poland, the middle gentry predominated, lords of one or two villages together with their own estate lands. Since the seventeenth century, the general trend in Poland towards the formation of a powerful magnate class had made itself felt in the rise of several dozen noble families to ownership of multiple estates and domination of the political offices of the voivodeships of Kalisz and Poznań. The Archbishopric of Gniezno also owned a large number of villages, but in the late eighteenth century over 90 percent of the province's villages were still in the hands of the middle gentry. In Royal Prussia, land ownership among the gentry was more fragmented. A majority of nobles did not possess even one full village but only a share of its labor and land. Magnate holdings, although not entirely missing, as one assemblage of thirty-nine estates showed, were even less numerous here than in Great Poland.[19]

The szlachta's power rested on land ownership and legal jurisdiction over the peasantry, exercised either immediately over private serfs through the organs of patrimonial justice, or indirectly through gentry domination of the judicial system which governed royal domain serfs. But in their centuries-long erosion of royal power in Poland, the gentry had found means to appropriate state domain lands to their own profit and to acquire seigneurial rights over most of the small towns. Since they had frustrated the formation of a royal fiscal and judicial bureaucracy, all the public offices in the land were in their hands and were normally treated as prerogatives of the aristocratic notables resident in the various administrative districts of the Commonwealth. In the absence of any sizable standing royal army, the police and military powers of the state reposed in their collective hands, to be exercised by provincial military chieftains, by all or part of the gentry organized in a confederation, or individually, in gentry feuds such as that portrayed in Mickiewicz's Pan Tadeusz. Larger towns, such as Royal Prussia's three commercial centers, or Poznań and Kalisz in Great Poland, exercised self-government as Royal Cities, but except for Danzig they were subject to the aristocratic provincial authorities and the gentry-controlled local and Commonwealth diets.

The full measure of the Polish nobleman's privileges appeared in the liberum veto, by which a single deputy could annul the central parliament's legislation with the words nie pozwalam ("I do not assent"); and in the boast, empty in the mouths of all but

a very few, that the vote of his peers could some day place him on
the throne. Beyond this, the nobility ruled the Catholic church,
all of whose higher dignitaries, disposing of rich church incomes,
were drawn from aristocratic families.

Like their peers elsewhere in Poland, the szlachta in eighteenth century Royal Prussia and Great Poland claimed fancifully
that they, as an aristocratic ruling class, descended from the
lordly ancient Sarmatians, while the Polish burghers and peasants
were the progeny of lowly Ham, subject by destiny to noble rule.[20]
But the szlachta on the frontier also possessed a clear sense of
economic rationality, a "contract mentality," which reflected the
relatively more advanced economic circumstances in which they
lived and worked, in contrast to the old-fashioned "Sarmatian"
nobility in the south and east.[21] Although the magnates of Great
Poland followed a conservative, pro-Saxon and pro-Russian political
policy in the eighteenth century, the middle gentry were to be
found in the ranks of the "patriots," a moderately liberal, anti-
magnate tendency mirrored in the strong support the deputies of
the nobility of Great Poland showed for the reformed Polish Constitution of 3 May 1791.[22] Nevertheless, these attitudes were not
incompatible with the proudest assertion of the traditional
privileges of the Polish nobility. Certainly the frontier szlachta
clung tenaciously to the memory of these privileges after their unexpected conversion into Hohenzollern subjects.

An old Latin proverb, still current among the learned in
nineteenth century Poznań, said of the Polish Commonwealth that it
was heaven for the nobles, purgatory for the townsfolk, hell for
the peasants, and paradise for the Jews.[23] At least it is true
that little more could have been added to the freedoms of the noble
landlords or taken away from the rights of the peasant-serfs, who
were the great mass of the Polish population. Ostrowski's legal
commentary on the relations of landlords and serfs (1788), which
after 1793 the Prussian government accepted as a basic statement
of Polish common law, described the peasant-serf as "an item of
the landlord's property."[24] Serf holdings were the legal property
of the gentry and the peasants' tenure on them, as well as their
obligations to the landlord in exchange for cultivating them, were
a matter of private agreement between themselves and their lord; in
fact, the gentry defined the serfs' tenures, dues in kind or money,
and labor services according to the dictates of tradition and
economic expediency. Only peasant colonists--and this meant primarily German Hauländer--possessed hereditary tenure and clearly
limited obligations drawn up in a legal contract enforceable in

the courts, though even these privileged peasants suffered chicaneries and oppression at the gentry's hands. The great majority
of the Polish peasantry lived under conditions of legal insecurity
mitigated only by their landlords' interest in maintaining a
cooperative labor force and the peasants' readiness to run away if
conditions became intolerable. Although it was uncommon, Polish
serfs could be and were sold apart from the lands they occupied.[25]
Labor services on the lord's domain were heavy wherever estates
lay on the network of trade routes winding up at Danzig. A serf
tilling a full holding (ca. 35-60 acres) had to maintain two servants to work with two horses five or six days weekly for the
lord.[26] Serfs with only small plots worked continuously for the
estate, receiving supplementary food supplies in return. At best,
the serfs lived a life of rude sufficiency and traditional amusements, sanctified by religion and folk custom and watched over
paternalistically from the manor house; at worst, they suffered
destitution and lordly abuse. Beyond the office of village alder-
man or mayor, they had no political aspirations; riots and rebellions in the name of the restoration of the traditional order,
however defined, were rare in Poland. A good priest's word was
absolute while a bad priest merely demoralized the village. The
state belonged to the lords.[27]

The peasant-serfs tilling the fields of Great Poland and
Royal Prussia, though they fitted the common Polish pattern, enjoyed certain local advantages. The strong regional markets
benefited serfs with middle and large holdings, if only by permitting the conversion of a significant minority's labor services
to money rents; but this movement predominated on municipal,
church, and state domain land, and the private landlord switching
to money rents retained the option to return to the system of
field labor. Nonetheless, the economic expansion after 1721 endowed 65 percent of all peasant families, whether serfs or
Haulände r, with self-sufficient middle or large holdings by the
late eighteenth century; 17 percent of the peasants tilled garden
plots; 9 percent tilled a patch of land attached to a cottage; and
another 9 percent counted as landless wage laborers.[28] Royal
Prussia exhibited a greater disparity among peasant holdings: one-
third of the peasant farms qualified as large holdings, but almost 40 percent fell below the level of self-sufficiency. Probably most of the large holders were German colonists.[29]

If town life under the Commonwealth could be likened to
purgatory, the Catholic Poles were a minority among the frontier
burghers awaiting release. Table 1 roughly illustrates the
national composition of the urban population. These very

TABLE 1:   Estimated Population by Confession, ca. 1795

	Protestants	Catholics	Jews	Total
West Prussia				
Urban	131,500	50,000	2,500	184,000
Rural	239,500	221,000	3,000	463,500
Netze District				
Urban	23,000	21,000	14,000	58,000
Rural	24,000	42,000	10,000	76,000
Poznan District				
Urban	28,000	35,000	23,000	86,000
Rural	90,500	362,000	15,000	467,500
Total				
Urban	182,500	106,000	39,500	328,000
Rural	354,000	625,000	28,000	1,007,000
Total	536,500	731,000	67,500	1,335,000

SOURCES:[30]   Ilse Rhode, Das Nationalitätenverhältnis in Westpreussen und Posen zur Zeit der polnischen Teilungen (Poznań, 1926),
pp. 14, 25, 32, 38-39, 49, 53; Georg Dabinnus, Die ländliche
Bevölkerung Pommerellens im Jahre 1772 mit Einschluss des
Danziger Gebiets im Jahre 1793 (Marburg/Lahn, 1953), p. 73.

approximate figures show that Catholic burghers were in a clear
minority in West Prussia and the Netze district, while constituting
only a plurality in the towns of western Great Poland. Moreover,
while virtually all Protestants were Germans, Catholics were not
always Polish, though exposure to the cultural orbit of Polish
Catholicism exerted a strong Polonizing effect on German Catholics
in many parts of Poland. If we follow commonly held nineteenth
century estimates, about 5 percent of the frontier Catholics in the
eighteenth century must have spoken German, so that the German
bourgeoisie's strength was greater than the number of Protestants
would indicate.[31]

Except in Royal Prussia's three commercial centers, Poles held
most urban political offices. The Polish bourgeoisie were nevertheless economically weak. They were absent from the ranks of
Danzig's merchants and shippers and only minutely represented among
the central city's houseowners.[32] In Poznań, they stood together
with Germans in second place behind the Jews in the commercial
sphere: 307 of the city's 380 merchants paying the commercial tax
at the end of the eighteenth century were Jews, who controlled the
lion's share of the most lucrative wholesale trade. There were,
however, an equal number of Polish and German names among the owners
of the one hundred houses valued at 3,000 thalers or more, and many
of the city's master artisans were Poles.[33] A German account of
the town's economy written in 1845 declared that, while "all artisan trades, with the single exception of shoemaking, now contain

more German than Polish masters, seventy or eighty years ago the
opposite was true."[34] What held for master artisans probably
held for journeymen and apprentices as well, though only after
1848 did German artisans in the province of Poznań begin engaging
Polish instead of German apprentices in their efforts to cut
costs.[35] No doubt a large proportion of the city's unskilled
laborers and servants were Poles, like many members of the float-
ing, impoverished, and sometimes law-breaking urban underworld--
the "loose people" (luźni ludzie) or "wandering vagabonds"
(umherziehendes Gesindel).

   At the top of this social hierarchy stood the szlachta: in
1793 the fifteen finest houses in the Old Town were owned by
gentry families.[36] Thus within their own walls the Polish
bourgeoisie--the magistrates, merchants and tradesmen, apothecaries, doctors, lawyers, scholars, and urban priesthood--were
reminded by this show of wealth of their subordinate status in the
gentry Commonwealth. The nobility were certainly the Christian
merchants' best clients, and occasionally a bourgeois entrepreneur
could attain wealth in textiles or other ventures with the financial backing of noble-born silent partners.[37]

   Poznań, in 1793 a relatively thriving town of 7,000 Catholics,
2,000 Protestants, and 3,000 Jews, was no more the typical
frontier town than the venerably German and prosperous Danzig.
Most towns were much smaller: in the Poznań Kammer district in
1793, only 8 of 120 towns counted more than 3,000 inhabitants.[38]
Most were nothing more than stagnating sources of petty income to
their noble lords, more truly villages than towns. Many had solid
German majorities, some were predominantly Jewish. But Poznań's
example serves to show that in the eighteenth century an educated
and propertied Polish bourgeoisie existed side by side with the
German and Jewish burghers. Neither numerically nor financially
robust, confined by the szlachta's political monopoly in the state
to a narrow urban horizon, the Polish bourgeoisie in Great Poland
nonetheless produced at the end of the eighteenth century intellectuals and political writers of high stature: Stanisław Staszyc,
the brothers Śniadecki, and Józef Wybicki.[39]

   On the eve of Prussian domination, Polish society on the
nationality frontier encompassed a wide range of social groups and
political and cultural strengths and weaknesses. Even before the
extinction of the Commonwealth in 1795, the Poles were caught in a
flux of change, tending towards a diminution of the gentry's monopoly of freedom and power in favor of a reinvigorated monarchy,
greater influence on the part of the bourgeoisie and intelligentsia,
and more security and economic autonomy for the peasantry. The

bitter conflicts attending the promulgation of the Constitution of
3 May 1791 and the Kościuszko Uprising of 1794 were proof that this
flux had a dimension of political and social revolution. But the
fall of the Polish state stifled the resolution of these tensions
in the straightjacket of German and Russian absolutism.

The Germans on the Eighteenth Century Frontier

The German-speaking population of Great Poland and Royal
Prussia formed an archipelago of communities separated not only
geographically, but by differences in religion, social structure,
and political status. Although they certainly possessed a sense
of their national identity in contrast to the Poles and the Jews,
their principal concerns were their religious status and local
interests. No common bond united them among themselves, still
less with the German heartland to the west.

Protestant burghers and farmers constituted a sizable majority
of the population of the Prussian Province of West Prussia at the
end of the eighteenth century. In the Netze and Poznań Districts,
which together comprised the greater part of the post-1815 Province
of Poznań, every fifth villager and every third townsman was a
Protestant.

The strongest German bastion on the frontier was Danzig which,
including its suburbs, counted about 55,000 inhabitants in 1802.
According to the confessional census of 1799, over 90 percent of
its citizens were Protestants. Nearby, the town of Elbing housed
over 19,000 burghers, roughly 70 percent Protestant, while Thorn
upstream on the Vistula numbered 8,400 inhabitants, about half of
them Catholics.[40] Before the partitions, the German burghers in
these West Prussian towns expressed no regrets that their ancestors
had spurned the despotic overlordship of the Teutonic Knights and
subjected themselves to the Polish crown. As long as the aristocratic Commonwealth respected their privileges and local autonomy,
they were staunchly loyal to Poland. The Danzigers resisted their
Swedish coreligionists' claims in Poland in the seventeenth century
and supported Stanisław Leszczyński against the Saxons in the War
of the Polish Succession in the 1730s. Poland's last monarch,
Stanisław Augustus Poniatowski, was equally popular in the Baltic
port. The Danzigers paid little enough to the Polish Crown for
their town's freedom and their profits on the grain trade. The
Prussians could occupy and annex the city in 1793 only after an
armed struggle with the ill-matched Danzig militia.[41]

Elsewhere on the frontier, the town-dwelling Germans were both
more deeply sunk in provincial obscurity and more accustomed to
political subordination to the szlachta than the proud and

autonomous Danzigers. The spinners and weavers scattered across
the frontier, many descended from religious refugees, plied
their trades in old-fashioned piety and no great opulence. The
Prussian inspector Kunth, reporting in 1793 on Great Poland's
resources, wrote disparagingly that the German townsfolk "have
preserved the spirit of the last century intact, except that in
the heart of the land it has become even more primitive. . . ."
Only along the Silesian border did he find that, with all their
traditionalism, the Germans displayed "a certain sense of honor,
some involvement in the welfare of their towns, some love of
civilized manners and well-ordered domesiticity."[42] German
magistrates in sleepy small towns consulted the medieval codes--
the Sachsenspiegel and Magdeburger Recht--for guidance in settling thorny problems. The merchant and artisan guilds, where they
existed, included both Germans and Poles; they were more interested in fighting Jewish competition and staging holiday celebrations than in maintaining old standards of workmanship.[43]
German burghers cooperated willingly with Poles in town government. Among the six magistrates of the city of Poznań in 1793,
one spoke German, although three others--undoubtedly Polonized
German Catholics--had German names; eleven of the remaining
twenty-two town officials spoke German, though some of these may
have been bilingual Poles.[44]

In the countryside, the German-speaking population lived
either in compact Germanized regions, as in the Bishopric of
Ermland, the Vistula delta, and along the Silesian-Brandenburg
border, or in scattered Hauländer villages. In both cases, they
enjoyed the benefits of their free status, secure tenures, and
ample farms. The Hauländer were aggravated in the eighteenth
century by their noble landlords' frequent attempts to increase
their dues, not unnatural in light of the devaluation of Polish
currency in the seventeenth and eighteenth centuries. The
Catholic clergy strove with success to collect a tithe from
Protestant German colonists. But Polish taxes were low and the
German farmers did not need to fear military conscription. A
major reason for German settlement in eighteenth-century Poland
was precisely to escape the Prussian recruiters on the other
side of the frontier. The German peasantry's economic and
social status on the eve of the partitions was a favorable one,
whether judged by Prussian or Polish standards. The economic
efficiency of some of the German colonists impressed Frederick
the Great's officials as they toured Royal Prussia after the first
partition. Privy Finance Counselor von Brenckenhoff wrote to

Frederick of the lower Vistula basin: "The soil is everywhere good, very well cultivated and inhabited by purely Protestant German people living in very solid financial circumstances."[45]

The German Catholics worshipped freely, if not always in their mother tongue. The German Protestants, however, felt the repercussions of the Commonwealth's antidissident tendencies during the eighteenth century. In 1717, the central parliament, ordering all Protestant churches erected in Poland since 1632 to be razed, confined dissident Christianity to private chapels. This policy was only fitfully carried out in Great Poland and, as it would seem, not at all in Royal Prussia.[46] In the Poznań region, fifty Protestant churches closed their doors between 1717 and 1776, but five new churches were also built. The rebellious Catholic confederates of Bar threatened the Protestants during the turbulent years 1768-72. After the partitioning powers decreed a measure of toleration for dissidents in the Commonwealth, thirty new Protestant churches appeared in the Poznań region. But in 1737, when the antidissident laws were intact, there were eighty-eight Protestant communes in this area, served by sixty-five pastors. Numerous Silesian Lutherans migrated to western Poland after Frederick II's conquest of their homeland.[47] But very few Germans abandoned Poland to resettle in Germany during the eighteenth century, and then only during the Seven Years War, while the stream of new colonists, mainly Protestants, flowed uninterrupted to the end of the century.[48] Repression of Protestantism in Poland played no part in the Prussian government's justifications of the partitions, nor did Prussian administrators in the annexed Polish provinces after 1772 complain of Polish anti-Protestantism. Apart from the "bloodbath of Thorn," which was less an attack on Protestantism than a wedge opening the city to Catholic settlement, no memories of Polish religious persecution inflamed German opinion during the nineteenth century.[49] A German Lutheran minister in Berlin, writing on Poland in 1798, harshly condemned the government of the defunct Commonwealth but praised Poland's traditions of religious tolerance; the condition of German Protestants in Great Poland was "advantageous as nowhere else in Catholic Europe."[50]

The patrons of Protestantism in Great Poland were the small minority of Lutherans and Calvinists among the gentry, some of whom--the Dziembowskis, Unruhs, and Schlichtings--were German in language and cultural consciousness. A petition of 1764 to the Commonwealth parliament from Protestants in the voivodeships of Poznań, Kalisz, and Sieradz bore 115 noble signatures, 80 of them Polish. Some Protestant communes chafed under the domineering

patronage of local nobles. But usually the Protestant burghers
and farmers were left alone to practice among themselves a
homespun religion untouched by the German Enlightenment. Witch-
craft accusations were frequent; the last trial occurred as
late as 1773. When in 1793 these Protestants confronted the
church officials of the enlightened Prussian state, they viewed
them with suspicion, contrasting Prussian "worldliness" with
their own religious traditionalism.[51]

The German burghers and farmers on the eighteenth-century
frontier lived as a more or less privileged and well-to-do
minority. Because they lacked a politically enfranchised and
numerous aristocracy, they could play no active political role
beyond the confines of village or town. Fragmented in a myriad
of communities, they clung to their historic rights and, with
more diffidence than defiance, adapted to their Polish surroundings in order to live their insular lives in security. They
were undoubtedly an asset to the Polish Commonwealth, whose kings
and nobility had initiated and welcomed their settlement there.
They were not, as the Prussian government discovered, a race of
conquerors.

The Jews

According to the Latin proverb, Poland was the "paradise of
the Jews." Undoubtedly, the Jews, who had settled in Poland
to escape religious ostracism and persecution in the west,
wanted to believe that the Polish state would ensure them the
security they had failed to find elsewhere. There was reason
for these hopes, because from the time of Casimir the Great
(1333-70) until the extinction of the Commonwealth in 1795,
Poland's monarchs issued, reconfirmed, and extended privileges
which offered the Jews more religious freedom and royal guarantees
of protection against persecution than they enjoyed anywhere
else in Europe before the French Revolution.[52] Not only were the
Jews, as vassals of the Crown, a source of important revenues for
Poland's rulers; they were indispensible, first as minters and
financiers, later as merchants, to the economic life and development of the Commonwealth. They were loyal and peaceful subjects
who, because of their indifference to proselytizing, posed no
threat to Polish Catholicism. If Jewish chroniclers of the
seventeenth and eighteenth centuries wrote of "Poland the precious," and if the Jews displayed a "generally pro-Polish attitude"
until the partitions, it was because they never lost belief that
Poland's rulers would protect their existence.[53]

Although regulation of Jewish affairs never ceased to be a

regalian right, magnate domination of the Crown and the Crown offices in the seventeenth and eighteenth centuries delivered the
Jews into the hands of the szlachta. As the decentralization of
the Polish state progressed, the welfare of the Jews came to
depend on provincial governors and the local gentry. The Polish
Jews confronted widely divergent conditions, which created profound
regional differences in their ranks. In general, however, the
nobility, and especially the magnates and prosperous gentry, upheld
the monarchy's protective policies towards the Jews. Jewish merchants mediated the nobility's trade with Danzig, Jewish communities lent and borrowed money at rates advantageous to the
szlachta, Jews leased or managed many of the operations of noble
estates, while their presence in Poland strengthened the nobility's
control of the enserfed villages.

If the Jews had faced no opposition to their existence in
Poland, no royal privileges or noble protection would have been
necessary. But from the medieval beginnings of their settlement in
Poland, they confronted strong religious hostility among the
Catholic clergy and the pious laity. As they branched out from
financial affairs to commerce and handicrafts, they collided with
the Polish and German burghers engaged in these growing spheres of
the late medieval economy. There was no time in their history in
Poland when they were free of the threat of church-inspired attacks
or economically motivated riots aimed against them. This threat
always existed on the local level even though the Polish Jews were
far more secure from the menace of wholesale expulsion from the
state than were their coreligionists in Germany and most parts of
western and southern Europe.[54]

While sporadic local harassment was part and parcel of the
Jews' existence in Poland, nevertheless they flourished until the
mid seventeenth century. Their numbers rose greatly. New Jewish
communities sprang up following the lines of Polish political expansion in the east. In the fifteenth and sixteenth centuries, the
Polish Jews fashioned a theological tradition of Talmudic orthodoxy, peculiar to themselves and honored by Jews abroad, which
became the starting point for future permutations of Jewish culture in Poland such as the Hassidic movement of the eighteenth
century. But after 1648, the Polish Jews encountered fierce persecution in the course of the deluge of Cossack uprising, Swedish
invasions, and local anarchy which lasted fitfully into the
eighteenth century and which sealed the doom of the Commonwealth
itself. Murder and plunder, the uprooting and resettlement of
Jewish communities, and heavy debts incurred through extortion for

protection by the szlachta and Catholic church plunged Poland's
Jews into a long epoch of insecurity and painful recovery from
which they began to emerge only after the first partition. Social
tensions among the Jews in the south and east gave birth to
messianism and the Hassidic movement against which Talmudic orthodoxy waged a rearguard struggle. Yet by the end of the eighteenth
century, the Jews had made good their demographic and economic
losses of the preceding century and a half. In 1791, every tenth
citizen of the Commonwealth was a Jew, and despite bitter poverty
among the Jewish lower classes, a large share of Poland's foreign
trade, internal commerce, and artisan production was in Jewish
hands.[55] But the golden age of Polish Jewry's cultural development, social security, and internal solidarity had ended in 1648.

   The Teutonic Knights had forbidden Jewish settlement in
their lands, and during the centuries of Polish rule in Royal
Prussia restrictions on Jewish residence held their numbers to a
low level. But in Great Poland numerous Jewish communities took
root in the late Middle Ages which survived the vicissitudes of
the seventeenth and eighteenth centuries. The most important was
the Poznań commune, first mentioned officially in a document of
1399, though Jewish tradition maintained that the original synagogue arose in the mid thirteenth century. Symptomatically enough,
the town government accused the Jews in 1399 of desecrating the
Christian Host; a series of miracles attended the discovery of
this crime. The Jews never shook off their guilt in Christian
eyes, and lawsuits revolved around it in subsequent centuries. Not
until 1724 did the Jews and the town magistrates and church
leaders reach a settlement. The Jews agreed to make annual payments to a local convent in atonement for their forefathers' "outrage." But the tradition did not die there. In 1840 a Polish
priest wrote a book recounting the theft of the Host and the
miracles which followed; in the 1860s, Poznań Jews shared the
belief that the fourteenth-century incident had been manufactured
by the Catholic clergy to justify an anti-Jewish pogrom.[56]

   Despite this unpromising beginning, the Poznań Jews flourished
in the fifteenth and sixteenth centuries. They developed a
special "Poznań Rite" marking their religious practices off from
those of other Polish communes, maintained distinguished scholars,
and prospered in business until by the 1560s they numbered 3,000
souls, half the town's population.[57] But the advancing Counter-
Reformation brought them new harassment, particularly at the hands
of the seminarians of the Jesuit academy founded in 1573. The
riots sporadically launched against them until the end of the

seventeenth century caused the Jews heavy material losses and expenditures in legal defense. The most notable conflict occurred in
1687, when several hundred seminarians and their allies among the
townspeople stormed the ghetto, unleashing a pitched battle lasting
three days from which the beleaguered Jews were rescued only by
the intervention of the local nobility. A synonym among nineteenth-
century Poznań Jews for anti-Jewish riots was Schülergeläufe
("schoolboy runs").[58]

Royal protection, noble patronage, and economic prosperity
nevertheless allowed the Jews' number to increase until, by 1648,
they may have totaled 10,000 in Poznań alone. But the subsequent
Swedish invasion cost them heavily, both in lives lost and in the
accusation of having collaborated with the Swedes against the Commonwealth. The Swedes' harsh treatment of the Jews in Great Poland
made the charge unlikely, but it served to divert attention from
Polish compromises, especially on the part of the gentry and magnates, with the invaders.[59]

The Poznań Jews had only begun to recover from the seventeenth
and early eighteenth-century violence which beset western Poland
when in 1736-40, in a counterpart to the "Thorn bloodbath" of 1724,
a ritual murder trial staged against them by the town magistrates
ravaged their community. Defenders of the Jewish commune died
under torture. Fear and anxiety divided it. Only after the ex-
penditure of huge sums was the case dismissed in a royal court
after the Jews' pleas of innocence had been vouchsafed by the oaths
of a number of Polish noblemen.[60] But in the following half-
century, their circumstances improved. A royal commission regulated the Jews' indebtedness to the Catholic church in 1774, reducing the total sum from 950,000 to 690,000 Polish gulden, a sum
finally paid off only in 1870.[61] By 1793, the Jews numbered 3,021
of Poznań's 12,538 inhabitants. They dominated the town's wholesale trade both in textiles and agricultural products; they did a
large retail trade with the poorer Christian population, leaving
Poles and Germans to supply the szlachta with luxury wares; and they
pursued numerous artisan crafts, organized in guilds which excited their Christian rivals' hostility.[62]

Few sizable fortunes were to be found among the Jews of
Poznań or Great Poland. Their numbers were too great, the opportunities available to them too few, to rescue most of them from
threadbare existences in their ghettos. Their possessions perished
in the fires which periodically consumed their overcrowded, poorly
constructed quarters; when they spread beyond the ghetto, these
conflagrations ignited anti-Jewish riots.[63] The minority of Jews

who lived in the countryside eked out livelihoods as peddlers,
inn and tavern keepers, and dairy farmers, freer from the disadvantages of the ghettos but deprived of the benefits of social
and religious solidarity. But the example of Poznań shows that
these benefits were sometimes dubious. Between 1736 and 1774,
the commune's debts were so oppressive that it could not support
a rabbi. The political offices of the commune responsible to
the Christian authorities had become onerous and dangerous; tax
assessors were forced to accept the posts thrust upon them. The
poorer Jews often flaunted the religious law, gambled and engaged
in crime, while richer Jews sometimes paraded their wealth and
sought to escape their communal obligations. Untouched by
Hassidism, the commune's religious life had hardened into unsophisticated traditionalism. Salomon Maimon, the Polish Jew who
learned from Moses Mendelssohn in Berlin the first principles of
the Jewish Enlightenment (Haskalah), visited Poznań in 1776-77
but came to grief arguing against local superstitions. It was
generally believed that anyone touching a pair of antlers hanging
in the communal hall would die instantly. Maimon, inveighing
against the "Posener fools," defied this tradition and survived
unscathed, but found himself obliged by the resentment he had
stirred up to leave the city hurriedly.[64]

The Jews settled on the nationality frontier in the 1790s
lived in a close but ambivalent relationship with their Christian
surroundings. Their economic security rested on capital, business
techniques, and mercantile connections superior to those of their
Christian rivals and valued and protected by the Crown and local
nobility. Their corporate and legal autonomy, subject only to
the higher Crown officials, protected them from the hostility of
the Christian townspeople except in occasional extreme circumstances, from which the Crown and nobility rescued them, at a more
or less heavy price. Speaking Yiddish among themselves and
cultivating a Hebrew literary tradition, their dialect was
nevertheless understandable to the German Christians. They spoke
Polish with their business clients and with the nobility, magistrates, and Catholic church. But their dress, their social customs, their ghettos, and above all their religion separated them
by a great gulf from the Christian population with whom, apart
from economic dealings, their contacts were rare.[65]

Nationality Conflict in the Eighteenth Century

Although the frontier population counted those who spoke
Polish and those who spoke German, in one or another of the

dialectal and literary forms these languages then possessed, it would be a nationalist fallacy to make too much of this fact. In the eighteenth century, a shared language did not automatically confer a consciousness of political or even cultural community upon the inhabitants of Great Poland and Royal Prussia, and neither Polish nor German statisticians, in an age enamored of statistics, bothered to differentiate the population by this criterion. The Polish peasantry, generally illiterate, associated themselves with the dialect they spoke and with the narrowly circumscribed terri- tory in which they spent their lives. They thought of themselves as villagers in a given locality, speaking its language and look- ing upon it as their homeland. They could recognize that, in contrast to the speech of the Germans and Jews living in a nearby town, their language was Polish; but they knew that their Polish was different from that of the manor house or the city hall.[66] Similarly, urban illiterates and semiliterates identified primarily with their residential quarter and their occupations, and knew very well what a gulf separated them from the educated and propertied people speaking the refined version of their workaday tongue. Educated burghers, though they might speak the szlachta's polished language, could draw no political conclusions from that fact, faced as they were with their political nullity in the gentry's Common- wealth. Neither could a shared language erase the elaborate dif- ferences in mentality and social behavior separating burghers from aristocrats in eighteenth-century Poland.

Yet, if sharing a language did not necessarily join social classes politically or culturally, differences in language in- contestably raised barriers between the frontier Poles, Germans, and Jews, but not absolutely or in a fixed and unchanging manner. Any community of interest among the nationalities which created a need or desire for easy communication produced either bilinguality or linguistic assimilation. Jewish merchants or Jewish communal officials commonly spoke Polish, an unnecessary accomplishment for rabbis or artisans serving only the ghetto Jews. Poles and Germans cooperating in artisan trades, in commerce, or in town government found bilinguality, however ungrammatical, advantageous if not un- avoidable. It seems likely that bilinguality was a bridge to as- similation into a foreign nationality when religion was not a divisive factor and when a shared socioeconomic setting was strongly dominated by one language group. A Pole apprenticed to a German Catholic in a town whose artisanry was predominantly German might proceed beyond rudimentary bilinguality to acquire a sense of solidarity with his German colleagues, and a German wife and German

children. Or, as slowly happened among the numerous South German
Catholic colonists in the suburbs of Poznań, participation in a
religious and social life of a strongly Polish character could
lead through bilinguality to loss of command of German and full
assimilation into the Polish nationality.[67] Similarly, it was a
community of social and political interests that led to widespread
Polonization among the West Prussian German nobility in the seventeenth and eighteenth centuries.

Language did not therefore determine nationality. Neither
did language differences create insurmountable barriers to communication or assimilation among the nationalities. The crucial
factors dividing the frontier population into groups with distinctive concepts of themselves and their special interests were,
instead, religion and social status.

However conventionalized it may have been, religion was
nevertheless the unchallenged and pervasive rationale of existence
in eighteenth-century Poland. The most fundamental of all differences were religious. In this sense, Catholics, Protestants,
and Jews inhabited separate existential universes. The essence
of a Jew's character was his religion, from which followed his
social, economic, and political identity. Catholics and Protestants were divided not only by their differing conceptions of the
path to salvation, but by their participation in two unrelated
social systems, each revolving around their respective church
communities and differing calendars of holidays. The day had
not yet dawned when respite from work had any justification other
than religion. But the clearest proofs of the centrifugal force
exerted by the religions on their followers were the great infrequency of confessionally mixed marriages and the even greater
rarity of conversion from one religion to another.[68] The strongest
normative bonds fastened on Poles, Germans, and Jews were those
of religion.

At the same time, religion provided the scaffolding of ideas
and institutions enclosing and perpetuating the specific hostori-
cal identity of the group professing it. In the case of the Jews,
this identity and the religion which infused it were inextricably
intertwined mutual reinforcements. But surely it was no accident
that, in the sixteenth century, the Germans in Poland converted
massively to Lutheranism whereas the Polish nobility, after em-
bracing Calvinism in large numbers, found their way back to the
Catholic Church once they had gained control of the Commonwealth,
whose legitimization had always derived from the religion of Rome.
Catholicism in eighteenth-century Poland was heavily laden with

Polish traditions and historical associations, its clergy were
mostly Poles, its religious literature was part of a broader Polish
culture. Conversely, most Protestants were Lutherans, speakers of
German, professing a faith intimately associated with German cultural and political history.

To the Poles, both high and low-born, the idea was almost ir-
resitible, as an old saying put it, that co niemiec, to odmieniec
("Germans are dissenters"). The Poles commonly called Lutheranism
"the German faith."[69] But the German Lutherans could not fail to
perceive the massively Polish character of the Catholic church in
the gentry Commonwealth and, except perhaps in those few areas of
compact German Catholic settlement, conclude that Catholicism was
a Polish religion and that Catholics, even if they were not Polish-
speaking, were part of an essentially Polish culture. These associations of religion with linguistically circumscribed secular
culture left German Catholics and Polish Protestants in a kind of
limbo. But it was proof of the importance and essential soundness
of these associations that, in the nineteenth and early twentieth
century, German Catholics on the frontier opposed or stood passive
in the face of the German nationalist movement, just as Polish
Protestants were lost to the radical Polish nationalists.[70]

The lofty attitude of the Polish nobility towards their
German-speaking subjects can be summed up in the saying, co polak,
to pan--co niemiec, to cham: "a Pole is a lord, a German a vulgar
fellow."[71] The German farmers and burghers in Poland had earned a
reputation among the gentry for uncouthness (nieokrzesaność
niemiecka), stinginess, a vulgar preoccupation with business, and
social stiffness.[72] But the eighteenth century szlachta, inheri-
tors and bearers of Polish political tradition, had views as well
about the Germans as their political neighbors and rivals. German-
Polish political conflicts in the Middle Ages led a chronicler,
probably a Frenchman, to write in 1309 that naturale odium est
inter Polonos et Theutonicos. The influential political writer Jan
Ostroróg maintained in 1477 that "in their languages as well as in
other things nature has sown eternal discord and hate between them."
In the seventeenth century the poet Wacław Potocki reformulated an
old saying which, in modern times, inflamed nationalist passions:
Póki świat światem, nie będzie niemiec polakowi bratem--"As long
as the world is the world, the German will never be brother to the
Pole."[73] In the sixteenth and seventeenth centuries, the
szlachta's anti-Germanism throve on Polish-Hapsburg rivalries,
while the Saxon kings of Poland (1697-1763) tarnished the German
image in Polish eyes by their opportunism and neglect of the

Commonwealth. Ironically, prior to the partitions the Poles gave
little thought to their most dangerous German neighbor. Prussia
seemed a puny upstart compared to the vast and venerable Commonwealth; the lordly Polish magnates scorned the Junker squires.[74]

Polish burghers may have shared some of their noble masters'
prejudices about Germans, but they focused their hostility, and
envy, primarily on that Germanic industriousness and frugality
which was and still is proverbial in Poland. Polish peasants also
begrudged the prosperity and privileges of the German farmers in
their midst and composed ill-humored sayings in compensation. A
sure insult was to call a German a szwab (Swabian), just as the
word Polack was a venerable term of abuse and contempt in the
German language. The Polish peasants sometimes conceived Germans
in a sinister light. There was an old tradition representing
the Devil in "German dress," and some people held that when he
spoke or prayed, it was in German. Many popular Polish sayings
excoriated the Germans as "heretics" and rudely insulted
Martin Luther.[75]

The Catholic Poles had few good words for the religion of
the Jews. A pamphleteer, arguing for the civil emancipation of
the Jews, admitted in 1782 that Judaism "is a laughing stock and
prey to vilification."[76] On a secular level, too, Polish images
of the Jews were derogatory if not hostile. The szlachta, of whom
it was said "every landlord has his Jew," defended the Jews for
economic purposes, but scorned the Jews' struggle for survival,
their poverty, and dependence. Few sons of the nobility would
have idealized the Jews as Mickiewicz did in the character of
Pan Tadeusz's innkeeper Jankiel. Nevertheless, it was bourgeois
writers who voiced the bitterest secular opposition to the Jews.
Wherever considerable Jewish communities existed, the Christian
burghers waged a seemingly incessant struggle to limit Jewish
economic rights and opportunities. In 1617, a mass was celebrated
in Poznań after "the victory of the city against the Jews" in a
lawsuit. Later in the same year an entry was made in the town
register about "the Jewish locust, the dreadful beast, which
devours the flower of the city" (florem civitatis depascit).[77]
The crux of bourgeois economic complaints against the Jews was
that "they take the trade away from the city." Bourgeois writers
in the old Commonwealth held the Jews' poverty against them as
well, claiming it was their miserliness which prevented them from
clothing themselves and eating decently. The Polish peasantry
probably felt no more economic hostility towards Jewish merchants
and craftsmen than towards their Christian counterparts, if it
is true that "the Jews contented themselves with a lower profit

rate."[78]   But wherever Jewish tavernkeepers or moneylenders held
peasants in a condition of permanent indebtedness, the peasants'
religious antipathies towards the Jews could be powerfully reinforced by material resentment.[79]

The Jews, in their turn, had little comprehension for the cultural lives of the Christians in whose midst they lived. They had
no taste for secular Christian literature, whether Polish or German, which in any case their rabbis forbade them to read. The
value they placed on their scholarly traditions could hardly have
led them to esteem the illiterate traditionalism of the Polish
masses, while the religious and economic opposition they encountered among the Christian townspeople inevitably put the Jews on
their guard against them. No wonder that among the various segments
of the Christian population "Polish Jews generally identified with
the nobility" and "regarded the nobleman as a protector, more
rarely an oppressor." This was simply one instance of European
Jewry's tendency, particularly before the French Revolution, to look
to the Christian ruling classes for defense against the hostility
of the masses.[80]

It is difficult to characterize the feelings of the Commonwealth's Germans towards their Polish neighbors. Did thy, like
the Prussians, mock the social pretensions and political turbulence
of the szlachta, did they scorn the "superstitions" of the
Catholic clergy, and did they condescendingly pity the hard lot of
the Polish serfs?[81] The tradition-bound German Protestants undoubtedly shared in the anti-Semitic legacy of popular Lutheranism
and kept their distance from the Catholic "papists." Frontier
Germans, aware of their relative material well-being, may have
countered Polish resentment with sneering references to polnische
Wirtschaft ("Polish economy," a heavily ironical phrase). But
like the Jews, the Germans, despite their long residence in the
Commonwealth, were to some degree outsiders in a Polish land, and
if they could not form positive links with the Poles through
shared Catholicism, they led their insular lives avoiding hostile
relations with the Poles, whatever prejudices they may have
harbored privately towards them.[82]

The confrontation along the frontier of religions and languages, folkways and high cultures, and ethnically distinct social
and economic groups could not have failed to produce rich veins of
suspicion, prejudice, and hostility. But in the course of time the
nationalities accepted their interspersion as inevitable and
natural. Anti-Jewish tumults and Catholic attacks on Protestants
were the two forms in which the nationalities clashed violently in
the Polish Commonwealth. These were urban upheavals justified

religiously and, viewed over the long term, rarities. There is
no evidence of violent national struggles among the peasant
villagers.[83] Neither the nationalities' religious nor their
social and economic conflicts created unendurable strains among
them, or polarized them in any clear-cut political sense. ⎧Despite
its economic inequalities and cultural heterogeneity, frontier
society in the seventeenth and eighteenth centuries, when spared
the ravages of war, was relatively stable and peaceful. ⎫

"Sparta of the North"

Contemplating the state he had long served with distinction, the enlightened, reform-minded Baron Friedrich von Schrötter remarked at the end of the eighteenth century that Prussia was "not a country with an army, but an army with a country which served as headquarters and food magazine."[1] At the end of the Thirty Years War, Brandenburg-Prussia had been little more than a loose agglomeration of territories weakly governed by the Hohenzollern Electors in tandem with a provincial-minded nobility, dependent on mercenary troops and a negligible quantity in international affairs. The ambition of three energetic rulers transformed it into the autocratically ruled, militarized, and administratively rationalized Great Power whose 5 million inhabitants, 200,000 soldiers, and ample state treasure Frederick the Great bequeathed to his successor at his death in 1786.

Although the political and military powers of the Polish Commonwealth were dissipated through their devolution upon the nobility, while Prussia's were concentrated, as far as the nature of government in the eighteenth century allowed, in the hands of absolute rulers, in their social and economic structure the two states were not dissimilar. Like the szlachta, the Junker nobility of Brandenburg and East Prussia took advantage of the economic crises and conjunctures of the fifteenth and sixteenth centuries to amass estates, enserf the peasantry, weaken urban competitors, and establish themselves as a squirearchy profiting comfortably from domestic and foreign agricultural markets. They overrode other corporate interests to become monopolists of power in the system of provincial parliaments (Landstände) with which the Hohenzollern princes negotiated on such crucial matters as taxes and levies of recruits. In the sixteenth and the first half of the seventeenth century, the Junkers exploited their rulers' financial needs to extend their political influence over vital areas of princely policy, fiscal administration, justice, and foreign af-

31

fairs. They sought, after their own fashion, a political
primacy which, had they achieved it, might have stood comparison
with the triumph of the szlachta, about whom it may be said that
they succeeded utterly in realizing ambitions shared but only
imperfectly satisfied by other noble classes in northern and
eastern Europe, not only in Brandenburg-Prussia, but in Hungary,
the Austrian Crown lands, the Mecklenburg duchies, Livonia, and
Russia as well.[2]

The Junkers' failure finally to disarm the Hohenzollerns
can be ascribed to a jealous provincialism which prevented their
concerted political action, to the ravages of the Thirty Years
War and, perhaps most fundamentally, to the modest proportions
of their wealth and political talent. A noble state requires
great nobles, but the Junkers lacked counterparts to the Polish
magnates. Political ideas of the most varied sort flourished in
sixteenth century Poland, ultimately welding the szlachta
together around a Catholic-hued ideology of aristocratic repub-
licanism and "golden freedom." An escape into sovereign independence was far more difficult for the Junkers to conceive,
caught as they were under the stormy skies of the Hapsburg-
dominated Empire, with the dream of local security and the
Lutheran princes' model of peaceable and pious political economy
the only guideposts for most of them.

Stiff-necked and loath as many of them were to admit it,
the system of absolutism fastened on Brandenburg-Prussia by the
Great Elector, Frederick William (1640-88), the granitic king,
Frederick William I (1713-40), and his genial son, Frederick the
Great, benefited the Junkers in the short run as least as much,
and in the long run far more, than their liberties and omnipo-
tence did the Polish szlachta. From the end of the Thirty Years
War to the eve of the French Revolution, the Hohenzollern rulers
amassed a formidable army under their undivided control. Having
reduced the noble-dominated parliaments to docile nullities, they
created a corps of civil bureaucrats--governed by a protean, self-
amplifying administrative code--who outdid themselves in increasing the Crown's domainal and regalian incomes, in bending town
governments and guilds to the royal will, and in squeezing taxes
from the burghers and peasants. The progressive and enlightened
nature of royal absolutism was taught from the university lectern
to aspiring officials, jurists, clerics, and savants. The
Lutheran clergy preached not only salvation, but also respect for
the monarchy and modern economy to the hard-pressed peasant-
serfs.

Nor were the Junkers exempt from travail pour le roi de

Prusse. Their lands were taxed, though not very heavily. Their
access to the foreign grain markets was regulated in the monarchy's
interest of maintaining army stores and bread prices low enough to
ensure tax payments from towns and villages. Their sons were recruited into the army officer corps, at first against the will of
many parents. They were forced all too often, against their aristocratic inclinations, to gain a higher education and compete with
low-born bureaucrats if they chose to enter public life. They
lost all institutional controls over the royal will. But in return, particularly under Frederick thé Great, they received precious compensations. Above all, the monarchy confirmed them in
their rights as masters of the serfs who tilled their fields and
entrusted them, in the office of Landrat, with self-administration
in the principal spheres of rural government. The nobility alone
were able to salvage a vestige of judgment by their peers in the
civil courts. With the proper qualifications, they became the
preferred cadres in the upper civil administration as well, while,
especially during Frederick's wars, they embraced the officer corps
as their own. The absolute regime, though it fostered industry
and commerce in a mercantilist spirit, upheld the castelike dis-
tinctions of corporate (ständische) society, to the Junkers' great
advantage. After the Seven Years War ended in 1763, Frederick
established royally funded mortgage and credit societies for the
exclusive benefit of the noble estate owners. The state helped
the Junkers strengthen their financial positions and take advantage
of a long-term rising demand for grain in Western Europe at the
very time that the Polish export economy was faltering under
internal structural pressures and external political attacks,
launched most relentlessly in his own and his nobility's interest
by Frederick himself. Though they sometimes intrigued against the
Crown within the corridors of the military and administrative
bureaucracy, by 1786 the Junkers had become monarchists to the
core, and with good reason. Both as a squirearchy and as a
politically privileged class they were far better situated than
their forebears in the dark days of the Thirty Years War, while
the agonies of the fall of the Polish Commonwealth offered the
more thoughtful a lesson in the fragility of aristocratic government. [3]

It was not merely dynastic pride and emulation of Louis XIV
that impelled the Hohenzollern princes to create the absolute
Prussian monarchy. German political logic condemned any state
which was not politically centralized, financially strong, and
militarily bristling to the depredations of its rivals within,

and to the manipulation of the powers outside, the bankrupted
Holy Roman Empire. In the century before the accession of
Frederick the Great, Prussia's rulers labored internally to establish their system of royal autonomy and power, as Frederick William
I said, like a "rock of bronze" against which Junker intrigue and
opposition would be hopeless. In their foreign policy, they sought
territorial gains in western Germany, with little success, and
expansion towards the Baltic coast at the expense of Sweden, in
which by 1721 their efforts had been rewarded by the acquisition
of Stettin and the Oder mouth as well as Pomerania beyond to the
outskirts of Danzig.

No dreams of Prussian greatness could ignore the Polish Commonwealth, whose Vistula provinces divided East Prussia from the
Brandenburg heartland. Poland's forced concession of sovereignty
in East Prussia to its erstwhile Hohenzollern vassal in 1657 was
undoubtedly a diplomatic and military coup for the Great Elector.
The idea occurred to him, during that tense moment in Polish
history, to intrigue with the Commonwealth's foes and seize not
only Royal Prussia but also Great Poland. In this he was deterred
not only by his weakness as a minor German prince, but by another
consideration which loomed large in Prussian thinking until the
mid eighteenth century. Poland, provided it was not powerful
enough to menace Prussia or to revoke the settlement of 1657, was
a useful shield against Sweden and, after Sweden's eclipse as a
power in 1721, against Russia. It is true that schemes to dismember the Commonwealth were often discussed during the eighteenth
century among the future partitioning powers, even with the con-
nivance of Poland's Saxon ruler, August II (1697-1733). But, as
much as Prussia's rulers hankered after Royal Prussia, the prospect of Russia or Austria swollen with Polish spoils could only
evoke anxiety in Berlin. It was only after Frederick the Great's
seizure and conquest of the rich Hapsburg province of Silesia
against the combined arms of Austria, Russia, and France (1740-
48, 1756-63) that Prussia acquired the material base and international recognition as a Great Power to allow it to deal as an
equal with Austria and Russia on the Polish question.[4]

Frederick the Great and Poland

In Polish tradition and historiography, Frederick II looms as a
relentless and pitiless enemy of the old Commonwealth, a monarch
who diabolically opposed all attempts to reform the Polish constitution in the mid eighteenth century and the prime instigator of
the politically and economically disastrous partition of 1772.[5]
Frederick had no need to banish any sentiments of respect for the

szlachta empire in order to contemplate it in the cold light of
raison d'état; unlike his illustrious great-grandfather, he was
utterly devoid of such feelings. His interest in Poland was
wholly and nakedly territorial.[6] Yet, for this very reason, it
was a limited interest. From his years as crown prince until the
twilight of his reign, he focused his aggressive designs against
Poland on Royal Prussia, including Danzig, and the adjacent Netze
region. He expressed no intentions of annexing Great Poland, nor
did he look forward to the wholesale destruction of the Polish
state.[7] His motives were threefold: to gain a land bridge between
Brandenburg and East Prussia, to obtain a stranglehold on Poland's
export trade down the Vistula, and to acquire more tax-paying and
arms-bearing subjects. Although Danzig and Thorn eluded his grasp,
in his main ambitions he was not disappointed. To see him as the
chief architect of the first partition is to invest him with power
over Russian and Hapsburg policy which he hardly possessed. Rather,
to avoid entanglements alongside his sole ally, Catherine II, in
a war against Austria over Russian-Austrian Balkan rivalries from
which Prussia had nothing to gain, Frederick pressured his two
powerful neighbors to seek compensation not from the Turks but
rather from Poland, defenseless and, since 1768, torn by a civil
war strongly tinged with xenophobic, espcially anti-Russian, emo-
tions. For reasons of their own, and certainly without yielding
to Prussian compulsion, Austria and Russia concurred in Frederick's
ideas. When, in the spring of 1772, Prussian troops occupied Royal
Prussia and began pushing the line of Prussian annexation south
into the Netze district, Frederick could reasonably congratulate
himself for having avoided a new test of his exhausted resources on
the battlefield and for having strengthened his monarchy by a territorial acquisition of first-rate importance. The argument that
Poland must stand unimpaired as a buffer between Russia and Brandenburg-Prussia had lost its plausibility in the light of both
Frederick's alliance with Catherine and the massive advance since
1763 of Russian influence over the Commonwealth and particularly
over its ruler, the ill-fated Stanisław Poniatowski. Ignorant of
the still-unformulated ethics of modern nationalism, Frederick had
no reason to judge his Polish annexations any differently than his
seizure of Hapsburg Silesia.[8]

He was certainly cheered by his triumph over the Commonwealth.
Even before he was fully in control of the land he rebaptized as
West Prussia, he busily calculated the income the province would
pay into the royal coffers.[9] And after he had imposed a treaty on
Poland in 1775 which taxed Polish overseas exports heavily and thus

tended to divert Polish trade towards Prussia, he could describe
himself enthusiastically as "master of the Vistula" and "master
of Poland's commerce." Now--or so he thought--his kingdom had to
fear "neither famine nor shortage."[10]

If the partition was a heavy blow to the Polish Commonwealth,
in Frederick's opinion it was well deserved. It was, in the words
of his letter to Voltaire of November 1771, the result of "the
stupidities of the Potockis, Krasinskis, Oginskis and that whole
imbecile crowd whose names end in -ki."[11] Together with this
letter Frederick sent Voltaire a copy of a lengthy poem he had
composed to divert himself during the nerve-wracking preliminaries
to the first partition. "La guerre des Confédérés" showers his
scorn and acid wit on the Poles caught in the desperate and futile
turmoil of the civil war provoked in 1768 by the formation of the
Confederation of Bar. Poland Frederick calls "a land of fools,
madmen, and war," the Poles a people deranged by "folly" and
fanatical attachment to the "false zeal" of a benighted Catholicism.
"They loved too well their lady Mary, and their country anarchic
and lawless." Of "la Sottise" he wrote:

> She contemplates Poland with pleasure,
> No different than at its creation,
> Coarse, stupid, without education,
> Governor, Jew, serf, minister, drunkard,
> Vegetating, all of them lived without shame.

In the poem's closing lines, Peace, having descended to earth, lectures the Poles coldly:

> Open your eyes, the Devil ensnares you!
> Long have you thoughtlessly offered the napkin
> To your powerful neighbors.
> One fine day you may well discover
> These neighbors dividing the cake.
> Such are the fruits of your extravagance,
> Of your intrigues, the issue of madness.
> For a peace dictated to you who are vanquished
> Console yourselves in the arms of Bacchus.[12]

In his Histoire de mon temps (1746) Frederick delivered a
classic Prussian judgment on Poland and the Poles.

> That kingdom is caught in an eternal anarchy. Conflicting
> interests separate all the magnate families. They put
> their own advantage above the public good and unite among
> themselves only to consider cruel and atrocious means of
> oppressing their serfs, whom they treat like cattle.
> The Poles are vain and haughty when favored by fortune,
> abject in defeat; capable of the greatest baseness when
> money is to be gained thereby; but after getting it, they
> throw it out the window. Frivolous, they have neither
> judgment nor firm opinion. Without any justification,
> they adhere to political factions and then abandon them.
> Because of their irrationality they get mixed up in the
> worst kinds of political affairs. True, they have laws,
> but no one obeys them because of the lack of agencies
> to enforce them. In this kingdom, reason has become the

vassal of women; they intrigue and decide about
everything, while their men worship the bottle.[13]

Frederick's contempt for Poland arose from his aversion, as
the enlightened, disciplined, and autocratic ruler of an increasingly powerful and well-organized state, to the Commonwealth's
aristocratic constitution, to its inability to defend itself, and
to the wealth and cultural dominance within it of the Polish
Catholic church. The political impotence of the kings of Poland
was an affront to his monarchist convictions.

Attitudes similar to Frederick's were common in eighteenth-
century Germany. The earliest references to Poland in German
popular and high literature alike were tinged with superiority and
irony: Poland was a land of ox-drivers, wolves, and people in bear
skins; the numerous lower Polish nobility were lampooned and denied
equality of status by seventeenth-century noble German writers and
visitors in Poland. In the period after the mid seventeenth century, expectations in Germany of the collapse of the Commonwealth
were ever more widely expressed in print. "Turbulent" (verwirrt)
became a standard adjective to describe things Polish, "Polish
freedom" a mockery, while "the wild proceedings of the Polish
parliament provided a popular and proverbial comparison for every
kind of uproar and disorder."[14] Silesian scholars amused themselves at Poland's expense by reciting reges exreges, curia furia,
nobiles mobiles, clerus non verus, jura obscura.[15] Lutheran
Germans castigated the Poles for the "Thorn blood bath" of 1724,
a proceeding enlightened Germans condemned equally for its
ferocity and obscurantism.[16]

The more strongly German Protestants embraced the Enlightenment and royal absolutism, the greater was their hostility to the
Polish Commonwealth. Hence in Prussia, that militarized autocracy
which had inscribed the slogans of the Enlightenment on its own
banner, the first partition of Poland appeared as a progressive
and praiseworthy event. Influential German publicists outside
Prussia, notably Wilhelm Ludwig Wekhrlin and Christian Wieland,
applauded the partitioning powers. The Stürmer und Dränger, the
German admirers of Rousseau, and also German Catholics, had no
reason to celebrate the triumph of a state whose structure and
spirit they condemned. But only the well-known poet and journalist
Christian Schubart left a tribute to Poland in the first German
Polengedicht, a few verses published in the Deutsche Chronik
(1774) expressing in classical imagery the tragedy of "Polonia" at
the loss of "her children."[17]

The Conversion of Royal Prussia into West Prussia

By the time Russia, Austria, and Prussia sealed the first
partition, the armed resistance of the szlachta to foreign interference in Poland, organized in the Confederation of Bar, had
spent itself in skirmishes, mainly in the east, against Russian
troops. At the Diet of Grodno in 1773, the terrorized representatives of the Polish nobility ratified at bayonet-point the Commonwealth's losses. Demoralized and embittered, the proud "Sarmatians" in the annexed territories offered no resistance to the arrival of their new overlords.

Frederick was able to occupy Royal Prussia and the Netze
district almost without firing a shot. In September 1772 the
Prussian government issued a proclamation justifying the partition.
Here, in Frederick's name, Brandenburg-Prussia's title to Royal
Prussia and the adjoining Netze region was solemnly though implau-
sibly expounded as a right of inheritance usurped in the thirteenth
century by the Teutonic Knights and in the fifteenth century by the
Polish Republic. In feudal language carefully distinguishing the
various statuses of the annexed subjects, the Besitzergreifungs-
Patent called for loyalty to the Hohenzollern monarchy without
reference to mother tongue or nationality. In return Frederick
promised "Our true and obedient subjects" that

> . . . We are firmly determined, and hereby assure,
> that We will protect and administer them in their pos-
> sessions and rights in the spiritual and secular realm,
> and in particular grant the adherents of the Roman-
> Catholic religion free exercise of their faith, and in
> general rule the land in such a manner that the reason-
> able and right-thinking (vernüftige und wohldenkende)
> inhabitants can be happy and satisfied and without any
> reason to regret the change.[18]

Two weeks after the publication of this patent, in a ceremony in
the great castle of the Teutonic Knights at Marienburg (Malbork),
the assembled high nobility and clergy and the deputies of the
lesser nobility, lower clergy, towns, and villages swore fealty
to the Prussian monarchy. This large multitude of former Polish
subjects then listened to a speech pronounced in German by Minister
von Rohd and subsequently translated into Polish. He praised "the
hand of the Almighty for fastening this seal on the greatness"
of Frederick II who, in vindicating his dynasty's claims to the
newly won territories, "brought them like a lost sheep back
into his flock, to which originally they belonged and in which
likewise they had originally been born." In the spirit of the
ancien régime he summed up his lengthy exhortation to obedience by
explaining that "the bond which unites a father with his children
is the same which holds together the body of a great state." At

the end of his address, he quoted a passage from Horace, an apos-
trophe to the glory of Rome which he altered to express the hope
that the West Prussians would recognize the Hohenzollern state
as their "great and happy fatherland."[19]

It was thus on a traditional basis of dynastic right, confirmation of social privilege, and recognition of the legitimacy of the
Catholic religion that the Prussian state fastened its rule on
Royal Prussia and the Netze district. This did not prevent
Frederick from ordering his officials to place the new territories
"on a Prussian footing" as soon as possible. The Prussian administrative system expanded into the partition zone with no concessions to local autonomy. Unlike their counterparts in Brandenburg, the West Prussian nobility were denied the right to nominate
from among their own ranks those whom the government appointed to
the vital local rural office of Landrat. The Prussian conscription (Canton) system was promptly introduced, along with the taxes
on peasants and noble lords which financed it. The Prussian government confiscated, with compensation, the rights of the szlachta
to the income from former Polish Crown estates and incorporated
these lands into the system of royal domains. Similarly, the
estates of the Catholic church were taken into the royal domain,
the upper clergy receiving henceforth only a fixed percentage of
their yield at the time of confiscation. To strengthen its hold
on the new province, the government strove to fill vacancies in
the church hierarchy with men dedicated to the Prussian cause
while the Protestant church fell wholly under the supervision of
the Berlin Consistory.

Polish common law enshrining the rights of landlords over the
enserfed villagers remained in force, but Prussian administrative
and civil law ruled all other spheres. The Prussian judicial
system was introduced, including patrimonial estate courts presided over by jurists paid by the landlords and certified by the
state. The serfs gained a limited right of appeal from these
courts to royal courts, though whether they often exercised it is
questionable. The personal freedom and limited labor services of
the domain peasants remained unchanged, as did the unfree condition
and unlimited dues of the private serfs. The self-government of
the towns buckled under royal confirmation of magistrates and regulation of guilds, the interference of the powerful urban tax
assessor--the Steuerrat, appointed by the provincial administration
--and the arrival of a small army of excise-tax collectors under
the supervision of the well-hated, French-staffed Régie in Berlin.[20]

In little more than a decade, the semifeudal wooden scaffold-

ing of public life under the Polish Commonwealth was torn down
and replaced by the well-manned, solid brick bastions, overflow-
ing with regulations and red tape, of the military-bureaucratic
Prussian state. Not a protest was heard, not an arm raised
against this replay of the revolution of absolutism. This was
proof not only of Prussia's ability to absorb a population of
nearly 600,000, but to do so profitably. By 1773-74, the government collected an income from the province of 1.72 million thalers,
of which 1.3 million was spent in outlays in the province while
the remainder flowed into the royal treasure.[21]

Frederick's zeal as a ruler did not end with mere budgetary
"plus-making." From the reports of his high officials and from
his own observations during his annual tours, he formed a low
opinion of the material and spiritual culture of the province.
"The common man," he was told in 1774, lives in the "most miserable circumstances"; "the cities, which do not deserve the name,
are extraordinarily bad."[22] The poor country people "are fed
worse than cattle," or so Kammerdirektor Vorhoff told him in
1775.[23] He himself observed in 1773 that beggars were excessively
numerous in West Prussia, in 1775 that burghers and peasants
alike were lacking in "industriousness, cleanliness, and orderli-
ness," in 1776 that "the people are too sluggish and lazy and have
no wish to work and make money," in 1780 that "stupidity and
negligence" prevented the peasants from properly husbanding their
farms.[24] The conclusion he had already drawn in 1772 was that
his erstwhile Polish subjects must acquire "a Prussian character."[25]

Frederick's long-standing scorn and mockery of the Polish
szlachta colored his attitude towards the West Prussian nobility
from the moment they became his subjects. His distrust showed
itself in his refusal to permit them county diets (Kreistage) or
to fund a provincial credit society (Landschaft). It was heightened
when he learned that many of the Polish nobility leased their West
Prussian estates and took up residence in Warsaw, revealing their
unwillingness to work for the king of Prussia while violating the
mercantilist principle that cash should not flow out of the
state.[26] He was ready to confer official posts on Polish nobles
who commanded the German tongue and showed a spirit of discipline
and loyalty. In 1776 he established a Cadet Academy at Kulm
(Chełmno). Most of its sixty students were sons of the Polish
gentry. In the following decades the academy succeeded in
channeling many Poles, lacking prospects of becoming solid gentry
landowners, into the Prussian officer corps.[27] But the aloofness
and attraction to Warsaw of many of the Polish gentry and magnates

irritated Frederick and led him to discriminate from the beginning
against the Polish szlachta as a whole. Thus in 1772 he decreed
that, among the landlords, Germans (Teutsche) should pay 5 percent
of their net profits in land taxes, but that Poles (Stockpolen)
should pay 10 percent.[28] In West Prussia he relaxed his policy,
rigid in his other lands, of forbidding middle-class purchase of
estates, decreeing in 1772 that if the Poles wished to sell their
lands "from spite or feelings of resistance," he would gladly see
"rich Danzig merchants" take their places.[29] The following year he
forbade his administrators to lease róyal domain estates to
Poles.[30] He complained of the szlachta's susceptibility to bribe-
taking and agreed with Privy Finance Councillor von Brenckenhoff
that their "chief passions" were "drink, love affairs, and personal
financial interest."[31]

By 1777 he had taken the decision, pregnant with consequences
for the subsequent history of Prussian Poland, to commit state
money to the purchase of Polish estates in order to sell or lease
them to Germans. As a beginning he ordered 120,000 thalers spent
"to get rid of the bad Polish stuff (schlechtes polnisches Zeug)";
he added that "the German noblemen are to be maintained in their
estates, since they are altogether good and orderly."[32] A few
months later, he wrote to West Prussian Provincial President von
Domhardt, saying that those Poles with estates in both West Prussia
and Poland would have to declare for one or the other state and
liquidate their holdings accordingly within four years. "I would
gladly get completely rid of the Polish stuff, because they will
never fit themselves into our constitution or into our system."[33]
He fumed against the szlachta with increasing venom, speaking in
1783 the already traditional words of insult, "slovenly Polish
economy (liederliche polnsche Wirtschaft)."[34] In the same year he
urged his officials once again to buy up szlachta estates "so that
gradually we will get rid of all the Poles."[35]

Apart from their sojourns in Warsaw, their not unnatural
regret at the loss of their Polish citizenship, and their in-
comprehension of a regime conducting its affairs in a foreign
spirit and language, the Polish nobility gave Frederick no cause
for wrath. At bottom, what he objected to in them was their
spiritual and material independence of the Prussian state and their
traditional Polish way of life. Because they would not devote themselves to the service of the Prussian state, he wished to "get rid"
of them. But since West Prussia was unthinkable without a local
class of large landowners, he arrived naturally at the thought that
the "bad" Polish nobles should be replaced by Germans. This was

not so much because he valued Germans above other European
peoples--it is notorious that he did not--but rather because
German Junker sons and bourgeois capitalists were ready at hand.
They would, Frederick thought, respect and support the Prussian
state while managing their estates more productively than the
szlachta. It was as an enlightened German absolutist, not as
a modern nationalist, that Frederick initiated the replacement,
slowly and by legal methods, of Polish landlords by Germans.
But to the degree that the Polish gentry submitted to Prussian
citizenship, mastered the German language, and acquired a
"Prussian character," Frederick was happy to accept their services.
Shortly after the partition he instructed Kammerpräsident von
Domhardt to employ Polish-speaking officials, which meant German-
speaking Poles, wherever possible in the new province.[36]

Between 1772 and 1806, the West Prussian estate-owning
class changed radically. In 1772 only 13 percent of the noble
families of Pomerelia, the heartland of Royal Prussia, were unquestionably German in language. But after the turn of the
nineteenth century the statistician Holsche counted 161 German
and 353 Polish estates in the larger, but still mainly old-
Polish area of the province of West Prussia. The market value
of the German estates exceeded that of the Polish.[37] Between
1763 and 1806, the export grain trade was increasingly favorable
for Brandenburg-Prussian landlords. This was true after 1772 in
West Prussia as well. A flurry of speculation in estates and
a spurt of technical and financial innovations occurred in these
years, accompanied by increased exploitation of serf labor and
the rise and fall of gentry families. At the same time, many
szlachta families liquidated their holdings and moved, for
political and cultural reasons, to the old Commonwealth. Others
failed to adjust economically to the new conditions and fell
into bankruptcy. Still others, particularly after Frederick's
successor granted the West Prussian nobility a mortgage credit
society (Landschaft) in 1787, came to terms with their new overlords and profited from the grain trade until the imposition of
the Continental Blockade in 1807. Simultaneously, German Junkers
and domain lessees moved into West Prussia and carved out a position of economic strength equal if not superior to that of the
szlachta. Undoubtedly the most anti-Prussian of the Polish
nobility left the province before the 1790s, since support for
Kościuszko's uprising against the partitioning powers in 1794 and
for the Polish breakaway from Prussia in 1806-7 was notably weak in
West Prussia. The stifling of the szlachta's political autonomy
under Prussian absolutism, the emigration of some Polish nobles,

and the assimilation into Prussian public life of others, together
with the introduction into the estate-owning ranks of a large
German element greatly weakened the Polish character of West Prussia even before 1815. This accomplishment of the Frederickian
system was not lost on the Prussian government in its confrontation
with the Polish nobility in other parts of the state after the
second and third partitions and indeed throughout the nineteenth
century.[38]

While Frederick was inclined to dismiss the szlachta as the
corrupted victims of their own political and social traditions, he
betrayed his debt to the Enlightenment in his condescending belief
that the Polish common people could become "human beings and useful
members of the state."[39] But he had no high opinion of them as he
found them. Even at the end of his reign, in an interview with
West Prussian Regierungspräsident von Schrötter, he showed himself
"extremely prejudiced" against both the Polish nobility and common
people, saying of the latter that they consisted mostly of "ordinary thieves and criminals."[40]

Despite his misanthropic cholers, which he vented by no means
only against the West Prussians, Frederick had a plan to change the
character of the Polish commoners. On the one hand, the serfs
needed release from the "hard Polish footing," from their "Polish
slavery." Access to royal courts, written limitations of labor
and other dues, and gradual abolition of serfdom itself were the
measures he envisaged, though failed to realize fully in his reign.
But as things stood in 1772, he did not believe that the "inhabitants of the Polish nation will understand and appreciate the bles-
sings intended by the abolition of personal serfdom (Leibeigen-
schaft)." He went on to reveal his solution to this dilemma:
"The surest way to impart to these slavish people better ideas and
morals will always be to mix them gradually with Germans (mit der
Zeit mit Teutsche[n] zu meliren), even if in the beginning only two
or three to a village."[41]

Here Hohenzollern tradition dovetailed with the problem of assimilating the Poles into the Prussian state. Frederick's forebears had pursued a policy of "populating" (Peuplierung) their
lands with foreign colonists, whether non-Prussian Germans or such
refugees as the French Huguenots. Now Frederick proposed to "populate" West Prussia, but with "Protestant people," with German
farmers who, by the example of their industriousness and prosperity,
would help the Polish "common man to acquire a Prussian character,"
as would also the "German schoolmaster" whom Frederick wanted to
settle in every village and small town. Nor was this mere talk.

Frederick committed sizable funds towards the recruitment of
German peasant colonists, particularly in land-hungry South Germany.
During his reign he settled as free farmers, well-endowed with
land, over 3,200 families in his Polish province. Smaller numbers of artisan-colonists migrated to the West Prussian frontier
and many schoolteachers settled there as well, though not in
every town and village.[42]

Frederick's interest in "German schoolmasters" was free of
any intent to Germanize the Poles linguistically. He recognized
that "Catholic-Polish schoolmasters" would be needed in many areas
and instructed the Bishop of Ermland to train them.[43] But he
demanded that, both in the teaching ranks and among the clergy,
all native Polish speakers know German and that Polish pupils
learn the rudiments of German. In fact this result was rarely
achieved in formal instruction because of the infrequency of
school attendance in the eighteenth century, the paucity of schools,
and the incompetence of many teachers. It is true that Frederick
had no respect for Polish culture, denying that it had ever produced a literature worthy of the name.[44] But he leveled similar
charges against German literature, and assumed, for his own part,
that the language of a cultured man was French. German he accepted as the unavoidable medium of communication--not only, as
he once said disparagingly, with his horse, but in Prussian government and public life generally. Hence the Poles would have to
learn it. What they did with their own language seems to have been
a matter of utter indifference to him, although he recognized that
Polish children would have to be instructed at the elementary level
in their native tongue.

Frederick's policy of mingling the Poles with Germans, like
his settlement of German estate-owners in West Prussia, sprang
not from nationalist convictions but from the desire to impress
upon the "slavish" Poles a "Prussian character." This depended
less on language than on political allegiance and obedience, and
on productive, thrifty, and enlightened behavior in private life.
Frederick attached no significance to the mere fact of German
or Polish ethnic-linguistic identity. He would have well understood the query of the Austrian Emperor Francis I when informed
that one of his subjects was a patriot: "But is he a patriot for
me?" Nevertheless, in his conviction that the Poles in West
Prussia would become more "human" by assimilation into Prussian-
German social and political life, he dismissed the cultural and
political distinctiveness of the Poles and set a goal of Prussianization, though not linguistic Germanization, which strongly influenced future generations of Prussian statesmen.

In the first partition, Prussia acquired for the first time a relatively large and socially variegated Jewish population. The attitudes which informed Frederick II's policies towards the West Prussian Jews, like his attitudes towards the Poles, shone in his reflected glory long after the end of his reign.

Martin Luther bequeathed to his religious followers a hostility toward the Jews which, although essentially determined by the Jews' unwillingness to convert to Christianity, was also strongly colored by medieval agrarian hatred of "usurious" and "parasitical" urban merchants and financiers. Although few of his followers in the period before the French Revolution attacked the Jews as fiercely as Luther himself had done, most Protestant states in Germany strove to limit to a minimum the number of Jews they tolerated within their borders, whence the Jewish migrations of the sixteenth and seventeenth centuries to Poland. The Jews who remained in Germany comprised a decentralized constellation of more or less inconspicuous communities of "privileged" townspeople, many trading their financial and business expertise for the not always reliable protection of local princes.[45]

Although they had converted to Calvinism in the early seventeenth century, the Hohenzollern princes of Brandenburg-Prussia respected and upheld the Lutheranism of their subjects. In his efforts to "populate" and develop his lands, the Great Elector allowed the settlement in Berlin in 1671 of fifty families of "protected Jews" (Schutzjuden), but the edict he issued on this occasion bore as part of its title the words "on condition that they maintain no synagogues."[46] Thereafter other Jews were granted protection within the Prussian state, but on onerous financial terms and only with the most grudging acceptance of their religious practices. In 1750, Frederick II issued a "General Jewish Regulation" which defined the Jews' status in Prussia in principle until the issuance of the Edict of Emancipation of 1812. Frederick's legislation distinguished between "regular" and "extraordinary" Jews, according to their wealth and utility to the regime. "Regular" Jews could pass their status on to one or, sometimes, to two or three sons; "extraordinary" Jews were subject to expulsion from the state at a moment's notice and could guarantee their offspring nothing more in the way of civil rights.[47] In the eighteenth century, only the poorest Jews needed to feel insecure in their residence in Brandenburg-Prussia, but neither Frederick's predecessors, nor the enlightened absolutist himself, made any efforts to counteract the hostility of Protestant

tradition towards the Jewish religion. Indeed, the Prussian
government lent its imprimatur to the publication in 1711 of
Johann A. Eisenmenger's virulent book, Entdecktes Judenthum (Jewry
Uncovered), a basic source for the literature of eighteenth and
nineteenth century anti-Semitism.[48] Frederick himself, as is well
known, "shared with Voltaire an enlightened contempt for [the Jews']
'religious superstitions', for their irrational ceremonial laws,
and for their orthodox rabbis." In this attitude, he had fallen
behind the sympathies of his own progressive intelligentsia, who
in 1771 elected Moses Mendelssohn to membership in the Prussian
Academy of Sciences, only to have their royal patron refuse the
enlightened but pious Jew admission to that particular commune of
the republic of letters.[49]

Like his forebears, Frederick tolerated the Jews strictly
for their utility to his kingdom. They served as partners, not
always willingly, in some of his mercantilistic ventures; they
assisted the royal treasury, sometimes in none too honorable roles,
as in the flooding of western Poland with money counterfeited in
Berlin during the Seven Years War; and they handled a sizable proportion of the kingdom's wholesale trade and a major share of its
trade with Poland and the east. Frederick had no wish to see them
occupied in agriculture or the artisan trades, if only because
they refused military service and excited jealousy and turbulence
among the Christian population when engaged in direct competition
with them.

No wonder, then, that when Frederick learned of the existence
of some 25,000 Jews in his new Polish province, most of them
living meagerly as peddlers, artisans, and petty merchants, he unhesitatingly ordered Oberpräsident von Domhardt that "the impoverished Jews (Bettel-Juden) in the countryside as well as the
towns must be gotten rid of, one by one and without violence, [but]
the well-to-do commercial Jews . . . will be kept and engaged in
the trade with Poland."[50] As it turned out, many of West Prussia's
"Bettel-Juden" were vital to the local economy and could not easily
be replaced by Christians, so that despite Frederick's instructions,
by the time of his death only about 7,000 Jews had been driven
across the border into what remained of Poland. This was a
highly unsatisfactory state of affairs in Frederick's view. He
aimed at reducing the Jewish population in West Prussia to 2,000,
replacing what he habitually called the "Jewish ragtag" (Judenkrop)
with Christians from his western and central provinces.[51] In his
mass expulsion of poorer Jews--the first systematic expulsion
of any group from Prussia since the sixteenth century--and in his
harsh estimation of the Jews' social utility at a time when the

first Christian voices were being raised in favor of Jewish emancipation, Frederick reinforced traditions of anti-Semitism and provided by his own example a justification for anti-Jewish policies
to his conservative successors in the Prussian government during
the nineteenth century.

Prussia and the Second and Third Partitions of Poland

From the mid seventeenth century to the era of the French
Revolution, the balance of power in Central and Eastern Europe
shifted in favor of Russia, Austria, and Prussia at the expense
of Sweden, Turkey, and Poland. The collapse of Swedish power in
the Northern War of 1700-1721 made Prussia and Russia dominant in
the Baltic region. Equally important, it released Russian energy
for an assault on Turkey's Black Sea position shortly after
Austria's reconquest of Hungary (1699) placed the Turks on the
defensive in the Balkans. It seemed, in the mid eighteenth century, absolutely ineluctable that Russia and Austria would hammer
away at the Ottomans until one or the other had reached the
Bosporus. But what of Poland? In 1717 Russia wrung from the
Polish parliament a limitation of the Polish army to 24,000 men.
Henceforth there could be no talk of Poland as a great power. Instead, it seemed that the Commonwealth would fall intact into an
ever greater dependency on its mighty Russian neighbor. That it
did not, and that it vanished instead from the map of independent
states long before Ottoman Turkey collapsed, was the result not
so much of Prussia's and Russia's specific territorial claims to
Polish lands as of the nature of the rivalries which separated the
three absolute states surrounding Poland. Austria's and Russia's
maximal claims against the Turks were inherently conflicting.
Balkan gains for either power were, however, threats to Prussia's
relative strength. Given Austro-Prussian rivalry within the Holy
Roman Empire, neither German state could be indifferent to the
advantages of a Russian alliance. In this way, each of the three
states was dependent on the other two. In the interlocking Polish
and Turkish crises of 1768-72/74, the easiest way of reconciling
Russia's gains at the Turks' expense with the German powers' insistence on equivalent accretions of strength was through the first
partition of Poland, particularly since Poland's hostility to
Russia demonstrated its marginal value to Catherine as she sought
to roll back the Turks on her southern frontier. Better, from the
point of view of Petersburg, direct annexation and exploitation of
Polish lands to which, in any case, Russia laid traditional claims.
If Frederick gained in that transaction, Catherine could console

herself with the reflection that this injured Austrian interests
more than her own.

   Poland survived the first partition and found itself after
1772 much more firmly under Russian control than before. There was
no reason to suppose that in a few decades the Commonwealth would
be "hacked to pieces in the diplomatic slaughterhouse."[52] Why this
in fact occurred has been explained with great insight and
lucidity.[53] Here it is necessary only to recall the main outlines
of the second and third partitions, focusing especially on the
part Prussia played in them.

   In the 1780s Russia renewed its offensive against the Turks,
this time in an alliance with Austria which left Prussia in the
diplomatic cold. Catherine's involvement in war against the Ottomans inspired the progressive party among the Polish nobility,
stung by the first partition and by Russian overlordship, and
driven by a desire to reform and strengthen the Commonwealth, to
attempt a breakaway from Russian control. This occurred in the
convocation of the Four Years Diet in 1788. Its labors culminated
in the Polish constitution of 3 May 1791, a socially conservative
but politically progressive renovation of the Polish parliamentary
system within the framework of a projected hereditary, limited
monarchy. The diet approved a considerably strengthened standing
army, but disaster befell the Poles before it could be mustered
and equipped.

   Surprisingly enough, Prussia encouraged the Polish reformers
in their defiance of the Russians. Fearful of Austrian gains in
the Balkans and revisionist démarches in Germany, Frederick William
II and his ministers tried to fashion a front, including Poland,
Sweden, and England, to pressure Russia and Austria out of their
hostilities with the Turks and to restore peace on terms favorable
to Prussia in Germany. Moreover, Prussia hoped unrealistically
that in return for its Polish alliance, formally sealed in 1790,
Warsaw could be brought to hand over Danzig, Thorn, and part of
Great Poland. The Poles pressed forward in their reform program,
counting on Prussian backing on the inevitable day of reckoning
with the already enraged Catherine.

   The fate of the Poles was sealed, although they did not know
it, in 1790 when, after the formation of the Prusso-Polish alliance, Prussia forced Austria to withdraw from the Turkish
campaign. This was an unfortunate necessity from Viennna's vantage
point, dictated by internal unrest in the Hapsburg state and by
the problems raised in the west by the French Revolution. In 1792,
Russia emerged victorious from the Turkish war and in short order
contrived a Polish conservative opposition to the new constitution

which served as a pretext for Russian intervention in the Commonwealth. In a dramatic moment, the deputy of the Polish Diet, Ignacy
Potocki, appealed to Prussia to activate its alliance and assist
the Commonwealth in repulsing the advancing Russians. The Prussian
government refused in an egregious display of perfidy. Instead,
Frederick William II joined Catherine in overturning the constitution of 3 May 1791 and seizing the spoils of the second partition
of 1793, by which Prussia acquired Danzig, Thorn, and the voivodeships of Poznań and Kalisz.

Catherine, bent on a massive annexation of Polish lands, needed
one German partner to secure her gains, and this was the more than
willing Prussian state. Austria, tied down in war with France, was
fobbed off with promises of annexations in South Germany. In
Poland, the second partition inspired a last-ditch rebellion, led
by Tadeusz Kościuszko in 1794, to annul the fatal diminution
of the Commonwealth by defeating Russia and Prussia in the field.
Although Russia could have crushed Kościuszko alone, Prussia pulled
a major segment of its troops away from the anti-French front and
ultimately withdrew altogether from the coalition against France in
order to intervene in Poland and stake out a share of the third
partition in 1795, in which it finally received Warsaw and Mazovia
stretching northeast along the East Prussian border. This was
finis Poloniae. In the secret Petersburg convention of 1797, the
three partitioning powers agreed that the name "Poland" would
not be applied to the lands they had torn from the defunct Commonwealth.

After 1795, the Prussian state, thanks to Frederick William
II's unreflective but robust territorial appetite, had a vastly
different character from Frederick's realm. Half its extent consisted of annexed Polish lands, almost half its population of
recent subjects of the Polish king deposed in humiliation by the
same monarchs who fought the French to restore Louis XVI to his
ancient rights. And instead of "anarchical" Polish noblemen on
the other side of their eastern frontiers, the Prussians after
1795 had to accustom themselves to the presence, unnerving from a
German point of view, of Cossack legions.

Conservative Prussian historians, following the reasoning of
Heinrich von Sybel, have held that Prussia's participation in the
destruction of the Polish Commonwealth was a "question of power and
necessity," since annexation of Polish territories was preferable
to Russian domination of the whole of post-1772 Poland. Yet the
elimination of the Polish buffer between Russia and Germany allowed
the Tsarist Empire to exert an unparalleled influence over German
affairs in the period 1795-1856. Russia gained far more from the

second and third partitions than either Prussia or Austria or the
two German powers combined, as young Heinrich von Boyen, the
future Prussian military reformer, realized in 1794-95.[54]   This
fact alone calls into question the wisdom and necessity of Prussia's eager defection to Catherine's side in 1792. But before the
epoch of reforms associated with the Four Years Diet, Prussian
statesmen, formed in the Frederickian mold, had no faith in Poland
as a useful ally. And when, with the promulgation of the constitution of 3 May 1791, it appeared that Poland was beginning to shake
off Russian influence and renovate itself as a state, these same
statesmen privately expressed their apprehension even as they
publicly cheered on their allies in Warsaw. Foreign Minister
Count Ewald von Hertzberg praised the Polish reforms in an address
to the Academy of Sciences in Berlin, but wrote to the Prussian
ambassador in Warsaw:

> The Poles have delivered a mortal blow to the Prussian
> monarchy, creating a hereditary monarchy and bestowing
> upon themselves a constitution better than the English.
> . . . I suspect that because of this Poland will be-
> come dangerous to Prussia and sooner or later will wrest
> from us West Prussia, perhaps even also East Prussia.
> How are we to defend our state, open from Memel to
> Goschen [i.e., along its entire eastern border], against
> a numerous and well-governed nation?

Confronting this possibility, dangerous to Prussia in reality only
because of Frederick's participation in the first partition,
Hertzberg and Frederick William II opted for erasure of the
renascent Commonwealth from the map in league with Catherine.
General Field Marshal von Moellendorff, who commanded the occupation of South Prussia in 1793, later told a British diplomat that
"his country--and on this point every Prussian regardless of his
political leanings agrees--can never tolerate the establishment in
Poland of a good government."[55]

There was an ideological dimension to the Prussian government's defection from the Poles after 1791. Following the death
of Frederick the Great, the question of the further evolution of
the system of enlightened absolutism became increasingly acute,
not so much on account of the personal deficiencies of the soldier-
king's successors but rather because autocratic government was becoming impracticable on a rational basis as the complexity and
scope of the Prussian system increased. In the high civil bureaucracy, a movement towards limitation of the royal will in favor of
the "constitutionally" guaranteed rights of ministerial officials
represented a first stage in the conversion of the absolute monarchy into a "state of law" (Rechtsstaat) in which at least the
educated and propertied classes could exercise political rights

independent of, and if necessary in opposition to, the king. In
the 1780s and 1790s, this political issue crystallized around the
publication of the General Law Code (Allgemeines Landrecht), but
the outbreak of the French Revolution opened Prussian eyes to the
ramifications of a challenge to royal absolutism. Before 1806,
both Frederick William II and Frederick William III (1797-1840)
stuck to a conservative position, which meant that they opposed
any changes in the Frederickian constitution. It took the defeats
of Jena and Auerstedt in 1806 to open the gates to major social and
political reforms, carried out by the ministerial bureaucracy, in
Prussia.[56]

The political reforms of the Four Years Diet in Poland and the
ideological ferment accompanying them among the Polish nobility and
intelligentsia alarmed Frederick William II and his like-minded
advisers. Despite Prussian support for the Poles' reform efforts
since 1788, when Frederick William II ordered his troops into
Great Poland on the eve of the second partition he issued a public
proclamation justifying his decision on conservative ideological
grounds which were fundamentally genuine:

> The most earnest concern of the king and of [Poland's]
> neighboring Powers is aroused by the spread of French
> Democracy and the principles of that abominable faction,
> which prosyletizes everywhere and in Poland has already
> found so much access that not only are the projects of
> Jacobin emmissaries supported to the hilt, but revolu-
> tionary societies are formed which proclaim their program
> openly.
> Above all, Great Poland is infected with this dangerous
> poison and counts the greatest number of eager adherents
> of a misunderstood love of their country. Their connec-
> tions with French clubs must inspire a justifiable mis-
> trust in the king on account of the security of his own
> states. They impose on him the necessity of taking ef-
> fective countermeasures.[57]

Polish "Jacobinism" and "misunderstood love of country" flared up
even more prominently during Kościuszko's uprising of 1794. After
assisting the Russians in crushing this movement, after occupying
the lands of the third partition, and after having withdrawn from
hostilities on the western front, a feeling of relief swept the
Prussian court at having escaped a political and military situation
fraught with danger on all sides. Karl von Hoym, minister both of
Silesia, where peasant and artisan protests were serious in the
early 1790s, and of South Prussia, the scene of prolonged guerilla
fighting during Kościuszko's rising, wrote Frederick William II
after the conclusion of the peace of Basel of 1795, praising him
for having concluded "an honorable peace and thereby forestalled
in timely fashion any outbreak of unrest in the provinces."[58]
Undoubtedly, Prussia's participation in the final partitions of

Poland was one instance of a more general effort to defend the
Frederickian old regime against the novel socioeconomic, political,
and international menaces confronting it. But although the partitions destroyed the Polish Commonwealth, they did not stave off
the collapse of traditional Prussia in 1806. On the contrary, the
strains the military and civil administration of South and New East
Prussia placed on the Prussian state weakened its international
maneuverability and left it all the more vulnerable to Napoleonic
domination.[59]

Prussian Rule in South and New East Prussia, 1793-1806

At the time of the final partitions, Prussia's rulers had
no notion of the catastrophe they would suffer in 1806. Instead,
they took pride in their new acquisitions and, confidently anchored
in Frederickian traditions, began with determination to put the
new Polish provinces "on a Prussian footing." General Moellendorff congratulated the king on having won South Prussia: "no acquisition has been made in the past of such importance, rounding
out, consolidating, and lending as it does a true solidity to the
Prussian monarchy."[60] The king himself, touring the province,
wrote his son that "the new land . . . has some fine parts, but it
has been much neglected by bad cultivation and Polish economy
(economie Polonèse [sic])." The spirit in which the Prussian administrators approached South Prussia, where, as the king wrote,
"everything is 100 percent Polish (Stok-Polnisch)," pervaded a
report of the ministers von Voss and von Danckelman to the Crown
of December 1793. It expressed the enlightened authoritarianism,
the condescension towards the Poles, and the high regard for their
own mission characteristic of the late eighteenth-century Prussian
bureaucracy:

> The reasons for the previous decay of the province and
> the deterioration of its agriculture and industry lie
> in part in antiquated prejudices and profound ignorance
> linked with indolence; in part in the oppression of the
> common people and their attendant poverty; and in part
> also in the mistrustful, stubborn, and lackadaisical
> character of the nation as a whole. These basic flaws
> cannot be eradicated by even the most benevolent and
> salutary suggestions and decrees of the civil authorities
> as long as the nation, ignorant of the happiness a govern-
> ment seeking their general good prepares for them and
> for centuries unused to any sort of good order, misinter-
> prets the most honorable intentions and sees the most
> beneficial decrees in a false light. Consequently, they
> will have to be led toward their own good by compulsory
> laws. Thus we find it necessary to draft numerous police
> regulations. . . .[61]

Arduous though the task might be, the Prussians were determined to recast their extensive new Polish acquisitions in the

Map 2.--The partitions of Poland.

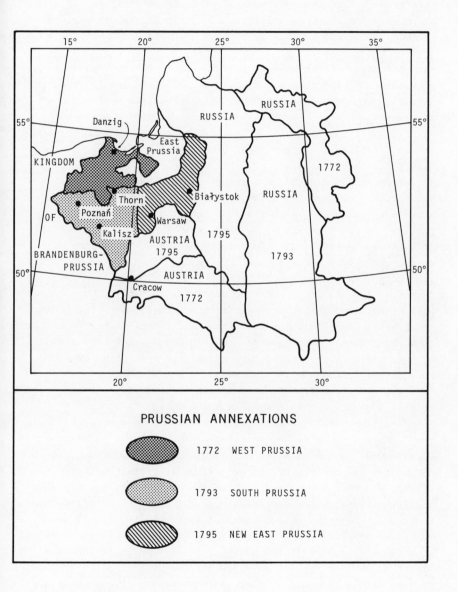

mold of enlightened absolutism. In a formal sense, they were re-
markably successful in this in the years before the Peace of
Tilsit (1807) annulled Prussian sovereignty over South and New
East Prussia. The cumbersome apparatus of the Prussian civil
administration, police, military, and judicial systems was erected
in short order and by 1806 functioned just about as well as in the
rest of the monarchy. Some improvements and innovations in traditional Prussian practice were carried out in the new Polish
provinces. Polish common law was superseded, except for the rights
of the gentry over the peasantry, by the provisions of the
Allgemeines Landrecht in its revised form of 1794. After some
hesitations, in 1795-96 former Polish Crown lands and the estates
of the Catholic church were confiscated with compensation and converted into state domains. The tax system of the vanished Commonwealth remained, but the levies on the szlachta rose. The Prussian government considered the Polish form of serfdom the harshest
prevalent within its boundaries and abolished whatever legal
vestiges seemed to smack of slavery, notably sale and transfer
of serfs among landlords. Some improvements in the status of
domain serfs were made as well, but on the whole the traditional
landlord-peasant relationship remained intact. Little state-
directed economic development occurred. Access of South and New
East Prussian merchants and manufacturers to the markets of the
old Prussian provinces was restricted until 1806 in order to shield
them from cheaper Polish goods. But in the crucial agricultural
sphere, grain exports through Danzig to the west were permitted
soon after 1795, and szlachta landlords profited considerably
from their release from Frederickian customs duties in the decade
of rising grain prices in Western Europe prior to 1806.[62]

Staffing the new Polish provinces with German officials over-
taxed the resources of the Prussian state. Numerous complaints
were lodged, even within the administrative system, about the lack
of ability and efficiency, the venality, rudeness, and "despotism"
of many who wore the king's coat in the east. Even the Minister
for South Prussia, Karl von Hoym, was tainted with scandal after
selling estates confiscated from Polish rebels in 1794-95 to his
favorites at bargain prices. This was the inauspicious beginning
of a pattern that persisted until 1918: service in the Polish
provinces was distasteful to Prussian officials, chiefly because
of the lower standard of living and the absence of a congenially
German atmosphere. The bureaucrats of a higher caliber sought,
usually with success, to avoid transfer there, while assignment
to the Polish east was a kind of punishment for incompetent of-

ficials. Even before 1806, contemporaries spoke of South Prussia
as the "Botany Bay of Prussian officialdom."[63] It followed that
disgruntled Prussian officials sometimes took their aggravation at
service in the east out on the local population. Minister von
Schrötter complained to his subordinates in New East Prussia in
1797 that among them were some who were guilty, in their dealings
with the Poles, of "the most disrespectful expressions and gross
behavior."[64] A year later, the new king, Frederick William III,
blamed his lower officials in the Polish areas for undermining the
population's respect for the Prussian state: "it is almost a proverb among them that the erstwhile Pole can only be ruled by the
whip, but I am convinced that the South and New East Prussians are
a good-natured and compliant people who do not deserve such treatment."[65]

If the Prussian government sought to integrate its new Polish
provinces as firmly as possible into the structure of the absolute state, this was a reflection of the historic drive of the
Hohenzollern rulers to weld their lands into an administratively
and judicially centralized whole. It did not mean that the Prussian government was indifferent to the problem of gaining the
acquiescence of its formerly Polish subjects to Prussian rule. The
extent of the new annexations and the great numbers of the Polish
and Jewish populations ruled out the high-handed attitudes of
Frederick the Great towards West Prussia. After 1793, it was
impossible to "get rid of the Polish stuff" or the "Jewish ragtag."
The acquisition of a large non-German population was the price of
the territorial expansion won in the final partitions. The
psychological assimilation of this population was an unavoidable
problem of first-rate importance to the Prussian state.

The traditional negative image of Poland and its inhabitants
harbored by Prussia's rulers complicated this. It would be
redundant to illustrate this attitude during the period 1786-1806.
It is enough to say that disdain for Polish ways and a strong
conviction of the superiority of Prussian-German civilization were
fundamental attitudes still shared very widely among the educated,
noble, military, and bureaucratic classes of Prussian society.[66]

Yet in the two decades after the death of Frederick II, a new
dimension to the Prussian and German conception of Poland and the
Poles emerged. Above all, the reforms of the Four Years Diet,
particularly the constitution of 3 May 1791, together with
Kościuszko's heroic attempt to ward off the destruction of the
Commonwealth, impressed the German political and intellectual
classes. They began to concede qualities of enlightenment,

patriotism, and a capacity for self-improvement to the Poles
which they had denied or belittled in the past. Since 1772, the
politically hamstrung but genial Polish king, Stanisław Augustus,
had become a rather popular figure in Germany, as had also the
talented Polish writer, Ignacy Krasiński. In the figure of
Kościuszko, however, liberal-minded Germans perceived a spirit of
political idealism which contrasted with the cynical and reactionary engagement of their own states in the final partitions and
the struggle against the French Revolution. Kościuszko became the
most celebrated Pole in German eyes since Jan Sobieski's relief
of Vienna from the Turkish siege of 1683. Although the Prussian
government suppressed the publication of an engraving of the
Polish leader in the influential Enlightenment journal, the
Berliner Monatsschrift, such portraits were widely sold throughout
Germany after the outbreak of the 1794 revolt.[67] The Polish
constitution of 1791, with its balancing of the principles of
popular sovereignty, aristocracy, and hereditary monarchy, had a
natural appeal to the moderately liberal and moderately conservative majority among politically minded Germans of the pre-1806
years. The Polish reforms appeared far more praiseworthy in German
eyes than the work of the French Jacobins.[68]

    As a result of these attitudes, there was little enthusiasm
among German political writers and intellectuals for the second
and third partitions, which they interpreted as the deplorable
outcome of an unprincipled power politics at the expense of a
state attempting to revive itself. Already in 1787, Johann
Gottfried Herder, a harsh critic of the "soulless machinery" of
eighteenth-century absolutism, diplomacy, and war, published in
his Ideen zur Philosophie der Geschichte der Menschheit his famous
and influential accolade to the peaceful and democratic qualities
of the Slavic peoples, together with the prediction that one day
they would escape foreign oppression and find an honorable and
autonomous political reorganization.[69] Herder's friend Kant, in
his essay "Eternal Peace," obliquely condemned the partitions.[70]
The very influential August Ludwig von Schlözer, editor of the
Göttinger Gelehrte Anzeigen, "posed the indignant question of how
the deeds of violence of the powers [against Poland] differed from
the atrocities of the Convention."[71] The widely read South German
publicist A. G. F. von Rebmann wrote of Prussian policy towards
Poland in the period 1788-93 that "a tyrant [Frederick William II]
incites the citizen of this land to war against another tyrant
[Catherine II], promises support, and then murders his own ally.
That's called--statesmanship."[72] In the aftermath of the third
partition, the first romanticization of Poland and Polish national-

ism appeared in German high literature, notably in the now-
forgotten poetry of Zacharias Werner, a Prussian official stationed
in South Prussia (1796-1805). Werner apostrophized Kościuszko's
virtues and foretold the inevitable rebirth of the Polish state,
establishing a genre of literary philopolonism in Germany which
reached a peak in the 1830s and 1840s.[73]

Despite their traditional anti-Polish biases, Prussian officials were not unaffected, in their policy towards South and New
East Prussia in the period 1793-1806, by the new and more favorable
currents of German opinion about Poland. They sensed what the
Poles had lost in the collapse of the Commonwealth. The Prussian
envoy in Warsaw, Buchholtz, calumniated the Poles in time-honored
fashion, yet admitted that the second partition must be "odious and
humiliating" to them.[74] South Prussian Minister von Voss wrote in
1800 that the "painful feelings" of the Polish nobility and clergy
should not be held against them. "What sort of loyalty and attachment to our own constitution could we expect of the progeny of a
nation which, without any feeling of commitment, forgot its previous constitution in an instant?"[75] Prussia could only strive to
win the loyalty of the rising generations of its Polish population
while conferring on the elders as many freedoms as possible.
Voss's predecessor, von Hoym, admitted that a certain Polish "national hatred" towards the Germans existed which Prussia should
strive to convert into "love and trust."[76] On numerous occasions
Prussia's governors spoke among themselves of the virtues,
political trustworthiness, and susceptibility to improvement of
the Polish common people.

Not Frederickian contempt, but rather a patronizing, conservative-minded conciliatoriness in an age of Jacobinism and
Bonapartism set the tone for the Prussians' efforts to secure their
new subjects' loyalty. The royal patent which officially announced Prussia's annexation of Great Poland and the cities of
Danzig and Thorn in 1793 loftily blamed the Poles, with their
"light-hearted" impulses towards political anarchy and Jacobinism,
for Catherine's and Frederick William II's invasion of their land.
But it also solemnly guaranteed the Poles' religious and material
privileges, following word for word Frederick II's patent of
1772.[77] Lavish banquets were staged to woo the Polish gentry
and aristocracy into social relations with Prussian officialdom.
Among the 1,500 guests at the Poznań festivities was the Prussian
king, who danced a polonaise with the Countess Chłapowska.[78]

There was widespread agreement within the government that
German-speaking Polish nobles ought to serve in the army and civil

administration, particularly as <u>Landräte</u>. This had the double
advantage of teaching the Polish gentry "order and obedience" while
enlisting their authority over the common people in support of
the Prussian state. A certain number of Poles did assist in the
administration of the new provinces, especially the Protestant
gentry. But lack of knowledge of Prussian law and institutions,
together with widespread ignorance of German and hostility towards
the new dispensation, held most of the Polish landlords aloof from
collaboration with their German governors.[79] A Cadet Academy
in Kalisz and a special light cavalry corps were created to win
over the politically turbulent landless Polish nobility, but
these institutions touched only a fragment of that numerous class.[80]
In the economic sphere, Minister von Hoym acknowledged the integra-
tive effect the establishment of state mortgage credit banks
would have, but none were created before 1806, primarily because
the Prussian state's finances were strained in the decade before
Jena and Auerstedt.[81] A bow in the direction of Polish culture was
made with the opening of the Warsaw Scientific Society in 1800,
but this was a disappointment to many of the Polish intelligentsia
because of its conservative and nonpolitical character.[82]

Although the Prussian government took over the management of
the estates of the Catholic church, it avidly sought to gain the
support of the clergy in the correct belief that they commanded
major influence over the Polish population's political loyalties.
Frederick William II ordered his officials to leave the system of
Catholic education intact and indeed to assist it in suppressing
"so-called Enlighteners who inspire democratic principles" in their
students.[83] But the Church's determination to maintain its administrative autonomy and iron control over education and marriage
policy greatly aggravated Prussia's enlightened Protestant officials. Hoym, longtime Minister for Silesia, told Voss in 1793
what he could expect in dealing with the Polish Catholic clergy:

> I have sown on this ungrateful soil for years and have
> harvested nothing but thistles. It is wholly in the
> monkish spirit to keep everything in an Egyptian dark-
> ness. All my simple efforts to make of the Polish Up-
> per Silesian clergy, schoolmasters, and children German-
> mannered people and to introduce new methods of instruc-
> tion have been frustrated by the upper clergy, who
> worked so long against them that I lost my determina-
> tion and strength.[84]

Hoym was not the last Prussian official to blunt his teeth on the
Catholic church, whose political and cultural autonomy in the
Polish areas constituted one of the Prussian government's knottiest
problems of <u>Polenpolitik</u> throughout the partition era.

Integration of the Poles demanded more than tying their noble

and clerical leaders to the state. At the deepest level, it was a
question of whether the Poles would divest themselves of their
traditional mentality and acquire a "Prussian character." To late
eighteenth-century Prussian officialdom, the national question was
essentially one of patriotism. What counted was neither language,
nor secular aesthetic or literary culture, nor religion, but rather
loyalty and devotion to the state. South Prussian Minister von
Voss argued to the king that to have retained the "Polish constitution" in the lands annexed in the final partitions would have
created a "state within a state" and encouraged the Poles to believe that they were still part of "the Polish nation."[85] Such a
state of affairs would have contradicted one of the strongest tendencies of Prussian history, which was the formation, by means of
"absolute" political centralization, of a unified whole from
originally widely disparate parts. Before the partitions, the
problem was one of integrating various German lands. After 1772,
and especially after 1793, it was compounded by the nationally
foreign character of the state's new subjects. In 1798 the leading ministers proposed a solution to this problem in a memorandum
to the king:

> To destroy the Polish language by fiat and compulsion
> has never been, and never can be, the object of the Prussian
> government. To wish to deprive a nation, even after it has
> ceased to exist politically, of its language means to seek
> to take from it its way of perceiving the world, its style
> of thought, its scientific and religious culture, however
> considerable or inconsiderable it may be. This is a co-
> ercion of conscience of the most painful sort, a completely
> impracticable idea which, were it attempted to carry it
> out, would produce infinitely harmful consequences. . . .But
> every true and ardent Prussian harbors the wish that his
> fellow subjects in West Prussia (where already so much has
> been done with such success to this end) and his new
> fellow subjects in South and New East Prussia will be bound
> ever more closely to the Prussian state through duty, loyalty,
> and love, and will cease to be Poles and become ever more
> true and genuine Prussians. This can be best promoted if
> at least the Prussian officials in those provinces willingly
> learn the Polish language while, so far as it is possible,
> every former Pole willingly learns the German language.
> Thus they may share among themselves their knowledge and
> their ideas. The Prussian will learn to know the land
> where he ought, and indeed wishes, to do good. And the
> former Poles will see in the Prussian no longer an unknown
> foreigner, towards whom he is suspicious, but his fellow
> subject and friend. Hence the Prussian government encour-
> ages and promotes the learning of Polish by its officials
> and is most happy indeed to see the former Pole learning
> German.

In the few years before its collapse in 1806, the Prussian
government failed to create the educational facilities for this
ambitious program of bilingualization. Despite royal and
ministerial edicts calling for the establishment of Polish language

teaching courses in Prussian universities and secondary schools,
nothing substantial was accomplished, presumably because of lack
of sufficient funds and acceptable bilingual instructors.
Nevertheless, the Prussian authorities sought out bilingual Germans
and Poles for service in the Polish provinces, where Polish and
German were both taught in the elementary schools and communication
with German officialdom and the courts in the Polish language was
permitted.[87]

The Prussian government made little progress in spreading a
knowledge of German among the Poles, again because of limited
time and funds. German language instruction was, however, introduced in preexisting Polish Catholic secondary schools. Poles
seeking university training for secondary teaching were restricted
to study at Prussian universities and hence to a German curriculum.
Such a policy, or so official reasoning supposed, would promote a
"growth of patriotism" and "further nationalization (Nationalisier-
ung)" in a sense favorable to Prussia.[88] In general, the Prussian
government underplayed Polish language study in secondary and
university education in favor of a more exclusive concentration
of study in German.[89]

Prussian educational policy raises the question whether, despite the generous phrases of the memorial on bilinguality of 1798,
there was not an underlying tendency towards Germanization in
Prussian Polenpolitik in the years 1793-1806.[90] The supposition
that this may have been the case seems to be strengthened by the
government's efforts to dispatch German farmers and artisans as
colonists to South and New East Prussia, even though far fewer
German pioneers settled on Polish soil in these years than in West
Prussia during Frederick II's reign.[91] Similarly, the sale of confiscated Polish estates to Prussians and the leasing of state
and church domains primarily to Germans hints at a policy of building up a local German landlord class to counterbalance the szlachta,
although no official programmatic statements with that intent have
been discovered.[92]

No doubt, the Prussian authorities sought a "transformation"
(Umbildung) of the Polish character along Prussian-German lines,
not only in a political, but also in a socioeconomic and cultural
sense. Ignorance of the German language, according to a report of
1794, impeded the formation of a "community (Gemeinschaft) among
the Polish and German inhabitants." But it was only through such
a community that "the vices, commoner among the Polish than the
German residents, of drunkenness, lack of industry, and a tendency
towards indolence and vagabondage can gradually become less widespread."[93] No doubt most Prussian officials believed, as Voss

wrote in 1796, that "unity of laws, customs, morals, benefits and
burdens, and, if possible, language forges the strongest national
bond among large populations."[94] Before 1806, it was generally
assumed in Germany, even by those who were critical of the partitions, that Polish independence was a thing of the past. Political
centralization, accompanied by the adoption of a single state
language, was a general European trend in the eighteenth and early
nineteenth centuries. Even had the Prussian government repudiated
its own powerful traditions of political integration, it could not
have created a semiautonomous Polish political region subordinated
to Berlin by a personal union symbolized in the Prussian king without having aroused the hostility of Austria and Russia.

Thus it was natural to strive towards the conversion of the
Poles into Prussians in the political sense of nationality congenial to the Prussian mind in the years before 1806. To be a
Prussian, whether as a nobleman, bureaucrat, intellectual, clergy-
man, burgher, or peasant, implied certain patterns of social and
economic behavior, a certain mentality not characteristic of
traditional Poland. It was natural for the Prussians to expect
their Polish subjects gradually to acquire in some degree those
characteristics and that mentality. To do so required some knowledge of the German language as an indispensible means of communication with the Prussian state and German society. The Prussians
did not suppose that the Polish language, Polish cultural traditions, or the positive dimensions of Polish social life would
perish through these processes of assimilation and adaptation. But
they did insist that the Poles locate their political identity in
the Prussian state.

Prussianization, however, is not Germanization. As an explicit official policy, Germanization should be defined as intensive settlement of Germans in Polish regions accompanied by
systematic and forceful efforts, justified in nationalist terms, to
undermine the Poles' cultural autonomy, economic strength, and
national consciousness. Not until after the collapse of the
Frederickian state did the possibility of such a course slowly
dawn on the Prussian government.

The Poles in South and New East Prussia

The reactions of the Poles to the fall of the Commonwealth
and their passage under the Prussian scepter in the years 1793-95
were complex and contradictory. The Prussian annexation of 1793
occurred in the face of no more Polish resistance than had that of
1772. The szlachta in Great Poland, deprived of any central

leadership by the Commonwealth government, were unprepared to act
on their own. Yet Moellendorff wrote the king from the field in
1793 that the Polish nobility, clergy, and burghers in South
Prussia were "refractory" and in many cases Jacobin-minded.[95] But
the second partition appeared to be a fait accompli, and the
Poles soon began adapting to their new circumstances. Some of the
magnates sold their estates and retired either to the rump Commonwealth or, lacking any faith in Poland's future, to Russian
Poland. Łukasz Bniński, who chose the latter course, said "I
would rather live freely under the broad skirts of the Russian
Tsarina than suffer in the tight breeches of the German Fritz."[96]
Most of the landed nobility turned their thoughts towards obtaining the best possible terms of existence within Prussia. In May
1793 they swore homage to Frederick William II in a great ceremony
in Poznań. One of their spokesmen, Ziemięcki, referring to their
oath of loyalty, declared that "this is indeed a great sacrifice,
for it is made by a nation which from time immemorial gave itself
its own laws, chose its own kings--nay, more: chose its own kings
from amongst its own ranks. This nation gives Thee, King, a most
precious jewel in sacrifice, with deep feeling and yet without a
murmur or any resistance whatever."[97] Later, after having received Frederick William II's promises to uphold their religion
and privileges, the South Prussian nobility submitted a petition
to the king reiterating their "unalterable loyalty" and humbly
requesting, among other things, that they be allowed to retain
their crown domain leases, that they be granted a mortgage credit
bank on the West Prussian model, that they trade freely with
Prussia's other provinces, that their sons be enrolled in cadet
schools, and that they be employed actively in the South Prussian
administration.[98] They promised that "our generation, for the most
part, and the next generation in its entirety will prepare itself
by a proper education in the use of the language of the land."[99]

No doubt the South Prussian gentry hoped to obtain far-
reaching autonomy and self-administration for their province, and
were disappointed when they failed to get it. Yet many served in
the Prussian bureaucracy "eagerly and energetically," as Voss
wrote the king in 1793, and stayed at their posts until 1806.
For many others, the years of high grain prices after 1795 were
remembered fondly as "the golden Prussian times." A flurry of
palace construction in Great Poland testified to the well-being of
many of the gentry in the decade before 1806.[100]

Other members of the szlachta found accommodation to Prussian
rule more difficult and galling. Patriotic verses circulated

covertly during 1793 bitterly denouncing the "treason" of the noble
leaders at the homagial ceremonies, where they had tamely bent
their necks to "the yoke of the west."[101] The tax increases and
economic disruptions accompanying the second partition, paired with
the loss of local legal, civil, and police functions, were serious
provocations to a great many members of the middle and lesser
gentry and to numerous Polish professionals and officials of noble
origins.[102]

Thus when, in March 1794, Kościuszko raised the banner of
revolt in Cracow, many of the South Prussian nobility were ready
to join in support. So too were some of the common people.
Kościuszko's promise to restore the constitution of 3 May offered
a better political future to the Polish bourgeoisie than did
Prussian absolutism. The Prussian government's increase of the
salt tax after the second partition, together with its puritanical
restrictions on card-playing and Sunday dancing in the taverns,
aggravated the petty bourgeoisie and rural population. Beyond
this, the Prussians' image in the average Pole's eyes was negative.
A Poznań district official wrote Minister Wöllner that the common
people in South Prussia thought of the Prussian kings as "harsh and
glowering warriors."[103] According to a Prussian army officer in
South Prussia, "even the people of lower race," having heard of
Kościuszko's rising, "reckon that in a month everything will be
different here."[104]

The 1794 rising occurred mainly in the land of the rump
Commonwealth, where Russian and Prussian troops besieged Warsaw and
battled Kościuszko in the field. But by September 1794, a contingent of South Prussian nobility had openly declared their support and begun engaging in sabotage and guerilla attacks on the
Prussian occupiers of the province. For some time, only the garrisoned towns were secure in Prussian hands, despite the promises
of the more conservative Polish noble Landräte and the clergy to
hold the common people in the countryside with them in loyalty to
Frederick William II. Although at the end of September 1794 Józef
Dąbrowski, Kościuszko's lieutenant, entered South Prussia with
6,000 men, he did not wish to risk his soldiers in a pitched
battle. When Russian forces began to grind down Kościuszko's
troops outside Warsaw, Dąbrowski withdrew. Soon thereafter the
rising was bloodily suppressed east of the Prussian borders.[105]

In South Prussia, perhaps several thousand persons had engaged in active resistance to Prussian rule. The leaders were
middle and lesser gentry, the mass of the followers were "barefoot"
nobles, peasants, and rural laborers. They were assisted in vari-

ous ways by sympathetic lower clergy and certain monasteries. In
the aftermath of the rising, it was difficult to identify all
the rebels. Yet 387 Poles, chiefly nobles, were arrested and
sentenced to a total of 300,000 Reichsthalers in fines, resulting
in the confiscation of many estates later distributed among the
friends of Minister von Hoym.[106]

Apart from these punishments, the Prussian government avoided
harshness in its policies towards its Polish provinces following
Kościuszko's defeat and the third partition. It pursued instead
the conciliatory approach--within Frederickian limits--described
above. The events of 1794 did not persuade the Prussians, nor did
they in fact prove, that a majority of the Polish gentry, bourgeoisie, or common people were actively or irreconcilably opposed
to Prussian citizenship. The Poles in West Prussia had stood almost entirely passive during Kościuszko's rising, indicating that
in time Prussia's policies of integration could perhaps also succeed in South and New East Prussia.[107]

The Poles demonstrated no further opposition to Prussian
rule before the state's collapse in 1806. It may be true, as
Michał Ogiński wrote after 1815 of the szlachta during the South
and New East Prussian period, that "having been reduced to a
condition of degrading inactivity and complete [political] nullity,
they only awaited the favorable moment when they could shake off
their bonds."[108] But while they may have looked to external
deliverance, particularly at Napoleon's hands, they were unwilling
to pursue a revolutionary policy of raising the Polish common
people in the towns and villages in a war of national liberation
by promises of political enfranchisement or, most important, full
abolition of serfdom. The dilemma of Polish nationalism was
evident at the moment of the fall of the old Commonwealth. To the
szlachta, the fulfillment of their national goals consisted in the
restoration of a Polish state in which they would enjoy substanti-
ally the same social and political preeminence as had fallen to
them before 1795. The masses of the Polish town population and
peasant serfs could not be moved to support the gentry in a rebellion against foreign rule on these terms. Hence, the Polish
nobility and noble-born intelligentsia had either to resign themselves to awaiting the restoration of the state in the aftermath
of a central European war or make the social and political sacrifices which might engage the common people in support of a szlachta-
led rebellion. Otherwise, the Polish upper classes had no choice
but to adapt themselves as best they could to foreign domination.
Not before the mid nineteenth century would economic and cultural

changes place the Polish bourgeoisie or working classes in a position to formulate a political program of their own. When that
moment arrived, it would be a crucial question whether they would
put the creation of a Polish national state before their grievances
against the nobility.[109]

The Germans and Jews in South and New East Prussia

In 1793-95, Prussia acquired not only masses of new Polish
subjects, but a major proportion of the Commonwealth's Germans and
Jews as well. Although it pained the patricians of Danzig to surrender their Polish privileges, in general the German burghers, and
especially those who were Protestants, welcomed their passage under
Prussian rule. They expected, reasonably enough, that a German
government would favor them in the distribution of urban offices
and pay more attention to their economic and religious interests
than had the Commonwealth authorities. They struck no nationalist
notes in their greetings of the new regime, but rather most sub-
missively praised Frederick William II in various festivals staged
in the towns of Great Poland. The burghers of Meseritz
(Międzyrzecz) hung a banner on their town gates through which the
Prussian king entered in 1793, announcing: "To our King--to our
Father. He has become Father and we will be his obedient children."[110] The reaction of the German Hauländer to Prussian rule in
Great Poland was to withold those dues and services to the
szlachta and Catholic clergy which they believed had been unjustly
imposed on them.

Although the Prussian government regarded the many Germans in
South Prussia and the few who lived in New East Prussia as valuable
subjects, it did not take any systematic pains to strengthen them
against either the Poles or the Jews. The state compelled the
Hauländer to continue paying the tithe to the Catholic clergy until
1806. The new regime upheld most of the rights of the Polish
gentry over their numerous patrimonial towns inhabited by many
German burghers. The petition of the merchants of Poznań requesting limitations on Jewish commercial and settlement rights, access
to the whole of the Prussian market, and state-funded credits was
not satisfied before 1806 on a single point. The German textile
industries of Great Poland suffered from inclusion in the Prussian
market and exclusion from the broad Polish and Russian hinterland.
Only in appointments to town offices and in the provincial administration did the government show favor to local Germans, but even
then bilinguality was a prime qualification which could be met by
Poles as well as Germans.[111]

The Jews also ceremonially welcomed their new Prussian overlords in South Prussia. In Meseritz they decorated their houses
and erected a gate of honor for the royal procession. In Poznań,
arrayed in what a Prussian writer called their "Turkish dress,"
they met the king on the outskirts of town. In the city, they
illuminated their ghetto and synagogue and staged a musical
concert ending in cries of "long live Frederick William."[112]

The Prussian government contemplated its multitudinous Jewish
population in the Polish provinces with mixed feelings. Some high
officials, like Bismarck's maternal grandfather, Mencken, expressed a strong Frederickian hostility towards the Jews. They
"injured" local commerce, he wrote, and "have the most negative
effect on the [Polish] national character"; their "disproportionate" numbers should therefore be decreased. Frederick William III
instructed Minister von Voss to restrict Jewish economic influence
in Warsaw and search for "indirect" means to persuade the Jews to
convert to Christianity.[113]

More widespread was the belief among the high Prussian
bureaucracy that the Jews were potentially useful citizens whose
status was in great need of reform. By the end of the eighteenth
century, the Jewish enlightenment movement, an intellectual, social,
and political revolt against insular Jewish traditionalism and
Christian prejudice, had won supporters among Prussian intellectuals and officials. A turning point was the publication in 1781
of Christian Wilhelm von Dohm's Über die bürgerliche Verbesserung
der Juden (On the Civil Improvement of the Jews). Dohm argued
that the Jews' poverty and pursuit of "unproductive" occupations
was a consequence of the traditional restrictions fastened upon
them. They ought to be allowed to engage freely in industry and
agriculture, to be released from discriminatory taxes, and to be
encouraged in social and intellectual intercourse with the
Christian population. The Jews' religion should not be viewed as
a reason for opposing their assimilation into Prussian society.[114]

The governors of South and New East Prussia agreed with the
notion of Jewish "improvement," but subordinated it characteristically to their Frederickian conception of raison d'état.
Minister von Hoym, who explicitly endorsed Dohm's work, urged that
the Jews be fully exposed to "all enlightenment," especially
through the creation of schools with "rational" teachers who could
teach them "proper religious ideas and make them useful to the
state as soldiers."[115] After lengthy consideration, a General
Jewish Regulation for South and New East Prussia appeared in 1797
which represented a compromise between Frederickian and reformist
ideas. On the one hand, it aimed at a reduction in the Jewish

population by the expulsion of all Jews not resident in the new
provinces at the time of the Prussian occupation. The remaining
"protected" Jews could not marry before the age of 25, and then
only if they had an established occupation or fortune. Exemption
from military service was granted only in exchange for the traditional tax. On the other hand, all occupations in commerce, the
artisan trades, industry, and agriculture were opened to the Jews,
with the exception of money-lending, itinerant commerce, and sale
of liquor on credit. Jews could now reside in any city and own
houses outside the traditional ghettos. Finally, their communal
responsibility in fiscal matters vanished, and in all civil and
criminal suits they became subject to the regular Prussian
courts.[116]

The South and New East Prussian Jews were conservative Polish
Jews and not entirely grateful for these innovations. They especially feared losing their communal legal privileges, fearing
reprisals in town courts from the Christian burghers. But they
found that Prussian justice was administered fairly. The Prussian
authorities turned a deaf ear to Christian complaints about
Jewish competition. In one instance, the Poznań Department
rejected an anti-Jewish petition filed by Christian artisans with
the observation that "if the Christian handworkers cannot sell at
the Jews' prices, the main reason is that they spend their morn-
ings in the groghouses and their afternoons in the beer halls."[117]
In 1803, a great fire destroyed the ghetto in Poznań. The
Christian magistrates urged the complete expulsion of Jews from the
city after this incident, but Minister von Voss archly rejected
the proposal in the name of "enlightenment and toleration."
Nevertheless the Jews clung to their traditional school system and
evaded or rejected all Prussian efforts to introduce "rational"
teachers and concepts. The confrontation with the German Jewish
reform movement lay in the future for the Polish Jews.[118]

Prussian Defeat and Polish Rebellion, 1806-7
On 14 October 1806 Napoleon routed the main body of the
Prussian army at the battles of Jena and Auerstedt. This unexpected and humiliating catastrophe spelled the end of the absolute
Prussian state in the form into which Frederick the Great had
molded it. In the Treaty of Tilsit of July 1807, Napoleon stripped
Prussia of its western provinces, imposed a crushing war indemnity
upon it, and limited its army to 42,000 men. But the Prussians'
losses were the Poles' gain: Frederick William III also relin-
quished South and New East Prussia, which were reconstituted as the

Grand Duchy of Warsaw, a Polish state ruled by the Saxon dynasty
in alliance with France. Thus, little more than a decade after
the third partition, Poland reappeared in abbreviated form on the
European map. But the Grand Duchy was inextricably tied to
Napoleon's fortunes. After his defeat in Russia, it was occupied
by the Tsarist army. At the Congress of Vienna the lands of the
old Commonwealth were redistributed among the revived and victorious partitioning powers. Prussia's eclipse as a great power and
the restoration of a Polish state in the form of the Grand Duchy of
Warsaw were only transitory episodes, but they cleared the ground
for a redefinition of Prussian-Polish relations after 1815.

The last chapter in the history of old Prussia's Polish
provinces was hardly a vindication of Berlin's domestic
Polenpolitik, though neither was it a triumph the Poles owed only
to themselves. Despite the surface calm which had prevailed in the
eastern provinces for over a decade, when Napoleon commissioned
the Polish emigré leaders Dąbrowski and Wybicki to call their
countrymen in Prussia to arms, saying "I will see if the Poles are
worthy of being a nation," a new rebellion against Prussian rule
broke out, centered in South Prussia.[119]

This uprising was a spontaneous reaction of the Poles to the
breakdown of the civil and military authority of the Prussian
state and to the entry in November 1806 of French troops into
South Prussia. Already after Jena and Auerstedt the Prussian
officials in the Polish provinces vetoed the idea of arming the
population for defense against the French, fearing the Poles
would stage an insurrection instead. When Dąbrowski and Marshall
Davoust arrived in Poznań with the French forces, the Poles
greeted them enthusiastically. Napoleon's reception in Poznań
and Warsaw in January 1807 was tumultuous. The German officials
in the province were paralyzed. They stayed at their posts under
French orders, but monitored by the Poles and the invaders. Later
in January a Polish Executive Commission emerged and the Prussian
system collapsed, its frightened servants fleeing to the secure
ground of the German heartland. Regiments for a Polish army were
formed under French prodding. Thus the scene was quickly set for
the Poles' commitment to the Napoleonic future.[120]

Not unnaturally, some members of the Prussian government and
bureaucracy railed bitterly against the apparent ingratitude and
perfidy of their erstwhile Polish subjects. Yet in fact most of
the South Prussian Poles stood by passively or found themselves
forced into action by the French and their Polish allies as the
pillars of Prussian authority tumbled down around them. The West

and New East Prussian Poles hardly lifted a finger to influence the
great events in their midst.[121] It is true that Prussian rule was
strongly resented in Warsaw. A Prussian report from the former
Polish capital of November 1806 stated that the desire for a
restored Polish state was universal, that the landed nobility would
act towards this end if convinced of the inability of Prussia to
defend itself, and that the most dangerous social elements in any
national rising would be the petty szlachta, the unemployed youth,
and the Warsaw "rabble."[122] Later on, the Warsaw artisans were
said to have greeted Napoleon with "bestial joy."[123] Yet there
was virtually no Polish violence against the Prussians, but only
demonstrations of satisfaction that the partition regime had
failed. Insofar as the common people participated in these events,
it was as spectators whose natural interest in the collapse of the
socially rigid old order was sanctioned for national reasons by the
clery, the politically active nobility, and the intelligentsia.[124]
Justus Gruner, the Poznań Kammerdirektor who lived through the
rising in South Prussia, wrote that the active Polish insurgents
counted a certain number of gentry "Republicans," genuinely and
honorably motivated by commitment to the Commonwealth past, a
dangerous but dwindling generation of men. He distinguished another group of "fortune hunters," drawn especially from the lesser
and ruined gentry, and a sizable number of noble-born "glory
seekers," political adventurers chafing under Prussian discipline.
Most of the landed gentry, though not yet reconciled to Prussian
rule, had respected Prussian "order and prosperity" and were only
dragged along in support of the rising by the hotheads and by
what Gruner considered the most dangerous group of all: "fanatical
women." "They are," he wrote, "the chief insurgents and true
ringleaders. . . .They suckle and raise their children on hate and
rage against the Prussians and divest themselves of every female
virtue to satisfy their most unwholesome fanaticism." This was
not to be the last Prussian diatribe against the patriotism, which
grew stronger as the nineteenth century progressed, of upper-class
Polish women.[125]

The South Prussian rising demonstrated the willingness of
some of the Polish gentry and intelligentsia to commit themselves
actively in support of the Napoleonic new order, especially by
volunteering for military service. It also revealed the unwillingness of the rest of the nobility and the Polish common people to
stand in defense of the Prussian state. This only proved that
under Prussian rule the Poles had not become Prussians. It did not
prove that on the strength of their own convictions the South

Prussian Poles had launched a national uprising, or that,
should the star of Napoleon fall, the Poles could not come to
terms with Berlin.

Prussian Reform, Polish Rebellion

In August 1799 the Prussian Finance Minister von Struensee confidently declared to the French chargé d'affaires in Berlin that "the creative revolution was made in France from below; in Prussia it will be made slowly and from above."[1] Struensee was reckoning without the reactionary inertia which had overtaken Prussian absolutism since Frederick's death. Yet, in the aftermath of Jena and Auerstedt, the liberal wing of the Prussian bureaucracy and military quickly seized control and, in a renowned epoch of reforms (1807-19) decisively altered the structure of the state, enabling it to recover its power and join triumphantly in the overthrow of Napoleon.

During the reform era, the high civil bureaucracy forced upon Frederick William III concessions granting it a near coregency and shielding itself from autocratic caprice to such a degree that the period 1807-48 can be called the age of bureaucratic rather than royal absolutism.[2] Simultaneously, reform of the cabinet structure and the provincial civil and judicial administration brought to completion the centralization of the state striven towards by Prussia's rulers since the seventeenth century. The founding of Berlin University and the many improvements carried out in the Prussian schools ensured for the rest of the nineteenth century a flow of well-trained and cultured graduates, most of them from bourgeois families, into the prestigious and politically crucial spheres represented by the upper bureaucracy, the judiciary, and the higher educational establishment.

These were changes which most directly benefited the civil bureaucracy, Prussia's dominant political group in the first half of the nineteenth century. The disgrace of 1806 cost the aristocratic and politically powerful army officer corps some of its traditional privileges. It was opened to recruitment of commoners and subjected to stiffer technical entrance requirements. While universal military service began to draw the entire able-bodied

male population into direct engagement in state life, a system
of reserve forces arose in which bourgeois officers disputed the
Junkers' exclusive claim to the honors of military leadership.

The Prussian nobility suffered further losses. After 1807
landownership became the right of all citizens. The bourgeoisie
could now purchase noble estates, as some of them had been doing
under various pretenses since the mid eighteenth century. In the
most significant of the Prussian reforms, serfdom was abolished.
Some of the peasants gained as freeholds the lands they had previously tilled as serfs. All won legal release from compulsory
labor services on their former lords' estate lands. The creation
of an unrestricted market in land, abandonment of state manipulation of grain prices, the replacement of serf labor by wage labor,
and the separation of peasant holdings from estate land revolutionized the Prussian countryside. There arose a socially mixed
class of estate owners and a class of free peasant farmers (those
who as serfs had tilled medium-size and large holdings). Both
turned for their wage-labor to the multitude of former serfs on
small holdings or cottage plots, who gained no farms of their own
from the emancipation.

Prussia's bureaucratic reformers set urban life on new
bases. The Town Ordinance of 1808, lifting the heavy hand of
Frederickian offialdom, created elected town councils which became the political schools of the private bourgeoisie. The Trades
Ordinance of 1811 complemented this vital political change by the
abolition of guilds and monopoly privileges in the urban economy.
In 1812, the Jews of the Prussian heartland gained civil equality
which, though subsequently hedged in, at least opened all trades
and private occupations to them.

The capstone to these major social and political reforms in
the programs of the guiding ministers, Baron vom Stein and Prince
Hardenberg, was meant to have been a consultative assembly,
granting representatives of the nobility, the educated and
propertied bourgeoisie, and the well-to-do peasant farmers an
advisory voice in the royal government. This became a vital issue after Frederick William III's promise, announced during the
War of Liberation in 1814, that his subjects would be rewarded in
their sacrifices by the conferral of a constitution. The atmosphere of reaction following the Congress of Vienna delayed the
fulfillment of this promise until the Revolution of 1848. Bowing
to Restoration conservatism, the Prussian ministers and Crown
settled in 1823 on a system of provincial assemblies with highly
limited powers elected on class franchises enormously advantage-

ous to large landowners. In this modest form the parliamentary
principle sank roots in Prussian soil.[3]

The Prussian reform ministers had striven to humanize the
stiff and authoritarian system of Prussian absolutism by attacking
caste privilege in the name of cultured individualism. At the same
time, because they stood at the helm of the state, they aimed to
restore Prussia's military strength and great-power status. The
link between these concepts of individualism and state power was
the nation. The reform minister von Altenstein wrote in 1807 of
the pre-1806 regime that "there was no nation in the state, there
were not even real provinces, but rather only particular social
orders (Stände) in the various provinces, each with special
interests, without any point of unity. . . ."[4]

These words rejected the decentralized, caste-bound, and
privilege-ridden society of the European old regime of which
princely absolutism had become both the powerful armature and,
despite its enlightened tendencies, the hostage. In its place,
Altenstein, like countless statesmen and political thinkers throughout Europe during the era of the French Revolution and Napoleon,
put the concept of the nation, and not for any sentimental reasons.
The Prussian reformers hoped to awaken, through progressive reforms
and official appropriation of the ideology of nationalism, a
popular patriotism in Prussia such as the revolution and Napoleon
had sparked in France and England's long centuries of war with its
continental foes had called forth among its people. But were the
Prussians a nation, and could the Prussian monarchy claim to be a
national state?[5]

At the end of the eighteenth century, Herder had exalted the
nation as an ethnic-linguistic-cultural organism independent of the
state. Imbedded in his writings were sharp protests against the
political particularism and absolutist authoritarianism of eighteenth-century Germany. The nation, or Volk, should not be ruled
as a mass of passive subjects. Moreover, "the most natural
[political] state comprises one nationality with one national
character." Herder's ideas were later developed both by the
German romantics and by democratic nationalists of a Mazzinian
temperament. Although some of his conservative followers insisted
on the national character of particular German states or regions,
Herder's greatest legacy was to those who sought the political
unity of all Germans.[6]

For the Prussian monarchy, intent upon constituting itself
from top down as a nation, the question in the first half of the
nineteenth century was whether the social classes it sought to

recruit in its support--the private bourgeoisie and intelligentsia, the artisans and the peasants--would accept Prussia as a national state, or whether a larger sense of German nationalism both within Prussia and elsewhere in Germany would overwhelm it.[7] In 1815, the Prussian government faced the task of integrating into the fabric of the state the new territories it gained at the Congress of Vienna. It was committed to the complex and time-consuming process of peasant emancipation and a moderately liberal program of industrial development. It was financially exhausted and politically pinned between the aristocratic and bureaucratic sup- porters of Metternichian conservatism and the more feeble chal- lenges of constitutional liberalism and democratic, greater-German nationalism. During the 1820s the Prussian bureaucracy embraced a conservative authoritarianism against which the forces of liberalism, nationalism, and popular radicalism finally exploded in the Revolution of 1848.

Such was the setting in which the Prussian government con- fronted the Polish question and its Polish subjects in the four decades after Jena and Auerstedt. But meanwhile, great events shook Polish society. The Grand Duchy of Warsaw demonstrated that, given the right constellation of international forces, the events of 1795 need not have spelled, as so many had despaired, finis Poloniae. The Congress of Vienna was inevitably a sore disappointment. Yet, at no time from 1815 until the restoration of a Polish state after World War I did Polish nationalists abandon the hope that, in the wake of a European war, statehood would be regained by means of the intervention of whichever victorious powers desired the weakening of one, two, or all three of the partitioning states. Above all, the Poles looked for sup- port to France and England. After 1815, this diplomatic orienta- tion intertwined with the thought of domestic insurrection against the partitioning governments, for which Kościuszko had given the Poles a model.

The issue of insurrection was clouded until the 1830s by the nature of the settlement of the Polish question at the Congress of Vienna. By 1815, the European cabinets were prepared to con- cede the necessity of recognizing the claims of what they referred to as "Polish nationality." Since the great powers could not agree in 1815 on the perpetuation of Polish independence, they seized on the idea of more or less far-reaching autonomy for the Poles in Russia, Austria, and Prussia. This especially suited Tsar Alexander I, who acquired in 1815 the greater part of the Grand Ducy of Warsaw as an addition to Russia's gains in the eighteenth-century partitions. He organized his western Polish provinces as the Kingdom of Poland, endowed with an oligarchical constitution and szlachta parliament, considerable legal-administrative and cultural autonomy, and a Polish army under Russian supervision. Austria and Prussia also made significant concessions to their Polish subjects' cultural and local political interests in the fifteen years after Waterloo.

This system of limited autonomy did not survive the revolutionary year 1830. In Russian Poland, where serious frictions with Petersburg had accumulated, the revolutions in France and Belgium and the prospect of revolution in Germany fired the courage of the liberals and radicals to raise in insurrection. Spearheaded by the Polish army, but launched with the hope of Western aid, its aim was to restore Poland in its borders of 1772 once again to full independence. Nicholas I's army crushed the rising with some difficulty, whereupon the autonomy and self-administration of the now defunct Kingdom of Poland yielded to a severe Russian military-bureaucratic regime. Similar, though less extreme, measures struck the Poles in Austria and Prussia.

In the 1830s and 1840s, revolutionary sentiment was strong among the thousands of Polish exiles in Western Europe. In the homeland, underground agitation among the common people aimed at a rising under the leadership of the radicalized lesser nobility and intelligentsia. The Polish masses were to be rewarded for taking up arms against the partitioning governments by gaining freedom from serfdom, especially in Russia and Austria, and by acquisition of their lands as freeholds or, for the landless, by grants of land. Some who espoused this strategy hoped to coordinate it with the next wave of western European revolutions; others argued for trusting in the nation's own powers.

Opposed to these revolutionaries were the conservative and wealthy Polish aristocrats and their followers among the gentry and intelligentsia. This group rejected insurrection but recommended a strategy which called for moderation towards the partitioning governments in the hope of recovering the system of pre-1830 autonomy sanctioned by the Congress of Vienna. Meanwhile, they passively and silently anticipated a general European war which would lead the great powers to restore a Polish state, the larger the better. Scattered among this second camp were those who devoted themselves to promoting education and the national cultural tradition in the homeland. They sought to organize the peasantry and townspeople in economic and self-help associations, to ensure the economic survival of the gentry, and to draw the Polish

clergy into the national movement. By the 1840s, Polish nationalists of this sort began to be called practitioners of "organic
work."[8]

Prussian *Polenpolitik* and the Grand Duchy of Poznań, 1815-31

The Polish uprising in South Prussia provoked righteous
indignation in those Prussian statesmen who defended the pre-1806
regime and resignation to what seemed the inevitable in those who
criticized it. But, in any case, the Prussian government could
spare no energy from its struggle for survival against the French
to prevent its Polish subjects from going over to Napoleon.

Nonetheless, before the Peace of Tilsit in 1807 formally
stripped Prussia of Polish lands it had acquired since 1793, the
reform ministers engaged in a debate on the Polenpolitik to be followed in the future should the Polish provinces be retained or
later reconquered. This debate was sparked by Justus Gruner, the
Poznań Kammerdirektor and witness of the uprising, who in the
first months of 1807 energetically forced his views on the beleaguered Prussian court. In his scathing characterizations of
Polish history and culture and in his harsh condemnation of the
moral and political failings of the Polish nobility, Gruner's pen
equalled, if it did not surpass, Frederick the Great's.[9] Blaming
the szlachta and clergy for the risings of 1794 and 1806-7,
he wrote that "for the next hundred years" the nobility would revolt if given the chance, since they had a "justifiable right" to
oppose the partitions.[10] Gruner saw no way of amicably reconciling the szlachta with the Prussian state, and so proposed, although he confessed his "heart trembled," the "Germanization"
(Verdeutschung) of South Prussia.[11] By this he meant a deliberate
uprooting of the Polish gentry and their replacement with Germans.
This could be achieved by denying credits to the heavily indebted
Poles, raising their taxes 50 percent or more, and abolishing
their urban revenues. Participants in the rising of 1806-7 should
be executed or exiled, while the government in Berlin should promote the "transplanting" of Germans to South Prussian soil. No
marriages, after a period of fifteen years, should be permitted
without proof of a knowledge of German. No Pole should be admitted to public service without the same qualification. South
Prussia must become "a genuinely German province."[12]

Unlike Frederick the Great, Gruner had good words to say
about the Polish common people. He urged Frederick William III
to undertake "the restoration of the Polish bourgeoisie and
peasantry" through gradual peasant emancipation and urban develop-

ment. For this "rebirth of the Polish nation" the masses would be
"eternally grateful."[13] Though he outlined no school program, the
thrust of his reports was clearly in the direction of linguistic
Germanization, the obstacles to which he did not consider.

Though an old-Prussian official, after 1812 Gruner became involved in a secret society aiming at the unification of Germany.[14]
This was not inconsistent with his Polish program, whose nationalist radicalism and antiaristocratic populism foreshadowed attitudes
which later became widespread in German bourgeois nationalist
circles. But in Gruner's own time, Prussia's rulers recoiled from
his prescriptions. First to refute them was Prince Antoni Radziwiłł, an uncle-in-law of Frederick William III and a conservative
aristocrat who strove throughout his life for conciliation between
the Polish gentry and the Prussian court. He dismissed Gruner's
reports as the reflection of "the Germans' habitually contemptuous
way of thinking about the Poles." Radziwiłł believed the Poles
could be won to the Prussian side by Frederick William III's assumption of the title of King of Poland and by granting them
aristocratic self-government under the Prussian sceptre.[15]

Similarly, Altenstein penned a memorandum for Hardenberg's use
in March 1807 which condemned Gruner for aiming at "the complete
extirpation" of the Poles. Altenstein praised the Poles' "national
pride" and proposed that in the future the Prussian government
should engage the Polish gentry in local and central administration, while Frederick William III should assume the title of "King
of Great Poland." Frederickian influences were evident in Altenstein's approval of German colonization, which set the Poles "a
good example," and in his stress on German language instruction,
although not at the expense of Polish, in order that "the progress
of German culture" and "German morality" should be comprehensible
to the Poles. Not "extinguishment and extermination" of the Polish
national character, but rather its "ennoblement" was Altenstein's
aim. This would lead the Poles "imperceptibly" to abandon the
distinction between Prussians and themselves.[16]

Baron vom Stein, the greatest of the Prussian reformers, did
not fail to consider the Polish problem in his famous Nassauer
Denkschrift of June 1807. Like Frederick II and Gruner, he had no
high opinion of the old Commonwealth or of the szlachta, whose
"fickleness, instability, dissoluteness, and taste for turbulence"
he solemnly condemned. But he also denounced the partitions and,
like Altenstein, credited the Polish nobility with many virtues,
including the capacity "to sacrifice themselves for fatherland and
freedom." The goal of the Prussian regime must be to encourage

the development of the "individuality" of Polish culture through
education, social reform, and the involvement of the upper classes
in local self-administration. Stein also endorsed Radziwiłł's
proposal to revive the name of Poland among the Prussian king's
titles and suggested the appointment of a Polish Statthalter, or
viceroy, with an attendant Polish council in Warsaw.[17]

The attitudes of the Prussian reform ministers unquestionably
signaled a break with the authoritarian and centralizing
Polenpolitik of the years before 1806. Though not free of traditional Prussian anti-Polish prejudices, the reformers rated the
prospects of Polish-Prussian collaboration much more highly than
did their predecessors. But they assumed the finality of the
partitions and wrote not a word of the possibility of a restored
and independent Poland.[18] Implicitly, they agreed with Gruner
that it lay in the "nature" of the Prussian state to impose "its
own constitution" on its Polish lands.[19] At best, they wished to
involve the szlachta in the provincial administration, without conceding that this should vary from general Prussian norms. And
they were convinced that the Poles would not become acceptable
Prussian subjects until they had mastered the German language and
embraced German culture and social values as their own.

Between the Peace of Tilsit and Napoleon's expulsion from
Germany, the Polish question played a minor role in official Prussian thinking. At the Congress of Vienna, Frederick William III
and Hardenberg thought so little of regaining the full extent of
Prussia's pre-1806 Polish territories that they stirred up one
of the congress's crises by joining Russia in a belligerent gambit.
Its object was to obtain for Prussia the whole of Saxony, which
had stood with Napoleon, and virtually all of the Polish Commonwealth lands for Russia. English opposition to such Russian
aggrandizement and Austrian resistance to such an access of Prussian power in Germany found Talleyrand's support. After a brief
war scare among the allies, a compromise left the Prussians with
a large slice of Saxony and with the Rhineland and most of Great
Poland as well. Prussia's rulers had been ready to trade their
claims to Warsaw, Thorn, and Poznań for Leipzig and Dresden. In
1815 they took control of Great Poland, and the Rhineland too, as
consolation prizes.[20]

In the Final Act of the Congress of Vienna, the signatory
powers, including Austria, Russia, and Prussia, agreed that the
Poles should receive "representation and national institutions"
from the governments under whose rule they now found themselves.

Prussia agreed that its share of Great Poland should be ruled as
the "Grand Duchy of Poznań" (Grossherzogtum Posen). In a separate
treaty with Russia complementing the Vienna act, the Prussians concurred that "the Polish subjects of the two contracting parties
will receive institutions ensuring the maintenance of their nationality according to those forms of political life which each of the
governments finds it suitable to confer upon them."[21] These
declarations became the subject of endless and acrimonious debates
between the Prussian Poles and the Berlin government.

Frederick William III displayed outward magnanimity towards
his returned Polish subjects, many of whom had been heartily glad
in 1807 to escape his control. The oracular words of his proclamation to the population of the Grand Duchy on 15 May 1815,
like the Vienna treaties, were recalled again and again by the
Prussian Poles:

> You too have a fatherland, and together with it you
> have received proof of my regard for your attachment
> to it. You will be incorporated in my monarchy without
> having to relinquish your nationality. You will have
> a place in the constitution I intend to bestow upon
> my loyal subjects, and you will receive, like the other
> provinces of my state, a provincial ordinance [i.e., a
> diet].

After assuring the Poles that their religion and private property
would be scrupulously protected, Frederick William III declared
that "your language, together with German, will be used in all
public functions." Hoping to make a fresh start, he added that
"it is my sincere wish that what occurred in the past will have
been completely forgotten." "Great experiences," he concluded,
"have matured you."[22]

From 1815 until the outbreak of the rebellion against Tsarist
rule in Russian Poland in November 1830, the Prussian government
attempted to administer the Grand Duchy in a conciliatory spirit.
The hierarchy of administrative and judicial offices reaching its
peak in Berlin was imposed on the Duchy. But Prince Radziwiłł
received the office of Statthalter in the expectation that he
would mediate the central government's interests and the Polish
gentry's wishes. A liberal-minded German official sympathetic to
the Poles took office as Provincial President (Oberpräsident).
Some Polish nobles became Landräte, others took posts in the
central administration of the Duchy. The gentry's rural judicial
and police authority and their patrimonial powers in the noble-
owned towns remained intact. Finally, in the provincial diet,
first convened in 1827 with the powers of expressing opinions and
submitting petitions on royal policy in the Grand Duchy, they
wielded a majority.[23]

MAP 3.--The Prussian East after 1815. Distribution of the
nationalities according to the Prussian language census
of 1910. Source of census data: Polish Encyclopedia,
vol. 2, no. 3, Territorial Development of the Polish
Nation (Geneva, 1921), pp. 435ff.

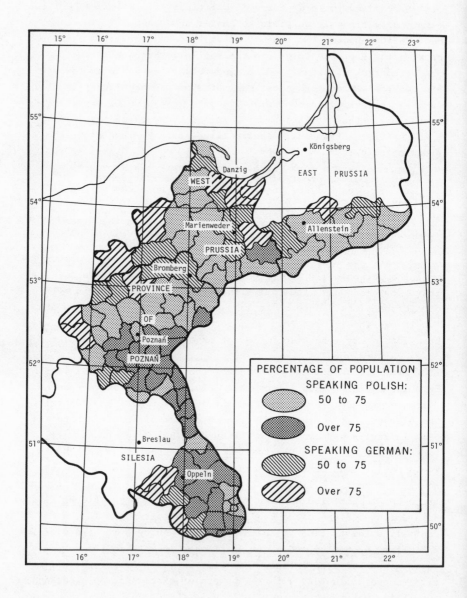

The Polish gentry were in parlous economic straits in the
aftermath of the Napoleonic wars. Burdened by debts contracted
before 1806, depleted by loans to the Grand Duchy of Warsaw, confronting depressed grain prices and hit by bad harvests, many of
them needed state credits to escape ruin. The government responded with the establishment in 1821 of a mortgage and credit
society for large landowners (Landschaft). It rescued the landlords from bankruptcy and provided a vital financial support for
the capital investments forced upon them in the decades before
1848 by peasant emancipation.[24]

Already in 1807, the Grand Duchy of Warsaw had proclaimed the
personal freedom of the Polish peasant-serfs, but the question of
establishing their title as freeholders to their serf plots remained unresolved after 1815. The edicts of 1811 and 1816 committed the Prussian government to the regulation of this problem
throughout its realm. In 1821 it absolved the Grand Duchy's
Hauländer of all obligations to their former lords and bestowed
their farms upon them as freeholds in return for a long-term cash
settlement with the gentry. In 1823, the more complex procedure
of endowing the former serf population with freeholds began,
not to reach its conclusion until 1858. These peasants were
divided into two categories, according to the amount of farmland
(technically owned by the lord) they were cultivating as of the
year 1819. Those who, after compensating their lords by varying
combinations of land, money, or continued labor services for a
limited period, could emerge from this process of "regulation" in
possession of self-sufficient medium-size or large holdings were
enfranchised as freeholders under the edict of 1823. They accounted for roughly 40 percent of the serf population.[25] For the
rest, regulation by the Prussian state meant the loss of whatever
security of tenure they had possessed as small-holding serfs.
Now they were their landlords' tenants-at-will, obliged to work
as cottagers on the estate land, liable to eviction if the gentry
found it advantageous to incorporate their lands into their
estate domains. As elsewhere in the Prussian state, settlement of
the land-tenure question following personal emancipation meant
the creation of a stratum of self-sufficient, though technically
backward, peasants alongside a larger class of laborers intended
to serve both the landlords and richer peasants. Until the
second half of the nineteenth century, most of these laborers
were lodged as cottagers on small plots of noble-owned land.
Although the Polish gentry were fearful of the economic consequences of peasant regulation, the process proved to be favorable

to them. Estate land increased from 53 percent to 57 percent
of the Duchy's total arable between 1816 and 1858. The landlords
still possessed a pool of cheap labor, which could be exploited
more efficiently under the threat of eviction than under the old
regime of serfdom. Separation of lords' from peasants' land
allowed more rational exploitation of the new estates. State
credits, together with monetary compensation from the regulated
peasants, provided the landlords with capital for equipping themselves as capitalist entrepreneurs.[26]

Just as gentry interests were taken into account in public
administration and agrarian reform, so also in the sensitive
area of education and language policy the Prussian government
made conciliatory gestures. In principle, Polish was accepted
as an official language in communications with the bureaucracy
and in judicial processes. Elementary education was conducted
in the pupils' mother tongue. The Catholic teachers' seminaries
were Polish institutions. In the secondary-level gymnasiums,
Polish was the language of instruction in the lower forms, while
in the higher forms German was adopted for Polish students in
the hope of perfecting their command of the language they would
need to use at the universities. Even then, certain advanced subjects continued to be taught in Polish. The Prussian state expended large sums in improving the Grand Duchy's educational system. In addition to several gymnasiums, 984 elementary schools
were built between 1815 and 1839, bringing the Duchy's total to
1,673 schools encompassing a majority of its school-aged children.[27]

In 1822 Education Minister von Altenstein made an official
statement of the government's language policy which, after its
subsequent publication, served the Poles as an eloquent reproach
in later years of national conflict. Denying any need to "Germanize" Polish students, praising the cultured nature of the
Polish language, and calling only for the teaching of enough
German to enable the Poles to participate in public life, Altenstein warned the Grand Duchy's officials:

> Religion and mother tongue are the most sacred pos-
> sessions of a nation. In them its whole mentality
> and style of thought are grounded. The government
> which recognizes, respects, and protects them may be
> sure of winning the hearts of its subjects; but a
> government which shows itself indifferent to them, or
> even allows attacks upon them, embitters and dis-
> honors a nation and makes of its members untrue and
> bad subjects. He who thought that it would contribute
> essentially to the cultural development of the Polish
> nation if it were Germanized, at least in speech,
> would find himself greatly in error.[28]

The Poles and the Grand Duchy, 1815-31

In 1815, the Polish gentry in Prussia were financially exhausted and, like their brothers in Russia and Austria, defeated
in their hopes of regaining independence. They were resigned to
coming to the best terms possible with the government in Berlin,
and made more sanguine by the royal promises of 1815, which were
liberally interpreted to them by Prince Radziwiłł.[29] They accepted and took advantage of the concessions and opportunities extended to them before 1831 by the Prussian government. But, at
the same time, they were unsatisfied.

Polish politics in these years were gentry politics. Prince
Radziwiłł might have been the focus of an aristocratic "court
party," but he lacked energy and adroitness and also the active
support of the szlachta, among whom the country squires and
gentlemen far outnumbered the occasional magnate. Polish students,
mostly sons of the gentry attending the Berlin and Breslau universities, might form small secret patriotic societies, while
radicalized veterans of the Napoleonic campaigns might seek to
maintain an underground Masonic movement.[30] But these efforts of
the 1820s were feeble and without significance. The political
center of gravity among the Prussian Poles reposed in the Grand
Duchy's squirearchy. The creation of county and provincial diets
in the 1820s provided them with an institutional framework for
political action.

The convocation of the first diet in 1827 gave the Polish
gentry, who won twenty of the twenty-four mandates in the dominant
"knightly" estate, a chance to air their grievances about the
political evolution of the Grand Duchy since 1815. They had already been disappointed that a widely discussed plan to create a
separate Polish division in the Prussian army, supported by the
cabinet and certain Polish veterans, had collapsed shortly after
1815 because of royal and military opposition.[31] Now they drew
up petitions expressing their alarm about the use of the German
language in the upper gymnasium forms and about the many German
officials in the Duchy's civil administration unable to speak
Polish. Although the government subsequently made concessions on
these points, a fundamental question had arisen which was debated
until the Revolution of 1848. What had Frederick William III
meant when he told his Polish subjects in 1815 that "you too have
a fatherland"? The Polish gentry wished to understand by this
that the Grand Duchy of Poznań was their fatherland.[32] They spoke
fulsomely of the quintessentially Polish character of the Duchy,
"the oldest branch of a once great, powerful, and flourishing

tree."[33] It was within the bounds of the Duchy that the szlachta
wished to cultivate the "nationality" the Prussian king had assured them they would not need to abjure. This term "narodowość"
carried a high charge. Addressing the Provincial President in
the diet, Prince Sułkowski invoked the Poles' "longing for nationality": "If only this jewel be preserved for us, nothing will
adequately express our joy, and our proper fidelity and honorable
respect for the king will be transformed into unalterable love
and attachment to both the king and the state itself."[34] Nationality meant, in the first instance, language. Hence the great
importance these diets attached to educational matters. Polish
should be the language of instruction for Polish students throughout their secondary education--not only for practical purposes,
but for the advancement of the national culture. For the same
reason, in the 1840s the provincial diet petitioned, though in
vain, for the establishment of a university in Poznań.

The Polish nobility's traditions of political action were too
strong to confine the meaning of nationality to a purely cultural
level. Preservation of their nationality seemed to them impossible
without political autonomy and self-rule, if not in their own
national state, then in the Grand Duchy. One of the deputies
introduced a resolution, rejected by the majority as hopelessly
radical, demanding sovereignty for the Poznań Duchy in a loose
union with the Prussian crown: "Our nationality is gravely
threatened and, nationality lost, all is lost."[35] The influential
and moderate Prince Sułkowski tried unsuccessfully to persuade
the Berlin government to make the Statthalter, assisted by a
Polish Grand Ducal cabinet, the real head of the Duchy's administration.[36]

Instead, the Poles witnessed an influx of German officials
and the increasing use of the German language in public life and
secondary education. The Crown replied to the diets that no
obstacles stood in the way of Polish access to official positions
in the Duchy, on condition that the Poles mastered the German
language and trained themselves in Prussian law and administration.
The gentry's response, though not hostile, was unenthusiastic.
They wanted to serve in Polish, not Prussian, institutions. When
Prussian officials accused the Poles of boycotting military and
civil service for reasons of national pride and exclusiveness,
they were not entirely wrong.[37]

The history of the Grand Duchy from 1815 to 1831 ended on a
contradictory note. Peasant emancipation and dependence on the
German market linked the Poles' fortunes to Berlin. In the Duchy

they accepted many administrative posts and organized their political life around the provincial diet. Yet the local administration rested in mainly German hands, and not the most competent or
sympathetic at that. Polish complaints about the arrogance, in-
comprehension, and hostility of the provincial authorities were
numerous.[38] The principal apologist of the Prussian bureaucracy
admitted that German officials disdained service in the Grand
Duchy and that venality, mediocrity, and authoritarianism were
commonplace.[39] Polish aversion to Prussian service only compounded this problem. But already before 1831 patriotic militancy
had acquired a moral value among the szlachta outweighing conciliatory tolerance or courtly national diplomacy. In 1827 supporters of a strongly worded petition against the use of German
in the gymnasiums threated the opposing deputies with duels.[40]

The Polish gentry began to devote their talents to
political opposition while the generous sentiments the Prussian
king had expressed towards the Poles in 1815 were translated by a
sullen bureaucracy into suspicion and haughty superiority. At
the heart of the matter lay the fact that even those generous
sentiments had been equivocal. A month before Frederick William
III's proclamation of 1815, his ministers coolly advised him:

> The Grand Duchy of Posen represents an integral
> part of the Prussian monarchy and will be organized
> accordingly; the nationality of its inhabitants
> should be taken into account to the degree that this
> is compatible with our primary goal. . . .The province
> should not forget that it has given Your Excellency
> justifiable reasons for mistrust; it must therefore
> take steps to prove its fidelity beyond any doubt.[41]

The government in Berlin saw the Polish deputies' oppositional
stance in the diets of 1827 and 1830 as no proof of "fidelity."
Prussian mistrust then rose to the level of paranoia during the
insurrection of 1830-31 in Russian Poland.

Prussian *Polenpolitik* and the Province of Poznań, 1830-47

The Prussian Poles played no part in the outbreak of the
1830 rising, whose origins lay in the complex web of Russian-
Polish relations in the Congress Kingdom of Poland. The prospect
of a general overthrow of the "Vienna system" opened by the revolutions in France and Belgium spurred the Russian Poles, swayed
more by the vision of independence than by the likelihood of
defeat, to revolt.

The insurrectionary leaders in Warsaw wished to confine
their struggle, initially at least, to Russian Poland. They proclaimed their nonbelligerency towards Prussia and Austria and

refused any encouragement to those who argued for extending the
rebellion beyond Tsarist borders. Nevertheless, many Austrian and
Prussian Poles crossed their frontiers and joined in the increasingly desperate fighting, which was only quelled after mid 1831.
From the Grand Duchy of Poznań some 1,600 Polish civilians and
1,400 Poles in Prussian military service defied the Berlin government's closure of the eastern frontier to engage in the anti-
Russian campaign.[42] These were significant numbers, but they were
not a mass exodus of adult males among the Grand Duchy's Polish
population, which in 1825 numbered altogether roughly 625,000.[43]
The szlachta took the initiative in aiding the insurrection:
Polish army officers persuaded enlisted men to follow them; landlords recruited their estate employees and laborers. Smaller
numbers of townspeople, students, and peasants joined independ-
ently.[44]

    The rising in Warsaw greatly alarmed the Prussian govern-
ment, already tensely on its guard against the possibility of
war with France on the Rhine and in the Low Countries, and fearful
of the eruption of liberal revolution in Germany itself. Frederick
William III wrote bitterly of the "treacherous and fanatical
Poles," while Clausewitz sourly wrote to his wife, "These people
[the Poles] have so many delusions and never comprehend anyone's
interests but their own."[45] It came as a great relief when the
Polish regime in the Congress Kingdom foreswore an attack on
Prussia. Had the revolt spread into Prussian Poland, or had
Prussia found itself fighting on Russian soil, the diplomats and
generals in Berlin were convinced that war with France on the
Rhine must have ensued. Instead, Prussia proclaimed formal
neutrality towards the Polish insurrection. It greatly reinforced its troops on the eastern frontiers, securely garrisoned
the Grand Duchy of Poznań, and covertly lent what diplomatic and
material aid it could to the Tsarist government to hasten the
rebels' downfall.[46]

    This insurrection put an end to the grudging efforts of
Frederick William III's government to conciliate the Poles in
the Grand Duchy. Official Prussian opinion, wavering since 1807
on questions of Polenpolitik, crystallized now in a sense thoroughly hostile to the Polish nobility and clergy. It was at this
time that the military-diplomatic doctrine appeared, maintaining
on geopolitical grounds that restoration of a Polish state would
necessarily undermine Prussia as a great power. In 1831 Clausewitz gave classic expression to this widely held view:

        For some years it has been necessary to regard the
        Poles and the French as natural allies. German

> power, lying between these two states, opposes that
> natural alliance. . . .Woe to us if Russia were to
> lose control of Congress Poland and cede its Polish
> provinces of Lithuania, Volhynia, and Podolia to the
> Poles. The Poles and the French would then shake
> hands at the Elbe.

Breaking free of Russian domination, the Poles would inevitably
contest control of West Prussia and the Grand Duchy of Poznań
with Prussia.[47] In retrospect it is clear that this view greatly
exaggerated both the rapacity of French designs against Germany
and the ability of an independent Poland to wage war against
Prussia with a defeated and vengeful Russia at its rear. Nevertheless, Prussia's trauma during the Napoleonic period made this
perspective plausible, especially to political conservatives like
Clausewitz and his colleagues in the Prussian government who expected the triumph of revolutionary liberalism to unleash war
throughout Europe.

In its domestic policy towards the Grand Duchy of Poznań,
the Prussian government reverted after 1830 to the anti-Polish
traditions and mentality of Frederick II and Justus Gruner. This
shift was symbolized in the appointment in December 1830 of
Eduard Heinrich Flottwell as Provincial President, a post he held
to 1841. Flottwell inaugurated a Polenpolitik which had immense
influence on the subsequent relations of Germans, Poles, and Jews
in the Prussian east. There was little that was original in his
views or program; what counted were the concrete steps he took.
Nor did he act in isolation. The king and the Berlin ministries
supported him for a decade, and many leading Prussian statesmen
endorsed his views.[48]

Frederickian policy rested on a contemptuous mistrust of the
Polish nobility. They were to be denied full Junker privileges
while the common people were to be held in passive subjection and
led to adopt "German manners." The statesmen of the Reform Era
assumed that, given a privileged and active role in the state, the
Polish nobility and clergy would respond with Prussian loyalty.
At the same time, the Polish townspeople and peasantry were to be
freed from noble domination and encouraged to educate themselves,
improve their economic practices, and take a minor but real role
in public affairs. From the Prussian point of view, neither of
these orientations had been effective. Frederickian policy in
practice had amounted to bureaucratic containment of the nobility
and continued fiscal-feudal exploitation of the common people.
The uprising of 1806-7 was the result. Reform-inspired practice
between 1815 and 1830 had favored the szlachta without fully
abandoning the bureaucratic, centralizing, and Prussianizing

tendencies of the old regime. The outcome was gentry opposition
and participation in the Russian Polish rising of 1830-31.

Flottwell's policies represented a new synthesis aimed at
extricating the state from the impasse it had reached. He echoed
Frederick and Gruner, as well as contemporary official opinion, in
rejecting collaboration with the Poles. He believed the older
members of the gentry had accustomed themselves to frequent changes
of rule and would, given the chance, thoughtlessly break with
Prussia to reassert their historic claims to independence. Meanwhile, "Most of the male youth among this nobility have been
duped by the academic swindles of fatherland and freedom, which
unite in the illogical head of a Pole with the proud insolence of
a Sarmatian magnate in the most marvelous way. . . ."[49] Even if
many of the Polish aristocracy and gentry saw the advantages of
Prussian rule, Flottwell believed they were terrorized into
political silence by hotheaded sons, fanatically patriotic wives,
and reckless nationalist adventurers among the lesser and ruined
nobility.[50]

Flottwell similarly attacked the Polish clergy for their
"hypocrisy," "benightedness," "coarseness," ignorance, and "egotism," betraying in these epithets a Protestant aversion to
Catholicism widespread among Prussian officials.[51] He especially
deplored the church's political influence over the common people.
The Poznań-Gniezno archbishop's tours of his diocese were "tri-
umphal marches".[52] Support for the 1830 rising had been preached,
he claimed, from the Grand Duchy's pulpits.[53]

Flottwell did not suppose that the Polish common people felt
any great attachment to the Prussian state. But he believed
that the peasants in process of freehold regulation would not
risk their gains in nationalist opposition. The artisans and
urban workers, on the other hand, struck him as potentially rebellious because of the German competition they faced, their
hostility to Prussian military service, their obedience to the
church, and their susceptibility--especially after a round of
patriotic songs in the tavern--to rush to insurrectionary arms.[54]
Since collaboration with the gentry was impossible, "because they
will demand a completely unlimited national and political autonomy," Flottwell strove to disarm them completely.[55] He revoked
their right to nominate candidates to the office of Landrat.
Thereafter, until the end of Prussian rule, these key officials
were Germans, frequently drawn from outside the Duchy. Radziwiłł
was dismissed and the office of Statthalter abolished. German
became the exclusive language for internal affairs in the civil

administration. The gentry's influence in their local bailiwicks
was undercut by speeding up the process of peasant regulation and
by replacing the landlord-appointed rural police agents by German
lower officials. These District Commissioners, a class of Prussian officials peculiar to the Grand Duchy, combined normal
police duties with surveillance of the Polish nationalist movement. In the diets of 1834 and 1837, Flottwell pressured the
German majorities in the urban and peasant estates to oppose the
Poles' protests and so blocked their appeals to the Crown. In
1831, a Revised Town Ordinance appeared, granting the Duchy's
towns many of the same rights of self-government the Ordinance
of 1808 provided for the burghers of the Prussian heartland. In
1833 Flottwell abolished the gentry's seigneurial rights over
the towns. As for the church, in 1833 all remaining cloisters were
liquidated, while state-supervised seminaries were attached to the
Duchy's gymnasiums. These, however, were only glancing blows at
the Archdiocese's autonomy in matters of priestly and teacher
training.[56]

While striking out at the nobility and clergy, Flottwell
tried to please the Polish common people by upholding their right
to deal with the civil authorities and courts in the Polish
language, by his peasant emancipation and town government policy,
by building many new schools and roads, and, in 1833, by abolishing
the guild system which had prevented the entry into master status
of many poorer Polish craftsmen. This was the kind of promotion
of the Polish bourgeoisie and peasantry Gruner had recommended.

A third and crucial dimension to Flottwell's strategy, also
adumbrated in earlier Prussian practice, encompassed the active
promotion of German interests in the Duchy and a concentrated effort to lend to it a German rather than Polish character. Since
Prussian interest required the province to be merged "inseparably"
into the state, Flottwell concluded that "an inner fusion of the
two nationalities" must occur. "Their complete union can, however, only be achieved through the decisive predominance of German
culture."[57] Accordingly, Flottwell revived the Frederickian
policy of German peasant colonization, strengthened German-language
secondary education, invigorated the German-speaking community
through his town and guild reforms, and strove to win the Jews to
the German side. But a loyal population of German burghers and
peasants in the Grand Duchy was not enough. A crucial social
component of the Prussian state was still lacking: a Junker landlord class.[58] With special state funds, Flottwell purchased bankrupted Polish estates and sold them to Germans. He also sold, to

Germans only, estate-sized parcels of royal domain land. These
measures, reinforced by a tendency in the 1830s and 1840s among
Germans outside the Duchy to take advantage of its relatively low
land prices to buy estates there, inaugurated the growth of a
sizable class of German landlords.[59]

Flottwell's regime outraged and embittered the Polish upper
classes. Their hopes for home rule vanished. Their fatherland,
Frederick William III admonished them in 1832, was the Prussian
monarchy, not the Grand Duchy. They were not Poles, Flottwell
said, but Prussians.[60] They found themselves thrown completely
on the defensive. In the diets of 1834 and 1837 they protested
the advancing exclusion of their language both from public administration and secondary education, but on the former issue the
German deputies refused to support them, while on the latter the
Crown rejected a moderate Polish-German compromise petition.
Stung in their national pride, the Poles in Prussian service
resigned their posts in large numbers. This only tightened the
German grip on the Duchy's bureaucracy.[61]

Under these galling circumstances, Polish nationalists confronted three options. One was to prepare secretly for a new
war of national liberation and unification. Propagation of this
idea was undertaken above all by the Polish Democratic Society in
France, whose members were drawn from the thousands of Poles who
had emigrated to Western Europe after the failure of the insurrection of 1830. Bathed in the prestige of martyrdom, this revolutionary wing of the "Great Emigration" exerted considerable influence on the Polish homeland until the uprising of 1863-64.
Their program, set forth in the Poitiers Manifesto of 1836, called
for raising the Polish peasantry against the partitioning powers
with promises of land and personal freedom. Although the Democratic Society inveighed against the Polish aristocracy and prosperous gentry, its leaders in exile depended on the homeland
nobility to recruit the common people. This dilemma was compounded
in the case of Prussian Poland by the fact that peasant emancipaton
and freehold regulation had been preempted by the Prussian government. Only the small-holding, nonregulated peasants offered social
revolutionary potential, but this class in particular was in the
gentry's grip. Although in 1839 a secret committee of the Democratic Society was formed in the Grand Duchy, its influence among
the landlords and common people was slight.[62]

A second option was to follow the lead of the exile community
grouped around Prince Adam Czartoryski. From his Parisian palace,
Czartoryski cautioned the homeland aristocracy and gentry to rely

on the interest of the west in the restoration of Poland when,
through diplomacy or war, the opportunity arose. While Czartoryski's camp engaged in private diplomacy in France and England,
its adherents in the homeland were counseled to engage in legal
political opposition on the basis of the Vienna agreements while
avoiding any revolutionary unsettling of the nobility's landholdings. This orientation was congenial to the gentry in the Grand
Duchy but, given the Prussian government's anti-Polish stance,
unpromising.

These conditions favored the rise of the Organic Work movement in Prussian Poland. In the mid 1830s, local gentry clubs
arose to promote modern agricultural practices and provide
social amusements. Technical journals were published. Later, an
outstanding organizer appeared on the scene in the person of Dr.
Karol Marcinkowski, a son of the Poznanian bourgeoisie, trained as
a physician in France with Czartoryski's help. Between 1838 and
1843, he persuaded the gentry to donate money for the construction
of the Bazar Polski in Poznań, a hotel with conference rooms and
shops. It was a national symbol, signaling the beginning of the
Polish nobility's efforts to promote Polish urban interests and to
create for themselves a central focus in the Grand Duchy for their
political and cultural activities. The Polish Casino, a social
club attached to the Bazaar, became a venerable gentry institution.[63]

After the accession of Frederick William IV in 1840, the Prussian state, and the Grand Duchy along with it, plunged into a
rapid flow of political events and economic crises which culminated in the Revolution of 1848. At the coronation ceremonies at
Königsberg, the erratic new king, already on good terms with the
leading aristocrats of the Grand Duchy, lent a sympathetic ear to
a denunciation of the Flottwell regime formally delivered in an
eloquent speech by Count Edward Raczyński. Persuasively contrasting the Prussian government's promises of 1815 with the Germanizing
tendencies of the 1830s, Raczyński won from Frederick William IV
the response: "Your nationality is not to be undermined."[64] In
1841, Flottwell left the province. Official support of German
colonization ended and the use of the Polish language in public
administration was extended. In 1842 a liberal school language
ordinance, which remained in effect for the next thirty years,
satisfied the Poles' basic complaints about Prussian educational
policy in the Duchy.[65] Chairs in Slavic literature and philology
were created at the Berlin and Breslau universities. The forma-

tion in the same year of a separate Catholic section of the
Ministry of Education placed supervision of Polish elementary
schools in the Grand Duchy in the hands of the Polish clergy. The
government also liberalized its press and private association
policy and permitted Polish political emigrés from Russia to
reside unhindered in the Grand Duchy.[66]

Frederick William IV instructed his officials to respect the
Poles' nationality and avoid any appearance of favoring the German population in the Grand Duchy. Despite his fanciful dreams
about German unification, this ruler possessed a caste-bound
mentality which preferred the vision of the Polish nobility joined
with the rest of his aristocratic subjects in upholding his
throne to any idea of populist German or Prussian nationalism
directed against the szlachta, in whose "better impulses" he,
unlike his father's government, trusted. Moreoever, like such
enlightened officials of the late eighteenth and early nineteenth
centuries as Altenstein, Frederick William IV had no doubts about
the powers of attraction of German civilization. He wrote the
provincial president of the Grand Duchy in 1841 that "the natural
result of an undisturbed historical development will be the suf-
fusion of the Polish element in the province with a Prussian
spirit and German culture. . . ." In an analogy later deplored
by German nationalists, he concluded that "the French government
has only succeeded in making good Frenchmen of the Alsatians by
permitting them to remain Germans."[67]

The king's officials could not rise to such levels of high-
mindedness. Both Minister of Interior von Rochow and Provincial
President von Arnim posited an ineluctable struggle in which
German culture and Prussian discipline would overcome Polish backwardness and disorder. Arnim wrote grimly that "only when the
entire Polish organism is filled with German blood will it cease
its efforts to break loose from the body with which it has been
joined against its will."[68] Yet these ministers agreed that a
discriminatory and provocative Polenpolitik, such as Flottwell
had pursued, could only be self-defeating.

The Polish nobility welcomed Flottwell's departure. After
a social boycott of Prussian functionaries of ten years' duration,
they were glad to establish personal relations with the new provincial president and with the king, who ceremoniously visited
Poznań in 1841. Their confidence was buoyed by the government's
concessions over language and educational policy. Yet they had
not unlearned their habits of political opposition. More important, in the 1840s it became clear that an ideological rift was

opening between the Poles and the Prussian regime. They had not
abandoned their hope of seeing the Grand Duchy become an island
of Polish nationality within the Prussian sea. The issue arose
at the diet of 1841, when German liberal deputies from the urban
estate introduced a bill calling for the creation of an all-
Prussian parliament. The Polish deputies, fearing this would integrate the Duchy more fully into the Prussian state, opposed the
measure, not on its intrinsic merit, but "as Poles." Raczyński
declared in the diet: "For 25 years we have not abandoned the
standpoint that we are not Germans, not Prussians, not some kind
of mongrels of Polish extraction, but Poles under the sceptre of
the king of Prussia; for 25 years we have resolutely opposed amalgamation with the Germanic nation." To send Polish deputies to a
central Prussian parliament would amount, the arch-conservative
Raczyński said, to the Poznanian Poles' repudiation of their ties
with the Russian and Austrian Poles in favor of "Rhinelanders and
Westphalians."[69]

But as the Prussian constitutional question grew more critical after 1840, the Poles began to reconsider their position. They
concluded that, if the Prussian monarchy and bureaucracy would not
grant them the national rights they believed the 1815 settlement
had promised them, then they must look to a "system of freedom,"
that is, to the German liberal movement which seemed to promise
them a future of self-administration and cultural autonomy. In
the diet of 1843 the Poles supported a German petition for a central Prussian parliament, while the Germans underscored their
support of the Poles' linguistic rights, which were still subject
to the chicaneries of the lower bureaucracy. Although the government's reaction to these petitions was an outraged rejection, the
Poles and Germans persisted at the diet of 1845 in pressing for
a variety of liberal measures whose official condemnation was a
foregone conclusion. Like the rest of the monarchy, the Duchy
was heading towards a revolutionary confrontation whose first formal expression was the United Diet in Berlin, called by the
financially pressed government in 1847.[70]

The Polish gentry's turn towards liberalism seemed duplicitous
to many Germans, who thought of the szlachta as "Sarmatian magnates." But since the Gordian knot of serfdom had been cut, re-
lieving the Polish nobility of their onerous role as feudal ex-
ploiters of their own common people, this political step was a
logical one, foreshadowed already in the Poles' broad support of
Napoleon. After peasant amancipation, the nobility could rest
secure in their own economic base as they sought popular backing.

At the same time, liberal parliamentarism appeared as the only
promising means of reversing the Germanizing tendencies of the
Prussian bureaucracy.

Frederick William IV's concessions allowed the Poles to
create a lively political and cultural press, aimed both at the
upper classes and the common people. Emigrés from Russian and
Austrian Poland collaborated with the local intelligentsia to make
the Grand Duchy in the years 1840-46 the most advanced of all
centers of Polish culture. A major accomplishment in the realm
of Organic Work was the foundation in 1841, under Marcinkowski's
leadership, of the Society for Academic Aid to the Youth of the
Grand Duchy of Poznań (TNP).[71] This organization consisted of
county fund-raising committees. These elected a provincial committee which distributed part of the funds in scholarships to
young Polish applicants. The remainder of the money collected
was deposited in an "iron fund," the interest from which in the
future became the major source of scholarship money. The Society
became an archetype for subsequent socioeconomic and cultural
organizations. In it, the intelligentsia played a major executive role, but its chief organizers were Catholic priests, who
in this way and with the Archbishop's approval began their crucial
role in the nationalist movement. The gentry donated most of the
funds. The scholarships were granted to children of the petite
bourgeoisie, the prosperous peasantry, estate officials and
servants, and a smaller number of urban and rural workers. These
students, who were chosen for their command of the literary Polish
language and their interest in Polish history and literature, attended secondary schools and Prussian universities where they
trained as merchants and businessmen, teachers and scholars,
doctors, lawyers, and technicians. They took their places in the
ranks of the Duchy's Polish bourgeoisie and intelligentsia and
proved themselves, in the years between 1841 and 1914, valuable
supporters and leaders of the national movement. By 1851, 455
students had already completed their secondary or university
training, at a cost of nearly 300,000 marks; by 1914, 3,500
students had been educated with the Society's aid. The TNP thus
promoted with success the emergence of an educated and professional,
nationally conscious bourgeoisie of common origins in Prussian
Poland.[72]

To a number of Poles in the Grand Duchy, legal action offered
no attraction. On the contrary, in the early 1840s the revolutionary pulse began again to beat strongly throughout Polish
society. The Democratic Society in Versailles, which counted

several hundred adherents in the Duchy, began planning a general
uprising in all three partition areas. In Poznań, a bookseller
organized a secret "Union of the Working Classes," the first
instance of a plebeian quasi-socialist movement in Prussian
Poland. The brilliant and radical Eduard Dembowski and Henryk
Kamieński preached a doctrine of popular revolt aimed squarely both
at the Polish landlords and the partitioning government. Conflicts within the international Polish revolutionary movement
forced the Democratic Society's hand, and a rising was hastily
scheduled for early 1846. Betrayed by anxious gentry to the
Prussian police, most of the prospective leaders were arrested in
the winter of 1845-46. Only in Galicia did the insurrection takes
its course. But it was quickly transformed, to the despair of
all Polish nationalists, into a bloody peasant jacquerie aimed at
the local Polish nobility. The Austrians crushed the rising, but
at the price of the annexation of the Free City of Cracow.[73]

        In the Grand Duchy, the abortive rising of 1846 led to the
resumption of a harsh Polenpolitik which manifested itself in the
strangling of all but the clerical-conservative Polish press,
the closing of various local Polish organizations, and the sus-
pension of Polish administration in the Landschaft bank. In
1847, 254 Poles were brought to trial in Berlin for participation
in the attempted insurrection.[74] Throughout 1846 and 1847, the
Duchy's German police combed town and village alike for Polish
revolutionaries. Contemporary sources indicate that this confrontation with the Prussian authorities considerably intensified
anti-Prussian sentiment among the Polish common people. On the
eve of 1848, frustration and bitterness prevailed among the Polish
upper classes and suspicion and economic deprivation among the
masses, while the revolutionary leadership sat in Berlin's Moabit
Prison.[75]

Germans and Jews in the Grand Duchy of Poznań, 1815-48
        During the nineteenth century, the Polish nobility, towns-
people, and villagers continued to think of the land of the Grand
Duchy as their homeland, their native soil, part of the larger
geographical, social, and cultural fatherland (ojczyzna) to which
they, in their varying ways, felt attached. To travel west into
Prussia and Germany was to leave the homeland behind. The settlement of 1815 placed the Germans and Jews in a more equivocal relation to the Grand Duchy. Their rootedness in this largely Polish
environment, their Bodenständigkeit, depended, once they were free
to migrate to the purely German parts of the monarchy, on the ad-

vantages, both material and psychological, they could reap for
themselves by living in the Duchy. In the course of centuries,
they undoubtedly had developed a native feeling for their areas
of settlement in western Poland. But for the Germans, and later
also for the Jews, if local conditions grew intolerable, they
could migrate elsewhere in Prussia without having to feel that
they were exiles in a wholly foreign land.[76]

Between 1815 and 1848, all three nationalities felt the
impact of the Duchy's incorporation into the Prussian state and
the government's reform legislation. The estate owners made the
transition to capitalist agriculture fairly smoothly. Compensation paid by their regulated serfs and state credits enabled them
to equip their farms anew. Unregulated but emancipated serfs
provided a cheap labor source. Technical societies and literature
showed them how to crop the traditional fallows. Although grain
prices on the Prussian market and abroad slumped in the 1820s and
bad harvests plagued the 1840s, they found a good market in wool
and invested heavily in sheep-raising, while they also profited
from distillation of liquor. The peasantry endowed with freeholds
lacked capital and expertise and only managed to hang on to their
farms, which they sought to make as self-sufficient as possible.
The lot of the masses of unregulated peasants was hardest of all.
Many kept their traditional small holdings in return for labor on
the local estate, but others lived miserably as poorly paid and
badly housed cottagers and laborers.[77]

Reincorporation into Prussia dealt a hard blow to the Duchy's
towns. In 1822, Russia closed its frontiers to textile imports
from Prussian Poland. The Duchy's once-flourishing cloth manufacturers, unable to compete on the Prussian market with Silesia,
Saxony, and the Rhineland, never recovered from this loss, and
by the mid nineteenth century the textile industry had withered
irredeemably. The province lacked the raw materials for metal-
lurgical industries. Local capital was mainly in gentry hands
and flowed into agriculture. Railroads built in the 1840s transported most agricultural products outside the Duchy to preexisting
processing plants. Urban entrepreneurial talent was scarce. No
wonder that the Duchy's 131 small towns slumbered in small-scale
artisan production, local trade, and market gardening well beyond
1848. Only Poznań and Bromberg (Bydgoszcz), the province's two
administrative centers, throve modestly on the patronage of the
bureaucracy and military. The provincial capital's population
doubled from 1818 to 1849, but its 39,300 souls made it nothing
more than a medium-sized preindustrial city in a sea of villages
and tiny market towns.[78]

The province's population altogether increased from 780,000
in 1818 to 1,352,000 in 1849, but the proportion of townspeople to
villagers remained steady at roughly 1:3. Nevertheless, this was
rapid growth. It was caused by earlier marriages occurring among
the emancipated peasantry--a general phenomenon throughout the
Prussian east--and by German immigration to the province after
1815. But the Duchy was by no means overpopulated. Though
slightly larger in area, its population did not equal even a third
of mid nineteenth-century Belgium's.[79]

The numerical and occupational distribution of Poles, Germans,
and Jews within the Duchy's population in 1848 did not differ
radically from that of the 1790s. In the mid nineteenth century,
60.7 percent spoke Polish, 33.6 percent were German-speaking
Protestants and Catholics, 5.7 percent were Jews.[80] In the countryside, except in the Germanized border counties, the private
estate owners were still mostly Polish gentry. Judging by the
languages spoken by village mayors, in the 1830s roughly two-
thirds of the peasantry were Poles.[81] In the towns, confessional
figures from 1840 for the District of Poznań (the more Polish half
of the Duchy) show that 41 percent of the population were Catholics,
both Polish and German; 34 percent were German Protestants; and 25
percent were Jews.[82] A large majority of the wealthier merchants,
both wholesale and retail, continued to be Jews. The most lucrative and highly skilled artisan trades were in German hands,
though many Poles and Jews were also handicraftsmen. Apprentices
and journeymen tended to share their employer's nationality. Poles
predominated among unskilled workers, while all three nationalities
were represented in the poverty-stricken ranks of occasional
laborers, vagabonds, and beggars.

Yet, since Great Poland had fallen under Prussian domination
at the end of the eighteenth century, the balance of demographic
and economic power had shifted perceptibly in favor of the German-
speaking population. In 1848, a numerous class of Prussian officials resided in the Duchy, from lowly post employees and district
commissioners to the provincial president and his staff. Sizable
army garrisons had sprung up. The Prussian government, assuming
control of former Polish Crown lands, leased or sold them to
Germans. Flottwell's regime settled many German peasant colonists.
German Junkers and bourgeois purchased estates in the Duchy,
until in 1848 roughly 30 percent of the private estate land was in
their hands.[83]

The predominantly German textile artisans of the eighteenth
and early nineteenth centuries were forced out of work and emigrated

either westward or to Russian Poland, where many helped to
establish the great textile center of Łódź. But other Germans
migrated to the Duchy to become artisans, market gardeners, shopkeepers, technicians, and professionals, relying on the official
establishment's patronage, taking advantage of the province's
need for capital and expertise, and riding the upward swing in
overall population growth. Until about 1870, the population of
Prussia's thinly settled eastern provinces grew very rapidly
despite the absence of industrialization. Many Germans from
Prussia's relatively overpopulated central and western provinces
moved to the east. The one-time mayor of the West Prussian town
of Marienwerder (Kwidzyń) wrote of these years,

> As long as agriculture and those small-scale urban
> trades and crafts which served the needs of agri-
> culture were the chief forms of earning a living
> in Germany, the eastern provinces were willingly
> sought out. In this new territory, one could
> quickly attain a good income--better in fact than
> in the rest of Germany.[84]

As a result of these migrations the non-Jewish German-speaking
population in the Duchy rose between 1825 and 1849 by 41 percent,
almost twice as rapidly as the Polish population. This allowed
the proportion of Germans in the Duchy's population to rise in
the same period from 30.8 percent to 33.6 percent, while the
Poles' share fell from 62.9 percent to 60.7 percent.[85]

    The Jews, whose strongest economic positions were in com-
merce, suffered some heavy losses after the resumption of Prussian rule and the subsequent closure of the Russian market to the
Duchy's trade. Jewish merchant-entrepreneurs in textiles went
out of business, and wholesalers dealing with what now was Russian
Poland were forced to resort to smuggling, which some developed
into a virtuoso art.[86] Prussian regulations forbade Jewish migration from the Duchy to other provinces in the period 1815-48, but
evasion was possible. Some of the province's wealthier merchants
managed to move west, while Galician and Russian Jews crossed il-
legally into the Duchy. But the majority, confined with the Duchy,
increased their numbers between 1825 and 1849 by 18 percent.
Their 76,800 souls in 1849 represented the Poznanian Jews' absolute
maximum between 1793 and 1914 and put them in the first rank in
numbers among the Prussian provinces' Jewish communities. But, in
proportion to the non-Jewish German and Polish populations, the
Jews began to lose ground steadily after 1815. In 1825, they
comprised 6.3 percent of the total provincial population; in 1849,
despite their increase, this figure had fallen to 5.7 percent.[87]

    During the first half of the nineteenth century, Jewish
society was ruled by its rabbis who, although sometimes at odds

with the richer merchants, tended towards solidarity with them.
Below these religious and secular notables were the several strata
of the Jewish common people, most of them living on the edge or in
the midst of poverty. In 1849, of the employed or income-receiving
population, 10 percent were bankers and financiers, wholesalers,
specialty retailers, inn and hotelkeepers "for the cultivated
classes," rabbis, educated professionals, and communal officials.
Below them, 52 percent were either artisan masters--very many of
them in the clothing trades, two of every three working without
paid laborers--or petty merchants, brokers, tavern-keepers, and
traveling salesmen. Below these, 27 percent were employed as ap-
prentice and journeymen artisans, day laborers, and servants.
And, at the bottom, 11 percent lived on alms or begging. It was an
economically troubled society. The property-owning notables were
responsible for heavy communal debts incurred mostly before the
partitions of the Commonwealth. The Jewish proletariat, wrote
Flottwell in 1832, lived in "indescribable misery."[88]

    In 1807, the Germans of Great Poland turned their backs on the
Hohenzollern monarchy and dutifully paid their taxes to support
Napoleon and his allies. They became obedient Polish subjects of
the Grand Duchy of Warsaw.[89] In 1815, as the Prussian regime was
reestablished in the newly christened Grand Duchy of Poznań, the
Germans staged celebrations, as they had in 1793, in honor of
their new masters.[90]
    For the Duchy's Germans to think of themselves as Prus-
sians, and not merely Prussian subjects, it was necessary that
they share in the life and fortunes of the state. But after 1815
the Prussian government, increasingly hostile to the liberal constitutional movement in Germany, confined the political rights of
the Duchy's Germans to representation in the consultative,
szlachta-dominated county and provincial diets and, for the
propertied townspeople, limited self-government after 1831 in
elected city councils. Most of the province's native Germans
were urban or rural commoners. The conservative and aristocratic
Prussian monarchy sought to keep them in political leading
strings while molding them into "good Prussians."
    Education was one means to this end. By the 1840s Prussian
schoolmasters had succeeded in teaching the German pasants and
urban lower classes, who as late as 1833 spoke what a Prussian
official called "a highly corrupted Kashubian-Low German dialect,"
to understand spoken and written High German.[91] The schools
taught the German common people the elements of Prussian and Ger-

man history and instructed them in the rights and the duties
of Prussian citizens. But tying the Germans to the state through
bonds of religion proved to be difficult. The Protestant Lutherans
found their communes supervised by outsiders appointed without
their consultation and wedded to a theological rationalism foreign
to their traditions. They objected to the merger of the Lutheran
and Calvinist faiths in Prussia promoted by the Crown and bureaucracy after 1817. In the 1840s, the government imprisoned dissenting Lutheran pastors in the Grand Duchy. Because of the
church's control by the military-bureaucratic monarchy, and its
stress on subordination to secular authority, the Lutheran
German common people began in this period "to regard the pastors
as something in the nature of gendarmes in black."[92] The government ignored the German Catholics, who supported the Polish-
dominated Archdiocese in its struggle with the state over mixed
marriages in the 1830s. Polonization of German Catholics continued
well beyond 1848.[93]

The state's release of the German peasantry from the rents
and obligations traditionally owed their Polish lords no doubt
earned their gratitude. But it was tempered by the monetary
compensation they were required to pay and by the taxes and military service the Prussian government fastened upon them. The same
can be said of the many German burghers freed after 1833 from
subjection to Polish landlords. Abolition of guilds was unpopular
among the German artisans, while the German merchants and old-
fashioned entrepreneurs resented loss of the Russian market and
competition from Silesia and the western provinces.

Before 1848 the German common people in town and villages
alike accepted the Prussian regime passively. During the bad
harvests and attendant urban economic crises of the 1840s, which
the state did little to alleviate, they had few reasons to be
proud of being Prussians or members of the German nation. The
wealthier Germans who were engaged in private business in the
towns and active in urban government began after 1831 to find
their political voices, but what they said was unpleasing to official ears. They opposed the state's commercial policy, called
for an all-Prussian parliament and broad civil liberties, criticized the caste spirit of the aristocratic monarchy, and in the
provincial diet supported numerous Polish petitions in linguistic
and educational questions. They had, in short, by 1848 entered
the stream of Prussian-German liberalism.[94]

In the three decades after 1815, the royal bureaucracy in the
Duchy became an increasingly solidly German corps, recruited

largely from outside the province. After 1830, it acquired a collective mentality which persisted to the end of Prussian rule. This was a compound of bureaucratic egotism, which assumed the state administration's superior political objectivity and competence in contrast to the mass of private individuals it was destined to govern, together with a strong conservative-monarchist orientation. To these traits common to all Prussian officialdom, many of the Duchy's bureaucrats joined a pervasive suspicion of Polish revolutionary impulses and political disloyalty, a contempt for the character and culture of the Polish upper classes, and a paternalistic, authoritarian attitude towards the Polish common people. Towards the province's German population, the bureaucracy assumed the lofty stance of unquestionable authority which provoked throughout Prussia so many accusations of "bureaucratic despotism."[95]

By the 1840s, the Duchy's increasingly numerous German landlords began, like the liberal bourgeoisie, to formulate a political program of their own. Already Flottwell had encouraged them, in the diets of the 1830s, to denounce the Poles' allegedly treasonous tendencies. In the diets of the 1840s, the Duchy's Junkers defied the liberalism of both the Polish gentry and the German bourgeoisie. Feeling their growing economic strength, they chafed under the shadow of the szlachta. The abortive Polish revolutionary attempts in the winter of 1845-46 gave them the political opening they sought. They submitted various petitions to the provincial administration calling for a resumption of Flottwell's policies, especially state-sponsored buying out or even expropriation of the Polish gentry and settlement of Germans in their stead. They demanded suppression of Polish private associations, packing of elective bodies with Germans, further restrictions on the Polish language, and official support for private German political and socioeconomic organizations. These proposals were rejected by a government unwilling to have its policies dictated by private interest groups. But they illuminate an aggressively anti-Polish, conservative, and outspokenly Prussian-German patriotic mentality among the Duchy's Junkers who saw their own advantage in the political and economic decline of the Polish gentry. It was a mentality which, like that of the bureaucracy, persisted to the fall of the monarchy in 1918.[96]

The Grand Duchy of Warsaw was a Napoleonic satellite. For the Jews of Great Poland, this was a fact of great importance since the Code Napoléon, adopted as civil law in the Grand Duchy in 1808,

placed them, for the first time since their ancestors' medieval
migrations to Poland, in a status of full civil equality with
the rest of the citizens of the state. But before they had time
to react to this startling change, a decree of 1809 postponed
the Jews' emancipation for ten years, during which the Polish
government hoped that at least the upper classes would embrace
the Polish language and commit themselves to Polish political
goals. Meanwhile, as of old, exceptional taxes continued to be
levied on the Jews, while they were asked to pray for the success of Polish and Napoleonic arms.[97]

Such was the ambiguous status of the Jews when the Prussian
government established the Grand Duchy of Poznań. In a reaction
not unlike that of the Poles in 1809, the Prussians in 1815
balked at extending the civil equality granted the Prussian Jews
in 1812 to the populous Jewish communes of the Duchy. This was
primarily because they feared migration of the Jewish proletariat
to central and western Prussia and because they were unsure of the
Jewish upper classes' attachment to German culture and the Hohenzollern monarchy. Hence, until 1833 the Jews were confined to the
Duchy, excluded from civil and political equality, and governed
under the laws of the Grand Duchy of Warsaw which, in social and
economic matters, favored the wealthier Jews at the expense of
the poor.[98]

Nevertheless, by 1815 the Duchy's Jews confronted legal
emancipation as a possibility. This intensified the debate over
the Haskalah movement into which the Jews of Great Poland had been
drawn in the second half of the eighteenth century. Adoption of
the German literary language and abandonment of strict Talmudic
law governing social life and contacts with Christians, as the
increasingly numerous proponents of "Enlightenment" urged, would
make Jews more acceptable to the Prussian government and hasten
the day of legal equality. This promised an end to the age-old
insecurity of the Jews by granting them full citizenship, exemption from restrictions on marriage, occupation, and place of
residence, and abolition of exceptional taxes. Civil equality
was unquestionably in the Jews' secular and material interest.
Yet, it carried with it a possibility which appeared as a threat
to the adherents of traditional Talmudic Orthodoxy. If the Jews
were assimilated culturally, politically, and economically into
Prussian-German society, what would remain of Judaism as a self-
contained social community whose purpose was the preservation of
the Jewish law and the Jewish people, distinct by their religious
destiny from all others? Could assimilation even be reconciled
with the traditional religion?

This dilemma confronted all traditional European Jewish communities in the nineteenth century. In the communes of the Grand
Duchy, the Jews split into traditionalist and reform factions
whose disagreements came to light especially over the election of
rabbis. A crucial issue was Jewish education. Reformers, supported by the wealthier Jews, argued that Jewish students should
attend Prussian schools to obtain their secular education, and
that the traditional Talmudic schools should provide religious
education only. The traditionalists opposed attendance in state
schools. But by 1815, after several decades of contact with
German Jewry, many of the Jews of Great Poland found this position
benighted and self-defeating.[99]

Following the Polish insurrection of 1830-31, the Prussian
authorities, spurred on by Provincial President Flottwell, presented the Duchy's Jews with a fundamental choice. Seeking to
draw them into the life of the state on the side of the German
nationality, an edict of 1833 promised "naturalization" to all
Jews possessing a certain sum of capital or a secure profession
who adopted German dress, spoke German fluently, and sent their
children to public German schools. Naturalization meant full
civil equality, as well as the right to pursue any occupation.
Only naturalized Jews could apply for the right to emigrate from
the Duchy. In place of military service, naturalized Jews paid a
special tax until 1845, when this was abolished and service became compulsory.

The attractions of naturalization were irresistible to the
upper classes, including even many traditionalists. Akiba Eger,
the highly Orthodox chief rabbi of Poznań, solemnly led his followers into the ranks of the naturalized Jews. Full-scale
Orthodox Jewish schools survived until the 1870s, but attendance,
except for religious studies, declined as the Duchy's Jews gradually accepted Prussian education. The Jews trimmed their beards,
abandoned their caftans, and began to speak High German instead of
Yiddish. Their religious lives remained intense throughout the
nineteenth century. But after 1833 they assimilated, following
the lead of the propertied classes, into the social, literary,
and political culture of the Prussian state. In 1847, the non-
naturalized Jews obtained the same status as their naturalized
brothers. The revolution of 1848 conferred complete civil and
political equality, including the right of free internal migration,
on all Prussian Jews.[100]

After 1833, the naturalized Jews, having taken the first step
towards integration into the Prussian state, faced the question of

their political position in the Duchy. As townspeople this
meant, until 1848, their role in urban politics. Christian anti-
Semitism was still a strong force after 1815. The diet of 1827
unanimously rejected Jewish emancipation, called on the Jews to
"civilize" themselves first. After 1833, the Jews' financial
strength was such that they could have elected strong contingents,
or even majorities to many town councils, had not the Prussian
government limited their electoral rights and had not town governments, as in Poznań itself, contrived to refuse them seats in
the councils. By the 1840s, however, it was evident to both the
Poles and the Germans that the day of full Jewish equality could
not be far away. Each side began tentatively to seek the Jews'
support. In 1845 a Polish majority voted to admit Jews into the
Poznań town council. In the diet of the same year, both the Poles
and the German urban delegates called for final Jewish emancipation, though with the ulterior motive, openly admitted on the
German side, of enabling the Jews to emigrate.[101]

The Jews themselves, suspicious of Christian anti-Semitism,
approached the political arena with great caution. Before 1848,
they did not take sides in the conflicts between Germans and
Poles. Only on the eve of the revolution did they consider
electing Jewish candidates to urban offices. Still strongly influenced by traditions of obedience to their own religious leaders
and by Talmudic dictates to honor the Christian authorities, they
were remote from doctrines of liberalism or democracy. They felt,
as one wrote of his youth in Poznań, "a good Prussian, old conservative, one might say religious-dynastic patriotism" which
"filled the Jews with confidence that the government would honorably uphold law, peace and the practice of religion."[102]

The Revolution of 1848 in the Grand Duchy of Poznań

In March 1848 Prussian absolutism resigned its monopoly of
political power under threat of popular revolution. Amid the
turbulence of the fall of Louis Philippe and Metternich and the
collapse of royal absolutism in the lesser German states, Frederick William IV yielded to the long-standing opposition of the
educated and propertied middle classes by promising constitutional
government and Prussian leadership in German unification. By
these means, he sought to weld the middle and upper classes
together in opposition to the social radicalism, real and potential, of the urban and rural common people, a radicalism which
was the political articulation of the suffering and dislocations
visited upon them by the economic breakdown of the old regime and
the halting beginnings of industrialization.

As in 1806, so too in 1848 the paralysis of the central government in Berlin led to a Polish revolution in Poznań. But no Napoleon guaranteed this revolution. From its convulsions issued, not a restored Polish state, but an unprecedented political struggle among the Poznanian nationalities and a definitive estrangement between the Polish upper classes and the Prussian government.

The first weeks of the revolution in Germany were tense with the anticipation of imminent war. Rumors circulated of impending French attacks on the Rhine, or a Russian invasion to restore the crumbling ancien régime. Better grounded than these popular fears was the belief, widely shared by German liberal nationalists, that, although Russia might tolerate constitutional reform in the various German states, the creation of a powerful, unified Germany would so upset the traditional European balance of power that Russia could not fail to intervene in defense of its own mighty international position. An assault by Nicholas I's armies on the German revolution seemed but a question of time. Heinrich von Gagern was not the only German liberal who welcomed the prospect of victorious war with Russia as a bridge towards national unification.

German liberal Russophobia went hand in hand during the 1830s and 1840s with an unprecedented enthusiasm for the Polish cause. This was born not only of an admiration for the Poles' revolutionary struggles, such as Kościuszko had first inspired in Germany; particularly after the insurrection of 1830-31, the belief grew that German unification on a liberal or democratic basis--before 1848 few supposed unification would be accomplished by conservative means--required the restoration of Poland. This view presupposed a common German and Polish interest in the greatest possible weakening of Russian strength and influence in Europe. Since Polish revolutionary nationalists were the Tsar's bitterest and most active enemies, it was natural that German nationalists should hope to add impetus to their own movement by supporting the Poles. Moreover, German liberals opposed not only Russian, but also Prussian and Hapsburg autocracy. They perceived little danger to the interests of the German nation in the loss of the Grand Duchy of Poznań and Galicia, which they regarded as essentially Polish lands, to a restored Polish state. Many were equally willing to see West Prussia ruled again from Warsaw. They judged the partitions of the Polish Commonwealth as the cynical, criminal acts of the very absolutism they fought in the name of the German people. Restoration of Poland in the borders of 1772 would

erase German responsibility for these misdeeds while making possible the birth of a popularly governed, unified German state.
The question of sovereignty over the Vistula delta paled next to
such momentous prospects, just as the traditional social and
cultural problems of Polish-German coexistence seemed to retreat
before the coming age of democratic national self-determination.[103]

No wonder that the breakthrough of the German constitutional
and national movement at the expense of the traditional absolute
regimes in March 1848 coincided with a wave of pro-Polish sentiment and the expectation that Poland would soon be restored in a
victorious German-Polish war against Russia. In Berlin, the
Polish revolutionaries imprisoned since 1846 obtained release
and paraded in triumph through the streets. Their leaders, the
military strategist Ludwik Mierosławski and the democratic intellectual Karol Libelt, seized this excited moment to proclaim in an
address to the German people, "You know that the time has come in
which the fateful deed of the partition of Pland must be expiated.
But it is also a time in which, for the security of a free Germany, an independent Poland must be created as an outpost against
the pressure of the Asiatics."[104] Simultaneously, in Poznań the
Polish nobility, intelligentsia, and bourgeoisie took advantage of
the paralysis of the Prussian administration to create a Polish
National Committee which announced its aim as "the independence of
the whole of Poland."[105] A few days later, Mierosławski arrived
in the Grand Duchy to recruit a Polish army, whose numbers quickly
swelled to 10,000. This force, he hoped, would soon invade Russian Poland in concert with a revolutionized Prussian army and a
Polish contingent similar to his own from Galicia. Throughout the
predominantly Polish districts of the Grand Duchy, local Polish
representatives of the National Committee, mainly noblemen, ignored the authority of the Prussian officials and helped raise men
and money for Mierosławski's venture. Proclamations of the
National Committee promised economic relief to the peasants who
joined the national liberation force, abolished legal class dis-
tinctions, and assured the Germans and Jews equality and national
toleration in the new Polish state.[106] It seemed that the Prussian Poles were prepared as never before for the moment of liberation.

The drift of Prussian and German revolutionary politics
favored the Poles. On 28 March, the liberal nationalist
Camphausen-Hansemann ministry took office in Berlin. The new
foreign minister, Harry von Arnim, anticipated war with Russia
and the restoration of Poland. The revolutionary all-German pre-

Parliament met between 31 March and 3 April, condemned the Polish
partitions, described Polish restoration as "a sacred duty of the
German nation," and provisionally exempted the Grand Duchy from
participation in the National Assembly which was to decide the
constitutional and territorial structure of the new Germany.[107]
At the same time, the United Prussian Diet reconvened, and it too,
on 2 April, solemnly called for the restoration of Poland.[108] So
as not to lose complete control of events in the Grand Duchy, the
Prussian government appointed General Wilhelm von Willisen royal
commissioner with plenipotentiary powers to agree with the Poles
on the Duchy's military and civil reorganization. Willisen, a
veteran of the German War of Liberation against Napoleon, was the
only high Prussian army officer ever entrusted with Polish affairs
who felt a strong sympathy with Polish national aspirations. He,
too, expected war with Russia and the creation of a Polish state
joined in friendship with a liberalized Prussia and Germany.[109]

Despite this surge of action and opinion, neither was an anti-
Russian war fought nor a Polish state reestablished. Nicholas I
shrewdly avoided aggression against Prussia or Austria. He contented himself with gradually massing over 300,000 troops in Russian Poland, an action which posed a formidable challenge to the
west. The Russian Poles, caught in the vise of a relentless
military-bureaucratic occupation, had no chance to revolt. The
Galician Poles were immobilized by the opposition of the nobility
and the common people bloodily brought to light in 1846. France
and England, though sympathetic to the Polish cause, feared a war
with Russia into which it was likely that they would be drawn.
Frederick William IV himself, despite the policies of his ministry,
was dead set against war with Russia. In the end, his word alone
governed the Prussian army, whose leadership in any case shared
his sentiments. The engines of war having thus misfired,
Mierosławski and the Prussian Poles found themselves trapped in the
Grand Duchy and dependent on the further course of the revolution
in Prussia and Germany.[110]

Misled by the monarchical regimes' concessions to national
and constitutional reform during the March Days, German liberal
nationalists, and especially those in Prussia, failed to follow up
their first successes with efforts to seize complete control of
state power. Instead, they placed their trust, to the scorn of the
revolutionary republican and socialist Left, in the constitutional
conventions, especially the German National Assembly in Frankfurt
am Main and the Prussian National Assembly in Berlin. These were
elected and convened in mid 1848 with the presumed authority to

dictate to the still-intact monarchies the new political and
territorial structure of the German nation. This tactic, which
proved fatal to liberal nationalist hopes, left the old regimes--
even where, as in Prussia, they were fronted by liberal minis-
tries--a freedom of action quickly seized upon by antirevolutionary circles at court, in the military, and in the unreconstructed
bureaucracies. Finally, military force and monarchical fiat
crushed the moderate and radical revolutionary movements in both
Prussia and Austria. In early 1849 Frederick William IV shattered
the pretentions of the Frankfurt assembly by rejecting the
imperial crown it offered him. Prussian troops defeated the
popular armed protests of May 1849 against this counterrevolution-
ary stroke. A subsequent Prussian effort to unify Germany on
terms favorable to monarchical conservatism foundered on Russian
opposition and the intractable problem of reconciling Prussian and
Austrian interests in Germany. Finally, in 1851, the prerevolu-
tionary status quo returned in the reconstitution of the monarchist-
particularist Germanic Confederation of 1815.

The fate of the German revolution determined the course of
events in the Grand Duchy of Poznań. Before the convocation of
the national assemblies, the Prussian government, over whose
policies the king exercised final control, could deal as it saw fit
with its subjects in the Grand Duchy. Thereafter, whatever the
assemblies decided about the Grand Duchy could be accepted or ignored by the Prussian government, over which neither the elected
delegates in Berlin nor those in Frankfurt possessed any powers
of coercion.

Despite liberal nationalist opinion and Arnim's foreign
policy, the Prussian government never planned seriously for war
with Russia. Frederick William IV and his closest advisers, far
from wishing to reopen the international Polish question, were
determined to maintain Prussian sovereignty in the Grand Duchy.
The establishment of the Polish National Committee and the formation of Mierosławski's legions had created a revolutionary situation in the Grand Duchy. But the Poles had not yet demanded
independence from the government in Berlin. A Polish delegation,
headed by Archbishop Przyłuski and representing majority opinion
in the Polish National Committee, confined itself cautiously in
an audience with the king on 23 March to a request for linguistic
equality and administrative autonomy. The next day, a royal rescript appeared vaguely promising "national reorganization" of
the Duchy.[111]

In the meantime, the Poles' revolutionary initiatives, the
breakdown or paralysis of the local German administration, the

rumors of war and Polish independence, and the royal talk of "national reorganization" forced the Duchy's Germans and Jews into action. The Germans, especially the large Protestant majority, followed three paths. In the provincial capital, the apparent strength of the Polish revolutionary movement inclined the private bourgeoisie towards collaboration with the Polish National Committee. But the Poles, not wishing to compromise their freedom of action, refused to seat the Germans in their own ranks. Hence a separate German National Committee arose which soon fell under the control of nationalist officials and teachers who, although they conceded Polish demands for equality in the Duchy, opposed its secession from the Prussian state. In the predominantly German northern, western, and southern border counties, the Prussian administration remained intact, forming a rally point for burghers and peasants alarmed by the prospect of Polish rule. From the end of March, the towns and villages in this area began petitioning the Berlin government insistently for detachment of their districts from the Grand Duchy and their inclusion in the future German national state. Finally, the Germans scattered elsewhere in the province and surrounded by Polish majorities attempted either to flee to solidly German areas or to ride out the revolutionary waves as unobtrusively as possible.[112]

For the Jews, the March Days of 1848 were a decisive turning point. The Polish National Committee proclaimed full Jewish emancipation and civil equality. But memories of szlachta oppression, fear of the Polish masses, social and cultural affinities with the Germans, and the political loyalism the Prussian government had encouraged them to express since 1815 led them, by joining and supporting the various German national committees, to commit themselves openly to the German national movement in the provincial capital and Germanized counties. Only in the Polish heartland of the Duchy did they veil their sympathies in passivity.[113]

In early April, after any immediate threat of war with France or Russia had passed, the Prussian government began to reassert its shaken authority in the Grand Duchy. Its first object was to disarm Mierosławski's legions. General von Willisen, the emissary of the moderate liberal ministry, attempted this with promises to the Polish National Committee of home rule. But the Duchy's Prussian army command, encouraged by Frederick William IV and ever more stoutly supported by the local Germans and Jews, aimed to smash the Polish forces in the field. Greatly outnumbered, lacking any foreign aid, and unsure of the social consequences of an un-

expected victory over the Prussians, Mierosławski's noble-born
officers lacked the will to wage revolutionary war. On 11 April,
Willisen negotiated a compromise reducing the number of Polish
legionnaries in return for promises of "reorganization." Not
content with that, the Prussian army attacked the Poles. Several
pitched battles resulted, with considerable losses on both sides,
before the Poles were driven, on the 9th of May, to capitulate.
Meanwhile, Frederick William, impressed by the German-Jewish out-
cry against inclusion in a Polish-dominated Grand Duchy, announced
on 14 April that it would be partitioned, "reorganization" now ap-
plying only to the Polish districts.   These were defined in a
series of "demarcation lines" which, by early June, had staked
out for the Germans virtually the whole of the Duchy except for
a central region from the east of Poznań to the Russian border,
tentatively baptized the "Grand Duchy of Gniezno." At this point,
more Poles found themselves in the "German" districts than in
their own. The Polish National Committee, compromised in its passivity by Mierosławski's hapless resistance and humiliated by the
success of the conservative party in the government in confining
"reorganization" to a mere fragment of the Grand Duchy, dissolved
itself on 30 April. The Polish revolution defeated, the Prussian
police and civil officials returned to their posts in the van of
the triumphant Prussian army.[114]

The future of the Duchy now hinged on events in Germany. At
Frankfurt, the question was no longer restoration of the Polish
state, but whether the Poznanian Germans should become part of a
unified Germany. Not surprisingly, a large majority of the
delegates thought so, endorsing "demarcation" and Polish self-
administration only in the "Gniezno Duchy." This act of "national
egoism" on the part of the Frankfurt delegates has often been condemned.[115] No doubt, far too much of the Duchy was claimed for
the German nation. Nonetheless, the Frankfurt constitution extended linguistic, cultural, and local self-administrative rights
to non-German minorities which were far more liberal than any
the Poles in fact ever possessed under Prussian rule.[116]

The German state the Frankfurt constitution was meant to
govern was never born. The future of the Grand Duchy therefore
depended finally on the course of the revolution in the kingdom
of Prussia. The majority in the Prussian National Assembly, more
intent on curbing Hohenzollern absolutism than on the attainment
of German unity, recognized that the army's defeat of the Polish
revolution signified a triumph for their opponents at court, in
the bureaucracy and among the Junkers. The Germans in the Duchy

who rejoiced at the Poles' defeat appeared to the liberal and
democratic delegates in Berlin as accomplices in reaction. Hence,
on 29 October 1848, the assembly voted by a majority of one to retain the Grand Duchy in its pre-March limits and to fulfill the
royal promises of national equality made in 1815. This decision
did not weaken the Duchy's ties with the Prussian state. But,
taken together with the general liberalization of Prussian government aimed at by the assembly's majority, it offered the Poles
the prospect of national liberties no less considerable than those
the Frankfurt constitution extended.

The National Assembly's Polenpolitik was one among many
reasons for the royal coup d'état of November 1848. The delegates
were forcibly dismissed. On 5 December 1848 Frederick William IV
proclaimed a royally dictated, conservative-monarchist constitution. This document, later revised in a still more conservative
sense until attaining its final form in 1850, made no mention of
the Grand Duchy of Poznań and included no guarantees of national
minority rights. In effect, Frederick William III's pledges of
1815 were annulled. Henceforth, in the conservative Prussian
view, Polish claims to separate national rights had no basis in
law. For this reason, the Polish deputies in the Prussian
parliament (Landtag) refused in 1850 to swear the oath of allegiance to the constitution and resigned their seats in protest. It
was a futile gesture. After 1848, it was tacitly admitted throughout Europe that the 1815 Vienna settlement had lost its legitimacy.[117] In the 1850s, what was now simply called the Provinz
Posen, like the rest of the Prussian state, fell once again under
bureaucratic repression. Elections were rigged in favor of official candidates, the press censored, political associations
prohibited. The revolution of 1848--the "spring of nations"--had
frozen over.

The Legacy of 1848 to the Poznanian Nationalities

The Poles' political leaders--the gentry, noble-born intelligentsia, bourgeois activists, and clergy--could take no credit
for the outbreak of the revolution. Yet its advent on a European
scale heralded not merely deliverance from the repression that
had descended on the Grand Duchy since 1846, but an opportunity
for the restoration of Polish independence. The failure of a
war against Russia to materialize dashed the hopes of conservative
Polish nationalists. Only the prescription of the more radical
wing of the Emigration remained: recruitment of the Polish masses
with promises of social reform in a war of national liberation.

Because of circumstances peculiar to Russian and Austrian Poland,
this strategy could be attempted only in the Grand Duchy of
Poznań. But here the process of peasant regulation had satisfied
a sizable minority of former serfs. To endow the disenfranchised
majority with farms raised in the minds of the Polish gentry the
specter of seizure of their estates. Mierosławski, the only man
able and willing to lead a Polish revolutionary army in the Duchy,
was an emigré from Russian Poland, contemptuous of the landlords'
egotism but prevented by his own noble origins and fear of social
anarchy from making a realistic appeal to the economic interests
of the masses. The pressure of patriotic opinion led the Duchy's
nobility to aid Mierosławski with men and arms. But at heart
they doubted his prospects of success and feared his organization
of the common people. One of their principal spokesmen, Count
Tytus Działyński, wrote the Berlin authorities on 27 March, warn-
ing against a precipitate suppression by the Prussian army of
the revolutionary ferment in the Duchy:

> The troops will prevail wherever they show them-
> selves, but these triumphs will cost the lives,
> first, of the Germans who live in the province, then,
> of the Jews, and finally of the entire nobility. The
> only hope lies in the immediate formation of Polish
> regiments under the command of General Willisen; the
> disorder must be organized. . . .[118]

The Polish gentry looked to a sympathetic Prussian general, not to
Mierosławski, for defense of their lives and their interests. The
Polish National Committee's promises of reductions in regulated
peasants' compensation payments and of land "from the national
domains" to landless fighters disquieted the gentry. The
turbulences of Mierosławski's legions alarmed them. They foretold his defeat and, when it came, did not mourn him.[119]

In March and April, the Poles learned how unlikely a Polish
restoration through European war actually was. They contemplated
as well the cost of social revolution, and refused to pay the
price. They were left with the strategy they had conceived during the pre-March years: negotiations with the Prussian government, in alliance with the German liberals, for national equality
in the Duchy, paired with a program of Organic Work to improve
the cultural and economic conditions of the Polish masses and
simultaneously to tie them politically to the upper classes.

The Poles' defeat at the hands of the Prussian monarchy
between 1848 and 1850 was, ultimately, a consequence of the
failure of the popular constitutional movements in Prussia and
Germany. In the sphere of Organic Work, however, the revolution
marked a new stage with the creation in late 1848 of the Polish

League (Liga Polska). This strictly legal organization, strongly
supported by the gentry, clergy, and intelligentsia, aimed to enlist in local branches the whole of the Polish-speaking population. When in 1850 the government dissolved it, the league had
already recruited over 35,000 members. Its efforts to promote a
popular press, establish financial cooperatives, and develop the
Polish urban economy provided a model stressing mass participation in the Organic Work movement which was to have great importance.[120]

The Prussian constitution of 1848-50 provided the Polish
nationalists with a powerful new tool in their work of popular
organization. Elections to the lower house of parliament exposed
the common people to the language of national conflict, liberalism,
and national self-determination. The Landtag deputies could not
control the royally appointed ministries or impose legislation
upon them. Yet, despite an oligarchical application of universal
male suffrage, Prussian parliamentarism allowed the gentry, clergy,
and intelligentsia to assemble and propagandize the masses
legally.[121] The Poles seized this opportunity to create an
elaborate system of precinct, county, and electoral district
(Wahlkreis) committees charged with organizing voters' assemblies.
These, at least in theory, democratically selected the names of
Polish Landtag candidates. In fact, the committees were dominated until the end of the nineteenth century by large landowners,
conservative clergymen, and noble-born urban professionals. The
voters merely ratified the names of those members and allies of
the upper classes proposed as candidates by the committees. Yet
this system of "electoral authorities" (władze wyborcze) not only
deepened the common people's national and political consciousness,
but represented a kind of surrogate government within Polish society. At the apex of the committee system stood the "Provincial
Electoral Committee of the Grand Duchy of Poznań." This was a
kind of parliament of notables which, in tandem with the parliamentary delegations whose members it had previously certified as
"legal" candidates, formulated the "official" ideology and parliamentary strategies to which the entire Polish population was ex-
pected--and in large measure did--subscribe. Until 1909, this
system, which after 1870 managed elections to the Imperial
Parliament (Reichstag) as well, substituted for a political party
among the Prussian Poles. National solidarity was its guiding
principle, both in its agitation among the Polish masses and in
its parliamentary deputies' confrontations with the German
parties and Prussian and Imperial governments in Berlin. The

success of this system was evident in both the strict discipline
of the parliamentary delegations and the unusually high frequency
of Polish voting.[122]

In the aftermath of the revolution, the Polish upper classes
committed themselves solidly to the tactics of political legality
and Organic Work. But how deeply had the revolutionary crisis
stirred the common people? A Prussian police report listed 659
Poles active in the various local branches of the Polish National
Committee. Among these, 277 were small merchants and artisans,
191 were estate owners and managers, 66 were landed peasants, 59
were teachers and state officials, 46 were priests, and 20
were free professionals.[123] In Mierosławski's legions, most of
the soldiers were either landless peasants and estate servants--
many of them impressed into service by the gentry--or urban
workers and artisans. A smaller number were landed peasants and
their sons.[124] After Mierosławski's defeat, the reoccupation of
the province by the Prussian army and bureaucracy led to German
reprisals against Polish activists, such as floggings and scuffles,
and to desecrations of Polish churches. Contemporary reports
indicate that these events excited and embittered the Polish
common people in the Duchy's many small towns and villages.[125]
Of the many thousands who joined the Liga Polska, a majority were
peasants and tradesmen. Poles of all classes voted heavily in the
elections of 1848 and 1849.[126] But while the events of 1848 undoubtedly stirred the Polish masses, relatively few took active
steps in defense of the Polish revolution in the Duchy. Those who
did so, by joining local committees of Mierosławski's legions, remained under gentry control. No coherent movement emerged pursuing distinctively popular social or political ends in opposition
to the traditional Polish leadership. But many of the Polish common people showed themselves willing to support the national cause
by legal means. Already in 1848, it was clear that the Polish
townspeople were more volatile than the villagers. Reflecting
on the revolution, a gentry publicist, Władysław Kosiński, wrote
in 1861:

> Among the lower bourgeoisie, the artisans of the small
> towns, squeezed by German and Jewish competition, hatred
> of the national enemy takes the place of a more positive
> and idealistic patriotism. . . .Having little to lose
> and everything to gain, the readiness for insurrection is
> natural among them. . . .But the landed peasant in the
> Grand Duchy is, in his own way, an aristocrat and con-
> servative, deeply rooted in a materialism out of which
> he cannot easily be led except by religion. . . .In 1848,
> therefore, he was hardly to be budged. . . .This class
> of the common people, only recently admitted to land
> ownership and, in general, prospering from it, is

distrustful and cannot shake itself loose from the
idea: I know what I've got, but I don't know what
awaits me.[127]

The Duchy's Protestant Germans--merchants and artisans, officials, peasant farmers, and large landowners--faced two novel
situations as a result of the March revolution in Berlin and the
Polish revolution in their midst. While the possibility arose that
the Duchy would revert to Polish sovereignty as part of a renascent
Polish state, the apparent collapse of absolutism in Germany offered them their first chance to articulate freely and without
bureaucratic guidance their own constitutional and national convictions. Under these circumstances, 1848 proved a milestone in
the development of the national movement among the Protestant
Germans. At first haltingly but in the end unequivocally, they
declared themselves solidly against separation of the province
from the Prussian heartland. They committed themselves to the
idea that their settlements in the Grand Duchy formed an inalien-
able part of the German nation. To a degree, they were led to this
conclusion by a defensive, even fearful, reaction against the
Polish revolutionary movement. "The Sarmatian knocks at our door,
the Russian stands armed at our frontier": so spoke their deputy
at the German pre-Parliament on 31 March.[128] Certainly war and
revolution threatened their security. To fall under Polish rule
would deprive them of the economic and political advantages they
enjoyed under the Hohenzollern scepter. Despite the Polish National Committee's conciliatory promises of future brotherhood,
the Germans feared becoming a persecuted minority. To avoid that,
they did not hesitate to urge the military suppression of the
Polish movement and to work hand in hand with the anti-Polish conservative court party in Berlin and Frankfurt.[129]

Once the threat of a Polish restoration was past, the Duchy's
Germans turned to the constitutional issues of the revolution.
The conservatives formed a provincial branch of the Prussian
"Union for King and Fatherland," which won the support of Junkers,
peasant farmers, and officials. The liberals joined the Constitutional Club in Poznań and the Citizens' Union in Bromberg, which
spoke for the private German bourgeoisie. In the fall of 1848,
an effort was made to unite the whole German population in an
organization called the German Brotherhood (Deutsche Verbrüderung).
Its program, beyond exhortations to German economic and cultural
self-help, demanded intensified German peasant colonization and
the formation of a well-funded corporation to purchase land for
sale to Germans from outside the province. Division of opinion

over the Prussian and Frankfurt constitutions crippled the never
very robust Brotherhood. By 1850, German liberals had already
begun making common cause with the Poles against German conservative Landtag candidates. Polenpolitik split the German parties.
The liberals supported Polish demands for national rights, since
the Poles favored liberalization of the Prussian constitution,
while the conservatives upheld the government's campaign against
Polish "separatism." As long as the specter of Polish revolution
lay dormant, the province's Protestant Germans remained divided
politically into two camps.[130] The revolution of 1848 united
them in a common national self-consciousness which insisted upon
preservation of Prussian sovereignty in the Duchy, but it split
them on the Prussian and German-national constitutional question.

The revolution's invocation of the popular will embroiled
the Duchy's German Catholics in a dilemma. They were joined
through religion with the Poles in a community of interest. In
the Grand Duchy the government threatened to partition the
Archbishopric of Poznań-Gniezno in the course of "reorganization"
and "demarcation." A village of German Catholics, led by a German
priest, petitioned the government in 1848:

> By speech we are Germans; but the manners, customs and
> habits in which we have been born and raised are of a
> Polish character, and we would contrast very greatly
> with the rest of the Germans in Germany. . . .In that
> which concerns the Catholic religion, we do not have the
> best impression of Germany. . . .We therefore request the
> carrying out of a reorganization which will secure and
> uphold our Polish nationality. . . .[131]

Nearly every Catholic commune in the province petitioned the
government against demarcation.[132] Yet the German Catholics'
ignorance of the Polish language prevented their active participation in the Polish national movement. So long as their religion
was their first concern, and so long as conservative German
nationalism in Prussia showed an anti-Catholic tinge, the province's German Catholics were consigned either to a conciliatory
role in nationalist politics or to political paralysis.

Like the Protestant Germans, the Jews, when confronted with
the possibility of a reversion to Polish sovereignty, declared
themselves openly for the Prussian state. Their decision, not unnaturally, embittered the Poles. In retaliation, the Polish
League proclaimed a boycott of German and Jewish firms. But the
Poles could not provide alternative services, while a counterboycott staged by Jewish wholesalers brought the income of the
Polish landlords to an embarrassing halt. The wealthier Jews, at
any rate, could withstand such onslaughts against their economic
positions, though the boycott issue did not die in 1848.[133]

Despite these and other tensions, the Jews did not emerge from
the revolutionary years as anti-Polish German nationalists. Complete civil equality for the Jews was an important constitutional
issue in 1848. The Jews of the Grand Duchy, like their coreligionists throughout Germany, gravitated towards the moderate left
into the liberal clubs and associations. Although the royal constitution of December 1848 confirmed the full emancipation of the
Jews proposed by the Berlin National Assembly, anti-Semitism had
flared up during the revolution on the conservative right. In the
post-1848 reaction, official practice discriminated against Jews
in a variety of ways. Hence the Prussian Jews supported the
liberal opposition. In the province of Poznań, as supporters of
the German liberal movement they collaborated with the Poles
throughout the 1850s. But Polish-Jewish cooperation was strictly
a marriage of convenience. If the liberal movement in Prussia
could not prevail in the decades after 1848, the Jews ran the risk
of finding themselves isolated between two hostile camps--trium-
phant German conservatives on one side, Polish nationalists on the
other.[134]

By 1850 the political relations of the nationalities in the
province of Poznań had become hard-edged. Yet the Poles, Germans,
and Jews had not fallen into murderous aggression against each
other. Violence did indeed accompany the revolution in the Grand
Duchy. A small number of Jews and Poles were killed in pogroms
and reprisals for actual or anticipated pogroms. Privately armed
Germans assaulted Poles in the aftermath of Mierosławski's defeat.
Polish legionaries and Prussian soldiers killed each other in
battles and skirmishes. Yet these incidents all occurred in connection with the Prussian suppression of the Polish armed forces in
April 1848. Apart from them, the revolutionary year passed in
security of life and property. Nor did these acts of violence
permanently color the nationalities' views of one another. Except for the German conservatives, the political leaders of all
three nationalities went on record during the revolution in favor
of equal rights for Poles and Germans and conversion of the Prussian state into a liberal constitutional monarchy.

Bismarck and German Nationalism

Believing that "if there must be revolution, it is better to
make it than suffer it," Otto von Bismarck, Prussian Minister-
President since 1862, seized upon the army, the most potent weapon
in the arsenal of Prussian absolutism, to unite north and south
Germany, in the course of three wars, in the Prussian-dominated
German Empire of 1871. Having defied the Prussian parliament in
the execution of his policy, Bismarck broke the lance of post-
1848 German liberalism.[1]

The creation of the Bismarckian empire brought to a close the
century-old duel between Prussia and Austria for hegemony within
Germany. In one sense, Bismarck was the final executor of the
will of a line of Prussian statesmen who advocated, largely on
the basis of traditional Prussian raison d'état, a military solution to the problem of German unity. Yet Bismarck embarked on his
radical course primarily because he grasped that if the Prussian
monarchy failed to act on the national question, it would surrender
the initiative not so much to the Hapsburg Empire, itself caught
in the toils of liberal and national challenges, as to the professional and capitalist middle classes in Prussia and throughout
Germany.[2]

Bismarck's triumph undoubtedly did confer upon Prussia and
the new Reich a national prestige and legitimacy widely accepted
among all social classes. The Prussian aristocratic-bureaucratic-
military ruling class not only retained its dominance within
Prussia itself, whose oligarchical and semiabsolute political
structure the federalist principle shielded from Reich interference; it extended its influence over the non-Prussian states
through the Prussian-controlled executive, military, and administrative offices of the Empire. In the "feudalization of the
bourgeoisie," the Prussian aristocracy fastened its social and
political values upon important elements of the propertied and
educated middle classes.[3]

Idealization of Polish national solidarity. Priest, nobleman and peasant under the mottos "pray and work" and "liberty, equality, fraternity." At right, an aristocratic shade of the partitioned Commonwealth symbolizes Polish statehood. (Praca, 1898)

Pre-War Conservatives.

Poznanian Provincial President Dr. Philipp Schwatzkopff

Dr. Eduard Likowski, Archbishop of Poznań

Dr. Wolf Feilchenfeld, Chief Rabbi of Poznań

Polish National Democrats in Paris during World War I. Seated in center is Roman Dmowski. Standing, second from right, is Marian Seyda.

The Founders of the Eastern Marches Society: Kennemann, Tiedemann, Hansemann.

Generalleutnant
Karl Grolmann

Oberpräsident
Eduard Flottwell

Staatsminister
Johannes von Miquel

Reichskanzler Fürst
Bernhard von Bülow

Oberpräsident
Wilhelm von Waldow

Die verantwortlichen staatlichen Vertreter einer kraftvollen Ostmarkenpolitik.

The Architects of Official Germanization Policy: an icon of the
H-K-T Society (1913)

The Prussian Colonization Program: Ideal and Reality.

Statues of German Peasants adoning the Commission's Headquarters
in Poznań. (Above)

Scene from a Village of German Colonists (1911) (Below)

Bismarck's violent methods created a German national state fatefully wedded to the semiabsolute Prussian monarchy which dominated it. Having established the Empire against the opposition of Prussian agrarian and German particularist conservatism, Bismarck ran the risk after 1871 of falling into dependence on the moderate National Liberal Party and the more doctrinaire German Progressive Party, the pillars of middle-class liberalism and nationalism. Yet, determined to diminish the influences of what he conceived to be the anti-Prussian forces of German Catholicism, represented by the Catholic Center Party, Bismarck was compelled to rely upon the liberal parties in the anti-Catholic Kulturkampf of the 1870s. The liberals hoped that this alliance would transform the Imperial government into a ministry responsible to the Reichstag, but Bismarck evaded this outcome in the "refounding" of the Empire in 1878-79. The conservative parties joined in a pro-Bismarckian alliance with the National Liberal Party. The bases of this alliance were support of agrarian and industrial tariffs as defenses against the "long depression" which had begun in 1873, opposition to parliamentarization of the Reich, and support for the proscription (1878-90) of the nascent but burgeoning socialist movement in Germany. In the 1880s, Bismarck added a new dimension to this alliance by official promotion of overseas expansion. He sought both to ensure foreign trade outlets for German industry and to invest the ruling classes and parties in Germany with the prestige of empire.[4]

By 1890, Bismarck had grown accustomed to dividing the German parties into "friends of the Reich" (Reichsfreunde) and "enemies of the Reich" (Reichsfeinde). Among the former stood the German Conservative Party, supported by the Prussian agrarian-military-bureaucratic nobility and the North German Protestant peasantry; the Free Conservative Party, representing other conservative interests, particularly outside Prussia; and the National Liberal Party, purged in the 1880s of its oppositional liberalism and representing socially conservative, bourgeois nationalist interests and opinion, especially in industry and the professions. The Reichsfeinde were first and foremost the supporters of the militant Social Democratic Party, representing the industrial workers and radical intelligentsia; secondly, and less unequivocally, the Catholic Center Party, supported by the Catholic peasantry, bourgeoisie, and large numbers of Catholic workers; and finally the Progressives, speaking for Protestant and Jewish middle-class professionals, antiprotectionist businessmen, and ideological liberals. In the Reichstag elections of 1890, the parties

"friendly to the Reich" won 135 seats, the "unfriendly" parties
217.[5] These figures symbolize the limits of the Bismarckian unification of Germany.

Bismarckian *Polenpolitik*: Tradition Radicalized

Having defeated the revolution of 1848, the Prussian government attempted in the 1850s to paralyze the liberals and
nationalists. The parliament was packed with a conservative
and bureaucratic majority, while the police harassed and muzzled
the opposition. But the international flux stirred up by Russia's
defeat in the Crimean War and the unification of Italy revived
Austro-Prussian competition for domination of Germany. William I,
successor after 1858 to the madness-stricken Frederick William IV,
abandoned domestic repression in the hope of winning the support
of German national opinion for Prussian foreign policy. This led
in short order to a bitter constitutional conflict, in which the
Progressive-dominated parliament asserted its claim to codetermina-
tion of domestic policy in Prussia. Bismarck, appointed Prussian
Minister-President in 1862 to blunt the Landtag's onslaught, rescued monarchical power through the creation of the German Empire
against a liberal opposition which waned with each of his military-
diplomatic triumphs.

Against this background of international upheaval and domestic
crisis, the problems of internal Polenpolitik could not claim
much of the Prussian government's attention. But the revolution
of 1848 in the Grand Duchy of Poznań had banished whatever doubts
remained in the ministries of Berlin about the Polish nobility
and clergy. Before 1848, even so resolute an enemy of the Polish
gentry as Flottwell believed that, given sufficient exposure to
German discipline, culture, and prosperity, they would gradually
acquire a loyal Prussian mentality. After the revolution, the
Prussian government abandoned all such hopes. The Poles, as a
report of the Ministry of the Interior put it in November 1849,
were the captives of their "longing to break away." "They cannot
be won by any concessions"; it was therefore of no concern to the
government if they felt embittered by Prussian rule.[6] Provincial
president von Bonin in 1862 wrote bluntly that "there can be no
more talk of fostering the Polish element, of any effort to ensure its existence."[7]

What then was the Prussian state to do with its Polish subjects? Provincial president von Puttkammer provided the Manteuffel
ministry with a classic answer to this question. Of the Polish
national movement ("Polonism") he wrote in 1851:

It is and will remain an element hostile to the Prussian
government, no matter the form in which it may choose to
appear. To conciliate it [ihn versöhnen] is impossible.
To extirpate it [ihn ausrotten] is inhumane (as well as
impossible; at least it would take generations to do so).
Therefore, nothing remains but to confine it energetically to the subordinate position it deserves.[8]

So strong were the Prussian state's traditions of centralization,
so normative was its concept of a specifically Prussian Staats-
nationalismus, and so deeply rooted was the belief in the impossibility of coexistence with an independent Poland that, given the
Polish gentry's evident rejection of these principles, nothing remained to the Prussian government but to suppress "Polonism" as a
farmer rids his fields of weeds. It is noteworthy that Puttkammer's negative train of thought led him to the idea of the "extirpation" or, as the term ausrotten also suggests, the "extermination" of Polish society as a politically distinctive formation
within the Prussian state, though he shrank from saying how this
might be done.

The policy of containment and suppression of Polish nationalism which the government adopted after 1848 implied as a corollary
the necessity of the "Germanization" of the Province of Poznań, a
goal first explicitly advocated by Justus Gruner. In the 1850s
and 1860s, the word Germanisierung, hitherto seldom encountered in
the Prussian political vocabulary, became a routine expression of
the positive content of official policy.[9]

"Germanization" could, in one sense, be understood as suppression of "Polonism": the more politically passive the Polish
population, the more secure the province under its Prussian administration. Until 1858 the Prussian government applied its
reactionary policies with special rigor to Polish political agitation, electioneering, and press and associational life.[10] But with
the opening of the "New Era" in 1858 the government could not deny
the Poles the civil liberties it granted its German subjects,
particularly since the Progressive opposition in the parliament
upheld the Poles' equal treatment in public life as part of a more
general defense of the constitutional Rechtsstaat. Before 1871 a
parliamentary majority in favor of anti-Polish "exceptional laws"
did not exist. Moreover, the Prussian courts enforced the Poles'
rights to communicate with state agencies in their native tongue,
as guaranteed in the edict of 1832, and the employment of Polish
as a language of instruction in elementary education, as provided
by the edict of 1842.[11] The tools available to the government
for the suppression of "Polonism" were therefore limited. In its
secondary-school policy, it concentrated on channeling students

into new gymnasiums in which German was the predominant language
of instruction, so that by 1870 only two which employed Polish to
any considerable degree remained.[12]

In the field of elementary education, the Prussian government felt greatly cramped by the authority and autonomy of the
Archbishopric of Poznań-Gniezno. This thoroughly Polish institution, through its control of Catholic elementary school supervision and its teachers' seminaries, lent the elementary schools a
Polish character which, the government believed, discouraged Polish
children from learning German and fostered Polonization of
German-speaking Catholics.[13] Prussian officials were equally
frustrated by the participation of the Polish clergy in political
life, both as organizers among their parishioners and as elected
parliamentarians. In these roles, the clergy were undoubtedly
highly effective. Yet their actions were in no sense illegal.
Only archdiocesan regulations could force the clergy to abstain
from politics, but since 1848 Archbishop Przyłuski had strongly
supported the POlish national movement. In 1866 Bismarck negotiated with the Vatican the appointment to the Poznań-Gniezno see
of Count Mieczysław Ledóchowski, a conservative Ultramontane who,
hoping to advance the interests of Pius IX, imposed a ban on
clerical participation in elections in the Province of Poznań.
The priesthood's immobilization cost the Poles eight of their
twenty Landtag seats in the elections of 1866.[14]

Official support of German interests in Poznania represented
another strategy of Germanization. But in a Landtag debate of
1850, Manteuffel rejected a Poznań German's call for governmental
aid to his compatriots in the province, saying that "if the German
nationality requires the protection and leadership of the state
administration to advance its interests, then it has no future
ahead of it."[15] Similarly, Bismarck's prime concern was to combat
the political influence of the Polish gentry and clergy. In a
cabinet report of January 1863 to the king, he wrote that the
state's goal of Germanization was attainable "only through the
suppression [Verdrängung] of the Polish element."[16] To the degree
that Polish interests were injured, it could be argued that German
interests benefited. This was clearly the case with the state's
handling of the Polish-dominated provincial credit society for
large landowners (Landschaft), whose funds had been frozen in 1847.
Not until 1857 did the government make credit once again available
to the province's estate-owners, this time through the Neuer
Kreditverein under a thoroughly German management. Although the
Polish members of the defunct Landschaft obtained credits from the

new society after 1859, in the preceding decade many had succumbed
to debts and bankruptcy. Having to sell their estates in whole or
part, they sold mainly to Germans. In this way, the German share
of the province's estate land expanded by more than 100,000 hectares between 1848 and 1861.[17]

Karl von Horn, whom Bismarck appointed provincial president in
1862, wrote bluntly that the extension of German estate land was
"a very practical means of Germanization."[18] Horn's predecessor
had urged the government to revive Flottwell's state-funded
estate purchasing agency. But this was unnecessary during the
prosperity of the 1860s which in itself encouraged Germans to buy
land in the Province of Poznań.[19] In general, as long as economic
and demographic trends in the Prussian east benefited local German
urban and agricultural interests, state intervention in their behalf lacked urgency. Consequently, official Polenpolitik between
1850 and Bismarck's accession to power remained essentially negative, hostile to "Polonism" but offering no new means of combatting
it. Bismarck, fertile in political designs as he was, soon blazed
new trails towards the Germanization the Prussian government had
already agreed was necessary.

Bismarck's attitudes towards Poland and the Poles were remarkable not for their originality but rather for the vehemence
with which he expressed them and the ruthlessness with which he
acted upon them. He fully accepted Clausewitz's thesis of the
incompatibility of Prussian and Polish national interests. He
never wavered in the convictions he expressed in 1848 as a young
and reactionary parliamentary deputy outraged by German liberal
sympathy for the Polish cause.

> The national evolution of the Polish element in Posen
> can have no other sensible goal than preparing the
> restoration of an independent Polish state. One may
> wish for the resurrection of Poland in its borders of
> 1772, as the Poles do, though they do not admit it
> openly; one could give back to Poland all of Posen,
> West Prussia, and Ermland. In that case, the best
> sinews of Germany would be severed, millions of
> Germans would fall prey to Polish arbitrariness. Thus
> one would gain an uncertain ally, covetously awaiting
> any sort of trouble on Germany's part in order to tear
> away from it East Prussia, the Polish part of Silesia,
> The Polish regions of Pomerania. On the other hand,
> one might wish to restore Poland in narrower limits,
> giving it only the decidedly Polish part of the Grand
> Duchy of Posen. In that event, only he who is
> completely ignorant of the Poles would doubt that they
> would be our sworn enemies so long as they had not
> conquered from us the mouth of the Vistula and, beyond
> that, every Polish-speaking village in West and East
> Prussia, Pomerania, and Silesia. Only a German who

> allowed himself to be guided by tearful compassion
> and impractical theories could dream of establish-
> ing in the immediate neighborhood of his own father-
> land an implacable enemy always ready to externalize
> his feverish domestic turbulence in war and, in any
> serious complication we might find ourselves in, to
> fall upon us in the rear.

Bismarck went on to argue that Russia had no interest in threatening Germany's eastern borders. But even if it did, "we do not
need the Poles to shield us against Russia, since we ourselves
are shield enough."[20]

As a Prussian conservative, Bismarck supported German unification only to the degree that it would strengthen the Prussian
state. Unlike his liberal nationalist opponents, he did not
reckon on the probability of armed conflict with Russia over
the unification of Germany. Rather he believed that, given the
fundamental compatibility of Russian and Prussian interests
(cemented by the partitions of Poland) and Russia's Balkan rivalries with the Hapsburg empire, the one form in which the Tsarist
state would accept German unification was the conservative Prussian solution which he advocated and finally reached. After 1871
Bismarck aimed to exert the weighty power of the German Empire
to prevent Austro-Russian clashes in the Balkans. Bismarck's
"honest brokerage" would give the Russians no cause to wage war
on the Prussian-dominated state over Balkan issues. Since
Bismarck's Germany in its turn had no territorial designs on
Russia or the Balkans, it could have no motive for an aggressive
policy towards the Tsarist empire. If German-Russian relations
could be cast in this mold, it made sense for Bismarck to declare,
as he did in 1894, that "if I have the choice, I will always prefer to deal with the Tsar in Petersburg rather than with the
szlachta in Warsaw."[21]

Yet, as Bismarck's argument of 1848 reveals, he had reasons
apart from the desirability of Russo-Prussian harmony to oppose
the restoration of Poland or a conciliatory domestic Polenpolitik
which, in his view, would only encourage the Prussian Poles'
hopes of independence. Bismarck shared in full measure the traditional conservative Prussian distrust in the political capacities
of the Polish gentry. In his view, the old Commonwealth had
perished justly, the victim of the political egotism and economic
incompetence of its nobility. One of Bismarck's most tenaciously
held and oft-stated beliefs in the realm of Polish affairs was
that no genuine solidarity bound the Polish common people to the
nobility and clergy. The szlachta's despotism had undermined the
subservience and loyalty of the common people to their masters.

The Catholic clergy exploited the masses' religiosity to enlist
their support for the national movement of the Polish gentry aimed
at restoring the Commonwealth. But, as he said in 1867 in the
North German Reichstag, to resurrect the old Commonwealth would
require the destruction of three Great Powers only to hand over a
non-Polish majority to the rule of a Polish gentry whose legitimacy was dubious even in the eyes of the Polish masses.[22] The
szlachta, not content with the historic borders of 1772, would
press to extend them, for example into Silesia, by invoking the
bonds of language. The result of a Polish restoration would be
domestic strife and foreign war. Ultimately, the partitioning
powers would recover their strength and solidarity and dismember
Poland once again.[23]

Convinced that Polish national aspirations were anachronistic
and chimerical, Bismarck occasionally permitted himself the hope
that the Poles would perceive this too and accept the consequences
by becoming loyal Prussians. In his North German Reichstag
speech of 1867, he paid tribute to the energy they invested in
their national movement, but quoted Schiller's line to them: "what
you lost in the crucial moment no eternity can restore [Was du
vom Augenblicke ausgeschlagen, bringt keine Ewigkeit zurück]".[24]
Yet his more fundamental conviction was that the Polish gentry
and clergy would never be more than Prussian citizens "on twenty-
four hours' notice," ready to revolt whenever an opportunity to do
so arose, irresistibly attracted to all anti-Prussian international
combinations, always ready to make common cause within Prussia
and the Empire with Bismarck's political opponents, particularly
in the liberal and Catholic camps.[25]

Bismarck was never interested in offering political concessions to the Prussian Poles to gain their loyalty for his regime.
It was up to them to demonstrate their allegiance. It was one of
Bismarck's fundamental maxims that only repression of the Polish
national movement would convince its leaders of the hopelessness
of their cause and incline future generations of Prussian Poles
to become Polish-speaking Prussians. In his political practice,
he remained faithful to the sentiments he expressed in a letter
to his sister written in 1861, while Prussian ambassador to
Russia: "Flay the Poles until they despair of life! I have all
sympathy for their position, but if we wish to endure, we can do
nothing else but extirpate them." Bismarck meant that the Poles
should be deprived of all national autonomy and forced to accept
citizenship under the partitioning governments, not physically
destroyed. Yet he concluded this passage with the sanguinary

remark, "It is not the wolf's fault that God created him as he is, but nevertheless we kill him whenever we can."[26]

Before his appointment as Prussian Minister-President in 1862, Bismarck's involvement in Polish questions was peripheral to his diplomatic activities. Satisfied with the Prussian government's repressive domestic Polish policies, Bismarck's only practical concern was to combat the influence at court of certain "old liberals" who argued, particularly during the Crimean War, for a prowestern orientation involving the possibility of a Polish restoration in the wake of a resounding Russian defeat. Since Frederick William IV judged the Polonophile projects of Christian Bunsen, a spokesman for this group, as "the bunglings of a madman," Bismarck's exertions did not need to be great.[27]

Between 1862 and 1871, the Polish question played a minor but noteworthy part in Bismarck's diplomatic calculations. The outbreak of the Polish insurrection of 1863 in the Congress kingdom, although confined by the Polish rebels as in 1830 to Russian soil, allowed Bismarck, through the negotiation of the short-lived Alvensleben Convention with the Petersburg government, to underscore Prussia's solidarity with Russia's anti-Polish stance. At the same time, the Alvensleben Convention forced a breach in Russo-French relations useful to Bismarck in his subsequent diplomacy. The insurrection, despite the modest support it found among the Prussian Poles, gave Bismarck an opportunity to denounce the Poznanian gentry. Since, Bismarck argued, the revolt aimed in the last analysis at restoring Poland in the borders of 1772, it threatened the existence of the Prussian state. Active support for it, which Bismarck claimed to detect among the nobility and clergy, therefore constituted treason against Prussia.[28] In 1864, after the suppression of the revolt, Bismarck's administration placed 148 Prussian Poles on trial in Berlin and succeeded in gaining 93 convictions on treason and lesser charges. The court ruled out the argument of the Poles' advocate, the eminent liberal Rudolf von Gneist, that their activities had been aimed against a foreign state whose defense against treason was no business of Prussia's.[29]

During the Polish revolt of 1863 as well as at the time of the wars of 1866 and 1870, Bismarck entertained the idea that, should Russia lose control of its Polish provinces or enter into war with Prussia, the establishment of a Prussian-dominated Polish state in the area of the former Russian partition zone might become unavoidable. Such a notion was no proof of Polish sympathies. On the contrary, it revealed Bismarck's belief that "in any event

it is a lesser danger to attempt to conquer and rule Congress
Poland than to have it as an independent neighbor."[30]   Fortunately
for Bismarck, Russia tightened its grip on its Polish lands after
1864. Since Petersburg made no efforts to hinder his policy of
German unification, a revolutionary widening of Prussian domination in Poland, a step to which he was highly averse, remained
locked in Prussia's arsenal of military-diplomatic possibilities.[31]

   After the formation of the German Empire, Bismarck faced the
delicate task of assembling a coalition of political supporters
both in Prussia and on the Reich level. At the same time, he was
anxious to stabilize the Empire's international status and ward
off the threat of renewed war with Austria or France. At home, he
could rely on the liberal parties to support him against anti-
Imperial "particularist" groups. Chief among these, in the early
1870s, was the German Catholic church and the Catholic Center
Party. Abroad, his chief concern was to isolate France while
drawing Austria and Russia into a conservative alliance with the
German Empire. This constellation of problems led Bismarck into
the Kulturkampf of the 1870s, in which the autonomy of the Catholic
church, especially in educational matters, was sharply curtailed,
the loyalty of the Center Party to the Reich challenged, and
hostility to Catholic France forged into a dogma of the new
Empire.

   Despite the liberals' cultural secularism and Bismarck's
Protestant conservatism, they could agree in uniting against
Catholic influence in education. They demanded that the schools
uphold the legitimacy of the solution of 1871, the unity of the
Reich, and the ideal of Imperial German nationality. Bismarck
himself, who wrote in 1858 that "there is nothing more German than
the development of rightly understood Prussian particular interests," did not hesitate to speak after 1871 of "Prussian nationality" and "German nationality" as interchangeable concepts.[32]   The
National Liberals and Progressives hailed Protestant Prussia as
the most advanced state in Germany and agreed with Bismarck that
the core of the German nation-state was--and should be--Prussian.[33]

   The constitution of 1871 contained no clauses guaranteeing
the national rights of non-German minorities, nor did the liberal
parties insist on their inclusion. Bismarck's and his allies' sus-
picions of irredentism along the new Reich's frontiers outweighed
all appeals to national toleration and equality. After 1871
Bismarck and the liberals observed a distinction between the
"language of state" (Staatssprache) and the "popular language"
(Volkssprache), insisting that imposition of the former did not

imply a desire to extinguish the latter. Nevertheless, the
conviction grew in both conservative and liberal circles that
"nationality follows language."[34]

Bismarck's and his partners' insistence on the exclusively
German national character of the Empire spelled serious danger
for the Prussian Poles. The Polish parliamentary delegations
protested, in the name of the treaties of 1815 and the "idea
of nationality," against the inclusion of the Province of Poznań
in the North German Confederation and subsequently in the German
Empire.[35] After 1867 Polish nationalist opposition to the Prussian government was exposed to condemnation not only in the
traditional terms of Prussian raison d'état; since Prussia claimed
responsibility for the leadership of the German nation, opposition to Prussian interests, as defined by the conservative
Prussian ruling class, necessarily became opposition to German
national interests. In this respect, the position of the Poles
resembled that of the Hanoverian or Saxon particularists. But
the Poles were further removed from the Reich by their non-German
culture and language. Moreover, they were fervently Catholic,
hence to be counted among the "international" and "Ultramontane"
coalition of enemies Bismarck supposed he faced after 1871.

These circumstances led Bismarck and his advisers in the
Prussian government into a sharp attack on "Polonism." One of
the prime objectives of the Kulturkampf itself was to undermine
the Polish character of the Archbishopric of Poznań-Gniezno
and to carry through the Germanization of education in the Polish
districts.[36] Hundreds of Polish priests refused to submit to the
governmental controls of the May laws of 1872 and in consequence
lost their ministries. Many were imprisoned for their opposition,
icnluding, finally, in 1876, Archbishop Ledóchowski himself.
Archiepiscopal appointments became the objects of intense negotiations between the Prussian government and the Vatican even as
Bismarck ended the Kulturkampf in a compromise with the German
church. By 1886, archbishops of a conservative German national
temperament presided over the West Prussian and Silesian districts,
keen on suppressing nationalist activism among the Polish clergy.
In 1886 the Vatican appointed to the Poznań-Gniezno see the first
German archbishop in its history. To the government's disappointment, Archbishop Dinder, a political moderate who spoke fluent
Polish, refused to advance Germans into the upper echelons of the
hierarchy or to Germanize its internal language of administration.[37]

The May laws abolished the Catholic Section of the Prussian

Ministry of Religion and Education and replaced priests with state-
appointed laymen in the local supervision of elementary schools.
These measures, although part of Bismarck's broader attack on the
Catholic church in Prussia, drastically reduced the Polish clergy's
influence on lower education throughout the Polish-speaking east.
Bismarck was keenly interested in the anti-Polish thrust of these
changes. In a cabinet meeting of 1 November 1871 he declared with
unusual invective that "the influence of the local clergy [in
Poznanian lower education] hinders the use of the German language,
because the Slavs and Romans, in their alliance with Ultramontanism,
try to preserve primitiveness and ignorance; all over Europe they
are fighting Germanism, which seeks to spread enlightenment."[38]
In the upper chamber of the Landtag, he defended the secularization
of school inspection with an attack on the Polish clergy, saying
that by their hostility to the teaching of German to Polish children they maintained the Polish common people in ignorance of the
true and beneficent character of the Prussian state.[39]

Bismarck thus delivered several telling blows to the Polish
clergy both because they were Catholic and because they were active in the Polish nationalist movement. But the Prussian government's new Polenpolitik was fundamentally secular in inspiration
and intent. "From the Russian border to the Adriatic Sea,"
Bismarck warned in a cabinet meeting of October 1871, "we are confronted by a Slavic agitation working hand in hand with the
Ultramontanes and reactionaries; we must openly defend our national
interests and our language against such hostile activities."[40]
Bismarck believed that, in Prussian Poland, Polish veterans of the
insurrection of 1863 and the Paris Commune were subverting the
system of Organic Work institutions.[41] In his anxiety to stabilize
the international position of the Empire, his suspicion of the
revolutionary intentions of the Poznanian Poles grew acute. He
threw down the gauntlet in the debate over the school inspection
question: "This Polish agitation thrives perhaps only because
of the benevolence of the government but, I can assure you, there
will be no more of it."[42]

In the course of 1873 and 1874, a series of administrative
decrees substituted German for Polish as the language of instruction in all secondary and elementary schools of the Province of
Poznań. The Polish language henceforth figured only as an aid to
learning German and in teaching religion to Polish Catholic pupils.
So that Polish children would properly understand their religious
education, instruction in Polish grammar continued in the lower
classes of elementary school only.[43] In 1876, the Landtag ap-

proved a law which made German the sole permissible language in
public administration, in the courts, and in all official political bodies, annulling the Poles' right to use their own language
in dealings with these institutions.[44]

From the Polish point of view, these were exceedingly harsh
measures. The propagation of Polish literary culture lost all
state support and threatened to collapse if the Poles could not
find private means to carry it on. For the Polish common people,
Germanization of official affairs meant paying for translators.
The Germanization of education, particularly given the over-
crowdedness and underfunding of the elementary schools which
most of the Polish children attended, reduced to a minimum the
social and cultural advantages they derived from public education
under the Empire. If they learned German, usually in a rudimentary and inelegant fashion, they learned little else. A bilingual
education stressing German alongside Polish could hardly have accomplished less.[45]

The Germanization laws of 1872-76 were certainly proof of
Bismarck's determination to put an end to official "benevolence"
towards the Poles. By abolishing clerical influence on lower
education and by substituting German schoolmasters for the Polish
instructors who withdrew or were dismissed from the Poznanian
school system after 1873, Bismarck and his allies believed they
had established the basic preconditions for the Germanization of
the Prussian Poles. In the debate on the language bill of 1876,
the National Liberal position was that "by the propagation of the
German language the law will bring about the conversion of the
foreign-speaking population to bilinguality; thus it is a stepping
stone towards Germanization."[46] In subsequent debates, the
Progessives made it clear that they too, while avoiding the term
"Germanization," believed that through learning the German language
fluently and sharing in the cultural and material benefits of
German society, the Poles would assimilate psychologically and
politically into the German nation.[47] Bismarck thought of
Germanization in more negative and traditional terms. Breaking
the gentry's and clergy's influence over the Polish masses would
deliver the politically passive and socially subservient common
people to the guidance of the German upper classes. The Poles
would then either vegetate harmlessly in their villages and small
towns or, if they sought social or political advancement, they
would be drawn into a web of Prussian institutions and Germanized.[48]

The Kulturkampf and the Germanization laws of the 1870s

outraged the Poles and brought a mass of new recruits into the
nationalist movement.[49] By the 1880s it was clear that government
policy needed stiffening if Germanization was to succeed. Meanwhile, the political constellations prevailing both in Prussia and
on the Reich level had changed fundamentally as a result of the
crises and conflicts of the 1870s which Bismarck had resolved in
the conservative parties' favor during 1878 and 1879. Henceforth,
until the collapse of the German Empire in 1918, Prussian Polenpolitik was formulated by an openly conservative and antiliberal
government reliably supported in the Prussian Landtag by the combined forces of the agrarian Conservatives, Free Conservatives,
and National Liberals. This coalition, unrepresentative of the
Prussian population as a whole, stayed in parliamentary power in
Prussia thanks to the oligarchical three-class voting law of 1850.
Aware after 1881 that the Reichstag housed an increasingly large
number of critics of its discriminatory policies towards the Poles,
particularly in the Progessive, Center, and Socialist parties, the
Prussian government rejected the Imperial parliament's competence
in domestic Polish questions. Conversely, a hostile attitude
towards Prussian Polenpolitik came to be adopted by all those who
opposed Prussian conservatism, whether their motives were liberal,
confessional, or revolutionary.

Bismarck's last decade in power was tense and embittered.
At home, it was overshadowed by the Great Depression and dominated
by Bismarck's efforts to solidify the conservative-nationalist cartel
through suppression of the socialist movement, the turn towards
overseas expansion, and official patronage of anti-Semitic agitation. Abroad, Bismarck strove against increasingly slim odds to
hold Russia and Austria together in the Three Emperors' Alliance
despite his partners' Balkan rivalries. The political consolidation and rising nationalism of the Third Republic in France boded
no good for Bismarck's Germany, nor did Anglo-German colonial frictions.

Under these circumstances, Bismarck felt no compunction in
continuing an aggressive Polenpolitik. Launching attacks against
the Poles had become a standard and predictable part of the
Imperial and Prussian governments' conservative-nationalist
policies. Harsh treatment of the Prussian Poles complemented
Russia's repression of its own Polish-speaking subjects. Austria,
which alone of the partitioning powers granted a measure of
national autonomy and cultural freedom to the Poles, inspired an
ingenious Bismarckian thesis. Since, in the event of war between
the allied German powers and Russia, Austria would be compelled to

raise the international Polish question to maintain the loyalty
of the Galician Poles, Bismarck argued that "the weakening of
the Polish element in our state" meant "the strengthening of
our alliance with Austria."[50] Whatever territorial revisions a
victorious Austria might wish to make in the Polish lands would
upset the stability of the German Empire less to the degree that
Prussia had already broken the political will of its own Polish
subjects. This argument dovetailed with Bismarck's musings, during moments of crisis in German-Russian relations during the
1880s, about the possibility of the reemergence at Russia's expense of a Polish state in the Congress Kingdom region under
Austrian or German auspices. Thus it justified Bismarck in continuing to "flay the Poles" in the Prussian east.[51]

In 1883, Prussian officials began summarily expelling Russian
and Austrian subjects who had settled permanently in Berlin and
the eastern provinces. At first, the victims of these measures
were mostly Jews. In the fall of 1885 the expulsions reached a
high point. They now included Russian and Galician Poles living
in Prussia as small farmers, urban and rural workers, as well as
Jewish businessmen. By the end of 1885, 32,000 persons had been
driven out of the Reich on short notice, at a high economic cost
to themselves and without having violated German law. Two-thirds
of them were Poles, the remainder Jews. This was an action unprecedented in nineteenth-century Europe during a time of peace.
It put a great strain on German-Russian relations and drew the
Hapsburg government's fire as well. General Hans von Schweinitz,
at the time German ambassador in Petersburg, described it later
as "an imprudent and unnecessarily cruel measure."[52]

These expulsions expressed the hostility of German businessmen and nationalists in the eastern provinces towards the un-
naturalized Jews and Poles in their midst, a hostility the
local bureaucracy shared and urged on Berlin. Bismarck fully approved the measures, saying in 1885 that he had complained for
years about the foreign influx.[53]

The expulsions of 1883-85 signaled the start of a new governmental attack upon the Poles. It was a characteristically aggressive Bismarckian reaction to new social and demographic problems
in the eastern provinces. The economic crash of 1873 coincided
with a crisis in Prussian agriculture, as cheaper Russian and
especially American grain imports began to drive prices down on
the German market. This crisis, which the agricultural tariffs
of 1879 were meant to surmount, lingered on until higher duties,
together with the recovery of German industry after 1896, granted

Prussian estate agriculture a contrived, but nonetheless genuine,
recovery. In the Prussian east, dependent as it was on agriculture, the long depression had unfavorable demographic consequences
for the Germans in the predominantly Polish regions and above all
in the Province of Poznań. Unemployment and bankruptcy drove many
Germans as well as Jews to emigrate to central and western Germany.
The Poles too migrated in large numbers to western Germany and the
United States, but nevertheless the demographic balance turned
after 1873 in the Poles' favor. For despite the drain of westward
emigration, falling rates of mortality combined with a birthrate
much higher than that of the Germans or Jews to produce both an
absolute and a relative expansion of the Polish-speaking population. Because of emigration, the Poznanian population rose relatively slowly between 1871 and 1890--from 1,584,000 to 1,752,000;
but the Poles increased their proportion of the total population
from 61 percent to 63.6 percent. The German-speaking population,
excluding the Jews, fell from 35.1 percent to 33.9 percent of the
whole, while the percentage of Jews dropped from 3.9 percent to
2.5 percent. The German population increased absolutely in the
1870s and 1880s by 7 percent, but since the number of Jews fell
absolutely by 28 percent, the increase of Germans and Jews counted
together was cut to only 3 percent. By contrast, the Polish population grew absolutely by 15 percent.[55]

From 1815 to the mid 1870s, the population of the Prussian
east as a whole had grown faster than that of the central and
western provinces, primarily because of earlier marriages and
greater fertility among peasants freed from serfdom. Once central
and western Germany had begun to industrialize, it was inevitable
that the surplus population of the eastern villages would migrate
to the west to avoid the consequences of rural overpopulation and
impoverishment. The agrarian crisis of the 1870s triggered this
westward migration, which continued at a more or less rapid rate
into the 1930s.[56] Had industrialization flourished in East and
West Prussia, Pomerania, and Poznania, the "flight from the
east" (Ostflucht) would have been correspondingly smaller. But
this would have entailed a weakening, if not the economic destruction, of the system of east-Elbian large estates. Prussia would
have been compelled to open its frontier to Russian grain imports
to gain access for its eastern industries to the Russian market
for manufactures. Moreover, in an industrializing setting,
extensive grain cultivation would have come under great economic
pressure to yield to livestock and intensive market farming. But
this threatened the social base of the Prussian aristocracy, the

"knightly estate" (Rittergut). Despite the Ostflucht the Prussian government took no steps to promote eastern industrialization. It concentrated its energies instead on shoring up, through
tariffs and fiscal-commercial arrangements favoring the large
landowners, the traditional agrarian structure in the east. In
the Polish regions, this policy favored not only the German
Junkers, but the Polish gentry as well. It injured local commercial and manufacturing interests, which were still largely
German and Jewish interests. Had the large estates been parceled
out to the local peasantry, emigration to the west and overseas
would have slowed down, population density in the east increased,
and a larger rural base for local industrial development created.[57]
But such measures would have undermined the Junkers. And since
the Poles outnumbered the Germans among the eastern peasantry,
wholesale parcellation of the large estates would have tipped the
demographic balance even farther in their favor.

In the 1880s, the Prussian government and the German press
became aware of the national ramifications of the depression and
the demographic trends in the Polish areas. An alarming specter
of "Polonization in the east" and "the retreat of the Germans"
arose in German nationalist minds.[58] At the same time, the liberal
parties, strongly entrenched in the eastern cities, began to
criticize the system of large estates which, by their very existence, aggravated the economic problems of the German urban-
industrial sector. In September 1885 the influential National
Liberal Party raised the banner of "inner colonization," in which
the state would settle peasants on the parceled-out lands of
economically faltering eastern estates.[59] This represented a
veiled attack on the conservative aristocracy which dovetailed
with the Progressives' and Social Democrats' long-standing criticism of the Junkers.

The expulsions of 1885 aroused the protest of Bismarck's
political enemies. In January 1886 the Reichstag voted, by a
majority of Progressives, Centrists, Poles, and Socialists, to
censure the Prussian government for having carried them out. This
unprecedented political slap in the face stung Bismarck keenly.
He vowed to obtain "a splendid satisfaction" and set about it by
opening a new and radical anti-Polish campaign.[60] It was also
one which held out the prospect of diverting German opinion hostile to the large-estate system away from the Junkers and toward
Bismarck's and the Prussian conservatives' old foes, the Polish
nobility.

In 1886, Bismarck's compliant majority in the Prussian Landtag approved the creation of the Royal Prussian Colonization Commission, headquartered in Poznań and funded for a twenty-year period with a total of 100 million marks. Its purpose was to buy financially toppling Polish estates in Poznania and the adjacent Polish regions of West Prussia and parcel them out to German peasant colonists. Bismarck had been interested in reviving the Frederickian and Flottwellian traditions of German colonization since the early 1870s.[61] So in 1886 it was easy for him to approve the proposals to create a settlement agency submitted by high officials in the Province of Poznań. Bismarck personally opposed parcellation and would have preferred simply to lease or sell estates bought from Poles to Germans, thereby swelling the ranks of the conservative Junkers. But peasant colonization was the price of the National Liberals' support of the new commission, and Bismarck, eager to make good his defeat in the Reichstag, agreed to pay it.[62]

In its first years of existence, the Colonization Commission succeeded in buying out a number of hard-pressed Polish noblemen. It seemed to be accomplishing the goals Bismarck had set for it: ". . . to put it bluntly, to expropriate the Polish nobility" and bring to an end the "cancer-like spread of Polonization" in the east.[63] This formidable program of German colonization was certainly Bismarck's most significant innovation in Prussian Polenpolitik, since it held out the hope of breaking the political backbone of "Polonism" in general, at least as Bismarck and his allies defined it. The Colonization Commission's work would not only counteract the Ostflucht, but unequivocally promote the Germanization of the Polish districts. This, following upon the Germanizing language laws of the 1870s and Bismarck's success in 1886 in persuading the Vatican to appoint a German archbishop to the Poznań-Gniezno see, pointed towards a complete victory in Prussia's century-old struggle with the Polish gentry and clergy. Perhaps sensing this, Bismarck tried to press the attack even harder. In the Prussian cabinet he raised the question "whether measures analogous to the Anti-Socialist Law . . . could not be sought against the Polonizing activities of the press and the private associations in the Polish areas."[64] His advisers must have dissuaded him from pursuing these ideas. But in the course of 1886 and 1887 a flurry of minor laws and edicts tightened state control over education in the Polish regions, created special German "continuation schools" for Polish youths, to be attended from the time of their departure from elementary school until their induction into the army, and removed Polish language instruc-

tion entirely from the elementary and secondary curriculum.[65]
By the end of Bismarck's last campaign against them, the Poles
appeared to be completely surrounded and pinned down by the
Prussian state's heavy artillery of Germanization.

Polish Society 1850-90:
Capitalism, Organic Work, and Political Crisis
     In the second half of the nineteenth century, the fast-
paced industrialization of Germany dragged the Poznanian economy
along in its wake. Between 1850 and the mid 1870s, many estate
owners reaped high profits thanks to rising grain and wool prices,
an abundant supply of cheap farm labor, and the completion of the
railway network linking the province with western Germany and the
Baltic ports. But the agrarian crisis which coincided with the
long depression of 1873-96 forced the abandonment of sheep-
raising because of cheaper wool imports. As grain prices fell,
the onset of rural migration to the west resulted in a rise in
the cost of agricultural labor. The tariffs on foreign grain
imports adopted between 1879 and 1902 ultimately reserved the
rapidly expanding German market to the east-Elbian estates.
Nevertheless, the era of easy profits was over. Poznanian landlords had to rationalize their financial affairs, diversify their
crops (especially through the cultivation of sugar beets), and
replace workers with machines wherever possible. By 1890, most
were making this transition, but many had been driven into bankruptcy or had been forced to sell part of their estate land to
salvage the rest.[66]
     The small and medium-sized farms created before 1848 in the
Prussian regulation process slumbered through the 1850s and 1860s.
Division of holdings among heirs threatened some members of the
self-sufficient peasantry with decline into the ranks of the
dwarf-holding day laborers. Lack of credit at moderate rates and
technical ignorance prevailed into the 1870s. But the long depression did not hit the peasantry, producing for their own and for
strictly local needs, as hard as it did the large landowners,
dependent as they were on sales outside the province. Urbaniza-
tion after 1870 strengthened local demand for peasant products.
Cooperative banks and technical societies for peasant farmers
arose. Westward migration eased pressure on village lands. Many
peasant sons worked only temporarily in the west, returning home
to buy new lands or to expand their patrimonial holdings. Thus
the peasantry weathered the crisis while managing to supply the
local market more profitably and efficiently.[67]

The rural working class considerably outnumbered self-sufficient farmers and their families. It was in turn divided into a
minority who owned or leased small plots and a landless majority.
In either case, the crucial factors for this, the province's
largest social class, were the prevailing rural wage rate and the
availability of alternative employment outside agriculture. Wages
rose during the depression, both in an absolute and real sense.
More important, the Poznanian towns offered new possibilities for
work after 1870 while the central and west German industrial areas
absorbed hundreds of thousands of rural emigrants from the province. Others, in a process which came to be called Sachsengän-
gerei, migrated seasonally to western agricultural regions whose
own rural proletariat had left the land. These Sachsengänger
returned home and used their savings to strengthen their small
holdings or acquire one for the first time. The wage-earning opportunities made possible by German industrialization spared the
province what otherwise would have been serious rural overpopulation and impoverishment. The rural proletariat's standard of
living, though low by contemporary German standards, was higher
in 1890 than it had been one or two generations previously.[68]

The province's towns preserved their somnolent character after
1848. In 1871, the proportion of townspeople to villagers was no
different than in 1815. In the 1850s and 1860s, fees levied on
outsiders as the price of city residence, the Prussian government's
revival after 1848 of guildlike restrictions on artisan trades, and
the feebleness of local industrial development left the province's
burghers little more to do than supply each other's and the
peasantry's traditional needs. Symptomatic was the fact that the
absolute numbers of the Poznanian artisanry reached a peak for the
period 1793-1914 in the year 1871. In these decades, the only real
urban business prosperity fell to agricultural brokers and wholesalers.[69]

After 1871, liberal business laws, investments by large landowners in agricultural processing plants, the creation of local
small-scale credit facilities, and the slowly rising purchasing
power of the province's villagers allowed the urban economy to
expand modestly. Between 1871 and 1890, the population of the
towns rose by 18 percent, that of the countryside by 8 percent.
A process of concentration began as family workshops yielded to
small firms employing five to ten hands while more and more agriculturally related factories arose. Before 1890 these developments were still in their beginning stages, but they showed the
direction industrial growth would take. It could perhaps have

been more rapid in the absence of the regime of agricultural
protectionism after 1879. In reaction, Russia returned to counter-
tariffs, relaxed since 1848, which stifled the eastward trade in
agricultural and manufactured goods of the province's towns and
other cities of the Prussian east.[70]

The Poles suffered some economic blows in the post-1848
decades. Debts and, after 1873, falling profits forced many
Polish estate owners to sell out to Germans. In the thirty years
after the revolution, the ratio of Polish-owned to German-held
private estate land fell from 70:30 to 55:45.[71] The number of
German peasant farms in the province had been rising slowly
since 1815. By 1881, only a little less than two-thirds of the
land cultivated in holdings smaller than 150 hectares was still
in Polish hands. Although the Poles migrated westward in large
numbers, they continued to comprise a large majority of the
province's farm workers. In the towns, they gained new positions
in small business and added to their numerous contingents in the
artisan and shopkeeping trades, but before 1890 they were financially much weaker than the Germans and Jews.[72]

Altogether, the expansion of the German-speaking population,
even discounting Jewish emigration after 1848, outstripped that of
the Poles until 1871. Germans and Jews in 1825 had accounted for
37.1 percent of the population (30.8 percent and 6.3 percent
respectively); in 1871, they comprised 39 percent (35.1 percent
and 3.9 percent). But after 1871 the long depression and the
Ostflucht favored the Poles. It turned out that 1871 had been
the Germans' demographic high point between 1793 and World War I.
By 1890, the proportion of German Protestants and Catholics had
slipped to 33.9 percent of the total population, that of the Jews
to 2.5 percent.[73] Between 1875 and 1895, the Catholic population
in the towns of the Regierungsbezirk of Poznań increased at three
times the Protestant rate. While the Catholic villagers increased
at the same rate after 1871 as before, a considerable exodus of
rural Germans must have occurred in the 1870s and 1880s. Despite
the Prussian government's extensive colonization efforts between
1886 and 1914, by 1910 the Protestant country people in this half
of the province were no more numerous than they had been in 1871.[74]

In a raw demographic sense, the Poles were in a stronger
position vis-à-vis the Germans and Jews in 1890 than they had been
in 1850. But this was primarily because of their greater fertility
and attachment to their native soil. The economic strength of
the gentry at the end of this period was shaky, the incomes of the
peasantry and bourgeoisie modest, while urban and rural poverty

was much greater among the Poles than among their German-speaking
neighbors. In Polish society itself, stratification and economic
inequalities were extreme. In 1882, six of every ten Poles were
rural laborers. Of all persons with officially counted occupations, 11 percent were self-employed agriculturists. Most of
these were small-holding peasants; only a thousand or so, in a
total population of about one million, were large estate owners.
Only 6 percent of the Polish population were self-employed in
industry, artisan trades, and commerce. Most of these were very
small businesses, scattered about the province's many towns and
villages. Their employees (8.6 percent) barely outnumbered them.
The intelligentsia--educated professionals, clergymen, schoolteachers, and state employees--accounted for 3.4 percent of all
employed persons in Polish society. Domestic servants and occasional laborers comprised almost 12 percent, more than the
landed peasantry and gentry or the educated and propertied
bourgeoisie.[75]

The Poles' most enduring accomplishment in the four decades
after 1850 was the creation of a set of Organic Work institutions
which strengthened Polish society economically while they integrated into the gentry-dominated national movement sizable contingents of the urban and rural common people. The political and
confessional crises of these years, most of them initiated by
Bismarck's government, played into the Polish nationalists' hands.
Their successes in socioeconomic organization and popular nationalist agitation offset their inability to resist the radicalization
of official Polenpolitik in the arena of parliamentary politics.

In the aftermath of the revolution of 1848, the only privately organized Polish national organizations were the Marcinkowski Scholarship Society and scattered local economic and social
associations among the gentry. The Prussian Reaction prevented the
founding of new, centrally organized associations until after 1858.
Nonetheless, the experience of the revolution had turned many of
the Polish gentry and intelligentsia, political conservatives and
radicals alike, towards an Organic Work strategy which they were
eager to pursue.

The first province-wide organization to be established after
the end of the Reaction represented, characteristically enough,
the interests of the gentry. The Central Economic Society
(Centralne Towarzystwo Gospodarcze--CTG), formed in 1861, consisted of county associations which elected and supported a
provincial executive commission. It published a high-quality

agronomic journal and arranged annual conferences at which, behind closed doors, the gentry could hear lectures on scientific
farming, discuss their economic and political interests, and
socialize among themselves. The CTG became a popular and effective institution, its county branches a focus for local action,
its leadership a source of political influence.[76]

In the 1850s and 1860s, priests, 1848 democrats, and landowners competed in forming local associations among the Polish
peasantry, aimed at spreading technical and commercial enlightenment and acquainting the villagers with Polish history and culture.
In 1873, the patriotic and conservative-minded landlord
Maksymilian Jackowski captured the leadership of the peasantry
for the gentry's Central Economic Society by creating within the
CTG the office of "patron" of the province's peasant societies
(Kółka rolnicze). Jackowski centralized the existing societies
and added more than two hundred new locals to the provincial
web before his death in 1905. Altogether some 10,000 farmers, a
sizable minority of Polish peasant proprietors, joined the
provincial union created by this energetic squire.

A CTG member or the local priest administered each local
society, while one of the peasant members acted as president.
Every county acquired a vice-patron, again a CTG member and
usually a well-known noble landowner. At the central level, the
patron and his staff published a journal and arranged annual
meetings of peasant society presidents and their local and county
mentors which became occasions of political importance and
nationalist pride. These congregations of traditionally dressed
peasants, some of whom gave homespun addresses to the assembled
gentry, clergy, and newspapermen, symbolized the peasantry's
support of the national cause and the idea of the national solidarity of all classes, even though the subjects under discussion,
like the organization as a whole, were nominally nonpolitical.
The creation and leadership of the peasant societies, which on
the local level were often popular and active organizations, was
undoubtedly a triumph for the gentry and their clerical allies,
even though in 1890 the thornier question of organizing the
masses of the small holders and landless workers remained to be
confronted.[77]

In the towns after 1848, national activists, particularly
physicians and lawyers, labored to form merchants' and artisans'
organizations with purposes similar to those of the peasant
societies. Before 1871, they made little headway because of the
competition of nationally mixed guildlike organizations. These

faded in importance after the legislation in 1869 of "freedom of
trade" (Gewerbefreiheit). The national polarization stirred up by
Bismarck's policies created an opening for Polish urban organizers,
particularly those associated with the petit bourgeois "populist
movement" which emerged after 1871.[78] By 1890, forty Polish "industrial societies" (towarzystwa przemsłowe) counting 3,700 members
were functioning in the Poznanian towns. Five years later they
formed a central association and began publishing a nationalisti-
cally colored professional journal.[79]

The organization of the greatest economic importance to
Polish society was undoubtedly the "Union of Cooperative Societies
of the Grand Duchy of Poznań and West Prussia," formed by nineteen
preexisting savings and loan cooperatives in 1871. Like the peasant associations, the cooperative union acquired a patron who
acted as executive financial director and founder of new banks. In
1873, this office was assumed by Father Augustyn Szamarzewski, who
guided the Union until his death in 1891, establishing a tradition
of priestly leadership in the cooperative movement. In 1885, he
succeeded in founding a central bank for the system which ultimately became the most powerful financial institution the Prussian
Poles possessed. By 1890, seventy-one banks had arisen, counting
over 26,000 shareholding members and holding 12 million marks
in deposits, 4 million marks in share capital and reserves.

This cooperative network expanded greatly in subsequent years.
It was well-managed and succeeded in avoiding dependence on German
sources of capital. Although they could turn to a variety of
state-funded or private German banks, the Polish farmers and
bourgeoisie preferred the Union system. It offered the villagers
profitable alternatives to traditional high-interest personal loans
and represented a major source of venture capital for small urban
entrepreneurs. Although the clergy were often the banks' founders
and directors, full-time professionals came to replace them in
day-to-day management. Thus the Polish middle class gained new
strength, while for all those involved in the system nationalist
sentiment accumulated with the deposits.[80]

The Germanization of public education in the 1870s invigorated
a movement which had begun in the 1850s to establish private
Polish lending libraries throughout the province. Primers and
works of popular Polish literature were required if the clergy and
nationally conscious parents were to teach the national language
and culture to Polish children now attending German schools. The
liberal wing of the national movement took the initiative by
founding the "Society for Popular Learning" in 1872. Because of

ideological differences among Polish liberals and clericals in the
1860s and 1870s, Archbishop Ledóchowski forbade the clergy to take
part in this association, while the Prussian government immediately prohibited Polish public school teachers from joining any
Polish cultural or socioeconomic organization. In 1878, the
liberals composed their quarrels with the clergy, whose assistance
as local activists and whose public endorsement of the libraries
were essential to the movement's success. In 1880 the system
was reorganized as the Society of Popular Libraries (Towarzystwo
Czytelni Ludowych--TCL). Thanks in large part to the clergy's
efforts, by 1890 almost 1,000 libraries were scattered across the
province and throughout other areas of Polish settlement in the
Prussian east. In the late 1880s, the Society's leadership was
distributing from 17,000 to 39,000 books annually. Their content
was respectful to religion, conservative politically and socially,
but as nationalistic as Prussian officialdom's eagle eye for
"Polish agitation" would permit. In subsequent years, the typical
library came to hold several thousand volumes drawn upon by five
or six hundred borrowers. Thus the popular library movement,
managed by priests and intellectuals and funded largely by the
gentry, represented yet another pillar of Polish national
consciousness and solidarity.[81]

     In the sphere of politics, in the period 1850-90 the Prussian
Poles confronted the radicalization of official Polenpolitik even
as they witnessed, after the suppression of the great uprising in
Russian Poland of 1863-64 and the foundation of the German Empire,
the apparently permanent eclipse of all prospects for the restoration of a Polish state. In attempting to master these changes, the
traditional leaders of Polish society in Prussia wound up in a
political dead end, exposed to the challenges of new and more
radical forces in their midst which appealed to middle- and
lower-class social groups until then politically passive or
voiceless.
     After the revolution of 1848, the gentry recovered from their
disappointments and, dutifully elected by the Polish common
people, took their seats in the Landtag in Berlin. In 1859, after
the end of the Reaction, the liberal and nationalist gentry founded
a newspaper which long remained the predominant voice of the Polish
upper classes in Prussia. In its first edition, the Dziennik
Poznański declared itself "the organ of Polish nationality in the
limits of the rights guaranteed it by the Vienna treaties and of
the freedoms deriving from the constitution of the land." It

spoke up for political and religious liberty, equality among social
classes, and "organic progress."[82]

Opposed to the national-liberal group, which dominated both
the Polish parliamentary delegation (Koło Polskie) in Berlin and
the local system of "electoral authorities," stood a clerical-
conservative, Ultramontane camp. Hostile to social and political
liberalism and despondent over the future of Poland, this group,
influential among the richer noble families, looked to the consolation of religion and the lead of Pius IX and his emissary in
Poznania, Archbishop Ledóchowki. This caused certain internecine
disagreements in Polish society, brought to a crisis and finally
resolved during the Kulturkampf.[83]

The insurrection in Congress Poland of 1863 engendered much
sympathy and a good deal of covert financial support from the
Poznanian gentry. But no efforts were made to stir up revolt in
Prussian Poland. Not even very many volunteers crossed the
frontier to join in the struggle. Of those who did, 175 are known
to have been killed, and 44 banished to Siberia. The Berlin trial
of 1864 convicted 93 Poznanians for having supported the rising on
Prussian soil.[84] A government report on the Poznanian reaction
to the revolt seems credible, allowing for Prussian prejudices:

> The worst elements of the present movement [favoring
> the rising] are the half-bankrupted small Polish
> estate owners and lessees, the bookkeepers and in-
> spectors on the estates, the fanaticized poorer arti-
> sans in the towns, and a large part of the lower clergy.
> The greater part of the Polish nobility lends this
> business only a reluctant support.[85]

When it became evident that the western powers would limit their
intervention to mild diplomatic protests in Petersburg on the
Poles' behalf, the Poznanian gentry resigned themselves to the
insurrection's extinguishment by "the Muscovites."

Even before the outbreak of the rebellion, the Polish
Landtag deputies in Berlin had provoked a series of debates in
which they protested their treatment at the Prussian government's
hands. The gentry liberals put their case thus: In 1815 the Great
Powers agreed the Poles should have distinctive "national institutions" within the partitioning states and also within the geographical limits of 1772; Prussia ought therefore to grant the Poles
separate political institutions in both the Grand Duchy of Poznań
and West Prussia. Hope for the restoration of Poland was not incompatible with the demand that the treaties of 1815 be enforced.
Such hope, said the uncompromising Władysław Niegolewski, was the
Poles' "gospel."[86] The German liberal majority, though not un-
sympathetic to the Poles, argued that the Polish provinces had

joined Prussia not through violence but legally, by virtue of
the 1815 treaties, which incorporated them in the Prussian
state in a "real," not "personal" union. The Poles' "national
institutions" were those granted them and Prussia's other citizens
by the constitution.[87]

The Polish parliamentarians were unable to abjure the hope
of a Polish restoration even as they protested their adherence
as Prussian citizens to the letter of the law. Bismarck seized
upon this fact to accuse them of a "treasonable" mentality, a
belief which became unshakable among German conservative nationalists after 1871. The Poles defended themselves against this
charge in a North German Reichstag debate in which they attempted
fruitlessly to persuade the German deputies to exclude the Grand
Duchy of Poznań from the new German national state whose constitution was being drawn up. "It lies in the principle of nationality
and the right of self-determination," said Kazimierz Kantak,
"that a nation which claims this principle for itself and its own
development as a state must admit the same right to other nationalities."[88] Niegolewski defined the "principle of nationality" in
these terms: "It consists simply in this, that every nation possessing its own customs and language and, moreover, its own
history wishes to have an independent existence and not to be subject to a foreign state." The Poles, Niegolewski declared, grant
the Germans the right to form a state according to this principle
but the Germans, illogically, refuse to reciprocate. So the
Poles must fall back on the rights assured them in 1815.
Niegolewski allowed himself the hope that "when the principle of
nationality rises fully to the consciousness of the German people,
then the historical necessity of the restoration of Poland will
emerge as well!"[89]

The Poles could not have spoken otherwise and still remained
nationalists. Yet their appeals to national equity did them no
good in German eyes, fixed on German interests which, as Bismarck
and his allies defined them after 1871, required the sacrifice
of Polish national claims for the sake of the unity of the Reich
and its good relations with Russia. Thus had reigning German
opinion on the Polish question turned full circle since 1848.

The Kulturkampf and Germanization laws of the 1870s produced
an especially bitter reaction among the Polish national liberals
because, in supporting these measures of Bismarck's government,
the German liberals were openly abaondoning whatever concern
they had evinced since 1848 for the Poles' national interests.
It availed them nothing to warn in their parliamentary protests

that attacks on the religion and on the language spoken by part of
the citizenry of the state contradicted the ideology and spirit of
liberalism. What injuries, Kantak declaimed in 1872, had the
Poles committed against the state to justify such discriminatory
treatment? Denying any revolutionary intentions among his countrymen, he protested that "we have turned our attention to practical
life. Education and work are our slogans too." Yet the Prussian
government denounced the Poles' legal activities as "agitation"
and suppressed the remnants of their national rights.[90]

Bismarck's assault on the Catholic church spurred the Poznanian clerical party to action. In 1872, a daily newspaper, the
Kuryer Poznański, appeared as an ideological alternative to gentry
liberalism. It called for defense of the church and denounced the
threat to the Poles' faith posed by liberalism in general. The
lower clergy ignored Ledóchowski's ban on political activism and
organized with their lay allies numerous protest meetings against
the Germanization laws. The clergy supported the collection of
petitions, some with as many as 300,000 male signatures, condemning
the government's actions. The Poles, and particularly the common
people, could not fail to interpret the government's attacks on
their religion as well as their language as assaults upon their
nationality. The clergy's opposition acquired the glow of national
heroism. The church's national leadership, cast in some doubt by
the Ultramontanism of the preceding years, was fully restored.[91]

This discomfited the Polish national liberal camp, whose
leaders could boast of no success in averting the blows suffered
by Polish society in the 1870s. The clerical-conservatives took
advantage of their rising national stock to force their viewpoint
not only on the institutions of Organic Work, as for example the
Society for Popular Libraries, but equally upon the parliamentary
delegations in the Landtag and Reichstag. Rather than attempting
to win over the German liberals with invocations of the principle
of nationality and the treaties of 1815, the Poles' political
leaders slowly turned during the 1870s and 1880s towards collaboration with the Catholic Center Party. This amounted to an adoption
of an antiliberal social conservatism stressing the traditional
religiosity of the Polish people and the hierarchical, agrarian
nature of Polish society. It followed from this that a better
tactic for the Poles, especially after Bismarck had abandoned the
Kulturkampf, might be to seek to come to terms with the conservative elements in German and Prussian society. The Polish gentry,
like the Centrists and Prussian Junkers, supported agricultural
protectionism and legislative defense of agrarian interests in

general. They opposed socialism, which in the 1880s began to
flicker feebly in the province of Poznań, as strongly as Bismarck
himself.

In the 1880s, the Polish parliamentary delegations inched
towards a position of conservative "loyalism". They hoped that
after William I and Bismarck had passed from the scene, which
could not be far in the future, the Prussian state would cease
its attacks upon them and perhaps even restore some of their
national rights in the spheres of education and language policy.
This program finally crystallized as official Polish strategy after
1890. It owed its triumph, which was to be brief, not only to the
failures of national liberalism in the 1860s and 1870s, but to
the example of the Galician Polish nobility who, in return for
their support of Hapsburg conservatism, had won enviable national
and social privileges in their own land. Moreover, in the 1880s
the underground Polish revolutionary movement had revived, especially in exile and in Russian Poland. It spoke a language not
only of national but also social upheaval, frequently couched in
Marxian or Russian populist-revolutionary terms. This language
was offensive not only to agrarian-conservative but also national-
liberal ears. To these reasons for the Poznanian upper classes'
turn towards "loyalism" in the 1880s yet another must be added:
the slow emergence in their own midst of a populist political
movement representing the Polish petite bourgeoisie and common
people.[92]

The rise of populism in Prussian Poland was not a simple
function of popular hostility to the Prussian regime. But such
hostility increased after 1848, with politically important consequences. According to fragmentary Prussian evidence, the Polish
educated and propertied classes avoided social contacts with the
German bureaucracy and landowners of the province of Poznań
rather consistently after the revolution. By 1886, the district
president in Bromberg could write that "the opposition between
the two nationalities emerges more sharply every day and leads to
the breakdown of even the most harmless intercourse."[93] Bismarck's
Polish policies contributed to the formation in educated Polish
circles of an emotionally charged and highly negative image of
German civilization and Germans in general, an image which pervaded the widely read and morally authoritative post-1863 literature created by Józef Kraszewski, Eliza Orzeszkowa, Henryk
Sienkiewicz, Bolesław Prus, Stefan Żeromski, and Władysław Reymont.
In contrast to the now patronizing, now scornful ridicule with
which earlier Polish writers had lampooned German philistinism,

authoritarianism, and money-grubbing, the writers of the period
1863-1914 tended to view the Germans, especially the Prussians, as
the embodiment of moral and political evil. They became the Poles'
hereditary enemy, more dangerous than the Russians because of their
political and economic strength and discipline. Bourgeois Polish
writers, persuaded of their own nation's need for Organic Work
and a rational and scientific conception of society and politics,
counseled their readers to acquire some of those "Germanic traits."
But they did not mean that the Poles should lose their "national
virtues" of emotional and moral sensitivity, heroism, and love of
political liberty. In fact, it was precisely these attributes
which would grant the Poles victory over their oppressors in the
future.[94]

This Germanophobia the educated Prussian Poles absorbed
through their reading of the post-1863 classics and their own
experience of Prussian rule. It inspired, along with more idealistic nationalist feelings, their political action and their
avoidance of all but the most necessary social, economic, and
cultural interchanges with their German-speaking neighbors. It
could hardly have been otherwise. While the Germans were forging
their national myths of Bismarck's greatness, the Poles shuddered
at what seemed to be the "Iron Chancellor's" unremitting and un-
fathomable malevolence towards them.[95]

One can only wonder to what extent the Polish common people
accepted the anti-German stereotypes of post-1863 Polish literary
culture. Certainly readers of the political press and frequenters
of Polish libraries were exposed to them. But there is evidence
of a more deep-seated hostility of the Polish common people to the
Prussian regime and their German neighbors. In the years 1861-62,
heavy-handed police inspections of "Polish agitation" led to
several tumults between Polish workers and local Germans in which
the Poles delivered themselves of one of their favorite insults,
calling their antagonists "you Prussian dog's-blood."[96] It is
not improbable that a Polish priest actually did say in public,
upon hearing of Frederick William IV's death, that "if he croaked,
so he croaked, the German dog's-blood. . . .When a German dog's-
blood croaks, a second one takes his place."[97]

During the Kulturkampf, Polish villagers resorted to violence
to defend their dissenting Polish priests and oppose the "official"
priests, usually Germans, who came to take their place. In some
cases, they barred the newcomer's access to the parish church, for
which they got jail sentences and fines. In others, they beat
"official" priests, or boycotted them. Father Moerke, appointed to

the parish of Powidz in 1877, never saw his parishioners, who attended the services of a neighboring Polish priest. When Moerke
died in 1882, the villagers exhumed his coffin and dropped it in a
lake.[98]

By 1875, an eminent Polish ethnologist could write that the
common people in Poznania, under the impact of the Kulturkampf
and Bismarck's anti-Polish legislation, were abandoning their
former supercilious tolerance of the German-speaking peasantry
and adopting instead an attitude of suspicion and active dislike.[99]
Official reports on Polish public opinion in 1886 and 1887 found
"even among the lower classes of the Polish population, among
peasants and workers, a lively and excited national feeling and
even a mood of exasperation."[100]

True, the Polish common people served obediently in the
Prussian army despite the occasional insults of their German commanders. And many of the poorest had a genuine respect for the
economic solidity and psychological tranquility they perceived
in Germany society. Jakób Wojciechowski, son of a hard-pressed
and unsuccessful landless laborer, willingly sought out employment with Germans. In his remarkable autobiography, he paid
tribute to his masters' benevolence and interest in teaching him
their language, which he was eager to learn for its practical value
in getting him better jobs.[101]

Nevertheless, a psychological gulf separated the Poles from
their German and Jewish neighbors. It contained a traditional
component of animosity which grew larger on account of the
Prussian government's repressive policies. Among the best proofs
of the lack of intimate bonds between Poles and Germans are
the sparse data on religious conversions and interconfessional
marriages. During eight years between 1832 and 1847, only 146
conversions of Catholics to the Evangelical Church occurred in the
government district of Poznań. In the same years, the 446 conversions of Protestants to Catholicism bear witness both to the
Catholic church's opposition to mixed marriages and the readiness
of a small number of Germans to enter into a largely Polish
milieu.[102] In 1889 the Catholic clergy in the western half of the
province reported that in the preceding decade 426 mixed marriages
were performed with the Church's dispensation, 1,459 without it,
the latter of course in Protestant churches. Bearing in mind that
a certain number of these mixed marriages occurred in predominantly
German counties and thus among German Catholics and Protestants,
an annual average of fewer than 200 mixed marriages in a population
of almost one million underscores the rarity of intermarriage
among the nationalities.[103]

The Polish common people's attitudes towards Germans and the Prussian regime were not incompatible with acceptance of the political leadership in Polish society of the gentry and clergy. Nevertheless, in the 1870s and 1880s a modest bourgeois challenge arose. It was voiced by Roman Szymański, the leader of the populist movement (ruch ludowy) until his death in 1908. Szymański, the son of a provincial cloth-dyer, took a university degree in the 1860s. In 1871 Jackowski and other national-liberal noblemen offered him the editorship of a new daily newspaper they wished to publish to circulate their views among the Polish townspeople. Szymański accepted. The journal--Orędownik [the Advocate]--appeared, but before long its editor began calling for greater representation of Polish burghers in the executive organs of the system of electoral authorities. Szymański urged the Polish bourgeoisie to wake up politically and defend the Polish national cause, particularly in urban elections. He admitted the political indolence and inexperience of the Polish townspeople. "Our middle classes will need the help, advice, and direction of the upper classes for a long time yet," he wrote in 1887.[104] Despite his Catholic orthodoxy and invocations of national solidarity, Szymański's gestures at bourgeois independence irritated his gentry employers. In 1873 they withdrew their financial support. Szymański found bourgeois funding for his journal and carried on, becoming a well-known writer, speaker, and organizer of political meetings in the province. His importance or the number of those who shared his temerity to question the gentry's political dominance should not be overestimated. In 1886, the circulation of his paper was only 800, while that of popularly written rivals funded by the gentry exceeded 10,000.[105] Still, Szymański's populism was the first independent political movement among the nineteenth-century Poznanian bourgeoisie. It won support from urban Organic Work activists and educated professionals of bourgeois origins, merchants, artisans, and small-scale manufacturers. These were groups whose numbers and prosperity were on the rise after 1870.[106]

Bismarck's anti-Polish campaigns provoked a crisis of national confidence among the gentry. They were gratified to find a Reichstag majority speaking up for them and denouncing the expulsions of 1885, but their Landtag deputies were helpless before Bismarck's onslaughts. They could only reiterate their innocence of revolutionary intentions, whether nationalist or socialist, and wonder aloud why they, dutiful citizens as they were, were being placed under an official "ban" and subjected to "a war of extermination."[107]

Worse yet, when the Colonization Commission was ready to buy Polish estates, many among the gentry were prepared to sell. The debts of even nationally prominent and militantly anti-Prussian noblemen were too great, and the offers the commission made too tempting, not to lead a rash of sales which created the impression that before long the Polish gentry would have allowed itself to be expropriated and uprooted. The greater part of the nobility held aloof, while a group of activists among them founded a Polish Land Bank (Bank Ziemski) intended to refinance gentry debts. But neither the financially pressed Poznanian gentry nor the Russian and Galician nobility lent the bank much support. Before 1890 it accomplished little.[108]

The Polish press denounced the Colonization Commission while the gentry fired up the machinery of the electoral authorities to stage protest meetings and contest the elections of 1887. But the Poles' agitation lacked spirit and they lost parliamentary ground to the Germans and Jews. Instead of changing the electoral system's managers, the county representatives in 1888 confirmed in their offices the five estate owners, two priests, and the gentry-born newspaper editor and manufacturer previously seated on the Provincial Election Committee. This was too much for Szymański. Resigning his seat on the Poznań city electoral committee, he wrote gloweringly that "the leadership of the nobility and clergy, [who] until now have passed for the natural protectors of the middle and lower classes, turns out to be fruitless."[109]

In these straits, the gentry politicians finally decided a change in tactics was in order. After Bismarck's dismissal by William II in 1890, they initiated an ostentatious policy of "loyalism." Ironically, this is what Szymański wanted them to do, only without the aristocratic flourishes which annoyingly recalled the old szlachta-Commonwealth both to the skeptical bourgeois Polish mind and the suspicious Prussian consciousness. From the Poles' unaccustomed ventures in Prussian loyalism of the early 1890's unexpected political storms were to blow up.

Germans and Jews, 1850-90

The prosperity of the province's agrarian economy from the 1850s to the mid 1870s profited Germans and Jews more than it did the Poles. The wholesale trade in agricultural products remained largely in Jewish hands. Germans and Jews handled virtually all the province's trade beyond its borders, to the east, to the west, and south to Silesia. The province's tighter integration into the industrializing Prussian and Imperial German economy created com-

mercial and industrial opportunities which its German-speaking
population, thanks particularly to their preexisting capital
reserves and access to west German credit, were the first to exploit. Importation into the province of factory-produced wares
threatened the existence of many German and Jewish handicraftsmen,
as it did that of their Polish counterparts. But Germans and Jews
in artisan trades capable of adaptation to an industrializing
economy, of which there were many, were in a better position than
their poorer and often technically less skilled Polish rivals.
Undoubtedly, most of the modern industrial and commercial firms
which began to appear in the province in the 1870s, including
agricultural processing plants and distilleries as the biggest and
most profitable among them, were owned by Germans or Jews.[110]

Similarly, German farmers, and especially the large landowners, gained not only acreage at the Poles' expense after 1850.
The local Junkers had a secure supply of credit, unlike the Polish
gentry, while profits earned outside the province in business or
farming in these first decades of German industrialization often
were translated into possession of a Poznanian estate. The local
bureaucracy had assisted the German peasantry since the end of the
1820s in the formation of technical education societies. State-
supported savings banks had existed since the 1840s, and in the
1860s the cooperative savings and loan movement, centered initially in the towns, found organizers among the province's Germans.
The crisis of the long depression struck Germans and Poles alike,
but the Polish gentry and villagers lacked financial resources
equivalent to the Germans' to allow them to weather the storm
equally well.[111]

These economic circumstances underlay the relative expansion
of the German Protestant and Catholic population between 1849 and
1871.[112] But the westward migration of the 1870s and 1880s accompanying the long depression reversed this demographic trend.
In these difficult years the German farm worker began to abandon
the province. So too did many small farmers and poor artisans.

Jewish migration out of the province rose steadily after the
1848 revolution finally permitted it. From 1849 to 1871, the
Jewish population declined absolutely by 19 percent; in the next
two decades, it fell by 28 percent. At the mid nineteenth century,
the Poznanian Jews were more numerous (76,800) than at any time
under Prussian rule, or perhaps in their entire history. By 1890,
they numbered only 44,000. First to depart were the ghetto poor.
They were followed by artisans ruined by industrial competition,
especially in the textile and clothing trades, and by the weaker

members of the commercial and shopkeeping class. Jewish settlements in villages and small towns emptied faster than those in the
middle-sized and larger cities. Here the Jewish retailers and
commercial bourgeoisie, extending their already strong economic
positions in the 1860s and 1870s, held on more confidently,
buoyed up by the larger size of their communities, their political
influence, and their cultural and religious activities.[113]

The occupational census of 1882 showed the Jewish population
to be ever more concentrated in commercial and small-business
ownership: 41 percent were self-employed in commerce, 22 percent
self-employed in industry and handicrafts. Single-family operations dominated both these categories, as the smaller percentages
of salaried or wage-earning persons counted within them (17 percent and 10 percent, respectively) reveal. Of the remaining 10
percent, 7 percent were professionals in secular and religious
callings, a dwindling 3 percent in the servant and unskilled
working class. Three of every five Jews worked in a commercial
trade, one of every three in manufactures.[114]

The German social structure stood between the urban Jewish
and the predominantly rural Polish pattern. Over half the German
population (51 percent) worked in agriculture. Farm owners--
Junkers and peasants alike--accounted for 14 percent, rural workers
for 37 percent of the German population. Of the remainder, settled
mainly in the towns, 22.5 percent were engaged in industry and
handicrafts (owners, 9 percent, workers, 13.5 percent). The large
number of German officials swelled the professional category to
12 percent, whereas only a relatively few Germans were engaged in
commerce (3.5 percent). At the bottom of the social scale, 11
percent were servants and unskilled workers.[115] Before 1890, only
three groups possessed any political importance: the Junkers and
the more prosperous peasantry who followed their lead; the private
urban bourgeoisie, comprising manufacturers, well-to-do artisans,
merchants, and educated professionals not employed by the state;
and the state officials, led by those in the higher civil administration but counting also military officers, middle and subaltern bureaucrats, policemen and railway men, and primary and
secondary schoolteachers

Unlike the Poles, after 1848 the German Protestants and
Catholics were under no compulsion to defend their nationality.
The Prussian state, seeking to suppress "Polonism" and to Germanize
the province, acted in their name. The Polish language lost all
public or official relevance for speakers of German. After the

Germanization of the educational system, the Poles gradually became more or less bilingual while Germans and Jews fluent in
literary Polish dwindled in number to the point where they were
considered a rare curiosity, though not the more esteemed for their
rarity. In their contacts with the Poles, the Germans came to assume they would be understood and addressed in their own tongue.
Critics of Prussian linguistic policies later maintained that the
Poles' enforced bilinguality gave them an economic advantage over
the Germans, who could not study Polish systematically anywhere
within the lower or higher Prussian school system.[116]

The state provided the province's Germans and Jews with a
German national educational and political system, while their
integration into the Prussian and German economy linked them to
social developments in the German heartland. Prussian _Polenpolitik_
was designed to allow them to live as if they had no Polish neighbors. Although there were, throughout the partition period,
roughly two Poles for every one German speaker in Poznania, the
Prussian government strove to make this fact irrelevant, both for
its functionaries and for the local German population.

In the four decades following the revolution, the Poznanian
Germans and Jews elaborated the political ideas they had embraced
before 1848 into two socially and ideologically distinct political
movements. The German and Jewish urban bourgeoisie and educated
professionals firmly embraced Prussian-German liberalism. The
Junkers and rich farmers, persuading and pressuring the peasantry
to join with them, allied with the high bureaucrats, whose political signals to their subordinates were likewise efficacious, in
support of Prussian-German conservatism. The strength of liberals
and conservatives varied with the political context. In the
country and provincial diets, whose prerogatives were local and un-
controversial, Junkers and Polish estate owners sat in control.
Town councils, governed by the Prussian three-class voting law,
were strongholds of Jewish businessmen and German manufacturers and
artisans. So, too, were the semiofficial chambers of commerce.
In the Prussian Landtag, the liberals' tax-paying strength allowed
them to dominate the urban mandates, while the Junkers commanded
those rural districts where they outnumbered the Polish gentry.
Reichstag elections, conducted by universal male suffrage, gave the
agrarian-bureaucratic bloc an advantage over the liberals, who
countered by bargaining for mandates in those districts where their
votes could decide between a German or Polish victory.

Before the Reich-level political crisis of 1878-79, both the
liberals and conservatives contented themselves with local organi-

zations which languished between elections. But in 1890, the
liberals, who previously had supported the National Liberal Party,
trekked into the camp of Bismarck's left-liberal opponents, forming a province-wide organization of the Deutsche Freisinnige Partei
to which they subsequently remained stubbornly faithful. Their
cause was defended in respectable bourgeois fashion by a provincial
liberal press guided by the Posener Zeitung, established in 1806.
In 1879, a group of agrarian and bureaucratic notables funded the
publication of the province's first conservative daily, the
Posener Tageblatt, which pleaded the cause of agricultural protectionism. In 1884, the same circles set up the German Central
Union of the United Conservatives of the Province of Posen.
This was an upper-class organization concerned mainly with election
strategy and defending agrarian interests before the local civil
administration. Before 1890, neither liberals nor conservatives
took special pains to recruit the German common people. They
either counted blandly on their support or ignored them.[117]

There was no question after 1848 of the liberals' or conservatives' Prussian loyalty and support of German unification under
Prussian auspices. Nor were they divided before 1879 by economic
issues, since the state's free-trade policies were agreeable to
agrarians and burghers alike. Thereafter, a serious rift opened
between them, as the liberals began attacking the regime for
favoring agrarian interests at the expense of trade with Russia
and the eastern commercial-industrial economy in general. This
economic opposition compounded the two parties' preexisting
hostilities over social and constitutional issues. Liberals
attacked aristocratic privilege while they smarted under the
haughtiness and hectoring meted out to them by local military
commanders and high officials. Until 1866, they opposed the
government's reactionary manipulation of the Prussian constitution.
The conservatives reacted with stiff-necked monarchism and social
exclusivity.[118]

Anti-Semitism was also an issue. The province's Jews threw
themselves behind the liberal movement after 1848, fearing in
the 1850s and 1860s official repudiation of Jewish emancipation
and dismayed after 1879 at the emergence in Germany of anti-
Semitic agitation to which Bismarck and his allies lent more or
less open support.[119] The provincial bureaucracy either ignored
the Jews or discriminated against them, as for example in seeking,
unsuccessfully, to limit Jewish enrollment in the gymnasiums or,
more successfully, to prevent appointments of Jews as state and
city officials and as public schoolteachers.[120] Within the

liberal movement, Protestants and Jews cooperated on the basis of
common political and socioeconomic interests, but it was a marriage
of convenience overshadowed by centuries of Christian-Jewish urban
tension. On the social level, "Germans of the Christian faith kept
completely away from the Jews."[121]

In their views on Prussian Polenpolitik and the Polish national movement in Poznania, the starting point of liberals and
conservatives alike was opposition to the "breakaway" (Losreissung)
of the province and its inclusion in a restored Polish state. The
argument of the conservatives on this question followed Bismarck's
point for point.[122] Before 1871, the liberals still reckoned with
the possibility that German unification would involve war with
Russia. In the Polish debates of 1862 and 1863, they fulminated
against Tsarist autocracy and sympathized with the rebellious Russian Poles. The Progressive leader Schulze-Delitzsch declared
that Germany and Poland, organized as national states, would be
"natural allies" bound together by common hostility to Muscovy.
But he also insisted that Prussia's formerly Polish provinces
"have succumbed definitively to a process of Germanization" and
under no circumstances could the German nation surrender them. By
"Germanization" he meant a "natural" and ineluctable movement of
civilization and culture from west to east, a process into which
the Prussian Poles were peacefully being drawn, just as a steady
flood of German settlers was making of Poznania "not merely a
Prussian possession, but a German possession, a quintessential
part of German life." Schulze-Delitzsch gave expression to
the nationalist pathos and defensive-mindedness of the German
liberal movement, saying that if the Poles "broke away," "Prussia
would not merely be poorer by one province; no, rather a valuable
member of Germany would be thereby torn away, and once again the
mutilation of our already so damaged and violated national body
would begin."[123] The Poznanian Progressives shared these views,
whose rigidity and condescension grated on Polish nerves, even
though German liberals, unlike the conservatives, attempted to find
a conciliatory tone in addressing the Poles. A Poznanian liberal
reminded the Poles of "the poet's" (Schiller's) dictum, "The
history of the world is the judgment of the world": through its
own faults, Poland lost the right of national independence, and
Germany was justified in absorbing those Polish lands it prevented Russia from seizing.[124]

The Poznanian German liberals and conservatives both approved
Bismarck's efforts to bend the Polish Catholic church to German
control and his Germanizing language decrees of the 1870s. On the

conservative side, the Junkers fully shared the state bureaucracy's traditional anti-Polonism which inspired these measures.
To the liberals, linguistic assimilation of the Poles and their
exposure to secular German culture were the very heart of Germanization and the precondition of what Heinrich Rickert, a prominent
left liberal from West Prussia, described in an 1886 debate as
"the reconciliation of the nationalities."[125] These goals overrode the Poles' claims to a national right to employ their
language in schools and public life. Liberals either ignored
discussing these claims or referred the Poles to the use of their
language in religious instruction. But, when in 1887 teaching of
Polish was abolished altogether, the liberals raised no protests
in the parliamentary chambers.[126]

It was Bismarck's last campaign against the Poles, beginning
in 1885 and culminating in the creation of the Colonization Commission, which finally divided the province's Germans over official Polish policy. The Junkers had called on the state to
uproot the Polish gentry since before 1848.[127] Bismarck was
strongly urged into action in 1886 by the Poznanian bureaucracy,
whose proposals no doubt had been aired among local German estate
owners. Poznanian Junkers defended the colonization bill vociferously in the Prussian Landtag. Rejecting liberal objections that
the bill amounted to an unconstitutional "exceptional law" aimed
against one part of the population alone, Heinrich von Tiedemann
declared that its objective was nothing less than the "maintenance
of the state," threatened as it was by future Polish rebellions.
If, to this end, Poles ought to be rejected as colonists, even
though their taxes supported colonization, such an outcome was
legal because of the higher needs of the state. Such ideological
recklessness had acquired a quality of indubitable Bismarckian
respectability by the 1880s.[128]

Although they favored peasant colonization at the East
Elbian estate owners' expense, the left liberals voted against
the Colonization Act not only because it conflicted with the
principles of equality before the law and freedom of internal
settlement; they also objected, as Rudolf Virchow put it, to the
government's arrogation to itself of "the right to say who is and
who is not a German." The Colonization Commission would discriminate not only against Poles, or those whom it decided were Poles;[129]
it would, Virchow correctly predicted, also favor conservative-
minded Protestants at the expense of German Catholics, Progressives, and Socialists. In fact, such legislation, excluding part
of the population of the state from the ranks of the nation, set a

grim precedent in German history, prefiguring the "racial laws" of
the National Socialist regime.[130]

The Poznanian Progressives were similarly incensed at the expulsions of 1883-85, not only because of their brutality in
general, but especially because of their anti-Semitic focus. Jewish protest meetings assembled in Poznań, but the Jewish members
of the Freisinnnige Partei remained true to their principle of not
speaking politically as Jews, but rather simply as German citizens.
They upheld their party's condemnation of the expulsions as arbitrary measures directed against minorities unjustifiably branded
as disloyal and dangerous by the Prussian regime.[131]

At the end of Bismarck's chancellorship, nationality relations in the east were tense. The Polish nationalists, embittered
by the Germanization laws, oscillated between anxiety, despair,
and rage. The German conservatives in Poznania did not bother to
hide their belittling contempt for the Polish movement even as
they expressed exaggerated fears of its treasonable powers. Towards their bourgeois liberal critics, the conservatives restrained
with difficulty, in the interest of an elusive German national
solidarity, the "drastic" expressions and "sharp tone" in which
under Bismarck it had become fashionable for the military-minded
Prussian-German upper class to defend its privileges.

The Poles and German liberals occasionally collaborated,
particularly between 1850 and 1866 and again after 1879, to defeat
German conservative candidates in Landtag elections. In town council elections compromises were not uncommon giving the Jews the
seats in the first tax bracket, the German Christians those in
the second, and the Poles those in the remaining third. After
1886 German liberals often voted with the Poles against official
Polenpolitik in the Landtag in Berlin.[132]

Nevertheless, the Poznanian Germans had lost what little touch
they earlier had with Polish society and culture. They viewed
the Poles' national organization with mistrust and more or less
vivid apprehensions. Among German conservatives, Frederickian and
Bismarckian judgments of the szlachta and Polish civilization had
become stereotyped and automatic. In educated bourgeois German
circles, little remained of the pre-1848 romanticization of the
Poles. German literature after the mid nineteenth century dealt
with German-Polish relations with increasing Polonophobia. Gustav
Freytag, author of the most widely read German novel of the nineteenth century, Soll und Haben (1855), treated the Polish upper
class in this and his other works with scorn and sarcasm, the

Polish common people with insular condescension. From the 1880s,
authors of lesser talents turned out Ostmarkenromane, nationalist
potboilers rendering the Polish-German question in melodramatic
tones.[133] No doubt, the German bourgeoisie in the province of
Poznań had a more balanced view of their Polish neighbors, but
German politicians in the east could not hide their sense of
national superiority. The Germans' private contacts with the
Polish population were diminishing. The Poles seceded from
nationally mixed organizations and created a set of social and
cultural institutions--for example, the Polish theater in Poznań
(1875)--independent of German society. The growth of the Polish
commercial and industrial bourgeoisie occurred amid boycott
slogans aimed at Germans and Jews. Whether or not the boycott
worked, the appearance of new Polish business rivals inevitably
weakened the German bourgeoisie's economic ties with the Poles.

     The capitalist development of the province and the Germaniza-
tion of education, contrary to many Germans' expectations, did
nothing to bridge the traditional social, cultural, and political
divisions among the nationalities. These were growing wider
as the Prussian government sought to hasten the "process of
Germanization." To this end it seized upon means which deeply
divided German society. By disaffecting the Polish masses,
Bismarck's regime offered the Polish nationalists new possibilities
for political and economic conquests. The stage was set for the
spiraling conflict of the prewar decades.

The Crisis of Government under William II

In the 1880s the parliamentary base of Bismarck's regime was
the cartel or "rallying" (Sammlung) of agrarian-aristocratic,
bureaucratic, and conservative bourgeois interests, expressed in
a coalition of the German Conservative, Free Conservative, and
National Liberal parties. This alliance rested on the assumption
that the interests of heavy industry and Prussian estate agriculture were not only of roughly equal importance in the Imperial
German economy, but also that tariff protectionism served the two
equally well. The cartel parties upheld the Bismarckian constitution in exchange for tariff rates favorable to both the heavy
industrialists and the Junkers.

The cartel system, or what was also called Sammlungspolitik,
represented a balancing of the three dominant interests in Imperial
Germany. In the forefront stood the Prussian state and the
German Empire Bismarck had bestowed upon it. This imperfectly
parliamentarized, still strongly authoritarian, military-
bureaucratic political system was socially grounded, after the
1870s even more than before, in the Prussian royal household and
the nobility and landed gentry who supplied most of its high officials and military leaders. To these ranks were joined those
members of the educated and propertied bourgeoisie whose social
and political mentality met the conservative standards set by the
noble-born official establishment for admission to their privileged
circles.

Despite the great strength of their positions at court, in
the army, and in the bureaucracy, the Junkers could not ignore the
Prussian Landtag and Imperial Reichstag, whose legislative powers
bore directly on the Prussian nobility's economic interests and
privileges. Since they could marshal only sizable minority delegations in the Berlin assemblies, the Junkers were compelled to
ally themselves with the conservative bourgeois interests repre-

sented in the National Liberal Party. Insofar as the state
depended for its own self-perpetuation on new sources of income,
it fell into political dependence on the parliaments; insofar as
the Prussian nobility could not force the monarchical regime to
safeguard their interests autocratically, their social and economic
survival hinged on parliamentary votes; and insofar as the conservative bourgeoisie sought economic protection and entry to
official ruling circles, it was forced to demonstrate its indis-
pensability to the regime in parliamentary politics.

Thus were the three dominant political elements in Prussia
and Imperial Germany intertwined. For any one of them to desert
the others called the Bismarckian system into question. Refusal
by the government to cooperate with the parties in the parliaments
raised the prospect of a monarchical coup d'état and the consolidation of a radicalized popular front against absolutist rule. Withdrawal of the National Liberals or the conservative parties from
the cartel coalition would force the government to look for support among the "enemies of the Reich." Collaboration with the
proscribed and militantly oppositional Social Democrats was impossible in principle. But falling into dependence either on the
left liberal Progressives or the Catholic Center Party could only
lead to constitutional, economic, and ideological concessions to
them contradicting the aims and interests of Bismarck's Germany
and those groups upon whose support he had stabilized it in the
course of the 1870s. Here lay the importance in the following
years of the maintenance of the cartel system and of the balancing
of industrial and agrarian interests which was its vital precondition.

Yet between the 1870s and 1914, industrialization and urbani-
zation cast a heavy shadow on the social and economic landscape
of traditional Germany, whose dominant features had been the
village, the manor house, and the small town. The Reich population grew from 42 million in 1873 to 67 million in 1913. The
proportion of city dwellers rose from 36 percent to 60 percent
of the whole. Industrial output increased fourfold until by 1914
it was the greatest of any European state. Equally significant
was the declining role of agriculture in the national economy.
While in 1873 the value of agricultural output stood to that of
large-scale industry in a relationship of 38:32, by 1895 the
figures had reversed themselves. Similarly, net investments in
agriculture and industry were of equal extent in 1879. But in
1910 more than four times as much new investment capital flowed
into industry as into agriculture. By the eve of World War I,

Imperial Germany had completed the passage from <u>Agrarstaat</u> to
<u>Industriestaat</u>. Although the social, cultural, and political
desirability of this transition was hotly debated in the 1890s,
the watershed had already been crossed by the beginning of that
decade.[1]

The beneficiaries of these years of industrialization were
the industrial and commercial middle classes. Their numbers,
wealth, and self-confidence rose considerably, especially after
the long depression of 1873-96 gave way to almost two decades of
erratic but cumulatively immense industrial expansion. The East
Elbian landlords, on the other hand, emerged from the depression
under a mountain of debts. Despite grain tariffs and state subsidies, their income rose only slowly in the two prewar decades.
After the mid 1870s, Imperial Germany was a net importer of grain.
Despite tariffs, foreign cereals poured into the domestic market
and held prices relatively low, though not as low as they would
have been without import duties. Not until 1912 did farm prices
rise again to the levels of the early 1870s. In relation to the
business-owning classes, the Junkers were steadily losing economic
ground.[2]

As the urban economy grew, so too did the number of industrial
workers and commercial-industrial white-collar employees. The
<u>Ostflucht</u> which, paired with rural-urban migration in west and
south Germany, supplied the expanding cities with new manpower,
continued to drive the price of rural labor up while it accentu-
ated the demographic shift within the Empire away from the old
Prussian provinces towards the west. After 1870, the social pillars upon which the traditional Prussian state rested--estate
agriculture worked by a settled peasantry, commerce in agricultural
products, handicrafts and industry oriented to governmental
demand--began to crumble. Simultaneously, industrialization
created a modern and dynamic urban society--but a society still
subject to the political domination of the old Prussian ruling
classes.[3]

The fundamental issue of Imperial German and Prussian politics
after 1890 was whether this domination could last. The enrichment
of the industrial and commercial bourgeoisie raised the question
whether it would remain content with junior partnership in a cartel
system upholding the fulsome privileges of the monarchy and aristocracy. The "flight from the east" and the "flight from the
countryside" weakened the popular basis of conservative authority
while the political interests of the expanding big-city lower
middle class bore no obvious relation to those of the haughty and

imperious Bismarckian ruling class. Repressive laws and police
action could not prevent working-class socialism from becoming
as early as 1893 the numerically preponderant movement in German
politics. It raised the specter of social revolution against
Junkers and capitalists alike even as it threatened to paralyze
the inner workings of the Reichstag and--should the three-class
electoral law ever fall--the Prussian Landtag as well. Could the
Bismarckian system preserve its beneficiaries' prerogatives and
authority in the face of such social and political challenges?

The answer depended in no small degree upon William II. Two
years after his accession, this ambitious, but dilettantish
ruler dismissed Bismarck in the midst of a parliamentary crisis
in which the cartel parties in the Reichstag lost their majority
while the Anti-Socialist Law and the Reinsurance Treaty with
Russia lapsed. The Kaiser appointed General Leo von Caprivi as
Bismarck's successor with the intention of dictating to him the
new lines of Prussian and Imperial policy. But the pressures of
Reichstag politics quickly forced Caprivi to commit himself to a
political program which broke decisively with several Bismarckian
precedents. To counter the Franco-Russian military-diplomatic
entente which took shape after 1890, Caprivi sought the Reichstag's
approval of army expansion. In the midst of an industrial depression aggravated by grain shortages, Caprivi abandoned the cartel
strategy by offering the National Liberals and the parties to
their left commercial treaties with Austria-Hungary, Rumania, and
finally also Russia which promised German industry cheaper access
to those markets in return for lower duties on their agricultural
exports to the Reich.

By 1894, this policy had proven a success for Caprivi.
Reichstag majorities had voted for both the army reforms and the
commercial treaties. But meanwhile the socialist movement had
taken advantage of its legal status after 1890 to extend its
membership impressively and organize a potentially formidable
trade-union adjunct, simultaneously reaffirming its implacable
ideological opposition to bourgeois society. Worse still,
Caprivi drove the Prussian agrarians into a shrill and demagogic
public opposition by his reductions in farm tariffs. Conservative
intrigue against Caprivi in the bureaucracy and at court at last
in 1894 inspired the Kaiser to replace him with the aged and compliant Prince Chlodwig zu Hohenlohe-Schillingsfürst.

Caprivi's makeshift policies had threatened to draw the
monarchy into dependence on the middle-class parties and to
undercut the Junkers' economic interests. Despite his longing for

popularity with the masses, William II would not break politically
with his aristocracy. To have done so definitively would have required elimination of the Junkers' massive influence at court, in
the ministerial and provincial civil bureaucracy, and in the military. They could only have been replaced by the educated and
propertied bourgeoisie, against whose pretensions to power Bismarck
had erected the Empire and into whose hands William II had no
reason to wish to deliver himself. On the contrary, in 1894 and
1895 he lent an ear to reactionary deliberations over the possibility of a constitutional coup d'état aimed at the socialists
and the Reichstag electoral law. Realizing at length the perils
to his Imperial legitimacy posed by such a course, he turned to a
group of high officials whose prescriptions for strengthening the
Empire suited both his own ambitions and the interests of the
upper classes.[4]

The appointment in 1897 of Count Bernhard von Bülow as
Imperial foreign secretary signified the entry of the Reich into
serious competition with the other Great Powers for territorial
aggrandizement in Asia and Africa. Admiral Alfred Tirpitz's appointment as Reich naval secretary in the same year soon made it
clear that German Imperial expansion would be promoted by the
building of a great high-seas fleet, a new weapon William II
keenly wished to add to the Hohenzollern arsenal. To the powerful Prussian minister of finance, Johannes Miquel, fell the task
of reassembling the aristocratic-bourgeois cartel as the base of
domestic political support from which Wilhelminian imperialism
(Weltpolitik) could be launched. German industry, having entered
into the post-1896 boom, was not irrevocably committed to Caprivi's
commercial treaties. In exchange for agreement to support higher
grain tariffs, it obtained the agrarians' approval of Tirpitz's
bills commissioning it to build the German navy. The "alliance of
rye and iron" of 1879 reemerged amid imperialist fanfare in a form
profitable to industrialists and Junkers alike.[5]

Between 1890 and 1897, German politics had passed through a
crisis. Faced with political and economic contradictions within
the cartel, William II and his advisers vainly sought a purely
domestic escape from this impasse first in a turn towards the left
under Caprivi and then towards the right in 1894-95. Even had
William II wished to dispense with conservative backing, the
bourgeois parties were too divided among themselves to form a solid
bloc shielding the monarchy both from the aristocratic right and
the socialist left. Menaced in the rear by the socialist movement,
these parties had no heart for a liberal assault against the mon-

archy and its aristocratic allies. Given their penchant for
empire and tariffs as well as their antisocialist phobia, the
National Liberals and many Progressives and Centrists as well
could be tempted after 1897 to support a neo-Bismarckian cartel.
Autarchy and imperialism were to unite the aristocracy and
bourgeoisie behind William II's "personal regime," blocking the
socialists off from power at the cost to the bourgeois parties
of further parliamentarization of Prussia and the Reich. They
paid this price in the hope of Imperial prosperity and the social
and political patronage of the monarchical regime. But, as it
happened, in 1897 William II and his agrarian and industrial
supporters only "exported the internal crisis and so took the road
which led to diplomatic isolation, war and the collapse of the
monarchy."[6]

Germany's foreign policy between 1897 and 1914 functioned as
a test of the legitimacy of the Wilhelminian system of domestic
politics. If the Kaiser and his aristocratic servants could not
translate their claims to a unique military virtue into glorious
and economically profitable Imperial triumphs--triumphs which in
turn might be expected to counteract proletarian hostility to
bourgeois society and inspire enthusiasm for a "people's empire"
(Volkskaisertum)--then the bourgeoisie's political support and
economic subsidy of the monarchy and the agrarian conservatives
could only be a bad bargain. But it soon became apparent to the
agrarian right that their political and economic future depended
on the monarchy's foreign policy successes, if only because
failures raised the question of the political utility of the
monarchy which shielded their privileges. So long as the Kaiser
and his aristocratic aides monopolized the direction of foreign
and military policy, a moderate diplomatic defeat could be expected to weaken bourgeois commitment to a cartel whose financing, in the form of army and navy expansion bills, cost commerce
and industry relatively more than it cost the Junkers. In official
and bourgeois circles, it became axiomatic that a disastrous
military or diplomatic setback would fan the fires of socialist
revolution and so imperil the Wilhelminian status quo, if not
expose the monarchial regime to destruction.

William II's government found itself compelled after 1897
to seek out foreign policy triumphs and to avoid with exaggerated
sensitivity setbacks which a politically more stable system could
have weathered without alarm. If official policymakers yielded to
diplomatic caution or the temptations of unheroic compromise with
the other European powers, they exposed themselves to the charges
of weakness which radical nationalist and imperialist pressure

groups among the agrarians and middle class were ever ready to hurl
at them. But even the less aggressive-minded agrarians and
bourgeoisie, having perceived after 1897 the degree to which William II and Bülow staked the empire's authority on its foreign successes, could not wish military or diplomatic failure on the regime
without facing the prospect of struggling with the socialists to
divide a discredited monarchy's legacy.[7]

Although Imperial Germany had as good a claim to overseas aggrandizement as any European power, in retrospect it is clear that
Wilhelminian foreign policy undermined the regime it was intended
to strengthen. After Bismarck had tied the Empire to Austrian
fortunes, in the alliance of 1879, it was inevitable that Germany
gravitate towards Vienna in the Austro-Russian rivalries over the
Balkans. Cartel politics, based as they were on shielding the
East Elbian landlords from the competition of Russian agricultural
exports, only widened the diplomatic gulf between the Reich and
the Tsardom. Construction of the Grand Fleet robbed Germany of
the chance that, in the event of war in defense of Austrian
interests on the Russian front, England might hold France neutral
on the western front. Instead, England moderated its colonial
rivalries with both France and Russia so as to counter the challenge to its own imperial position and domestic security raised by
the German navy. The Reich's diplomatic "encirclement" was plain
to see after the first Morocco Crisis of 1905-6. The second
Morocco Crisis of 1911 revealed Germany's dependence on the Triple
Entente for the acquisition of overseas territories conceded even
in Berlin to be of only second-rate importance. In supporting
aggressive Austrian policies in the Balkans after 1908, William II
and his advisers gained nothing but the desperate resolve to exploit the July crisis of 1914 to break through the ring of their
foreign enemies and seize "world power" (Weltmacht) status by
arms. Thus would they revive the flagging confidence of the
bourgeoisie in the Wilhelminian state and trample on the revolutionary hopes of the ever more numerous Social Democrats.[8]

The gamble of the Prussian ruling class in 1914 proved fatal
to its authors. Yet they were driven to risk it by their apprehension in 1914 that the Wilhelminian political system was on the
verge of breakdown. Under Bülow's chancellorship (1900-1909) the
cartel had collapsed because of diplomatic failures and the agrarians' refusal to share tax increases for arms expenditures equally
with the middle classes. Bülow's successor, Theobald von Bethmann
Hollweg, attempted in the years 1909-11 to allay English suspicion
of German naval aims by a soft-spoken foreign policy while he

pursued a conservative domestic policy supported without enthusiasm in the Reichstag by agrarians and Catholic Centrists. These
strategies drew the fire of the imperialist pressure groups and
the condemnation on domestic grounds of the National Liberals and
Progressives. In the Reichstag elections of 1912, the Social
Democrats won every third vote, increasing their support since
1907 by more than a million votes. The National Liberals and
Progressives registered smaller gains while the conservative and
Center parties lost ground. The economic rationale for collaboration among the cartel parties against the left grew less persuasive
as fiscal conflicts continued to strain conservative-bourgeois
political relations. Dissatisfaction with William II and Bethmann
Hollweg was loud on both the right and the left. Further defeats
of the government would have encouraged the increasingly publicized
inclination among National Liberals and Progressives to make
temporary and tactical common cause with the socialists in a
campaign to subordinate the Kaiser and Chancellor to parliamentary
controls.

Such was the domestic scene from which the monarchy's conservative leaders escaped in entering World War I. A successfully
waged war, they thought, would establish German hegemony in Central
and Eastern Europe, break the barriers to German overseas expansion, and salvage the social and political hierarchy Bismarck had
imposed upon Germany. In early 1914, the Duke of Ratibor expressed
himself bluntly on the political situation in Germany to Jules
Cambon, the French envoy in Berlin: "The commercial and bourgeois
classes are gaining the upper hand at the expense of the military
and agrarian classes. A war is therefore in order to restore the
old relationships between them. . . .The wars of '64, '66 and '70
consolidated the military and agrarian parties." A war now, he
concluded, was "necessary to put things back on the old tracks."
During the July crisis, Ernst von Heydebrand und der Lasa, the
leader of the German Conservative party, expected that war would
"strengthen the patriarchal order and temperament" in Germany,
while even Bethmann Hollweg imagined it would "heal domestic
relationships in a conservative sense."[9] The same motives that
inspired Bismarck to forge a Prussian-dominated German Empire
in the fires of war led his successors in 1914 to look to war to
preserve it.

Wilhelminian *Polenpolitik*: Old Wine, New Bottles
    The argument of the preceding pages underlines the element
of continuity in Prussian and Imperial German domestic politics

during the Bismarckian and Wilhelminian eras. In this perspective,
Wilhelminian imperialism does not figure as a radical departure
from Bismarckian practice, but rather as a means Bismarck's successors seized upon to perpetuate the balance of social and political forces upon which he had stabilized the Reich in the 1870s.
It was Bismarck himself who in the 1880s set the Empire on the path
of imperialism, not so much for the sake of colonies as to consolidate conservative and bourgeois support for his regime in opposition to free-trade liberalism, "particularistic" Catholicism,
and internationalist socialism.

     Similarly, Wilhelminian Polenpolitik, particularly in the
period 1894-1914, represents an elaboration in practice of the
implications of Bismarckian policy towards the Prussian Poles and
the frontier provinces generally. It is true that Bismarck approached the domestic Polish question in a traditional spirit.
Suppression of the Polish nationalist movement was his prime concern because of the threat he believed the Polish gentry and
clergy posed to the territorial integrity and security of the
Prussian state. In his view, that threat could be neutralized by
stripping the Poles of all control over the public life of the
frontier regions while stamping these areas and their inhabitants
with the strongest German character possible. In championing the
establishment of the Royal Colonization Commission, Bismarck's
object, as he said himself, was to "expropriate the szlachta"
and so cut through the root of "Polish agitation" in Prussia.

     At the same time, Bismarck admitted the desirability of re-
placing a few thousand Polish estate owners with a multitude of
German peasant colonists. Thus he conceded it to be a legitimate
goal of the Prussian state to convert the frontier regions, by
means of colonization, into areas of ethnic German predominance.
This program of positive Germanization his heatedly nationalist
and anti-Polish allies in the bureaucracy and the National Liberal
Party imposed upon him. Nevertheless, his acquiescence in this
objective marks a fundamental change in the nature of Prussian
Polenpolitik. After 1886, without abandoning the essentially
negative goal of the suppression of "Polonism," the Prussian
government accepted the responsibility for increasing the frontier
German population at the Poles' expense. This could be justified
in terms of traditional raison d'état: German majorities on the
eastern borders would both protect the Empire from any future
territorial claims made by a renascent Polish state and strengthen
the frontier regions' loyalty to the Reich.

     But official championship of Germanization through coloniza-

tion served another function as well. It enabled the Prussian
government to appropriate the slogans of conservative, völkisch
German nationalism, as they were formulated by such influential
publicists as Treitschke and Paul de Lagarde. These posited
ethnic homogeneity as a vital need of the German national state.
They called for expansion outward of the limits of German
settlement as proof of the biological strength and political
greatness of the German nation. These slogans found widespread
acceptance among the educated and properties classes after 1880.
The popular ideology of Wilhelminian imperialism derived in large
measure from them. To the degree that the conservative ruling
establishment in Germany claimed to act upon and realize the
aspirations both of German nationalism and German imperialism, it
found itself impelled to assume the mission of advancing the
German nationality on the eastern ethnic frontier. In launching
the colonization program, Bismarck made this mission official.[10]

His successors during the Wilhelminian epoch pursued this
mission too--with the exception of the man who replaced him.
Caprivi, for reasons that will emerge below, attempted a policy
aimed at conciliating the Polish aristocracy in Prussia. His efforts ended in failure, but not before provoking bitter opposition
in official circles and among conservative and nationalist
political groups. His successors made haste to return to Bismarckian orthodoxy. But in the two decades preceding the outbreak of World War I, Polish political opposition to the Prussian
regime and the Poles' demographic and economic positions in the
east gained steadily in strength. To suppress "Polonism" and
promote Germanization, the Prussian government seized upon increasingly radical means. Its struggle against the Prussian
Poles reached a height of intensity, unmatched even by Bismarck's
campaigns, during the period of Bülow's chancellorship (1900-1909).
By 1914, Prussian Polish policy depended upon means which glar-
ingly contradicted the principles of the German "state of law"
(Rechtsstaat). It represented both a massive attack on the very
existence of the Prussian Poles as a culturally and ethnically
autonomous segment of the Reich's population and a strenuous
effort to push the ethnic German border eastwards. This model
of officially promoted Germanization, posited upon the ideas of
a Polish menace to the German nation and the necessity of the
geographic expansion of the German people eastward, became one
of the most fateful of Imperial Germany's legacies to Hitler's
National Socialist regime.

The Caprivi Era: 1890-94

The threat of war overshadowed Caprivi's chancellorship. The
cornerstone of Prussian foreign policy since the end of the
eighteenth century had been cooperation with Russia. By 1890,
German opposition to Russian designs in the Balkans, Bismarck's
alliance of 1879 with Austria, and Russo-German commercial rivalries had opened a decisive breach between Berlin and Petersburg.
Between 1891 and 1893, Germany's encirclement in World War I was
adumbrated by the emergence of the Franco-Russian military and
diplomatic entente.   In response, William II and Caprivi sought
closer ties to England, strengthened Germany's position in
central and southeastern Europe through Caprivi's trade treaties,
and prepared for military challenges by approving the Schlieffen
plan and pushing the army expansion bill of 1893 through the
Reichstag.[11]

Caprivi had no prior interest or experience in the problems
of Prussian Polenpolitik, but he recognized that, if war should
break out between Germany and Russia, the international Polish
question would inevitably reopen. The Kaiser, far from being
alarmed by the diplomatic turbulence of these years, foresaw a new
era of Prussian triumphs in the east. In a conversation of 1892
with his intimate adviser, Philipp zu Eulenburg, he exulted in
rumors of pro-German opinion among the Polish aristocracy in
Russian Poland:

> They are completely filled with the hope of being
> liberated from the Russian yoke, and in the event
> of a war with Russia the whole of Poland would
> revolt and come over to my side with the express
> intention of being annexed by me.

To Eulenburg's suggestion that the Poles would collaborate with
Prussia only in order to pave the way to the restoration of a
"Polish Empire," the Kaiser replied self-confidently:

> No. They have given that up. The educated elements
> are aware of their own weakness. They want to come
> under Prussia. . . .In case of need we would make
> Poland into an Imperial Territory (Reichsland).
> Alsace and Lorraine have proved the value of such
> an arrangement.[12]

Such were the sanguine expectations that allowed William II
to describe himself to Eulenburg as "pro-Polish" (polenfreundlich)
in 1892. Caprivi, responsible for the details of domestic policy,
realized that something more than grandiose words would be required to make possible Polish-German collaboration at Russia's
expense. The harshness of Bismarckian policies towards the Prussian Poles constituted an almost insuperable obstacle to such collaboration, even granting that Tsarist repression of the Poles

in Russia had fully estranged Polish sympathies from Petersburg.
Caprivi was aware that the aristocratic leaders of the Poznanian
Poles, driven to desperation by Bismarck's attacks upon them,
were interested in better relations with Berlin.[13] In his turn,
Caprivi stood in need of Reichstag votes, but could not reckon
on the support of the Polish delegation without making concessions
to them. Above all, diplomatic considerations inclined Caprivi
to abandon Bismarck's policy of forcing the Poles into doctrinaire
opposition to Berlin. He justified his position in a memorandum
of 18 November 1893 addressed to the Prussian cabinet:

> We must seek to avoid [in case of war with Russia]
> having the opinion of the Prussian Poles favorable
> to the Russian side. . . .The present attitude of
> our Polish aristocracy is conditioned by the fact that
> they may no longer count on French opposition to
> the Tsardom. They must for the moment place their
> hopes in us. . . .Our concession of a few hours a
> week of Polish instruction in the schools is a price
> worth paying to hold them on our side. . . .In my
> opinion, the Prussian Poles are becoming divided among
> themselves. . . .The Polish middle class has gone into
> opposition against the Polish aristocrats. It lies
> in the government's interest to intensify this divi-
> sion. The support of the aristocratic part of the Polish
> population may be turned to good account in our foreign
> policy as well as in our domestic policies of strengthen-
> ing and preserving the state. The aristocratic camp
> within Polish society is led by Archbishop Stablewski
> and the majority of the Polish Reichstag delegation.
> But Stablewski can only maintain his (certainly not
> selfless) program of support of the government if
> he can demonstrate to his countryment some kind
> of tangible success.[14]

During the Caprivi era, the Prussian government did in fact
make a number of concessions to the Prussian Poles which were
both intended and understood to signify a retreat from Bismarck's
policy of uncompromising hostility. Upon the death of Archbishop
Dinder in 1890, the government began to press the Vatican for
appointment of another German to the see of Poznań-Gniezno. But
in 1891 it bowed to the wishes of the local hierarchy and Rome in
approving the consecration of the politically prominent and
popular Father Florian Stablewski. The new archbishop thereupon
publicly paid homage to the state and harshly denounced Russia
and Russian policy towards the Poles.[15] Between 1891 and 1894,
teaching of religion in Polish was restored in the Poznanian
elementary schools. So too was limited instruction in the Polish
language itself.[16] The government conceded to the system of
Polish cooperative banks self-auditing rights, withholding of
which might have dealt with Poles a heavy economic blow. In 1890,
the government reopened the eastern frontier to seasonal immigration of Polish rural laborers from Russian and Austrian Poland.

This was more a concession to the East Elbian Junkers and Upper
Silesian industrialists than to the Polish gentry, who nevertheless benefited greatly from it. Caprivi's regime allowed the Poles
to participate in the estate parcellation and peasant colonization
programs established under the Prussian Rentengüter legislation of
1890-91. This produced the ironical spectacle of state-aided
Polish land settlement occurring simultaneously with the Colonization Commission's efforts to uproot the Polish gentry and settle
German peasants in their stead. Finally, in 1891 the government
appointed as provincial president Baron Hugo von Wilamowitz-
Möllendorf, a conservative Poznanian landlord with a reputation
for fairmindedness towards the Poles.[17]

The Poles, in their turn, backed Caprivi's legislation in the
Reichstag. Despite their agrarian interests, they voted for
Caprivi's trade treaties, the objects of the Junkers' bitterest
political opposition. It was thanks to Polish votes that Caprivi's
hotly contested army bill of 1893 finally gained a majority, in
recognition of which William II conferred a royal decoration upon
the Poles' delegation leader, Józef Kościelski.[18]

Caprivi's fall from office in 1894 was only peripherally
related to his conciliatory Polish policy. With the ratification
in that year of Caprivi's Russo-German trade agreement the threat
of war in the east receded, eliminating the principal ground for
his policy of rapprochement with the Poles.[19] In any case, the
government's concessions had proven inadequate from the Poles'
point of view. The populist movement in Poznania had begun to
attack the Polish conservatives for their loyalty to a regime
which upheld the Germanization and colonization laws of the 1870s
and 1880s. Even before Caprivi's dismissal, the Polish conservatives had admitted defeat and returned to parliamentary opposition
to the government, whereupon William II delivered a speech in
Thorn calling the Prussian Poles' loyalty into question.[20]

There is no evidence suggesting that after 1894 Caprivi
wished to extend further concessions to the Poles. He seems to
have contemplated their ultimate political designs with suspicion
and to have sought their cooperation with a minimum of relaxation
in the oppressive system of offical Polenpolitik. In any case,
Bismarck's colonization program, the capstone of that system, was
enshrined in law. Throughout Caprivi's tenure in office, the
Prussian Landtag was secure in the control of the conservative
and National Liberal parties, unwavering in their hostility to
the Poles. Restoration to the Poles of the official use of their
language and abolition of the Colonization Commission could only

come about through legislative action. But as long as the
Prussian three-class electoral system prevailed, the artificially
overrepresented cartel parties could veto any such efforts. The
Prussian bureaucracy remained a stronghold of Bismarckian sentiment in Polish matters. Caprivi was able to secure the reintro-
duction of Polish classes at the elementary school level only
because some high officials feared that the conservative effect
of religious instruction would be lost on Polish children if they
were required to study it in a language they did not understand.
The general principle of employment of German as the sole language
of instruction in public education stood unassailed and unassail-
able.[21]

      The views of Oberpräsident Möllendorf, who came under public
attack by nationalist groups after 1894 for his alleged pro-
Polonism, illuminate the mentality of the upper bureaucracy during the Caprivi era. In a memorial of November 1895 addressed to
the Prussian minister of interior, Möllendorf conceded that the
Poles sought to form a "state within the state," in contradiction
to the centralizing principles of the Prussian government. But he
maintained that "ruthless struggle with and forcible suppression
of everything Polish will not make Germans of the Poles." It was
necessary to make the Poles aware of the benefits they derived
from "a just and benevolent administration." But when Möllendorf
came to specify his priorities in domestic Polenpolitik, linguistic
Germanization came at the head of the list. Not content with
making German the sole language of instruction in the schools,
he recommended a prohibition of the use of Polish in all public
meetings and assemblies. "If this stipulation were realized, the
exclusivity of Polish organizational life would be dealt a most
decisive blow." In Möllendorf's view, the institutions of Organic
Work, which constituted "the basis of the Poles' national
solidarity and separation from the rest of society," could not
function if deprived of the public use of the Polish language.
They would atrophy as the Poles accustomed themselves to participation in mixed Polish-German organizations conducting their affairs in German. Likewise, Möllendorf staunchly supported the
Colonization Commission's strategies of fragmenting the area of
solid Polish landholdings by the creation of German peasant en-
claves and strengthening the German urban population by systematically encircling the towns in Polish agricultural districts with
villages of German colonists. He favored the establishment of
social contacts between the bureaucracy and the Polish landowners and intelligentsia in the Province of Poznań. But he in-

sisted on the German character of the Poznanian administration, recommending that Poles be admitted to high official positions only in the thoroughly German regions of the Reich where they would more quickly acquire a Prussian character and mentality.

Möllendorf imagined himself to be speaking from a position of "official objectivity" (obrigkeitliche Objektivität). In 1899, he was replaced by a man expected to follow a harder line towards the Poles. Yet it is clear that he himself was a captive of the traditional Prussian view that, as long as the Poles maintained their separate cultural and political mentality, they could not be reliable Prussian and German citizens. Möllendorf not only affirmed Bismarck's strategies, but spoke up for their radicalization, blind to the fact that the Prussian government's system of repressive laws only intensified the Polish "exclusivity" he deplored.[22]

William II abandoned Caprivi at the end of 1894 to make peace with the chancellor's agrarian enemies. Although the Prussian conservatives concentrated their political fire on Caprivi's tariff policies, they attacked him as well for his concessions, marginal though they were, to the Prussian Poles. At the same time, Caprivi's Polish policy came under assault from a different quarter. Already in 1890 the German government's exchange with England of territorial claims in East Africa for the North Sea island of Heligoland had provoked bitter opposition in bourgeois nationalist and imperialist circles. Out of that opposition arose the Pan-German League (Alldeutscher Verband). By 1894 it had become a highly vocal and visible propaganda organization urging upon the government, while popularizing among the educated and propertied classes, its policies of expansionist völkisch nationalism and imperialist conquest.[23] The Pan-German League took a keen interest in the Polish problem in Prussia which, from its point of view, constituted the Imperial German analogue to the struggles of the Hapsburg Germans against the Czechs, Slovenes, and Italians. In 1894 the League's founder and one of its guiding spirits, Alfred Hugenberg, arrived in Poznań as a young official attached to the Colonization Commission. He organized a local branch of the League and soon established himself as its expert on the domestic Polish question and as an influential voice in the formulation of official Germanization policy as well. In April 1894, Alldeutsche Blätter, the League's journal, opened a public campaign against Caprivi's Polish policies and demanded official adoption of a set of proposals aimed at speeding up the Germanization of the Polish provinces.[24]

Simultaneously, agrarian opposition to Caprivi flared among
the Poznanian Junkers. In 1893, disgruntled members of the
German Conservative Party founded the Bund der Landwirte (Farmer's
League) in Berlin. It soon enlisted the support not only of
the East Elbian large landowners but of the landed peasantry
both in the Prussian east and in large parts of south and west
Germany as well. Under Junker control and closely tied to the
German Conservative Party, the League became one of the most powerful pressure groups in Imperial Germany. It provided the conservatives with a well-organized mass base even as it radicalized
traditional Prussian conservative ideology and political practice.
Until the protectionist Bülow tariff of 1902 went into effect,
the League's chief aim was to agitate for higher farm duties, but
it trimmed this propaganda in a gaudy veil of antisocialism,
strident nationalism, antiparliamentarism, and anti-Semitism. In
the province of Poznań, local organizations of the League quickly
emerged and gained an influential following.[25]

While some Poznanian conservatives channeled their opposition
to Caprivi through the German Conservative Party and the Bund der
Landwirte, others grew persuaded that a distinctive assault should
be launched on the chancellor's Polish policies. In September
1894 three of the province's Junkers led almost two thousand
German Poseners and West Prussians to Bismarck's residence at
Varzin where they listened to the ex-chancellor denounce Caprivi
and the Poles. Heartened by their success, the leaders of this
pilgrimage founded in November 1894 in Poznań the Verein zur
Förderung des Deutschthums in den Ostmarken (Society for the
Support of the Germans in the Eastern Marches). Known from 1899
as the Ostmarkenverein (Eastern Marches Society), this organization quickly rose to prominence both in the Prussian east and
throughout the Reich for its tireless and strident attacks upon
the Prussian Poles and its unrelenting pressure on the Prussian
government to escalate its policies of Germanization. Its
organizers were Ferdinand von Hansemann, son of the founder of
the Disconto-Gesellschaft, one of Germany's great commercial
banks; Hermann Kennemann, a Junker of common origins, owner of
vast landholdings in the eastern provinces and an anti-Polish
agitator since the 1860s; and Heinrich von Tiedemann, a retired
Prussian major and gentleman farmer. From the initials of their
names arose the polemical Polish term hakata to refer to the
society they founded and hakatyści to refer to its members; the
latter term found a German equivalent in Hakatisten.[26]

At first the Eastern Marches Society attracted the support

of many Poznanian estate owners, including some of the leaders of
the Conservative party and the Bund der Landwirte. But the new
society's enthusiasm for peasant colonization and its opposition to
seasonal immigration of Polish farm workers from Russia and Austria
irritated the Junkers and caused them to withdraw to their own
aristocratic and agrarian strongholds. Personal rivalries also
played a part. The Poznanian Bund der Landwirte became the preserve of the flinty retired army major and local estate owner
Ernst Endell, who single-mindedly refused to subordinate his followers' economic interests or political privileges to the demands
the Hakatists voiced in the name of the German nation. The
Ostmarkenverein, in its turn, fell under the imperious control of
Tiedemann, jealous not only of Endell but of the Pan-German League,
whose followers he accused of "confusion and impotence" and whose
local representative, Hugenberg, he called "a raving idealist."[27]

By the end of the year 1900, the Hakatists had recruited approximately 20,000 members, about half of them in the provinces of
Poznań and West Prussia. State officials, schoolteachers, and
Protestant pastors formed the majority of the society's followers.
Protestant German farmers and estate owners, businessmen, artisans,
and workers were only sparsely represented in its ranks, Jews and
German Catholics virtually not at all.[28] It proclaimed itself an
organization devoted to the practical strengthening of German
society in the east by such means as the creation of scholarship
programs, public health institutions, and labor exchanges for
businessmen. But, in fact, the Ostmarkenverein functioned
primarily as a propaganda agency, effectively disseminating its
program through its journal, Die Ostmark, upon which the great
German nationalist daily press came to lean heavily in its
coverage of the domestic Polish question. The society acquired
a curious but vital role in relation to the Prussian government
and its administrative agencies. On the one hand, it acted as a
pressure group, recruiting support for its views in the Berlin
ministries, in provincial bureaucratic offices, and in the
Reichstag and Landtag. By private lobbying and public agitation
it tried to influence both the political parties and the Prussian
government to support its views on the Polish question. On the
other hand, the Ostmarkenverein's influence and organizational
vitality gained a great deal from official support. Without the
Prussian government's endorsement of the society's aims and
activities, membership recruitment among officials and schoolteachers undoubtedly would have been far less successful than in
fact it was. These were the groups which supplied most of the

Eastern Marches Society's local activists. So, while the Hakatists
owed much of their political weight to the Prussian government's
patronage, they also exerted considerable influence on the formulation of official Polish policies, directly through pressure on
the ministries and parliaments and indirectly through the populari-
zation of their views among the readers of the conservative and
nationalist political press.[29]

The Years of Hohenlohe's Chancellorship, 1894-1900

Under Chancellor Hohenlohe's somnolent eye, Eulenberg,
Miquel, Bülow, Tirpitz, and their allies in the ministries and
among the political parties restored the cartel system and set
the stage for Germany's imperialist ventures. Caprivi's successors
were well aware of the unpopularity in conservative and nationalist circles of his Polish policies. They heard the clamor of the
Hakatists and the agrarian and Pan-German press for a return to
Bismarckian methods, methods which in any case they as graduates
of the Bismarckian school of politics approved. Resumption of an
aggressive Polenpolitik was a logical corollary of a domestic
policy based on the cartel parties and a foreign policy aimed at
arousing mass support for the Wilhelminian monarchy. At a Prussian
cabinet meeting of 1897, Miquel spelled out his strategy:

> Political divisions [among the conservative and bourgeois
> parties] must be relegated to the background and the
> basis for agreement sought in the economic field. At
> the next elections, national questions could also be
> raised. We must strengthen national sentiment by treat-
> ing the Poles harshly, and this even against the Center
> Party.[30]

Between 1895 and 1900, the Prussian government steadily
sharpened its anti-Polish policies. This was not capitulation to
the demands of nationalist pressure groups. On the contrary,
the Prussian minister of interior, Wolfgang von Köller, chose, in a
Landtag debate of 1895, to endorse publicly the Ostmarkenverein's
"defensive" resistance to the "Polish threat" in the east. In
this way, the government deliberately accepted the nascent Eastern
Marches Society as an ally and, by pronouncing its purposes
good and opening it to the membership of public officials, strengthened it.[31]

In these years, the government renewed its pressure on the
Poles in two familiar ways. First, it sought to weaken the
national cohesion and strength of Polish society directly by the
resumption of expulsions of nonnaturalized Poles from the eastern
provinces, rejection of Polish applicants to the Rentengüter
parcellation and peasant settlement programs, suppression of

private tutoring in Polish, administrative harassment of the
Polish cooperative system, and similar petty but, from the Poles'
point of view, galling measures.[32]   Second, in 1898 the Landtag
voted to supply the Royal Colonization Commission with another one
hundred million marks.   While this represented a deepening commitment by the government and the cartel parties to Bismarck's goal
of expropriating the Polish gentry, it was also a tacit admission
that achieving the goal was proving more difficult than had been
expected.   Although the Commission had been able to buy considerable amounts of Polish estate land in the first few years after
its establishment, by the early 1890s the Poles had developed a
system of private land parcellation societies to which financially
hard-pressed large landowners could turn instead of to the government's well-hated colonization agency.   The Polish press had begun
to brand sellers of land to the Commission as national traitors.
Since the Polish parcellation banks could count on selling, at
relatively high prices, farm-sized plots or smaller holdings to
the land-hungry Polish peasants, they could afford to outbid the
Commission.   The Polish landlords, assured of high prices for their
estate land by selling to their countrymen, thus found a means
of reconciling profits and patriotism and turned their backs on the
Commission.   In its search for colonization land, the Commission
was forced to look to the German Junkers, many of whom, like their
Polish counterparts, wished to cleanse themselves of debt by
parcelling off a portion of their holdings so as to put the remainder on a sound financial footing.   The competition that
developed after 1890 between the Commission and the Polish land
banks had the effect of driving land prices up steeply.   While in
1886 the Commission paid an average of 568 marks per hectare, by
1901 it was paying 801 marks, considerably more than the price of
estate land elsewhere in East Elbia.[33]   This tempted the local
German estate owners, many of whom--unlike the Polish gentry--
felt no political or national attachments to the frontier lands,
to sell out and move to a new property in one of the solidly
German eastern provinces.[34]   Ironically, by the end of the 1890s
the Colonization Commission was dismembering more German than
Polish estates.   While it continued to pursue its program of
peasant settlement, the Commission had also become an official
relief agency for the Junkers in the Polish provinces.[35]

     In the business of peasant colonization itself, the Commis-
sion had run into unexpected problems.   The supply of experienced
peasant farmers with the capital necessary to launch a new existence in the east proved before the end of the 1890s to be limited.

Many German colonists, once settled, looked continuously to
the Commission and the state for financial support. Finally, the
cost of settling each peasant family turned out to be much higher
than originally expected, while the relatively easy financial
terms upon which the colonists assumed their farms meant that the
Commission's return on its investments was very low. Hence the
necessity of replenishing its funds in 1898, at which time the
twenty-year term on its activities established in 1886 was prolonged indefinitely. But, however unexpectedly the colonization
program had changed its character, and whatever the difficulties
the Commission confronted, neither the government nor the cartel
parties wavered in support of what they claimed was the Prussian
state's best means of countering, in the words of the 1886 Colonization Bill, "efforts to Polonize" the eastern provinces.[36]

The vitality of the Polish nationalist movement after 1890
reflected demographic and socioeconomic trends in the Prussian
east which, in their political effects, favored the Poles over
the Germans.[37] The Prussian government found that suppression of
the Polish nationalist movement and reduction of the Polish
masses to a state of passive Prussian loyalty were becoming madden-
inly elusive goals. Without abandoning them, Caprivi's successors
inaugurated what seemed to them a defensive strategy of material
and political support of the frontier Germans. This shift in
emphasis, indirectly evident in the services the Colonization
Commission rendered the Junkers and in the government's endorsement of the Eastern Marches Society, became explicit in the budget
of 1898. The government obtained from the compliant Landtag approval of the creation of a special "disposition fund" of 400,000
marks annually, to be expended at the discretion of the provincial
presidents in Poznań and West Prussia in support of the economic
and cultural interests of the local German population. This was
the beginning of an expensive program of state subsidization of
German educational, religious, and cultural organizations in the
east. A few years later came an ambitious building program to
modernize the frontier cities and adorn them with theaters and
operas, libraries, and new centers of secondary and technical
education. These policies favored Prussian officialdom and the
German bourgeoisie in the Polish regions. They had the public
endorsement of the National Liberal Party and its representative
in the Prussian government, Johannes Miquel. It was above all
Miquel who secured official sanction after 1894 for programs of
direct and positive aid to the frontier Germans. Indeed, in a
ministerial conference of 1897 he announced grandiosely, "It

is time once again to take up in full measure the mission of the
Prussian state: the strengthening of the German nationality and its
expansion eastwards."[38]

Miquel's program of direct state support for the frontier
Germans had been widely discussed in ministerial and crown councils after 1896. Some conservative opposition arose among officials who preferred to concentrate the state's efforts on control
of the Polish population by police agencies and repressive laws
while supporting the German cause in the east primarily by strengthening the economic and political power of the Junkers. But the
Kaiser was a convinced believer in Pan-German and völkisch ideas
of the Germanic racial mission to struggle with and overcome the
Slavs in Central Europe. He was disillusioned if not embarassed
by his overtures to the Polish nobility during Caprivi's chancellorship. Hence he swung his weight in Miquel's favor. The fiscal
appropriations of 1898 were evidence of the government's decision
to pledge itself publicly to the economic and political advancement of the frontier Germans. So too was an administrative order
of the Ministry of Interior of the same year calling on middle-
ranking and high officials in Poznania and West Prussia to participate actively in private associations devoted to German interests
on the frontier.[39]

So began the Prussian government's fusion of traditional
Polenpolitik with the ideology and aims of Wilhelminian Weltpolitik.
For almost a century following the partitions of the 1790s, the
government in Berlin had concentrated first on the neutralization
and then on the suppression of the Polish nationalist movement.
The colonization program, although it was meant to serve this
traditional end, soon acquired the dual function of repairing
German demographic losses in the east caused by peasant and working-class emigration and ensuring the survival of the frontier
Junkers by refinancing them in the process of peasant settlement.[40]
By accepting in 1886 a program of German peasant colonization at
the Polish landlords' expense, Bismarck conceded to the German
nationalists the Prussian state's interest in increasing the
German population in the east as an issue separate from the
threat of Polish revolution and irredentism. According to the
ideology of bourgeois nationalism as it was formulated by such
publicists as Treitschke and enshrined in the programs of the
National Liberals, the frontiers of the Empire ought to encompass
a wholly German population. It was an index of the vitality of
the German Volk, and also of the state representing it, whether
the German population increased and expanded territorially or

whether it shrank before the rising demographic tides of its
neighbors.

These ideas, and the social Darwinist concepts which underlay them, were the common coin of the Pan-German League and
Wilhelminian imperialism after 1890.[41] It followed from them
that conversion of the Polish regions of Prussia into ethnically
German strongholds became a nationalist goal regardless of the
attitude of the Poles towards the Prussian state. Their assimilation into a Germanic wave swelling eastward was inevitable if
Germany was to realize its historic potentiality and prove itself
a nation of the future.

In the course of the 1890s, Prussian Polish policy began to
pursue these ideological ends. The Prussian state, which had
shouldered the interests of the German nation, now assumed
responsibility for the German population living on the ethnic
frontier. What before had been the prosaic fortunes of a peripheral population of German peasants, burghers, and Junkers now
acquired a new and portentous significance. Their future both
symbolized and literally stood for the future of the Germanic
people. They were Imperial Germany's bulwark against what
William II in 1895 called "the Slavic-Czech invasion which
threatens us all in the highest degree."[42] At the beginning of the
twentieth century the Prussian government had sworn itself to guide
them to victory over the Poles in the struggle for domination of
the "eastern marches." Success would represent a first pledge for
the fulfillment of Prussia's "mission" to promote once again, as
nineteenth-century nationalists supposed it had in the days of the
Teutonic Order, the expansion of the German nationality into the
east.

Bülow's *Polenpolitik* 1900-1909

Bernhard von Bülow, opportunistic though he was, believed
profoundly in the importance of Prussia's eastern mission. He
was a forceful exponent of Treitschkean nationalism and symbolized
in his own person Wilhelminian imperialist claims and aspirations.[43] Trained as a diplomat under Bismarck, he posed ever
afterwards as an executor of the Iron Chancellor's political will.
Yet on occasion Bismarck had found Bülow's political ideas, if not
repugnant, at least reckless. Writing to Holstein in 1887 on
German policy in the event of war with Russia, Bülow suggested the
possibility of a Polish restoration under Hohenzollern auspices
in the Congress Kingdom region, but added that the outbreak of war
ought to be taken advantage of "to expel en masse the Poles from

our Polish territories." Bismarck's marginal comment on this idea
was that "one should not commit such eccentric thoughts to paper."[44]

When after 1900 Bülow assumed responsibility for Prussian
Polish policy he spoke out frankly for "the Germanization of our
eastern marches." Only thus might Prussia "remain what it is and
always must be: a [German] national state."[45] Unlike Bismarck,
Bülow did not believe that it was only the anachronistic and self-
serving strivings of the nobility and clergy that prevented the
mass of the Prussian Poles from affirming their Prussian-German
loyalty. "Great-Polish agitation" had, in Bülow's view, slipped
into the hands of a middle-class movement whose tireless and uncompromisingly anti-German propaganda had made disloyalty endemic
among all classes in Prussian Poland.[46] The Poles could not
abandon the goal, dictated to them by their own history, of
national independence. By their political agitation and social
and organizational "exclusivity" they "forced" the frontier
Germans to abandon their homes and move west.[47] The differential
between Polish and German birthrates in the east compounded the
problem. By reproducing, as Bülow said to the press in 1902, "like
rabbits," the Poles threatened the eastern provinces with a "Slavic
flood."[48] Bülow admitted privately that the frontier Germans could
not by themselves counter the Polish pressures on them.[49] "The
same process is taking place in our eastern provinces," he reported ominously to the Prussian cabinet on 13 June 1900, "that
occurred in Austria, where predominantly German lands underwent
Slavicization."[50] It was therefore the Prussian government's
task to create a numerical majority of Germans in Poznania and to
extend German landholdings at the Poles' expense. Only so could
the Poles be brought to understand that, whether or not a Polish
state reemerged on Russian or Austrian soil, Prussian Poland had
become part of Germany and was forever lost to them.[51]

Urgency was lent to Bülow's Polenpolitik by demographic and
economic shifts in the eastern provinces favorable to the Poles.
"The danger is all the greater," Bülow declared in the cabinet
meeting of June 1900, "since we cannot count on pursuing a common
policy with Russia against the Poles."[52] In the event of war,
Russia could be expected to raise, however insincerely, the prospect of Polish independence to rally the Poles' loyalty. Following
Bismarck's logic, Bülow concluded that this threat required the
earliest possible Germanization of Poznania and Polish West
Prussia to ensure their retention by Prussia whatever such a war's
outcome might be. A hard Prussian line against its own Polish subjects would also assure Petersburg that it need not fear Prussia's
manipulation of the Polish question to Russian disadvantage.[53]

In his memoirs, Bülow claimed that he had never advocated "repression" of the Poles in the spheres of education and religion. In fact, his memorial to the Prussian cabinet of 3 July 1901 recommended not only prohibition of the use of the Polish language in public assemblies but also complete elimination of Polish from elementary education.[54] It was in pursuit of the latter goal that Bülow's government first clashed with the Prussian Poles. Beginning in 1900, Konrad Studt, the Prussian minister of religion and education, ordered the replacement of Polish by German in the teaching of religion in the middle and upper forms of Poznanian elementary schools. This order automatically abolished Polish-language instruction at all levels, since it had been tolerated after 1898 only in those schools where religion continued to be taught in Polish.[55]

Before the Prussian school authorities could apply this policy to all Poznanian schools, Polish resistance broke out, above all in the town of Września (Wreschen). With the encouragement of their parents, Polish children staged a "school strike," refusing to recite or otherwise participate in German-language religion classes. Teachers' canings of striking students led to public tumults and stiffened Polish opposition. As the strikes spread to other localities, the government staged a trial against the participants in the Września disorders, gaining convictions and harsh sentences. This affair outraged Polish society in Prussia and abroad. But the Prussian authorities did not retreat and finally broke the strikes, above all by refusing year-end promotions to striking children.[56]

Conversion of religion classes from Polish to German occurred at a slower pace after 1903. But the example of the massive and successful Polish school strikes in Russian Poland during the revolution of 1905 recharged the Poznanian atmosphere. Language conversions ordered for the 1906-7 school year met with spontaneous strikes, beginning in June 1906, which were quickly organized and propagated throughout the Polish regions of the province by Polish nationalist organizations, the Polish press, the Catholic clergy, and local activists and notables. This strike wave crested in November 1906, when approximately 70,000 Polish children in 950 elementary schools were refusing to participate in German-language religion classes.[57] Although in the course of 1907 the Prussian authorities succeeded in breaking the strike, Studt's subsequent resignation and the abandonment of further language conversion orders until the eve of the war indicated that the government looked upon its most recent suc-

cesses in Germanizing education as costly. The strikes of 1901-7
proved that nationalist militance and discontent with Prussian rule
was deeply felt among the Polish common people. Despite his loyalist inclinations, Archbishop Stablewski had found himself compelled
to condemn Prussian school policy publicly. Although he did not
unequivocally endorse the strikes, his protests showed that the
Catholic church refused to be discredited in Polish eyes by standing passively aside in the nationality conflict. Stablewski's
advocacy of Polish-language religious instruction lent moral support to Polish nationalism which undercut whatever advantages the
government hoped to derive from its school language policies.[58]

Bülow's regime stood firm in its claim that Germanization of
religion classes was both legal and desirable. Bülow himself,
when he deigned to comment upon them, denounced the strikes as the
manipulation by implacable Polish nationalists of innocent children intended to stir up in them, and among the Poles generally, a
"spirit of rebellion."[59] Bülow was stung by Stablewski's breach
with the government. When soon afterward the Archbishop died, the
chancellor refused to confirm the appointment of the man the
archdiocese recommended as his successor, Bishop Edward Likowski.
Until 1914, the government recognized Likowski only as admini-
strator of the Poznań-Gniezno archbishopric, despite Likowski's
explicit condemnation of the strikes and his conservative loyalism. In his policies towards the Church, as in those towards
education, Bülow gave the Poles, sensitive as they were about their
Polish-Catholic identity and the Polish character of the Poznanian
archbishopric, reason for bitter resentment.[60]

Privately, some members of Bülow's administration condemned
Prussian school policy and the government's harsh suppression of
the strike. In a letter of March 1907 to Studt, Reich Secretary
of the Interior Arthur von Posadowsky-Wehner described the Prussian government's position on the strikes as "ethically weak."
He added that "it is an illusion to assume that one can Germanize
Polish children by forcing German-language instruction on them."[61]
But Posadowsky's counterpart in the Prussian cabinet, Theobald
von Bethmann Hollweg, opposed all concessions to the striking
children and their parents. Conciliatory gestures would only
strengthen Polish "radicalism."[62]

At that moment, Bethmann was looking beyond the school strikes
towards the promulgation of two laws whose impact on Polish
nationalist opposition both he and Bülow expected to be devastat-
ing. One of these laws was the Expropriation Act, approved by
the Prussian parliament on 3 March 1908. It was meant to extri-

cate the Colonization Commission from an embarrassing crisis
which threatened to bring its work to a standstill. After
twenty years of colonization activities, the Royal Commission
could boast of substantial accomplishments. Almost 14,000 German
colonists and their families had been settled on self-sufficient
farms ranging from 10 to 20 hectares.[63] Altogether the Commission had purchased more than 325,000 hectares in the predominantly Polish regions of Poznania and West Prussia.[64] Colonization
officials were proud to point out that settlement of these lands
had displaced over 40,000 Poles who had inhabited them previously.
The Commission claimed that the German population of towns in
the colonization regions grew and prospered while in noncolonized
districts it was retreating before the "Slavic flood."[65]

   Although its prime goal was peasant colonization, since 1898
the Commission had purchased numerous private estates unsuitable
for immediate colonization and leased them as state domains to
German managers. Its "residual estate" (Restgut) program put
financially ailing Junkers on a sounder, if more modest, economic
footing and made some new estates carved out of Polish landholdings available to German purchasers. A system of Raiffeisen
cooperative societies, founded and directed from Poznań by Alfred
Hugenberg in the years 1900-1903, extended credit to colonists
and other German farmers. Hugenberg's cooperatives worked closely
with the Colonization Commission, his own employer from 1894 to
1900. In 1904 he could take credit for the establishment in
Poznań of the Mittelstandskasse, a bank whose purpose was to refinance the debts of German farmers and so protect them against
the blandishments of Polish parcellation societies. The Colonization Commission welcomed its formation. In 1908 the Prussian
government granted it credits of 125 million marks,strengthening
it greatly as an ally of the Royal Commission.[66]

   The lands purchased and settled by the Colonization Commission
and those refinanced by the Mittelstandskasse were thought to
have been secured in lasting German possession since, in the event
of their sale, both the Commission and the bank had the right of
first purchase. This condition was permanently attached to
colonization and refinancing contracts to prevent subsequent
sales to Poles. German eastward expansion in the twentieth
century was to be an irreversible wave.[67]

   By 1907 the Prussian government and the Royal Commission
claimed that the 388 million marks invested in the colonization
program since 1886 had been well spent.[68] The rate at which the
"Slavic flood" was advancing westwards had diminished, particularly

since 1898. Bülow was proud to announce that the Royal Commission had by 1908 settled as many colonists in the east as had Frederick the Great in the course of his long reign.[69]

Yet the infuriating fact remained: between 1882 and 1907, Polish landholdings in Poznania and West Prussia expanded, at German expense and despite official colonization, by 52,000 hectares.[70] In the decade since 1896, the figure was higher still (75,000 hectares). Bülow had to admit that "the Poles are waging the struggle for the land with extraordinary energy."[71] The Royal Commission's fundamental problem was that, with increasingly few exceptions, it could no longer buy Polish land. Polish estate owners, when driven to sell their land in whole or in part, turned to Polish banks or parcellation societies. Since 1900, a bank specializing in refinancing the Polish gentry's debts at lower interest rates had helped forestall the crises which in the 1880s and 1890s had driven desperate landlords to the hated Commission. The prosperous condition of East Elbian agriculture after the late 1890s reinforced the Poles' desire to maintain possession of their estates. Nor could the Commission acquire much land from Polish peasant farmers. Although sometimes tempted to sell by soaring land prices, like the gentry they could turn to parcellation or refinancing banks which guaranteed the retention of their land in Polish hands.[72]

Thus after 1898 the Colonization Commission had no choice but to turn to German estate owners for its land. The competition of Polish parcellation banks and the rising profitability of eastern agriculture drove the prices the Commission had to offer higher and higher. In 1901, it paid on an average 801 marks per hectare; in 1907 the price was 1,508 marks.[73] The price of estate land in the colonization districts was so high that the temptation to sell out and buy a new estate elsewhere in the Prussian east was almost irresistible to many of the precariously rooted Poznanian Junkers. Not only had the colonization program become enormously expensive; it began to dawn on the government that, if the program continued unchanged, it would produce a paradoxical result wholly at odds with the sociopolitical constitution of the Prussian state: as Bethmann Hollweg put it in a cabinet report of 1907, "the decimation of German large landholdings because of the impossibility of purchasing land from the Poles."[74] But it was precisely upon a class of loyal Junkers that the Prussian state had attempted since the partitions to build its domination of Prussian Poland.

The Poles' successes in combatting the colonization program enormously aggravated the Prussian government, the Royal Commis-

sion, the Eastern Marches Society, and the Pan-German League. At
first it appeared that Polish parcellation was the chief obstacle
confronting the Commission. It was, after all, the high prices
land-hungry Polish peasants were willing to pay for small plots
which drove up the cost of estate land in the colonization area.
As early as 1901 Miquel advocated a law against Polish parcellation with the argument that, since it prevented the realization
of the aims of the 1886 colonization law, it ought to be illegal.
The Eastern Marches Society and Pan-German League and their
partisans in the government and Colonization Commission took
up his idea and agitated publicly and privately for it. The
government hesitated to set the precedent of state interference
on political grounds in the sale or transfer of private property.
In 1904 it obtained instead a law from the Landtag authorizing
county officials to refuse building permits in cases where their
issuance would hinder the colonization program. The law of 1904
prevented Poles from constructing houses and farm buildings on
plots of land obtained through parcellation. But this measure
did not bring Polish parcellation to a halt. Purchasers of land
parcels could, however inconveniently, inhabit preexisting buildings obtained with the plots, while nothing prevented parcelled
land from being incorporated into the holding of adjacent Polish
farmers. If in some cases the 1904 law discouraged estate parcellation, the result was to turn Polish land banks towards purchase
and sale to Polish buyers of whole German farms, raising the
specter of the liquidation through sale at high prices of entire
German villages in the east.[75]

The law of 1904 was aimed at forcing Polish estate owners
to offer their holdings to the Colonization Commission by
eliminating the alternative of turning to a Polish parcellation
bank. In practice, this tactic failed to work. Moreover, because
of the rationalization and heightened profitability of Polish
estate agriculture and the creation of Polish debt-refinancing
institutions, the number of Polish estates offered for parcellation was diminishing. Since the late 1890s it had been primarily
German estates that Polish parcellation banks had sought to purchase and subdivide. To block their activities did not therefore
ensure the Colonization Commission an ample supply of Polish estate
land.

This was the setting in which the idea of expropriating Polish
estate land by state fiat for the purpose of German colonization
emerged. In all likelihood, it was Hugenberg and his radically
minded associates in the Royal Commission who first hit upon the

idea of expropriation. The Eastern Marches Society raised the
question in its journal in 1900, but then abandoned any further
public discussion until 1907.[76] Forcible expropriation of the
Polish gentry was a far more radical step than the Prussian government had yet taken. Above all, a law sanctioning expropriation of
land for political reasons would not only constitute an "exceptional law" infringing the civil rights of one segment of the
population; it would also set a precedent for the expropriations
of the property of other groups: the German Junkers, for example,
whose estates the socialists hoped to nationalize. The Catholic
Center Party, upon whose support in the Reichstag Bülow depended
between 1900 and 1907, opposed all exceptional laws in principle.
Despite occasional frictions arising from their divergent national
orientations, the Center patronized and attempted to defend the
Poles against discriminatory Prussian legislation. Bülow's government could not introduce an anti-Polish expropriation law in the
Landtag without risking the Center's defection to the opposition
in the Reichstag.

But by 1906 Bülow had grown weary of collaboration with the
Center. After the Reichstag elections of January 1907, he turned
to an ideologically motley majority of Progressives, National
Liberals, and Conservatives who, as the "Bülow bloc," supported
him on the Reich level during the years 1907-9. While this
political reshuffling eliminated one obstacle to the passage of an
expropriation act, a still more serious one remained: Could the
Prussian Conservatives, for whom the legal inviolability of land
ownership was such a crucial question, be persuaded to support
the Polish gentry's forcible dispossession?

By 1907 the directors of the Colonization Commission were
convinced that success hinged on obtaining Polish estate land
through expropriation. Only thus could further fragmentation of
German estate land in the east be prevented, an assured quantity
of Polish land acquired, the upward trend of prices halted, and
the Commission's existing settlements of colonists "rounded out"
and "rationally" extended.[77] At the end of 1906 the National
Liberal Party, the Hakatists, and the Pan-German League started
to campaign publicly for expropriation.[78] Most importantly, the
Prussian cabinet finally accepted the necessity of equipping the
Royal Commission with expropriation powers, not to placate
nationalist political organizations, but as the only practical
means by which the colonization program could avoid a collapse in
defeat.[79] Such an outcome, given the importance officially attached to the government's struggle to Germanize Prussian Poland

since Bismarck's time and before, was wholly unacceptable. It
would not only have required the government's withdrawal from
the "struggle for the land" in the east but would have called into
question the anti-Polish bases of the entire system of Prussian
Polenpolitik. If the Prussian government abandoned its struggle
with one of the long-execrated "enemies of the Reich," the
credibility and effectiveness of its campaigns against the others
could not fail to suffer.

The necessity of keeping the colonization program afloat
outweighed any scruples in the minds of the Prussian ministers
about fastening "exceptional legislation" on the Poles. There
is no evidence that William II or Bülow worried that expropriation violated the Poles' civil rights and so was unconstitutional
and illegal. Count Ladislaus von Szögyényi, the Austrian ambassador in Berlin, tried in 1907 and 1908 to stop William II's government from adopting an anti-Polish expropriation law. He argued
that such a radical step would greatly antagonize the Austrian
Poles and weaken their support in the Reichsrat and in the
Austro-Hungarian joint parliamentary delegations for the Hapsburg
regime and the German-Austrian Dual Alliance. Szögyényi's point
was recognized in Berlin as a serious one. Yet he found that both
Bülow and the Kaiser were unshakably committed to expropriation.
William II, in particular, "supports the most ruthless action and,
so far as the Poles are concerned, holds to the principle 'bend
or break'."[80] In his interviews with Szögyényi, Bülow unheroically
justified his support for the expropriation bill by invoking
the "determined wish of the Crown, the Prussian ministers, and
the governors of all the eastern provinces."[81] Bülow, Szögyényi
reported ruefully to Austrian foreign minister Count Aehrenthal,
had "driven himself in a corner." To avoid losing popularity in
nationalist circles, he could not resist seizing upon Polish expropriation, even though "not even in Russia" were nationality
conflicts fought with such weapons.[82]

Of Bülow, Szögyényi wrote in February 1908 that "it is really
unbelievable how openly his actions, and especially his disastrous
Polenpolitik, are attacked in all circles, even among the high
ranks of the military."[83] But in the Prussian cabinet only the
representatives of the Ministry of Justice raised any principled
objections to an anti-Polish expropriation bill. These they
were willing to withdraw if the law were framed in such a way as
to be applicable to German as well as Polish landowners, though
it went without saying that only Polish land would be expropriated.[84] The minister of finance, Georg von Rheinbaben, a spokes-

man for heavy industrial and imperialist interest groups under
whom Hugenberg served as assistant and "expert on eastern questions" from 1903 to 1907, frankly admitted the "exceptional" nature
of the expropriation bill. But he added that "since we are dealing
with a question of our national existence," constitutional objections to expropriation were irrelevant. This Treitschkean line of
reasoning, employed already in the 1886 parliamentary debates on
the colonization question, encountered no objections in Bülow's
cabinet.[85]

The prime question facing the Prussian government was whether
the Conservatives would stand behind expropriation. For in this
connection, as Bethmann Hollweg conceded, "the government will
have to make its decisions basically according to the wishes of
the Conservative Party."[86] The Conservatives' leader, Ernst von
Heydebrand und der Lasa, finally agreed to support expropriation,
but only on terms guaranteeing his Junker followers' special
interests.[87]

In principle, the Conservatives opposed expropriation. But
the party had long and vociferously supported the government's
campaigns against "Polish agitation," including the colonization
program from which the Poznanian and West Prussian Junkers
derived substantial benefits. The Conservatives were no more prepared than the government to admit the defeat of the Royal Commission, whose highly publicized struggle with the Poles had
diverted bourgeois nationalist hostility away from East Elbian
landlords in general and towards the Polish estate owners in
particular. In 1907-8 the Conservatives were also loath to put
the emerging Bülow bloc in jeopardy by defeating an anti-Polish
bill they knew the government was under pressure from within and
without to introduce.

To ensure that expropriation would not in the future be
turned against himself and his followers, Heydebrand demanded that
it be clearly formulated as an anti-Polish exceptional law and
accompanied by "energetic anti-Polish policies up and down the
line, especially limitations on the Polish press by way of
Reichstag legislation."[88] The government agreed. Expropriation
powers were granted the Royal Commission as a provision of the
Prussian Colonization Law submitted to the Landtag at the end of
1907. This law authorized the Commission to expropriate, for
purposes of carrying out its anti-Polish settlement program alone,
a maximum of 70,000 hectares in the provinces of Poznań and West
Prussia. To ensure that its expropriation decisions were agreeable to the Junkers, the Commission was obliged to admit to its

directorate delegates of the Poznanian and West Prussian chambers of agriculture.[89]

In other respects, too, the 1908 colonization bill took account of Junker interests. Beyond increasing the Commission's funds for peasant colonization by 125 million marks, the Landtag supplied it with 25 million marks for the purchase of domain land, 50 million marks for purchasing, refinancing, and selling to Germans on highly favorable terms ailing German estates and farms, and 75 million marks to be paid to German estate owners as subsidies for employing German instead of Polish agricultural workers.[90]

In this form, a majority of German Conservatives in the Landtag and Upper House joined the National Liberals and Free Conservatives in voting for expropriation on 20 March 1908. Not only the Poles, the Progressives, and the Catholic Centrists, but also an influential minority of Prussian Conservatives condemned and refused to support the 1908 law.[91] Already in November 1907, the Polish, Czech, and Slovene delegations in the Austrian Reichsrat had heatedly denounced the Prussian expropriation bill. After its passage, it came under harsh attack in the French and English press.[92]

In the end, Bülow hesitated to push forward with the application of expropriation, fearing both its domestic and foreign repercussions. He comforted himself by imagining that its very possibility hanging like a "sword of Damocles" over the Poles' heads would "make them see reason" and abandon their intransigent opposition to the Prussian government.[93] This was a fatuous hope. Although the government did not apply the expropriation law until 1912, and then only on a very small scale, its passage greatly radicalized the Polish nationalist movement in Prussia. At the same time, the government had raised the expectations of German nationalists that expropriation would bring about a decisive turn in the Germans' favor in the "struggle for the land." When in the years following 1908 this failed to occur, the Prussian government found itself subjected to withering attacks from the nationalist Right. In the expropriation issue, the government finally succeeded in pleasing no one. Instead, it multiplied the ranks of its critics and opponents and so assisted in undermining its own authority.[94]

Expropriation was only one part of a two-pronged attack Bülow's government mounted against Polish nationalism in 1907-8. The debates stirred up by the expropriation issue gave Bülow a favorable opportunity to strike a blow against "Polish agitation" which he had contemplated at least since 1901: prohibition of the use of the Polish language in public assemblies. This measure also served as a substitute for the suppression of the Polish nationalist press demanded by Heydebrand but likely to meet with decisive opposition in parliament and the courts.

In the Reichstag session of 1907-8 a general revision and liberalization of the laws governing private associations was underway. To its draft of the new Associations Law the Imperial government added a provision empowering Prussian officials to require public meetings staged by Polish organizations to be conducted in the German language, except in the case of meetings held in connection with Reichstag and Landtag elections, where use of the voters' mother tongue was guaranteed by Imperial law.

The anti-Polish "muzzle paragraph" of the Associations Law embarrassed the Progressives, who in 1907 had emerged from long years of opposition to join the Conservatives and National Liberals in support of Bülow. Assured of the Conservatives' and National Liberals' support of the controversial language paragraph, Bülow forced the Progressives to abandon their liberal scruples and accept it too. Otherwise, they ran the risk of scuttling the reform, which they had long advocated, of the association laws and toppling the bloc itself, thus landing themselves once again in sterile opposition. Despite some misgivings, the Progressives voted for the bill after having amended it to exclude for twenty years those counties where Poles comprised 60 percent or more of the population. They expected the Poles to thank them for this change, claiming that had their party rejected the law in its revised form Bülow would have only engineered the passage of a harsher anti-Polish language bill in the Prussian parliament.[95]

Reich Secretary of Interior Bethmann Hollweg defended the language paragraph in the Reichstag debates with two not altogether congruent arguments. On the one hand, since "the essence of our existence as a state is German," there could be nothing exceptional or illegal about requiring the use of the German language at all public meetings. On the other hand, Bethmann declared, the state always had been and still was happy to tolerate public manifestations of loyalty, even when couched in foreign tongues. There was therefore no need to impose German on all public meetings, but only on those of the Poles--and not because they spoke a foreign language but because they were allegedly disloyal subjects. Who could deny the Poles' "separatist desires," their dreams of a "Jagiellonian Empire?"

> Do we not see how Pan-Polonism (Grosspolentum)
> spreads, not only here in our midst but in the
> lands of our neighbors too? Can we not see that
> a great wave of powerful and elementary national
> passion is swelling up and threatening to engulf
> us?[96]

The language paragraph, which would hinder "inflammation of the
broad Polish masses by Pan-Polish agitators," was, Bethmann
argued, a simple dictate of self-defense.[97]

Like the expropriation act, the "gag law" greatly provoked
the Poles without really crippling their oppositional activities.
The Progressives' amendment suspended the language law's validity
in twenty-six of the forty-two counties of the Province of Poznań
and in twenty-one other counties in Upper Silesia and in West and
East Prussia. Elsewhere Polish nationalist organizers and agitators could make intensive use of public meetings during election
campaigns. By organizing broadly defined "private" political
clubs under the liberalized provisions of the 1908 Association Law,
it was relatively easy to assemble sizable audiences for Polish-
language meetings even in heavily German counties and regions.
The language law of 1908 did not therefore stifle "Polish agitation." On the contrary, it provided Polish nationalists with
one more instance of the Prussian government's anti-Polonism which
made their own appeals to the "broad Polish masses" all the more
persuasive.

The discriminatory laws of 1908, following upon the school
strikes and raising the highly publicized "struggle for the land"
to a new pitch of intensity, were Bülow's last attacks on the
Poles. Thereafter, he struggled with the diplomatic and military-
financial crises which ultimately split the Reichstag bloc and
forced his resignation in mid 1909. But in Poznań, Prussian officials, their hands strengthened by the legislation of 1908,
kept steady pressure on the Poles. Wilhelm von Waldow, provincial
president since 1903, reported to the Prussian Ministry of Interior in May 1909 on "successes in our eastern marches policy."
These he defined in strictly numerical terms as German gains at
the Poles' expense in population, property ownership, and political
representation. Assuming hostility to Prussian rule to be pervasive and ineradicable among the Poles, Waldow altogether dis-
counted the radicalizing effect of Bülow's campaign against them.
They figured in his thinking only negatively, as a quantity to be
diminished. This he sought to achieve not so much by assimilating
them into the German nationality as by displacing them physically
and settling Germans in their stead. Germanization, in Waldow's
view, had less to do with the Poles than with the ground they

stood on. This conception, sanctioned by Bismarckian practice and
widely shared in official and nationalist circles during Bülow's
chancellorship, justified depriving the Poles of national toleration and stripping away their civil rights as Prussian and Reich
citizens.

In 1909 Waldow contemplated the Poles' expropriation with
high hopes. He rejoiced in the relative growth in the German
population of the Province of Poznań revealed in the censuses of
1900 and 1905: from 38.07 percent tó 38.32 percent of the total
population. The expansion of the Polish population which had
alarmed Prussian policymakers and German nationalists since the
1870s appeared to have been brought to a halt. Waldow attributed
this gratifying fact to the action of the Colonization Commission.
But he praised his own efforts to replace Poles with Germans in
the local bureaucracy. He had added 3,200 Germans to the provincial post and railway administration since 1907, while holding the
number of Polish workers hired to 795. By stiffening the regulations governing command of the German language, the proportion of
Poles in the secondary schools had fallen from 26.8 percent in 1902
to 25.1 percent in 1908. Similarly, "sharper demands on national
behavior" had caused the proportions of Poles in the provincial
teacher-training seminaries to fall from 60 percent in 1898 to 10
percent in 1908.[98] Waldow was also happy to report that since 1900
over 600 provincial place names had been officially Germanized.
The most notorious case was the rebaptism of the sizable town of
Inowrocław as Hohensalza. Similarly, 1,249 personal surnames had
been Germanized since 1905. Finally, while since 1905 only 330
Germans had emigrated from the province, over 3,800 Poles had left,
mainly to seek their fortunes in the United States.

Waldow had to admit that German population growth since 1900
had been achieved by artificial means:

> A large part of our success in raising the numbers of
> the German population is the result of gains through
> immigration and not natural population increases. Ex-
> panding the corps of German officials, creating new
> state offices and enterprises with German personnel,
> eliminating Polish employees from those institutions
> amenable to state influence--these and similar
> measures have their limits. One can hardly reckon on
> a continuation of the gains of the last years.[90]

In the long run, Germanization of the province depended on intensive peasant colonization. Only by vigorous exercise of its expropriation powers could the Royal Commission obtain the colonization land it needed. But Waldow insisted on the importance of
settling not only German peasants, but German rural workers and
artisans as well. Only such a "German lower class rich in

children" could counteract the greater fertility of the Polish
population and eventually eliminate the German estate owners'
"nationally undesirable" dependence on Polish seasonal laborers.[100]
The crucial questions here were whether sizable numbers of Germans
from outside the colonization districts would volunteer to settle
there as rural workers and whether the local Junkers, even if offered subsidies to this end, would pay the higher wages such
workers would inevitably demand.

Waldow's report demonstrates how those Prussian officials most
involved in executing official policy had abandoned the Bismarckian
perspective that identified the Polish nobility and their hangers-
on as the principal obstacles to the state's Germanization
policies. Instead, because the creation of an unchallengeable
German numerical majority in the Polish provinces had become the
primary object, the focus of the government's concern shifted to
the demographic vitality of the Polish population as a whole and,
especially, to the fertility, land hunger, and modest wage demands
of the Polish peasants and rural workers. Ultimately, it was
these large groups that lent the colonization regions their Polish
character. It was their demographic and territorial expansion
that threatened to Polonize adjacent German lands. By 1909 the
Prussian government's only means of counteracting the national
consequences of their demographic strength lay in buying up Polish
farms and smallholdings, expropriating the Polish estates which
employed them as laborers, and creating a rival class of German
worker-colonists as a labor force for the Junkers. But to level
the sharp point of Prussian colonization policy directly at the
Polish rural masses, whose disaffection from Prussian rule had
already been made plain during the school strikes, threatened to
drive them into a nationalist opposition far more dangerous to the
Prussian state and social order than that of the Polish middle
and upper classes.

Bethmann Hollweg's Chancellorship, 1909-14

Bülow's fall from office temporarily neutralized the Polish
question as an issue of Prussian cabinet and parliamentary
politics. The conservative parties' refusal to submit to a modest
degree of direct taxation to finance the increasingly heavy costs
of the Imperial fleet had split the Bülow bloc and undermined the
cartel strategy of which an aggressive domestic Polish policy was
part and parcel. Bethmann Hollweg willingly accepted the necessity,
incontestable from the government's point of view since the Caprivi era, of basing his parliamentary policies first and foremost

on Conservative support. Because the liberal parties would not
accept fiscal reforms favoring agrarian interests at their own expense, Bethmann found himself dependent in his Reichstag policies
on a shaky coalition of Conservatives and Catholic Centrists (the
"blue-black bloc"). This state of affairs lasted until after the
Reichstag elections of January 1912. The enormous gains of the
Socialists in this contest heightened Bethmann's desire, which had
animated him since his appointment as chancellor and Prussian
minister-president, to revive the alliance Bismarck had mediated
between the National Liberals and Conservatives. But these
parties had lost so much ground in the 1912 elections that, even
if they could agree on common economic policies, they still required Center support to attain a majority in the Reichstag. In
fact, since the liberals and conservatives remained at loggerheads
after 1912, Bethmann had no choice before the outbreak of the war
but to stumble from one desperate improvisation to the next,
seldom escaping dependence on Catholic votes.

On the Reich level, where he confronted his greatest political problems, Bethmann had nothing to gain from continuing or
intensifying, as Prussian minister-president, Bülow's harsh
political assaults on the Poles, even though the traditional Con-
servative-National Liberal majority stood fast in the Landtag and
could be expected to cooperate in forging new links in the chain of
Prussian Polish policy. Attacking the Poles would weaken Catholic
support for Bethmann's Imperial policies. It would not help to
resolve the Reich-level disputes between Conservatives and National
Liberals. It would make cooperation between the Progressives and
the parties to their right more difficult and it would provide the
Socialists with yet another stick to beat the government with.

If Bethmann sought to tone down the strident campaign Bülow
had set in motion against the Poles, it was not because he rated
Germanization of the eastern marches less highly than his predecessor. As Prussian minister of interior he had played a major
role in drafting the expropriation law. As Reich interior secretary he defended the 1908 "gag paragraph" before the Imperial
Parliament. The apprehensions he voiced on the latter occasion
about revolutionary Polish nationalism were genuine. In a private
conversation with Szögyényi in 1910 Bethmann said that, while he
wished to be "objective and avoid any sharp attacks on [Prussia's]
Polish-speaking citizens," he could not ignore "the danger of Great-
Polish agitation, whose unswerving goal, however much it might be
denied, was the restoration of the Polish Empire."[101] Bethmann
candidly set forth his view in a ministerial conference of 1907.

"Pacification" of Poznania and Polish West Prussia would be
achieved "only when the local German population has been
secured in both its political and economic ascendency over the
Poles; only then--and not before--will the process of assimilation begin." The surest means to this still distant goal was
the colonization program, which Bethmann endorsed unreservedly.[102]

As chancellor, Bethmann shared Bismarck's and Bülow's Germanizing objectives, but sought to realize them without stirring up
political opposition which might undercut his policies on other
fronts. In the aftermath of the passage of the Expropriation Act,
this was a difficult tactic to pursue. Bülow's government, in
which Bethmann occupied a prominent place, had argued forcefully
during 1907 and 1908 that only through the exercise of expropriation powers could the Royal Commission--the all-important
vehicle of Germanization--accomplish its ends. This argument was
noisily seconded and unceasingly repeated by the Eastern Marches
Society, the Pan-German League, and the nationalist politicians
and journalists who followed their lead in Polish affairs. But
the debates of 1907-8 had revealed solid Catholic hostility and
considerable Conservative ambivalence towards forcible expropriation of Polish estates. Passage of the Expropriation Act had
weakened the domestic position of the Hapsburg government, an effect which enforcement of expropriation in practice could only
intensify. In Poznania, Bülow's anti-Polish legislation inspired
the more radically minded Polish nationalists to launch an open
campaign to wrest control of the social and political institutions
of Polish society from the hands of the demoralized traditionalists. The spearhead of this campaign was the National Democratic
Society, organized in 1909 as the first genuine political party,
as opposed to the nationally solidary system of "electoral
authorities," to have emerged among the Prussian Poles. The
National Democrats, identified in German conservative and nationalist circles as the most dangerous type of "Great-Polish agitators,"
immediately threw the Polish conservatives on the defensive. In
1909, National Democratic prospects of winning control of Polish
society and of recruiting the Polish common people under their
militant banners were strong. By acting upon its expropriation
powers the Prussian government would, at least in the short run,
only make them stronger still.[103]

Under these circumstances, Bethmann decided to resist German
nationalist pressures for application of expropriation. In 1910
he told Count Bogdan von Hutten-Czapski that "it could only be in
the government's interest to treat the moderate [Polish] circles

in a not unfriendly manner, so as to strengthen them in their difficult position vis-à-vis the irreconcilable National Democrats."[104] Already in 1909 the Polish parliamentary delegations,
still dominated by conservative and moderate nationalists, had
begun to lend Bethmann selective support with their votes which,
as in the case of his 1909 Reichstag financial reforms, the chancellor sometimes genuinely needed. In a Prussian cabinet meeting
of March 1911, Bethmann remarked irritably that "immediate expropriation would satisfy only the Hakatistic and Pan-German
press;" but his government could not afford to lose the Center's
or even the Poles' support.[105]

        Nevertheless, with his characteristic fatalism and pessimism
Bethmann conceded to Szögyényi the difficulty of resisting
nationalist agitation. He predicted that sooner or later the government would find itself required to apply the expropriation law
on a small scale as a token "that it is determined, now as before,
to carry through with its program of supporting the Germans in
the eastern marches."[106] But he sought to stave off that moment
as long as possible. In fact, in the years after 1908 the Colonization Commission continued to acquire estates on the open
market. So long as it possessed a reserve of still unsettled
land, Bethmann could argue that there was no urgency in unsheath-
ing the sword of expropriation. In January 1910 he was even able
to persuade the Kaiser to announce through his Cabinet Councillor
von Valentini that "he wished to permit expropriation only as an
ultima ratio, in particular as a reply to provocation from the
Polish side."[107]

        By 1911 it was clear that Bethmann had no intention of satisfy-
ing the radical German nationalists' long-standing, increasingly
impatient expectation that the government would energetically
employ its expropriation powers to shatter Polish resistance in
the "struggle for the land." In the spring of that year, the
Eastern Marches Society greatly intensified its public agitation
in favor of expropriation. It harshly attacked Bethmann's Catholic-
conservative minister of agriculture, Baron Clemens von Schorlemer,
accusing him of bland indifference to German national interests.
Schorlemer, who already in January 1911 had commented privately
that "this shadow government of the Eastern Marches Society is
starting to get very uncomfortable," replied in an Upper House
speech of May 1911 with a sharp denunciation of the anti-Polish
organization's pressure tactics.[108]

        In the province of Poznań Schorlemer's counterattack upon the
Eastern Marches Society inspired a group of conservative-minded

German estate owners to circulate a petition among the local
German population, and particularly among the Junkers. It
upheld the government's decision to postpone application of the
Expropriation Act and disputed the Eastern Marches Society's
claims to speak for the entire German population of the eastern
borderlands. Chief among the organizers of this action were the
son-in-law of former Provincial President von Wilamowitz-Möllendorf, the chairman of the provincial Chamber of Agriculture, and
Major Endell. These highly respectable figures quickly came
under a heavy fire of Hakatistic propaganda. The petition movement collapsed, but not before having made its point that there
were influential opponents of expropriation among the eastern
large landowners.[109]

    Thus by mid 1911 a breach had opened between radical and
conservative German nationalists. To strengthen the government's
position in this controversy, in September Bethmann replaced
Waldow, whose outspoken Hakatism had ceased to be an asset, with
Dr. Philip Schwartzkopff, under state secretary in the Prussian
Ministry of Religion and Education. Waldow was an influential
advocate of expropriation. His succession by Schwartzkopff, a
religiously minded Poznanian estate owner and a bureaucratic conservative of the old school, signified Bethmann's open repudiation
of the Eastern Marches Society in particular and Bülow's anti-
Polish intransigence in general. Beyond tightening his control
over the provincial bureaucracy, Bethmann's appointment set the
stage for a low-keyed policy of cultivating government support
among the Polish conservatives. It aimed to win Polish votes
in the Reichstag and stiffen the conciliation-minded Polish
traditionalists' resistance to the rising influence of the National
Democrats.

    Bethmann and Schwartzkopff realized that, if they offered
the Poles even a partial dismantling of the already existing
machinery of official Germanization policy, the Hakatists'
denunciations of the government for conducting a Caprivi-style
"policy of conciliation" would convince Prussian and German conservative nationalists opposed to the Eastern Marches Society's
demagogic radicalism but committed to the substance of Bismarck's
and Bülow's policies. Bethmann himself felt the same commitment
and had no intention of abolishing any of the fundamental institutions or legal expressions of official Germanization policy. But
by avoiding any new provocation of the Poles, by dissociating the
government from the Eastern Marches Society, and by establishing
social and other politically neutral contacts between Schwartz-

kopff's local administration and the Poles, Bethmann and his new
provincial president hoped to weaken Polish opposition to the
government. Simultaneously, they intended to steer German opinion
away from the inflammatory slogans of the Hakatists and towards
support of the government's unemotional pursuit of colonization,
Germanization of education, and the advancement of the eastern
Germans' economic and cultural interests.[110]

Bethmann's and Schwartzkopff's strategy mirrored their con-
servative-aristocratic yearnings for tranquillity and their
bureaucratic distaste for noisy partisan politics. But their
tactics were not only inadequate to the pacification of the
Poles, whose opposition to Prussian rule was deeply rooted in the
government's discriminatory Germanization system itself; they
erred more fundamentally in believing that the anti-Polish substance of Prussian policy could be separated and dispassionately
pursued apart from the aggressive rhetoric in which it had been
swathed since the mid nineteenth century. Prussian Polish policy
since Bismarck's time had been an integral part of a system of
socially conservative, antidemocratic nationalist politics. That
system had become radicalized, in its rhetoric as well as in its
practice, in proportion as domestic challenges to it multiplied.
Moreover, its component parts had become mutually interlocking.
Prussian Polenpolitik was one of the monarchy's defenses against
social and political democratization. It could not be de-
escalated when, as was increasingly the case in the years before
1914, challenges to William II's regime were multiplying and when
the imperialist foreign policy intended to counter them was en-
countering unremitting frustration.

The Second Morocco Crisis of 1911 proved this point. From
this long and tense confrontation with France and England, Bethmann's government, despite its warlike gestures, emerged with
imperial trophies which, from the German Right's point of view,
were disappointingly small. Bethmann failed to silence the Left
by an imposing display of German power, resolution, and international success. Instead, the chancellor's foreign policy provoked the Socialists' denunciations by its sword-rattling, and their
scorn by its compromised rewards. The Conservatives concluded
that the protection of their domestic interests and the realization of their sanguine foreign-policy expectations required a
government more ruthless than Bethmann Hollweg's. In the Reichstag
debates on the Morocco settlement of November 1911, Heydebrand's
withering criticism of Bethmann's diplomacy signified the Conservatives' open rejection of his leadership. Although William II

kept Bethmann in office, the chancellor had henceforth to pay
a high price for Conservative support. Even then, Heydebrand
and his followers complied only grudgingly.

The Morocco debates in the Reichstag ended on 11 November.
On 14 November spokesmen for the Colonization Commission raised
the question of expropriation in a Prussian cabinet meeting. The
advocates in the government of a hard-line Polenpolitik undoubtedly
recognized that Bethmann's censure in the Reichstag presented
them with a favorable opportunity to force his assent to expropriation. At that moment Bethmann could not afford to become embroiled again in the Eastern Marches Society and its allies in
a propaganda war over Polish policy. Finally he and Schorlemer
agreed that four Polish estates, totally 1,700 hectares, should
be expropriated. In all likelihood the government's decision
was immediately leaked to the Eastern Marches Society and Pan-
German League. It was not to be officially announced until after
the forthcoming January 1912 Reichstag elections, so as not to
jeopardize the electoral alliances already forged between the
German liberals and conservatives in Poznań. The cabinet would
have to vote again on the actual date of expropriation, a circum-
stance that offered Bethmann the possibility of delaying or even
perhaps circumventing altogether its actual execution.

In fact, nationalist pressure exerted within the administration and by the conservative parties soon forced Schorlemer to
concede, in the Landtag debates on the 1912 eastern marches
financial bill, that expropriation would occur before the end
of the year. On 15 October 1912, during the excitement stirred
up by the First Balkan War--an event interpreted by German nationalists as a menacing victory of Pan-Slavism--the Prussian government made public its decision to expropriate the four Polish
estates. It could not resist attempting to offset the impact on
German opinion of an unfavorable foreign policy development by
striking a blow at the Prussian Poles.

This expropriation action, which immediately became enmeshed
in lengthy litigation in the courts, did nothing to tip the
balance in the "struggle for the land" in the Germans' favor.
The area involved was insignificant. But the government's expropriation options were limited. Sometime after 1908 Waldow
had drawn up a partial list of Polish estates which, for political
reasons, he recommended not be expropriated. The list covered
only ten counties, yet spared the sizable total of 124,000 hectares from confiscation. On the one hand, Waldow argued, the
lands of politically passive or conservative Poles should be left

untouched, to avoid creating political martyrs. On the other hand, lands owned by prominent Polish nationalists and opponents of the government ought also to be spared, to avoid inflating their prestige in Polish society. It is likely that the Royal Commission and the government took a similar view of the problem, even though it ensured the retention in Polish hands of great blocs of land in the colonization districts. The victims of the 1912 action were persons of no social prestige or political importance in Polish society, but this did not prevent the Poles from staging massive protest meetings against the expropriation of their lands.[111]

It was foreseeable and inevitable that expropriation would stiffen and radicalize Polish opposition to the Prussian government. Similarly, the Hapsburg government's relations with the Galician loyalists underwent a predictable crisis, emerging intact but weakened, as Szögyényi and Berchthold, who learned of the Prussian expropriation decision in the newspapers, bitterly pointed out to Bethmann. But the Prussian government was unprepared for the assault the Reichstag launched upon it in January 1913 in the form of a hostile interpellation which ended in a majority vote of Socialists, Catholic Centrists, and Poles censuring Bethmann's application of the 1908 law. Barely two months after his condemnation by a conservative-led majority in the Reichstag, Bethmann suffered the humiliation, which in a fully parliamentarized system would have forced his resignation, of having his policies denounced by a left-center majority. But, as in the aftermath of the Saverne case later in the same year, the Kaiser retained in office the politically lamed and harried chancellor despite his lack of solid parliamentary backing.[112]

The political repercussions of expropriation were sufficiently negative to stiffen Bethmann's resolve to avoid it in the future. Szögyényi reported in January 1913 that the chancellor "has assured me categorically that no further expropriations are in sight."[113] A year later Berchthold instructed the Hapsburg consul in Breslau to sound out Schwartzkopff on the prospects of future expropriations. The consul reported that, while the Oberpräsident admitted the Eastern Marches Society was pressuring the Royal Commission to demand expropriation of three particular Polish estates, Schwartzkopff said that Bethmann was convinced expropriation could only produce harmful results. It would almost certainly not occur again under his chancellorship. Schwartzkopff admitted there were "too many heavy-armored (panzer-platten) patriots" in Prussia to permit repeal of the Expropriation Act. He added "in strict confidence" that the Kaiser's position on the

Polish question could not be pinned down in advance "since he
often lets himself be influenced by peripheral and irrelevant
circumstances."[114] Thus a situation was not unimaginable in
which Bethmann might again find himself forced to sanction new
applications of the expropriation law, though clearly after 1912
he was opposed to this.

Because of the political controversy surrounding it, expropriation, though an important symbolical issue of Prussian
Germanization policy, failed as a practical instrument for
providing the Colonization Commission forcible access to Polish
lands. After 1908, as before, the Commission settled its
colonists primarily on lands acquired from Germans. To avoid the
"decimation" of the eastern Junkers which Bethmann warned against
in 1907, the government was obliged to hold peasant settlement to
a slow pace. Aware that this would aggravate the extreme nationalists, Bethmann took pains to satisfy the special interests
of the eastern landlords. In May 1912 the government obtained from
the Landtag 100 million marks to extend its program of refunding
financially wobbly German estates beyond the two original colonization provinces into East Prussia, Upper Silesia, and Pomerania,
areas now declared to be threatened by "Polonizing tendencies."
In fact, offering to refinance the Junkers in these provinces
amounted to a lucrative public subsidy for them and a political
bribe by Bethmann's government to maintain the Conservative
party's parliamentary toleration, if not its loyalty.[115]

In May 1913 the government steered another "Eastern Marches
Appropriation" through the Landtag. Seventy-five million new
marks flowed into the Commission's peasant colonization fund, 50
million fewer than were granted for this purpose in 1908. But
130 million additional marks were appropriated for the refinancing of existing German peasant farms and the subsidization of farm
workers' holdings in Poznania and West Prussia. The Landtag
added another 25 million marks to the refinancing program for
estate owners in the colonization provinces. Altogether, while
these appropriations upheld the Germanization goals of the
colonization program, they also strongly benefited the Poznanian
and West Prussian Junkers, both as debtors and as employers of
rural laborers.[116]

Although the eastern marches appropriations of 1912 and 1913
struck at the Poles' civil rights and economic interests, the
Prussian government and the German nationalist parties regarded
them as economically productive investments on behalf of frontier
Germans menaced by "the Slavic flood" rather than discriminatory

attacks on the Poles. Bethmann did not believe passage of these
bills posed any obstacles to his and Schwartzkopff's policy of
treating the Poznanian Poles in a "not unfriendly manner," a
policy which in the fall of 1913 they decided to put to a public
test.

In August, William II took up residence in his recently
constructed neogothic imperial castle in Poznań. He had come to
review the locally headquartered Prussian Fifth Army Corps. His
visit also provided an occasion for the Germans of Poznań to express their Hohenzollern enthusiasms by decorating their houses
and turning out in full force to greet his parade through the
city. The political high point of the emperor's visit was a
banquet staged at the castle on 28 August, to which 355 of the
province's high officials and notables in political and social life
were invited. Schwartzkopff, assisted by Hutten-Czapski, had seen
to it that 36 Poles were among the guests. Of these, 21 held high
positions in the Catholic church, in the provincial self-administration system, or at court. The others were socially prominent
and politically conservative aristocrats. At the time of the
Kaiser's visit to the province in 1902 even those Poles holding
high offices in the self-administration network had boycotted the
imperial ceremonies in protest against the government's ruthless
suppression of the school strikes. Thus the banquet of 1913
vindicated, though on a modest scale, Bethmann's and Schwartzkopff's
belief that some at least of the "moderate" Poles--Schwartzkopff
privately even called them "lukewarm Poles"--could be persuaded to
cooperate with the government in pursuit of an "understanding"
(Verständigung) among the nationalities.[117] But in the Kaiser's
toast, the government's one-sided conception of such an understanding emerged all the more clearly because the sentiments it
expressed were intended, unlike William II's Hakatistic pronouncements of the Bülow years, to be conciliatory:

> May the province's inhabitants--regardless of
> their nationality and confession--be drawn closely
> together through the bond of love for the beautiful
> homeland [Heimat] they share and through common
> loyalty to king and fatherland. May they take unto
> themselves and enjoy the blessed fruits of German
> culture.[118]

Even conservative-minded Poles, as Polish press commentaries on the
Kaiser's words made clear, bridled at the suggestion that their
homeland's happy destiny lay in its Germanization, all the more
since so many of the "blessed fruits of German culture" were being forcibly imposed on it and its Polish inhabitants at the
expense of its indigenous Polish culture. The Polish populists

and National Democrats exploded with indignation not only over the
Imperial toast but also at the "treason" of the aristocratic
banquet-goers, against whom a sizable Polish crowd had rudely
demonstrated in the city's streets. Altogether, the Polish
conservatives' participation in the Imperial ceremonies tarnished
their image among the Polish bourgeoisie and common people without
gaining for themselves or their compatriots anything more than
another confirmation of the Germanizing mentality of Prussia's
governors.

Despite the negative treatment of the royal banquet in the
Polish press, Schwartzkopff did not despair of what he called his
"milder conception of the Polish question." He still believed in
1914 that the Polish moderates could be steered out of "the tow
of the rabble-rousers," provided the government was patient and
avoided such "imbecilities" as expropriation.[119] But, if Bethmann
still shared these sanguine hopes, he greatly jeopardized their
realization when in March 1914, bowing to the pressure of the
Hakatists, the Pan-German League, and the radical nationalists
in the bureaucracy, his cabinet introduced in the Landtag the
draft of a new "Parcellation Law." Had the outbreak of war not
forestalled its enactment, this measure might have dealt the Poles
a painful double-edged blow in the "struggle for the land." In
the first place, the draft proposed that no farm land be parcelled,
either by a parcellation society, a bank, or a private broker,
without the consent of the local district president, who would be
obliged to veto all such transactions if they conflicted with
official colonization policy. Here, in effect, was the general
prohibition of Polish parcellation activity demanded by radical
nationalists since the turn of the century.[120] Secondly, the draft
provided that in sales of landholdings ten or more hectares in
size which had not been in the seller's possession for ten years
or more, the Royal Commission might intervene and take the place
of the prospective purchaser if the lands so obtained were required for colonization purposes. Here Bethmann's government
responded to the Eastern Marches Society's and Pan-German League's
long-standing calls for arming the state with an Einspruchsrecht
or right of preemptive purchase by which Polish land transactions,
especially those preceding parcellation actions, might be turned
to German advantage.[121]

Advocacy of this Parcellation Law was proof that the
colonization program had reached a critical impasse. Since the
Poles refused to sell land freely to the Royal Commission and expropriation of Polish landowners had become politically hazardous,

Bethmann and his advisers saw no means other than forcible intervention in Polish land sales of providing the Royal Commission with
Polish lands for peasant settlement, without which colonization
must either further erode German large landholding in the east or
cease altogether. Neither of these possibilities was politically
tolerable, given the social base and political ideology of the
Prusso-German state. If to forestall them the search for an
"understanding" with the conservative Poles had to be sacrificed,
Bethmann was clearly willing to do so.

   Yet it is not certain the Parcellation Law would have passed
the Landtag in the form in which it was proposed. The Conservatives objected to the fact that it was not framed as a specifically anti-Polish measure. Conceivably, therefore, it could in
the future be turned against their own landholdings by German
advocates of "inner colonization" or agrarian socialism. The
National Liberals criticized the ten-hectare limitation and
feared the Poles would find legal means of evading the law's
effect--for example, by attaching a condition to the sale of
their land that the state could not meet, such as the stipulation
that it be sold only to a Polish purchaser.

   The bill did in fact get bogged down in a parliamentary commission. But, had the war not intervened, it is certain that some
more or less effective law further hindering Polish parcellation
and land transfers would have found the approval of the Conserva-
tive-National Liberal majority. After all, it had never since
Bismarck's time failed to support the government's anti-Polish
legislation. Despite his self-proclaimed, if implausible,
scruples about "exceptional laws," Bethmann could have rejected
the Landtag's revisions of this bill only at the cost of provoking
a new German nationalist campaign against him.[122]

   As the 1914 Landtag debated the Parcellation Law, the
Ministry of Religion and Education approved the request of the
school inspector in the city of Poznań for the abolition of the
last vestiges of Polish-language instruction in grammar and
religion, confined since the turn of the century to the city's
first two elementary school grades. This measure provoked loud
and bitter protests. The specter of a final campaign against
Polish-language instruction throughout the province arose, and with
it the possibility of new school strikes.[123]

   Symbolically, in the midst of these new anti-Polish offen-
sives Schwartzkopff died while hunting on the estate of a Polish
aristocrat. His successor, Johann von Eisenhardt-Rothe, was a
politically obscure protégé of Bethmann not likely, according to

what Schorlemer told Hatten-Czapski, to continue Schwartzkopff's
conciliatory gestures towards the Polish aristocracy.[124]   But
Eisenhardt-Rothe had no time to show his colors before the
shadow of war descended on the province.

The war reopened the international Polish question. Inevitably, the Central Powers and the Russians began to manipulate
Polish hopes for independence as a means of advancing their own
mutually hostile territorial designs. On 31 July, as the German
army mobilized against Russia, William II received Hutten-Czapski
and grandiosely told him, "It is my decision, should the Lord God
confer victory on our arms, to restore an independent
(selbstständige) Polish state, in alliance with which Germany will
be forever secured against Russia."[125]   The war with Russia which
had haunted Prussian political thought throughout the nineteenth
century having finally come, it was natural that William II
should have seized upon one of the principal defensive strategies
the men of Bismarck's generation had devised to weaken the Russians' assaults and forestall their reoccurrence. In exchange
for a truncated, satellite state, such as the Central Powers
ephemerally created in the "Kingdom of Poland," proclaimed in
the Russian partition area in November 1916, the Poles could be
persuaded, or so it was hoped in Berlin, not merely to "work for
the King of Prussia" but to die fighting the Russians for him.

The German government was slow in translating William II's
enthusiasm into a concrete policy. Unlike the Tsarist regime,
which at the war's outset bid publicly for Polish support with
vague promises of "self-government," Bethmann's ministry gave
the Prussian Poles no signs pointing to German championship of
a Polish restoration or to a relaxation of Prussia's discriminatory domestic policies.[126]   The one concession to Polish sensitivi-
ties made in Berlin at the beginning of the war misfired. On 31
August, William II finally confirmed Bishop Likowski's election of
1907 as Archbishop of Poznań-Gniezno. But whatever mollifying effect this might have had was lost with the publication on 12
August of the aged and archconservative Likowski's first pastoral
letter. Amid denunciations of Russian "barbarism," it called
for loyal Polish service in the cause of the victory of German
arms. In the Polish version of his letter Likowski expressed the
hope that William II would reward the Poles' war-time sacrifices
by abolishing the "exceptional laws which have struck our society
painfully." But his missive was received, as a Catholic historian
has observed, "with great mortification by Polish society," since

it appeared to be the price of his appointment and enjoined on the
Poles their armed support of the very German nationalism which had
oppressed them at home for decades.[127]

By the time the Archbishop's letter was published, the
eastern provinces had fallen under a state of siege which brought
local political life to a standstill. Military and police officials subjected all meetings to an intense and hostile scrutiny,
the press succumbed to rigid censorship, political leaders and
activists were drafted and sent to the front. The internal
security of the eastern marches guaranteed, Bethmann Hollweg's
government plunged into the war whose course would determine the
future of Prussian Polenpolitik.

During the 1890s, the Imperial German economy escaped the
grip of the post-1873 depression and entered a period of unprecedented growth and prosperity lasting to the outbreak of
World War I. In Poznania, estate agriculture, the province's
economic linchpin, recovered its profitability. This occurred
in part as a result of technical rationalization already begun in
the 1880s. But even the technically most advanced estates yielded
meager dividends until farm commodity prices began their steep
ascent from the depressed state into which they had been plunged
by Caprivi's commercial treaties to the high levels of the
decade preceding the war to which they were driven by official
export subsidies, the Bülow tariff of 1902, and intensified demand
exerted by the rapidly expanding German population.[1]

During these years, intensive application of chemical fertilizers and widespread adoption of mechanical reapers, steam plows,
and steam-driven threshers enabled the province's estate owners
to double or triple their yields per acre of potatoes and cereals
(mainly rye).[2] By 1909 the province's grain shipments abroad and
to other parts of the Empire not only had doubled since 1887; they
also represented in absolute terms the largest such "export surplus" of any of the Reich's provinces.[3] At the same time, the
large landowners invested heavily in their preexisting distilleries.
By 1907 the sales of spirits and liquors produced by 543 establishments, owned for the most part by estate owners, netted 31 million
marks annually. This sum was exceeded among the province's other
processing and manufacturing industries only by sugar production,
whose output reached an annual value of 40 million marks in the
years 1910-13.[4] Cultivation and refining of sugar beets, marginal
enterprises in the 1880s, comprised a major agricultural industry
on the eve of the war.[5] In the sphere of livestock raising, the
province's estate owners compensated for the Reich-level decline
in domestic wool consumption by considerably expanding their herds
of beef cattle.[6]

Bank credit from both private and state-funded sources became increasingly available to the large landowners after 1894.
But rationalization of estate agriculture in these years was
funded no less by the profits the Polish gentry and German Junkers
reaped through land sales to the Colonization Commission, Polish
parcellation banks, or private speculators. The land hunger of
the Polish peasants and Sachsengänger combined with the Royal
Commission's demand for colonization land to drive the average
price of land per hectare up from 568 marks in 1886 to 1,600 marks
at the end of 1912.[7] Large landowners plagued by debts could
either liquidate their holdings entirely, so as to reestablish
themselves with adequate working capital on smaller estates; or
they could sell part of their land to put the remainder on a
sounder financial footing. For prospective land purchasers,
especially among the peasantry, this inflation of land prices,
which rose much more sharply than commodity prices, was a burden.
But for debt-ridden large landowners, it was a blessing. In its
political effects it favored the Poles, enabling them to solidify
their economic positions in the province. Among the Junkers,
it encouraged full-scale liquidations and resettlement on lower-
priced estates outside the province as well as an overheated
speculation in estate land of which the Colonization Commission
was the principal victim.[8]

As a result of land sales to the Royal Commission and private
parcellation societies, the percentage of arable land farmed in
units of 100 hectares or more fell from 58.5 percent in 1882 to 46
percent in 1907.[9] Altogether, between 1886 and the outbreak of
the war the Prussian state resettled 16.2 percent of the province's
arable while private parcellation redistributed another 16.8 percent. The Colonization Commission establishes 21,714 new farms in
these years, while 4,920 new holdings were set up under the state's
Rentengüter legislation of 1890-91. Meanwhile, between 1890 and
1914, private, mainly Polish, parcellation created 25,500 new
farms; 46,200 pieces of land were attached to neighboring farms,
leaving 22,700 Restgüter, or farms and estates shorn of part of
their land through parcellation.[10]

While the large landowners streamlined their holdings and
rationalized their operations, both the absolute numbers of the
landed peasantry and the proportion of the province's farmland
they tilled rose steeply. In 1882, there were 48,500 farms of 5
to 100 hectares accounting for 29.3 percent of the total arable;
by 1907, the number of these peasant holdings had risen to 63,800,
their share of the arable to 47.3 percent.[11] At the same time,

both the profitability and productivity of peasant farming increased. The expansion of cooperative and state-funded bank
credit eliminated the necessity of recourse to usurious private
lenders. Public and private technical education spread, relatively inexpensive horse-driven machinery became available and
the prices netted by market garden crops and livestock (especially
swine and poultry) steadily rose.[12]

The province's rural working class benefited least from the
agricultural prosperity of the two prewar decades. Wages rose
more slowly than either land or commodity prices.[13] As a result,
emigration of the rural poor to the industrial districts of
central and western Germany as well as westward seasonal migration in search of higher agricultural wages persisted, at the high
rates established in the 1880s, to the outbreak of the war. This
outflow of labor drove up local wage rates only slowly. It was
countered, at least as far as unskilled rural labor was concerned,
by the annual influx of low-paid seasonal laborers from Russian
and Austrian Poland.[14] But emigraion of the province's surplus
rural population assured most of those who remained behind a
livelihood which, though low by contemporary German standards,
was free of unemployment or the threat of pauperism. Savings
from local and seasonal labor in the west enabled some of the
province's landless villagers to acquire dwarf holdings of their
own: the number of farm plots smaller than five hectares rose
between 1882 and 1907 from 114,500 to 139,000.[15]

Despite the expansion of the peasant farming sector in
relation to that of the large estates, the province's rural population grew only slowly after 1890. Between 1890 and 1910 the
population of the province as a whole increased much less rapidly
than did that of the Prussian state, even though the birthrate
among the Poznanian Poles far exceeded the Reich average. Neither
the province's agricultural nor its urban economy could absorb
the full increments in the population's natural growth after 1870.
In the four decades before 1910, net emigration from the province
totalled 545,000, a figure which slightly exceeded the absolute
net growth of the whole provincial population in the same period.[16]

The Province of Poznań exported to the western parts of the
Empire not only rye, vodka, and sugar, but men and women as well.
That fact does not diminish the importance of the rising productivity and incomes of the province's agriculturalists in the
years after 1890. By counteracting pressures towards fragmentation of peasant landholdings and by forcing agricultural wages
slowly upward, heavy rural emigration was an important precondi-

tion of the province's agricultural prosperity in the prewar decades. The robust condition of the province's rural economy led in its turn to the rapid growth and economic development of the province's towns.

In the 1870s and 1880s, the urban population had begun to expand slowly at the expense of the countryside, while capitalist enterprises emerged in the midst of the towns' old-fashioned artisan workshops and commercial counting houses. With the passing in the 1890s of the shadow of the long depression, increased demand on the part of the farming population for capital and consumer goods; heightened demand elsewhere in the Reich for the province's agricultural products; the Prussian state's heavy investments in the colonization program, in urban building projects, and in the enlargement of the bureaucracy and military establishment--all combined to accelerate urban growth, promote industrial development, and raise urban incomes.[17]

While the town population increased 18 percent between 1871 and 1890, in the next twenty years it grew 42 percent. Because the rural population rose only 11 percent in the latter period, the urban-rural ratio shifted rapidly in those years from 29:71 to 35:65.[18] Although the population of the provincial capital rose from 69,000 in 1890 to 157,000 in 1910--part of this increase being the result of suburban annexations--most of the province's urban demographic growth occurred in its many small towns. In 1910 only one-third of its urban population lived in cities counting more than 25,000 inhabitants, of which there were only four. Migration from the countryside to the towns was so heavy that by 1907 43 percent of all town dwellers were village-born.[19]

The province's industrial development, after 1890 as before, depended on the goods supplied and required by the agricultural sector, and especially by the large estates. Not only sugar refining and liquor production but grain and timber milling, tanning and meat packing, brickworking, and manufacture of farm machinery and chemical fertilizers prospered in these years. Most of the province's corporately organized capital was invested, primarily by estate owners, in these industries, which employed many of the province's largest work forces. The construction industry also boomed, while many new firms appeared in various consumer goods industries. Between 1875 and 1907 the number of industrial enterprises employing fifty or more workers rose at a rapidly accelerating pace from 72 to 352, those employing eleven to fifty workers from 395 to 1,373, and those with six to ten workers from 511 to 1,810.[20]

Many of the smaller firms that emerged during these decades
of low-level industrialization grew out of artisan workshops
financed by savings and local bank loans and transformed by
mechanization. But many more artisan masters were driven to the
wall, if not altogether out of business, by the competition of
local and west German factory-organized production. By the eve
of the war, few artisans working with hand tools and only a few
employees could maintain their traditional place as primary
manufacturers. Those who failed to acquire power-driven machinery
and larger work forces either closed up shop and hired themselves
out as skilled wage-earners, or found themselves increasingly
dependent on small retail orders, repair work, or selling of
factory-produced goods in their own line of trade. In general,
conversion of artisan workshops into independent and modern
manufacturing operations was most difficult in the textile
crafts, clothes-making, machine building, tool-making and
most metalworking trades. It was relatively easier in construction, food processing, and wood and leather working.[21]

Between 1875 and 1907 the number of "industrial" establishments in the province employing from one to five workmen declined
absolutely by almost 25 percent. In 1875 such artisan workshops
comprised 83 percent of all manufacturing operations, but by 1907
this figure had slipped to 52 percent.[22] In the prewar years,
two-thirds of the province's artisan masters lived in villages or
in towns with populations under 5,000; 58 percent labored without
hired help while another 13 percent employed only unskilled apprentices; only about half owned the houses they lived in. Nevertheless, although the artisans had lost their central role in the
province's industrial life and lived in circumstances often little
better and sometimes worse than those of skilled laborers, they
remained a numerous and politically significant group. The census
of 1907 listed 41,000 persons self-employed in industry. A large
majority of these were artisans working without hired help.[23]

The Wilhelminian era witnessed the first stages in the formation of an industrial working class in the province of Poznań.
The number of wage-earners in industry and the artisan crafts
doubled from 61,000 to 122,000 between 1882 and 1907. More
significantly, while the number of those employed in artisan
workshops declined absolutely, workers engaged in labor forces of
six to fifty and fifty or more hands increased in equal measure
their proportions within the industrial and manufacturing working
class--from 23 percent in 1882 to 49 percent in 1907.[24] This
process of concentration underlay the emergence of these decades

of trade-union and working-class political movements. Their
growth suffered from the dispersion of the province's agriculturally
oriented industry across the countryside and among the small towns.
Here, as well as in more strictly urban industries, a high proportion of the workers were recruits from a peasantry and farm worker
class unused to political or economic resistance. But as the post-
1870 rise in real industrial wages began after 1900 to be threatened by more rapidly rising food and consumer goods prices, small-
scale strikes occurred with greater frequency. The hardships of
seasonal unemployment were compounded after 1890 by several reces-
sions. Nevertheless, the incomes and standard of living of the
skilled industrial and artisan workers, thanks in part to the
prewar strike movement, followed the upward trend of the provincial
economy in these decades.[25]

Commercial development mirrored that of industry. On the one
hand, the province's vigorous agricultural and industrial growth
promoted the expansion and prosperity of the more capital-strong
wholesale houses, especially those with good connections in the
Silesian and west German markets. Banks, both private and cooperative, flourished. So too did transport firms and the state-managed
railroads. Rising incomes and urban growth benefited old established retailers, restaurateurs, and hotel-keepers but allowed many
new entrepreneurs to join their ranks. But the concentration of
capital and business accounts among the more successful wholesale
and retail firms, as well as the expansion of the banking network,
drove many traditional brokers, lenders, and shopkeepers into
penury or out of business altogether. These trends are reflected
in the slight increase between 1882 and 1907 in the number of
those self-employed in commerce and transport (from 16,750 to
19,100) as opposed to the sizable increase of salaried employees
in private commerce (from 9,000 to 24,000) and transportation
workers (from 7,000 to 20,000).

Germanization policy combined with the growth of the cities
and towns to increase the number of middle and high-ranking state
and municipal officials. University-trained "free professionals"
such as doctors, lawyers, engineers, and journalists multiplied
and so, too, did teachers and clergymen. Prussian statistics
lumped these occupations together, but their collective increase
from 30,000 in 1882 to 51,000 in 1907 illustrates the growing
strength of these politically crucial groups.

Table 2 summarizes the occupational changes accompanying
the province's economic development from the 1880s to the prewar
years.

TABLE 2: Province of Poznań: Occupational Shifts, 1882-1907

Occupational Group	1882 Absolute Number	% All Employed	1907 Absolute Number	% All Employed	% Change 1882-1907*
A. Agriculture					
Self-employed	74,229	11.7	95,943	11.6	+12
Wage-earners	321,086	50.8	405,553	49.2	+ 8
B. Industry and Handicrafts					
Self-employed	43,183	6.8	40,928	5.0	-23
Wage-earners	60,915	9.7	122,412	14.8	+84
C. Commerce					
Self-employed	15,604	2.5	17,444	2.1	- 6
Wage-earners	8,960	1.4	24,216	3.0	+148
D. Transport					
Self-employed	1,135	0.2	1,668	0.3	+29
Wage-earners	6,861	0.8	19,935	2.4	+174
E. Household Servants and Occasional Laborers					
Wage-earners	70,915	11.3	44,915	5.4	-54
F. Officials and Professionals Salaried and Self-employed	30,466	4.8	51,284	6.2	+51
		100.0		100.0	
TOTAL A-F					
Self-employed	164,614	25.9	207.267	25.1	0
Wage-earners	468,737	74.1	617,031	74.9	+14
Total	633,351	100.0	824,298	100.0	+12
G. Rentiers and Pensioners	34,235		93,823		+156
H. Unemployed Family Members	997,447		1,046,259		-13
TOTAL A-H Provincial Population	1,665,028		1,963,480		+18

SOURCES: Die Ergebnisse der Berufszählung vom 5. Juni 1882 im preussischen Staate. Preussische Statistik, vol. 76 III (1885), table 3, p. 242; Berufs- und Betriebszählung vom 12. Juni 1907. Statistik des Deutschen Reichs, vol. 206 (1910), table 3, pp. 226-31.

*In excess of the rate of total population growth (1882-1907: + 18%).

These figures show the increases in the peasant farmers' ranks
which ran parallel to the decline during these years in the sheer
mass, if not the economic strength, of the large estates. In 1907,
over 40 percent of those the census listed as rural laborers were
members of peasant farmers' families--wives, children, siblings,
and other relatives--fully employed in working the family farm. Of
the remainder, 12 percent were wage laborers owning small holdings
of their own or deputants and cottagers residing on estate-owned
parcels. The large estates also employed 7,500 stewards, overseers, accountants, and clerks and 8,300 house servants. This
left 40,000 unmarried farm hands (10 percent) and 134,000 other
landless farm workers (33 percent). Self-employed farmers together
with their working family members comprised 52 percent of all those
occupied in agriculture in 1907. A large majority of the remaining
48 percent constituted the internally differentiated labor force
serving the large estates. These proportions illustrate the
roughly equal numerical importance of the peasant-farming and
large-estate sectors.[26]

Table 2 also illustrates the principal trends at work in the
nonagricultural sectors of the provincial economy: concentration
of ownership among the capital-strong firms in industry, commerce,
and transport; expansion of the university-trained upper bureaucracy and liberal professions; the rapid formation of a factory-
employed industrial working class; proliferation of salaried
employees in commerce; contraction in the ranks of the artisanry;
and rapid decline in the numbers of domestic servants and ill-
paid occasional laborers.

A notable rise in personal income, obliquely but accurately
mirrored in tax records, accompanied the province's economic
growth in the late nineteenth and early twentieth centuries.
The number of persons paying taxes on personal incomes in excess
of 3,000 marks annually--an income supporting a solidly bourgeois
way of life--rose between 1852 and 1875 from 2,185 to 4,904, and
between 1875 and 1911 to 23,200.[27] Dividing the population into
classes of taxpayers together with their family dependents
yields the more precise picture given in table 3.

These figures reflect an expansion of aristocratic, bourgeois,
and petty bourgeois incomes that far outstripped the inflationary
price trend of the Wilhelminian years. Although in 1910 a majority
of the population earned less than 900 marks--an income supporting
the family of an agricultural day laborer or semiskilled worker in
no great comfort--working-class incomes were rising nonetheless.
Moreover, these figures take no account of the agricultural pro-

TABLE 3:   Provincial Population according to Tax Brackets, 1896-
           1910

	Percentage of Population	
Taxed Income of	1896	1910
Over 3,000 marks	1.9	3.9
900 to 3,000 marks	17.9	33.2
Under 900 marks	80.2	62.9

SOURCE: Encyclopédie Polonaise, Vie économique de la Pologne
     prussienne (Fribourg, 1917), p. 194.

duction for home consumption of many peasants and workers raising
livestock and tilling garden plots, which yielded additions to
the family larder raising the value of their actual income above
the 900 mark level.

     Between 1901 and 1910, the state income taxes paid by the
Poznanian population rose from 3.7 to 6.4 million marks annually
--the highest proportional increase in tax revenues among all
the Prussian provinces in these years.   In the same period,
savings-bank deposits doubled.   Similarly, the number of commercial and industrial enterprises paying the Prussian business tax
(Gewerbesteuer), levied on yearly net incomes above 1,500 marks,
rose between 1903 and 1912 from 16,794 to 22,809, or by 36 percent.[28]   These and the foregoing figures and analyses show that
during the Wilhelminian era the population of the Province of
Poznań completed its passage across the threshold of agrarian
and industrial capitalism.   Although the estate owners, urban
entrepreneurs, and educated classes reaped the largest profits
from this transition, the rising incomes of farmers, small businessmen, and workers were equally crucial elements in the political
conflicts of the prewar decades.

Demographic Changes among the Nationalities, 1890-1914
     During the depression-ridden 1870s and 1880s, overseas
emigration and the Ostflucht to central and western Germany
held the growth of the province's population to its slowest
rate between 1815 and 1914.   Although each of the three nationalities contributed heavily to these emigration waves, the Poles'
high birthrate allowed their numbers at home in the province to
expand fairly rapidly at the Germans' and Jews' expense.   Absolute Jewish losses undercut the Germans' meager gains to hold
combined German-Jewish growth in these two decades to only 3 percent, while the Polish population rose 15 percent.
     Despite the launching of the colonization program to combat

these demographic trends, they persisted through the 1890s. Although overseas emigration tapered off in this decade, the Ostflucht intensified. The provincial population as a whole began
to grow more rapidly than during the preceding decades. But,
again, it was the Poles who gained most, increasing their numbers
during the 1890s by 9.5 percent. The Jews' 20 percent decline
counteracted the Germans' 4 percent gain to hold composite German-
Jewish growth to 3 percent.

Perception of the durability of these demographic patterns
favoring the Poles alarmed Prussian officials and German nationalists and contributed powerfully to the radicalization of the
state's Polenpolitik after 1898. The tempo of peasant colonization
quickened after 1900 while Oberpräsident Waldow purged the bureaucracy and state-dominated local institutions of Poles in order to
make room for Germans recruited both within and outside the
province. These measures combined with the province's economic
recovery and growth after the mid 1890s to turn demographic trends
in the province to the Germans' advantage in the decade 1900-1910.
Some 180,000 Poznanians migrated west in these years, but since
official policy and economic prosperity induced 81,000 persons from
outside the province--mostly Germans--to settle there, net emigration fell off considerably.

Between 1900 and 1905, the German population rose 7 percent;
in the next five years, 6.5 percent. On the other hand, in both
these periods, the Poles added 5 percent to their numbers, while
the Jewish population lost first 14 percent and then 13 percent
through emigration. As a result, combined German-Jewish gains
were held to 6 percent in both periods. Considering the government's great exertions on behalf of the frontier Germans, these
were very modest successes. They barely balanced German losses
in the 1890s, as table 4 illustrates.

TABLE 4:   Province of Poznań: Population Growth, 1890-1910

| | 1890 | | 1910 | | % Change |
	Number	% of Pop.	Number	% of Pop.	1890-1910
Poles	1,112,650	63.6	1,352,650	64.7	+22
Germans	594,650	33.9	720,650	34.0	+21
Jews	44,300	2.5	26,500	1.3	-40
Total	1,751,600	100.0	2,099,800	100.0	+20

SOURCE: Appendix, tables A1 and A2, below.

Despite official Germanization policies, the Poles actually
increased their proportion of the population during these years,

principally because, once again, Jewish losses cut German-Jewish
total gains. But by 1910 the Jewish population had grown so small
that it could not much longer negatively affect the German-Polish
demographic balance. Intense official intervention in the province's economic development demonstrated that the Poles' natural
demographic advantage over the Germans could be overcome. On the
other hand, by 1909 Waldow had admitted that the efficacy of his
bureaucratic tactics had reached its limit. More importantly,
for technical and political reasons the pace of official colonization began to lag after 1907.[30] It is doubtful whether the Germans' slight gains over the Poles in the decade 1900-1910 carried
over into the subsequent four prewar years. It is certain that,
without a vigorous revival of official colonization and the
launching of other massive state-sponsored German settlement programs, the German population of the province could not have shifted
permanently and decisively to the Poles' disadvantage. The Poles'
rate of natural increase--twice that of the Germans as late as
1911--was so high that they could sustain heavy losses through
the Ostflucht and still increase their population in the province
at a relatively rapid pace. The Ostflucht drained the province
not only of the Jewish urban and German Christian rural masses,
but enticed many skilled workmen, educated professionals, and
propertied burghers among the Germans and Jews to emigrate west
as well. Between the onset of the Ostflucht in the 1870s and the
eve of the war, the German-Jewish population grew by only 21
percent, the Polish population by 40 percent. The full scale of
the Germans' demographic dilemma can only be grasped by considering that, had Poznanian industrial development rivaled that of
western Germany, the whole population surplus of the Poznanian
Poles unassimilable by local agriculture would have entered the
local industrial labor force rather than gravitating, as it did
in large part, to Westphalia, Berlin, Saxony, and the Rhineland.
In that event, the Poles' demographic gains after 1890 would
have been much greater than in fact they were.[31] But by concentrating on displacing the Polish rural population through German
colonization while minimizing official support for urban industrial
development, the Prussian government simultaneously attempted to
strike at the agrarian root of Polish demographic strength and
encouraged the dispersion of the Poles' population surplus outside the province.

     In the decade after 1900, this tactic was at least partially
successful. Thanks to the colonization program, the German-speaking rural population of the province increased 11.5 percent, the

Polish villagers by only 6.5 percent. But perpetuation of this
trend required a steady commitment to intensive colonization which
the government was politically unable to maintain. As things
turned out, this decade of German rural gains merely compensated
for previous losses between 1870 and 1900.[32] Nor could the
Prussian government prevent Polish villagers from migrating to the
province's towns and taking jobs in the expanding urban industrial
and commercial sectors. In fact, one of the most striking aspects
of the province's social development after 1890 was the very rapid
expansion of the Polish urban population at the Germans' and Jews'
expense, illustrated in table 5. Between 1895 and 1910, the Polish

TABLE 5: Province of Poznań: Urban Population by Nationality,
          1895-1910

Year	Poles	Germans	Jews	Total
1895	44.5%	48.5%	7.0%	100.0%
1910	48.9%	47.6%	3.5%	100.0%

SOURCE: Lech Trzeciakowski, Walka o polskość miast pozñanskiego na
         przełomie XIX i XX wieku (Poznań, 1964), p. 217; Karol Rze-
         pecki, Ubytek żydów w Księstwie poznańskiem (Poznań, 1912),
         table A; Statistisches Jahrbuch für den preussischen Staat
         (1913), p. 21. These figures are based on official language,
         not confessional, censuses.

town population rose absolutely by 46 percent, while the Jews'
numbers fell in the same proportion. The number of Catholic and
Protestant Germans increased by 29 percent. But reckoning Jewish
losses against German gains reduced the total German-speaking increase to 23 percent. By 1910, despite the claims of the Colonization Commission and its apologists that German peasant settlement
would ensure the maintenance of the Germans' traditionally strong
positions in the province's towns, the Poles stood within an ace
of gaining a majority of the urban population.[33]

Occupational and Social Shifts among the Nationalities

        The preceding pages analyzed demographic relations among the
Poznanian nationalities after 1890 as a function, on the one hand,
of the interlocking economic development of the province and the
Reich and, on the other, of natural demographic factors, migra-
tional patterns, and official Germanization policy. A finer focus
on this problem, and a clearer view of the part each of the
nationalities played in the province's economic development, will
emerge from an analysis of the changes in the distribution and

economic strength of the nationalities in the province's principal occupational groups. Table 6 summarizes these changes as they were reflected in the censuses of 1882 and 1907.

TABLE 6: Distribution of Nationalities among Principal Occupational Groups, 1882-1907 (%)

Occupational Group	Self-Employed			Wage and Salary Earners		
	Poles	Germans	Jews [=100%]	Poles	Germans	Jews [=100%]
A. Agriculture						
1882	62.3	37.5	0.2	76.8	23.2	----
1907	62.6	37.4	----	73.4	26.6	----
B. Industry						
1882	49.8	41.8	8.4	53.5	43.8	2.7
1907	58.5	38.3	3.2	64.2	34.8	1.0
C. Commerce						
1882	29.9	26.7	43.4	36.6	33.4	30.0
1907	44.6	33.6	21.3	53.7	34.0	12.3
D. Domestic Servants and Occasional Laborers						
1882	----	----	----	70.0	29.2	0.8
1907	----	----	----	59.0	40.4	0.6
E. Public Officials and Free Professionals						
1882	39.1	58.4	2.5	----	----	----
1907	31.2	67.2	1.6	----	----	----

SOURCES: Cf. table 2, above, which gives the absolute numbers of the groups analyzed here.

The absence of any significant shifts among the self-employed agriculturalists (mostly peasant farmers) indicates that, in the highly politicized "struggle for the land," the number of new Polish farms created through private parcellation in these years

cancelled out the increase of the German peasantry brought about
by the state's colonization program. But not only did the relative proportions of Poles and Germans among the farming population
remain virtually unchanged; so too, did the amount of agricultural
land controlled by each of the two nationalities (see table 7).

TABLE 7: Estimated Distribution of Arable and Forest Land, 1913

Holding Size in Hectares	Polish	% Change 1881-1913	German	% Change 1881-1913
Over 150	568,000	-21%	755,000	-22.5%
Under 150	806,000	+23%	620,000	+54.5%
Total	1,374,500		1,374,500	

SOURCES: Eugen von Bergmann, Zur Geschichte der Entwicklung
    deutscher, polnischer und jüdischer Bevölkerung in der Provinz
    Posen seit 1824 (Tübingen, 1883), pp. 361-65; Stanisław
    Borowski, Rozwarstwienie wsi wielkopolskiej w latach 1807-1914
    (Poznań, 1862), p. 283; Vie économique de la Pologne prus-
    sienne, pp. 22, 36-37.

The shrinkage of German privately owned large holdings was greater
than these figures would suggest, since the Prussian state's extensive forest reserves and domain land actually expanded in the
prewar decades. The data on smaller holdings show that, while the
sheer number of German and Polish farmers increased in equal
measure, the Germans, typically disposing of larger savings than
the Poles and strongly supported by the Royal Commission and other
German financial institutions, bought bigger farms than the
Poles.[34]

    On the eve of the war, the nationalities were deadlocked in
their competition for landowning primacy, neither one clearly
winning or losing. But since Polish estate land was no longer
willingly offered to the Colonization Commission, further expansion of German peasant holdings depended on continued fragmentation
of German estate land, to which the state was politically opposed.
Prospective Polish buyers of peasant holdings, finding both Polish
and German estate land increasingly unavailable, were turning to
the purchase intact or parcellation of German peasant land, bidding
prices up to levels German small farmers found hard to resist.[35]
Unless the Prussian state could impose radical controls on Polish
land acquisition, it was likely in 1914 that, in the future, the
Poles would turn the balance of landholding in their favor, particularly if the post-1890 economic upswing yielded to a depression
in which land prices fell while German westward migration returned
to the levels of the 1880s and 1890s. Although the government

proposed legislation to the 1914 Landtag aimed at the stringent
curtailment of the Poles' right to buy farmland on the open
market, whether the bill would have passed into law and accomplished its purposes remain open questions.

The rural working class, in 1907 as in 1882, counted three
Poles to every German. The absolute numbers and relative proportions of German farm workers were rising, primarily because the
reservoir of cheap Polish farm servants and laborers upon which
German farms could draw in the 1880s began to dry up, forcing
the German peasants' wives and children into full-time engagement
in running the family farm.

The Polish villagers who could not be absorbed into the
agricultural labor force swelled the ranks of the burgeoning
industrial working class, increasing their proportions of this
second-largest occupational group from 53.5 percent in 1882 to
64.2 percent in 1907.[36] The Poles' advance was nearly as great
among artisan masters and industrial entrepreneurs (from 49.8 percent to 58.5 percent). Many Poles stepped into the places of
German and Jewish artisans and small manufacturers who quit the
province and migrated west, often because of having been under-
sold by Polish rivals content with lower profit margins. But
many other German workshops and factories--some of them well
established before 1890, others newly founded--prospered on a
scale seldom attained among Polish businessmen.

In 1901, 53 percent of the province's state-certified artisan
masters were Poles. But even in the government district of
Poznań--the province's more populous and more Polish half--German-
speaking artisan masters in both the towns and villages, though
a numerical minority, paid more than twice the business taxes of
their poorer Polish counterparts.[37] Polish artisans likewise
worked with fewer hired workers and with less power-driven
machinery than did the Germans. In the sphere of industry proper
--among relatively highly capitalized manufacturing enterprises
employing more than a handful of workers--the German position
after 1900 was very strong. Germans and Jews controlled two-
thirds of all capital located in such firms in the prewar decade.
They owned more than half the province's distilleries, including
all the larger ones, half the construction firms and grain mills,
60 percent of the dairies, 80 percent of the breweries, and 90
percent of the sugar refineries. Altogether, in 1907, of 1,708
urban firms employing eleven or more workers, 79 percent belonged
to Germans or Jews, only 21 percent to Poles.[38]

In commerce, nearly half of all Jewish-owned enterprises

were liquidated between 1882 and 1907. Polish commercial operations multiplied by two-thirds, German firms by 40 percent, so that
by the eve of the war the Poles had replaced the Jews as the
numerically largest group among commercial proprietors. But, as
in industry, the German and Jewish positions were financially the
strongest. Among the Jews, many owners of medium-size or large
retail and wholesale businesses not only held their ground but
prospered. In the prewar decade the provincial capital's Jewish
community, strongly engaged in commerce and the professions, paid
a quarter of the city's share of state income taxes though comprising only 4 percent of the population. A comparable situation
prevailed in most of the province's other towns, as the widespread
phenomenon of Jewish control of the first of the three municipal
voting classes attested. [39] On the other hand, far more Poles than
Germans or Jews joined the rapidly expanding ranks of commercial
employees, a group which contributed many activists to the province's nationalist movements.

State policy succeeded in increasingly notably the proportion
of Germans among public officials and professionals (from 54.4 percent to 67.2 percent). But the rise in the number of Poles engaged in these occupations signified a strengthening of the uni-
versity-educated Polish intelligentsia, particularly since in these
same years many Poles in state service were either dismissed from
their posts or transferred to positions outside the province.
Nevertheless, a large majority of Poles in this sphere comprised
state-employed workers, subaltern officials, elementary school
teachers, and Catholic clergymen. On the eve of the war the
number of Poles in the liberal professions was still small. In 1912,
58 of the provincial capital's 128 medical doctors were Poles; so,
too, were 28 of the 65 private attorneys and 4 of the 13 apothecaries. [40] But in the entire government district of Bromberg,
the Poles could muster only 47 medical doctors, 6 veterinarians,
15 apothecaries, and 13 lawyers and notaries. [41]

Just as the Poles gained most among the three nationalities
in the province's demographic growth between 1890 and the eve of
the war, increasing their proportion of the total population
slightly and their numbers in the towns very considerably, so
too did they derive the greatest collective advantage from the
province's economic expansion in the prewar decades. Not only did
Poles occupy a large majority of the tens of thousands of new
jobs which opened up in industry and commerce; among the ranks of
the province's self-employed, they increased their proportions

considerably.[42] Even as in the countryside the Poles kept pace
with the officially promoted expansion of the German landed
peasantry, in the towns the Polish middle classes grew rapidly.
Small-scale Polish-owned artisan workshops, industrial firms,
and commercial establishments sprang up at the same time that
comparable operations in German or Jewish hands were undergoing
liquidation or expansion. But while among the Poles a numerous
petite bourgeoisie was forming, the solid German and Jewish
middle classes were growing richer. The figures in table 8 offer
a clear picture of the relative strength in the prewar years of
the Polish and German-Jewish business proprietors in the province's
large and small towns. While the Germans' edge over the Poles

TABLE 8:   Urban Industrial and Commercial Employers, 1907

Number of Workers Employed	German-Speaking Employers	Polish-Speaking Employers
None	9,527	10,619
1-5	11,043	9,188
6-10	1,553	674
11-50	1,076	311
51-100	168	32
101-500	95	16
Over 500	6	4
	23,468	20,844

SOURCE: Max Broesike, "Deutsche und Polen der Provinz Posen im
    Lichte der Statistik," Zeitschrift des Königlich Statistis-
    chen Landesamts 25 (1912): 388.

among employers of five or fewer workers was slight, the large
majority of bigger employers were Germans.

        Yet the Polish middle classes were gaining not only in num-
bers but also in financial strength. Between 1895 and 1910, the
business taxes they paid increased from 18 percent to 27 percent
of the total collected in the towns of the Poznań government
district.[43] In the same years, they increased their state income tax payments by 25 percent, their payments of the tax on
estates (Vermögenssteuer) by 33 percent, and their real estate
taxes by 6 percent.[44] German and Jewish urban wealth far exceeded the Poles' even in 1910. But it was symbolic of the
broader economic trends among the nationalities after 1890 that
the Poles reaped the financial gains reflected in these tax payments during a period of advancing prosperity not only for themselves, but for the Germans and Jews as well.

7. "EACH TO HIS OWN":
   THE POLISH NATIONALIST MOVEMENT, 1890-1914

Between 1886 and 1914, the Prussian government attempted, by
a variety of more or less discriminatory and irritating measures,
to impede the demographic growth and economic development of
Polish society in Poznania. In the "struggle for the land," the
government strove to uproot the Polish gentry. This policy also
aimed, though the government did not trumpet the fact aloud, at
driving Polish rural laborers displaced by German peasant colonization off the land and so, given the limits of urban employment
in Poznania, into emigration in large numbers from their Polish
homeland. Laws and regulations sought to prevent Polish peasants
and workers from purchasing farms and plots carved from parcelled
estate land. In the towns, both the civil and military bureaucracy boycotted Polish businessmen and professionals in awarding
government contracts for goods and services. Waldow and his
lieutenants forbade soldiers and public officials to patronize
Polish restaurants and shops. Many Polish state employees were
transferred out of the province. Others failed to attain promotions or were dismissed because they did not meet the government's
increasingly "sharp demands" on their "national behavior." New
appointments to publicly funded jobs were reserved for Germans
despite the fact that Polish taxes contributed to the creation of
such positions in no small degree.[1]
     Simultaneously, the government tried to strengthen the
Poznanian Germans' economic and demographic positions through its
many programs of aid to the German Junkers, peasants, rural workers,
civil servants, and the urban middle classes. In view of these
officially conferred advantages their national rivals enjoyed and
the governmental discrimination they labored under, the Poles'
economic and demographic advances between the 1880s and the outbreak of the war appear all the more remarkable. The significance of these advances does not consist merely in the fact that
the Poles increased numerically after 1890 at the Germans' expense,
or that the Poles gained more ground than the Germans in the

"struggle for the land," or that Polish society grew richer in
relation to German society. More importantly, its economic
development in these decades strengthened the capacity of Polish
society both to oppose the government's Germanization programs
and to pursue the more positive political, social, and cultural
goals its national leaders had set for it in the course of the
nineteenth century.

By 1914, the Polish nationalist movement could count for
leadership and financial backing on a richer gentry and a more
numerous and better educated clergy than ever before. It had
gained a great many new political activists and financial supporters from the ranks of the increasingly prosperous and numerous
industrial-commercial bourgeoisie and professional intelligentsia.
The rising numbers of the petite bourgeoisie and of workers in
industry and the skilled trades provided the nationalist movement
with a burgeoning, increasingly vocal and volatile constituency
in the towns. In the villages, the peasant farmers began to
assert a political will of their own. Even the rural laborers,
less poverty-stricken than in the past, somewhat better schooled,
and, above all, stirred up by the agitation of the nationalists
and provoked by official Germanization policies, began to find
their political voices.

The Caprivi Era and the Defeat of Polish Loyalism

"I do not think it should matter whether a Prussian prays to
his God in German or Polish, whether he toasts his king in Polish
or German. . . .Today there are only two parties: the state-
supporting party of order and the state-destroying party of
revolution." Thus Józef Kościelski, leader of the Polish loyalist
movement, sought in a Landtag speech of June 1891 to persuade
Caprivi's government and the Prussian conservatives to abandon
Bismarck's radical hostility to the Polish nationalist movement
in Prussia.[2] "The existence of Poles on the eastern borders is
not what weakens Germany," Kościelski later told his no doubt
skeptical German colleagues; "rather, it is the attempt to
Germanize them. Give that up and you will immediately gain in
strength." To William II Kościelski wrote that the Prussian Poles,
if granted full civil equality and exercise of their basic
national rights, would cleave to the Hohenzollern monarchy even
if, as Kościelski could not refrain from hinting, growing
hostility between Germany and Russia should lead to war and the
establishment of an autonomous, Hapsburg-governed Polish state
in the area of Galicia, the Congress Kingdom, and the Russo-

Polish borderlands. In his Polish subjects William II could have, if he willed it, a "loyal watch on the Vistula" (<u>eine treue Wacht an der Weichsel</u>).[3]

Bismarck had driven the Polish politicians into tactical bankruptcy. The traditional national liberalism of the gentry and the ultramontanism of the Polish Catholic upper clergy and their aristocratic allies succeeded only in providing pretexts for Bismarck's anti-Polish campaigns of the 1870s and 1880s. The failure of the Poles' leaders to avert the blows Bismarck rained upon them and their countrymen produced despair in their ranks. They felt a twinge of panic as the populist movement, fired by Szymański's demands for bourgeois representation in the system of Polish political institutions, gained adherents among the townspeople. As Bismarck's days in office grew numbered, the younger members of the gentry, led by Kościelski, launched a bid for the political favor, first, of the short-lived Emperor Frederick III and then of William II. By convincing Bismarck's successors of their irrevocable commitment to Prussian citizenship and their antirevolutionary social conservatism, the Polish loyalists hoped to gain the relaxation or even annulment of official Germanization policies. This would rescue the upper classes' political prestige in the eyes of the common people and blunt the criticisms of the populists.

In need of Reichstag votes and apprehensive of war with Russia, Caprivi accepted the Polish loyalists' political support, which provided the margin of victory for several of the chancellor's military and tariff bills between 1891 and 1894. But the concessions Caprivi made to the Poles' national interests, minimal though they were, aroused bitter opposition in German nationalist and agrarian-conservative circles, contributing to Caprivi's dismissal and setting the stage for the resumption of an aggressive <u>Polenpolitik</u> under the direction of Miquel and Bülow.

Loyalism fared no better among the Poles, although Caprivi's initial concessions, and especially Stablewski's appointment as archbishop, aroused considerable enthusiasm. Even skeptical Poles found the prospect of deliverance from the official wrath Bismarck had focused upon them seductive. But as it became clear that Caprivi intended to leave the foundations of Bismarckian policy in the spheres of education, public administration, and German colonization intact, the Poles' optimism yielded to frustration and anger. The populists repudiated their early advocacy of loyalism and began to attack Kościelski and the Polish Reichstag delegation as "compromisers" and "collaborators" with the national enemy. During the Reichstag elections of 1893, in which the

issue was army expansion, Szymański and his allies assaulted
the nobility and upper clergy with unprecedented bitterness.
They charged that the Polish deputies' poorly rewarded alliance
with Caprivi strengthened the Prussian monarchy while it injured
the political interests of the Polish common people, whose still
unsophisticated national consciousness required stiffening
through militant agitation against the government. The gentry
politicians' vain and servile pursuit of official favor only misled workers and peasants about the threat the government posed
to their nationality.[4]

Paradoxically, the populists condemned the upper classes
for pursuing a policy that they had themselves urged upon the
Polish parliamentarians. In the election campaign of 1893,
Szymański and his allies agitated, noisily and sometimes violently,
for the unseating of loyalist deputies and the election of
populist tribunes. Election campaigns and parliamentary politics
should heighten national solidarity and convey the Poles' sharp
protests against official Germanization policy. But the essential
tasks lay at home, above all in the propagation of Polish culture
among the masses and the economic strengthening of the middle
classes and peasantry. The system of electoral authorities
ought to bow to populist direction and the objectives of the
Organic Work movement ought to be pursued with redoubled zeal.
To the degree that the gentry and clergy shared these goals, the
populists welcomed them as allies. Their sense of deference
towards the upper classes was acute and prevented their sporadic
political rebellions from acquiring the form of irreconcilable
class conflict. The populists, representing the still economically
weak and numerically thin Polish bourgeoisie, could not hope to
direct a nationalist movement encompassing the whole of Polish
society without benefit of the financial aid and the social and
political authority of the estate owners and priesthood.

The campaign of 1893 revealed both the populists' limitations
and the enormous influence of the established leaders over the
common people. Populist protest meetings found support in a mere
handful of towns. Only in the capital city did a populist
candidate--Szymański himself--attempt to unseat an incumbent loyalist deputy. So great was the authority of the gentry-dominated
system of electoral committees which endorsed the loyalist's re-
election that, even in the province's principal populist stronghold,
Szymański was heavily defeated. In the runoff election between the
Polish loyalist and a German candidate, the populists, bound by
the principle of national solidarity, suffered the further humili-

ation of having to support their erstwhile antagonist. After the
election, Szymański presumed to call into question Archbishop
Stablewski's independence of the Prussian government and commitment to the Polish cause. The clergy retaliated with stinging
denunciations of the populists in town and country parishes alike.
Patron Jackowski mobilized the peasantry organized in his Agricultural Circles against the populists, whom he described to his
toil-worn audiences as town-dwelling "loafers."[5] The conservative establishment lumped Szymański and his allies, despite their
vehement antisocialism, together with the handful of Polish and
German Marxists attempting to organize the province's urban workers
in the early 1890s.

In the face of the traditional leadership's assault upon
them, the populists retreated into their editorial offices, professional clubs, and singing and gymnastic societies to ponder their
next political moves. Though defeated on the issue of loyalism--
the Polish Reichstag delegation, duly reelected, returned to
Berlin to vote for Caprivi's army bill--nevertheless the populists
had gained urban support and a clearer ideological perspective
from the internecine political strife of 1893-94.[6]

In the spring of 1894, after Kościelski and his colleagues
in the Reichstag had helped vote Caprivi's highly controversial
commercial treaty with Russia into law, both the Poles and the
Prussian government resigned from further political collaboration.
Among the Poles an influential minority of gentry and clerical
politicians had been critical of loyalism from the start, demanding
full restoration of the Polish language in public education and
abolition of the colonization program as pledges of the government's seriousness in accepting the Poles' parliamentary support.
As Caprivi's concessions grew more marginal and as the populists
attempted to use the issue of loyalism to drive the upper classes
onto the defensive, the voices of this minority group gained in
authority. Finally, the loyalist politicians suffered a decisive
blow when their support of Caprivi's antiagrarian commercial
policy, whose capstone was the Russian agreement of 1894, was denounced by the Polish landlords.[7]

Kościelski's resignation of his Reichstag seat symbolized the
Polish Reichstag delegation's passage into opposition. Loyalism
had failed the Poles because its means contradicted its ends: the
goals of liberal-democratic civil equality and national toleration could not be attained by appeals for monarchical favor based
on antirevolutionary aristocratic-clerical conservatism when
Prussian conservatism itself repudiated those goals. Nor could

the Polish gentry hope to maintain their political authority and ward off challenges from below by pursuing a parliamentary tactic requiring support of reduced agricultural duties which would undercut their own still-shaky economic base.

The Prussian government's resumption of an aggressive Polenpolitik after 1894, and especially the unprecedentedly radical initiatives of Bülow's regime in this sphere, confronted the Poles with an acute political crisis. Recasting of official Polish policy as a component, not merely of Prussian and Reich-level Sammlungspolitik, but of the imperial governing class's völkisch-hued imperialism magnified the symbolic character of the Polish question as an issue of domestic German politics. The more intense the domestic German political pressures became which impelled the Prussian monarchy towards a policy of conservative reaction and social imperialism, the harsher official Polish policy could be expected to become. If, under these circumstances, the Poles' parliamentary spokesmen joined forces with the German left-wing opposition, they exposed the community they represented to heavier German nationalist reprisals. But as long as the Prussian government had no need of Polish votes, as was the case in the period 1894-1909, any effort on the Poles' part to solidarize with the monarchy on conservative principles would fail because of the increasingly vital role of anti-Polish nationalism in official ideology and practice.

The Polish upper classes found themselves helpless to prevent by conservative tactics the radicalization of offical Polenpolitik after 1894. Yet at the same time they were isolated by their own social conservatism from the liberal and socialist German opposition to William II's regime, which in any case could do nothing in the short run to relieve the Poles' dilemma. Consequently, within Polish society the center of political gravity shifted away from parliamentary questions to the problem of organizing national resistance on the local level. In this sphere, the conservative gentry and clergy found themselves pitted against the increasingly effective competition not only of the populists, whose ranks swelled from year to year as the Polish bourgeoisie grew in wealth and numbers; they also faced a powerful new movement which ultimately swallowed up the older populist tradition and, in its bid for political control of Polish nationalism in Prussia, drove the traditional aristocratic leadership entirely onto the defensive.

The Rise of the National Democrats

In the 1880s, in Russian Poland and among Polish political émigrés in western Europe, the Polish revolutionary movement, dormant since 1864, revived. Sharply critical of the socially conservative Tri-loyalism espoused during the 1870s and 1880s by the aristocratic politicians in Kraków, Warsaw, and Poznań, this new generation of Polish revolutionaries drew its inspiration both from nineteenth-century Polish democratic tradition and from revolutionary Russian populism, Marxism, and Western European anarchism. Its agitation for restoration of an independent Polish state rested on revolutionary appeals to the Polish common people aimed not only against the partition regimes, but also against the Polish nobility and their allies who, to preserve their social privileges, had repudiated national independence and were seeking partnership with the Russian, Austrian, and German ruling classes.

This attack made a powerful impression on the educated Polish youth of the 1880s and 1890s. Even when they did not fully share its social-revolutionary implications, it helped to justify their rejection of the ineffectual conservatism of the aristocracy and upper clergy, to focus their protest against the increasingly menacing policies of Russification and Germanization aimed against Polish society from Petersburg and Berlin, and to frame their own hopes of national independence. Among the sons and daughters of the bourgeoisie, the liberal intelligentsia, and the lesser nobility, a minority embraced the cause of proletarian revolution. A larger number responded by radicalizing the tradition of "positivistic" liberalism and Organic Work. Their program called for the elimination of the anachronistic, caste-bound aristocracy from the leadership of Polish society and its replacement by an economically vigorous, scientifically minded middle class who would take in hand--illegally if necessary--the political and economic organization of the workers and peasants under the banners of democratic nationalism. Condemning all political and economic dependence on the partition regimes, they sought to concentrate and strengthen Polish society within itself. They focused especially on the development of an autonomous Polish industrial and commercial bourgeoisie, a numerous secular intelligentsia without aristocratic pretensions, a prosperous, nationally militant peasantry, and an industrial working class organized along national lines. What distinguished this generation of Polish nationalists from their nineteenth-century predecessors was their keener, more aggressive, and secularly defined political sense. They accepted and welcomed, particularly in the years prior to

the outbreak of the Russian revolution of 1905, a fundamental
struggle with the clerical-conservative aristocracy for political
leadership within Polish society even as they preached a sharp
hostility to the partition regimes, the Jews, and the Marxist
revolutionary movement. They did not seek to ignite an uprising
aiming at national liberation. But, unlike the Tri-loyalists and
earlier advocates of Organic Work, they placed the ideal of
national independence in the foreground of their propaganda in
an effort to draw Polish society away from accommodation with the
partition powers and prepare it for the day when international
developments would make a Polish restoration possible.

These ideas attained their authoritative formulation in the
pre-1914 writings of Roman Dmowski (1864-1939). They furnished
the ideological basis for the National Democratic movement, whose
beginnings date from the secret Liga Narodowa (National League)
which Dmowski and his allies in Russian Poland organized in 1893.
After the turn of the century, in each of the three partition
areas powerful National Democratic parties emerged whose broad
strategies were formulated and coordinated by the three parties'
collective leadership acting through the League, which successfully maintained its clandestine existence throughout the prewar
years. National Democratic organization reflected the movement's
aspiration, proclaimed in the title of Dmowski's journal, Przegląd
Wszechpolski [Pan-Polish Review], to the leadership of all Polish
society across the boundaries of the partition regimes.[8]

In Prussian Poland, Dmowski's ideas fell on fertile soil.
Independent of his influence, the younger generation of university-
educated professionals had begun to collaborate with liberal-
minded sons of the gentry in publishing between 1894 and 1896 the
Przegląd Poznański [Poznań Review]. Pronouncing the strategy
of loyalism oriented towards parliamentary action in Berlin
bankrupt, it urged the upper classes to concentrate on nationalist
agitation among the common people. Success in that enterprise
required cooperation with Szymański and the populists, not their
anathematization. In 1896, Dmowski conferred with the Przegląd
Poznański group. Several years later, between 1899 and 1901,
the League enrolled its first members from Prussian Poland. This
inner circle, whose numbers slowly expanded in the following years,
set to work preparing the ground in Poznania, West Prussia, and
Upper Silesia for the organization of a formally constituted
National Democratic Party.[9]

In Poznań, the headquarters of the new movement, the National
Democrats at first comprised no more than a handful of well-

educated, polished agitators. The political impulses of the
Polish shopkeepers, artisans, and urban workers had all too frequently found expression in crude xenophobia, anti-Semitism, and
antiaristocratic, anticlerical sloganeering which the upper classes
had little difficulty in discrediting. But the debacle of loyalism
and the radicalizing impact, demonstrated in the school strikes, of
Prussian Polenpolitik on Polish public opinion rendered the traditional politics of the upper classes obsolete. To win popular
support and respect, the gentry and clergy needed to adopt a more
radical and uncompromising nationalist vocabulary and strengthen
their ties with the bourgeoisie and common people.

To the populists, the National Democrats offered prestigious,
articulate leadership and an ideology which, though it accepted
the primacy of the educated and propertied classes, regarded the
common people as the center of gravity of Polish society, their
material welfare and nationalist self-awareness as the chief objects of political action. To the gentry and their clerical allies, the National Democrats proposed a vigorous agitation among
the workers and peasants. Although it would require some economic
concessions to them, it would exempt the large estate system and
the church from radical criticism while concentrating on countering Germanization threats, strengthening Organic Work institutions, and involving the common people more intensively in the system of electoral authorities.

Having staked out their ground between the two principal
Polish political camps, the National Democrats quickly gained con-
verts from both sides. They recruited almost the whole of the
younger generation of the rapidly growing professional and commercial-industrial middle class, upon whom the unsophisticated provincialism of the old populist movement exercised little attraction. To a lesser degree the National Democrats also won the
support of the younger middle gentry, whose scientific education,
economic self-confidence, and awareness of the political isolation of the magnates and old-fashioned nobility made them receptive
to the new movement. Many young priests found the National
Democrats' concern for the nationalist fervor of the common people
complementary to their own interest in maintaining Polish Catholic
religiosity.[10]

The National Democrats scored their first public success in
1901 when, with the support of Szymański's populists, the ND
leader Bernard Chrzanowski won a Reichstag by-election in the
city of Poznań. The radicalization Bülow's Polenpolitik produced
among Polish political activists came to light in the nomination

through the system of electoral authorities and subsequent vic-
tories in the general Reichstag elections of 1903 of seven Polish
deputies representing populist, National Democratic, and "progressive szlachta" opinion. The antipopulist clerical conservatives
salvaged only five seats of their previous near-monopoly. By 1904
the Poznanian National Democrats had grown numerous enough to form
a secret organization among themselves, complete with a formal
program stressing their Pan-Polish and independence-oriented brand
of elitist populism.[11] In the following year, the aristocratic
old guard, led by Kościelski, staged a counteroffensive against
the rising influence of the National Democrats. Under Kościelski's
leadership, an organization called Straż [The Sentinel] appeared,
intended as a nonpartisan amalgamation at the local, county, and
provincial level of Polish nationalist activists for agitational
and organizational purposes not already met by the network of
Organic Work institutions. National Democrats had become so
prominent in the circles Straż aimed to organize that they quickly
captured the new society's leadership. Defeated, the conservative
gentry withdrew their support. This, together with Archbishop
Stablewski's ban on priestly membership, prevented Straż from fulfilling its projected role.[12]

In 1906, Szymański agreed to a formal merger with the National
Democrats. He sold his populist newspapers, chief among them
Orędownik, to a newly formed publishing company in which National
Democratic notables held a controlling interest. While Szymański
continued to edit Orędownik until his death in 1908, he agreed to
tailor his policy to that of a new daily, the Kuryer Poznański,
edited by Marian Seyda, the National Democrats' chief ideologist in
Prussian Poland. Henceforth, the Kuryer, addressing the educated
middle and upper classes, represented authoritative ND positions,
which Orędownik and the provincial populist press translated into
their accustomed homely, often scurrilous idiom. Szymański's
earlier doubts about the National Democrats, focusing upon what he
feared were secretly cultivated revolutionary tendencies, were
dispelled by Dmowski's opposition to Polish efforts to launch
either a socialist revolution or a national breakaway from Tsarist
rule during the Russian revolution of 1905. In driving the National Democrats in Russian Poland towards the aristocratic and
clerical right, that upheaval hastened the Prussian ND's open
commitment to the strictly legal tactics which had acquired dog-
matic validity among the Prussian Poles since the revolution of
1848.[13]

That commitment came to light during the Poznanian school
strikes of 1906-7. In response to the first wave of sporadic,

locally inspired strikes, the National Democrats took the lead
among exasperated parents and local Polish notables, provincial
populists, and nationally minded priests in systematically propagating a general school strike throughout the province of Poznań.
Like their allies, the National Democrats hoped massive protest
would reverse Prussian school policy. At the same time, they welcomed this highly favorable opportunity to fan popular opposition
to the Prussian regime and channel it into heightened mass support
for the ND movement. But even as they encouraged the strike,
they took care to represent it as a legal protest against a viola-
tion of Polish society's rights not only as they were defined by
the church but as they were guaranteed--although ultimately the
Prussian courts held differently--under Prussian-German constitutional law.[14]

The Reichstag election of 1907 revealed the National Democrats'
success, during the embittered Bülow era, in taking command of
Polish nationalist protest and subordinating populist and
"progressive szlachta" opinion to their own movement. Of eleven
Polish deputies elected from Poznania, seven were ND spokesmen or
sympathizers, two were anticollaborationist (but also anti-ND)
conservatives, while only two were clerical conservatives willing
to speak up for "compromise" with the government if the opportunity for it somehow arose.[15]

The Expropriation Act and anti-Polish "muzzle paragraph" of
1908 put new wind in the National Democrats' sails, even though
the government justified these measures in no small part by the
"menace to state security" posed by the emergence of the Polish
"democratic party." The parliamentary speeches of the conservative Polish deputies appealed to Frederick William III's promises
of 1815, to the Germans' respect for civil equality, to the Poles'
innate conservatism and desire "to live, work, and die" within the
bounds of the Prussian state, to the "divine world-plan" which
decreed the free development of all nationalities. But their
words, high-minded and pathetic though they were, fell on the deaf
ears of Bülow's Reichstag majority and the Landtag cartel.[16]
The desperate efforts of the Polish aristocracy to exploit their
connections at court and among the conservative Junkers to bring
about a withdrawal of the anti-Polish initiatives or their defeat
in the Bundesrat and Herrenhaus came to nothing.[17] Meanwhile, the
National Democratic deputies contented themselves with sharp protests against the unconstitutionality of the exceptional laws,
admonitions that Polish loyalty could only follow from civil
equality and freedom, and taunting references to the restoration

of Polish statehood sometime in the future. "Dreams are free'"
Chrzanowski said, quoting Bülow himself, but adding that their
national aspirations in no way prevented the Poles from fulfilling
their duties as Prussian citizens.[18]

The National Democrats' chief response to the anti-Polish
laws of 1908 occurred not in Berlin, but in the Poznanian towns
and villages. As at the time of the general school strike, so
also now they organized and mobilized popular indignation, staging numerous protest meetings and strengthening their reputation
as the common people's most energetic and militant national
tribunes. In 1909, in the aftermath of this agitational campaign,
the National Democrats felt sure enough of their strength to
organize themselves publicly as a formal party, registered from
1910 as the Towarzystwo Demokratyczno-Narodowe [Democratic-
National Society--TDN] but popularly referred to as National
Democracy (endecja). Although this step represented the logical
culmination of their efforts since the late 1890s, it drew heavy
criticism from the conservative camp, which accused the TDN of
violating the sacrosanct principle of national solidarity by
dividing Polish society into warring parties. Sensitive to the
charge, the National Democrats affirmed their solidarity with
Polish society in its relations with the state and the German
population but insisted on clear-cut political organization and
debate among the Poles themselves.[19]

Public marshaling of the National Democrats' forces acted as
a counterweight to the reemergence during 1909 of "compromising"
tendencies among the Polish conservatives. In the Reichstag, the
Polish delegation had the satisfaction that year of casting the
deciding votes in the defeat of Bülow's proposed financial
reforms and so of assisting the Conservatives and Catholic
Centrists in driving him from office. The Poles then joined the
"blue-black bloc" in ratifying Bethmann Hollweg's tax program
favoring agrarian interests. Further collaboration with Bethmann's regime promised the Poles protection against expropriation
and new anti-Polish legislation. The Polish conservatives leapt
at this prospect, especially since it coincided with their own
economic interests. For the National Democrats, the decision to
compromise with Bethmann was harder to make. To maintain good
relations with the Catholic Centrists required the Poles to soft-
pedal their campaign against the Center's traditional dominance
in Polish Upper Silesia. This contradicted the National Democrats' "Pan-Polish" strategy of rallying all Prussia's Polish-
speaking population under their nationalist banners. Moreover,

while challenging Center control over Polish voters would not
alter the Catholic party's principled opposition to anti-Polish
exceptional laws, tactical cooperation with the German Conservatives in the Reichstag would not dissolve the Junkers' motives for
continuing to support the Prussian government's Germanization
policies.   Nor did Bethmann himself hold out any promises of
fundamental changes in those policies.   On the other hand, the
TDN's endorsement of "compromise" would require muting of its
antigovernmental agitation and solidarity at home with its conservative Polish rivals.   To maintain a free hand in canvassing
Polish mass support at the Center's and the Polish conservatives'
expense, the National Democrats finally decided in 1909-10 to
persevere in what they called their "sharp policy" of nationalist
protest and self-sufficiency.[20]

This decision not only antagonized the Polish conservatives,
who denounced the TDN's "negativism" as a politique du pire; it
provoked desertions from the National Democrats' own ranks of
prominent politicians whose assessment of the prospects of "compromise" was more sanguine than that of the movement's leaders.[21]
In Poznania, the conservatives attempted to drive the TDN onto
the defensive through the formation in 1910 of the Związek Narodowy
[National Union] a gentry-dominated political party which tried
to drum up bourgeois support.   An adjunct called the Stronnictwo
Ludowe [Populist Party] sought petit bourgeois and working-class
backing.   In 1911, the estate owners organized themselves in the
Kasyno Obywatelskie [Citizens' Casino], a political club coordinating the conservatives' policy towards the government and their
ND opponents.[22]   Election campaigns grew more bitter as conservatives and National Democrats sought to pack the Polish parliamentary delegations with their own supporters.   The TDN staged a
"secession" in a Reichstag by-election of 1910 in the city of
Poznań, urging Polish voters to ignore the "official" candidate,
whose nomination had been approved by the conservative-controlled
provincial electoral committee, in favor of an "illegal" ND
candidate.   The voters followed the TDN's lead, ratifying the
first successful revolt against the directors of the Polish
electoral authorities since the system's establishment.   A compromise negotiated between the TDN and the Kasyno Obywatelskie
over distribution of nominations in the general Reichstag elections of 1912 did not prevent the conservatives from staging an
unsuccessful "secession" of their own.   Altogether, ND spokesmen
and sympathizers captured six of the province's eleven Polish
Reichstag seats in 1912, while only three declared collaboration-
ists were returned.[23]

The government's exercise of its expropriation powers in
the fall of 1912 played directly into the National Democrats'
hands. Not only did this incident present them with a splendid
opportunity for staging massive protest rallies; it also dashed
the hopes of all but the most doctrinaire conservatives that
compromise with Bethmann's regime would shield the Poles from
Hakatistic assaults. Schwartzkopff's attempt on the occasion of
the Imperial banquet of 1913 to rally the Polish conservatives
around the monarch ended in a fiasco. The authoritative conservative press organ, the Dziennik Poznański, repudiated the
strategy, if not the patriotic intentions, of the handful of
aristocratic "castle-goers." In the elections of 1913 to the
Prussian Landtag, hitherto a bastion of Polish conservative
strength thanks to the disproportionate weight of estate owners'
votes under the three-class franchise, the National Democrats
reaped the rewards of their anticollaborationist stand in the
election of three ND party-members. In 1914 popular indignation
with Schwartzkopff's Polish collaborators, picked up and amplified
by ND propaganda, forced the resignation from the provincial
electoral committee of two important executive officers whose
places were taken by National Democrats.[24] On the eve of the
war, control of the political institutions and parliamentary
strategies of the Poznanian Poles was slipping from conservative
hands. The National Democrats, who had wagered on the irrevers-
ibility of Bismarckian Polenpolitik and the receptivity of Polish
society to their own nationalist militance, were collecting on
their bets.

The Balance of Political Power
within Polish Society on the Eve of World War I

The Poznanian National Democrats' swift rise from the obscurity of their turn-of-the-century drawing-room and university politics to command of a formidable movement standing in 1914
at center stage in Polish political life dazzled and alarmed both
their Polish and their German opponents. The National Democrats
seemed to embody a will to power whose juggernaut course would
not stop short of dictatorial control of Polish nationalism in
Prussia, a goal which--at least in Poznania--they appeared on
the verge of attaining when the war broke out. Since then both
German and Polish historians have painted a similar picture of
the TDN's tendencies and prewar strength.[25] Yet closer analysis
of Polish political life in the prewar years reveals that the
National Democrats were obliged to share power with influential
and well-entrenched rivals. In their ascent the National

Democrats made fundamental concessions to their opponents'
economic and ideological interests which in important respects
strengthened the hand of the traditional leaders of Polish society.
These concessions would have been unnecessary if the National
Democrats had aimed to drive their aristocratic and clerical rivals
from the field of politics altogether. But that was not their intention. They sought instead to force the conservatives into an
alliance whose object was to heighten, according to ND prescriptions, both the common people's national loyalty and their acceptance of upper-class leadership. The measure of the National
Democrats' success will lie, therefore, not only in their strength
as an organized movement but also in the degree to which they imposed their own ideas and strategies upon the gentry and clergy.

Even after its organization in 1909 as a proper political
party, the National Democratic movement rested in the hands of a
relatively small number of activists. In 1912, the National
Democratic Society claimed 500 active members, most of them
residents of the province of Poznań. But at the party's annual
assembly of 1911 only 150 appeared. Karol Rzepecki, the TDN's
chief organizer, claimed its ranks numbered educated professionals,
merchants, manufacturers and artisan masters, workers, and landowners and peasants in roughly equal proportions.[26] This was the
social composition the TDN wished to have. But among 80 persons
identifiable by name and occupation as ND activists in the period
1911-14, 47 percent were journalists, writers, physicians, and
lawyers--in other words, members of the professional intelligentsia. Another 28 percent were businessmen and artisan masters,
while 14 percent were large landowners and priests. No peasants
turned up in the press or police records as ND spokesmen. In the
remaining 11 percent, trade union officials outnumbered industrial
workers. If this sample is representative, three-quarters of the
movement's organizers and leaders were drawn from the propertied
and educated middle classes.[27]

During the Wilhelminian years, the system of Organic Work
institutions flourished. The record of the Polish cooperative
banking network was particularly impressive. Between 1890 and
1914, the number of local banks rose from 71 to 208, membership
from 26,553 to 129,448, deposits from 12,530,000 to 271,000,000
marks.[28] The Society for Popular Libraries (TCL) increased the
number of its local lending institutions in these years from 1,000
to 1,662, so that by 1914 the average library counted five to six
hundred borrowers and several thousand volumes.[29] The Polish

Scholarship Fund (TPN) could by 1913 draw on the interest of
nearly two million marks to support the secondary and advanced
education of 500 students annually.[30] National Democrats came
to figure prominently among the leaders and organizers of these
important institutions. But, as in the past, the clergy played
a major administrative role while the gentry remained the chief
financiers of both the TCL and TPN. Given the nature of the
purposes they served, these organizations were unsuitable as
vehicles for the extension of the National Democrats' influence,
even had the ND position within them been stronger than it was.

Other Organic Work institutions the National Democrats succeeded in capturing. ND notables took control of the Sokół
gymnastic movement, which in 1910 counted 40 locals and some 800
regular participants.[31] The National Democrats won over the
artisan-dominated "industrial societies" and the merchants' and
commercial employees' associations, of which on the eve of the
war there were altogether 261 with a combined membership of over
14,000.[32] Yet another ND stronghold was the Polish trade-union
system (Zjednoczenie Zawodowe Polskie--ZZP), established by ND
organizers in the years after 1901 to provide Polish workers in
Poznania and West Prussia, Upper Silesia, and the Ruhr valley
with an alternative to the German Socialist Free Trade Unions.
In this goal the ZZP's founders were largely successful, particularly in Poznania where by 1913 the Polish unions had recruited
approximately 12,000 members, a third of them from the building
trades.[33] These organizations--from the Sokół to the ZZP--the
TDN could count on to support its policies and candidates for
office. From their ranks a certain number of TDN members and
activists arose, just as through them the National Democrats
radiated their influence outward into society. Still, these associations had their own purposes independent of the TDN and very
few of their members took many pains to agitate on its behalf.[34]

The National Democrats played a major part in organizing and
providing speakers for the innumerable mass meetings held after
the turn of the century in protest against the successive escala-
tions of official Polenpolitik. Yet these meetings were normally
staged under the auspices of the local electoral authorities and
were occasions for displays of national solidarity and antigovernmental outrage rather than ND partisanship. While the National
Democrats' conspicuous roles in these protest meetings undoubtedly
earned the TDN popular support, it sought to amplify this through
mass meetings, of which there were fifteen in the three years 1911-
13, specifically devoted to advertising its own accomplishments
and ideology.

Still more crucial to ND propaganda was the press. By 1914 the Kuryer Poznański had reached a daily circulation of over 7,000, the Orędownik over 11,000. The National Democrats had also acquired the old anti-Semitic populist daily Postęp [Progress], whose prewar circulation rivaled the Kuryer's. Four well-established provincial ND dailies supplemented those of the capital city, while the magazines published by the Organic Work associations close to the TDN spread its message as well. Altogether, the National Democrats' daily and periodical press must have attained a circulation of 50,000 or more by 1914.[35]

In little more than a decade, the hard organizational work of the several dozen activists who formed the inner nucleus of the ND movement had raised a solid and elaborate, if not all-encompassing, structure alongside the system of electoral authorities and Organic Work institutions. The Polish conservatives, strongly entrenched in both those spheres, showed little inclination or talent for combatting the National Democrats openly on the field of party politics. While the Kasyno Obywatelskie proved its value in crystallizing the conservative gentry's strategies in provincial and parliamentary politics, it remained a private political club. The conservatives' efforts to organize the intelligentsia and bourgeoisie in the Związek Narodowy and the common people in the Stronnictwo Ludowe fizzled because of half-hearted leadership and the negativism of a propaganda consisting mostly of attacks on the TDN.[36] Among themselves, the gentry were a well-disciplined phalanx. While some one hundred stiff-necked conservatives belonged to the Kasyno, nearly all the province's Polish estate owners had by 1914 joined the Central Economic Society (CTG). Although an agronomic society, the CTG forcefully voiced its members' social and political claims through its influential and outspokenly conservative leadership.[37] By the eve of the war, sympathy for the ND movement had dwindled among the landlords. The TDN's attempt, in the aftermath of expropriation and the Imperial banquet of 1913, to organize its estate-owning supporters publicly in the Centrum Obywatelskie [Citizens' Center] yielded only fifty signatures on the stillborn party's founding manifesto.[38] Most of the gentry subscribed to the anti-ND, guardedly "collaborationist" and socially conservative views expressed by the dignified Dziennik Poznański. Its daily circulation of about 3,000 in the prewar years indicates that traditional conservatism did not lack support among the intelligentsia and educated middle classes.[39]

The tradition of gentry leadership of the landed peasantry which "Patron" Jackowski had founded survived his death in 1905.

Well-funded CTG organizers extended the system of "agricultural circles" (kółka rolnicze). By the end of 1913, Jackowski's successor could report the existence of nearly 350 active circles with a combined membership of 14,500, or almost two-thirds of the province's self-sufficient peasant farmers. At circle meetings and in the association's journal, the identity of peasant and gentry economic interests and the political primacy within Polish society of the farmers, great and small, formed an ideological leitmotiv agreeable to the prosperous peasantry's ears.[40]

In the circle system, the conservatives possessed a powerful bloc of popular support. While they could boast of no such organized following in the towns, an influential minority of businessmen and professionals joined them in their opposition to the National Democrats. Similarly, the old-established clerical-conservative populist press maintained a readership rivaling that of Orędownik and Postęp even as it sharply attacked the TDN and sang the gentry's praises.[41]

The Catholic clergy's role in organizing the common people complicated the political confrontation between conservatives and National Democrats. In reminding the villagers and town workers of their "holy obligation" to vote according to the electoral authorities' instructions, to join and support the institutions of Organic Work, and to honor the concept of Polish Catholic national solidarity, the clergy clearly served conservative interests to the degree that control of Polish politics rested in the gentry's hands. But as the National Democrats gained influence within the system of electoral authorities, the clergy were obliged by their own principles of "legality" to recommend support of ND candidates. While a few priests became ardent supporters of the ND movement, Bishop Likowski denounced it in an archdiocesan assembly of 1908 as "a branch of a subversive party in Warsaw." The bishop warned the clergy, forbidden since Stablewski's 1905 ban on priestly membership in political parties to join the TDN's ranks, not to subscribe to the local ND press.[42]

The church hierarchy's hostility to the National Democrats harmonized with the sentiments of many parish priests, especially in the countryside and small towns. After 1909, an important segment of the clergy, led by Likowski himself, supported the conservatives in their polemics with the TDN. A small number of priests maintained secret membership in the ND movement, but most of the lower clergy were loath to embroil themselves in the controversies stirred up by the rise of the National Democrats. Endorsing the "legal" candidates during elections whether they were

National Democrats or not, these priests concentrated on strengthening the common people's religiosity and national consciousness
through organizations and a press which together formed a growing
bloc of what might be called clerical populism distinct both from
gentry conservatism and National Democracy.

This orientation manifested itself in the Union of Polish
Catholic Workers' Societies (Związek Katolickich Towarzystw Robotników Polskich--ZKTRP), a network of mutual-aid and social clubs
built up by the clergy, primarily among the rural workers, in the
years after 1891. Originally inspired by Leo XIII's call for
priestly involvement in the secular lives of the working class,
these associations multiplied rapidly in the politically agitated
decade prior to the war, until by 1914 they numbered 271 with a
total membership of 31,140. Although even then they comprised only
a minority of the rural workers, they represented the single
largest occupational association in Polish society. Under firm
priestly control, these societies recruited lay leaders from
the membership and so provided the farm laborers and small-holding
peasants and workers with the first organization they could regard
as their own in any sense. The Union's clerical leaders undertook
to represent its members' economic interests to the estate owners
in biannual conferences with the CTG. Although, predictably
enough, the gentry conceded little in these negotiations, and
while Prussian law prevented the Union from threatening to strike,
the ZKTRP still represented an important first step towards
rural unionization.[43]

The ideology animating the ZKTRP and its weekly journal
(Robotnik [The Worker]) stressed the working class's significance in the Polish nationalist movement and the legitimacy of
its economic demands. It did not abandon the overarching ideal of
national solidarity with its rejection of class struggle. A similar message reached an even broader mass audience through the
Przewodnik Katolicki [Catholic Guide], a cheap, skillfully written
popular weekly published from 1895 under the archdiocese's auspices. Here, too, the Polish common people found themselves encouraged to value their own political importance and to bestir
themselves in political life, especially in legal protest against
the state's Germanization policies. By 1904, the Przewodnik's
circulation reached 64,000; a decade later, it was undoubtedly
considerably higher. The Przewodnik and the ZKTRP's Robotnik
together formed the single largest ideological bloc within the
province's Polish press. After 1890 the clergy, apprehensive of
their parishioners' susceptibility to socialism, Germanization, and

secularization, had ceased relying on automatic obedience in the
political realm and instead began actively indoctrinating the
Polish workers and common people with a popular nationalist
Catholicism. The result by 1914 was that the priestly nationalists and their followers had become an important independent
force which neither the conservative nor the ND camp could afford
to antagonize or ignore.[44]

The national Democrats, speaking mainly for the more
secularized and class-conscious Polish burghers and urban workers,
thus were only one among three major ideological blocs within
Polish society. Opposed to their well organized and vigorous
party stood the economic strength, social prestige, and traditional political preeminence of the gentry, tightly organized
among themselves and commanding an agrarian-conservative movement
supported not only by the landed peasantry but also by a majority
of the rural workers who, on the clergy's instructions, obediently
followed their local squires' lead.[45] The conservatives occupied
a powerful position within the system of electoral authorities,
which through the years they had come to regard as the equivalent
of their own party structure. In the upper clergy and among the
local priesthood they counted powerful allies whose own institutional base was more widely ramified and highly respected than any
other in Polish society. Polish religiosity thus tended to
strengthen the agrarian conservatives' political hand. To the
degree that Catholic populism drew upon that religiosity to
strengthen the common people's national consciousness and inhibit
the spread of secular ideologies, it heightened Polish national
solidarity. It also forced the ideologically more well-defined
ND and conservative camps to formulate realistic bids for the
allegiance of the increasingly politicized but still strongly
Catholic rural workers.

The emergence and consolidation of these three camps ac-
corded with the economic development of Polish society in the prewar decades. The ND movement drew strength from the growth and
enrichment of the bourgeois intelligentsia, the industrial-commercial and white-collar middle classes, and the skilled urban
working class. But the agrarian conservatives profited greatly
from the wave of agricultural prosperity of the years after 1896
upon whose crest the Poznanian urban economy was swept forward.
In 1914 the National Democrats had no reason to anticipate the
imminent replacement within Polish society of agrarian economic
predominance by that of urban industry and commerce. On the
contrary, the towns could be expected to remain economically

dependent on the farming community for years to come. At the
same time, it was capitalist development in both the towns and the
countryside which underlay the crystallization of working-class
political movements. And, while the National Democrats counted
on the support of the urban trade-union movement (ZZP) and might
hope that the rural workers organized in the ZKTRP would prefer ND
candidates to rigid aristocratic conservatives, nevertheless class-
based worker organization posed a long-term threat to the urban
middle classes no less than to the aristocratic-clerical camp.

These circumstances forced the National Democrats into a
complex ideological and tactical balancing act. Capturing the
loyalties of the educated and propertied middle classes and self-
employed petite bourgeoisie could at best have won them the status
of junior partners to the agrarian conservatives. Hence the
TDN's bid for the urban workers' backing through appeals to their
class interests and national sensibilities--a safe enough tactic so
long as it directed Polish working-class opposition against German
employers. But already before 1914 the ZZP had begun to organize
and strike against Polish employers, trapping the TDN occasionally
in a dangerous cross fire.[46] In any event, the TDN could not rest
content with urban support but, in view of the still primarily
agrarian character of Polish society in Poznania, required peasant
and rural worker backing as well.[47] That was impossible to win
against the determined resistance of the village clergy. The TDN
had to trim its sails to suit the church. It also had to show
itself friendly to the landed peasantry's and the estate owners'
economic interests, not only because any other course would have
been politically self-defeating but also because the Polish
bourgeoisie vitally depended on the economic strength and patronage of the countryside.

To overcome these obstacles, the National Democrats followed
the classic nationalist strategy. Minimizing divisive issues
within Polish society, they concentrated their fire on the enemy
beyond the gates--on the Prussian government and the manifold
threats of Germanization. Claiming to represent the people's will
to liberation from national oppression, they sought to gain control
of Polish politics, not through a frontal assault on their conservative rivals' social privileges or traditional political and cultural prestige, but through attacks on their capacity to conduct
Polish society's national defense, attacks which did not shrink
from insinuations of treason. In the years before 1909, the
National Democrats found encouragement for this policy in the unrelenting character of official Germanization policy and in the

conservatives' inability to shield Polish society from its blows.
After 1909 the mildly conciliatory tendencies of Bethmann's
policies and the possibility of Polish cooperation with anti-
Hakatistic forces in German society threatened the National
Democrats' political momentum. The TDN strove to hold the Polish
conservatives on the defensive by concentrating a heavy propaganda
campaign against their collaborationist tendencies. Although
Bethmann's acquiescence in a hard-line Polenpolitik after 1911
defeated collaboration, the focal point of Polish politics on
the eve of the war remained a recrimination-filled debate on the
question of the conservatives' national militance and virtue.

The National Democrats could hardly fault their rivals for
lukewarm denunciations of Prussian policy. Even Prince Ferdynand
Radziwiłł, the most conciliatory-minded of Polish politicians,
described the government's object in a Reichstag speech as "the
destruction of the Polish nationality" in Prussia. The National
Democrats' lament that "the endeavor to Germanize us flows from
the very being of the Prussian state and from the thousand-year
history of the German population's pressure on the east" found
echoes among the conservatives, equally persuaded of the ineradicable character of the age-old Germanic "push to the east"
(Drang nach Osten) now threatening the Poles with "extermination"
and their homeland with conversion into a "Slavic cemetery."
By 1914, both camps agreed the Poles' worst enemies were the
Eastern Marches Society and its agents within the government.
Filled with a "Satanic hatred" of all things Polish, the Hakatists'
malevolent influence held the government chained to its Germanizing
course.[48]

The conservatives clung tenaciously to their historically
deep-rooted sense of Polish identity. Like their forefathers, they
refused to regard themselves as "Polish-speaking Prussians" or "to
give up all aspirations to a separate national life." This "would
be suicide, but we do not wish to die."[49] The program of the TDN
gave pride of place to the "principle of national separateness"
(odrębność narodowa), which required single-minded devotion to
Polish identity in opposition to the Prussian state and to German
society.[50] The conservatives honored that principle as well,
as a widely distributed, pathos-suffused antiexpropriation manifesto signed by a large majority of the gentry, including the most
conservative, showed:

> We large landowners of the Grand Duchy of Poznań
> and West Prussia affirm that we have no intention of
> abandoning the lands of our birth. We will nurse in
> our hearts and our families and in our people our
> national and religious ideals with a fervor which

persecution can only intensify and with a love stronger
even than the hatred of our enemies. He who is expropriated will devote even more energy to the work of the
national enlightenment of our people.
    Love is stronger than death. Love for our continually
abused fatherland swells our breasts and our hearts sing
a hymn of unshakable faith in our triumph over the spirit
of destruction which seeks to eliminate the Polish nation,
with its thousand years of service to Christian culture,
so as to smooth the path for materialism and Protestantism.[51]

The National Democrats could not demand more national fervor
of the conservatives. Nor did they demur when the conservatives
proclaimed, more soberly, that in their "heavily besieged fortress"
the Poles' salvation could only lie in "closing ranks under the
double standard of cross and fatherland." The National Democrats
sang the praise of national solidarity no less loudly, solemnly declaring that "class egotism and exclusivity are the negation of
our very being."[52]

    Both camps agreed that Polish national survival demanded
freedom from German economic domination. Except insofar as they
depended on demand for their products within the German market,
the gentry and peasant farmers had largely attained this goal
through the Polish banking and cooperative system. They could
pride themselves on their relatively high level of technical efficiency. They insisted uncompromisingly on maintaining the
German Empire's system of high agricultural duties. But they met
with no resistance to this from the National Democrats who, although they had inherited from the older populist movement certain
free-trade impulses, had come around to the position that Polish
industry and commerce would benefit from tariff-protected agricultural prosperity even if the masses had to pay more for their
bread and meat.[53] In return for this support of the Polish
agrarians, the National Democrats won conservative endorsement of
their anti-German boycott campaign, epitomized in the slogan
swój do swego po swoje, meaning "each to his own [nation's mer-
chants] for his own [nation's goods]." In fact, the conservatives
called for more rapid industrialization. They criticized the
tendency among the prosperous bourgeoisie to withdraw their capital from business and buy land in an attempt to "live nobly."
Ignorance of farming led such parvenus to economic ruin. The
agrarians argued that a stronger Polish urban economy could absorb a larger part of the high profits gained since 1896 in farming, easing pressure on land prices while offering jobs to Polish
workers who would otherwise be lost in the Ostflucht.[54]

    In 1913, two books appeared under the Church's imprimatur at-
tacking the TDN. Written by local priests, they argued, mainly on

the basis of references to the earlier writings of the Russian
ND leaders Dmowski and Balicki, that the National Democrats had
abandoned Christian morality in favor of a "pagan" ethics of
"national egoism." These clerical polemicists condemned the ND
movement for advocating control by "public opinion" of the social
and political behavior of the Polish clergy, for sowing hatred of
the clerical-conservative upper class among the common people,
and for striving to establish a political "tyranny" reducing the
traditional leadership to silence.[55] Poland ruled by National
Democrats would be, in Father Geppert's damning phrase, "a
Borussia of the Hakatists et consortium in red and white dress."
Father Hozakowski wrote that "educating the Polish masses in a
national spirit will not be a guarantee of the future of our
Catholic Polish society without maintaining their Catholic consciousness as well." To reject in favor of ND slogans the Church's
formula--"first religion, then nationality"--amounted to a self-
conscious "break with Catholicism."[56]

The TDN could not ignore these grave charges. Szymański
had aroused clerical hostility by ineptly insinuating that the
Poznanian church's political conservatism derived from subservience to the Prussian government. In Russian Poland, particularly
before the revolution of 1905, a genuine conflict existed between
the radical nationalism of the ND movement and the church's extreme social and political conservatism. But in Prussia the
government's sporadic efforts to bring the Poznań-Gniezno archbishopric under German control and its Germanizing-Protestantiz-
ing policies in the archdiocese had, long before the Kulturkampf,
forced the Polish clergy into alliance with secular Polish nationalism. Even though a sizable majority of the Polish clergy no
doubt shared in some degree Geppert's and Hozakowski's misgivings
about the ND movement, the priesthood's active support of the
institutions of Polish nationalism in Poznania was beyond doubt.
The legacy of Szymański's and the Russian National Democrats'
anticlericalism had become a liability to the TDN. In response to
the church's propagandistic salvos of 1913, Marian Seyda formally
abjured it. Acknowledging the importance of Catholicism as a
component of Polish national identity, he praised the clergy's
national activism, which energetic ND protests against Germanizing
pressures on the church were only meant to shield. He disclaimed
"dictatorial" tendencies among the National Democrats, stressing
their desire to rally the common people under the banner of national solidarity and within the "legal" political institutions
of Polish society. On the crucial issue of Catholic orthodoxy,

Seyda explicitly assigned Dmowski's and Balicki's provocative works
to the realm of historical curiosities and immunized the TDN from
further moral scrutiny by declaring that

> the "guideline of our public activities" is always the
> "advantage of the general national cause"--and this is
> a specifically Polish goal. But the ethical measure
> of our means of action is the Christian principle of
> justice, which is a universal ethical standard and one
> which accordingly governs both our private and our
> public lives.[57]

If by 1914 conflict between the conservatives and National
Democrats over economic and religious issues had lost its polemical
edge, debate over the nationalist indoctrination of the common
people and the political democratization of Polish society still
caused the ideological fires in both camps to burn brightly.
Following upon the "principle of national separateness" in the
TDN's 1909 program came the "democratic principle" which defined
the "broad popular masses" as the heart of the nation. Patroniz-
ingly lamenting "the ignorance and passivity of our masses,"
their "poverty, inefficiency, and indolence," the National Democrats demanded of the educated and propertied classes that they
sacrifice, when the need arose, their material interests to those
of the common people and "admit them, in reality and not merely
nominally, to the leadership of national affairs." At the same
time, ND propaganda revealed its makers' determination to hold
"the masses" on a tight political leash in its stress on the ND
mission of educating the people to "moral health," to "true Polish
citizenship," to "sharing responsibility" and "cooperation" with
the other classes of society. Criticizing those "populist" intellectuals who affected the peasant dialect to parade their ties with
the masses, Seyda wrote archly that "we must continually strive
to raise the people's culture to a higher level and certainly not
lower our own culture to the level of the people."[58]

The conservatives apostrophized the common people no less
fervently than the National Democrats, as these lines from a run-
of-the-mill Dziennik Poznański article illustrate:

> Despite our people's sense-directed lives, under their
> "thick outer shell, lined by toil and baked by the sun"
> lies a wellspring of noble feelings. Their hearts are
> capable of loving and commitment to ideals. . . .We must
> familiarize ourselves with the people, . . . seek out the
> buried treasures in their souls through love and trans-
> form them into national values.
> The Satan of socialism bares his teeth, jeers at our
> powerlessness, rubs his hands, and casts his nets. We
> must defend our weaker brothers! . . . Our large land-
> owners must work among the people with dedication so
> that, having attuned themselves to the people and awakened
> in them their "humanity," they shall one day have the
> right to say: "the people shall go with me, and in my
> name they shall shed blood and tears."[59]

Despite their evident uncertainty about the common people's
humanity, the conservatives insisted on calling themselves democrats. They appealed to their record since 1848 to prove that
"every authority we have created rests on the will of our society
insofar as society wishes, by taking part in public meetings and
elections, to express its will. . . .In this respect our society
is no less democratic than any democratic party in Europe."[60] The
common people were free to rise to positions of leadership within
that system, just as a worker's son could rise to the same heights
in the church as "the son of a prince or a rich man."[61] The
people had no right to reject the legitimacy of those authorities
or oppose to them leaders or institutions speaking in the name
of the common people alone. Like the National Democrats, the
conservatives advocated a democracy guided by themselves from
above in which the common people--in conservative parlance, "our
younger brothers," in the ND phrase, "our youngest brothers"--
would shoulder the defense of upper-class interests.[62]

The conservatives occasionally sensed the peasants' and
workers' brooding social resentments and dreaded their crystallization into political opposition or physical violence. The
reality of this threat was proven, in the Poznanian conservatives'
eyes, by the revolution of 1905 in Russian Poland. Referring to
the leader of the 1846 peasant massacres of the Galician gentry,
one of the landlords' worst memories, the Przegląd wielkopolski
wrote of 1905 that "there were times when the fear was justified
that the bloody twilight of Jakób Szela's time would descend
again on the Piast lands. Slogans of national independence and
political freedom were misunderstood by the people as incitements
to class war."[63] Here lay the root of the conservatives' hostility
to the ND movement in Poznania. Like Szymański's populists before
them, the National Democrats stirred up the common people's
class-hatred of the traditional clerical-conservative leadership
merely to earn an easy living from politics and gratify their
personal political ambition. What was true of Szymański's time
still held: "The worker did not know the szlachta, nor the intelligentsia; he felt inferior to the priest. So it was easy for
him to understand the slogan: Down with the landlords, down with
the priests, down with the learned doctors." The National Democrats plied their self-serving trade with the same rhetorical
tools. But if they succeeded by such demagogic means in driving
the conservatives from political life, their own "takeover" would
prove ephemeral. Having stirred up the demons of class-hatred
and party strife, the National Democrats would perish along

with Polish society under the waves of socialism and bloody
anarchy.[64]

In hurling these inflammatory charges at their ND rivals,
the conservatives revealed both a deep-rooted social defensiveness
and bitter anger at the TDN's challenge to their political preeminence. Undoubtedly ND agitation attacked the conservatives.
But it did so "legally," within the system of electoral authorities
and Organic Work institutions, reinforcing popular acceptance of
the legitimacy of the system itself and of the leading role in it
of the educated and propertied classes. ND propaganda ruthlessly
denounced socialism as "godless materialism" and its Polish adherents as national renegades. It did not aim its assaults on the
Polish conservatives against their economic privileges and power
over the common people; rather, it condemned their political egotism, their "caste spirit," which led them to claim leadership of
Polish society independent of the people's will.[65]

An ND speaker warned a meeting of artisans and workers against
joining the conservatives' ill-fated People's Party, saying,
"Behind this organization stands the Polish szlachta, which has
never had anything to spare for the common people." But Karol
Rzepecki, one of the conservatives' most biting critics, then
rose to add that "it never occurred to the National Democrats to
damn the entire szlachta. Members of the szlachta with democratic convictions have always been welcome to them."[66] At another
meeting, an ND worker-activist complained that "the szlachta still
think they can do what they like with the common people"; but National Democracy "has taught us that we are Poles and have certain
rights as such."[67] At a TCL meeting, a local estateowner who
had donated 100 Polish grammars to poor children inspired the same
worker to make a speech ending with the cry, "Honor to such a
Polish patriot."[68]

The National Democrats sometimes mocked their conservative
rivals by addressing them in language befitting feudal lords.
Seyda's Kuryer denounced the szlachta's aloofness, saying of the
provincial capital that "it is a completely morbid abnormality
that in the same city a Chinese wall should separate the social
lives of persons of noble origins from those with bourgeois
roots."[69] But the fundamental ND strategy in fighting the conservatives was to consolidate mass support so as to advance ND
spokesmen in the system of electoral authorities and elect ND candi-
ates to parliament. They tried to hold the conservatives off
guard by magnifying and harshly condemning their "collaborationist"
efforts--in reality confined to a demonstration of good will to

Bethmann and Schwartzkopff--to "bargain with the government behind the back of Polish society."[70] Seyda denounced the conservatives' attendance at the Imperial banquet of 1913 as "an
unheard-of and enormous national sin," a "pro-Prussian conspiracy"
of "the most influential party among the large landowners,
grouped around the Kasyno Obywatelskie and living as a closed
caste cut off and completely separate from the rest of society."[71]

The National Democrats' hostility to "collaboration" and
"compromise" with the Prussian authorities was not just tactical;
it also reflected the strength of their commitment to the ideal
of Polish independence. They repeatedly demanded the restoration
of Polish statehood as straightforwardly as possible, even
though they paid many fines and suffered many jail sentences for
doing so. In the Kuryer Seyda wrote:

> It is perhaps not immoral that a nation desires an in-
> dependence which it possessed for nine centuries and
> which it today feels capable of maintaining. This is
> all the more so since it lost its independence through
> acts of violence, because it is a nation which long
> was a bulwark of Christianity and a pillar of western
> culture, and because it stands today in many ways on a
> higher spiritual level than do the states and nations
> which partitioned it.[72]

The international Polish question was not dead nor would it die
so long as the Poles in all three partition areas maintained
their sense of unity and their vitality as a self-contained
national community. One of the TDN's prime slogans was "spiritual
independence (niezawisłość duchowa)." This the Prussian Poles
could attain through self-enclosure in the highly organized
structure of their own "society (społeczeństwo)," a word that in
vital ways served the Poles as a substitute term for the state
they no longer possessed.[73]

"Spiritual independence" required maintenance of a purely
Polish way of life--in speech, manners, marriage, religion, and
culture. It required reduction to the absolute minimum of any
economic and, more importantly, political dependence on German
society. The "collaborationist" mentality, as the TDN defined it,
worked against these goals. Moreover, given the unalterable
Hakatism of the Prussian ruling classes, no amount of "compromise"
with them could restore the Poles' national rights. Their only
realistic political hope lay in the democratization of the Prussian constitution, which the Polish Landtag deputies, including
the conservatives, consistently though fruitlessly supported
whenever the issue came to a vote.[74] It seemed to Seyda that,
despite the apparent strength of Prussian conservatism, "Prussia's historical role is in principle already fulfilled.

. . .The further development of Germany must by the force of
events proceed towards the gradual exclusion and obliteration of
Prussian characteristics."[75] The Poles' task lay in gathering
their forces and riding out whatever storms might blow over them
until democracy and national toleration prevailed in Germany--or
until, as another ND argument ran, war liberated the Poles from
German rule.

For it also appeared to the National Democrats that "German
militarism and chauvinism" were leading "with ineluctable cer-
tainty" towards a war for "world domination."[76] In the meetings
of the Liga Narodowa between 1912 and 1914, Seyda and the other
Prussian National Democrats sided with Dmowski's Russian delegation in favoring a Tsarist victory in case of war with Germany
and Austria. They endorsed Dmowski's argument that Polish
autonomy within the Russian Empire was at least a possibility,
whereas Hapsburg Polonophilia could not prevail over Imperial
German opposition to Polish self-government.[77] The TDN could express its pro-Russian orientation, which was less a result of
Russophilia than of Germanophobia, only very obliquely in print.
But the National Democrats made it clear that, far from fearing
European war, they faced it in the conviction that Germany would
lose and Poland gain from it. Perhaps the Prussian National
Democrats' most fundamental characteristic was their sanguine
faith in the growing strength of the Polish nation. From it
they drew the resolution to resist their German antagonists
well expressed in Seyda's response to the expropriations of
October 1912:

> Between us and them--that whole Prussian world--there
> always was a chasm. Today flames are rising up out of
> it, flames we do not fear in the least. Let the fires
> burn higher! Who will be overcome, who will be destroyed
> --tomorrow will show.[78]

Such battle-ready optimism was completely lacking among the
Polish conservatives. Their faith in the future restoration of
Polish independence derived from nineteenth-century Polish-
Catholic romantic messianism. While real, it was mystical and
passive: "The immortality of the nation's soul is an unknowable
mystery, just as is the ascension of God-man from the grave."
In the long run, the will of God would coincide with the "logic
of history" in resurrecting the Polish state as part of a general
triumph of democracy and national self-determination over monarchical absolutism. But, in the short run, the Polish future
appeared bleak. If German militarism unleashed war, Poland would
be devastated without hope of liberation. Nor did the conserva-

tives place any faith in Russian patronage of the Polish cause.
On the contrary, they feared the Tsarist Empire stood on the
verge of a social revolution which would engulf and destroy their
political counterparts in Russian Poland.[79]

The conservatives were caught in a painful dilemma. They
had no wish to suffer the material losses and the political aggrandizement of their more radical rivals that inevitably would
attend the restoration of Polish statehood through war and revolution. But their inclination to accept the status quo in a spirit
of Tri-loyalist resignation collided both with the anti-Polonism
of the Prussian government and the anticollaborationist strategy
of the National Democrats. Although their own analysis of the inherently aggressive nature of Prussian Polenpolitik condemned collaboration with the government to futility, they argued that the
National Democrats' defiant nationalist militance amounted to
nothing more than a self-serving policy based on the adage "the
worse, the better," whose only tangible result was to heap coals
on the Hakatists' fire.[80] The conservatives justified their willingness to entertain the idea of "compromise" by arguing that
"it is a duty to consider what, even if it does not bring our
land a positive advantage, will at least minimize what afflicts
it." The Poles ought to demonstrate to the Prussian government and
to German society that

> we are not waging a struggle with the state, but rather
> with the false direction of its policies. Our struggle
> with the government will cease when its policies towards
> us are based on the dictates of justice and political
> equality. If the government does this, it will see that
> it can rely upon the Polish population.[81]

If the government made a gesture of compromise in the Poles'
direction, as Bethmann did in appointing Schwartzkopff and as
Schwartzkopff did in attempting to rally the szlachta around the
throne, the Poles had the obligation of reciprocating, if only
to discredit Hakatistic claims of Polish disloyalty and to show
that "the Polish people are peaceful, religious, respectful of
authority, and grateful to him who renders them justice."[82]

The conservatives' inclination towards "compromise," defeated by Bethmann's inability to steer Prussian Polenpolitik
into calmer waters, ultimately reflected their pessimism about
the prospects of Polish independence. It followed that only
through a frank and positive acceptance of Prussian citizenship
could the Poles hope to escape official persecution. A century
of Prussian rule had proved, however, that what the Prussian
government demanded of the Poles was not merely loyalty as citizens, but acceptance of an increasingly exclusively and ethnically

defined Prusso-German nationality, of which even the Polish conservatives were incapable.

Despite their ideological and tactical differences, the
National Democrats and the Polish conservatives paid homage in
equal measure to the principle of national solidarity. This required both camps to recognize the "sovereignty" of the system
of electoral authorities and the obligation of every parliamentary
deputy to cast his votes according to the majority will of the
Polish delegations. In principle, the will of the Polish voters
in each district, expressed through the nominations of precinct-
level preelection assemblies, determined candidacies for Reichstag
and Landtag seats. The body which definitively established the
names of "official" candidates was the provincial assembly of
county delegates, numbering forty-two in all. When a district's
several nominating assemblies proposed more than one candidacy, the
vote of the provincial delegates' assembly decided which one best
represented the electorate's choice. At the ensuing election,
Polish voters were obliged to cast their ballots for the candidate
ratified by the delegates. General acceptance of the delegates'
decisions was the rule. Only one successful "secession" occurred
in the system's long history.

The acid test of the National Democrats' and conservatives'
relative strength in Poznanian politics on the eve of the war was
the degree of their influence in the provincial assembly of county
delegates. Not only did this body determine parliamentary candidacies and thus the ideological-tactical orientation of the Berlin
delegations; since its members were themselves elected through a
pyramid of precinct and county assemblies, its political composition mirrored Polish political opinion in the province, at least
so far as it could be crystallized on the county level. The
provincial delegates' assembly also elected from its midst the four
executive officers of the provincial electoral committee, who could
mobilize the system of committees and assemblies they presided over
in ad hoc protest campaigns or for other agitational purposes.

In the provincial delegates' assembly of 1912, whose main
task was to ratify candidacies for the Reichstag elections of
that year, National Democratic and conservative influence was
roughly equivalent. On the controversial question whether a TDN
activist or a National Union conservative represented the voters'
choice in one divided district, the delegates split 20-20, with
one abstention, on the first ballot. The second ballot decided
the issue in the TDN's favor, 22-19. On another decision pitting

the National Democrats against a conservative, the latter prevailed 19-17 with several abstentions. In the assembly of 1913
which determined Landtag candidacies, the conservatives mustered
blocs of nine to thirteen votes in opposition to ND candidates
while the National Democrats commanded minorities of eleven and
twelve votes against the nomination of anti-ND conservatives.
Here a pattern evident in the 1912 proceedings emerged more clearly.
Neither the TDN nor the conservatives possessed stable majorities.
A bloc of delegates standing between the two factions held the
balance, swinging its weight back and forth and partially satisfy-
ing the interests of each while denying to both clear-cut control
of the assembly. In the delegates' meeting of 1914 the centrist
votes favored the National Democrats, whose candidate for a seat
on the provincial electoral committee prevailed by a majority of
twenty-nine. That decision amounted to a censure of the conservatives' part in the unpopular Imperial banquet of 1913. But
the presidency and one other seat on the executive committee remained in conservative hands.[83]

Analysis of the prewar parliamentary delegations also confirms the presence of a centrist bloc mediating between the ND
and conservative extremes. Of the eleven Reichstag deputies
elected from the province in 1912, four were acknowledged leaders
of the ND movement, three were conservative partisans. Two were
priests, Catholic populists endorsed equally by the ND and conservative press, and two were popular independents wooed by
both parties. Among the nine Landtag deputies elected in 1913,
three were ND spokesmen, one was a conservative, and the remaining five were nonpartisan nationalists acceptable to both factions.[84]

The Nationalist Movement
and the Polish Common People
on the Eve of World War I

Despite the gloomy expectations of many conservatives, the
National Democrats neither fastened a political "dictatorship"
on Polish society nor dissolved its national solidarity in a
maelstrom of party strife and class conflict. On the contrary,
in 1914 the TDN still represented a minority force in Polish
politics, though a well-organized and highly influential one.
They could not outflank their conservative rivals without the
support of Catholic populists and nonpartisan centrists, for
which the TDN paid the price--to the Catholics of concessions to
Poznania's deep-rooted clericalism and, to the independents, of
acceptance of compromise and pluralism within the nationalist

movement. Even as the National Democrats assaulted conservative
"collaborationism" they found it necessary to uphold the agrarian
economic interests upon which the gentry's social and political
prestige depended.

The ND movement nevertheless broke what had become by 1890
the political monopoly of the szlachta conservatives and their
clerical allies. Although the National Democrats represented
primarily the interests and claims to power of the educated and
propertied middle classes, they recruited a strong following in
the towns by agitating among the petite bourgeoisie and workers
as tribunes of popular democracy and threatened to do the same
among the peasants and rural laborers, given the chance. The ND
movement forced the conservatives to tighten their grip on the
peasantry through intensified appeals to their common agrarian
economic interests and to the threat posed to manor and village
alike by the Prussian government's colonization program. The
clergy followed suit, adding a social and political dimension
to popular Catholicism, stressing defense of the national faith
against its Germanization.

The rise of the National Democrats strengthened the leadership of the national movement not only by the addition of its own
activists but also by driving more members of the gentry and
clergy into political action. Through the mass organizations each
of these groups sponsored, a growing number of workers and
peasants rose to leadership positions in public life. The numbers
of political and Organic Work officeholders estimated in table 9
show that by 1914 all classes of Polish society contributed sizable
contingents. The gentry, the clergy, and the educated and

TABLE 9: The Polish Nationalist Leadership in 1914

Occupation		Number	%
Estate Owners		571	18.7
Peasant Farmers		305	10.0
Priests		869	28.5
Urban Middle Classes			
Artisans/Industrialists	237		
Merchants	225		
Professional Intelligentsia	303		
Commercial Clerks	72		
Middle-Class Women	45		
		882	29.0
Rural and Urban Workers		442	13.8
TOTAL		3,049	100.0

SOURCE: See note 85, below.

propertied bourgeoisie dominated Polish public life in roughly
equal measure: agrarian conservatives (estate owners and peasants)
provided 29 percent of Polish society's national activists, while
the ND camp and the clerical populists, dividing between themselves the leadership of the workers' contingent, could claim approximately 35 percent each.

Because they honored the concept of national solidarity and,
despite their internal political quarrels, regarded themselves as
allies in the defense of the same national community, these three
thousand activists constituted, especially from the German point
of view, a single and formidable nationalist phalanx. They could
count on a high degree of organized support within Polish society.
By 1914 the network of professional and cultural Organic Work
institutions counted a membership of 82,000 men and women, or
roughly one-quarter of all the province's Polish-speaking adults.
Among men alone, perhaps as many as 60 percent had joined one or
another of these organizations. Membership in the Polish cooperative banking and marketing system was higher still: in Poznania
alone, roughly 100,000.[86]

The Poles participated after 1900 in thousands of political
meetings while the nationalist press they read had by 1914 reached
a combined circulation in the province of well over 100,000.
Yet the common people showed their loyalty to the national movement and its leaders best by their voting record. In the Reichstag
election of 1912, 93 percent of all eligible Polish voters cast
their ballots for Polish national candidates, while another 3 percent voted for the Socialists.[87] The nationalists had succeeded
in mobilizing virtually the entire Polish electorate in their
support. In view of the national movement's treatment of Reichstag elections as demonstrations of Polish national solidarity
and antigovernmental protest, the very high frequency of Polish
voting justifies the conclusion that by 1914 Polish nationalism
had penetrated the humblest cottages and urban workshops.[88]

It was, as its leaders intended it to be, a socially conservative and clerically hued nationalism. Nevertheless, in
their efforts to uphold the national political and cultural
traditions to which they had fallen heir, the gentry, clergy,
and bourgeois intelligentsia had moved the common people into
political action. While they encouraged the peasants and workers
to speak in tones of respect for the propertied and educated
classes, in the nationalist movement they provided the common
people with a forum in which ultimately they could, speaking
their own language, find their own voice for the grievances they

felt not only against German society but against the Polish upper
classes as well.

Before 1914, few Polish workers and peasants had progressed
that far. During the school strike of 1906-7, the families of
more than one-quarter of the province's Polish elementary school
children supported their classroom protests. Nearly 150,000 adults
signed a petition against Germanization of religion classes. But
the strike attained its massive proportions through its systematic
organization and propagation by the nationalists. It was aimed
against the Prussian government, inspired by religious sentiment
as well as national outrage and thought by most Poles to be a
legal protest.[89]

If the school strikes were not expressions of spontaneous
social-revolutionary sentiment, neither did the socialist movement
find a strong following among the Polish masses. In the Reichstag
election of 1912, while the province's electorate cast 343,000
votes for Polish nationalist and German conservative, liberal, and
clerical candidates, only 13,000 votes fell to the socialists, at
least half of them cast by Germans. Many obstacles confronted the
spread of socialism in Poznania. The province lacked large industrial centers, while the politically active members of both the
Polish and German intelligentsia were engaged in the nationality
conflict. The Prussian authorities hindered the formation of
socialist trade unions and party organizations by numerous
chicaneries, while the Polish nationalist movement anathematized
socialism and steered Polish workers into the ZZP and ZKTRP. At
a large ND meeting in Ostrowo a police agent reported that

> a certain Moryson said it was a good thing that Social
> Democracy existed, because it tried to improve the
> common people's lot. At this there arose a great
> commotion, hissing and whistling, until Moryson had to
> be removed from the hall.[90]

In addition to these problems, the socialist movement was
divided in itself. Since 1893 a separate Polish Socialist Party
(PPS--Polska Partia Socjalistyczna) had existed as a subsidiary
to the German SPD. Only in the vicinity of Katowice in Upper
Silesia did the PPS acquire any considerable popular support. In
Poznania, its members numbered only fifty as late as 1912. The
provincial SPD organization, to which until the end of 1913 PPS
activists also belonged, counted just over one thousand members
in 1914, while by the end of 1912 about six thousand workers had
joined Socialist trade unions. Since 1903, however, the SPD had
fallen increasingly under German control, until by the eve of the
war its leadership and organized following were concentrated mainly
in the heavily German northern counties of the province.[91]

In 1913, the PPS broke its financial and organizational ties
with the SPD. Although the two parties had, at least in theory,
agreed since 1893 on the Poles' right of national self-determination, the Polish Socialists in Germany gravitated towards Józef
Piłsudski's "revolutionary wing" of the PPS in Russian Poland.
From 1912 the German PPS supported Piłsudski's strategy of launch-
ing an armed rising with Austrian backing to liberate Russian
Poland in the event of war between the German monarchies and the
Tsarist state. The SPD condemned this plan as adventuristic.
The deeper roots of the PPS-SPD rift precipitated by this issue
lay, on the one hand, in mounting anti-Polish tendencies within
the German labor movement, deriving in part from resistance among
Polish workers in the Ruhr district to unionization under
Socialist banners. On the other hand, the PPS gained little from
its alliance with the SPD. The growth of the ZZP demonstrated
the Polish workers' receptivity to nonsocialist appeals both to
their national and to their class consciousness. To overcome
their own numerical weakness the Polish Socialists dropped their
German connections and increasingly emphasized the ideal of
national autonomy in their propaganda. But adoption of this tactic required the PPS to beat the ZZP at its own game, which before
the war it showed no promise of doing.[92]

The weakness of the PPS's following and agitation in the
province of Poznań meant that, from the Polish common people's
point of view, socialism was synonymous with the SPD. Despite
its bilingual propaganda and endorsement of Polish-speaking candidates in Polish districts, the SPD nevertheless inevitably projected a German image. The SPD's secularism, easily misrepre-
sented by its opponents as militant atheism, together with its
inability to formulate plausible economic appeals to the rural
workers and small-holding peasants, further reduced its appeal
in the eyes of the Polish villagers.[93]

By 1914 the Poznanian Poles, both rich and poor, had withdrawn in hostility, resentment, and national self-absorption
from all but the most unavoidable and formalized contacts with
German society. Instances could be cited of amicable, though
still highly patriarchal, relations between German landlords and
Polish farm laborers; of mutual respect among German urban
employers and their Polish workers; of camaraderie among the
common people of both nationalities; of Polish patronage of
German and Jewish commercial establishments in preference to those
of their own countrymen; of Polish subscriptions to German

liberal newpapers.[94] But these would be individual cases un-
characteristic of the broader pattern. Moritz Jaffé, scion of a
long-established Poznanian Jewish family, wrote in 1909 that "in
the close confines of today's city of Posen, Germans and Poles
treat each other like foreigners."[95] The organized lives of the
nationalities had grown almost completely disengaged. In the
1870s nationally mixed artisans' and commercial associations were
common, but by 1914 the only important organization in which Poles
and Germans freely collaborated on a basis of at least formal
national equality was the Socialist trade-union network. Apart
from their participation in the Germanized school system, against
which they vented their antagonisms in the school strikes, and
apart from their increasingly hostile confrontation with German
society within the public political institutions of the province
and state, the Poles retreated into the well-articulated structure of their own national society, doing their best to minimize
their economic dependence on their German and Jewish neighbors.

The superficiality of Polish-German social relations
emerges from the sparse data on intermarriages distinguished not
on the basis of confession but on that of the declared nationality
of the marriage partners. Such information exists only for the
population of the provincial capital, but even that relatively ur-
bane atmosphere intermarriage between Poles and Germans was highly
exceptional. In 1905/6, 97.3 percent of all new Polish husbands
chose Polish wives; in 1911/12, this figure had risen to 98.5 percent. The proverbial, though overrated, susceptibility of German
men to Polish women was declining: in the same period the percentage of those who took Polish wives fell from ten percent to 9
percent.[96]

Even the common bond of religion had broken under the pressure of the nationality conflict. The conservative Dziennik
Poznański, which had no interest in exaggerating such matters,
wrote in mid 1912 that "in every sphere of social, political, and
religious life a gulf separates Polish from German Catholics."[97]
The National Democrats insisted upon a Polish boycott of social
contacts with the German population until the Poles had attained
civil and national equality. While Schwartzkopff managed to
establish social relations with some of the Polish aristocracy,
a better indication of the Polish upper classes' attitude emerges
from the Dziennik's mournful statement in response to the application of the Expropriation Act:

> Obviously, nationality relations in our districts will
> sharpen to an impossible degree. A deep and unprecedented
> division between the two nationalities inhabiting these

areas is opening, for the awareness of the wrong that
has been done prevents any kind of intimacy.[98]

In the political realm, the long-standing collaboration of
the Poles and German liberals against the German conservatives
came to an end with the formation in 1907 of the Bülow bloc,
which was accompanied on the provincial level by the negotiation
of electoral compromises among the German parties against the
Poles.   In the following years these compromises were with some
difficulty maintained and extended from Reichstag and Landtag and
local communal elections.   In reaction, the Polish electoral
authorities adopted the principle that, on first ballots, Polish
voters would support only Polish candidates, although in runoffs
between German candidates the Poles should attempt to swing the
balance in favor of the less hostile of the two.[99]

In Polish political meetings and in the nationalist press,
characterizations of German society and of the local German
population grew increasingly hostile and one-sided.   The old
adage that "the German will never be brother to the Pole" drew
cheers from massive crowds.[100]   Both the National Democrats and
the Catholic populists systematically propagated the view that no
German heart was free of Hakatistic prejudices and hostility to
the fundamental character, rights, and interests of Polish society.
The Polish conservatives might disavow any desire "to sow and
spread hatred towards their persecutors or towards those nationally
foreign to them, for that is permitted neither by Christian nor
by Polish hearts."[101]   But to stir up the Polish common people's
resentments against German discrimination was part of the National
Democrats' program of fostering "spiritual independence" among
them.   Should the Poles, asked the Kuryer, try to divide the
Germans into friends and enemies?   "What a waste of time!   We
have our own work cut out for us.   Here we are--and there are they.
What is ours, we have to increase, enrich, and improve."   A Pole
who helped advance German interests was "dishonest to his own
society."[102]

Anti-Semitism played a vital role in populist and National
Democratic propaganda and agitation.   The Polish nationalist
movement's increasingly raucous hostility to the Jews was a major
reason for the German liberals' dwindling political collaboration
with the Poles after 1907.   In its most primitive form, Polish anti-
Semitism expressed ancient fears of the Jews as ritual murderers
and ruthless, hate-filled conspirators against every Christian
Polish interest.   So, for example, even the relatively mildly
anti-Semitic Dziennik Poznański left its readers free to accept
the Tsarist regime's charges of ritual murder in the sensational

Beilis case tried in late 1913 in Kiev. The ND and populist press
positively encouraged acceptance of Beilis's guilt.[103] This type
of anti-Semitism propagated the idea that the Jews were the secret
financiers and political wire-pullers behind the scenes of the
Socialist movement and the HKT Society. It served as the emotional
backdrop to the TDN's and populists' unremitting economic attacks
upon the Jews, who in this connection were excoriated as a "ter-
rible plague" upon the Polish lands and as "the sole reason why our
middle class . . . cannot arrive at the wealth and comfort it
desires."[104] The editor of the scurrilous newspaper Postęp, a leading National Democrat, lectured an audience of Polish villagers
in 1914:

> Many Poles are still patronizing the Jews, because they
> think they can buy better goods more cheaply from them than
> from Polish establishments. But the Jews are leeches, they
> are a cancer on the body of the Polish community. The Polish
> kings supported the Jews, to the ruin of the Polish people.
> And to show their gratitude the Jews now fight against the
> Poles. The Poles can have no pity on the Jews. After all,
> the Jews get rich off the Poles, then they go to Berlin and
> set up German newspapers that attack the Poles.[105]

The National Democrats' anti-German boycott hurt the Jews economically while demoralizing them psychologically. Unquestionably it
was a major factor in their emigration westward. Marian Seyda
exulted in this: "What it means to be liberated from the Jewish
yoke can only be appreciated within all of Polish society by the
Prussian Poles."[106] Although the Polish conservatives were not
engaged, as the TDN's backers were, in direct economic competition with the Jews, the gentry's tendency to view the Jews as
cultural and economic "Germanizers" and as anticlerical liberals
encouraged them to minimize their conflicts with the TDN by endorsing the boycott campaign.[107] The Catholic populists in their
turn unhesitatingly supported the boycott and condemned the Jews
who, as Father Kłos, editor of the Przewodnik Katolicki, put it in
his memoirs, "laughed at our faith and all we hold sacred."[108]

    The Polish nationalist movement's anti-German and anti-Jewish
propaganda expressed, even as it intensified, the Polish population's grievances against the state and against German society
generally. It reinforced the Poles' tendency to withdraw into
their own social and cultural universe and economic and political
organizations. This strengthened the Polish common people's acceptance of the legitimacy of the traditions and institutions of
the aristocracy, clergy, and middle classes. But, if the peasants
and workers were won for the nationalist movement, their assertion
within it of their own social and political interests would inevitably reshape it.

Before World War I, most of the Polish peasants and workers
in Poznania accepted their role as obedient foot soldiers in
the nationalist army commanded by the educated and propertied
classes. Yet· some of them had begun to demand an independent
voice for themselves within the nationalist movement. For example, Polish workers organized in ZZP unions and other workers
sympathetic to the ND movement campaigned energetically on behalf
of the National Democrats' "secessionist" candidate, the ZZP
leader Nowicki, in the Poznań city Reichstag by-election of 1910.
Nowicki won broad support among the Polish common people in the
provincial capital as one of their own kind, the first worker
to seek high office in the Polish nationalist movement. But when
groups of working-class campaigners tried to gather support for
Nowicki in the city's rural suburbs, they ran into the hostility
of conservative-minded priests and estate owners, who denounced
them variously as "socialists," "horned devils," "pigs," and
"dogs." In one case, a priest rallied the peasants against them:
"Get your sticks, boys, take these fellows out of the village and
flay them so they'll never get back to Poznań." In another,
Nowicki's campaigners brawled with his rural opponents "like in a
revolution," as a conservative county committeeman wrote to the
Provincial electoral committee. A Polish landlord threatened to
dismiss any of his laborers who voted for Nowicki. Nevertheless,
Nowicki's partisans' two-fisted agitation in the villages reinforced the working-class support he already possessed in the city
and assured his victory in the election.[109]

Again, in 1909, in a small town near Poznań the members of
the local Polish Catholic Workers' Society decided, with their
priest-patron's encouragement, to run a working-class candidate
of their own for one of the three seats on the city council commanded by the town's Polish voters. The electoral committee,
dominated by merchants and artisans, blocked the workers' plan,
nominating three of their own colleagues as the "official" candidates. The workers protested hotly against what they stigmatized
as the petit bourgeois "aristocracy's" political monopoly. One of
the committeemen replied: "Go to the devil! Let that peasant,
that priest of yours, vote for you." The workers then declared
a boycott of the election and the three Polish "aristocrats"
went down to defeat at the Germans' hands.[110]

Incidents such as these were not uncommon in the prewar years.
They were certain to multiply in the future. They illustrate the
bitter resistance the Polish common people confronted in their
efforts to play an autonomous role in Polish national politics.

But in these two political contests, at any rate, the "youngest brothers" in Polish society carried the day.[111]

8   MISSIONARIES IN THE EAST:
     THE EASTERN MARCHES SOCIETY, THE STATE,
     AND THE JUNKERS

In its New Year's message of 1912, the Eastern Marches Society invoked "the spirit, which we have always preached, of national comradeship (völkische Gemeinburgschaft) among the Germans of the eastern fighting provinces."[1] The Hakatists liked nothing better than to imagine themselves apostles of that spirit: high-minded champions of German culture and civilization in the east, Teutonic Knights in frock coats, rallying the frontier Germans under their banners of national brotherhood and self-defense.

From the moment of its founding in 1894, the Eastern Marches Society (OMV) disclaimed any aggressive designs against "our Polish-speaking fellow-citizens."[2] The menace of "Great-Polish agitation" and the national breakaway it allegedly preached was real enough, but the might and vigilance of the Prussian state could restrain it. The colonization program equipped the government to reverse the "Polonization" of the east threatened by the demographic and economic trends of the 1870s and 1880s. The Eastern Marches Society aimed not to combat the Poles, but to overcome what it saw as a harmful and deplorable national passivity among the frontier Germans. Caprivi's coquetry with the Polish nationalists and his slighting of Prussian agrarian interests showed to the OMV's founders that the government could stray from its national post in the east. Unquestionably, they aimed in 1894 to pressure Berlin into resuming an energetic Bismarckian Polenpolitik. But they set their sights higher. "This society," they announced in 1896,

> arose from the conviction of thousands of patriotically minded people that, as the experience of a century has shown, the activity of the government alone will not suffice to master the danger facing the Germans in the east. The assistance of the whole German nation is required, especially in the economic realm. Many tasks defy solution by the government. They can be fulfilled only by the completely free and independent action of our organization.[3]

Above all, the OMV sought to "promote and fortify German national

consciousness through the numerical expansion and economic
strengthening of the German population in the east." The Hakatists
took the network of Polish Organic Work institutions as their model
and aimed to provide the frontier Germans with an analogous set.[4]

By 1914 the Eastern Marches Society commanded one of the
largest and most active German political movements in the east. It
was an acknowledged power in German national politics, rightly
claiming considerable influence over German public opinion and
widely regarded as an irresistible pressure group dictating
Prussian Polish policy from behind the scenes in Berlin. The
Hakatists distinguished themselves in their own time and have
since figured in modern historiography not as idealistic patriots
defending the frontier Germans' interests, but rather as a clique
of powerful agitators who, while provoking a mean hatred and exaggerated fear of the Poles far beyond their own circles, imposed
upon a reluctant Prussian government an ever harsher Polenpolitik.
Contemporary German and Polish historians alike continue to
emphasize the OMV's heavy responsibility not only for the radicalization of pre-1914 Prussian Polish policies, but also for setting
the German political stage for National Socialist aggression
against Poland.[5]

It is crucial to recognize, however, that official Germanization policies before World War I were the work of the Prussian
monarchy's aristocratic-bureaucratic governing class, supported by
the prestigious and "state-conserving" National Liberal and Conservative parties. The radical character of Prussian Polenpolitik
was not merely the result of völkisch pressure exerted by the
Eastern Marches Society, but flowed from the heart of Prussian
monarchical conservatism as Bismarck and his allies had refashioned
it.

After 1894 the Prussian government called the OMV into the
service of its Germanization policies. Official support helped the
new organization grow strong. During the Bülow era, no pressure
from the OMV was necessary to launch the government's anti-Polish
campaigns. They followed from the strategy of Wilhelminian
imperialism, from the advancing crisis of the colonization program,
and from the government's efforts to disarm the increasingly militant Polish nationalist movement. Until 1908, the OMV played the
role, highly useful to Bülow and his allies, of recruiting popular
support for the government's anti-Polish initiatives. The one
instance in which the government might be said to have yielded to
Hakatistic pressure was in enforcing the Expropriation Law in 1912,
but even here Bethmann acted primarily to offset German foreign

policy rebuffs, not to gratify the OMV. The parcellation bill
of 1914, though demanded for a decade by the Eastern Marches
Society, owed its introduction by the government to the necessity of holding Bismarck's colonization program afloat and could
well have been proposed had the OMV never existed.[6]

The OMV exerted its greatest influence in Prussian and
Imperial German politics not as a pressure group, but as a
propaganda organization. Soon after its founding Tiedemann
established its central office in Berlin, not only to lobby the
government and parliaments but also to recruit the "whole German
nation" in support of the frontier Germans' special interests.
There the society published its monthly journal, Die Ostmark,
which aimed at a nationwide audience. The OMV established itself
as a kind of Eastern Marches press agency. It supplied the major
nationalist dailies throughout Germany with reports on the successes and tasks of official policy, alarmist accounts of the
Polish nationalist movement, and inspirational tributes to the
eastern Germans' powers of resistance. From Berlin, too, it
organized local OMV branches in central and western Germany.

By 1913, the Hakatists numbered nearly 48,000, organized in
over 400 local societies, 92 of them counting some 8,000 members
outside the five eastern provinces.[7] Die Ostmark circulated in an
edition of over 60,000. Hundreds of German newspapers received
the OMV's press releases, regularly published by such major
journals as the Tägliche Rundschau, Rheinisch-Westfälische Zeitung,
and Hamburger Nachrichten. The editors of these newspapers and
many other journalists outside the Eastern Marches were OMV
members.[8] The Pan-German League, whose Alldeutsche Blätter
circulated in an edition of 10,000 before the war, looked upon the
OMV as a political brother-in-arms. In Poznania, it retired from
the organizational field in favor of the OMV, while in its Reich-
level agitation it pronounced the Hakatists' purposes unreservedly
good.[9] So, too, did the other major right-wing propaganda organizations of Wilhelminian Germany. The Eastern Marches Society
represented not the dimmest constellation in the nationalist-
imperialist galaxy formed by the Bund der Landwirte, the
Deutschnationaler Handlungsgehilfenverband, the Pan-German League,
the Army, Navy, and Colonial Leagues, the Antisocialist League,
the anti-Danish Nordmarkverein, and others. These groups, which
tended to support and reinforce each other, spread the OMV's influence far beyond its own organizational boundaries. Taken
together, they represented a powerful bloc of political support
for the Conservative and National Liberal parties, a few of whose

deputies could always be counted on to champion their various
interests in parliament.[10]

Like its counterparts, the Eastern Marches Society won a
strong following in the academic world. Schoolteachers, university students, and professors enthusiastically spread its message as local organizers and speakers. Some of Imperial Germany's
best-known scholars and political writers sat on its councils or
lent their names to its pronouncements, including among many others
Treitschke (until his death in 1896), Gustav Schmoller, Adolf
Wagner, Ernst Haeckel, Dietrich Schäfer, Ernst Hasse, Felix Dahn,
Reinhold Koser, Erich Marcks, Karl Lamprecht and, in the 1890s,
Max Weber.[11] Such men stamped with an imprimatur of intellectual
respectability the ideology which it was the OMV's most significant accomplishment to have brought into focus from disparate
sources and energetically advocated in German nationalist circles.

Outside the eastern provinces, the German bourgeoisie and upper classes regarded the Polish question in Prussia and the interests of the frontier Germans with considerable indifference.
In these circles, the liberal tradition of Polenfreundschaft
was by 1890 virtually dead. Its theoretical premises, grounded in
the egalitarian doctrine of natural rights in general and the
universal right of national self-determination in particular,
fell victim to the triumph in nineteenth-century bourgeois political philosophy of historical realism in its Hegelian and Treitschkean forms. Prussian raison d'état and post-1848 national
liberalism converged in the propositions, equally evident to Bismarck and Treitschke, that Poznania and West Prussia were indispensable sinews of the German national state, that the Poles were
historically unfit for self-government, and that the Germanization
of the Polish provinces was a dictate of national self-defense.
After 1871 these ideas won at least the passive approval of a
majority among the Protestant middle and upper classes. In any
event, the Bismarckian-Treitschkean critique of the Polish problem
in Prussia left its solution to the state, acting through its
military and police forces, its bureaucratic and educational apparatus, and, after 1886, the Colonization Commission as well.

The OMV, attempting to rally popular backing outside the east
first for its campaign against Caprivi's national "aberrations" and
then for the stiffening of the government's crisis-ridden Polenpolitik, found it necessary to formulate a comprehensive critique
of the "Eastern Marches question," justifying before German
public opinion its crucial importance. Although little was new in

the OMV's analysis, it was nevertheless the first full-scale
theory of German-Polish conflict to enter the mainstream of
German politics. This was a fitting accomplishment for the first
political organization in German history to concern itself exclusively with the Poles and the German-Polish borderlands.

HKT propagandists had to combat at the outset what they took
as the common German view, namely that the Ostmark, by which
they usually meant Poznania and the adjoining Polish West Prussia,
was nothing more than "a joyless Sarmatian steppe," a "foreign
land" to which it was the fate of mediocre bureaucrats to be
transported while its native German population strained to "retreat to the far west, where things are beautiful."[12] But it was
difficult to represent these lands as integral parts of the German
social and cultural universe. The frontier Germans' conservative
insularity and lack of opulence, the Jews' prominence in the towns,
the recent origins--often bourgeois--of the Junkers, and the transi-
ence of the estate-owning and official classes left most Germans
outside the Polish provinces with a vague and patronizing view
of their eastern compatriots. Even the Pan-German theorist Ernst
Hasse admitted the Poznanian Germans, apart from old-settled
peasants, lacked firm and settled roots (Bodenständigkeit).

> The Poseners and West Prussians have no group identity
> (Landsmannschaften). The East Prussian is proud to
> call himself an East Prussian, likewise the Silesian a
> Silesian, and they are recognizable as such. But who can
> tell by speech or character a Posener or a West Prus-
> sian?[13]

The borderland Germans' homely obscurity and undistinguished
national culture did not detract in the Hakatists' eyes from the
fundamentally German character of their native soil. The OMV
appropriated and popularized the theses of nineteenth-century
German historians not only that the German title to the lands of
Great Poland and Danzig-Pomerania antedated the Poles' claims to
them, but also that, despite centuries of Polish rule, the frontier
owed whatever degree of civilization it could boast of to German
influence and action. Thus, or so the argument ran, Goths inhabited these lands before the Slavs settled in them. The historic
Polish state was founded by Germanic warriors above the heads of
the bucolic and unpolitical natives, who had German Christian
missionaries to thank for liberation from their accustomed though
barbarous paganism. Urban civilization and literary culture
the medieval Poles received from German hands; Protestantism
they rejected to their own loss. The Polish Commonwealth won
independence only because of the medieval Germans' unhappy fixa-
tion on Italy; it preserved it only because of the impotence and

division forced on Germany by Hapsburgs and Bourbons. But the
Poles abused their liberty and could not husband their resources.
They brought the partitions on themselves; Prussia only reclaimed
the Germans' lost patrimony. The OMV leader and editor of the
right-wing <u>Posener Tageblatt</u>, Emmanuel Ginschel, minced no words:

> This once-German land, which under Polish rule sank
> into misery and neglect, has been conquered for the
> German people by sword and plow. It has been ferti-
> lized by German blood and sweat, and owes its culture
> to Germans. For these reasons, we are the masters here.[14]

The Eastern Marches Society combined the contempt and incomp-
rehension with which Frederick II and Bismarck had viewed Polish
political and social life with their championship of Prussian
eastward expansion in a synthesis whose importance lay in its
claims to provide a "scientific"--which in Imperial Germany meant
a historical--rationale for Prussian rule over the frontier. In
a speech of 1901 to the Borussia student corps, William II said
that "the essence of a nation consists in delimiting itself
against that which surrounds it, in expressing its folk-personality
according to its specific racial character."[15] Although the OMV
avoided racial terminology, in holding that the Poles owed the
positive elements of their history and culture to German influence,
it denied to them the capacity or right to develop their "folk-
personality" autonomously. From this followed not only their sub-
mission to German rule, but to cultural, linguistic, and socio-
psychological Germanization as well.

Hakatist writers interpreted the history of the Prussian Poles
since the partition in two stages. Until 1871, the <u>szlachta</u>
and clergy had followed the deep-rooted inclinations of their
Polish hearts in revolutionary plotting and dreaming, in "the dangerous work of conspiracy and international conflict."[16]
Meanwhile, the fruits were ripening of the "hereditary fault of
Prussian Eastern Marches policy--encouragement of the Poles'
economic and cultural advancement." Left to themselves and their
own national leaders, the Polish bourgeoisie and rural masses
would have continued to slumber in the "helotry" in which the
Prussian government found them at the time of the partitions. But
peasant emancipation and Prussian schooling enabled them to follow
the lead of those among the upper classes whose deeper exposure to
German society and culture taught them the value of economic
development and peaceful cultural and political organization. The
Germans had themselves to blame for the Poles' successes after
1871 in the Organic Work movement and in the nationalist awakening
of the common people. On the war's eve Otto Hoetzsch admitted of
the Poznanian and West Prussian Poles that

through the modernization of their economic and
intellectual life, this Polish people appears to be
ripe for its own national state. To this end, the
Poles seem to be preparing their separation from
the German Reich--not, however, by force. Rather,
after the Germans have been deprived of their economic
base and driven out of the Polish areas of Prussia,
and when they have established their own economic
power securely in these regions, then the Prussian
Poles will seek to connect themselves with their
Russian and Galician brothers.

If then Germany found itself at war with Russia, the Prussian
Poles' "breakaway" would surely follow.[17]

The emergence of the National Democrats quickened Hakatist
hopes that the Poles would betray their revolutionary designs.
In the years after 1909, HKT propaganda systematically exaggerated
ND influence, but without conceding the sincerity of the Polish
conservatives' professions of loyalty. The Polish nationalists
were all without exception "Prussians on short notice (auf
Kündigung)."[18] The OMV showed a grudging admiration for the
Poles' national perseverance and dedication. Dietrich Schäfer
wrote, "One can understand the Poles historically, and precisely
a good German can conclude: 'If I were a Pole, I would do no less;
I too would refuse to give up the dream of the restoration of the
Empire (Reich) of my fathers.'"[19]

Polish nationalist militance justified the OMV's guiding
principle that "the Polish question cannot be solved on peaceful
lines, but only through struggle (Kampf)."[20] The Germans could
triumph only by taking the offensive with unwavering governmental
support. In a memorial to Bülow of 1902, the Hakatists wrote:
"However shameful for us Germans the admission might be, we have
to reckon with the eastern Germans' lesser powers of national
resistance and try to offset this disadvantage through a correspondingly stronger intervention of the state."[21]

HKT propaganda intoned the old National Liberal slogan
"Nationality follows language" as it demanded unceasingly further
repression of the Polish language, not only in the schools but
in the church, press, public meetings of all sorts, and in business
life. While experience discredited the strategy of forcible
linguistic Germanization, the OMV argued that the state should
prevent the Poles from parading their national separatism in the
public use of their language.[22]

Although it urged the Prussian government to strengthen its
arsenal of specifically anti-Polish laws and regulations, HKT
propaganda's heaviest emphasis fell on official aid to the
frontier Germans. Germanization of the Poles, Hugenberg wrote,
would remain a "utopian fantasy" so long as the Germans' economic

and demographic strength in the Eastern Marches was not overwhelmingly strong. Only then would the Poles see the advantages of
of assimilation. Only then would the archdiocese of Poznań-
Gniezno switch to the German side to avoid abandonment of Polish-
hued Catholicism or conversion to Protestantism by assimilation-
minded Poles. As things stood in the prewar decade, the "strong
and healthy" Polish working class and the land-hungry Polish
peasants had every reason to follow the nationalists in driving
the Germans from the east and taking over their economic positions.[23]

Despite their original intentions, the Hakatists accomplished
very little in organizing private German self-help associations in
the eastern provinces. During Waldow's tenure as provincial
president, the district commissioners reported on business opportunities for Germans in their localities. Higher officials
passed this information on to the OMV, which volunteered through
its press to help west German entrepreneurs establish themselves
in such positions.[24] HKT propaganda preached from the start a
"counterboycott" of Polish business firms. Like the Polish TDN,
the OMV staged numerous public meetings after the expropriations
of 1912 to popularize the boycott movement but, as among the Poles,
the Germans' commitment was lukewarm.[25]

The Hakatists bluntly held the frontier Germans' prospects
in the "economic struggle" to be "hopeless" without massive state
aid.[26] Taking the position that "industry Polonizes," the OMV
attempted to pressure the government into heavier public investments in the towns. Besides building projects and expansion of
state agencies and military installations, it called for large
state credits to German mortgage loan banks and urban building cooperatives. The OMV strongly endorsed the Royal Commission's
strategy of promoting German urban prosperity through encirclement of towns with villages of German colonists.[27]

In the controversial question of eastern industrialization,
the Hakatists took the easy way out. One of the Society's economic
experts, the Danzig merchant and syndic Wilhelm John, argued that
only intensive industrial development in the eastern marches
could halt the "flight from the east" by creating the urban
prosperity and business opportunities which the eastern Germans
and Jews had been seeking since the 1870s in the west. Conceding
that the industrial working class would be predominantly Polish,
he argued that large-scale industrialization and the heavily
capitalized commercial sector it would create would benefit the
German middle classes and skilled workers most. The German

population would expand far more rapidly than it could in the
traditional agrarian setting of the eastern provinces. By their
numbers, wealth, and technical and cultural sophistication the
Germans in an industrializing Ostmark would Germanize it sooner
and more surely than the Colonization Commission could.[28]

Eastern industrialization and state subsidy of the large
estate system through tariffs, tax loopholes, freight reductions,
production bonuses, and the colonization program were incompatible.[29] Advocacy of heavy industrial development would have
forced the OMV into open conflict with the Conservative Party,
the Bund der Landwirte, and the Junkers' advocates in the
Prussian government. It would have swung the OMV into the free-
trade camp and driven state employees and functionaries out of
the Hakatist ranks, fatally depleting them in the eastern provinces.
In short, it was politically impossible.

The Eastern Marches Society had no choice but to entrust
this fate of the frontier Germans to the state's colonization
program. The greatest weakness of German society in the Polish
provinces was the lack of "a robust substructure." Polish rural
workers drove out their German counterparts. Industrialization
would not create a strong German working class. Nothing remained
but to colonize a numerous and self-sufficient peasantry.[30] To
their ill-disguised dismay, the Hakatists found that as World
War I approached, peasant settlement, the card they had bet all
their money on, was failing to pay off. Moreover, the Poles
were less to blame for this state of affairs than the Junkers,
the OMV's apparent allies.

The chief HKT theoreticians and eastern activists agreed
that "large estates Polonize." Whether German or not, they
employed Polish labor alone. They blocked the German peasantry's
expansion. They robbed the towns of a German rural clientele
and helped to Polonize them. From the Hakatist point of view,
the large estate system was the eastern Germans' Achilles' heel.[31]
But as long as the Royal Commission could buy out or expropriate
the Polish gentry, criticism of German estates was muffled. On
the expropriation issue, Justizrat Wagner put the OMV's case
succinctly at the 1907 Executive Committee meeting in Bromberg:

> The question is not what will happen to the Poles. The
> issue is not the Poles' rights, but entirely justifiable
> German claims. We want to force the Poles out of their
> landholdings in the eastern marches as completely as we
> possibly can. (Bravo!) If they can't make a living here,
> they're free to settle down somewhere else in the German
> Empire . . . where they will very quickly become German-
> ized.[32]

The rural working class was a source of strength to the frontier

Poles only so long as it could find employment on eastern estates
or settle on parceled plots. Even after the Poles had stopped offering land to the Royal Commission, the OMV could evade the problem Junker estates posed, but only if Polish parcellation were
prohibited and colonization revived through expropriation. State
subsidies to the Junkers after 1908 for settling German laborers
on their lands showed that the Colonization Commission and the
government recognized the problem and sought to solve it through a
compromise which would leave the German estate system intact.

Passage of the expropriation act appeared to the OMV's friends
and foes alike as a Hakatist triumph presaging the Poles' final
rout in the "economic struggle."[33] But the Junkers benefited most
from official Germanization policy after 1908, while peasant
and rural worker colonization languished and Polish land acquisition went unimpeded. Among themselves, the more radical Hakatists
began to curse the government and the German landlords. Leo
Wegener expressed "hearty contempt" for the Poznanian Junkers and
great aggravation at the soaring influence over the provincial administration and Royal Commission of Major Endell, the strong-
willed leader of the Bund der Landwirte.[34] In 1912 he complained
that Colonization President Gramsch "gives way to every large
landowner and in dealing with the bureaucracy he has always been
weak." Waldow's departure was a loss. Schwartzkopff worked in
"close contact" with the Bund and "hates all economic questions."
Hugenberg agreed: "Schwartzkopff as provincial president is bad!
He was one of the strongest opponents of expropriation and he is
keen on Restgüter."[35]

Reluctantly, the OMV decided in 1911 to break openly with
Bethmann's regime. The small-scale expropriations of 1912 hardly
repaid the loss of influence over the Poznanian bureaucracy which
their revolt cost them. By mid 1912 Wegener was desperate over the
conservative agrarians' domination of Schwartzkopff's administration. Tiedemann bewailed the transfer of a Poznanian Landrat:
"Since the departure of this indiscreet man he [Tiedemann]
no longer can find out anything about the Bund or the views of the
high officials."[36]

By 1914 the OMV's relations with the government in Berlin
and the bureaucracy in Poznania were weaker than they had ever
been. The Society welcomed the government's draft parcellation
bill of 1914 coolly, taking no credit for it and criticizing it on
many points. Like the other legions in the conservative-nationalist camp, the Eastern Marches Society was thoroughly disillusioned
with Bethmann and counted his days in office.[37] Yet the Hakatists

were ill-equipped to take the field against the government. It
was, Wegener wrote, a "scandal" how "miserably" the OMV's interests were represented in the Berlin assemblies.[38] The powerful
National Liberal Party prided itself on its "folkish standpoint"
in the eastern marches question and stood ready to support the
OMV's anti-Polish initiatives.[39] But in 1909 the National
Liberals joined the opposition to the Conservatives and to
Bethmann's regime. Had the OMV cut its ties with the conservative agrarians, it might have found stronger political representation of its program in Berlin. Why it could not do so will
emerge from a closer look at the conservative-nationalist camp
in Poznania in the prewar years.

        Bismarck's turn to protectionism and break with the left
liberals in 1878-79 divided the Poznanian Germans into two
sharply opposed forces. In 1880 the liberal bourgeoisie formed a
provincial branch of the German Progressive Party. Four years
later, the Junkers and high officials organized the Conservative
Union, an alliance of the agrarian, bureaucratic, and business
and professional circles separately represented elsewhere in
Prussia and the Reich by the German Conservatives (DKP) and
the Reichspartei.
        Since 1815 the Poznanian bureaucracy had coalesced into a
powerful and politically homogeneous force while the Junkers had
multiplied and prospered. Confident of their economic strength
and social prestige, the United Conservatives loftily claimed
political preeminence in local German society. Their interests
were clear: aristocratic-bureaucratic monarchism, high tariffs,
Polenpolitik in the Frederickian-Flottwellian-Bismarckian mode.
Between 1878 and 1890 they endured the discomforts of the long
depression believing Bismarck had irrevocably tied the state's
fortunes to their own. Caprivi showed them how easily the knot
could be undone.
        Prussian conservatism emerged triumphant from the Caprivi
era, but also profoundly changed. In 1892 the DKP grafted on
to its traditional aristocratic-authoritarian and Protestant
Christian ideology the anti-Semitic and antiindustrial slogans
of the nascent völkisch movement. In 1893 the Bund der Landwirte's
Junker leaders began massing the north German peasant farmers
under its protectionist and belligerently antiliberal banners.
The Bund and DKP, dragging the less influential Reichspartei
in their van, had inaugurated the German conservatives' search
for an antidemocratic mass base which finally led them, through

their alliance with the National Socialists, to self-destruction.[40]

The Caprivi era demonstrated that the Wilhelminian regime
could not govern against the Conservatives' opposition without being driven into a political dependence on the Catholic Center and
the liberals menacing the aristocratic-monarchical constitution
of Prussia and the Empire. Hence after 1894 the Conservatives
quickly regained their status as the government's indispensible
partners. The tariff of 1902 satisfied the Junkers' protectionist
demands, and the financial reforms of 1909-13 favored agrarian
interests. But although Bülow and Bethmann solicitously did their
bidding, the Conservatives' parliamentary strength steadily
diminished. In the Reichstag, the number of their tribunes fell
between 1893 and 1912 from 100 to 57. While the Reich electorate
expanded in these two decades by more than 60 percent, the absolute
number of votes cast for the conservative parties rose not at
all.[41]

The implications of these tendencies were fatal to conservative interests. The rapidly growing urban electorate was ignoring the DKP and Reichspartei in favor of the Socialists, Progressives, and National Liberals. But the Landflucht and east Elbian
Ostflucht condemned the numbers of the Conservatives' rural
supporters--the Protestant farmers and villagers--to stagnation.
In the democratically elected Reichstag, the Conservatives lost
ground absolutely; in the Landtag, a relatively declining rural
population and the growing wealth of the urban middle classes
eroded their strong positions in the first and second voting
categories. Recognizing these trends, the Conservatives sought
to counter them by championship of the völkisch and nationalist-
imperialist issues popular among the urban middle and lower
middle classes. But before World War I they were overtrumped by
the National Liberals and Progressives, who combined these issues
with an increasingly vigorous assertion of urban economic
interests at the aristocratic agrarians' expense.[42]

The Conservatives had to settle for the organized support the
Bund der Landwirte provided them in the rural districts of north
Germany and east Elbia. Although it did not extend their electoral
base, the Bund's recruitment by the war's eve of over 300,000
members gave the Conservatives control over the largest nonpro-
letarian pressure group in Germany. The Bund's increasingly vital
importance to the Conservatives as their chief guarantee of mass
support at the polls meant that in the two decades after 1893 the
leadership and political tactics of the DKP bent increasingly under

Bund influence. Before the 1890s bureaucratic, Protestant
clerical, and urban upper-class influence had loomed large alongside that of the noble estate owners in the DKP. By 1914, the
party of the Prussian conservatives had been transformed into a
vehicle first and foremost of the Junker landlords' and well-to-
do Protestant peasant farmers' narrow economic interests.[43]

In Poznania, the champion of these interests was the
energetic Major Endell, chairman of the provincial Bund from
1893 until his death in 1914. On the eve of the war, the Bund
possessed county-level and electoral district organizations
wherever sizable German populations existed. Local meetings
among its roughly 8,000 members were frequent.[44] Its influence
radiated far beyond these limits. By 1911 the Bund operated
thirty-eight large-scale agricultural purchasing and marketing
cooperatives in the province. Endell founded and directed the
Raiffeisen rural cooperative savings and loan bank association,
which by 1912 counted 305 local societies, 30,000 members, and
31 million marks in deposits.[45] Endell and his allies dominated
the provincial Landwirtschaftskammer, the agrarian equivalent
to the chambers of commerce, whose 210 local agronomic societies
and 12,000 members entered the Bund's constituency.[46]

By 1914 Endell spoke authoritatively for the Protestant
German farming community in Poznania. Endell participated equally
with United Conservative, Progressive, and National Liberal
leaders in negotiating the election pacts uniting the German
parties against the Poles in Landtag and Reichstag elections
after 1907. Endell's public endorsement of German compromise
candidates alone ensured them the Protestant farmers' vote. In
1907 over half of all the Poznanian Protestants plied agricultural
occupations. In the Bund, the Junker farmers and entrepreneurs,
local German society's richest and most prestigious members,
controlled the single most powerful German political organization
in the province.[47]

In electoral politics, the Bund formed the agrarian wing of
the local United Conservative Party, in whose leadership the
Junkers played a paramount, though not monopolistic, part. In
1912, three of the party's five executive officers were Bund
leaders, including Endell and Heydebrand, chairman of the Reich-
level DKP. The agrarians determined the party's parliamentary
candidacies, if only because it owed the four Reichstag seats it
won in the 1912 elections to the German rural vote, while the
Progressives' strength in the towns allowed it to elect Landtag
deputies only in country districts.[48]

Yet the United Conservative Party was more than an agrarian front. It was also the political arm of the Prussian and Reich bureaucracy. This wing provided the party with numerous influential activists. In Reichstag elections, it mustered the votes of the province's numerous regular officials, schoolteachers, Protestant clergymen, state-employed workers, and those among the private bourgeoisie who cast Conservative ballots not to express agrarian sympathies but rather to affirm the monarchical establishment generally. Among the seventeen members of the party's forty-man provincial directorate who in 1912 were not Poznanian estate owners, many were high officials, including the Regierungspräsidenten of Posen and Bromberg and a high-ranking member of the provincial president's staff. What held throughout Prussia and the Reich was true of Poznania: the Junkers could not dispense with their bureaucratic and urban allies without isolating themselves as a demographically stagnating agrarian interest group; but the governmental wing of the Conservative movement relied on the agrarians to compensate for liberal and socialist dominance in the towns by guaranteeing the election of Conservative deputies in the rural districts. Like their counterparts at higher levels, the United Conservatives represented a coalition of partners who could not desert each other.[49]

The breakup of the Bülow bloc, the center-left agitation after 1909 against conservative fiscal and political privileges, and the mushrooming strength of the SPD threw the Poznanian Conservatives onto the defensive. They pumped large sums of money into the local conservative-nationalist press and tried to combat Progressive and National Liberal influence in the towns by forming local voters' societies. In 1912, they held their first annual public convention (Parteitag). In the three prewar years they staged seven mass meetings in the provincial capital to defend conservative interests and excoriate their German detractors. Conservative Party agitation shed its traditional, complacently elitist character and, following in the Bund's footsteps, turned to local action and highly partisan large-scale public demonstrations.[50]

Landeshauptmann von Heyking expressed the German conservatives' prewar political pessimism and anxieties in a speech of 1911. "We are living in dangerous times: surrounded by enemies, without and within."[51] Repeatedly the Conservatives found themselves forced to defend the Kaiser's fulsome constitutional and military powers, the privileges of the Prussian aristocracy, the "old Prussian traditions" of "sober commitment to duty and subordination to authority."[52]

Farm tariffs, anthropomorphized as "the guardians of our
national toil," required constant vindication, especially as meat
prices began to rise steeply after 1911.[53] Yet the monarchy's
and Conservatives' enemies seemed only to multiply. Since 1909
the Progressives and National Liberals had attacked the Conservatives through the Hansabund, a commercial-industrial pressure
group, and the Bauernbund, an anti-Junker farmers' league. Both
organizations aimed to increase Junker taxes and weaken Conservative control over local government and the Prussian Landtag.
Neither found a strong echo in Poznania before 1914, but they
combined with the Socialist movement to conjure up before the
Conservatives' eyes the specter of isolation, defeat, and "the
demise of the Prussian state."[54]

The great question in the Conservatives' minds in these years
was "whether we shall succeed in the long run in maintaining the
monarchy against the democratic assault."[55] Moderate reforms de-
fusing bourgeois and socialist opposition to the aristocratic-
monarchical regime were not the answer. The prewar Conservatives
felt their backs against the wall and were in no mood to compromise.
Clinging to their privileges, they looked for deliverance to a
new Bismarck, to "the already almost legendary strong man at the
head of the Imperial government," as Landtag deputy von Gossler
put it to the accompaniment of "stormy applause."[56] The Conservatives embraced the mythology of German authoritarianism of which,
a few decades later, they were to be among the victims. The Bund's
national director, Gustav Roesike, declared at a meeting on the
Saverne affair that

> We can never agree to the kind of parliamentary rule
> that the democratic parties want. No people is less
> suited to that than the Germans. It is part of the
> German character that the nation goes the right way
> when it does its duty and when it has an energetic
> leader sure of his goals.[57]

Although the Conservatives refrained from assaulting Bethmann
by name, their cries for strong leadership, like Heydebrand's
oppositional parliamentary tactics, aimed unmistakably at forcing him from office. Paradoxically, on the war's eve the Conservatives were no less busy than the left-wing opposition erod-
ing the Imperial government's authority, even though the
"legendary strong man" was nowhere in sight.

Such was the German conservative movement in Poznania, the
OMV's principal stronghold in the eastern marches. Despite their
nationwide propaganda campaigns, the Hakatists could not prevent
official Polenpolitik from sliding after 1908 onto conservative

tracks favoring Junker interests at the cost of massive peasant
colonization and other radical Germanization programs. Although,
as they said, "large estates Polonize," they did not break openly
with the Conservatives and the Bund der Landwirte as they did with
Bethmann and Schorlemer in 1911. Instead, they waited for
Heydebrand's conservative Fronde to overthrow Bethmann, hoping the
next chancellor would compensate for the necessity of maintaining
German large estates in the east by a renewed offensive against the
Poles.

The Ostmarkenverein could not break the Conservatives because
without the participation of employees and dependents of the state
in its ranks it would have faded into insignificance as a frontier
German political movement. At the end of 1907, it counted slightly
more than 11,000 members in the province. Of these 49 percent were
officials, clergymen, and elementary schoolteachers; 23 percent
were peasants, mainly colonists whose role in the movement was
largely passive; 22 percent were businessmen and artisans attracted
not only by the OMV's anti-Polish nationalism but also by its propaganda in favor of state aid to the towns; 2 percent were estate
owners, an indication that even in its years of greatest expansion
and prestige the OMV failed to recruit four out of every five of
the province's Junkers; and 1 percent were doctors and lawyers.[58]
Six years later, at the end of 1913, the OMV had added only 1,000
members to its ranks. The society's leaders privately bemoaned
this disappointing result of their recruitment efforts, which
boded no good for the future.[59] The occupations of these new
members are unknown, but the crucial importance of state servants
emerges clearly from the composition of the provincial executive
committee formed in 1912. Among these sixty-five OMV leaders,
there were twenty-two teachers, fourteen middle and higher officials, nine pastors or Protestant church officials, seven estate
owners, five businessmen, two journalists, and six in various other
private occupations. Altogether, 70 percent were state employees
whose participation in the OMV had been encouraged by state direc-
tives since 1895 and who after 1903 received salary bonuses for
doing so.[60]

Many officials, teachers, and pastors required no financial
inducements to join the OMV. By the nature of their duties and
their own convictions, they were agents of the Prussian state's
"mission in the east." But most of the Junkers and peasant
farmers looked to the Bund der Landwirte and United Conservative
Party to represent their particular interests. The Catholics,
the Jews, and a large segment of the Protestant bourgeoisie positively opposed the Eastern Marches Society.

Having failed to establish a local base independent of
the state, the OMV could hope to gain influence in frontier German nationalist politics only through collaboration with the
United Conservatives and so also with the Bund der Landwirte.
Antagonization of either the state administration or the conservatives' two interlocking political organizations ran the risk of
forcing the OMV's state-employed members into a crisis of loyalty
and abandonment of the HKT cause. The Bund was suspicious of
the OMV from the start. Endell broke with it in 1895 in protest
over its propaganda against the Junkers' employment of Russian
and Galician Polish seasonal labor. Only after the OMV dropped
this issue and reassured Endell and the Prussian government
that the point of its political lance was leveled at the Poles
and not at the system of German large estates did the Bund,
the Conservatives, and the state accept it as a political ally.[61]
In the period 1897-1908 the OMV served the Prussian government
and the Conservatives as a useful junior partner in Bülow's
nationalist-imperialist campaigns against the Poles, especially
since the Hakatists hoped to forge an urban nationalist bloc in
the east in opposition to the German liberals.

The expropriation issue ruptured the anti-Polish alliance
of the state, the Bund, the Conservatives, and the Hakatists.
After gaining the government's assurances that expropriation would
be applied only to Polish lands, and then only in consultation
with the frontier Junkers, Heydebrand succeeded in swinging the
DKP and the national leadership of the Bund behind the 1908 law.
But in Poznania, Endell and his followers bitterly resisted it,
fearing it would strengthn the Polish nationalists' hand in
organizing the common people and, in the long run, undermine
the eastern Junkers' control over their lucrative Polish labor
force.

The government and the Royal Commission hoped passage of the
expropriation bill would halt the soaring price of estate land
in Poznania. But the local Junkers, profiting greatly from the
post-1894 inflation of land values, explicitly opposed the "general fall in prices" they too expected the new law would cause.
Heydebrand and Waldow urged Endell to support the government's
draft. Waldow overconfidently reported to Bülow in the fall of
1907 that the Poznanian Bund had been won over. In fact, Endell
complained to Waldow about the local officials, no doubt Landräte,
who pressured German estate owners to drop their opposition to the
law. "Great violence," Endell melodramatically declared, "is
being done to the individual Bund members." Endell intransigently

submitted to the Prussian Herrenhaus a petition signed by 170
Poznanian Junkers, Bund members all, urging defeat of what they
believed was a dangerously radical measure.[62]

The expropriation debates exposed a fundamental conflict of
interest between the OMV, which was keen on uprooting not only the
szlachta but also the Polish villagers, and the frontier Junkers,
who depended on cheap Polish labor. In the years after 1908,
relations between the conservative agrarians and the Hakatists grew
increasingly frigid and hostile. The OMV's campaign in favor of
expropriation during 1911 did not prevent Bethmann from trimming
his policies to suit the Junkers, while it inspired the Poznanian
landlords, including Endell, to denounce, in their antiexpropriation petition of 1911, the OMV's claims to represent frontier German nationalist interests and opinion. Thereafter, until the
outbreak of the war, the Bund and the United Conservatives, like
Bethmann and Schwartzkopff, showed the Hakatists a cold shoulder.
The OMV lost its patrons in the local bureaucracy and in the
Colonization Commission. It had no influence in the leadership of
the Bund or Conservative Party. The province's German Conservative
parliamentary deputies paid it no homage.

On the eve of the war, neither the Bund nor the United Conservatives displayed any enthusiasm for harsh and noisy attacks on
the Poles. Their reaction to the expropriations of 1912 was dis-
tinctly cool. They viewed the parcellation bill of 1914 with a
mixture of indifference and suspicion. Their interest focused on
the larger issues of German national politics: above all, fiscal
and constitutional reform. Major Endell stated the Bund's position on the domestic Polish question tersely: "Only when the
German farmers in the east, both large and small, are effectively
ensured of their material existence under all circumstances will
they be able to defend the Ostmark successfully against all attacks on it."[63] Endell reduced Polenpolitik to unstinting state
support of German agrarian interests as defined by the Bund der
Landwirte.

The United Conservatives' views on the Polish question echoed
Bethman's and Bismarck's. During the debates sparked by the
Kaiser's visit of 1913, the Posener Tageblatt summed up local Con-
servative opinion thus:

> [What is at issue] is not an aggressive "life
> and death" struggle waged against the entire Polish
> population; it is not a question, so to speak, of
> exterminating the Poles (Ausrottung des Polentums).
> Rather the government's Polenpolitik is aimed only
> at the defeat of those Polish nationalist efforts
> and designs whose realization would be incompatible
> with the Prussian state-idea and with the security

> of the German Reich. Once again in Posen the
> Kaiser has encouraged the Poles in the friendli-
> est words to devote themselves to the common task
> of advancing and improving our narrower fatherland
> (engeres Vaterland)[i.e., Poznania] upon the founda-
> tion of German culture and merging the east ever
> more closely with the other parts of the German Reich.
> So long as the Poles reply to such an exhortation,
> which is an obvious prerequisite to any tolerable
> national peace in the east, with only the coolest
> and most emphatic refusal, they cannot expect that
> the state will not do everything in its own interest
> to fortify its borders.[64]

Germanization of the public life and institutions of the one-
Polish provinces followed from the Empire's character as a "uni-
tary German national state"; German colonization created the
fortifications which Polish "fanatics," "international Polonism,"
obliged the Prussian state to erect in its own self-defense.[65]
As the sharp-tongued Conservative Elard von Oldenburg-Januschau
told the Polish deputies during the expropriation debates, "If
you will not give us your hearts, gentlemen, then we must have
your land. . . ."[66]

The Poles saw rightly that the choice the German Conservatives
offered them was either voluntary or forcible Germanization. What
separated the Poznanian Junkers and Conservatives from the OMV
was their lack of interest in the Germanization of the eastern
marches and displacement of the Polish population as völkisch-
national ends in themselves. As the radical Hakatists and Pan-
Germans defined them, those goals could finally be attained only
through the liquidation of the system of large estates in the
east, and so also of the Junkers as a social class. It was
impossible for the Bund der Landwirte or the Conservative Party
to go along with this. They preferred to see German peasant
colonization grind to a half if the only alternatives were a
massive, politically all too suggestive expropriation of the
Polish gentry or further erosion of German large landholdings
through sales to the Royal Commission. They could afford to ignore the Hakatists' opposition to them on this crucial issue,
well aware that if the Eastern Marches Society dared to break
definitively with the Conservative camp, it would lose half its
members and most of its activists.

In 1914 the Hakatists' prospects were gloomy. Neither the
government in Berlin nor their conservative allies could be relied
on to promote Germanization of the east as they envisaged it. In
Poznania, OMV membership stagnated, its organizational life grew
desultory. The Hakatists' original hopes of uniting the frontier

Germans in a spirit of völkische Gemeinburgschaft had been disappointed by liberal hostility, Junker self-absorption, and the indifference of the German urban and rural workers.

The OMV's yearly celebrations (Deutsche Tage) continued to
draw large crowds of the HKT faithful, who also joined the German
Conservatives and liberals in the ubiquitous annual commemorations
of Bismarck's birthday and the Battle of Sedan.[67] Yet after 1908
OMV activists began to detect a spirit of indifference and "organizational ennui" among the Society's numerous local branches.[68] In
its widely distributed Eastern Marches Calendar for 1908 the OMV
admitted that

> there are many complaints that in the eastern
> provinces . . . the upper-class leaders of the
> German population--the large landowners and higher
> officials--apart from a few encouraging exceptions
> either hold themselves completely aloof from the
> Society, or at the most content themselves with
> paying membership dues without taking any part in
> the meetings and activities of the local Ostmarken-
> verein groups . . .[69]

The Hakatists' vision of national solidarity dissolved among the
harsh realities of the social and ideological fragmentation of the
frontier Germans. At a 1908 meeting in Danzig

> Herr Professor Hoffmann deplored the caste spirit
> which especially here in the east assumes such
> crass forms. This hinders the national develop-
> ment of the German people. It is no disgrace for
> richer or better educated people to sit together
> at the beer table with a man in a worker's blouse.[70]

At many meetings, not even all the local officers appeared. It was
"repeatedly observed" that

> outside the meeting the large landowners, the
> leaseholders on royal domains, or the notables of
> the town have sat at dinner, or over beer, or
> playing cards, without caring a whit for the as-
> sembly taking place right next to them.[71]

The outbreak of World War I offered the Hakatists a release
from this organizational malaise, firing their imaginations with
thoughts of grandiose German conquests in the east. Bethmann's
regime quickly committed itself to the annexation at Russian expense of a "Polish border strip" which would permanently extend
the German frontier eastward into Congress Poland. The Hakatists
and Pan-Germans were among this plan's chief proponents. As the
war proceeded, the idea arose in radical nationalist circles to
"resettle" the Poznanian and West Prussian Poles farther eastward,
in the German satellite Kingdom of Poland set up in 1916. The
Polish question in the Prussian east would be forcibly and
definitively resolved by the Prussian Poles' expulsion. Their
places would be taken by colonists drawn from both the Reich and

from German minority communities in the western lands of the Russian Empire. The German defeat of 1918 forestalled the execution
of this radical resettlement policy, which had steadily gained adherents among the parties and pressure groups of the nationalist-
imperialist right. It remained as a legacy to the National Socialists, who ruthlessly expelled from the lands of western Poland
the propertied and educated classes while forcibly recruiting
large numbers of Polish peasants and workers for semipenal labor
in west German industry.[72]

The Hakatists and Pan-Germans eagerly seized upon the idea
of expelling to the east the Prussian, and above all the Poznanian,
Poles. On 3 October 1914 Hugenberg wrote to the Berlin professor
Ludwig Bernhard, praising unreservedly his expulsion plan, which
went by the code name "land without people" (Land ohne Menschen).[73]
In a second letter Hugenberg declared portentously that execution
of the "land without people" scheme was Germany's highest objective in the war. Meanwhile, Bernhard and Wegener began pressuring
the Poznanian administration and the government in Berlin to
"improve" not only Germany's political boundaries in the east,
but its "ethnic frontier" as well.[74] On 15 December 1914, Bernhard
informed Hugenberg of the first fruits of these efforts: "No
doubt you have heard that the land without people idea has made
an impression on the Chancellor. Ganse [president of the Colonization Commission] has been ordered to provide the evacuations with
a legal rationale." Bernhard thought the expulsions could begin
once the German army had taken Warsaw.[75]

The Hakatists and their allies leapt at the prospect of
expelling the Poles with an enthusiasm revealing not only the depth
of their völkisch radicalism but also their frustration over their
waning political influence and organizational dynamism. "Land
without people," like many of the Hakatists' earlier anti-Polish
proposals, betrayed their debt to Bismarck, who in 1885-86 had
set the precedent of nationally inspired expulsions in the east.
As in the past, so too during World War I the government in
Berlin was free to resist the Hakatists' anti-Polish demands.
Whether in the wake of the conquests sealed by the Treaty of
Brest-Litovsk the Prussian-German ruling class would have long
resisted the right-wing nationalists' pressures for eastern "re-
settlements" is an open question. In the light of the Prussian
government's capitulation to such pressures before 1914, skepticism
is in order.

In the judgment of present-day German and Polish historians,
the Eastern Marches Society was ultimately nothing more than "an

extended arm of the state's German nationality policies in the
east (Deutschtumspolitik)."[76] It is true that its heavy recruitment of state servants drew the OMV into a galling dependency on
the government. The state alone could set in motion the Hakatists'
far-ranging anti-Polish strategies. But these strategies, as they
were spelled out by Hugenberg, Wegener, Vosberg, Bernhard, and
other covert or overt HKT leaders, differed fundamentally from the
policies the Prussian Conservatives and the government in Berlin
embraced.

The Hakatists were stirred by a vision of German national
community. Although they concentrated on realizing it at the
Poles' expense, it shed a hostile light on the class privileges
and "caste spirit" of the German agrarian and aristocratic-
bureaucratic ruling classes. Before 1914, the conservative
establishment was too strong for the OMV's völkisch yearnings to
determine the formulation and conduct of official Polish policy.
On the contrary, the government drew from the Hakatist arsenal
only such weapons as it found useful in defending its own
interests.

After 1918, the Prussian-German conservatives lost control of
the state. When finally it fell into the National Socialists'
hands, they pursued the goal of eastern German völkische Gemeinburgschaft which the Eastern Marches Society had first conceived
in its fusion of the anti-Polish Germanization policies of the
Prussian state with the antidemocratic mythology of late nineteenth century German bourgeois nationalism. But before 1918
the Prussian-German government had pronounced the Hakatists' goals
good and trimmed its policies to meet their demands at least in
part. Thus it stamped the OMV with a seal of respectability in the
eyes of the conservative and nationally minded German middle
classes, especially outside the eastern provinces. In the substance of its Polenpolitik, as in its initial patronage and later
appeasement of the HKT Society, the Prussian government legitimized
nationalist radicalism in conservative terms.

The Bismarckian empire bequeathed to the National Socialists
the strategy, championed by the Eastern Marches Society, of dis-
solving class conflict in an idealized German national community
expanding eastward. The price of Hitler's pursuit of this
imperialist chimera was not only the fierce destruction rained on
the land and peoples of Poland and Soviet Russia during World War
II; it was also the ruin and dismemberment of the German national
state.

The Progressives and the Polish Question

The Poznanian liberals of the pre-1914 decades were the
heirs of the Progressives and left-wing National Liberals whose
pressure on Bismarck to strengthen the Reichstag's constitutional
powers led him to abandon them as allies and proscribe them as
"enemies of the Reich" during the pivotal domestic crisis of
1878-79. Cast into the antigovernmental desert but still true to
free-trading "Manchesterism" and English-style parliamentarism,
the left liberals reorganized themselves on the Reich level in
1884 as the German Progressive Party (Deutsche Freisinnige Partei).
It was this oppositional wing of the liberal movement rather than
the more conservative National Liberal Party that commanded the
loyalty of the Poznanian German middle classes. Bismarck's
tariffs sharply contradicted their interest in free trade with
Russia and in east German industrial development. This, and
their hostility to Junker privilege, restrained the Progressives
from joining the National Liberals of central and western Germany
in their lucrative and prestigious junior partnership in the
Bismarckian regime.

After the elections of 1881, the Progressives were the
strongest opposition party in the Reichstag. By 1914 this distinction belonged to the massive SPD. After the Caprivi era the
Progressives commanded only a relatively small bloc of deputies
representing the views and interests of the liberal intelligentsia,
financial and commercial circles, and antiprotectionist manufacturers.[1]

Except for their ill-rewarded participation in the Bülow
bloc of 1907-9, the Progressives never escaped the oppositional
role Bismarck cast upon them. As the rise of the SPD forced the
government to seek a broader parliamentary base than the Con-
servative-NLP cartel afforded, it found coming to terms with the
more numerous and conservative Catholic Center easier than concessions to the Progressives. In opposition, the Progressives'
doctrinaire anti-socialism isolated them from the SPD.

As long as there was no prospect that the Progressives and
left-leaning National Liberals would join the Socialists in a majority coalition prepared to force social and constitutional reform
on the government, a vote for the left liberals was little more
than an ideological demonstration. After the collapse of the
Bülow bloc in 1909, and especially after the great gains of the
center and left parties in the elections of 1912, the formation
of such a grand coalition ("from Bassermann to Bebel") became a
distinct possibility, as the government and the conservative
parties nervously appreciated. The rift among the cartel parties
opened by Bülow's and Bethmann's tax reforms drove the National
Liberals leftward. Adopting the slogan "front against the right,"
the NLP and the Progressives, newly organized in 1910 after years
of schism as the Progressive People's Party (Fortschrittliche
Volkspartei), collaborated among themselves and with the SPD in
the runoff elections of 1912 against the Centrists and Conservatives. Although these tactical alliances were brittle, the 1912
elections showed that the Progressives had gained significantly in
popular support since 1907, while the NLP had at least lost no
votes through its shift away from the right.[2]

The prospect of Reich-level liberalization threw the survival
of the cartel parties' monopoly of power in the Prussian Landtag
in doubt. The three-class electoral law secured for the cartel
274 of the Landtag's 443 seats in the 1913 elections. But the
NLP's quarrels in Imperial politics with the conservative parties
made it more receptive to electoral reform in Prussia, conceded
already by Bülow in 1908 as necessary and cautiously advocated on
conservative terms even by Bethmann.[3] Rising incomes among the
industrial and commercial middle classes would combine with even
a moderate reform of the Prussian voting law to reduce the Conservatives' representation in the Landtag considerably. The same
effect would be hastened if the bourgeois parties and the Socialists
could force through the Reichstag a reduction in agricultural
duties. In Prussia as well as on the Imperial level, it was not
surprising that the Progressives anticipated the slow erosion of
William II's "personal regime," especially after its stewardship
had fallen to the uncharismatic and hard-pressed Bethmann
Hollweg.

While the Poznanian liberals found such prospects heartening,
their party loyalty depended very little on Progressive successes
or failures in Prussian and Imperial politics. This was especially true for the large number of Jews among them, for after 1880
only the Progressives could be counted upon among the nonsocialist

parties to provide a consistent defense of Jewish rights and
interests. The Poznanian Jews could not abandon the Progressives without facing the choice of supporting one of the other
bourgeois parties, which were either indifferent or more or less
hostile to Jewish concerns, or joining the Socialists, or retir-
ing from German politics altogether.

Between 1880 and 1914 the Progressives commanded the steady
support of the great majority of Germany's Jews.[4] After 1878
most of the National Liberals' numerous Jewish adherents followed
the party's dissident left wing into opposition and, in 1884,
fusion with the Progressives. In the 1890s, the Progressives began to suffer defections among their Jewish constituency to the
Social Democrats, especially in the large cities and industrial
districts of central and western Germany. But the SPD exerted
a stronger attraction on Jewish political activists, particularly
those with academic backgrounds, than on the Jewish electorate.
In the decade before 1914, while perhaps 40 percent of all Jewish
politicians were engaged in the Socialist movement, over 80
percent of the Jewish vote fell to the bourgeois parties, and
over 60 percent to the Progressives alone.[5] In Poznania the
vitality of Jewish religiosity, the bourgeois character of the
Jewish community, the weakness of the SPD, and the pressures
exerted by the nationality conflict combined to maintain unbroken the Jews' solid and active allegiance to the Progressive
Party to 1914 and beyond.

The Progressives' Jewish partisans expected the party to
be a "Jewish defense force" (Judenschutztruppe).[6] But they did
not wish it to be, nor of course was it, a specifically Jewish
party. The Progressive People's Party (FVP) organized in 1910,
like its left-liberal predecessors, was a secular organization
whose members were bound together by liberal conviction and German
national consciousness. Although most of the German Jews supported the FVP, a large majority of the Progressive electorate
and party leadership throughout the Reich were Protestants. Nor
were Catholics, especially those who agreed with the party's
insistence on a strict separation of church and state, absent
from the FVP's ranks. The Progressive movement's traditional
motto was "equal rights for all" (gleiches Recht für alle).
Insofar as the FVP claimed any social base, it was the "liberal
middle class" (liberales Bürgertum).[7] The party championed the
civil rights and equality of the Jews not as a distinctive
religious or ethnic group but as "German citizens of Jewish
faith" (deutsche Bürger jüdischen Glaubens), a description which

the great majority of the Jews of Imperial Germany willingly and
happily applied to themselves. The Progressives represented Jewish
social and cultural interests only to the degree that they were
shared throughout the Reich by the "liberal middle class" generally. Had the Jews entirely deserted the Progressive Party, it
would have lost perhaps 5 percent of its voting strength on the
Reich level, but its ideological and social character would have
remained completely unchanged.[8]

In Poznania, as elsewhere in Imperial Germany, the Jews supported the Progressive Party as German citizens and members of the
German nation whose right to practice their religion freely and
whose immunity from any civil liabilities for doing so were both
guaranteed by constitutional law. The Progressives fulfilled
their role as a "Jewish defense force" simply by upholding the
Jews' civil rights as German citizens. To this the party was
committed by its own egalitarian liberalism, regardless of whether
or not Jews voted for it or participated in its activities.

In Poznania, the Jews represented the richest and most
firmly rooted segment of the urban bourgeoisie. Although emigration to the west greatly reduced their absolute numbers after 1871,
on the eve of World War I the province's larger towns and cities
still possessed sizable Jewish populations. In 1910 the Jews of
the city of Poznań numbered 5,590. Bromberg counted a Jewish
community of 1,345; Inowrocław, 948; Lissa (Leszno), 802; Gniezno,
776; Kępno (Kempen) and Ostrów about 700.[9] Because of their
numbers and their economic strength, the Jews played a major role
in city government. Since Stein's municipal reforms of 1808, urban politics in Prussia had been liberal politics, at least so
far as the private bourgeoisie was concerned. In Bismarckian
Germany, the Progressive Party championed in the Reichstag and
Landtag the economic interests and claims to self-government of the
urban bourgeoisie, especially in east Elbian Prussia. It was
in the Prussian cities that the Progressives counted their strongest bases of support and their most active local organizations.
In Poznania, the Jews' involvement in urban politics thus led them
to look to the Progressives to represent them at higher political
levels and to join with liberal-minded members of the Protestant
German bourgeoisie to form local Progressive Party committees to
propagandize the liberal cause in the province and to run Progressive candidates in Landtag and Reichstag elections.

Not just the need to defend their civil rights led the
Poznanian Jews into active support of the Progressive movement;
the German left liberals were their natural allies in the promotion

of urban middle-class interests at the expense of royal absolutism
and agrarian conservatism. Conversely, the German Protestants
who headed the Progressive movement at the Reich and Prussian
levels, as well as those who were its partisans in the eastern
provinces, welcomed Jewish support. It broadened the party's
electoral base. In nineteenth century Poznania, no party claiming to represent the German-speaking bourgeoisie could hope to
flourish without Jewish backing.

The Poznanian Progressives were organized on two levels.
In the years after 1880 they established Freisinnige Vereine in
most of the province's towns with sizable German populations.
In 1893 representatives of these local organizations formed a
central executive committee known after 1910 as the Provincial
Association of the Progressive People's Party. It directed the
party's Landtag and Reichstag election campaigns throughout the
province and, in concert with the provincial capital's large and
active Freisinniger Verein, staged annual party conferences and
public meetings. The party possessed a strong advocate in the
Posener Neueste Nachrichten, whose daily circulation in the prewar
years reached 24,000. Although the Progressives accelerated
their agitation in the decade before 1914, they fell far behind
both the Polish nationalists and the German Conservatives and
Hakatists. The Progressives could boast of no such adjuncts to
their own party as the Poles' Organic Work institutions or the
DKP's Bund der Landwirte. Like the Progressives throughout the
Reich, the Poznanian liberals were a "party of notables"
(Honoratiorenpartei). Their strength derived from the prominence
of their prosperous and well-educated leaders in local social and
economic life, from the high quality of their press, and from
the appeal of their liberal-democratic ideology to the nonsocialist urban electorate. In Prussia, the Progressives could count
upon the three-class voting law to translate their economic
strength into numerous town council delegations and Landtag mandates. In Poznania, the weakness of National Liberal competition allowed the Progressives to dominate the first and second
voting categories in municipal elections and, in the Landtag
elections of 1908, to capture all seven of the province's urban
mandates.[10]

The Progressives elected many Jewish town councillors in
Poznania. But despite their voting strength in Landtag elections,
the Jews seldom stood for parliamentary seats. Only two of the
Progressives' seven Landtag deputies during the years 1908-
13 were Jews. Most of the party's Jewish partisans stoically

accepted this state of affairs. What counted to them was not the
religion of their deputies, but the reliability of their defense
of Jewish civil rights in the Landtag. If by running Jewish candidates the party weakened its appeal to German voters outside the
ranks of the party faithful, the Jews in Poznania were willing to
resign from such candidacies in elections where they might lead
the party into defeat.[11] But no such considerations deterred
Jewish liberals from playing major roles in the party's organizational life. Three of the five members of the FVP executive committee elected in 1910 were prominent members of the province's
Jewish community. One of them, Justizrat Michaelis Placzek, long-
standing chairman of the Poznań city council, also occupied one of
the three directorships of the capital city's Freisinniger Verein.
The society emphasized its multiconfessional character by electing as Placzek's colleagues a Protestant physician and a Catholic
school principal. Among the sixteen executive committeemen of
this most important of the province's Progressive locals, five
were active members of the local Jewish religious community. Most
of the rest were Protestants.   Among these sixteen, there were
three paid city officials, three merchants, three teachers (including one woman), two physicians, an architect, an attorney, a
newspaper editor, a postal official, and a shoemaker. University-
trained professionals and, to a lesser degree, merchants and
businessmen led the Progressive movement in the city of Poznań.
The addition of one state official to their ranks in 1914 only
underscored the Progessives' lack of support among the provincial
capital's large bureaucracy. The social and political gulf between
the private middle classes (Bürgertum) and Prussian officialdom
(Beamtentum) which the liberals resentfully denounced was real
enough.[12]

     In Imperial politics, the Progressives had reason to fear
being driven into the shadows by the swiftly growing socialist
movement. In the eastern marches, the Polish populists and National Democrats denounced them in increasingly harsh and anti-
Semitic tones. But the Progressives identified their principal
political adversaries as the "reactionary" parties in general
and the Prussian Conservatives in particular. Nothing embittered
the Progressives more than Bismarck's defeat of liberal government
in Germany and the perpetuation this entailed of the German bourgeoisie's socioeconomic and political subordination to the Prussian monarchy and its aristocratic sword-bearers, landlords, and
bureaucrats. "Under Bismarck the nation forgot how to think
politically. Any other opinion besides that of the leading
statesman was counted almost a crime." So spoke the Progressive

deputy and publicist Georg Gothein at a massive assembly staged
in Poznań in January 1914 by the Progressives to protest the
Prussian monarchy's arrogant exertion of its constitutionally unlimited military powers in the sensational Saverne case. This
incident, which unveiled the reactionary aggressiveness animating
William II's military entourage, touched the sorest nerves of the
Poznanian liberals. Gothein's audience of more than one thousand
listeners repeatedly interrupted him with what even the Conservative press described as "stormy and prolonged" applause as he
inveighed against "the spirit of the east Elbian Junkers, the
spirit that knows only lords and vassals." This was the spirit
which in the days of pre-Napoleonic Prussian absolutism had
harshly commanded the middle classes to "pay up and keep quiet."
The Junkers confined the reforms of Stein and Hardenberg to half-
measures, and in the aftermath of Bismarck's wars they bent the
monarchy, the Reich, and the nation to their will with ever
greater egotism. They set themselves above the nation as a race
apart, animated by a higher virtue peculiar to themselves alone.
But "there is no special honor for officers. Every man has the
same honor and needs only to act as an honorable man." Gothein's
attack on the systematic exclusion of Jews from the Prussian
reserve officer corps since the 1880s won resounding cheers.
So too did his closing sally: "Certainly we want the Kaiser's
coat to be respected--if it deserves respect. But the coat of
the private citizen must be respected too."[13]

During the years of Bethmann's prewar chancellorship, the
Progressives concentrated their ideological fire on parliamentary
reform. They advocated an oppositional coalition of the center
and left parties in the Reichstag which would trade support of tax
levies for constitutional liberalization. They redoubled their
propaganda in support of reform of the Prussian electoral law
"from the ground up." Though they stood for secret, direct, and
universal suffrage, they "reckoned with realities" in calling immediately upon Bethmann's government to redraw the boundaries of
voting districts in Prussia and to abolish open and indirect
balloting, reforms they thought attainable in the Landtag elected
in 1913. Prussian constitutional reform alone could bring about
the democratization of the Reich constitution and the other
changes, no less inimical to the "reactionary" parties, demanded
in the Progressives' prewar program: tariff reduction, abolition
of the Junkers' tax privileges, ending preferential treatment of
nobles and discrimination on religious grounds in the civil and
military service, secularization of school administration, intensive state-supported inner colonization in the east, abolition

of the Junkers' police powers, and repeal of the laws prohibiting rural workers from organizing unions.[14]

The introduction of universal and equal suffrage in Prussia would have permitted the SPD to send to the Landtag in Berlin a delegation nearly as powerful as its Reichstag counterpart. It would have abolished the privileges conferred on the Progressives in municipal politics by the oligarchical three-class system. In Poznania, it would have handed over many town councils and Landtag seats to the Poles. If these drastic changes seemed acceptable to the Progressives in the eastern provinces it was because the Bismarckian constitution excluded them from independent executive power even at the municipal level while discriminating against them socially and economically. The Wilhelminian government's reactionary enmity only fanned the Socialists' militance. In a liberalized Prussia the Progressives expected to see the SPD follow the path of reform and collaboration with the middle-class parties as it had already in Baden. Similarly, the Progressives held Wilhelminian Polenpolitik responsible for the radicalization of the national conflict in the east, from which their partisans derived nothing but losses. Relief was possible only through a fundamental reform of official nationality policy and that too required the dismantling of oligarchical monarchism in Prussia.

The Progressives condemned the idea that the state should Germanize the Prussian Poles and the lands of the eastern marches as a delusion of Berlin bureaucrats "with their heads in the clouds" and right-wing nationalists blinded by "the most idiotic sort of chauvinism."[15] This was, the liberals argued, a delusion a majority of the Germans in the east did not share. The government's aggressively anti-Polish Ostmarkenpolitik positively injured the economic and political interests of the very German population it grandly claimed to defend.

The Progressives had no quarrel with the state or the conservative parties over Prussia's sovereign right to rule the formerly Polish provinces. "The eastern marches are German property," declared FVP Reichstag deputy Dr. Wiemer at a well-attended Progressive meeting staged in Poznań in December 1912 to protest the government's expropriation actions. "We want to see the wings of the Prussian eagle soar forever over these lands." Wiemer added, "We certainly do not condemn the goal of maintaining and strengthening the German nationality in the Eastern Marches. That goal is thoroughly justifiable."[16] Nor did the Progressives dissent from the centralizing tendencies of traditional Polenpolitik. "The goal," wrote Georg Wagner, editor of the Posener

Neueste Nachrichten and a veteran Progressive leader in Poznań,

> must be to incorporate the eastern marches both in-
> wardly and indissolubly into the state as a whole.
> A firm and integrated state structure lies in the
> interest of the individual citizen as well as in the
> interest of the whole nation. Like any other German
> party, the Progressive People's Party regards this
> idea of the state as a basic principle. The means
> employed in the last decades to realize it, however,
> have been false, for they repel the Poles instead of
> drawing them towards the state. Through the use of
> exceptional [i.e., discriminatory] legislation, al-
> ways harmful to both state and society, they have
> turned the Poles into second-class citizens.[17]

The Progressives agreed with the German conservatives and
radical nationalists that the Poles ought to accept and value
citizenship in the German Empire. But the liberals denied that
the Poles needed to sacrifice their own nationality to do so,
just as they also denied that the Poles could be forced against
their will to become Germans. It was absurd, Delbrück argued,
not to recognize that the Poles constituted one of the historic
nations of Europe. Their will to maintain a national community
despite the destruction of the Polish state could be broken, if
at all, only by "ruining them utterly." Neither forcing the
German language upon them nor suppressing the use of their
mother-tongue would obliterate Polish national consciousness.
The Irish example alone refuted the equation of language and
nationality.[18]

The government's exclusion of Polish language instruction
from the public school curriculum merely heightened the Poles'
sense of discrimination at German hands while strengthening their
attachment to those Polish institutions--church, nationalist
cultural societies, press--which assumed the schools' job of
teaching and cultivating their mother-tongue. The more as-
siduously the state taught them German, the more willingly they
taught themselves to read and write their own language. Thus
the Prussian Poles became to a high degree bilingual. This conferred an advantage on them, as the Progressives frequently
pointed out, in their economic competition with the frontier
Germans, who were positively prevented by Prussian school policy
from learning their Polish competitors' and clients' language.[19]

The Progressives concluded that the Prussian government's
efforts to Germanize the Poles through the suppression of their
language in the schools and in other spheres of public life only
strengthened their national consciousness and anti-Germanism.
This was criticism as sound and embarrassing to the government
and the right-wing German parties as the Progressives' analysis
of the colonization program. The "struggle for the land" which

Bismarck launched in 1886 awakened the Polish gentry, economically
speaking, from their patriarchal slumbers and forced them to
become efficient producers. The government's increasingly desperate efforts to lay its hands upon Polish estate land through anti-
parcellation and expropriation legislation enraged and embittered
the Poles as perhaps no other assault upon the foundations of
their national existence could have done. Yet, the Progressives
argued, it was the Germans of the eastern marches, not the Poles,
whom the government's efforts to uproot the szlachta weakened and
demoralized. The Junkers proved so susceptible to the offers of
the Royal Commission, which they did not scruple to inflate by
threats of selling instead to the Poles, that the government finally found itself forced to bribe the Poznanian Junkers with refinancing programs and other subsidies not to abandon their posts
in the east. This amounted, as the Progressives' Landtag deputy
for the city of Poznań said, to "rewarding them for bad patriotism." The German landlords who felt an attachment to their local
homeland lost the respect of their Polish workers and the good
will of their neighbors among the szlachta. The German peasant
colonists upon whom the Royal Commission showered its abundant
favors were not natives of the eastern marches, but "outsiders"
from west and south Germany or from Russia or the Hapsburg lands,
resented if not scorned by the old-established Poznanian Germans.
The Poles these newcomers displaced migrated in large numbers to
the local towns, swelling the clientele of the Polish bourgeoisie
and driving German artisans and workers westwards. The German
commercial and professional bourgeoisie, the Progressives' main
constituency in the east, suffered most directly from the
crystallization of the Poles' anti-German hostilities in the
Polish boycott movement, whose accompaniment was an ever more nerve-
wracking anti-Semitism. Contrary to the government's and nationalists' claims, the patronage of newly settled German colonists
did not make good the losses the boycott inflicted on Christian
and Jewish German businessmen. The colonists transacted their
major financial affairs with government-funded banks while they
channeled their farm purchases and sales through Major Endell's
cooperative system.[20]

The Poznanian Progressives ascribed the political ineptitude
and economic inequity of official Polenpolitik to the ignorance
and prejudice of the Prussian bureaucracy and the self-serving
agitation of the radical nationalists. Georg Wagner, the eastern
marches' most biting left-wing critic of the government and the
Hakatists, described German Polonophobia in these terms:

Chapter Nine

> Just as many ultraradical workers go into a blue
> rage [Blaukoller] whenever they see a policeman,
> so also many hundred-percent Prussians suffer a
> similar attack, which I like to call the "Polish
> rage" [Polenkoller], whenever they meet a Pole
> or even simply observe Polish manners and customs
> or hear the sounds of the Polish language.[21]

The old-established Germans of the eastern marches, long used
to living among the Poles, were free of this unreasoning aversion
and hostility. It flourished among newcomers to the east, especially ambitious bureaucrats and members of the educated professions
inflamed by Pan-German rhetoric. It merged with the longstanding
Prussian suspicion that revolution seethed beneath the surface
of Polish life, however tranquil and law-abiding it might seem.
This complex of attitudes was responsible for the inability of
Bismarck and his allies to understand and tolerate the Polish
national movement, whose very existence they took--wrongly, in the
liberals' view--as a repudiation of the obligations of Prussian
citizenship. From these misapprehensions arose inevitably the
government's successive campaigns to eradicate "Polonism," in
which it was joined after 1890 by the bourgeois nationalists suffering from Polenkoller. Like the Poles, the German Progressives
attributed great and growing influence on the government to the
Eastern Marches Society, an organization which aroused both apprehension and contempt among the Poznanian liberals. Wagner ridi-
culed the Hakatistic notion that the frontier Germans needed an
organization to defend themselves against the Poles: "Nobody
is threatening Herr Hansemann's nationality. . . .Nobody is
trying to take the Ostmark away from us."[22] The HKT Society,
"an organization that pursues the worst sort of political in-
trigues" (die schlimmste Scharfmacherpolitik treibt), bent the
government's Polish policies to its will with increasing success.
Thanks to the support it won among lower and middle-ranking
bureaucrats, teachers, and pastors in the east, it could represent itself in Berlin, where there was little first-hand knowledge of conditions in the Polish districts, as the voice of the
most patriotic and reliable local German population.[23] The
Progressives protested that the Hakatists were not natives or even
permanent residents of the eastern borderlands. They were instead
career-making interlopers whose personal interest lay in stirring
up the national conflict to earn salary bonuses, promotions, and,
finally, transfers to better posts in the west. Deputy Kindler
illustrated this point by the case of Professor Hoetzsch, a
vociferous Pan-German publicist who, after his appointment to the
Royal Academy in Poznań, became a fiery HKT propagandist. If the

government wished to employ Hoetzsch "to spread German culture,
then he should be sent out to the colonies, not to us in Posen."[24]

The Progessives advocated a <u>Polenpolitik</u> which focused not on
the Germanization of the eastern marches but rather on the reconciliation of the Poles to Prussian-German rule. They denied that
the Polish nationalist movement worked first and foremost towards
a revolutionary breakaway.

> The Poles want to maintain their linguistic identity
> and improve their economic conditions. They cannot
> be reproached for this. The Germans do the same
> thing in Bohemia and in the Russian Baltic provinces.
> A nation that didn't wouldn't be worth its salt.[25]

The Progressives assumed, as most Poles did too, that a breakaway
from Prussian rule was conceivable only in the wake of a Russian
victory over the German powers. In that case, the Poles would
merely exchange German for Russian subjection. The Progressives
argued that the Poznanian Poles had solid reasons for preferring
to remain under German overlordship. They were more secure in
their Catholic faith in multiconfessional Germany than in Orthodox Russia. As farmers, they could not hope to profit more from
supplying the Russian rather than the German market. Given the
choice between free access to careers in the liberal professions
and in state service in Germany and Russia, the Progressives assumed not unreasonably that the Poles would lean to the west.

If the Prussian government were to abandon its sweepingly discriminatory Germanization policies and frankly and simply pursue
conciliation (<u>Versöhnung</u>) with the Poles, it could count on a
favorable reception in broad and influential circles in Polish
society. The Progressives were the most vocal supporters of
provincial president Schwartzkopff, who tried "to drive a wedge
into the Polish democratic agitation" by "winning the nobility,
at least a part of the clergy, and especially the peasants for a
policy friendly to the government." The Poznanian liberals admitted that exacerbation of the nationality conflict lay in the
immediate interests of the Polish National Democrats, intent as
they were on eliminating their German economic rivals from commerce, small-scale industry, and the liberal professions. But
the Progressives reasoned that restoration of the Poles' language
in education and public life, employment of Poles in state posts
in the east, toleration of Polish control of the Poznań-Gniezno
archdiocese, and abandonment of the specifically anti-Polish
dimensions of the colonization program would win the gratitude of
the great majority of the Prussian Poles and utterly isolate the
intransigents. In time, the Polish bourgeoisie would see that
citizenship in a German Reich which respected their national

identity was to be preferred to an uncertain future under
Russian domimation. They would see, too, that their economic
interests could be more profitably cultivated in the flourishing
setting of industrialized Germany than in the backward Russian
Empire.[26]

What "our poor eastern lands" needed, the Progressives
said, was an Ostmarkenpolitik that benefited both nationalities
equally. "Suppression of Polonism" and "Germanization of the
east" were both chimerical and pernicious goals. The Royal Commission ought to settle Polish peasants alongside Germans.
Workers' parcels and urban garden plots ought to be offered to all
comers. The old-fashioned, confessionally segregated and badly
funded elementary schools, in which many teachers confronted
classes of 100 pupils or more, ought to be replaced by well-
staffed secular neighborhood schools. Polish children should
be free to study their own language; German children should learn
at least the rudiments of Polish. The eastern provinces needed
universities and technical colleges to prevent the drift of the
middle-class youth westward and to provide east Elbia with its
own professionals and higher civil servants. It was eastern
industry, not the large estate system, that required governmental
subsidization. In short, the Progressives advocated policies to
raise the economic and cultural conditions of the eastern marches
to the level of central and west Germany. If that were achieved,
the Ostflucht would cease to drain the German population from the
east. Heightened prosperity paired with national toleration in
the political sphere would reconcile the Poles to German rule
just as it would incline them towards German culture, not as an
alternative but rather as a complement to their own national
identity. National conflict would give way to a mutually advantageous coexistence. Delbrück went so far as to argue that,
should a European war bring about a defeat of Russia by the German
powers, a satellite Polish state could be established in the area
of the Congress Kingdom and Galicia which would provide Germany
with a useful economic partner and strategic buffer against the
Tsarist empire without threatening the security of Prussia's
Polish provinces. Just as a majority of German Austrians willingly
resigned from citizenship in the German Empire, with which in any
case their own state maintained intimate ties, so too the Prussian
Poles could agree to remain loyal German citizens despite the
proximity of a revived Polish kingdom. The crucial point was that
both the Prussian Poles and their eastern brethren should perceive
more advantage in political and economic cooperation with Germany

and Austria than with Russia. If Prussia were to replace its
discriminatory Polenpolitik with a policy of national equality
and toleration, the Poles--both in Germany and Russia--would lean
to the Germanic west as their Galician countrymen did.[27]

The right-wing nationalists' defeat of Bethmann Hollweg's
modestly conciliatory Polish policy showed plainly that adoption
of the liberal and nationally neutral eastern marches policy the
Progressives advocated was unthinkable without the triumph of
parliamentary government in Prussia. The course of German politics
after 1908 gave the Progressives hope that William II's regime
would before long find itself forced to submit its semiabsolute
authority to parliamentary control. But in the meantime, no
abandonment of Prussia's Germanization strategy in the east could
be counted on. On the contrary, the parcellation bill of 1914
foretold its radicalization.

However confident the Poznanian liberals might have been of
the long-term triumph of their principles, in the short term their
prospects were disheartening. Both the Poles and the German conservatives and nationalists drew strength from the nationality conflict, the Poles thanks to their own efforts, the Germans thanks
to the government's heavy subsidy of their economic interests and
its highly partisan political patronage. But for the Progressives,
the polarization of the nationalities signified nothing but losses.

The "flight from the east" disastrously eroded the liberals'
social base in the frontier towns. This was true in both absolute
and relative terms. The Polish urban population, and the bourgeoisie in particular, grew rapidly from the 1880s to 1914. Government
policy enriched the Junkers, greatly expanded the ranks of state
employees, and counteracted the eastern "flight from the countryside" by settling thousands of German peasants from the west. But
between 1882 and 1907 the total of German Protestants and Jews self-
employed in industry and commerce declined by 18 percent. Joining
to these basic occupational segments of the private middle classes
the rapidly growing number of commercial employees, many of whom on
the Protestant side were inclined politically to the right, still
yielded an absolute decline of 2 percent. The Jews' losses viewed
separately were far heavier during these years: total population
fell by 50 percent, the total of commercial-industrial owners and
salaried employees, officials, and free professionals by 36 percent.[28]

The German and German-Jewish bourgeoisie's numerical contraction in these decades was to some extent the inevitable accompani-

ment of concentration of business ownership and capital. If these
groups were less numerous on the eve of the war, both their incomes and the scale of their business operations had grown considerably since the 1870s. But the competition of the Polish
bourgeoisie, reinforced by the boycott movement, taken together
with the expansion of the officially patronized German cooperative banking and marketing system, drove many German Christian
businessmen, and even more Jews, into economic capitulation and
emigration. There is no proof that the Prussian government
deliberately sought to displace the Jews from the Poznanian economy,
although some Jewish writers, judging from the tangible effects of
official policy, bitterly suspected that it did.[29] But the government did nothing to strengthen the Jews economically or even help
them find alternative means of employment in the east. The Polish
boycott, though erratically observed, undoubtedly took a heavy
long-term toll on all but the economically strongest of German
and Jewish commercial enterprises. A glimpse of the gradual collapse of the Jews' economic position within the Polish community
emerges from a police report of 1912 on conditions in the predominantly Polish town of Miłosław:

> In the last five years the Polish merchant class has
> grown considerably. The Polish villagers, constantly
> reminded in public and private assemblies of the
> slogan "each to his own," have learned to follow it
> in practice. For the most part, they buy only in
> Polish establishments. In these five years no less
> than eight Jewish businesses have fallen into
> Polish hands.[30]

The political effects of the shrinkage of the Progressives'
social base were blurred by the workings of the Prussian three-
class voting system. It was their wealth, not their numbers,
that won them numerous town council seats and all the province's
urban Landtag mandates. If, as the Progressives advocated, the
Reichstag electoral law were introduced in Prussia, many of these
positions would fall into the Poles' hands. Already the growth
of the Polish town population made it possible for the Poles to
capture disputed Reichstag seats, such as that representing the
provincial capital, without recourse to electoral alliances with
the Progressives, whose fading voting strength in Reichstag elections devalued their political stock. Breaking their traditional
ties with the Progressives, the Polish nationalists, particularly
in those districts controlled by the National Democrats, intensified their use of anti-Semitic slogans in bidding for the common
people's support. This turn of events combined with the Reich-
level maneuvers which led to the formation of the liberal-conservative Bülow bloc to persuade the Poznanian Progressives to ally with

the United Conservatives and, through them, with the <u>Bund der</u>
<u>Landwirte</u> and Eastern Marches Society in the electoral compromise
of 1907. This agreement governed not only the Reichstag elections of that year but also those of 1912 together with the
Landtag elections of 1908 and 1913. Although the compromise
benefited the Progressives in certain respects, it increased the
plausibility of the Poles' charges that they were merely Hakatists
in liberal disguise. Moreover, it forced them, despite the Jews'
great importance in their leadership and following, to join hands
with openly anti-Semitic German politicians.[31]

Anti-Semitism among the Frontier Germans

Bismarck's political campaigns of the 1870s against the
Catholics, Socialists, and left liberals took place amidst the
socioeconomic tremors set off by the onset of the long depression
of 1873-1896. That also was the setting in which anti-Semitism
emerged as an important issue in Prussian-German politics. It
was during the parliamentary elections of the crisis years 1878-
79 that anti-Jewish slogans became a permanent fixture in Imperial
German political life, however much their function and appeal
may have varied in the following decades.[32]

During the Wilhelminian era, three types of political anti-
Semitism figured importantly on the German political stage. The
first was the economically derived anti-Semitism of the traditional petite bourgeoisie and peasant farmers who, equating the
Jews with capitalism and liberalism, blamed them for the hard-
ships--real and imaginary--which industrialization visited upon
small producers, entrepreneurs, and salary earners. The second
was the political and racial anti-Semitism of the right wing of
the nationalist bourgeoisie, epitomized in such publicists as
the elderly Treitschke, Lagarde, and Hasse. It drew middle-class
attention away from the realities of domestic German parliamentary
politics, which its adherents interpreted pessimistically as a
struggle of Bismarck's weak-hearted epigones with the ever more
formidable dragon of socialism. The political configurations
created by advancing industrialism appeared to prevent the self-
styled "national" bourgeoisie from mediating or resolving this
struggle within the Bismarckian parliamentary system. They damned
parliamentarism and political democracy as the work of Jewish
liberals and socialists and called upon the military-minded Prussian-German ruling class to unsheath its sword in defense of the
threatened <u>Volk</u>. Enthusiasm for an authoritarian monarchy, overseas imperialism, expansion into the Slavic east, symbolic assaults upon "soulless" big capitalism in the form of various anti-

Semitic laws, and the suppression of the socialist movement
on anti-Semitic pretexts were the result of this political
mentality, widespread among the salaried middle classes and the
reactionary intelligentsia.[33]

Finally, there was the anti-Semitism of the conservative
upper classes. Industrial magnates and their apologists stigmatized trade-unionism and the SPD as Jewish inventions. The anti-
modernist academic establishment blamed the Jews for the medio-
crities and insecurities of "mass society" and the obliteration
of "personality" which it seemed to portend. These types of anti-
Semitism assumed importance only on the fringes of their respective settings and did not figure importantly in the politics of
big business or the universities, especially since the number of
Jewish capitalist magnates in Germany was negligible while the
anti-Semitic furor of the 1880s had led to the barring of Jews
from professorial appointment and the closing of the nationalist
fraternities to Jewish students.

There was, however, one form of upper-class political anti-
Semitism of great importance in Wilhelminian Germany. This was
propagated by the German Conservative Party, which first incorporated anti-Jewish slogans in its party program in 1892. After
the formation of the Bund der Landwirte in the following year, the
Prussian Conservatives commanded a formidable mass organization
which in the prewar decades made anti-Semitic agitation one of
its specialties. This freed the DKP to concentrate on less
demagogic issues in its campaigning among the educated and
propertied classes, where before 1914 a harshly anti-Semitic
vocabulary carried the stigma of vulgarity and social radicalism.

The Conservatives' anti-Semitism served three major ends.
The Bund employed it to steal the thunder of agrarian radicals
who paired anti-Jewish with anti-Junker slogans. Focusing the
peasant farmers' economic and social resentments on the "Jewish"
liberals and Socialists, the Bund's agitators reinforced the
conservative landlords' traditional political leadership of the
Protestant villagers. Secondly, the DKP and the Bund used anti-
Semitic arguments to defend the large estate system and particularly the tariffs which underpinned it. The "Jewish middleman,"
not the exclusion of cheap foreign farm products from the German
market, was to blame for the high prices the common people
paid for food in Imperial Germany. Finally, the Conservatives
seized upon anti-Semitic phraseology to defend their extensive
economic and political privileges against the increasingly ruthless criticism launched against them by the liberal and socialist
parties. The DKP and the Bund tried to represent themselves as

the sword and buckler of the "Germanic" middle classes against the
Jews and the other alleged enemies of Volk and Reich. To sacrifice the Conservatives' political privileges in the name of democracy, they argued, would open the floodgates to an anarchy in
which all patriots would perish alongside the Junkers.[34]

The Bund der Landwirte introduced systematic anti-Semitic
agitation into Poznanian German agrarian politics in the 1890s.
The founding of the Eastern Marches Society appeared to fore-
shadow the reemergence of anti-Semitism as a major issue in the
towns, a status it had lost after 1848. The HKT Society, animated
by völkisch and Pan-German sentiments, seemed the perfect vehicle
for inflaming not only anti-Polish but also anti-Semitic hostilities
among the German Protestant burghers and state employees.

In the years 1900-1902, anti-Semitic agitators from Berlin
staged a series of meetings in the northern, heavily German district of the province. These assemblies clearly revealed the susceptibility of the OMV's urban constituency to radical anti-Jewish
propaganda. Audiences of three to five hundred, composed overwhelmingly of members of the middle classes (Mittelstand), cheered
enthusiastically as anti-Semitic parliamentary deputies, including
the monomaniacal Count Pückler, heaped "filthy abuse" on the Jews,
accusing them of ritual murder and the "ruin of the artisans and
farmers" by "liberal legislation." Protests against these meetings were lodged with the Prussian authorities by Jewish communal
officials, who feared worse outbreaks of "the lower elements of
the popular masses" (niedere Volksmassen) than the vandalization
of the synagogue which twice occurred in Schneidemühl following
the "rabble-rousers'" assemblies.[35]

The liberal Berliner Tageblatt reported that Hakatists were
prominent in the anti-Semitic agitation in Schneidemühl. This
was probably true of anti-Jewish rallies staged elsewhere in the
province during these years, though Tiedemann and his associates
never formally endorsed them. In the elections of 1903 the Poznanian Conservatives, testing the local appeal of an issue which
in the 1898 elections had won considerable support on the Reich
level, ran an outspoken anti-Semite as the "German national" candidate in one district. While the Progressives voted with the Poles
against him, the Eastern Marches Society, tied already to the
Poznanian Conservatives' political fortunes, endorsed him.[36]

Whatever their views on the Jewish question may have been,
the HKT leaders found the anti-Semitic enthusiasms of the Conservatives and their own rank and file a political embarrassment.

Tiedemann and his friends sought to organize all the frontier
Germans in opposition to the "Polish threat." Support of the
anti-Semitic movement gained them nothing but the enmity of an
important segment of eastern German society while inflating the
importance of an issue which, because of its obsessive nature,
could only distract German attention from the Polish question.
To the more single-minded anti-Semites, the Poles figured as
potential allies agianst the "Jewish menace" rather than
dangerous national antagonists. "The government's Polenpolitik
is wrong," declared the Berlin journalist Wilhelm Bruhn in
Schneidemühl: "The Poles have a right to their homes here. They
shouldn't be repressed. They should be good Prussians and
cooperate with us against the Jews, because it's the Jews who are
the great danger."[37]

In the years after 1903, the Poles' bitter struggle with
Bülow's regime focused local German attention on the nationality
conflict. Preaching national solidarity, the Hakatists avoided
all anti-Semitic accents and routinely proclaimed the Progressives
their national comrades despite their "erroneous" views on the
Polish question. It is probable that Tiedemann discouraged anti-
Semitic agitation among his underlings, just as it seems likely
that the Prussian authorities placed obstacles in the way of further public anti-Semitic campaigning after 1903. In any event,
no more anti-Semitic meetings convened before the war. When the
Progressives joined the Bülow bloc in 1907, the German Conservatives took some pains to reassure the liberals' Jewish constituents of their good will towards them. Campaigning in Poznania
as a German national compromise candidate, the DKP leader Count
Westarp told the local liberals in 1908 that his party "fully
recognized the Jews' constitutionally guaranteed equality." In
the parliamentary elections of 1907-8 and 1912-13, the Conservatives avoided nominating anti-Semitic candidates and dutifully
voted for the two Jews whom the Progressives included among others
on their slate of deputies. The Progressives reciprocated by
voting for Conservatives in those districts allocated by the
compromise of 1907 to the DKP.[38]

Thus after 1903 the Conservatives and Hakatists sacrificed
anti-Semitic agitation in the name of German national solidarity,
above all to hold the Progressives on their side during municipal
and parliamentary elections. Nevertheless, anti-Semitism did not
disappear as one among the many prickly issues disturbing this
marriage of political convenience. The Prussian government
complacently persisted in barring Jews from positions as mayors

and salaried municipal officials, notaries and judges, gymnasium teachers and university professors, high civil officials and army officers. The Poznanian Jews had long been bitterly aware of how little the government valued their talents and services. They would have been scandalized had they known that Schwartzkopff, whose Polish policy they warmly supported in 1913, confided privately that "he advocated further expulsions from the state of non-naturalized Jews, since the eastern provinces have already got too high a percentage of Jews." The provincial president showed himself a captive of anti-Semitic mythology by adding that "the rate of natural increase among the Jews is already so high that all immigration of foreign Jews must be halted."[39]

The Jews condemned the government and the right-wing parties not only for these veiled forms of anti-Semitism; they held them responsible also for the one form of brazenly demagogic anti-Semitism which continued to flourish publicly until the outbreak of the war. This was the work of the Bund der Landwirte. Major Endell, it is true, supported the liberal-conservative compromise. He signaled his Junker and peasant followers to support the liberal compromise candidates in the elections after 1907, though in 1912 he openly denounced one of them for "Jewish shamelessness."[40] But in its local assemblies, the Bund attacked the Jews without restraint.

It is well known that the Bund's Reich-level leaders, and particularly its director, Gustav Roesicke, propagated a völkisch anti-Semitism whose racist intensity left little for the National Socialists to improve upon. Hans-Jürgen Puhle, the Bund's most recent historian, argued that its ideological radicalism was the handiwork of bourgeois agitators in its ranks who aimed it at the peasantry and small-town burghers; the Junker and bureaucratic conservatives active in the Bund countenanced its völkisch agitation as a political necessity but dismissed it among themselves for its intellectual crudeness and ethical faults.[41]

Roesicke's vehement anti-Semitism stands in no doubt. In March 1912 he displayed it to his Poznanian admirers at a Bund assembly in Lissa. But the proceedings of the Bund's provincial congress of 1912 throw into question Puhle's judgment of the Prussian Conservatives' relation to anti-Jewish propaganda. The congress's political centerpiece was an address pronounced by the local estate owner and retired captain von Levetzow in the presence of a large audience including high officials representing the provincial administration, the main dignitaries of the United Conservative Party, and numerous prosperous landlords. It was, in

the context of German politics in Poznania, a sensationally and
single-mindedly anti-Semitic speech, for which Levetzow was
repaid with "stormy applause." He raged against Jewish influence
at court and in the "blathering" Reichstag, at the "corrosive
Jewish spirit" of the press and German cultural life. He
pilloried "Jewish capital" for fixing farm prices to its own
advantage and for conspiring with the "Jewish" socialists against
the German workers. He insulted and mocked the Jewish members of
the Poznań city council. He upheld the Junkers as the German nation's champions against the protean Jewish menace but pessimistically concluded that "we have, unfortunately, left the age of
Junker rule [Junkerherrschaft] behind us and have entered an age
of Jewish rule [Judenherrschaft]. This fact represents, among
other things, an ethical loss as well."[42]

The Jews and the Zionist Movement

    The appearance after 1890 of anti-Semitism as a minor but
jarringly strident theme of German and Polish nationalist
agitation in Poznania alarmed the Jews. In response, an important
branch of the German Zionist movement arose. But the first to
take action were the Jewish notables in the Progressive Party,
the long-established leaders of the frontier Jews.

    Since the 1880s, anti-Semitism had been a principal concern
of the German liberals in Prussia and throughout the Reich. In
1890, the prestigious Progressive leaders Rudolf Gneist and
Heinrich Rickert, both Christians, organized the "Society for
Defense against Anti-Semitism." Arguing that discrimination
against Jews was unconstitutional and illegal, it sought without
notable success to combat anti-Semitism through the courts. The
heightened anti-Jewish agitation of the Caprivi era finally impelled the German Jews to break with the traditional policy of en-
trusting defense of their civil rights to their non-Jewish colleagues. In 1893, Jewish liberal activists founded the "Central
Union of German Citizens of Jewish Faith." Though never a mass-
based organization, the Central Union (CV) acquired powerful
influence among the German Jews in the years before 1914. Through
local meetings and the liberal press it countered anti-Semitic
propaganda and spread its own message. The CV emphasized the Jews'
civil rights and equality in their character as Reich citizens.
It made a strong point of stressing the German nationality, or
"German consciousness" (deutsche Gesinnung), of its members.
Formally independent of all political parties, it was in fact
closely aligned with the Progessives, though this did not prevent
it from attacking them when their parliamentary or electoral
strategies drew them into dealings with anti-Semites.[43]

In Poznania, the German anti-Semitic assemblies and electioneering of the years 1900-1902 spurred the Jewish liberals to stage
protest meetings leading to the formation of a provincial branch
of the Central Union. After the sensation caused by this first
assertion of specifically Jewish political interests in the eastern marches had subsided, the Poznanian CV lost momentum. In
the prewar years, it staged annual conferences at which the
Prussian government's discrimination against Jews in public service dominated the discussion. To restrain local anti-Semitism,
the CV did not engage in polemics with the German conservative
nationalists or the Poles. It adopted the strategy, which dovetailed with the local Progressives' stand in the nationality
conflict, of emphasizing the Poznanian Jews' German character
and loyalties while avoiding all anti-Polish accents.[44]

Polish anti-Semitism would decline in virulence as official
Polenpolitik conformed to liberal prescriptions. The political
triumph in Germany of liberal parliamentarism would end official
discrimination against Jews and discredit the agrarian conservatives' anti-Semitic demogoguery. In the meanwhile, the Jew's
best defense against anti-Semitism was to demonstrate their
complete social, political, and cultural integration in the German nation. A majority of both the Orthodox and Reformed Jews
in pre-1914 Poznania accepted these propositions and maintained
unbroken their allegiance to the Progressive movement.

The Reformed Jews, who called themselves "liberals" in
religion, agreed with Kommerzienrat Hamburger, one of Poznań's
outstanding merchants: "The Jewish Liberal Society is composed of
men who think German and feel German, and as members of the German nation are in no way hindered from exercising their Jewish
religion."[45] The Reformed Jews, heirs of the Jewish Enlightenment, controlled only 5 of the province's 24 rabbinical districts
and 12 of its 112 synagogue-communes. But even where Orthodoxy
prevailed, they formed an influential minority. In the provincial
capital, one of the city's two synagogues represented their views,
and half the Jewish communal council's seats were in their hands.
Most of the younger generation of businessmen and professionals
inclined towards liberal Judaism, which sought to fuse the essential theological and ethical teachings of traditional Jewish
religion with modern European high culture and its social and
political values. In the secular realm, the guiding concept of
Reform Judaism was assimilation. In 1913, a Poznanian speaker
put it thus:

> One of liberalism's chief demands is that we purpose-
> fully enter into the culture surrounding us. Then the

differences [of religion, ethnic background, and
historical experience] will vanish. So too will all
feelings of inferiority. Assimilation can occur without endangering our religious outlook if we are convinced that German culture is also our own culture.
Then each of us can be a good German of Jewish religion.[46]

The Orthodox Jews differed from the liberals not in their
categorical rejection of cultural and political assimilation, a
position they had abandoned after the Napoleonic wars. But
Orthodoxy insisted on preserving many more elements of Jewish
tradition in its merger with German culture than the Jewish
reformers found necessary or desirable. The Orthodox sought to
defend the traditionally strong authority of their rabbis
against elected communal councils. They followed the ritual laws
more scrupulously than the liberals thought reasonable. They
looked upon modern scientific thought and knowledge with suspicion. In Poznania, they clung fondly to their local quirks and
customs, proud of their regional individuality and indifferent
to the liberals' charges of benighted, old-fashioned provincialism.
They were proud of their intense religiosity and liked to think
of themselves as more genuinely Jewish than the rest of the German
Jews, whose Jewish character one of them, later a Zionist leader,
stigmatized as "unreal and watered down" in comparison with the
Poseners'.[47]

The Poznanian Orthodox communities were unquestionably foremost among the bastions of Jewish conservatism in Imperial Germany.
Traditionalism stamped their social and political style, despite
their allegiance to the Progressive movement. At the East German
District Conference of the Free Association for the Interests of
Orthodox Jewry, held in Poznań in 1912, a principal theme was
the collapse of centuries-old Jewish settlements in the eastern
provinces as the result of the Jewish Ostflucht. The delegates
lamented the disintegration of one of eastern European Jewry's
oldest and most solid communities. They discussed approaching
the government with the suggestion that Jewish emigrants from
the Russian Empire be settled in the places abandoned by westward-
moving Poznanian Jews, although since Bismarck's time official
policy had opposed naturalization of Russian and Galician Jews.
They denounced the "corrosive spirit of modern materialism"
and called for renewed devotion to the traditional Jewish law.
Speaking of the nationality conflict, Banker Loewy of Rawicz said,

The times are hard, especially for us Jews in the
eastern marches. Here the economic and political
relations are especially complicated. Nevertheless,
regardless of how these things have stood, we have
never hesitated to declare ourselves as Germans, al-

     though in doing so we have suffered heavy losses
     [lively applause].

Ignoring the Prussian regime's long record of anti-Jewish discrim-

ination, Loewy expressed the Jews' confidence in the government,

     which has always regarded us and our religious ef-
     forts with goodwill. Reverently we look up to the
     highest place in the state, to our exalted Kaiser,
     who is to us a shining example of the deepest inner
     religiosity.

The six hundred delegates responded to this speech with a <u>Hoch</u>! to

the Kaiser. Later they sent him a telegram expressing their loy-

alty, to which they received an appreciative reply from his

secretary.[48]

    Reaffirmation of their German national character and of

their traditional religious and political loyalties was the

principal response of the older Orthodox and liberal Jews of

Poznania to the resurgent menace of anti-Semitism during the Wil-

helminian years. The younger generations could not content them-

selves with cleaving to nineteenth-century tradition, and turned

in large numbers to Zionism.

    Theodor Herzl's publication of <u>Der</u> <u>Judenstaat</u> in Vienna in

1896 inspired his followers in the Reich to organize the German

Zionist Union (<u>Zionistische Vereinigung für Deutschland</u>) in 1897.

This society united secular-minded Jewish nationalists hostile to

liberal assimilationism with religious enthusiasts impatient with

Orthodoxy's resigned acceptance of the Diaspora and keen on Jewish

settlement in Palestine. By the eve of the war, the Zionist Union

counted some 9,000 members and 100 local branches throughout the

Reich. Many dedicated and talented activists spread its message

through local meetings, national conferences, and the Zionist

press. It was part of an international movement which by 1912

prided itself on having established in Palestine forty-one

Jewish colonies comprising altogether 10,000 settlers and 40,000

hectares of land. Herzl's aim of securing through negotiations

with the European Great Powers an internationally guaranteed self-

governing Jewish state, through still unrealized in 1914, appeared

increasingly plausible, particularly in view of the advancing

disintegration of the Ottoman Empire.[49]

    Although it focused its hopes on the traditional religious

ideal of the Jews' return to Palestine, German Zionism was first

and foremost a secular nationalist movement. It arose as a direct

response to the wave of anti-Semitism which swept through European,

and especially Imperial German and Austrian, nationalist circles

after the 1870s. The ideological violence and strong popular ap-

peal of <u>völkisch</u> anti-Semitism throughout German central Europe

threw into question the Jews' assimilation into German culture

and their political rights as Germans, genuine though their own
commitments to the German nation were. At the same time, the
emigration from pogrom-ridden Russia and from Eastern and Balkan
Europe of millions of unassimilated Jews inspired Western European
Jews to help them settle not in America but in the ancestral
homeland in Palestine. A Jewish state established there would
preserve rather than extinguish the emigrant masses' Jewish consciousness. It would also provide a haven for Jews settled elsewhere should anti-Semitism drive them into emigration. As traditional Orthodox religiosity weakened among the well-educated and
prosperous German Jews, they embraced the perspectives of the
European Enlightenment, Romanticism, and nineteenth-century
liberalism which had shaped the nationalist movements of t1e
Christian European nations. Their identification with liberal
German nationalism having been shaken by the anti-Semitic turn of
German bourgeois and upper-class conservative-nationalist
politics, many Jews began to regard themselves in secular historical and ethnic-cultural terms as members of a distinctive nation,
with the same right of national self-determination, the same
historic destiny of national rebirth and liberation, that other
European nations claimed for themselves.[50]

Before 1914, only a minority of the German Jews joined the
Zionists in their "return to Jewishness" (Rückkehr ins Judentum).[51]
The movement appealed most strongly to the younger generation
of the academically trained Jewish intelligentsia, a group whose
numbers increased rapidly after 1880. The anti-Semitic atmosphere of the German universities and the heightened official discrimination against Jews in public employment initiated by Bismarck's regime in the 1880s shook their faith in the assimilationist liberalism of their fathers. Some turned to the socialist
movement but many others, distanced by their bourgeois origins
from the SPD and stamped by their family life and religious education with a strong Jewish identity, embraced the Zionist cause.

On the larger stage of Wilhelminian politics, dominated
as it was by party conflict and foreign policy debate, Zionism
attracted little attention. But within the Empire's Jewish community it whipped up a storm of controversy. The Zionist Union
arose in 1897 amid the Association of German Rabbis' denunciations
of Herzl's movement as a distortion of Jewish messianism which
threatened to undermine the Jews' secular loyalties to their
fatherlands in the Diaspora. The Central Union of German Citizens
of Jewish Faith entered the fray, initiating a heated polemic
with the Zionists on the subject of "German consciousness" which

intensified as World War I approached. Both the Orthodox conservatives and Reformed liberals remained unrelentingly hostile to
the Zionists. Arthur Handtke, Reich chairman of the Zionist Union,
admitted at the 1912 congress in Poznań that "the great majority of
the Jewish notables, the leaders of the older generation, are still
our opponents." Yet, in the teeth of this opposition, the Zionists
steadily gained strength.[52]

In Poznań, Zionism was born in the midst of the agitation
which gripped the Jews after the turn of the century. In 1902
west German Zionist organizers staged meetings in the wake of the
launching of the local Central Union of German Citizens of Jewish
Faith. A Zionist gymnastic society formed the nucleus of the
Zionist Club established in the provincial capital in 1903.
From these headquarters the Zionists bid for influence in the
municipal and provincial politics of both the Jewish community
and the Progressive movement.

Among the Zionists' most energetic and articulate leaders was
the Poznań attorney Max Kollenscher, a cofounder of the local
movement and later a long-standing member of the Reich-level
Zionist Central Committee.[53] Kollenscher was born in 1875, the
son of a prosperous Poznań grain merchant. His family's Orthodoxy
was more ceremonial than fervent and, apart from some desultory
Hebrew studies with indifferent tutors, his education was wholly
German. After taking a degree in law at Breslau University, in
1898 he accepted a small-town legal post in a Poznanian courthouse.
In 1902, he passed the state legal examinations with honors, an
accomplishment that qualified him for an intermediate appointment
in a Berlin ministry. Because he was Jewish, he was advised by a
well-meaning senior official against pursuing a career in the
Prussian judicial service. He returned, as he had anyway intended,
to Poznań and launched a successful private legal practice.

Kollenscher's youthful politics were enthusiastically liberal.
To the end of the 1890s he regarded the "Jewish question" as
purely a "confessional matter." Although aware from an early age
of anti-Jewish discrimination in public and social life, he conceived his political obligation to lie in the pursuit of
"bourgeois democracy" above and beyond any consideration of Jewish
interests. After returning to the province from his studies, he
contented himself with writing occasional defenses of the Progressive Party for the local press.

But events forced him to ponder the implications of his Jewish identity more deeply. The Dreyfus Affair, pogroms in Russia,
anti-Semitic agitation in Reich politics and in his provincial

homeland, the slights he endured in Prussian service, the
spectacle of the Polish and German nationalist militance surrounding him--all combined to draw Kollenscher into the Zionists'
local discussions. He himself admitted that "people in Posen had
always felt that in some way or another the Jews formed a third
nationality." Yet it was painful for Kollenscher to acknowledge,
"We are not Germans, we are Jews."

He feared that commitment to Zionism would require, as he
said, "a break of all my relations with German culture." Since
his university studies of Darwin and the German positivists Büchner
and Haeckel, his Jewish religiosity had ebbed away completely.
His whole character as an educated and cultured man was German.
To repudiate this for the sake of a vision of Jewish statehood
in the Near East seemed to risk psychological self-destruction.[54]

But Kollenscher was "bound by iron chains" to his Jewishness (Judentum und Judenheit), which he felt "not as a burden but
as a necessary part of my self and my identity." His personal
relations and friendships had always been exclusively Jewish.
He thought it "natural" that this should be so. He was proud
of the exceptional vigor and solidarity of the Jewish community
in Poznania. He praised its "rootedness" and counted himself
happy to live in its midst.[55]

Such a distinctive Jewish self-consciousness, apart from all
religiosity, was at once evidence and proof of the Jews' separate
national character. In 1904 Kollenscher wrote,

> Our forefathers were not the old Arians and Teutons;
> the cradle of our ancestors stood on the Jordan. As
> much as some of the Jews of the German Empire may try
> to suppress what even they themselves know and feel to
> be Jewish within themselves, seeking at the same time
> other supports in alien manners and ways--nevertheless,
> nationality cannot be denied. The truth of this they
> will learn bitterly from the enemy's hatred in the racial
> conflict of our times; it will be taught to them too
> in brotherly fashion by their compatriots (Stammes-
> genossen) who have already awakened to their own
> identity.

Assimilation into the German nationality (Deutschtum) was historically and perhaps even biologically impossible. The Jews' acceptance and assertion of their own nationality was not a matter
of choice, but of ineluctability. "Yet," Kollenscher added, "we
do not repudiate German patriotism. Nationality has nothing in
common with patriotism."[56]

Like the other German Zionists of his generation, Kollenscher
resolved the apparent contradiction between Jewish and German
consciousness by affirming--not at all ungratefully--the imprint
of German culture upon him. His German "mother tongue," German

literature, and German art "have become our most secure and solid
possessions, which we wish never to relinquish." The Jews' German
cultural character and their participation in the destiny of the
German social and political community inspired in them a warm and
genuine German patriotism. "Patriotism, however, fixes itself
upon the state, and the state is not the exclusive possession of one
nation alone." As members of the Jewish nation, the German Jews
could and ought to be both patriotic German citizens and the
architects and pioneers of a Jewish state in Palestine whose existence, when it was established, would in no way conflict with the
interests of the German Empire. Kollenscher and his Zionist
allies echoed the universalism of early nineteenth-century democratic nationalism in saying, "We Zionists, who work for the rebirth of the Jewish people (Volk), take the keenest and most sincere interest in the progress of culture in all lands, just as each
of us seeks an active part in advancing the culture of his own
land of birth."[57]

The German Zionists defined themselves as German citizens of
Jewish nationality. Staatspatriotismus, not membership in the
German Volk, bound them to the German Empire. The question of
the realism and practicability of the Zionist program of Jewish
statehood was answered, for Kollenscher as for many other German
Jews, by Herzl's early successes in gaining Turkish and English
assent, if nothing more, to discuss the proposal formally. Final
victory was possible, if not inevitable, particularly if Zionist
colonization in Palestine continued to prosper.

Commitment to Zionism enabled Kollenscher and his allies, in
Poznania and throughout the Reich, to retreat from the perils of
German anti-Semitism to the higher and surer ground of their own
Jewish character. While Palestine shone forth in accordance
with traditional messianism as a future haven, they had found a
formula for their German loyalties compatible with their Jewish
identity. In Kollenscher, this resolution released a new flood of
political energy. If the Jew, he wrote, "can labor in the life of
other nations only under external limitations and with inner difficulty, because political and social barriers, disgrace, envy, and
hatred hold him down, as a Jew and Zionist a free and unlimited
field for work and creativity opens to him."[58]

Zionism meant devotion to Palestine. The Poznanian Zionists,
like their comrades everywhere, collected money to finance
Palestinian colonization. At the Zionist Union Congress of 1912,
the youthful enthusiasts succeeded in forcing passage of a resolution calling on all German Zionists to include emigration in

Palestine in their life plans. The older generation of "political
Zionists," which included Kollenscher and the Poznanian movement,
chose to interpret this as a call for more serious financial support of the colonization movement. They resisted the idea of
compulsory settlement in Palestine. The Zionist mission in Germany
was no less important than in the Near East.[59]

The Poznanian Zionists concentrated their main efforts
on agitation and organization within their own community. Through
frequent meetings of the Zionist Club and gymnastic society,
they pursued their goal of a "Jewish renaissance." Their teaching
of the Hebrew language and "our own national history" aimed to
instill national pride in the younger generation. In public
meetings and the press they attacked liberal assimilationism, and
above all Jewish conversions to Christianity, which they denounced
as "lack of religious character." While they resisted religious
identification with Jewish Orthodoxy or Reform, they campaigned
to restore to full vigor in synagogue services the ancient prayers
for return to Israel that nineteenth-century "German consciousness"
had watered down.[60]

Raising the cry "Democracy against the notables," the Zionists
campaigned in elections to Jewish communal councils, which supervised the finances and administration of Jewish religious, educational, and charitable institutions. In the Poznań elections of
1903 they scored some successes, but the formation of an anti-
Zionist liberal-Orthodox front prevented any repetitions in the
following years. Nevertheless, Kollenscher and his friends formed
a grandiose vision of the future political organization of the
Poznanian and German Jews. Under Zionist leadership, the communal
councils would greatly extend Jewish educational and social welfare
services while promoting the local Jewish economy through cooperative enterprises. Provincial and, finally, Reich-level councils
would be recruited through proportional representation of local
communes. A pyramidical structure of Jewish self-government
would arise within Imperial Germany. Apart from its tasks within
the Jewish community, it would represent the Jews in Prussian and
Imperial politics, acting not so much as a Jewish party as a powerful pressure group trading Jewish votes for the German parties'
support of Jewish interests.[61]

Thus would the Zionists succeed in "nationalizing the Jewish
people (Volk)" in Germany.[62] Before 1914, the joint hostility of
the Orthodox and liberal Jews greatly impeded their labors. In
Poznania, the Zionists failed to win control of Jewish communal
institutions while in the Progressive Party assimilationist

liberals overshadowed them. But in the Poznań communal elections
of 1914 Zionist candidates polled two to three hundred votes in
opposition to the liberal-Orthodox candidates' six to nine hundred.
In this large Jewish community, the Zionists had won the support of
every fourth adult male in little more than a decade.   Among the
youth, their strength undoubtedly was greater still.[63]

On the eve of the war, the Zionist movement's immediate prospects were good, despite its chilled reception among religious
traditionalists and Jewish liberals. The Zionists succeeded in
dissociating themselves wholly from their antagonists in the German
camp by denying the existence of any bond of national kinship with
them. This gave them a sense of national self-sufficiency and a
resolve, lacking in the Jewish liberals and Orthodox traditionalists, to protest the discrimination they suffered. At the provincial Zionist conferences held after 1906 and at the Reich Congress of 1912 in Poznań, they bitterly denounced Polish and German
anti-Semitism and the Prussian government's indifference to their
interests in the eastern marches. At their local meetings, they
alone among the many Jewish organizations in the province condemned
the anti-Semitic demogogy of the Bund der Landwirte.[64]

The Progressives on the Eve of World War I

The rise of Zionism did not undermine the frontier Jews'
traditional allegiance to the Progressive Party. The Zionists'
efforts to strengthen and stabilize the Jewish community upon new
organizational and ideological foundations promised to benefit the
Progressives by slowing the demographic erosion of their Jewish
constituency. The Zionists had no important strategic or ideological quarrels with the Progressives, whose advocacy of parliamentary liberalism and a nondiscriminatory Polenpolitik they fully
supported. The future held no hope of a time when the Poznanian
Jews would command the votes to stand alone in Prussian or Reich
politics. An alliance with the German party most sympathetic to
their interests was unavoidable.

The Progressives' horizons were cloudy in another direction.
In 1910, after two years of local organization, a provincial branch
of the National Liberal Party appeared on the Poznanian scene.
It won enough support in the provincial capital and the German
towns of the western and northern counties to compel both the
United Conservatives and Progressives to bid for its support. In
the Landtag elections of 1913, each of the two preestablished
parties ceded one of its seats to the National Liberals.

The new party attracted middle- and lower-ranking officials
and the Protestant bourgeoisie. It denounced Polish nationalism

and advocated fast-paced German peasant colonization regardless
of its decimating impact on German large landholdings. In
domestic German affairs, its guns were trained on the Conservative parties. It agitated against the Junkers' tax privileges
and supported a Prussian electoral reform weighing the middle
classes' and peasant farmers' votes more heavily.[65]

Provincial president Waldow and his lieutenants had attempted to discourage this National Liberal incursion. They
feared, rightly enough, that it would weaken the United Conservatives' influence among state employees and the monarchist-
nationalist townspeople who stood outside the Progressive camp.
By playing upon anti-Junker sentiments, the National Liberals
tried to lure the Protestant farmers away from the Bund der
Landwirte, though these tactics were unsuccessful before 1914.
Yet the NLP undoubtedly threatened to significantly erode the
Conservatives' popular support in Poznania.[66]

The appearance of the National Liberals menaced the Progressives as well. It blocked their prospects of expansion to the
Right and into the countryside at the same time that the gains
of the SPD, modest though they still were, undercut their appeal
among the German workers and artisans. To stave off constitutional
and social reform, the Prussian government and the conservative
nationalists could be expected to perpetuate Bismarck's tactic
of "flaying the Poles," despite its increasingly dangerous consequences for Junker interests in the east. Partly because
they recognized and welcomed these consequences and partly because
of their own nationalist fervor, the National Liberals stood ready
to support the government's anti-Polish campaigns.

The emergence of the National Liberal Party in Poznania
heightened the likelihood that, at least in the immediate future,
the nationality conflict would grow more intense.   The Hakatistic
demands of the new party in the eastern marches would strengthen
the government's inclination to fire new salvos at the Poles.
The Poles' anti-German reprisals, particularly the boycott movement, would acquire a sharper edge, while anti-Semitic agitation
would flourish on both the Polish and German side of the struggle.
The Progressives would suffer defections of their German Protestant
supporters to the National Liberals, while anti-Semitism and the
boycott would drive their Jewish adherents into emigration.   If
the Progressive movement did not collapse altogether, it would
stand in danger of becoming a mere relic of the German and Jewish
bourgeois past.   This end was not inevitable, but the weaker the
resistance to Wilhelminian imperialism in the heart of Germany,

the more certain became the defeat of the liberal German and
Jewish advocates of national coexistence in the eastern borderlands.

Frederick the Great set out to Prussianize the Polish nobility. Those who resisted—"the bad Polish stuff"—he aimed to "get rid of," putting German landlords in their place. The "slavish" Polish commoners he intended to transform into "human beings and useful members of the state" by "mixing them gradually with Germans." The impoverished Jewish "ragtag" he expelled from his Polish province, but the "well-to-do commercial Jews" he kept.

Such was the start of Prussian rule in partitioned Poland. Bismarck and the Wilhelminian statesmen who ended it acted on grimmer resolves. They proposed to expropriate and uproot the Polish gentry, Germanize the Polish church, bar the peasants from buying farmland, drive the laborers westward, and force the Polish language from public life. "If you will not give us your hearts," Oldenburg-Januschau told the Poles, "then we must have your land." During World War I the Hakatists inside and outside the government prepared to expel the Poles eastward from Poznania and West Prussia. A "land without people," awaiting German settlement, would forever shield the German heartland from "Polonization" and "Great-Polish agitation." Hitler gathered the harvest of Prussian nationality policy. "Germanization," he wrote in _Mein Kampf_, "can only be applied to soil and never to people."[1] During World War II, the National Socialist occupation regime in western Poland plundered and deported the Polish upper classes and forced the masses into helotry. Himmler's agencies filled the land with German colonists. Polish resisters were shot by the tens of thousands. The Jews, rich and poor, were exterminated.[2]

This shattering end to the nationality conflict in the German-Polish borderlands followed directly, if not inevitably, from Bismarckian and Wilhelminian Prussia's "mission in the east." Bismarck and his successors sought to drown Polish nationalism in a sea of German settlements swelling eastward. But their

claims to defense of the Prussian-German fatherland against the
"Slavic flood" were hollow. The "mission in the east" was an
imperialist strategy to hold the Bismarckian regime's domestic
enemies at bay. It was also a mantle covering a massive subsidy
of the Prussian Junkers, to whose interests not only the Polish
landlords but the German and Jewish bourgeoisie and the workers of
all three nationalities were offered up as sacrifices.

The cutting edge of Bismarckian and Wilhelminian Germanization policy was peasant colonization. Between 1896 and the end
of 1912, the Poles added 100,000 hectares to the land they tilled
in Poznania and West Prussia. Although they lost 60,000 hectares
to the Royal Colonization Commission and other German buyers in
the decade after 1886, by the eve of the war they had outstripped
their antagonists by a sizable margin in the "struggle for the
land." Bismarck in 1886 proposed to "expropriate the szlachta"
with one hundred million marks; by 1914 the colonization program
had cost the Prussian state almost one billion marks.[3] Its failure could be read even in the heavily biased language censuses.
Between 1890 and 1910, the Poles' share in the Poznanian population rose from 60.2 percent to 61.3 percent. The German Protestants and Catholics crept forward from 37.3 percent to 37.4 percent, but Jewish emigration condemned the whole German-speaking
population to proportional decline.[4]

Although it failed to Germanize the Polish borderlands, the
Prussian "mission in the east" succeeded in raising the nationality conflict to fever pitch. Since the eighteenth century,
Prussian Polenpolitik had provoked ever sharper Polish resistance,
culminating in the populist radicalism of the National Democrats.
Hakatism flourished in the east, but chiefly because the state
needed allies to "flay the Poles." The Poznanian Jews fled their
homeland or turned to Zionism to escape the mounting shadows
of anti-Semitism conjured up by nationalist radicals and fanatics
both German and Polish.

The nationality conflict in the eastern marches arose not
from the hatreds of the frontier peoples, but from the labors
of Prussia's rulers to Germanize the lands conquered in the partitions of Poland. Their appeals to the danger of Polish irredentism were fraudulent. The Prussian Poles strove for national equality and home rule, not revolutionary breakaway. Repression of
the Poles in the name of state security was no less unfounded
than the state's defense of the frontier Germans "against
Polonizing tendencies." The German bourgeoisie in the east, the
Jews, the German Catholics, and the Socialists all denounced

the government and its German nationalist allies for sowing
discord in their midst.[5]

The inescapable conflicts in the east were not national
but social. A century of capitalist development had broken
the traditional ties of occupation, class, and nationality. An
end to social upheaval and conflict could be gained neither
in the east nor in the German heartland through the ruin of
one or another of the frontier nationalities. Germanization
of the east could guarantee neither Junker privilege nor middle-
class security. Bismarck and his successors, the heirs of
Frederick the Great, launched the German state on a reactionary
flight into eastern expansion. It ended, under Hitler's command, in the destruction of the Jews, the devastation of Poland,
and a crushing defeat stripping the German nation of its
eastern outposts.

APPENDIX

Demographic Movements in
the Province of Poznań, 1815-1914

The Prussian government's reports on the total population of the
province of Poznań during the nineteenth and early twentieth
centuries were politically neutral enterprises. Their results
were undoubtedly reasonably accurate. So too were official
confessional statistics. But the quinquennial surveys, begun
in 1890, of the persons speaking German or Polish as their
mother tongue are of doubtful value, since the German officials
who conducted these censuses probably counted many bilingual Poles
as German-speakers.[1]

Because there is no acceptable series of official nationality
statistics, the numbers of the Poznanian Poles, Germans, and Jews
must be estimated. This requires altering the confessional
statistics to take into account the German-speaking Catholics
and the Polish-speaking Protestants. Language, though not the
sole criterion of nationality, was unquestionably a powerful
determinant of national consciousness. Certainly it is the
clearest distinction that can be drawn between the Poles and
Germans, though not of course between Germans and Jews. But the
numbers of Jews are accurately reported in the confessional
surveys.

Polish and German scholars agree that throughout the nineteenth century roughly 3 percent of all Protestants spoke
Polish. These were survivors of the Polish Reformation, conservative farmers settled in the southern counties of Odalanów
(Adelnau) and Ostrzeszów (Schildberg) bordering on Silesia.
Though exposed increasingly to Germanization pressures, they
preserved their Polish-language liturgy and voted for Polish
parliamentary deputies. As a group they cannot be counted as
Germans.

More controversy surrounds the German-speaking Catholics.
While linguistic and psychological assimilation into Polish
culture continued to occur throughout the nineteenth century,
the large majority of these Catholics considered themselves

Germans. They clung to their language and voted for German
Catholic Centrist deputies when given the chance. In 1883
Eugen von Bergmann estimated the proportion of German-speakers
among the province's Catholics in the preceding decades of the
nineteenth century at 6 percent, a figure Polish scholars have
tended to accept. The language census of 1910 reported that 10
percent of the Catholic community spoke German, a figure ap-
proximating earlier German nationalist estimates.[2]

TABLE A1. Absolute and Relative Changes in the Populations of
the Poznanian Nationalities, 1825-1910

	Poles (Absolute Number)	%	Germans (Absolute Number)	%	Jews (Absolute Number)	%	Total Provincial Population
1825	648,500	62.9	318,500	30.8	65,000	6.3	1,032,000
1849	809,000	60.7	448,000	33.6	76,800	5.7	1,334,000
1871	966,000	61.0	556,000	35.1	62,000	3.9	1,584,000
1890	1,112,650	63.6	594,650	33.9	44,300	2.5	1,752,000
1910	1,352,650	64.7	720,650	34.0	26,500	1.3	2,100,000

SOURCES: Eugen von Bergmann, Zur Geschichte der Entwicklung
deutscher, polnischer und jüdischer Bevölkerung in der
Provinz Posen seit 1824 (Tübingen, 1883), pp. 35, 44; Manfred
Laubert, Die preussische Polenpolitik von 1772-1914 (Berlin,
1920), p. 123; Leo Wegener, Der wirtschaftliche Kampf der
Deutschen mit den Polen um die Provinz Posen (Posen, 1903),
pp. 19-22; Karol Rzepecki, Ubytek żydów w Księstwie poznańskiem (Poznań, 1912), p. 4; Statistisches Jahrbuch für den
preussischen Staat (Berlin, 1913), p. 21.

The nationality statistics presented in table A1 are
employed throughout the text of this study. They represent a
compromise between the Polish and German estimates set forth in
the historical literature. The numbers of Jews follow the confessional censuses. The number of Poles is the mean of the
three most commonly suggested statistical definitions: (1) all
Catholics; (2) 94 percent of all Catholics and 3 percent of all
Protestants; (3) 90 percent of all Catholics and 3 percent of
all Protestants. The curve described by plotting the mean of
these three series on a graph at twenty-year intervals for the
period 1825-1910 parallels at a lower level the curve described
by the figures for all Catholics. This confirms Fritz Zitzlaff's
contention that "a shift among the confessions in favor of the
Catholics means quite simply a shift in favor of the Poles."[3]

The numbers of German-speakers (Protestant and Catholic) presented
in table Al are the statistical analogues of the Polish figures.
The widest range of variation among the three definitions of the
Polish and non-Jewish German population is only 5 percent of the
total population: in 1825, between 60.7 percent and 65.6 percent
of the population spoke Polish; correspondingly, German Protestants
and Catholics comprised between 28.1 percent and 33.0 percent
of the provincial population. The median figures adopted here
fall near the middle of this range of variation. Hence they do
not deviate from the maximal figures proposed by either Polish or
German scholars by more than a few percentage points, a fact that
in itself commends their acceptance.

TABLE A2:   Rates of Population Growth in Prussia and the Province
            of Poznań, 1825-1910 (%)

	Kingdom of Prussia	Province of Poznań	Poznanian Poles	Poznanian Germans	Poznanian Jews	Poznanian Germans & Jews
1825-1849	34	29	22	41	18	37
1849-1871	51	19	20	24	-19	18
1871-1890	21	10	15	7	-28	3
1890-1910	34	20	22	21	-40	17

SOURCES: As in table Al.

TABLE A3:   The Ostflucht: Emigration from the Province of Poznań
            to the Central and Western Provinces of the Prussian
            State and Overseas, 1824-1910

	Net Emigration (Excess of Out- over In-Migration)	Total Emigration to Other Prussian Provinces	Total Overseas Emigration
1824-1843	-115,068		
1843-1871	149,642		
1871-1880	62,840	54,558	18,160
1880-1890	203,273	113,558	122,160
1890-1900	179,732	147,582	64,595
1900-1910	99,057	148,715	31,400
1824-1910	579,476		
1843-1910	694,544		
1871-1910	544,902		

SOURCES: Eugen von Bergmann, Zur Geschichte der Entwicklung
           deutscher, polnischer und jüdischer Bevölkerung in der
           Provinz Posen seit 1824 (Tübingen, 1883), pp. 51-54;
           Julian Marchlewski, Stosunki społeczno-ekonomiczne w
           ziemiach polskich zaboru pruskiego (Warszawa, 1952), p. 197;
           Waldemar Mitscherlich, Die Ausbreitung der Polen in Preussen
           (Berlin, 1909), p. 24; Stanisław Borowski, Rozwarstwienie
           wsi wielkopolskiej w latach 1807-1914 (Poznań, 1962), Annex
           77.

NOTE: Two minor extrapolations have been made in the computation
        of these figures: (1) overseas emigration 1871-73 has been
        estimated in proportion to known figures for 1874-79; (2) im-
        migration to the province 1905-10 has been calculated in pro-
        portion to known figures for 1900-1905.   Note that emigration
        from the province to areas of the Reich outside Prussia was
        minimal.

Introduction
1. Witold Kula, Théorie économique du système féodal:
Pour un modèle de l'économie polonaise 16e-18e siècles (Paris,
1970); Jan Rutkowski, Historia gospodarcza Polski. Vol. 1
Czasy Przedrozbiorowe (Poznań, 1947); Andrzej Wyczański, Polska--
rzeczą pospolitą szlachecką 1545-1764 (Warszawa, 1965); Jerzy
Topolski, "Gospodarka," in Bogusław Leśnodorski ed., Polska w
epoce Oświecenia (Warszawa, 1971), pp. 171-212; M. M. Postan,
"Economic Relations between Eastern and Western Europe," in
Geoffrey Barraclough ed., Eastern and Western Europe in the Middle
Ages (London, 1970), pp. 125-75; Stefan Kieniewicz et al.,
History of Poland (Warszawa, 1968), chaps. 1-13.
2. On the social and political structure of the Commonwealth
see also, in addition to the works by Wyczański, Leśnodorski, and
Kieniewicz cited above, Antoni Mączak, "The Social Distribution of
Landed Property in Poland from the 16th to the 18th Century,"
Third International Conference of Economic History 1968 (Paris,
1968), 1:455-69; Andrzej Zajączkowski, "Cadres structurels de la
noblesse," Annales 18, No. 1 (1963): 88-102; Władysław Konopczyński
Dzieje Polski nowożtnej, vol. 1 (London, 1958); W. F. Reddaway
ed., The Cambridge History of Poland, vol. 2 (London, 1941),
chaps. 1-9.
3. Czesław Miłosz, The History of Polish Literature (London,
1969); Stanisław Cynarski, "The Shape of Sarmatian Ideology in
Poland," Acta Poloniae Historica 19 (1968): 5-17; W. I. Thomas and
Florian Znaniecki, The Polish Peasant in Europe and America (Chicago, 1918), 1:87-302.
4. Oskar Ritter von Halecki, Das Nationalitätenproblem im
alten Polen (Krakau, 1916); Polish Encyclopedia, vol. 2, no. 3:
Territorial Development of the Polish Nation (Geneva, 1921); see
also chap. 1, below.

Chapter One
1. Stefan Kieniewicz et al., History of Poland, p. 44;
Raphael Strauss, "The Jews in the Economic Evolution of Central
Europe," Jewish Social Studies, 3 (1941): 15ff.
2. On the political history of the medieval and early
modern Polish-German frontier and on the migrations to Poland of
Germans and Jews in these centuries see, in addition to the
general works cited in the Introduction, above, also Aleksander
Gieysztor, ed., Polska dzielnicowa i zjednoczona (Warszawa, 1972);
Albert Brackmann, ed., Deutschland und Polen: Beiträge zu ihren
geschichtlichen Beziehungen (München, 1933), chaps. 1-3, 6-8, 14-
15; Goettingen Research Committee, Eastern Germany vol. 2: History
(Wuerzburg, 1963), chaps. 1-3; Erich Schmidt, Geschichte des
Deutschtums im Lande Posen unter polnischer Herrschaft (Bromberg,
1904); Bruno Schumacher, Geschichte Ost- und Westpreussens
(Würzburg, 1959), chaps. 3ff.; Bernard D. Weinryb, The Jews of
Poland: A Social and Economic History of the Jewish Community in

Poland from 1100 to 1800 (Philadelphia, 1973); Jerzy Topolski, ed., Dzieje Wielkopolski. Tom 1. Do roku 1793 (Poznań, 1969), chaps. 7ff.

3.   "Great Poland" (Wielkopolska), comprising the northwestern regions of the Polish Commonwealth centering on the cities of Poznań and Kalisz, constituted one of several historic divisions of the Polish state. It was so named in contradistinction to "Little Poland" (Małopolska), comprising the lands around Cracow. After 1815, the term Wielkopolska gradually came to be synonymous with the Prussian Province of Poznań.
     On the Polonization of medieval German colonists in Great Poland see Erich Schmidt, Deutschtum, pp. 280 ff.; Felix Haase, "Der deutsche Katholizismus und seine Beziehungen zu Polen," in Brackmann, Deutschland und Polen, pp. 96ff.; Kieniewicz et al., History of Poland, pp. 200ff.

4.   Ilse Rhode, Das Nationalitätenverhältnis in Westpreussen und Posen zur Zeit der polnischen Teilungen (Poznań, 1926), p. 54. In addition to such direct attacks upon the practice of the Protestant religions, decrees were issued--for example, in Poznań in 1619--prohibiting Protestants from acquiring full political rights in Poland's towns. Cf. Gotthold Rhode, ed., Geschichte der Stadt Posen (Neuendettelsau, 1953), p. 38. Such measures not only encouraged conversions to Catholicism among the Germans in Poland but also ensured political predominance in the towns to the Polish and German Catholics. Nevertheless, as will be seen below, a sizable German Protestant minority survived in Great Poland to the end of the Commonwealth's existence.

5.   Haase, "Katholizismus," p. 104.

6.   I. Rhode, Nationalitätenverhältnis, p. 18.

7.   Schumacher, Ost- und Westpreussen, p. 187.

8.   I. Rhode, Nationalitätenverhältnis, p. 15. On the Polonization of Germans in Royal Prussia see also Max Bär, Westpreussen unter Friedrich dem Grossen (Berlin, 1909), 1:7ff., and Oskar Ritter von Halecki, Das Nationalitätenproblem im alten Polen (Krakau, 1916), pp. 65ff.

9.   Władysław Konopczyński, Dzieje Polski nowożytnej (London, 1958), 1:407.

10. Arthur Rhode, Geschichte der evangelischen Kirche im Posener Lande (Würzburg, 1956), p. 108; Kieniewicz et al., History of Poland, pp. 264ff.; Halecki, Nationalitätenproblem, chap. 5.

11. On the second wave of German migrations to Poland in the early modern period, see Erich Schmidt, Deutschtum, pp. 313ff.; Jan Rutkowski, Historia gespodarcza Polski (Poznań, 1947), 1: 232ff.; Topolski, Dzieje Wielkopolski, pp. 706ff., 795ff.; Walter Kuhn, "German Settlement in Eastern Europe from the Middle Ages to the 18th Century," in Goettingen Research Committee, Eastern Germany, pp. 94ff.

12. Topolski, Dzieje Wielkopolski, pp. 798-804.

13. A. Rhode, Kirche, pp. 100ff.; Kurt Lück, Der Mythos vom Deutschen in der polnischen Volksüberlieferung und Literatur (Poznań, 1938), p. 169. A venerable popular jingle, well known in the eighteenth century, raised the possibility of intermarriage in homely terms: "Hinter Schulze's Schuppen da giht's lustig zu, Tanzt der pul'sche Ochse mit der deutschen Kuh" (In back of Schulze's farm sheds, they're kicking up a row, The Polish ox is dancing with the German cow".) Quoted in Robert Arnold, Geschichte der deutschen Polenlitteratur von den Anfängen bis 1800 (Wien, 1900), p. 8.

14. On the Upper Silesian and East Prussian Poles, as well as the Kashubians, see the Polish Encyclopedia, vol. 2, no. 3: Territorial Development of the Polish Nation, 452ff.; Stefan Kieniewicz, Historia Polski, 13ff.

15. Polish Encyclopedia, vol. 2, no. 2: General Demography of Poland (Geneva, 1921), pp. 104-9.

16. The foregoing interpretation of the crisis of the Polish
serf-estate system represents a synthesis of the views presented
by Witold Kula, Théorie économique du système féodal; Jerzy
Topolski, "L'influence du régime des réserves à corvèe en Pologne
sur le développement du capitalisme (XVIe-XVIIIe siècles),"
Revista di Storia Dell' Agricoltura, Sept. 1970; Janina Leskiewicz,
"Les entraves sociales au développement de la 'nouvelle agriculture'
en Pologne," Second International Conference of Economic History
1965 (Paris, 1965), vol. 2; Leonid Żytkowicz, "Production et
productivité de l'économie agricole en Pologne aux XVIe-XVIIIe
siècles," Third International Conference of Economic History 1968
(Paris, 1968), vol. 2; Władysław Rusiński, "Hauptprobleme der
Fronwirtschaft im 16. bis 18. Jhd./ in Polen und den Nachbarländern,"
First International Conference of Economic History 1960 (Paris,
1960); Bernard D. Weinryb, Neueste Wirtschaftsgeschichte der Juden
in Russland und Polen (Hildesheim, 1972).
17. Jerzy Topolski, ed., Dzieje Wielkopolski, chaps. 27, 28.
18. Rutkowski, Historia gospodarcza Polski, 1:355;
Schumacher, Ost- und Westpreussen, pp. 235-36; I. Rhode,
Nationalitätenverhältnis, pp. 20-30.
19. Topolski, Djieje Wielkopolski, p. 847; Bär, 1:361.
20. Stanisław Cynarski, "The Shape of Sarmatian Ideology in
Poland," passim.
21. Topolski, Djieje Wielkopolski, p. 882.
22. Ibid., pp. 862-80.
23. J. Perles, "Geschichte der Juden in Posen," Monatsschrift
für Geschichte und Wissenschaft des Judenthums 13 (1864):281.
24. Jan Wąsicki, Ziemie polskie pod zaborem pruskim. Prusy
południowe 1793-1806. Studium historycznoprawne (Wrocław, 1957),
p. 255.
25. Jan Rutkowski, "Le régime agraire en Pologne au XVIIIe
siècle," Revue d'histoire économique et sociale 14 (1926), 15
(1927); Bär, Westpreussen, 1:309.
26. Topolski, Dzieje Wielkopolski, pp. 852-57; Rutkowski,
"Le régime agraire," 14:486ff.
27. W. I. Thomas and Florian Znaniecki, The Polish Peasant
in Europe and America (Chicago, 1918), 1:87ff.
28. Topolski, Djieje Wielkopolski, p. 855.
29. Rutkowski, "Le régime agraire," 15:85.
30. The approximate nature of the estimates contained in
this table must be emphasized. They are based on late eighteenth-
century Prussian sources cited by Ilse Rhode and Dabinnus. I have
estimated the Jewish rural population in the Netze and Poznań
Districts in relation to later known figures on the total Jewish
population of the post-1815 Province of Poznań. See Appendix,
table A1. The figures for West Prussia assume five members per
family. Compare the total population of the province (571,000) in
Leopold Krug, Betrachtungen über den National-Reichthum des
preussischen Staats und über den Wohlstand seiner Bewohner
(Berlin, 1805), 1:323. The figures for West Prussia include the
German Protestant population of regions formerly part of East
Prussia but added to the new Prussian province of Westpreussen
after 1772. Thus these estimates tend to magnify the number of
Protestants residing within the Polish Commonwealth before 1772.
The figures given for the Poznań District's urban population
comprise only 86 of the region's 120 towns. They do, however,
include the population of the district capital and the district's
other larger urban centers.
31. On the statistical admissibility of equating Catholics
with Poles and Protestants with Germans in the Poznanian sector
of the German-Polish frontier see the Appendix below.
32. I. Rhode, Nationalitätenverhältnis, p. 17.
33. Moritz Jaffé, Die Stadt Posen unter preussischer Herrschaft: Ein Beitrag zur Geschichte des deutschen Ostens (Leipzig,
1909), pp. 23ff.

34. "Vom Kaufmanns- und Gewerbestande des ehemaligen und jetztigen Posens," Provinzial-Blätter für das Grossherzogtum Posen (Lissa, 1846), 1:109.

35. Leo Wegener, Der wirtschaftlichen Kampf der Deutschen mit den Polen um die Provinz Posen (Posen, 1903), p. 146.

36. Jaffé, Stadt Posen, pp. 19-20.

37. Topolski, Dzieje Wielkopolski, p. 480.

38. I. Rhode, Nationalitätenverhältnis, p. 50.

39. Topolski, Dzieje Wielkopolski, pp. 881ff.

40. Total population figures from L. Krug, National-Reichthum, 2:62; confessional figures from I. Rhode, Nationalitätenverhältnis, p. 14.

41. Robert Arnold, Polenlitteratur, pp. 46ff.; Schumacher, Ost- und Westpreussen, pp. 225ff.

42. Report of Assessor Kunth, Berlin, 20 September 1793, in Rodgero Prümers, Das Jahr 1793. Urkunden und Aktenstücke zur Geschichte der Organisation Südpreussens (Posen, 1895), pp. 553-54, hereinafter cited as Das Jahr 1793.

43. Erich Schmidt, Deutschtum, pp. 413ff.

44. "Verzeichniss der städtischen Beamten bei der Uebernahme, 1793 Mai-September," Das Jahr 1793, pp. 491-92.

45. "Immediatbericht des Geheimen Finanzrats von Brenckenhoff, Driesen 1772, März 27," in Max Bär, Westpreussen unter Friedrich dem Grossen, vol. 2, Quellen, p. 14, hereinafter cited as Bär, Quellen. On the legal and economic status of the German rural population before the partitions, see Erich Schmidt, Deutschtum, pp. 313ff.; A. Rhode, Kirche, pp. 125ff; J. Rutkowski, "Le regime agraire," 14:504-5.

46. A. Rhode, Kirche, pp. 97-103.

47. Ibid., pp. 107-25.

48. Erich Schmidt, Deutschtum, pp. 376-412.

49. Arnold, Polenlitteratur, p. 45; see also chaps. 3-6; below.

50. Friedrich Herzberg, Süd-Preussen und Neu-Ost-Preussen (Berlin, 1798), p. 142.

51. A. Rhode, Kirche, pp. 108-114, 127, 131.

52. Philip Bloch, "Judenwesen," in Das Jahr 1793, pp. 591-605.

53. Bernard Weinryb, The Jews of Poland, pp. 200, 224; J. Perles, "Juden in Posen," 13:282; Louis Finckelstein, ed., The Jews: Their History (New York, 1970), chaps. 6-8.

54. Bernard Weinryb, The Jews of Poland, passim; Raphael Mahler, "Antisemitism in Poland," in Koppel S. Pinson, ed., Essays on Antisemitism (New York, 1946), pp. 145-172; Jan Rutkowski, Historia gospodarcza Polski 1:232-48.

55. Polish Encyclopedia, General Demography of the Polish Nation, p. 111 (Korzon's estimate for 1791)..

56. Perles, "Juden in Posen," 13:286-88.

57. A. Heppner and J. Herzberg, Aus Vergangenheit und Gegenwart der Juden und der jüdischen Gemeinden in den Posener Landen (Koschmin-Bromberg, 1909), p. 715.

58. Perles, "Juden in Posen," 13:294; G. Rhode, ed., Geschichte der Stadt Posen, pp. 52-56; Jacob Jacobson, "Zur Geschichte der Juden in Posen," in G. Rhode, Stadt Posen, pp. 252ff.

59. Weinryb, The Jews of Poland, p. 191.

60. Perles, "Juden in Posen," 14:168-72.

61. Heppner and Herzberg, Vergangenheit, p. 781.

62. Heppner and Herzberg, Vergangenheit, p. 733; Jaffé, Stadt Posen, pp. 162ff.; Bernard Weinryb, Neueste Wirtschaftsgeschichte der Juden in Russland und Polen, pp. 94ff.; "Generalbericht des Kammer-Kalkulators Zimmermann an den Grafen Hoym uber die Verhältnisse der Juden in Polen, Breslau, 1793 Mai 1," in Das Jahr 1793, pp. 605-9.

63. Heppner and Herzberg, Vergangenheit, p. 713.

64. Ibid., pp. 752ff., 810.
65. One Jewish historian claims that the Poznań Jews looked
upon the Christian urban population, on account of economic
rivalries, as their "Todfeinde (mortal enemies)." See Louis
Lewin, Die Landessynode der grosspolnischen Judenschaft (Frankfurt
a.M., 1925), p. 64. On the Jews' language and dress see Jaffé,
Stadt Posen, p. 163; Heppner and Herzberg, Vergangenheit, pp.
733ff., 804.
66. Thomas and Znaniecki, Polish Peasant, pp. 141ff. On the
regional culture and mentality of the Polish common people in
Great Poland, see the work of the pioneering Polish ethnologist,
Oskar Kolberg, Lud, Serya IX, W. Ks. Poznańskie (Kraków, 1875-77),
3 vols.
67. G. Rhode, ed., Stadt Posen, pp. 269-76.
68. For a more detailed discussion of the question of interconfessional marriages, see below, chaps. 4 and 6.
69. Lück, Mythos, p. 69.
70. See below, chaps. 3 and 7.
71. Lück, Mythos, p. 31. "Cham" means the Biblical Ham,
progenitor of the low-born.
72. Ibid., pp. 149, 287.
73. Ibid., pp. 23-24.
74. Arnold, Polenlitteratur, p. 100; Jósef Feldman, Bismarck
a Polska (Kraków, 1947), chap. 1; Władysław Konopczyński,
Fryderyk Wielki a Polska (Poznań, 1947), chap. 1.
75. Lück, Mythos, chaps. 3,4,7, passim.
76. Quoted in Mahler, "Antisemitism," p. 154.
77. Quoted in Happner and Herzberg, Vergangenheit, p. 724;
for similar entries from the seventeenth and eighteenth centuries,
see also p. 723.
78. Mahler, "Antisemitism," pp. 149-53.
79. Weinryb, Neueste Wirtschaftsgeschichte der Juden in Russland und Polen, pp. 131ff.
80. Quotation from Weinryb, The Jews of Poland, p. 242. See
also Hannah Arendt, Antisemitism (New York, 1968), chap. 2; and
Leon Simon, "Jewish Nationalism," in Royal Institute of International Affairs (RIIA), Nationalism (London, 1939), pp. 163-69.
Simon wrote of traditional European Jewry: "If the ghetto was the
Jew's prison, it was also his kingdom. There he could live his
own life and could nurse his sense of superiority to the Gentiles
to whom he was subservient. He had no wish to be like his neighbors; on the contrary, he wanted to be different from them--dif-
ferent not in religion only, but in language, in education, in
ethical outlook, in his memories and hopes, even in the externals
of dress" (165-66).
81. For a fuller discussion of Prussian attitudes towards
Poland and the Poles, see chap. 2, below.
82. Lück, chap. 8; Waldemar Gurian, "Antisemitism in Modern
Germany," in Pinson, pp. 218ff.; Wanda Kampmann, Deutsche und
Juden: Studien zur Geschichte des deutschen Judentums (Heidelberg,
1963), chaps. 2,3; A. Rhode, Kirche, p. 104.
83. Rutkowski, Historia gospodarcza Polski, 1:235ff.

Chapter Two
1. Quoted in Hans Rosenberg, Bureaucracy, Aristocracy and
Autocracy. The Prussian Experience 1660-1815 (Boston, 1966), p.
40.
2. See F. L. Carsten, The Origins of Prussia (Oxford, 1954);
Walter Görlitz, Die Junker: Adel und Bauern im deutschen Osten
(Glücksburg, 1957); Hans Rosenberg, "The Rise of the Junkers in
Brandenburg-Prussia 1410-1653," The American Historical Review
69 (1943-1944): 1-22, 228-42; Jerome Blum, "The Rise of Serfdom
in Eastern Europe," The American Historical Review 62 (1957), no.
4, pp. 803-37; M. Małowist, "The Economic and Social Development
of the Baltic Countries from the 15th to the 17th Centuries,"

Economic History Review 12 (1959): 177-89; Jan Rutkowski, "Le
régime agraire," 15:97ff.; Joachim von Braun, "Die ostdeutsche
Wirtschaft in ihrer vorindustriellen Entwicklung," in Herbert
Kraus, ed., Das östliche Deutschland (Würzburg, 1959), pp. 603-
45; Perry Anderson, Passages from Antiquity to Feudalism (London,
1974), pp. 213ff.
    3. See Rosenberg, Bureaucracy, Aristocracy and Autocracy;
Otto Hintze, Die Hohenzollern und Ihr Werk (Berlin, 1916), chaps.
2-8, and "Der österreichische und der preussische Beamtenstaat im
17. und 18. Jahrhundert," Historische Zeitschrift, 86 (1901): 401-
44; Leonard Krieger, The German Idea of Freedom (Chicago, 1957),
chaps. 1,2; Fritz Hartung, Deutsche Verfassungsgeschichte vom 15.
Jahrhundert bis zur Gegenwart (Stuttgart, 1950), chaps 6-8, and
"Der aufgeklärte Absolutismus," Historische Zeitschrift, 190 (1955):
15-42; Walter Dorn, "The Prussian Bureaucracy in the 18th Century,"
Political Science Quarterly, 46 (1931): 403-23, 47 (1932):75-93,
259-73; Henri Brunschwig, La crise de l'état prussien et la
génèse de la mentalité romantique (Paris, 1947), part 1; Johannes
Ziekursch, Hundert Jahre schlesischer Agrargeschichte: vom
Huburtusberger Frieden bis zum Abschluss der Bauernbefreiung (Bres-
lau, 1927); Horst Krüger, Zur Geschichte der Manufakturen und der
Manufakturarbeiter in Preussen. Die mittleren Provinzen in der
zweiten Hälfte des 18. Jahrhunderts (Berlin, 1958); Perry Anderson,
Lineages of the Absolutist State (London, 1974).
    4. W. Konopczyński, Fryderyk Wielki a Polska, chap. 1; Józef
Feldman, Bismarck a Polska, 34ff.; Max Lehmann, "Preussen und
Polen," Historische Aufsätze und Reden (Leipzig, 1911), pp. 83-99;
Otto Hoetzsch, "Brandenburg-Preussen und Polen von 1640-1815," in
Brackmann, Deutschland und Polen, pp. 185-206.
    5. See Konopczyński, Fryderyk Wielki a Polska, passim;
Stefan Kieniewicz and Witold Kula, eds., Historia Polski (Warszawa,
1958), 2:71-81; Topolski, Dzieje Wielkopolski, chap. 30; Topolski,
"Poglądy na rozbiory Polski," in Jerzy Krasuski et al., Stosunki
polsko-niemieckie w historiografii (Poznań, 1974), pp. 410-515.
    6. Martin Broszat, Zweihundert Jahre deutsche Polenpolitik
(München, 1963), pp. 26-33.
    7. Konopczyński, Fryderyk Wielki a Polska, pp. 57, 205ff.
    8. On the first partition, see H. H. Kaplan, The First
Partition of Poland (New York, 1952); R. H. Lord, The Second
Partition of Poland (Cambridge, Mass., 1915), pp. 46ff; Ludwig
Dehio, The Precarious Balance: Four Centuries of the European
Power Struggle (New York, 1965), pp. 124-30; Broszat, Deutsche
Polenpolitik, pp. 33ff.; Gerhard Ritter, Friedrich der Grosse
(Heidelberg, 1954), chap. 10; Walter Hubatsch, "Der preussische
Staat. Hauptprobleme seiner Entwicklung vom 16. bis zum
beginnenden 19. Jahrhundert," Jahrbuch der Albertus-Universität zu
Königsberg, 12 (1962): 132ff.; and the works cited in note 5,
above.
    9. See Bär, Quellen, Frederick's memoranda of 6 Oct. 1771,
1 April 1772, and 19 April 1772, pp. 6, 19, 22.
    10. Quotations in W. O. Henderson, Studies in the Economic
Policy of Frederick the Great (London, 1963), p. 134. On the
trade treaty of 1775, ibid., pp. 99ff.
    11. Quoted in G. Peiser, "Über Friedrichs des Grossen burleskes
Heldengedicht 'La guerre des Confédérés,'" Zeitschrift der
Historischen Gesellschaft für die Provinz Posen 18 (1903): 162.
    12. "La guerre des Confédérés. Poëme," Oeuvres de Frédéric
le Grand (Berlin, 1850), vol. 14, pp. 216-71. Quotations in text
from pp. 219 and 271.
    13. Quoted in J. Feldman, Bismarck a Polska, p. 72.
    14. Arnold, Polenlitteratur, p. 33 and chaps. 1-4, passim.
    15. Ibid., p. 33.
    16. Ibid., p. 45.
    17. Ibid., pp. 73ff., and Konopczyński, Fryderyk Wielki a
Polska, p. 155. Schubart's poem is reprinted in Arnold,

Polenlitteratur, pp. 78-79. European opinion was divided on the
first partition. In France, Voltaire and D'Alembert stood with
Frederick and Catherine, but Rousseau, Mably, Diderot, Reynal, and
the Physiocrats condemned their actions. The only European powers
expressing formal and public opposition to the partition were the
Ottoman Porte and the Vatican, the former because Poland was a
vitally important buffer against Russia and Austria, the latter
because of the passage of Polish Catholics under the rule of anti-
Papal Prussia and Russia. Cf. Arnold, Polenlitteratur, p. 76.
     18. "Besitzergreifungs-Patent," Berlin, 13 September 1772,
Bär, Quellen, pp. 72-75. Privately, Frederick admitted the
tendentiousness of his legal claims to Royal Prussia. Cf. Broszat,
Deutsche Polenpolitik, p. 33.
     19. "Reden des Etatsministers und Oberburggrafen von Rohd
bei der Eröffnung und dem Schluss des Huldigungsfeierlichkeit zu
Marienburg, 1772 September 27," Bär, Quellen, pp. 87-89. In the
original passage from the Carmen saeculare (lines 9-12), Horace
wrote urbe Roma in place of Rohd's patria nostra while Rohd added
the words et felicius to Horace's adjective majus. See Horace,
The Odes and Epodes, C. E. Bennett, trans. (New York, 1914), pp.
350-351.
     20. Bär, Westpreussen, vol. 1, passim; Reinhold Koser,
Geschichte Friedrichs des Grossen (Stuttgart, 1925), pp. 333-59;
Hubatsch, "Preussischer Staat," pp. 137ff.; Jürgen-Peter Ravens,
Staat und katholische Kirche in Preussens polnischen Teilungs-
gebieten (1772-1807) (Wiesbaden, 1963), pp. 14ff.
     21. See income from and the royal budget for West Prussia
during 1772-74 in Bär, Quellen, pp. 720-21.
     22. "Immediatbericht des Geheimen Finanzrats von Brenckenhoff,"
23 May 1774, Bär, Quellen, pp. 241-42.
     23. "Schreiben das Kammerdirektors Vorhoff an den Minister
von Massow," 8 June 1775, ibid., p. 288.
     24. See Frederick's memoranda of 8 June 1773, 7 June 1775,
7 June 1776, and 12 July 1780, ibid., pp. 200, 286-87, 309-10, 409.
     25. Frederick used the term preussische Landes-Art. See his
Kabinetts-Instruktion of 6 June 1772, ibid., pp. 41-43.
     26. Frederick's memorandum of 3 July 1780, ibid., pp. 407-8.
     27. Bär, Westpreussen, 1: 566ff.
     28. Royal order of 6 June 1772, Bär, Quellen, pp. 49-50.
     29. Royal order of 9 October 1772, ibid., pp. 116-17.
     30. Royal order of 25 March 1773, ibid., p. 190.
     31. Royal order of 25 September 1773, ibid., p. 218.
     32. Royal order of 2 March 1777, ibid., p. 335.
     33. Royal order of 8 June 1777, ibid., pp. 349-50.
     34. Royal order of 2 October 1783, ibid., p. 440.
     35. Royal order of 29 October 1783, ibid., p. 483.
     36. Royal order of 1 April 1772, ibid., p. 18.
     37. Dabinnus, Pomerellen, p. 51; I. Rhode, Nationalitäten-
verhältnis, p. 19.
     38. Schumacher, Ost- und Westpreussen, chap. 22; Görlitz,
Junker, 126ff.; Erhard Moritz, Preussen und der Kościuszko-Aufstand
1794. Zur preussischen Polenpolitik in der Zeit der Französischen
Revolution (Berlin, 1968), p. 113; Witold Jakóbczyk, ed., Dzieje
Wielkopolski. vol. 2. Lata 1793-1918 (Poznań, 1973), pp. 17ff.,
46ff. In a memorial to the Prussian government of March 1807, the
conservative Polish Prince Antoni Radziwiłł admitted the success
in West Prussia of "the Germanization system (System der
Verdeutschung)," but ascribed it, one-sidedly, to the West Prussian
Polish nobility's opportunity before 1795 to move to the post-1772
Commonwealth. See "Radziwills Denkschrift für den König," dated
Memel, 15 March 1807, in Kurt Schottmüller, ed., Der Polenaufstand
1806/7. Urkunden und Aktenstücke aus der Zeit zwischen Jena und
Tilsit (Lissa, 1907), p. 152.
     39. "Immediatbericht des Oberpräsidenten von Domhardt an den
König," 29 January 1773, Bär, Quellen, p. 178.

40. Schrötter defended the Poles against these charges
as far as Frederick's wrath could safely be challenged. But
afterwards he wrote, "I was glad that I did not let myself defend
the local nation too strongly against the charge that the common
man is too much inclined to theft, because on the same day I spoke
with His Majesty the watches of the three messengers in the Royal
lodgings were stolen." Schrötter's letter of 12 June 1784 to
Grosskanzler von Carmer, ibid., pp. 500-502.
41. Royal order of 1 April 1772, ibid., pp. 17-18.
42. See Frederick's memoranda of 6 June 1772, 9 October
1772, 14 December 1772, 8 June 1773, and 7 June 1776, ibid., pp.
42-43, 116, 159, 200, 309-10. See also, on Frederick's
colonization activities, Bär, 1:320ff.
43. Royal order of 20 January 1776, Bär, Quellen, p. 302.
44. Arnold, Polenlitteratur, p. 99.
45. Kampmann, Deutsche und Juden, pp. 41ff, 62ff.
46. Ibid., p. 71.
47. Ibid., pp. 75-77.
48. It was Berlin Hofprediger Daniel Jablonski (1660-1741)
who marshaled official Prussian support for Eisenmenger's giant
tract. He also organized Prussian missions to the Protestant
communes of Great Poland, but whether this involved circulation
of Entdecktes Judenthum among German Protestants in Poland is
unknown. See A. Rhode, Kirche, p. 104; W. Gurian, "Antisemitism,"
p. 219.
49. Kampmann, Deutsche und Juden, pp. 79, 104.
50. Royal instruction of 7 June 1772, Bär, Quellen, p. 49.
51. Royal orders of 15 November 1772, 27 April 1773, 8 June
1777, ibid., pp. 148, 195, 365; see also Bär, Westpreussen, 1:
429ff.
52. Dehio, Balance, p. 129.
53. Lord, Second Partition, passim.
54. Friedrich Meinecke, "Drei Denkschriften Boyens über Polen
und Südpreussen aus den Jahren 1794 und 1795," Zeitschrift der
Historischen Gesellschaft für die Provinz Posen 8 (1893): 307-19.
55. Quotations in Feldman, Bismarck a Polska, pp. 48-49;
see also Arnold, pp. 115-16. The distinguished biographer of
Frederick II, Reinhold Koser, argued that the final partitions
weakened old Prussia in the decade before its collapse following
its defeat at Napoleon's hands in 1806. See Koser's articles on
"Die preussische Politik von 1786 bis 1806," Deutsche Monatsschrift
für das gesamte Leben der Gegenwart 11 (1906-7): 453-80, 612-37.
This position, seldom adopted in Prussian-German historiography,
is, in my opinion, essentially sound. Cf. William W. Hagen, "The
Partitions of Poland and the Crisis of the Old Regime in Prussia
1772-1806," Central European History 9,2 (1977): 115-28.
56. See Otto Hintze, "Preussens Entwicklung zum Rechtsstaat,"
Forschungen zur brandenburgischen und preussischen Geschichte
32 (1920): 389-449; Rosenberg, Bureaucracy, Aristocracy and Autocracy, chaps. 6ff.; Brunschwig, Crise, part 2; Reinhardt Koselleck,
Preussen zwischen Reform und Revolution. Allgemeines Landrecht,
Verwaltung und soziale Bewegung von 1791 bis 1848 (Stuttgart,
1967), pp. 57ff.
57. "Declaration Sr. Majestat des Königs von Preussen
den Einmarsch Ihrer Truppen in Pohlen betreffend," dated Berlin,
6 January 1793, Das Jahr 1793, pp. 21-22.
58. Quotation in Wąsicki, Prusy południowe, 190. See also
Ziekursch, Agrargeschichte, 192ff. "South Prussia" was the
name applied to the Prussian province formed from the lands of
the partition of 1793. After the third partition, this province
was extended eastward to include Warsaw while yet another pro-
vince--"New East Prussia"--was created from the remaining annexed territory. See map 2, p. 53, for Prussia's gains in
the partitions.
59. Hagen, "Partitions of Poland."

60. "Vorschläge des Generals von Möllendorff zur Einrichtung der Provinz Südpreussen," dated Posen, 30 May 1793, Das Jahr 1793, p. 154.

61. Letters of Frederick William II dated Rawitsch, 16 October 1793 and Frankfurt a. M., 11 February 1793, Das Jahr 1793, pp. 103, 128; "Immediatbericht der Minister v. Danckelman und v. Voss, betreffend das Vorgehen beim Erlass von Polizeigesetzen für Südpreussen," ibid., pp. 415-16.

62. Jan Wąsicki, Ziemie polskie pod zaborem pruskim. Prusy nowowschodnie (Neuostpreussen) 1795-1806 (Poznán, 1963), pp. 53, 88, 129-33, 170, 193, 202, 261; Wąsicki, Prusy południowe, pp. 228, 251ff., 296, 316; Ingeburg Bussenius, Die preussische Verwaltung in Süd- und Neuostpreussen 1793-1806 (Heidelberg, 1960), pp. 121, 210-18; Kieniewicz, Historia Polski 1795-1918, p. 21; Otto Hintze, "Preussische Reformbestrebungen vor 1806," an essay written in 1896 and reprinted in Regierung und Verwaltung (Göttingen, 1967), pp. 504-29.

63. Quoted in Arnold, Polenlitteratur, p. 242.

64. Schrötter's rescript of 21 January 1797, in Ingeburg Bussenius, ed., Urkunden und Akten zur Geschichte der preussischen Verwaltung in Südpreussen und Neuostpressen 1793-1806 (Frankfurt a. M., 1961), p. 249.

65. Quoted in Richard Breyer, "Die südpreussischen Beamten und die Polenfrage," Zeitschrift für Ostforschung 4 (1955), no. 4, pp. 539-40. On the problems of the South and New East Prussian bureaucracies, see Bussenius, Verwaltung, pp. 56ff., 138, 186ff.; Bussenius, Urkunden, pp. 245ff.; Das Jahr 1793, pp. 774, 811.

66. Arnold, Polenlitteratur, chaps. 10, 11; Otto Tschirch, Geschichte der öffentlichen Meinung in Preussen vom Baseler Frieden bis zum Zusammenbruch des Staates (1795-1806) (Weimar, 1933), vol. 1, chap. 5; See Herzberg's work of 1798, pp. 104-200, for some particularly absurd and derogatory characterizations of Poland and the Poles; Breyer, "Beamten," p. 546.

67. Arnold, Polenlitteratur, pp. 128-31 and chap. 10, passim.

68. Herman Vahle, "Die polnische Verfassung vom 3. Mai 1791 im zeitgenössischen deutschen Urteil," Jahrbücher für Geschichte Osteuropas 19 (1971): 347-71.

69. Johann Gottfried Herder, Ideen zur Philosophie der Geschichte der Menschheit (1787), in B. Suphan, ed., Herders Sämmtliche Werke (Berlin, 1909), 14: 277-80. Note also Herder's analysis of the strengths and weaknesses of the Germanic peoples' military and political traditions, ibid., pp. 270-77.

70. Immanuel Kant, "Eternal Peace," (1795), in C. J. Friedrich, The Philosophy of Kant (New York, 1949), pp. 435-36.

71. Arnold, Polenlitteratur, p. 151.

72. Ibid., p. 238.

73. In Werner's case, enthusiasm for the Polish cause could not withstand exposure to the realities of Polish life. In 1804, with his major Polish poems behind him, he wrote: "Warsaw was far from being what I had dreamt it was; . . . that [Polish] freedom which I had enthusiastically embraced in Plozk and in whose honor, and that of the hero Kosciuszko, I had, in the company of some exalted Poles (no nation is more exalted than the Poles), composed a number of poems disgusted me through and through when I got to know its miserable apostles in Warsaw." Quoted in Bussenius, Verwaltung, p. 147. Werner's poems are discussed and reprinted in Arnold, pp. 227ff., 274-81.

74. Von Buchholtz's memorial, Warsaw, 27 January 1793, Das Jahr 1793, pp. 77-82.

75. "Immediatbericht Voss," Berlin 10 April 1800, Bussenius, Urkunden, p. 279.

76. Quoted in Wąsicki, Prusy południowe, pp. 182-83.

77. "Patent an die Einwohner von Südpreussen," Berlin 25 March 1793, Das Jahr 1793, pp. 42-45.

78. "Bericht über des Königs Aufenthalt in Posen," Posen, 10-14 October 1793, Das Jahr 1793, pp. 98-99. The Poles' reputation as talented dancers was born in Germany at the end of the eighteenth century. Goethe, no Polonophile, declared "they have an inborn grace." Quoted in Arnold, Polenlitteratur, p. 82.

79. Hoym's memorial, Breslau, 21 December 1794, Das Jahr 1793, p. 776; Wąsicki, Prusy południowe, pp. 129-131, 317, and Prusy nowowschodnie, pp. 37, 45, 103.

80. Wąsicki, Prusy południowe, p. 234.

81. Bussenius, Verwaltung, part 2, chap. 2.

82. Wąsicki, Prusy południowe, p. 327.

83. Moellendorff's report to the Cabinets-Ministerium of 12 April 1793. Das Jahr 1793, p. 51; Royal order of 11 February 1793, ibid., p. 378.

84. Quotation in Ravens, Staat und Kirche, p. 78. On official policy towards the Catholic church between 1793 and 1807, ibid., pp. 76ff.

85. Voss's "Denkschrift über die Verwaltung Südpreussens," September 1794, in Bussenius, Urkunden, p. 62.

86. "Immediatbericht der Minister Finkenstein, Alvensleben, Goldbeck und Haugwitz," Berlin, 12 October 1798, Bussenius, Urkunden, p. 268.

87. See the documents on educational policy, ibid., pp. 230, 235ff., 367, 446; Wąsicki, Prusy południowe, p. 193, Prusy nowowschodnie, p. 245.

88. Voss's report of 7 November 1793, Das Jahr 1793, p. 683; report of South Prussian Kammer, 28 December 1793, on the Jesuit School in Poznań, ibid., p. 726.

89. "Reskript an die Kammer in Warschau," Berlin, 12 April 1799, Bussenius, Urkunden, pp. 448-49; Bussenius, Verwaltung, pp. 274-75. In the curriculum of the Royal Lyceum established in Warsaw in 1804, study of the German and Polish languages was compulsory through all six forms, but in the upper forms the only subjects not to be taught in German were Polish and French literature. In the presentation of vaterländische history the pupils would begin with the study of the Polish Commonwealth, pass through the partition period and conclude with the history of their new "fatherland," the Prussian state. See "Reglement für das Königliche Lyzeum," Berlin, 23 June 1804, Bussenius, Urkunden, pp. 466-69. In the Poznań Department, however, Prussian officials forbade the teaching of Polish history and geography on the grounds that these subjects were "too republican" for impressionable minds. See Das Jahr 1793, p. 727.

90. This is Wąsicki's general position, which is also argued more or less strongly in most of both the older and the more recent Polish historiography on the period.

91. Five hundred twenty peasant colonists and their families were settled by the government in South Prussia, 3,507 persons--colonists and dependents, but not all of them peasants--in New East Prussia. Wąsicki, Prusy południowe, p. 272, Prusy nowowschodnie, p. 146.

92. Wąsicki, Prusy południowe, pp. 225-28; Bussenius, Verwaltung, p. 293.

93. Quotations in Breyer, "Beamten," p. 547.

94. Voss's Denkschrift of 22 May 1796, Das Jahr 1793, p. 780. Goethe took a brief interest in the problems of assimilating the Poles into the Germanic cultural world, writing sometime between 1793 and 1795 an essay which Eckermann later entitled "Vorschlag zur Einführung der deutschen Sprache in Polen. Um eine höhere Cultur der niederen Classen zu bewirken," Goethe-Jahrbuch 13 (1892): 3-9. Goethe believed that after the partitions there would be an "internal war" as a result of differences in language and custom. Impressed as he had been on his journey to Cracow in 1790 by Polish poverty, he assumed the Polish common people would be receptive to sociolinguistic assimilation into the German world.

To accomplish this, he suggested that "popular theaters" be
staged in the Polish elementary schools representing the (presumably enviable) German style of everyday life. By a combination
of pantomime and simplified language instruction, these spectacles
would introduce the Polish children to the rudiments of German
while spurring them on to learn more as they grew older. This
genial proposal, since it was not published until 1892, came too
late to the Prussian authorities, who by that time had settled
on more rough-and-ready ways of teaching Polish students German.

95. Moellendorff's reports of February 1793, Das Jahr 1793,
pp. 25, 35.

96. Quoted in Wąsicki, Prusy południowe, p. 69.

97. Quotation ibid., p. 53. The Polish upper clergy made
similar protestations of loyalty.

98. Petition of the South Prussian nobility, May 1793, Das
Jahr 1793, pp. 84-87.

99. Quoted in Wąsicki, Prusy południowe, p. 57.

100. Voss's report to the king, 13 September 1793, Das Jahr
1793, p. 182; Wąsicki, Prusy południowe, pp. 49, 324.

101. Quotations ibid., p. 55.

102. Ibid., pp. 44-46; Moellendorff's Denkschrift of late
1793, Das Jahr 1793, pp. 768ff.

103. Report of Kriegsrat Dreyer, Posen, 9 November 1793,
Das Jahr 1793, p. 104. See also Moellendorff's Denkschrift of
late 1793, ibid., p. 769; Bussenius, Verwaltung, p. 177; Moritz,
p. 45.

104. Quoted in Moritz, p. 54.

105. Moritz, Kościuszko-Aufstand, pp. 76ff; Jakóbczyk, Dzieje
Wielkopolski, pp. 17-23. Not all the Polish recruits in the
Prussian army proved reliable in the South Prussian antipartisan
campaigns. The archconservative Ludwig von der Marwitz later
wrote of his experience in the fighting: "A half-dozen Polacks
deserted before the very eyes of the whole batallion." Quoted
in Moritz, Kościuszko-Aufstand, p. 90.

106. Moritz, Kościuszko-Aufstand, p. 196; Wąsicki, Prusy
południowe, pp. 185ff. Four monasteries lost their lands for
having hidden Polish rebels.

107. Moritz, Kościuszko-Aufstand, p. 113.

108. Quoted in Wąsicki, Prusy południowe, p. 147. The
Prussian envoy in Warsaw, von Buchholtz, wrote in 1797 that the
South Prussian nobles were generally dissatisfied with Prussian
rule and openly predicted the restoration of Polish independence.
See his letter to Hoym of 6 February 1797 in Bussenius, Urkunden,
pp. 251-53.

109. Jerzy Szacki, "L'Evolution du concept de 'nation' en
Pologne à la fin du XVIIIe et au début du XIXe siècle," Cahiers
d'histoire mondiale 9 (1965), no. 1: 59-79; Tadeusz Łepkowski,
"La formation de la nation polonaise moderne dans les conditions
d'un pays demémbré," Acta Poloniae Historica 19 (1968): 19-35;
Stefan Kieniewicz, "Le développement de la conscience nationale
polonaise au XIXe siècle," ibid., pp. 37-48.

110. See the reports on Frederick William II's reception in
Meseritz and Poznań in October 1793, Das Jahr 1793, pp. 97-99;
Wąsicki, Prusy południowe, p. 43.

111. See the petition of the Poznań Kaufmannschaft of 12 October
1793, Das Jahr 1793, pp. 581-82; table on organization of the
South Prussian towns, 16 January 1795, Bussenius, Urkunden, pp.
367-75; Ravens, Staat und Kirche, p. 107; Jakóbczyk, Dzieje
Wielkopolski, p. 28.

112. "Umständliche Erzählung der Huldigungsfeier in Posen,"
7 May 1793, Das Jahr 1793, pp. 53-57. See also the reports cited
in note 110, above.

113. Mencken's report from the end of 1796, Bussenius,
Urkunden, p. 207; "Kabinettsorder an Voss," Postdam, 26 April 1806,
ibid., p. 442.

114. Kampmann, Deutsche und Juden, pp. 98ff.
115. See Hoym's "Promemoria wegen der Verfassung der Juden,"
Breslau, 27 April 1793, Bussenius, Urkunden, pp. 434-35; Das Jahr
1793, editor's notes, 592.
116. "Generaljudenreglement für Süd- und Neuostpreussen,"
Berlin, 17 April 1797, editor's condensation, Bussenius, Urkunden,
pp. 436-37; Schroetter's Reskript, Berlin, 17 November 1799, ibid.,
p. 441; Wąsicki, Prusy południowe, pp. 292-94.
117. Quoted in Heppner and Herzberg, Vergangenheit, p. 785.
118. Ibid., pp. 786ff.; Perles, "Juden in Posen," 14: 207-10.
119. Napoleon's words quoted in Kieniewicz, Historia Polski
1795-1918, p. 32.
120. Bussenius, Verwaltung, p. 312; Schottmüller, Polenaufstand, p. 15 (text) and documents on the collapse of the Prussian
regime in South Prussia, pp. 33-35, 75; Jakóbczyk, Dzieje
Wielkopolski, pp. 46ff.
121. Wąsicki, Prusy nowowschodnie, p. 263.
122. "Bericht des Warschauer Kammerpräsidium wegen der
Stimmung im Bezirk," Warschau, 1 November 1806, Schottmüller,
Polenaufstand, pp. 12-13.
123. "Bericht des Oberfiskal Mosqua an den Kanzler v.
Schrötter über den Polenaufstand in Warschau," February 1807,
ibid., pp. 75-80.
124. "Bericht des Landrats v. Blomberg, Koniner Kreises,
über den Polenaufstand im Kalischer Kammer-Bezirk," ibid., pp.
52-57; "Bericht des Landrats v. Blomberg vom Kr. Konin über
die polnischen und französischen Truppen und die Stimmung in
Südpreussen," Königsberg, 21 January 1807, ibid., pp. 57-59.
125. "Denkschrift Gruners für den Konig. Bericht über den
Posener Polenaufstand. Vorschläge für die künftige Verwaltung
Südpreussens," Memel, 25 February 1807, ibid., pp. 34-51, 45-48.

Chapter Three
1. Quoted in Otto Hintze, "Preussische Reformbestregungen
vor 1806," Regierung und Verwaltung, p. 505.
2. Otto Hintze, "Preussens Entwicklung zum Rechtsstaat,"
Forschungen zur brandenburgischen und preussischen Geschichte
32 (1920): 442; Fritz Hartung, Deutsche Verfassungsgeschichte,
p. 252; Hans Rosenberg, Bureaucracy, Aristocracy and Autocracy,
chap. 9.
3. On the accomplishments and significance of the Prussian
Reform Era, see Franz Schnabel, Deutsche Geschichte im neunzehn
Jahrhundert (Freiburg im Breisgau, 1947), vol. 1, book 2, chap. 2;
Friedrich Meinecke, Das Zeitalter der deutschen Erhebung 1795-1815
(Leipzig, 1906), chap. 4; Walter M. Simon, The Failure of the
Prussian Reform Movement 1807-1819 (Ithaca, N. Y., 1955); Heinrich
Heffter, Die deutsche Selbstverwaltung im neunzehnten Jahrhundert
(Stuttgart, 1950), pp. 79-135; Reinhart Koselleck, "Staat und
Gesellschaft in Preussen, 1815-1848," in Hans-Ulrich Wehler, ed.,
Moderne deutsche Sozialgeschichte (Köln, 1968), pp. 55-85; Werner
Sombart, Die deutsche Volkswirtschaft im neunzehnten Jahrhundert
(Berlin, 1909), chaps. 12, 13; Theodore S. Hamerow, Restoration,
Revolution, Reaction: Economics and Politics in Germany, 1815-1871
(Princeton, 1958), chaps. 1-4; Gordon A. Craig, The Politics of
the Prussian Army 1640-1945 (London, 1955), chap. 2; Walter
Görlitz, Die Junker: Adel und Bauer im deutschen Osten (Glücksburg,
1957), pp. 172-211; Krieger, The German Idea of Freedom, pp. 139-
229; James J. Sheehan, "Conflict and Cohesion among German Elites
in the Nineteenth Century," in Robert J. Bezucha, ed., Modern
European Social History (Lexington, Mass., 1972), pp. 3-27; Wanda
Kampmann, Deutsche und Juden, chap. 8; Rosenberg, Bureaucracy,
Aristocracy and Autocracy, chap. 8; John R. Gillis, "Aristocracy
and Bureaucracy in Nineteenth-Century Prussia," Past and Present
41 (1968): 105-15.

4. Quoted in Koselleck, "Staat und Gesellschaft in Preussen, 1815-1848," p. 58.

5. Meinecke, Weltbürgertum und Nationalstaat, chap. 8; Walter M. Simon, "Variations in Nationalism during the Great Reform Period in Prussia," American Historical Review 59 (1954), no. 2, pp. 305-31; Krieger, Freedom, pp. 196-206.

6. Quoted in Alfred Cobban, National Self-Determination, p. 56. The italics are Herder's. See also R. R. Ergang, Herder and the Foundations of German Nationalism (New York, 1931).

7. Wolfgang Sauer, "Das Problem des deutschen Nationalstaates," in Wehler, Moderne deutsche Sozialgeschichte, pp. 407-36.

8. See, in addition to the works of Kieniewicz, Łepkowski, and Szacki cited above, Peter Brock, "Polish Nationalism," Peter F. Sugar and Ivo J. Lederer, eds., Nationalism in Eastern Europe (Seattle, 1969), pp. 310-72; Wilhelm Feldman, Geschichte der politischen Ideen in Polen seit dessen Teilungen 1795-1914 (München, 1917); Marian Kukiel, Czartoryski and European Unity 1770-1861 (Princeton, 1955); R. F. Leslie, Polish Politics and the Revolution of November, 1830 (London, 1956) and Reform and Insurrection in Russian Poland 1856-1865 (London, 1963); Henryk Wereszycki, "Polish Insurrections as a Controversial Problem for Polish Historiography," Canadian Slavonic Papers 9 (1967), no. 1, pp. 107-21.

9. Gruner's second Denkschrift, Memel, 1 March 1807, in Kurt Schottmüller, ed., Der Polenaufstand 1806/7, pp. 122-23; Gruner's third Denkschrift, Memel, 7 March 1807, ibid., pp. 140-42.

10. Gruner's second Denkschrift, ibid., pp. 126, 130.

11. Ibid., ;. 130; see also Gruner's first Denkschrift, Memel, 25 February 1807, ibid., p. 51.

12. Gruner's third Denkschrift, ibid., p. 144.

13. Ibid., pp. 145-48.

14. Simon, "Variations in Nationalism," p. 309.

15. Radziwiłł's Denkschrift of August-September 1806 in Schottmüller, ed., p. 6; Radziwiłł's report to the king, Memel, 15 March 1807, ibid., pp. 150-54.

16. Altenstein's Denkschrift, March 1807, in Schottmüller, pp. 165, 158-180 and passim. Schottmüller incorrectly assumed Hardenberg's authorship of this report. See Gerhard Ritter, "Die preussischen Staatsmänner der Reformzeit und die Polenfrage," in Brackmann, ed., Deutschland und Polen, pp. 218, 207-19 passim.

17. Nassauer Denkschrift, in Walter Hubatsch, ed., Freiherr vom Stein. Briefe und amtliche Schriften (Stuttgart, 1959), vol. 2, part 1, pp. 395-98.

18. Indeed, in 1814 Stein expressed his sharpest hostility to such a notion in a conversation with Tsar Alexander I. Stein quoted in defense of his position the cutting words of Stefan Batory, the distracted sixteenth-century Polish king: "Poland owes its existence neither to laws nor government, but to accident." Alexander responded with surprise to this deviation from what he called Stein's customary "liberalism." Feldman, Bismarck a Polska, pp. 73-74.

19. Gruner's third Denkschrift, Schottmüller, Polenaufstand, p. 135.

20. C. K. Webster, "England and the Polish-Saxon Problem at the Congress of Vienna," Transactions of the Royal Historical Society, 3d ser., vol. 7 (1913), pp. 49-102; Hermann Oncken, "Preussen und Polen im 19. Jahrhundert," in Brackmann, pp. 220-22.

21. The Vienna agreements on Poland are reproduced in Ludwik Żychliński, Historya Sejmów Wielk. Ks. Poznańskiego do r. 1847 (Poznań, 1867), 1:4-6.

22. "Odezwa królewska do mieszkańców W. Ks. Poznańskiego z 15 maja 1815," Żychliński, Historya Sejmów, 1:9-11.

23. On the administration of the Grand Duchy and the role played in it by the szlachta, see Manfred Laubert, Die Verwaltung

der Provinz Posen 1815-1847 (Breslau, 1923), pp. 31ff., 156ff.;
Franciszek Paprocki, Wielkie Księstwo Poznańskie w okresie rządów
Flottwella (1830-1841) (Poznań, 1970), chap. 1.   On the provincial
diet and the szlachta's political relationship to the government
in Berlin prior to 1830, cf. Żychliński, Historya Sejmów, 1: 39ff.
and passim.
     24. The Poles were properly grateful for the Landschaft.
They adorned the bank building with a bust of the Oberpräsident
who founded it. Żychliński, Historya Sejmów, 1:23.
     25. Stanisław Borowski, Rozwarstwienie wsi wielkopolskiej w
latach 1807-1914 (Poznań, 1962), pp. 43-49.
     26. On the agrarian reforms, see Stefan Kieniewicz, The
Emancipation of the Polish Peasantry (Chicago, 1969), chap. 4;
Władysław Rusiński, ed., Dzieje wsi wielkopolskiej (Poznań, 1959),
pp. 141-66; Witold Jakóbczyk, Studia nad dziejami Wielkopolski w
XIX w. (dzieje pracy organicznej), vol. 1, 1815-1850 (Poznań,
1951), pp. 8-20; Julian Marchlewski, Stosunki społeczno-
ekonomiczne w ziemiach polskich zaboru pruskiego (Lwów, 1903),
reprinted in Julian Marchlewski, Pisma wybrane (Warszawa, 1952),
1: 248-75.
     27. Laubert, Verwaltung, p. 253 and chaps. 21 and 22, passim;
Józef Buzek, Historya polityki narodowościowej rządu pruskiego
wobec Polaków. Od traktatów wiedeńskich do ustaw wyjątkowych z r.
1908 (Lwów, 1909), pp. 52ff.
     28. Altenstein's instruction to the Poznań Regierung, 23
December 1822, quoted in Siegfried Baske, Praxis und Prinzipien der
preussischen Polenpolitik vom Beginn der Reaktionszeit bis zur
Gründung des Deutschen Reiches (Berlin, 1963), p. 144.
     29. Hans Schmidt, Die polnische Revolution des Jahres 1848
im Grossherzogtum Posen (Weimar, 1912), p. 15.   On Radziwiłł's
views, cf. Żychliński, Historya Sejmów, 1: 22.
     30. Paprocki, Wielkie Księstwo Poznańskie, pp. 39, 52-56;
Jakóbczyk, ed., Dzieje Wielkopolski. Lata 1793-1918, chap. 5,
sec. 2.
     31. Hans Schmidt, 1848, p. 15; Buzek, Historya, p. 46.
     32. Speech of Prince Antoni Sułkowski in the provincial diet,
26 February 1830, in Żychliński, Historya Sejmów, 1:129-30.
     33. Sułkowski's speech in the Staatsrat in Berlin, 25 March
1828, ibid., pp. 82-83; cf. also the speech of the former
Napoleonic colonel, Niegolewski, in the provincial diet of 1827,
ibid., 1: 45-51.
     34. Sułkowski's speech in the provincial diet, 22 December
1827, ibid., 1: 77.
     35. Kossecki's speech in the provincial diet, January 1830,
ibid., 1: 117.
     36. Ibid., 1: 79-84.
     37. A practical difficulty confronted Polish university
students: they were required to learn Greek and Latin and master
the German language, while most of them chose to study Polish
literature and history as well. Ibid., 1: 48. On German accusations of boycotting, which Żychliński does not deny, cf. Laubert,
Verwaltung, p. 58; Żychliński, Historya Sejmów, 1: 90.
     38. Żychliński, Historya Sejmów, 1: 104, 108, 130.
     39. Laubert, Verwaltung, pp. 45-62.
     40. Żychliński, Historya Sejmów, 1: 45.
     41. Report of a conference of 7 April 1815 signed by Boyen,
Zerboni di Sposetti, Bülow, and (no doubt, uncomfortably) by
Radziwiłł as well. Quoted in Feldman, Bismarck a Polska, p. 68.
     42. W. Jakóbczyk, ed., Dzieje Wielkopolski, pp. 158-62.
Treitschke, in his Deutsche Geschichte, for polemical purposes
placed the number of participants from the Grand Duchy at 12,000.
Cf. Laubert, Verwaltung, p. 114.
     43. See Appendix, table A1.
     44. Jakóbczyk, Dzieje Wielkopolski, p. 161.
     45. Quotations in Henryk Kocój, Niemcy a powstanie listo-
padowe (Warszawa, 1970), pp. 14, 21.

46. Ibid., p. 15 and chaps. 3,4, passim.
47. Quoted ibid., p. 21; see chaps 1 and 7 for other contemporary Prussian expressions of these views.
48. On Flottwell's administration generally, cf. Paprocki, Wielkie Księstwo Poznańskie; Buzek, Historya, pp. 61ff.; Laubert, Verwaltung, pp. 113-24 and passim. See also the views on Polenpolitik during the 1830s of Frederick William III, ibid., p. 117; of General von Grolman, Paprocki, Wielkie Księstwo Poznańskie, pp. 95-96 and Feldman, Bismarck a Polska, pp. 75-76; of Flottwell's mentor, Theodor von Schön, ibid., p. 64; of General von Roeder, Laubert, Verwaltung, Anhang, pp. 1-13; of the Minister of Interior, Brenn (1832), ibid., pp. 13-19.
49. Flottwell's Verwaltungsbericht für 1831, dated 20 September 1832, reproduced in Laubert, Verwaltung, pp. 114-17. Quotation from p. 115.
50. Eduard Heinrich Flottwell, Denkschrift, die Verwaltung der Provinz Posen vom Dezember 1830 bis zum Beginn des Jahres 1841 betreffend (Berlin, 1897), pp. 8-10.
51. Laubert, Verwaltung, p. 115.
52. Letzter periodischer Immediatbericht von Grolman und Flottwell, 6 October 1840, in Laubert, Verwaltung, Annhang, pp. 20-27. Quotation from p. 25.
53. Ibid., p. 116.
54. Ibid., pp. 115-16.
55. Flotwell, Denkschrift, p. 5.
56. On Flottwell's administrative innovations, see the works cited in note 48, above. On his policy towards the provincial diets during the 1830s, Żychliński, Historya Sejmów, 2: 152ff., 196ff.
57. Flottwell, Denkschrift, p. 3.
58. Good indicators of the weakness of this class among the Duchy's Germans are provided by the fact that, of the Landschaft bank's members in 1821, only seven of eighty-one were Germans, and, in the diets of 1827 and 1830, twenty of the twenty-four seats reserved for large landowners were occupied by Poles. Buzek, Historya, p. 55; Żychliński, Historya Sejmów, 1: 41-42, 151-52.
59. Laubert, Verwaltung, pp. 179-201.
60. Żychliński, Historya Sejmów, 2: 4, 140.
61. Ibid., 2: 165ff., 202ff.
62. Stefan Kieniewicz, The Emancipation of the Polish Peasantry, chap. 8, and Społeczeństwo polskie w powstaniu poznańskim 1848 roku (Warszawa, 1960) [hereinafter cited as Kieniewicz, 1848], pp. 49-51.
63. On the "Organic Work" movement in Prussian Poland, see, above all, W. Jakóbczyk, Studia, vols. 1-3, passim; Wilhelm Feldman, Politische Ideen, pp. 128-39; Stanislaus A. Blejwas, "The Origins and Practice of 'Organic Work' in Poland: 1795-1863," The Polish Review, 15 (1970), no. 4, pp. 23-54; William W. Hagen, "National Solidarity and Organic Work in Prussian Poland, 1815-1914," Journal of Modern History, 44 (1972), no. 1, pp. 38-64.
64. Text of Raczyński's speech in Żychliński, Historya Sejmów, 2: 5-15, together with Frederick William IV's response, 15.
65. This ordinance provided for training bilingual teachers and instruction of children in elementary schools in their mother tongue, although a prime goal of the education of Polish children at this level was to impart to them a basic command of German. In the Duchy's three predominantly Polish gymnasiums, Polish was to be the language of instruction in the first four forms, German the language of instruction, except in religion and Polish history and literature, in the upper three. Buzek, Historya, pp. 80-84.
66. Ibid., part 1, chap. 5.
67. Quotations in Laubert, Verwaltung, pp. 129-30.
68. Arnim's Denkschrift for the king, 30 June 1841, ibid., Anhang, pp. 32-40; quotation from p. 36. Cf. also Rochow's Denkschrift of 5 June 1851, ibid., Anhang, 27-31.

69. Raczyński's speech in full, Żychliński, Historya
Sejmów 2: 43-48. Cf. also p. 40.
70. Ibid., 2: 122-23, 145-49, 207ff., 358-59.
71. Towarzystwo naukowej pomocy dla młodzieży Wielkiego
Księstwa Poznańskiego (TNP).
72. Jakóbczyk, Studia, vol. 1, chap. 4; vol. 2, chap. 1;
vol. 3, chap. 2.
73. Kieniewicz, Historia Polski 1795-1918, pp. 155-63;
Kieniewicz, 1848, pp. 61-113.
74. The social composition of the defendants: sixty-six
estate owners and their sons; forty-seven artisans; forty-one
villagers and estate servants; thirty-one members of the urban
intelligentsia; twenty-six estate lessees and officials; ten
priests; eight Prussian soldiers; twenty-five foreign subjects.
Kieniewicz, 1848, p. 115.
75. Hans Schmidt, 1848, pp. 50-53.
76. Jaffé, Stadt Posen, pp. 153-55.
77. Encyclopédie Polonaise, La vie économique de la
Pologne prussienne (Fribourg, 1917), pp. 3ff; Jakóbczyk,
Studia, 1: 59ff.; Borowski, Rozwarstwienie, chaps. 3-5;
Rusiński, Dzieje wsi, pp. 144-66; Kieniewicz, Emancipation,
chap. 7.
78. Czesław Łuczak, Położenie ekonomiczne rzemiosła
wielkopolskiego w okresie zaborów (Poznań, 1965), pp. 57ff.;
Marchlewski, Stosunki społeczno-ekonomiczne, pp. 338ff.;
Jakóbczyk, Dzieje Wielkopolski, chap. 4; Jaffé Stadt Posen, p. 150.
79. Borowski, Rozwarstwienie, pp. 63, 75; Heinz Rogmann,
Die Bevölkerungsentwicklung im preussischen Osten in den letzten
hundert Jahren (Breslau, 1936), pp. 22ff.
80. Cf., Appendix, table Al.
81. Laubert (Verwaltung, p. 153) cites official figures from
1836 on the Grand Duchy's Schulzen. Most were unable to read or
write. Of a total of 3,797, 762 spoke German only, 1,974 spoke
Polish only, while 1,061 were considered bilingual. Apportioning
the bilingual mayors equally among the nationalities, one arrives
at a total of 1,292 Germans and 2,504 Poles. The bilingual
designations may have been arbitrary or incorrect, however, and a
better notion of the distribution of Poles and Germans in the
countryside may be suggested by the unilingual counts. Bilinguals
included, the proportions of Germans and Poles were 34:66; bilinguals excluded--28:72.
82. Fritz Zitzlaff, "Die kleinen Städte," Ludwig Bernhard,
ed., Preussische Städte im Gebiete des polnischen Nationalitäten-
kampfes (Leipzig, 1909), pp. 12-16.
83. Buzek, Historya, p. 293.
84. Quoted in Zitzlaff, Kleine Städte, p. 11. See also
Rogmann, Bevölkerungsentwicklung, pp. 11-16; Eugen von Bergmann,
Zur Geschichte der Entwicklung deutscher, polnischer und jüdischer
Bevölkerung in der Provinz Posen seit 1824 (Tübingen, 1883), pp.
51ff.
85. Appendix, tables Al and A2.
86. Laubert, Verwaltung, p. 224.
87. Julian Bartyś, "Grand Duchy of Poznań under Prussian
Rule--Changes in the Economic Position of the Jewish Population
1815-1848," Leo Baeck Institute Yearbook (1972), pp. 191-204;
Appendix, tables Al and A2.
88. Quotation in Laubert, Verwaltung, p. 258. Bergmann,
Entwicklung, p. 41; Jaffé, Stadt Posen, p. 152; Bernhard
Preussische Städte, p. xiv; Wegener, Der wirtschaftliche Kampf,
p. 153. On the occupational structure of Jewish society in 1849,
cf. "Übersicht der Gesamtzahl der Juden und der davon in Geschäfts-
oder Gewerbs-Verhältnissen lebenden selbständigen Mitglieder, am
Ende des Jahres 1849," Tabellen und amtliche Nachrichten über den
preussischen Staat für das Jahr 1849 (Berlin, 1851), 1:296-99.

89. Jaffé, Stadt Posen, pp. 87-89.
90. A. Rhode, Kirche, p. 134.
91. Quotation in Wolfgang Kohte, Deutsche Bewegung und
preussische Politik im Posener Lande 1848-49 (Posen, 1931), p. 2.
It happened in law suits conducted in the German language between
Polish nobles and German commoners that, while the Prussian judge
could grasp the Poles' High German perfectly well, he required
a translator to understand the dialect of his "compatriots."
Jean-B. Neveux, "Une province polonaise de l'État des Hohenzollern:
la Wielkopolska et Poznan (1815-1840)," Revue Historique 230
(1963): pp. 377ff.
92. A. Rhode, Kirche, p. 144.
93. Kohte, Bewegung, p. 6.
94. Ibid., p. 608; Jaffé, Stadt Posen, pp. 181ff.;
Żychliński, Historya Sejmów, 2:125ff., 207ff.; James J. Sheehan,
"Liberalism and Society in Germany, 1815-1848," Journal of Modern
History, 45 (1973): 583-604; Heffter, Selbstverwaltung, chap. 4.
95. Kohte, Bewegung, pp. 8-9; Koselleck, "Staat und Gesellschaft in Preussen, 1815-1848," pp. 66ff.
96. Kohte, Bewegung, pp. 10-17; Adam Galos, "Hakata w
pierwszych latach istnienia (1894-1900)," in Adam Galos et al.,
Dzieje Hakaty (Poznań, 1966), pp. 27-28.
97. Lewin, Landessynode, p. 65; Heppner and Herzberg,
Vergangenheit, pp. 807-8.
98. Ibid., pp. 813-14; Laubert, Verwaltung, pp. 254ff.;
Perles, "Juden in Posen," 14: 210-14; Jaffé, Stadt Posen, pp.
162ff.; Kampmann, Deutsche und Juden, pp. 136-37.
99. Heppner and Herzberg, Vergangenheit, pp. 811-24.
100. Laubert, Verwaltung, pp. 256-60; Ignacy Schiper,
"Żydzi pod zaborem pruskim 1772-1807, 1815-1918 ," in Ignacy
Schiper et al., Żydzi w Polsce odrodzonej (Warszawa, n.d. [1935]),
pp. 556-60; Jacob Jacobson, "Zur Geschichte der Juden in Posen,"
in G. Rhode, ed., Stadt Posen, pp. 252ff.; Jaffé, Stadt Posen,
pp. 161-62; Heppner and Herzberg, Vergangenheit, pp. 824-34.
101. Żychliński, Historya Sejmów, 2: 313ff.; Jaffé, Stadt
Posen, pp. 181-83.
102. Moritz Lazarus, quoted in Jacob Toury, Die politischen
Orientierungen der Juden in Deutschland (Tübingen, 1966), p. 21.
103. On liberal and democratic German Polonophilia in the
Vormärz period and during the revolution, cf., Georg F. W. Hallgarten, Studien über die deutschen Polenfreundschaft in der
Periode der Märzrevolution (München, 1928); Kocój, Niemcy, chap. 5;
Lewis Namier, 1848: The Revolution of the Intellectuals (New York,
1964), pp. 59ff.; Arno Will, Polska i Polacy w niemieckiej prozie
literackiej XIX wieku (Łódź, 1970), pp. 15ff., 37ff., 80ff.;
Kohte, Bewegung, pp. 19ff., 49ff. On the revolution in general,
Rudolf Stadelmann, Soziale und politische Geschichte der Revolution von 1848 (München, 1948); Jacques Droz, Les révolutions
allemandes de 1848 (Paris, 1957); Friedrich Engels, Germany:
Revolution and Counter-Revolution (Chicago, 1967).
104. Address of 20 March 1848, Berlin, quoted in Hans
Schmidt, 1848, p. 65.
105. Proclamation of 23 March 1848, Poznań, quoted in
Namier, 1848, p. 34.
106. Hans Schmidt, 1848, pp. 88ff., 121-22, 144-45;
Kieniewicz, 1848, 182ff.
107. Namier, 1848, p. 87.
108. Hans Schmidt, 1848, p. 185.
109. Ibid., pp. 186ff. and chap. 4, passim.
110. Ibid., pp. 144ff.; Namier, 1848, pp. 67, 79.
111. Kohte, Bewegung, pp. 27-28; Kieniewicz, 1848, p. 161.
112. Kohte, Bewegung, pp. 27-49; Jerzy Kozłowski, Niemcy w
Poznańskiem wobec Wiosny Ludów (1848-1850) (Dissertation,
Uniwersytet im. A. Mickiewicza, Poznań, 1972), pp. 91-150.

113. Kieniewicz, _1848_, p. 182; Hans Schmidt, _1848_, pp. 150ff.;
Heppner and Herzberg, _Vergangenheit_, pp. 851-52; Jaffé, _Stadt Posen_,
pp. 193.
114. Namier, _1848_, pp. 93ff.; Hans Schmidt, _1848_, pp. 209ff.;
Kohte, _Bewegung_, pp. 77-106; Kieniewicz, _1848_, pp. 288ff.
115. Namier, _1848_, pp. 103ff. The decision of a majority
at Frankfurt to incorporate the greater part of the Grand Duchy
in the "German nation" was strongly influenced by the notorious
speech of Wilhelm Jordan, a left-wing delegate from Berlin, during
the _Polendebatte_ of July 1848. Scorning the "feeble-minded
sentimentality" of the Polonophile liberals (mainly south and
west Germans), Jordan insisted on the primacy both of German
national unity and German strategic interests which, in the case
of Poznania, required the retention of "the fortress Posen" and
its environs in the future German state. Speaking as a democrat,
Jordan showed no sympathy for the "feudalism" of the Polish
szlachta which, in his view, had caused the fall of the Commonwealth and which still lurked behind the national movement of
the Poznanian Poles. The fact is usually ignored, however, that
Jordan approved in principle of a Polish restoration, provided
that the new Polish state would be democratically ruled by the
Polish _Volk_ and that the Poles had proven their ability to develop
and manage a modern bourgeois economy. In this respect, his views,
which in their _Realpolitik_ otherwise closely resembled Bismarck's
(cf., chap. 4, below), diverged widely from Prussian conservative dogma.
          Jordan's conception of mid-nineteenth-century Polish national-
ism dovetails with some of the judgments of Marx and Engels on
the Slavic national revivals--with this difference, however, that,
as social revolutionaries, Marx and Engels wished to promote
actively revolutionary radicalization among both the Slavic
peoples and the Germans even at the expense of German national
unification and power. Hence, they condemned the Polish insur-
rectionists in Poznania for their lack of determination to mobilize
the Polish masses and resolutely attack the absolute and aristocratic Prussian state. If the Poles were able to promote
through their nationalist politics the advance of general proletarian revolution, Marx and Engels, in 1848 and thereafter,
were willing to support them whatever the consequences for bourgeois German nationalism. See Engels, _Germany: Revolution and
Counter-Revolution_, pp. 174-79, 210-211; Marx and Engels, _The
Communist Manifesto_ (New York, 1948), pp. 43-44; Solomon F.
Bloom, _The World of Nations: A Study of the National Implications
in the Work of Karl Marx_, pp. 45ff. and _passim_; H. Malcolm
Macdonald, "Marx, Engels and the Polish National Movement," _Journal
of Modern History_, 13 (1941): 321-34; Hans-Ulrich Wehler,
Sozialdemokratie und Nationalstaat (Göttingen, 1971), chap. 2.
Jordan's speech of 24 July 1848, is in the _Stenographischer Bericht
über die Verhandlungen der deutschen constituierenden Nationalversammlung zu Frankfurt am Main_ (Frankfurt a.M., 1848-50), pp. 1144-
52. It is interesting that one of the German delegates from the
Grand Duchy, pleading for his constituents' inclusion in the future
German state and defending Prussia's legal title to the Duchy,
declared that the German people's right to retain the Germanized
parts of Poznania had acquired in 1848 a new "legal basis" in the
awakening of the Poznanian Germans' "national consciousness and
will" during the Polish insurrection. Speech of Goeden (Krotoszyn),
24 July 1848, ibid., pp. 1137-34.
116. Kohte, _Bewegung_, p. 133.
117. Ibid., pp. 185ff.; Namier, _1848_, p. 111.
118. Quoted in Kohte, _Bewegung_, p. 52.
119. Kieniewicz, _1848_, pp. 203ff.
120. Jakóbczyk, _Studia_, 1: 101-84.
121. From 1849 until 1918, Prussian _Landtag_ and municipal

elections were governed by the "three-class electoral law," according to which in each electoral district all eligible voters were listed in descending order according to the amount of income tax they paid. Those few who collectively paid one-third of the total tax receipts were entitled to elect one-third of the Landtag or city council deputies; the relatively few who paid the second third likewise elected one-third of the deputies; the masses ended up in the third bracket. The law thus favored the Junkers and wealthy bourgeoisie at the expense of the ordinary townspeople, the peasantry, and the working class.

122. Zygmunt Hemmerling, Posłowie polscy w parlamencie rzeszy niemieckiej i sejmie pruskim 1907-1914 Warszawa, 1968, chap. 1; Lech Trzeciakowski, Rola rzemieślników w życiu politycznym," Zdzisław Grot, ed., Polityczna działalność rzemiosła wielkopolskiego w okresie zaborów (1793-1918) (Poznań, 1963), pp. 202ff.; Lech Trzeciakowski, Polityka polskich klas posiadających w Wielkopolsce w erze Capriviego (1890-1894) (Poznań, 1960), pp. 19-21.

123. Kieniewicz, 1848, p. 207.
124. Ibid., pp. 210-14.
125. Ibid., pp. 310ff.; Kohte, Bewegung, pp. 101ff.; Hans Schmidt, 1848, pp. 363-66.
126. Prussian officials claimed that 115 of the Duchy's 603 Catholic priests had been strongly engaged in Polish nationalist propaganda. Kieniewicz, 1848, p. 304; Kohte, Bewegung, p. 78.
127. Quoted in Jakóbczyk, Studia, 1: 102-3. Both Jacóbczyk and Kieniewicz accept Kosiński's judgments. Kieniewicz, 1848, 207-8.
128. Quotation in Namier, 1848, p. 85.
129. Schmidt, 1848, pp. 168ff.; Kozłowski, Niemcy, pp. 95-96.
130. Kohte, Bewegung, pp. 144-81, 206-8; Kozłowski, Niemcy, pp. 385ff.
131. Quoted in Kohte, Bewegung, p. 80.
132. Ibid., pp. 79-80.
133. Jaffé, Stadt Posen, pp. 214-15.
134. Toury, Orientierungen, pp. 53, 94ff.

Chapter Four
1. Bismarck to Field Marshall Manteuffel, 11 August 1866, quoted in Feldman, Bismarck a Polska, p. 248. On the domestic and national politics of the Prussian and west German middle classes in the 1850s and 1860s, see inter alia: Helmut Böhme, "Politik und Ökonomie in der Reichsgründungs- und späten Bismarckzeit," in Michael Stürmer, ed., Das kaiserliche Deutschland. Politik und Gesellschaft 1870-1918 (Düsseldorf, 1970), pp. 26-49; Hans Boldt, "Deutscher Konstitutionalismus und Bismarckreich," ibid., pp. 119-42; Eugene N. Anderson, The Social and Political Conflict in Prussia, 1858-1864 (Lincoln, Nebraska, 1954); Theodore S. Hamerow, The Social Foundations of German Unification 1858-1871 (Princeton, 1969-72); Heffter, Die deutsche Selbstverwaltung im 19. Jahrhundert, chaps. 6-8; Krieger, The German Idea of Freedom, chaps. 8, 9; Wolfgang J. Mommsen, "Der deutsche Liberalismus zwischen 'klassenloser Bürgergesellschaft' und 'Organisiertem Kapitalismus,'" Geschichte und Gesellschaft (1978): 77-90.
2. Hans-Ulrich Wehler, Das deutsche Kaiserreich 1871-1918 (Göttingen, 1973), pp. 32ff.; Michael Stürmer, "Konservatismus und Revolution in Bismarcks Politik," in Stürmer, Das kaiserliche Deutschland, pp. 409ff., 431ff. On Wehler's work, see the debate in Geschichte und Gesellschaft, 1975: 4, 1976: 1, 1978: 1.
3. Karl Erich Born, "Der soziale und wirtschaftliche Strukturwandel Deutschlands am Endes des 19. Jahrhundert," in H. -U. Wehler, ed., Moderne deutsche Sozialgeschichte, pp. 283ff.
4. Hans Rosenberg, "Wirtschaftskonjunktur, Gesellschaft

und Politik in Mitteleuropa, 1873-1896," ibid., pp. 225-53; Hans-Ulrich Wehler, "Bismarck's Imperialism 1862-1890," Past and Present, No. 48 (August 1970), pp. 119-55, and Das deutsche Kaiserreich, pp. 100ff.
    5. Electoral statistics in Koppel S. Pinson, Modern Germany (New York, 1954), pp. 572-73.
    6. "Nachtrag zur Oktober-Denkschrift des Ministeriums des Innern vom 5. November 1849," reproduced in Siegfried Baske, Praxis und Prinzipien der preussischen Polenpolitik vom Beginn der Reaktionszeit bis zur Gründung des Deutschen Reiches (Berlin, 1963), p. 209.
    7. "Oberpräsident v. Bonin an den Minister des Innern am 17. July 1862 (Auszug)," ibid., p. 219.
    8. Quoted in Feldman, Bismarck a Polska, p. 130. See also Baske, Praxis, p. 78.
    9. This was true of the rhetoric both of local administration in the province of Poznań and the central ministeries in Berlin, whether during the Reaction, the "old liberal" New Era or after Bismarck's appointment as minister president in 1862. Cf. Baske, Praxis, pp. 58, 79, 120, 123, 204-7, 225-26.
    10. Józef Buzek, Historya polityki narodowościowej rządu pruskiego wobec polaków, pp. 111ff.
    11. Baske, Praxis, pp. 186-88.
    12. Ibid., p. 169.
    13. Bonin's report of 1862 in Baske, Praxis, pp. 221-23; "Staatsministerium an den König am 21. Januar 1863," ibid., p. 226. The notion that the Poznanian elementary schools succeeded in teaching Polish children to speak German was refuted in the "Bericht des Provinzial-Schulrats Dr. Brettner vom 10. Juni 1858," ibid., p. 245.
    14. Ironically, Bismarck's attacks on the Polish church during the Kulturkampf undercut Ledóchowski's tentative loyalism and returned the archdiocese's leadership and clergy to an even more active national political opposition than they had pursued before 1866. Feldman, Bismarck a Polska, p. 292; Lech Trzeciakowski, "The Prussian State and the Catholic Church in Prussian Poland 1871-1914," The Slavic Review 26 (1967), no. 4, pp. 619ff.
    15. Quoted in Baske, Praxis, p. 38.
    16. Cabinet report of 21 January 1863, ibid., p. 226.
    17. Felix-Heinrich Gentzen, Grosspolen im Januaraufstand. Das Grossherzogtum Posen 1858-1864 (Berlin, 1958), p. 57; Baske, Praxis, p. 127.
    18. Quoted in Baske, Praxis, p. 123.
    19. Bonin's report of 1862, ibid., p. 224.
    20. Quoted in Feldman, Bismarck a Polska, pp. 95-96. In 1848, Bismarck failed to find a publisher for his article containing this passage. In 1886, during the debates on the establishment of the Colonization Commission, he had it reproduced in the progovernmental press as proof of the unwavering nature of his views on the Polish question.
    21. Quotation ibid., p. 367. See also Hans Rothfels, Bismarck, der Osten und das Reich (Darmstadt, 1960).
    22. Speech of 18 March 1867, Stenographische Berichte über die Verhandlungen des Reichstages des Norddeutschen Bundes im Jahre 1867, 1: 210-13.
    23. Bismarck expressed this view in 1883 in a conversation with Hohenlohe. Cf. Feldman, Bismarck a Polska, pp. 315-17.
    24. Ibid., p. 213.
    25. Speech of 28 March 1886, Landtag, Haus der Abgeordneten hereafter abbreviated [HdA], 1886, 1: 171.
    26. Quoted in Rothfels, Bismarck, p. 75, and Feldman, Bismarck a Polska, p. 138.
    27. Quotation in Baske, Praxis, p. 177; Feldman, Bismarck a Polska, pp. 109ff.

28. Speech of 16 February 1863, Landtag, HdA, 1862/1863, 1: 211.

29. Gentzen, Grosspolen, pp. 235-44.

30. Bismarck's conversation of February 1863 with Landtag deputy Behrendt, quoted in Feldman, Bismarck a Polska, p. 224.

31. Ibid., pp. 224-48, 265-66.

32. Bismarck's memorial of 1858 to the Prince of Prussia, quoted in Theodor Schieder, Das Deutsche Kaiserreich von 1871 als Nationalstaat (Köln, 1961), p. 23. See also Bismarck's speech 28 March 1886, Landtag, HdA, 1886, 1:166.

33. Schieder, Kaiserreich, pp. 29ff.

34. Schieder, Kaiserreich, chap. 3; R. W. Tims, Germanizing Prussian Poland: the H-K-T Society and the Struggle for the Eastern Marches in the German Empire 1894-1919 (New York, 1941), pp. 84ff. Heinrich von Treitschke's Berlin lectures popularized the idea of linguistic Germanization and the ideal of linguistic homogeneity within the borders of the Empire. Cf. Politics, ed. Hans Kohn (New York, 1963), pp. 129-32.

35. On the Prussian Poles' post-1848 parliamentary politics, see below, pp.142-50.

36. In his Landtag speech of 28 March 1886, Bismarck declared that it had been the threat to the unity of the Reich posed by the Prussian Poles which had forced him into the Kulturkampf. This position, which he later reaffirmed in his memoirs, obscured the domestic German and international motives of his anti-Catholic policies in the 1870s. But to recall those motives in the 1880s and 1890s served no political purpose, whereas laying responsibility for the Kulturkampf on the Poles' doorstep strengthened Bismarck's case for taking further repressive measures against them. Speech in Landtag, HdA, 1886, 1: 170; Bismarck, Gedanken und Erinnerungen (Stuttgart, 1898), vol. 2, pp. 123-41.

37. Lech Trzeciakowski, Kulturkampf w zaborze pruskim (Poznań, 1970), passim; Ks. Józef Nowacki, Archidiecezja poznańska w granicach historycznych i jej ustrój (Poznań, 1964), 2: 118ff.

38. Quoted in Trzeciakowski, Kulturkampf, p. 179.

39. Speech of 6 March 1872, Landtag, Herrenhaus, 1871/1872, 1: 202-5.

40. Quoted in Trzeciakowski, Kulturkampf, p. 178.

41. Quotation ibid., p. 179.

42. The phrase polnische Agitation was employed by Bismarck and like-minded German politicians to stigmatize the motives of the Polish upper classes in Poznania by suggesting that, however legalistic and pacific the Polish nationalist movement might appear, its purpose was to disaffect the Polish common people from the Prussian state and prepare them for revolt and "breakaway" (Losreissung--another highly charged term in the German nationalist political vocabulary). Bismarck's speech of 9 February 1872, Landtag, HdA, pp. 701, 698-702, passim.

43. Buzek, Historya, pp. 151ff.

44. Schieder, Kaiserreich, pp. 95-124; Buzek, Historya, pp. 163ff.

45. Hans Delbrück, Die Polenfrage (Berlin, 1894), pp. 12ff.; John J. Kulczycki, "Polish Society in Poznania and the School Strikes of 1901-07" (Ph.D. dissertation, Columbia University, 1973), pp. 35ff.; for a vivid account of the meager success of Prussian rural elementary schools in teaching Polish children German at the turn of the century, see Jakób Wojciechowski's chapters on his Poznanian childhood in Życiorys własny robotnika (Poznań, 1930).

46. Quotation in Schieder, Kaiserreich, p. 31; see also Trzeciakowski, Kulturkampf, pp. 184ff.

47. Speech of Heinrich Rickert, 30 January 1886, Landtag, HdA, 1886, 1: 228ff.

48. Speeches of 9 February 1872, ibid., 1871/1872, 2: 698ff., and 28 February 1886, ibid., 1886, 1: 173.

49. On Polish politics during the Kulturkampf, see below.

50. Bismarck's instructions to the German ambassador in Vienna, 1 February, 1886, quoted in Feldman, Bismarck a Polska, pp. 326-27.

51. Ibid., pp. 314-18, 333.

52. Quotation in Helmut Neubach, Die Ausweisungen von Polen und Juden aus Preussen 1885/86 (Wiesbaden, 1967), p. 224. On the expulsions generally, see Neubach, ibid., passim, and Richard Blanke, "Bismarck and the Prussian Polish Policies of 1886," Journal of Modern History 45, (1973), no. 2, pp. 211-15.

53. Neubach, Ausweisungen, p. 35.

54. On the post-1873 crisis in estate agriculture in the Prussian east, see Wehler, Das Deutsche Kaiserreich, pp. 45ff.; Hans-Jürgen Puhle, Agrarische Interessenpolitik und preussischer Konservatismus im wilhelminischen Reich (1893-1914). Ein Beitrag zur Analyse des Nationalismus in Deutschland am Beispiel des Bundes der Landwirte und der Deutsch-Konservativen Partei (Hannover, 1966), pp. 14ff.; Alexander Gerschenkron, Bread and Democracy in Germany (New York, 1966); Walter Görlitz, Die Junker, chap. 4; Werner Sombart, Die deutsche Volkswirtschaft, 396ff.; Encyclopédie Polonaise, La vie économique de la Pologne prussienne [hereinafter Vie économique], pp. 4ff.

55. See Appendix tables A1 and A2. In 1911, the annual rate of natural increase in the Polish population of the province of Poznań was almost twice that of the German-speaking population (20.75 per thousand and 11.76 per thousand, respectively). Since Poles did not marry earlier than Germans, while the infant mortality rate was only slightly higher among Poles than among Germans, the Prussian demographer Max Broesicke concluded that Poles desired larger families than did Germans and that perhaps Polish women were "naturally" more fertile than German women. In any case, in the 1870s and 1880s, even though infant mortality was probably higher among the Poles than in 1911, the Polish birthrate was probably still considerably higher than the German birthrate. It was emigration of the Polish rural and urban proletariat to west German industrial centers which prevented the Polish population in Poznania from increasing in relation to the German-speaking population faster than it actually did. See M. Broesicke, "Deutsche und Polen der Provinz Posen im Lichte der Statistik," Zeitschrift des Königlich Preussischen Statistischen Landesamts 25 (1912): 381-93.

56. Heinz Rogmann, Die Bevölkerungsentwicklung im preus- sischen Osten in den letzten hundert Jahren, pp. 22-23, 130ff. Between 1840 and 1933, 4.5 million inhabitants of Prussia's five eastern provinces migrated west in what came to be called after World War I the Ostflucht. Ibid., p. 100.

57. Ibid., pp. 189-96.

58. Neubach, Ausweisungen, pp. 33ff.; Feldman, Bismarck a Polska, pp. 311, 336ff.

59. Joachim Mai, Die preussisch-deutsche Polenpolitik 1885/87. Eine Studie zur Herausbildung des Imperialismus in Deutschland (Berlin, 1962), pp. 102ff.

60. Quotation in Blanke, "Bismarck," p. 232. See also Neubach, Ausweisungen, pp. 88ff. and Mai, Polenpolitik, chap. 5.

61. Trzeciakowski, Kulturkampf, p. 209.

62. Witold Jakóbczyk, "The First Decade of the Prussian Colonization Commission's Activities, 1886-1897," The Polish Re- view 17 (1972), no. 1, pp. 1-11; Blanke, "Bismarck," pp. 221ff.

63. Quotations from Bismarck's speeches of 28 February 1886, Landtag, HdA, 1886, 1: 173 and 15 April 1886, Landtag, Herrenhaus, 1886, p. 246. Bismarck's anti-Polish imagery grew more lurid with his advancing age. During the 1886 campaign he spoke privately of the szlachta as "a trichinosis" he wished "to rid the land of."

Quoted in Hans-Ulrich Wehler, Krisenherde des Kaiserreichs 1871-1918 (Göttingen, 1970), p. 187.
    64. Quotation in Mai, Polenpolitik, pp. 103-4.
    65. Of the continuation schools, Bismarck wrote in January 1886 that these "would promote the Germanization of the Polish working classes." Quoted in Mai, Polenpolitik, p. 115. Religious instruction continued to be offered to Catholic Polish children in the Polish language, even though the state school system abandoned the responsibility of teaching them to read and write in their mother tongue. The result of this contradictory state of affairs was that the burden of language teaching fell upon the shoulders of the clergy preparing their young parishioners for confirmation.
    66. Vie économique, p. 4ff; Jakóbczyk, Dzieje Wielkopolski, pp. 89ff., 374ff.
    67. Rusiński, Dzieje wsi, pp. 185-86; Marchlewski, Stosunki społeczno-ekonomiczne, pp. 417-24; Vie économique, pp. 182ff.; Borowski, Rozwarstwienie, chap. 5.
    68. Rusiński, Dzieje wsi, pp. 179ff.; Marchlewski, Stosunki społeczno-ekonomiczne, pp. 411ff.; Buzek, Historya, pp. 301-5; Ludwig Bernhard, Die Polenfrage: das polnische Gemeinwesen im preussischen Staat (Leipzig, 1910), pp. 434-36.
    69. C. Łuczak, Położenie ekonomiczne rzemiosła wielkopolskiego, pp. 23-26, and Życie gospodarczo-społeczne w Poznaniu 1815-1918 (Poznań, 1965), pp. 63-65, 101-6, 130-36; Borowski, Rozwarstwienie, pp. 63, 75; Jaffé, Stadt Posen, pp. 220ff.
    70. Łuczak, Przemysł wielkopolski w latach 1871-1914 (Poznań, 1960), pp. 16-19, 28, 46-51; Vie économique, pp. 158ff.; Leo Wegener, Der wirtschaftliche Kampf, pp. 143ff.; Borowski, Rozwarstwienie, p. 75.
    71. Buzek, Historya, p. 293; Broszat, Zweihundert Jahre deutsche Polenpolitik, pp. 63, 115.
    72. E. Bergmann, Zur Geschichte der Entwicklung deutscher, polnischer und jüdischer Bevölkerung, pp. 361-65; Buzek, Historya, p. 297.
    73. See Appendix, table A1.
    74. F. Zitzlaff, "Die kleinen Städte," in Berhard, Preussische Städte, pp. 12-16; Fritz Vosberg, "Die Mittel- und Kleinstädte der Provinz Posen," Ostland 2 (1913): 63-103; Statistisches Jahrbuch für den preussischen Staat (1913), p. 25.
    75. "Die Ergebnisse der Berufszählung vom 5. Juni 1882 im preussischen Staat. III: Landwirtschaftsbetriebe sowie Hauptberuf und Religionsbekenntnis der Bevölkerung," Preussische Statistik, Bd. 76, Dritter Theil (1885), p. 242. See also William W. Hagen, "The Impact of Economic Modernization on Traditional Nationality Relations in Prussian Poland 1815-1914," Journal of Social History (Spring, 1973), pp. 306-24.
    76. Jakóbczyk, Studia, 2: 90-91.
    77. Ibid., vol. 2, chap. 3, passim.
    78. On the populist movement, see below.
    79. Jakóbczyk, Studia, 2: 142, 3: 95.
    80. Vie économique, pp. 171-80; Lech Trzeciakowski, Walka o polskość miast poznańskiego na przełomie XIX i XX wieku (Poznań, 1964), pp. 120ff.; Bernhard, Die Polenfrage, pp. 373ff.; Jakóbczyk, Studia, 2:144ff.
    81. Jakóbczyk, Studia, vol. 2, chap. 2; vol. 3, chap. 4.
    82. Dziennik Poznański, 1 January 1859; Stanisław Karwowski, "Historya Dziennika Poznańskiego," Książka jubileuszowa Dziennika Poznańskiego 1858-1909 (Poznań, 1909), pp. 5ff.
    83. Wilhelm Feldman, Geschichte der politischen Ideen in Polen, pp. 209ff.; Nowacki, Archidiecezja, pp. 118ff.; Zdzisław Grot, "Kazimierz Kantak 1824-1884," in W. Jakóbczyk, ed., Wielkopolanie XIX wieku (Poznań, 1969), pp. 255-88; Jakóbczyk, Dzieje Wielkopolski, pp. 328ff.
    84. Gentzen, Grosspolen, pp. 194, 243.

85. Official report of March 1864, quoted ibid., p. 202.
86. Cf. the speeches of Niegolewski and Cieszkowski,
Landtag, HdA, 1861, 2: 829ff., and of Bentkowski, Prusinowski,
and Kantak, ibid., 1852, 4: 183ff.
87. Speeches of Vincke, Bonin, Schulze-Delitzsch, Haacke,
ibid., 1861, 2: 838ff., 1862, 4: 1838ff.
88. Verhandlungen des Reichstages des Norddeutschen Bundes,
speech of 18 February 1867, pp. 210-17.
89. Speech of 18 February 1867, ibid., p. 216.
90. Speeches Kantak (29 February 1872) and Wierzbiński (9
February 1872), Landtag, HdA, 1871/1872, vol. 2; Łubieński and
Jażdżewski (12 December 1873), Wierzbiński (21 January 1874, 5
May 1874), ibid., 1873/1874, vol. 1; Bniński (6 March 1872),
Landtag, Herrenhaus, 1871/1872, vol. 1.
91. Trzeciakowski, Kulturkampf, pp. 138ff, 221ff.
92. Jerzy Marczewski, Narodowa Democracja w Poznańskiem
1900-1914 (Warszawa, 1967), pp. 58ff.; Trzeciakowski, Polityka
klas posiadających, pp. 291ff.; Jakóbczyk, Dzieje Wielkopolski,
pp. 551ff.; Bolesław Danilczuk, Działalność SPD i PPS zaboru
pruskiego w Poznańskiem w latach 1891-1914 (Toruń, 1961), chap. 1.
93. Quotation in Neubach, Ausweisungen, p. 204. See also
Baske, Praxis, pp. 67, 209ff.
94. Gotthold Rhode, "Das Bild des Deutschen im polnischen
Roman des 19. und beginnenden 20. Jahrhunderts und das polnische
Nationalgefühl," Ostdeutsche Wissenschaft, no. 7 (1961): 327-66.
Polish writers tended to blame their countrymen for a philosophi-
cal and emotional sincerity which often caused their undoing.
Sienkiewicz wrote in Rodzina Połanieckich (1895), "If a German is
a pessimist, he writes whole volumes proving that life drives us
to despair--but at the same time, he drinks his beer, raises his
children, piles up his money, and sleeps peacefully under his
bedcovers. The Slav, however, either hangs himself or plunges
into a riotous life and finally expires in the mire into which he
deliberately descended." Quotation, ibid., p. 344.
95. Feldman, Bismarck a Polska, p. 374.
96. Quotation in Gentzen, Grosspolen, p. 121.
97. Quotation from police report in Baske, Praxis, p. 68.
98. Trzeciakowski, Kulturkampf, pp. 141ff.
99. O. Kolberg, Lud 9: 55. Kolberg noted also that the
Poznanian common people were more tolerant towards Jews than
their counterparts elsewhere in Poland, but that they tended to
regard "the Jew, dressing and behaving in a German manner,
practically as a German." Ibid., p. 54.
100. Quotation in Richard Blanke, "The Development of Loyalism in Prussian Poland, 1886-1890," The Slavonic and East
European Review 52 (1974), no. 129, p. 553.
101. Wojciechowski, p. 178 and passim.
102. WAPP. Oberpräsidium, syg. 5750: Kirche und Schulen.
103. Archiwum Archidecezjalne w Poznaniu. Akta Konsystorza
Jeneralnego Arcybiskupskiego Poznańskiego tyczące się: małżeństw
mieszanych. 1889. These figures are based on the reports submitted by twenty-three of twenty-four deaconries to the bishop of
Poznań. The reports on the city of Poznań are missing. On pre-
World War I mixed marriages in the capital city, see below, chap.
7.
104. Quotation in Blanke, "Loyalism," p. 558.
105. More persons read the Polish press than circulation
figures would indicate because of its passage from hand to hand
and its availability in inns and taverns. Additional circulation
figures for 1886: Dziennik Poznański--1,400; Kuryer Poznański--
750. Altogether, Prussian officials counted twenty-four Polish-
language dailies in the eastern provinces. Mai, Ausweisungen, pp.
173-74.
106. Lech Trzeciakowski, "Roman Szymański 1840-1908," in
Jakóbczyk, Wielkopolanie, 2: 341-61; Blanke, "Loyalism," pp. 557
ff.; Trzeciakowski, Kulturkampf, pp. 256ff.

107. Speech of Jażdżewski (15 January 1886), Reichstag, 1885/
1887, vol. 1; Stablewski (29 January 1886), Landtag, HdA, 118: 1;
Kościelski (15 April 1886), Landtag, Herrenhaus, 1886.
    108. Blanke, "Loyalism," pp. 555-56.
    109. Quotation ibid., p. 559.
    110. Jaffé, Stadt Posen, pp. 223ff.; Łuczak, Przemysł, pp.
58ff.
    111. Hermann Wagner, "Die Land- und Forstwirtschaft. Provinz
Posen," Die deutsche Ostmark: herausgegeben vom Deutschen Ostmarkenverein (Lissa, 1913), pp. 286ff.
    112. The non-Jewish German population increased absolutely
in these years by 24 percent, the Polish population by 20 percent.
See Appendix, table A2.
    113. Bergmann, Entwicklung, p. 41; Karol Rzepecki, Ubytek
żydów w Księstwie poznańskiem (Poznań, 1912), pp. 6-7; Bernhard
Breslauer, Die Auswanderung der Juden aus der Provinz Posen
(Berlin, 1909), pp. 3-13.
    114. Berufszählung 1882, Preussische Statistik, bd. 76 (1885),
p. 242.
    115. Ibid.
    116. A. Rhode, Kirche, p. 164; Delbrück, Polenfrage, p. 20.
Even when study of the Polish language was available to German and
Jewish students, as it was in Poznań's Friedrich Wilhelm Gymnasium
before the 1870s, few bothered to undertake it. Walter Breslauer,
"Jews of the City of Posen One Hundred Years Ago," Leo Baeck Yearbook 7 (1963): 229-37. Breslauer, generalizing from the documents
of his ancestors in nineteenth-century Poznań, wrote of the predominantly German gymnasium that "the general attitude of the
pupils (and their parents), including the Jews, seems to have been
one of dislike mixed with contempt for the Poles." Ibid., p. 233.
    117. Karwowski, "Historya Dziennika Poznańskiego," pp. 7ff.;
Aleksander Kramski, Untitled dissertation on German society in
the province of Poznań 1903-11 (Poznań, Uniwersytet im. A.
Mickiewicza, 1969), pp. 153ff., 180ff.; "Die Reichstagswahlen,"
Posener Neueste Nachrichten, 7 November 1911; Jaffé, Stadt Posen,
pp. 329ff.; "Das 50-jährige Jubileum des Posener Tageblattes,"
Posener Tageblatt, 13 May 1912; Trzeciakowski, Walka o polskość,
pp. 94-95.
    118. Gentzen, Grosspolen, p. 95; Jaffé, Stadt Posen, pp.
298-99; speech of Progressive leader, Heinrich Rickert, 30 January
1886, Landtag, HdA, 118, vol. 1.
    119. Toury, Die politischen Orientierungen der Juden in
Deutschland, pp. 110ff.
    120. Breslauer, Jews, pp. 234ff.; Herzberg and Heppner,
Vergangenheit, pp. 834, 863; Baske, Praxis, p. 129.
    121. Breslauer, Jews, p. 235.
    122. See, inter alia, speeches by v. Fincke (27 February
1863), Landtag, HdA, 1862/1863, vol. 1; v. Unruhe (18 March 1867),
Verhandlungen des Reichstages des Norddeutschen Bundes; Kennemann
(6 April 1886), Landtag, HdA, 1886, vol. 3; Tiedemann (7 April
1886), ibid.
    123. Speeches of Schulze-Delitzsch, Landtag, HdA, 1862, 4:
1843ff. and of 27 February 1863, ibid., 1862/1863, 1: 383ff.
    124. Speech of v. Sänger, 18 March 1867, Verhandlungen des
Reichstages des Norddeutschen Bundes. Cf. also speeches by
Waldeck and v. Sybel, 18 February 1863, Landtag, HdA, 1862/1863,
vol. 1; Rickert, 30 January 1886, ibid., 1886, vol. 1; Virchow,
7 April 1886, ibid., 1886, vol. 3. The decline of traditional
German liberal Polenfreundschaft was symbolized in the refusal of
the leadership of the Nationalverein, at its annual meeting of
1864, to put on the agenda a south German delegate's motion that
a Polish restoration would harm neither Germany's material nor
political interests. Gentzen, Grosspolen, p. 248.
    125. Quotation in Mai, Polenpolitik, p. 138.

126. Cf. speeches of Witt, 16 December 1873, Landtag, HdA,
1873/1874, vol. 1; Kohleis, 6 March 1872, Landtag, Herrenhaus,
1871/1872, vol. 1; Virchow, 7 April 1886, Landtag, HdA, 1886,
vol. 3. On local manifestations of Junker hostility to the Polish
gentry, see Feldman, Bismarck a Polska, p. 175; A. Galos et al.,
Dzieje Hakaty, p. 30.
127. In 1859, a group of Poznanian Junkers again petitioned
the government for resumption of state purchase of Polish estates
and their sale or leasing to Germans. Karwowski, "Historya
Dziennika Poznańskiego," p. 7.
128. Tiedemann's speech of 7 April 1886, Landtag, HdA,
1886, vol. 3. Bismarck justified his anti-Polish measures and proposals of 1885-86 by saying that "he who will not cooperate with
the state in its defense does not belong to the state and can claim
no rights from the state; he should withdraw from the state. We
are no longer so barbaric that we banish such people, but the right
answer to those who negate the state and its institutions is to
withdraw from them in every connection the official support of that
state which they negate." In fact, the expulsions of Poles and
Jews in 1885 did constitute a form of banishment directed indis-
criminately against peaceful residents of the Prussian state on
account of their ethnic-religious character. Speech of 28 February 1886, Landtag, HdA, 1886, vol. 1.
129. Bismarck promised that no Germans with Polish wives
would be settled by the Colonization Commission. Ibid.
130. Virchow's speech of 7 April 1886, Landtag, HdA, 1886,
vol. 3.
131. German Jews were also loath to take a political stand
as Jews for fear of giving their anti-Semitic opponents an opportunity to raise the specter of a separate, "antinational"
Jewish political interest. Toury, Orientierungen, pp. 131ff.;
Neubach, Ausweisungen, p. 153.
132. Toury, Orientierungen, pp. 97ff.; Baske, Praxis, p.
53; Bernhard, Preussische Städte, pp. xiv-xx; Jaffé, Stadt Posen,
p. 329.
133. Arno Will, Polska i polacy w niemieckiej prozie
literackiej XIX wieku, pp. 20ff. Inevitably, someone (P. O.
Höcker) finally wrote a novel entitled Polnische Wirtschaft
(Berlin, 1896). Ibid., p. 107.

Chapter Five
1. Hans-Ulrich Wehler, Kaiserreich, pp. 44-51; Werner
Sombart, Die deutsche Volkswirtschaft im neunzehnten Jahrhundert,
chaps. 12, 13; Fritz Fischer, Krieg der Illusionen. Die deutsche
Politik von 1911 bis 1914 (Düsseldorf, 1969), chaps. 1-4; Herman
Lebovics, Social Conservatism and the Middle Classes in Germany,
1914-1933 (Princeton, 1969), Introduction; David Landes, The Un-
bound Prometheus, chap. 5; J. H. Clapham, Economic Development of
France and Germany, 1815-1914 (Cambridge, 1961), chaps. 11-13.
2. Wehler, Kaiserreich, pp. 52-55; Alexander Gerschenkron,
Bread and Democracy in Germany (Berkeley, 1943); Hans Rosenberg,
"Wirtschaftskonjunktur, Gesellschaft und Politik in Mitteleuropa,
1873-1896" and "Die Pseudodemokratisierung der Rittergutsbesit-
zerklasse," in Wehler, Sozialgeschichte, pp. 225-53, 287-308;
Puhle, Agrarische Interessenpolitik, pp. 274ff.
3. Karl Erich Born, "Der soziale und Strukturwandel
Deutschlands am Ende des 19. Jahrhunderts," in Wehler, Sozial-
geschichte, pp. 271-86; David Blackbourn, "The Mittelstand in
German Society and Politics, 1871-1914," Social History 4
(Jan. 1977): 409-35.
4. J. C. G. Röhl, Germany without Bismarck: The Crisis of
Government in the Second Reich, 1890-1900 (Berkeley, 1967); J.
Alden Nichols, Germany after Bismarck: The Caprivi Era 1890-
1894 (Cambridge, Mass., 1958); Erich Eyck, Das persönliche Regiment
Wilhelms II. Politische Geschichte des deutschen Kaiserreiches

von 1890 bis 1914 (Zürich, 1948); Wehler, Kaiserreich, pp. 69ff.;
Hans-Jürgen Puhle, "Parlament, Parteien und Interessenverbände
1890-1914" and J. C. G. Röhl, "Beamtenpolitik im wilhelminischen
Deutschland," in Michael Stürmer, ed., Das kaiserliche Deutschland,
pp. 340-77, 287-311.
    5. Eckart Kehr, "Soziale und finanzielle Grundlagen der
Tirpitzschen Flottenpropaganda," in Wehler, Sozialgeschichte, pp.
389-406; Röhl, Germany without Bismarck, chap. 7; Wehler, Kaiserreich, pp. 149ff.; Holger H. Herweg, The German Naval Officer
Corps: A Social and Political History 1890-1918 (Oxford, 1973),
chaps. 1,2; Heinz Gollwitzer, Europe in the Age of Imperialism
1880-1914 (New York, 1969); Dirk Stegmann, Die Erben Bismarcks
(Köln, 1970), 59ff.; Geoff Eley, "Defining Social Imperialism:
Use and Abuse of an Idea," Social History, 3 (Oct. 1976): 265-90.
    6. Röhl, Germany without Bismarck, p. 10.
    7. Fritz Fischer, Griff nach der Weltmacht. Die Kriegsziel-
politik des kaiserlichen Deutschlands 1914/1918 (Düsseldorf, 1964),
chap. 1; Wehler, Kaiserreich, pp. 171ff.; Volker Berghahn, Germany
and the Approach of War in 1914 (London, 1973), passim.
    8. Fischer, Krieg der Illusionen, pp. 117ff. See also W. J.
Mommsen, "Domestic Factors in German Foreign Policy Before 1914,"
Central European History, 6 (1973): 3-43.
    9. Quotations in Wehler, Kaiserreich, pp. 198-99; see also
Fischer, Krieg der Illusionen, pp. 663ff.
    10. Treitschke, Politics, pp. 122ff., 283ff.; on Lagarde, cf.
Fritz Stern, The Politics of Cultural Despair: A Study in the Rise
of the Germanic Ideology (Berkeley, 1961), chap. 1; Henry C.
Meyer, Mitteleuropa in German Thought and Action 1815-1945 (The
Hague, 1955); George L. Mosse, The Crisis of German Ideology:
Intellectual Origins of the Third Reich (New York, 1964), part 1;
Gerard Labuda, Wschodnia ekspansja Niemiec w Europie środkowej:
zbiór studiów nad tzw. niemieckim "Drang nach Osten," (Poznań,
1963).
    11. Wehler, Kaiserreich, pp. 189ff.; Fischer, Krieg der Il-
lusionen, pp. 24ff.
    12. J. C. G. Röhl, "A Document of 1892 on Germany, Prussia
and Poland," The Historical Journal 7 (1964), no. 1, p. 147.
    13. In 1890-91, the Polish Reichstag delegation, under Józef
Kościelski's leadership, showed its readiness to cooperate with
Caprivi by voting in favor of the government's army and naval appropriations bills. William II publicly thanked Kościelski, whose
political opponents mocked him with the title "Admiralski."
Nichols, Germany after Bismarck, p. 127; Trzeciakowski, Polityka
klas posiadających, pp. 60ff.
    14. Quoted by Trzeciakowski, ibid., pp. 58-59. Whether
Caprivi actually pursued a policy of conciliating the Prussian
Poles has been questioned by Harry K. Rosenthal, "The Problem of
Caprivi's Polish Policy," European Studies Review 2, no. 3
(July 1972): 255-64. Rosenthal ignores Caprivi's memorandum of
1893, first published by Trzeciakowski, which both proves
Caprivi's intentions of conciliating the Polish conservatives
through concessions and the primacy of foreign policy considera-
tions among his motives for doing so.
    15. Harry K. Rosenthal, "The Election of Archbishop Stablewski,"
Slavic Review 27, no. 2 (June 1969): 265-75; Trzeciakowski,
Polityka, pp. 97ff.
    16. Buzek, Historya, pp. 212ff.
    17. Ibid., pp. 218-28; Trzeciakowski, Polityka, chap. 4.
    18. See below, chap. 7, for a fuller discussion of the Poles'
efforts to "compromise" with Caprivi's regime.
    19. Fischer, Krieg der Illusionen, pp. 91-92.
    20. Trzeciakowski, Polityka, p. 138.
    21. Buzek, Historya, p. 211; Trzeciakowski, Polityka, pp. 107-
11; Nichols, Germany after Bismarck, pp. 126-29.

22. Wilamowitz-Möllendorf to Köller, 23 November 1895, "Die Grundsätze für das Verhalten der Königlichen Staatsregierung gegenüber den Untertanen polnischer Muttersprache in der Provinz Posen." Deutsches Zentralarchiv, Ministerium des Innerns (Zentral-Büreau), Rep. 77, Tit. 871, no. 1 Jahr 1896.

23. Alfred Kruck, Geschichte des Alldeutschen Verbandes 1890-1939 (Wiesbaden, 1954), pp. 8ff.; Mildred S. Wertheimer, The Pan-German League 1890-1914 (New York, 1924), chap. 2.

24. Buzek, Historya, pp. 229-30; Trzeciakowski, Polityka, p. 137.

25. On the Bund in general, cf. Puhle, Agrarische Interessenpolitik, passim; on its establishment in the Province of Poznań, ibid., pp. 38ff. and Trzeciakowski, Polityka, pp. 95-96.

26. On the Ostmarkenverein generally, cf. Adam Galos et al., Dzieje Hakaty, esp. pp. 32-311; also Tims, Germanizing Prussian Poland, passim.

27. Quotations in Galos, Dzieje Hakaty, p. 135. Endell was not a born Junker, but rather the son of a wealthy merchant in Stettin. After a career as a Prussian army officer, Endell retired in 1885 to an estate he purchased on the outskirts of the city of Poznań. Tiedemann, too, was a retired army officer, as were many other activists in Prussian conservative-agrarian politics. Cf. the obituaries of Endell in the Posener Tageblatt, 17 February 1914, no. 80, and Posener Neueste Nachrichten, 18 February 1914.

28. Galos, Dzieje Hakaty, pp. 69-70, 102-3.

29. The Ostmarkenverein also conducted a vigorous national- ist and anti-Polish agitation among the frontier Germans. See below, chap. 8.

30. Cabinet meeting of 22 November 1897, quoted in Röhl, Germany without Bismarck, pp. 251-52. Italics in original. Miquel's reference to the Catholic Center meant that the govern- ment should not sacrifice the advantages to be gained from anti- Polish agitation to avoid irritating the Poles' German Catholic supporters.

31. Galos, Dzieje Hakaty, p. 73.

32. Buzek, Historya, pp. 235ff.

33. Ibid., p. 319. The profits awaiting the Polish parcellation banks can be surmised from the average free-market price during the years 1894-97 of 1,060 marks per hectare for land sold in plots of five to twenty hectares.

34. By the years 1910-12, the price of Poznanian land sold in parcels above 100 hectares in size exceeded the Prussian state average by roughly 15 percent. Vie économique, p. 54.

35. The Colonization Bill of 1898 made this function ex- plicit by granting the Royal Commission funds for the creation in the course of peasant settlement of Restgüter, a procedure that amounted to state-managed partial parcellation of estates for the benefit of their owners. Buzek, Historya, p. 310.

36. On the state's colonization program after 1890, cf. Witold Jakóbczyk, Pruska komisja osadnicza 1886-1919 (Poznań, 1976), passim, and "The First Decade of the Prussian Settlement Commission's Activities, 1886-1897," The Polish Review 17 (1972), no. 1, pp. 3-12; Buzek, Historya, chap. 19; Vie économique, pp. 16ff.; Bernhard, Polenfrage, passim; Mitscherlich, Ausbreitung, chap. 2; Wegener, Wirtschaftlicher Kampf, part 2; Julian Marchlewski, Zur Polenpolitik der preussischen Regierung: Auswahl von Artikeln aus den Jahren 1897 bis 1923 (Berlin, 1958) and Stosunki społeczno-ekonomiczne w ziemiach polskich zaboru pruskiego, part 5; Jakóbczyk, Dzieje Wielkopolski, pp. 456ff.; Deutscher Ostmarkenverein, Die deutsche Ostmark (Lissa, 1913), pp. 420-46.

37. On economic and demographic developments among the frontier nationalities, see below, chap. 6.

38. Quotation in Jakóbczyk, Studia, 3: 8. On the Prussian government's program of material support of the frontier German

townspeople (which came to be known generally as Hebungspolitik),
see Buzek, Historya, chap. 20; Lech Trzeciakowski, Walka o polskość
miast poznańskiego na przełomie XIX i XX wieku (Poznań, 1964),
chap. 2.
     39. Jakóbczyk, Studia, 3: 4ff.; Galos, Dzieje Hakaty, pp.
103ff.
     40. Colonization Commission officials realized they were at-
tempting to stem the Ostflucht, but they found, as one wrote in
the mid 1890s, that "it is not easy to reverse the migration movement towards the west that has lasted for centuries into one
towards the east." So far as Poznania was concerned, this would
have been a more accurate statement had its author substituted
"decades" for "centuries." Quoted in Jakóbczyk, "The First
Decade," p. 7.
     41. See the literature cited above, notes 10 and 23, and
also Wolfgang J. Mommsen, Max Weber und die deutsche Politik 1890-
1920 (Tübingen, 1959), chaps. 1-4.
     42. Quoted in Kruck, Alldeutscher Verband, p. 33.
     43. In his not altogether reliable memoirs, Bülow claimed
that "Treitschke's splendid study of the Teutonic Order lay for
many years on my desk." Bernhard Fürst von Bülow, Denkwürdigkeiten
(Berlin, 1930), 1: 565.
     44. Quotations in Fischer, Krieg der Illusionen, p. 88.
     45. Speeches of 26 November 1907 and 16 January 1908, Landtag,
HdA, 1907/1908, vol. 1.
     46. See Bülow's letter of November 1907 to the Polish con-
servative Franciszek Dzierżykraj-Morawski, quoted in Michał Pirko,
Bülow a sprawa polska (Warszawa, 1963), p. 316. Also Pirko,
Niemiecka polityka wywłaszczeniowa na ziemiach polskich w latach
1907-1908 (Warszawa, 1963), pp. 50ff.
     47. Bülow, Denkwürdigkeiten, 1: 562-63; speech of 26 November
1907, Landtag, HdA.
     48. Ibid. Leo Wegener recalled Bülow's notorious allusion to
the Poles' Karnickelfruchtbarkeit in a speech of 5 February 1910.
Cf. Bundesarchiv Koblenz. Nachlass Wegener, folio 47. See also
Poznanian Oberpräsident Rudolf von Bitter's alarmist report to
Minister of Interior Arthur von Posadowsky entitled "Vordringen
des Polentums in der Provinz Posen." Deutsches Zentralarchiv,
Ministerium des Innerns (Zentral-Büreau), Rep. 77, Tit. 871, no. 1.
Bitter warned of a "Polish wave" spilling westward from the
province of Poznań into Brandenburg, Silesia, and Pomerania and
"crowding out the German population," especially in the towns.
The Oberpräsident could think of no better countermeasure than in-
creased expenditures in the field of Hebungspolitik.
     49. Bülow, Denkwürdigkeiten, 1: 564.
     50. Quoted in Pirko, Bülow a sprawa polska, p. iii.
     51. Speech of 26 November 1907, Landtag, HdA.
     52. Quotation in Pirko, Bülow, p. iii.
     53. On Bülow's Polenpolitik generally, see in addition to
the works cited above Feldman, Bismarck a Polska, pp. 379ff.;
Broszat, Zweihundert Jahre deutsche Polenpolitik, pp. 120ff.;
Buzek, Historya, pp. 262ff.; Jakóbczyk, Studia, 3: 5ff.
     54. Bülow, Denkwürdigkeiten, 1: 563; Bülow's memorial quoted
in Pirko, Bülow, pp. 64-65.
     55. John Kulczycki, "Polish Society in Poznania and the
School Strikes of 1901-1907" (Ph.D. dissertation, Columbia University, 1973), pp. 46ff.; Rudolf Korth, Die preussische Schulpolitik
und die polnischen Schulstreiks. Ein Beitrag zur preussischen
Polenpolitik der Ära Bülow (Würzburg, 1963), pp. 61ff.

     56. Kulczycki, "School Strikes," pp. 73-120; Ludwik Gomolec,
"Strajki szkolne w Poznańskiem w latach 1901-1907," Studia i
materiały do dziejów Wielkopolski i Pomorza, vol. 3, (1957),
no. 1, pp. 118ff.; Zdzisław Grot, ed., Wydarzenia wrzesińskie w
roku 1901 (Poznań, 1964), passim.
     57. More than 50 percent of all Polish students receiving

religious instruction in German participated in the strike. According to official figures for 1906, 241,000 elementary schoolchildren in Poznania spoke Polish as their mother tongue.
Kulczycki, "School Strikes," pp. 177ff.
    58. The Catholic church responded to Germanization of
religious study in the public schools by extending the amount of
time Polish children spent in sacramental instruction. Thus, in
effect, the clergy increasingly took responsibility for teaching
Polish children to read and write their mother tongue. In
November 1907 the government acquiesced in the church's extended
sacramental instruction, conceding moreover that in the schools
religion would continue to be taught in the lowest forms in Polish.
That the strikes set a limit to the government's Germanization
policies is proven by the fact that, in 1913, 849 Poznanian
elementary schools offered Polish-language religious instruction
at all levels; in 1906, there had been 1,392 schools attended by
Polish children. Kuryer Poznański, 24 October 1913, no. 246;
Buzek, Historya, p. 469; Kulczycki, "School Strikes," pp. 187ff.,
303; Korth, Schulpolitik, pp. 120ff.
    59. Speech of 26 November 1907, Landtag, HdA.
    60. Kulczycki, "School Strikes," p. 302; Nowacki,
Archidiecezja poznańska, pp. 121ff.
    61. Quotation in Korth, Schulpolitik, p. 151. Posadowsky,
a conservative in this as in other spheres of German domestic
politics, resigned in mid 1907. Pirko, Niemiecka polityka, p.
122.
    62. Bethmann's views cited by Korth, Schulpolitik, p. 156.
    63. Figures from 1886 to the end of 1907. Buzek,
Historya, p. 327.
    64. Figures from 1886 to the end of 1906. Vie économique,
p. 28.
    65. Buzek, Historya, pp. 334–38.
    66. Albert Dietrich, "Die Besitzfestigung," Ostland--Jahrbuch
für ostdeutsche Interessen 1912: pp. 156–64; 1913: 215–25. Erich
Zechlin, "Die Polenfrage in Preussen, einschl. der Tätigkeit der
Ansiedlungskommission," ibid. 1912: 137–55; 1913: 198–214.
Friedrich Swart, "Das deutsche und polnische Genossenschaftswesen,"
ibid. 1912: 176–94. Leo Wegener, "Das Genossenschaftswesen,"
Die deutsche Ostmark, 447–57.
    67. The Colonization Commission held a small share in the
ownership of the farms it created and established a similar share
in the properties it assisted in refinancing in order to prevent
future sales to Poles.
    68. Buzek, Historya, p. 334. Colonists had repaid the Commission 9.4 million marks by the end of 1906.
    69. Speech of 26 November 1907, Landtag, HdA.
    70. Mitscherlich, Ausbreitung, p. 85.
    71. Speech of 26 November 1907, Landtag, HdA.
    72. On Polish parcellation societies and banks specializing
in refinancing of landowner's debts, cf. Buzek, Historya, chap.
19; Bernhard, Polenfrage, book 2; Ziemianin, 3 May 1914, no. 18.
    73. Buzek, Historya, p. 319.
    74. Protocol of Ministerial Conference of 16 January 1907,
Bundesarchiv Koblenz, Nachlass Hugenberg, no. 54, folio 1.
    75. Galos, Dzieje Hakaty, pp. 255ff.; Buzek, Historya, pp.
356ff. The consistency with which local officials enforced the
1904 law emerges from the Akta betr. Ablehnungen von Bauerlaubnis-
und Ansiedlungsgenehmigungsgesuchen. Polizeidistrikt Stenschewo,
1908–1913. WAPP, Landrat Posen-West, syg. 302. For an example
of German speculators' frequent practice of threatening to sell
their lands to Polish parcellation societies in order to drive up
the Colonization Commission's bids, cf. letter of Police President
von Knesebeck to the Commission, 28 December 1906, WAPP, Landrat
Posen-West, syg. 271. In this case the two speculators were
retired army officers. A Polish villager named Michał Drzymała

attempted to evade the 1904 law by living on his parcel of land in a gypsy wagon, but Prussian officialdom declared this illegal. This incident, widely reported in the Polish and western European press, provided Polish nationalists with more fuel for their agitation among the common people.

76. Pirko, Niemiecka polityka, pp. 97ff.; Galos, Dzieje Hakaty, pp. 255ff.

77. Colonization Commission President Blomeyer's statement, Ministerial Conference of 16 January 1907, Nachlass Hugenberg, no. 54, folio 1.

78. Galos, Dzieje Hakaty, p. 261; Pirko, Niemiecka polityka, pp. 103, 110ff., 134ff.

79. Ministerial conference of 15 July, 31 August and 6 November 1907, Nachlass Hugenberg, no. 54, folio 1.

80. Szögyényi to Aehrenthal, 15 January 1907. Oesterreichisches Staatsarchiv: Staats-, Haus- und Hofarchiv, Politische Abteilung III, Faszikel 180: Preussen III: preussische Polenpolitik. Enteignungsfrage 1907.

81. Szögyényi to Aehrenthal, 24 November 1907, ibid.; cf. also Szögyéni's report of 3 March 1908, ibid.

82. Reports of 15 January and 3 December 1907, ibid.

83. Report of 4 February 1908, ibid.

84. Cf. Minister of Agriculture Bernhard von Arnim's reservations voiced in the Ministerial Conference of 16 January 1907 and those of the Ministry of Justice reported in the conference of 15 August 1907. Nachlass Hugenberg, no. 54, folio 1.

85. Rheinbaben's report, ibid., 16 January 1907. In his defense of the Expropriation Act before the Landtag, Bülow justified it by appeals to "the state's duty of self-preservation." Arnim and Justice Minister von Beseler echoed this view. Speeches of 26 November and 29 November 1907, Landtag, HdA.

86. Bethmann's statement in Ministerial Conference of 16 January 1907, Nachlass Hugenberg, no. 54, folio 1.

87. Heydebrand's conversation of 6 November 1907 with Arnim, ibid. Not for nothing did the German press refer to Heydebrand as "the uncrowned king of Prussia." In this case, as in countless others, the Conservatives demonstrated their power to force their own position on the government, recalling the old Junker adage "Und der König absolut/Wenn er uns den Willen thut."

88. Report of Heydebrand's position, ibid., 16 January 1907. In his discussion of 6 November 1907 with Arnim, Heydebrand expressed concern that expropriated Poles would resettle on estates in solidly German areas of the Prussian east, bringing their "Polish agitation" with them. To forestall this, he recommended empowering the government with a general right to forbid any such nationally objectionable Polish land purchases. This proposal further strengthens our analysis of the Conservatives' nationalist radicalism in the sphere of Polenpolitik which traditional German historians have tended to deny or minimize. Cf. Hans Booms, Die deutschkonservative Partei (Düsseldorf, 1954), pp. 114ff. Puhle's argument dovetails with that presented here, Agrarische Interessenpolitik, pp. 257-60.

89. The publicly elected Landwirtschaftskammern were Junker strongholds. On the specific provisions of the Expropriation Act, see Buzek, Historya, pp. 311-13.

90. German estate owners were to receive state compensation for providing German rural laborers with cottages and small garden plots. This scheme, which contradicted the trend among east Elbian landlords to replace wage payments in naturalia with cash, failed to catch on. Nevertheless, by the end of 1913, several thousand workers had been settled in the east under its terms. Vie économique, p. 27; Kramski, pp. 77-78.

91. In the Landtag, one-quarter of the Conservative deputies withheld their votes. In the Herrenhaus, conservative opposition was stronger still, as the bill's passage 143-111

indicates. Landtag, HdA, 3 March 1908; Herrenhaus, 27 February 1908.

92. Szögyényi to Aehrenthal, 30 November 1907. Pirko, Niemiecka polityka, pp. 182ff.

93. Bülow's remarks quoted in Szögyényi's report to Aehrenthal, 24 December 1907.

94. On the German nationalists' pressures on the government after 1908 to carry out expropriation, see Pirko, Niemiecka polityka, pp. 271ff., and chap. 8, below.

95. On the Progressives' position on the anti-Polish language paragraph, see Payer's speech of 4 April 1908, Verhandlungen des Reichstages, vol. 232. The Poles urged the Progressives to vote against this paragraph even in its liberalized form. Cf. Brejski's speech of 4 April 1908, ibid. The left liberals supported this provision of the law with a bad conscience, yet their amendment undoubtedly weakened its anti-Polish impact. Eyck, Persönliches Regiment, p. 461.

96. Reichstag speech of 10 December 1907.

97. Reichstag speech of 4 April 1908.

98. Waldow's memorial, "Erfolge der Ostmarkenpolitik," Deutsches Zentralarchiv (Merseburg): Geheimes Zivilkabinet. Das Oberpräsidium der Provinz Posen. Rep. 89H II, vol. 2, 1851-1910. Waldow also prided himself on having increased the number of Evangelical elementary schools between 1903 and 1908 by 128; despite the Poles' much higher birth-rate, the number of Catholic schools rose by only 54 in the same period.

99. Ibid.

100. Ibid.

101. Szögyényi to Müller, n.d. (February 1910), fasc. 181.

102. Ministerial Conference of 16 January 1907, Nachlass Hugenberg, no. 54, folio 1. On domestic German politics and Bethmann's strategies and goals as Chancellor during the years 1909-14, see Berghahn, Germany and the Approach of War; Fischer, Krieg der Illusionen; Hans-Günther Zmarzlik, Bethmann Hollweg als Reichskanzler 1909-14. Studien zur Möglichkeiten und Grenzen seiner innerpolitischen Machtstellung (Düsseldorf, 1957); Eyck, Persönliches Regiment, chaps. 28-30.

103. On the Polish National Democrats, see below, chap. 7.

104. Graf Bogdan von Hutten-Czapski, Sechzig Jahre Politik und Gesellschaft (Berlin, 1936), 2: 42. Hutten-Czapski was one of the very few Polish aristocrats in Prussia who, without repudiating their nationality, regarded themselves as Prussians and committed themselves fully to Hohenzollern service. He used his influence at court in an effort to forestall application of the Expropriation Act and in general to turn Prussian Polenpolitik in a more moderate direction. For his appraisal of the expropriation question and Bethmann's Polish policies, see pages 36-64, passim.

105. Cabinet meeting of 30 March 1911, quotation in Pirko, Niemiecka polityka, p. 279.

106. Szögyényi to Aehrenthal, 20 March 1910, fasc. 181.

107. Quotation in Hutten-Czapski, Sechzig Jahre, 2: 37.

108. Quotation in Galos, Dzieje Hakaty, p. 268. On the HKT Society's public campaign against Schorlemer and Bethmann, ibid., pp. 267ff. On Schorlemer's Herrenhaus speech, Kuryer Poznański, 22 May 1911.

109. Die Ostmark, 1911, no. 9, "Der Fall von Heydebreck und Genossen"; Galos, Dzieje Hakaty, pp. 274-75; Hutten-Czapski, Sechzig Jahre, 2: 46-48. Hutten-Czapski, who took part in this petition campaign, wrote that "all the old-settled peasants and all the businessmen we approached were strongly in its favor. Even many colonists declared themselves in agreement with it. But it was difficult to win the officials and teachers, most of whom belonged to the Ostmarkenverein, and the more or less indifferent large landowners." Ibid., p. 48.

110. On Bethmann's and Schwartzkopff's views and tactics, cf. Hutten-Czapski, Sechzig Jahre, 2: 49-53; Posener Neueste Nachrichten, 20-21 September 1911; 29 September 1911; 1 October 1911; 31 May 1914; Posener Tageblatt, 20 September 1911; 31 May 1914; Trzeciakowski, Walka, p. 218; Łuczak, Przemysł wielkopolski, p. 83.

111. On Waldow's list, cf. Pirko, Niemiecka polityka, pp. 288-93. On Bethmann's acquiescence in November 1911 to application of expropriation, cf. Galos, Dzieje Hakaty, pp. 274-75; Tims, Germanizing Prussian Poland, p. 178; Hutten-Czapski, Sechzig Jahre 2: 53-54; on Schorlemer's acceptance and announcement of the expropriation decision, cf. Szögyényi's letter to Aehrenthal, 10 May 1912, fasc. 181; on the expropriations of October 1912, Posener Neueste Nachrichten, 15 October 1912; Die Ostmark, 1912, no. 11, "Die Anwendung des Enteignungsgesetz." Reich Foreign Secretary Kiderlen-Waechter told Szögyényi he learned of the Prussian government's expropriation action in the newspapers and apologized for its adverse effect upon the Hapsburg government's domestic policies. Szögyényi to Berchthold, 12 October 1912. Berchthold was furious that Bethmann had failed to inform him of a step which could not fail to weaken the Galician Poles' support of the Triple Alliance. Predictably, the Austrian Polenklub publicly denounced the Prussian government. Berchthold was able to persuade the Polish representatives at the meeting in November 1912 of the joint Austro-Hungarian delegations to support Vienna's fiscal proposals by promising to pressure the Prussian government to soften, if not reverse, its expropriation actions. Bethmann explained that no retreat was possible, but promised that no further expropriations were planned. See Szögyényi's and Berchthold's correspondence of October and November 1912, fasc. 181, passim.

112. On the antiexpropriation interpellation and votes, Verhandlungen des Reichstages, 287 (January 1913): 29-30.

113. Szögyényi to Berchthold, 19 January 1913, fasc. 181.

114. Consul Pitner to Berchthold, 29 January 1914, ibid.

115. Details in Dietrich, "Die Besitzfestigung," 1912, p. 113 (see note 66 above).

116. Zechlin, "Die Polenfrage in Preussen," pp. 198-99 (see note 66 above); Die Ostmark 1913, no. 5, "Das neue Ostmarkengesetz."

117. Pitner's report of 29 January 1914, fasc. 181.

118. William II's toast quoted in Posener Neueste Nachrichten, 29 August 1913. On the imperial visit generally and on Schwartzkopff's diplomacy among the szlachta, ibid., 23 and 26-29 August 1913, 31 May 1914; Kuryer Poznański, 30 August 1913. For examples of William II's "sharp tone" in addressing the Poles during the Bülow era, see his speeches of 5 June, 2 September, 4 September 1902 and 9 August 1905 in Johs. Penzler, ed., Die Reden Kaiser Wilhelms II (Leipzig, 1907), 3: 86, 121-27, 263-64.

119. Pitner's report of 29 January 1914, fasc. 181.

120. The HKT Society's legal expert Justizrat Wagner objected, however, that the government's draft would have left private individuals free to sell parcelled plots among themselves. Die Ostmark, 1914, no. 5, "Grundteilungsgesetz."

121. On the "parcellation law" generally, Orędownik, 27 February 1914; Dziennik Poznański, 10 July 1914; Galos, Dzieje Hataky, p. 280.

123. It is unclear whether Schwartzkopff participated in or approved of this radicalization of official school policy. Kuryer Poznański, 24 April 1914, and 12 May 1914; Dziennik Poznański, 24 April 1914; Posener Neueste Nachrichten, 24 April 1914 and 5 May 1914.

124. Hutten-Czapski, Sechzig Jahre, 2: 126-27; Posener Nueste Nachrichten, 13 June 1914; Die Ostmark, 1914, no. 7.

125. Quoted in Hutten-Czapski, Sechzig Jahre, 2: 145.

126. Werner Conze, <u>Polnische Nation und deutsche Politik</u>
im ersten Weltkreig (Köln, 1958), p. 49.
127. The local press published Likowski's pastoral letter
on 12 August 1914. For the Polish version, see the <u>Kuryer</u>
<u>Poznański</u> of that date. On Likowski's appointment, see Nowacki,
<u>Archidiecezja Poznańska</u>, 2: 121-23.

Chapter Six
1. Wholesale rye prices rose 60 percent on the Berlin
market between 1894 and 1912; in the period 1898-1913 the price
of pork rose 50 percent. Other farm commodity prices exhibited
similar trends. <u>Vie économique</u>, pp. 49-51.
2. In 1911, Poznania counted more steam plows and consumed more potash in the manufacture of chemical fertilizers
than any other Prussian province. Hermann Wagner, "Die Land-
und Forstwirtschaft," in Deutscher Ostmarkenverein, <u>Die deutsche</u>
<u>Ostmark</u>, pp. 275-78. Between 1881 and 1907, the number of horse-
drawn reapers and harvesters in use in the province rose from 210
to 6,227, steam-powered threshers from 972 to 6,130, steam plows
from 35 to 542. Stanisław Borowski, <u>Rozwarstwienie wsi wielko-</u>
<u>polskiej</u>, Annex 47. Average yields per hectare rose between
1879/1883 and 1909/1913 by a multiple of 2.3 for wheat, 2.5 for
rye, and 2.8 for potatoes. Ibid., Annex 42.
3. Grain sold outside the province doubled in volume
between 1887/1894 and 1906/1909, rising in the latter period to an
annual average of 400,000 tons. <u>Vie économique</u>, p. 52.
4. Czesław Łuczak, <u>Przemysł wielkopolski w latach 1871-</u>
<u>1914</u>, pp. 16-18.
5. Ibid., pp. 19-20. The province's sugar beet fields
expanded from 260 hectares in 1875 to 74,300 hectares in 1914.
<u>Vie économique</u>, p. 82.
6. The number of beef cattle rose between 1873 and 1913
by 65 percent, the total of horses, cattle and swine by 150 percent. Ibid., pp. 46-48.
7. Buzek, <u>Historya</u>, p. 319; <u>Vie économique</u>, p. 54.
8. German large holdings declined through sales to the
Royal Commission and parcellation societies by 220,000 hectares
between 1881 and 1913. The <u>szlachta</u> divested themselves of
150,000 hectares in the same period. Calculation from data on
German-Polish landholdings given in Bergmann, <u>Entwicklung</u>,
pp. 361-65; Borowski, <u>Rozwarstwienie</u>, 283; <u>Vie économique</u>, pp.
22, 36-37. Many German estates, few of which were latifundia,
were parcelled out completely; the <u>szlachta</u> tended to sell off
their outlying fields. <u>Die Ostmark</u>, 1914, no. 3, "Deutscher und
polnischer Grossgrundbesitz in der Provinz Posen"; <u>Dziennik</u>
<u>Poznański</u> (hereinafter DzP) 18 April 1914; <u>Posener Tageblatt</u>,
17 April 1914. The pre-1914 "mobility" of German large landholdings in the Prussian east, and especially in Poznania, was
notorious. See Arnim's, Bethmann's, and Blomeyer's complaints
on this score in the Ministerial Conference of 16 January 1907,
<u>Nachlass Hugenberg</u>, no. 54, folio 1.
9. Borowski, <u>Rozwarstwienie</u>, pp. 268-69.
10. Vie économique, pp. 16-17, 25-27.
11. A large majority of these peasant holdings fell in the
five-to-twenty hectare range. Borowski, <u>Rozwarstwienie</u>, pp. 268-69.
12. By 1907, many peasant farmers had equipped themselves
with seed drills, reapers, and steam threshers, a large majority
with horse-drawn threshers. Borowski, Annex 47. On the cooperative banking system, cf. chaps. 7 and 8, below. On the perils,
but also the limited degree, of rural usury in the 1880s, cf.
"Der Wucher auf dem platten Lande in der Provinz Posen," in
Schriften des Vereins für Sozialpolitik, vol. 35: <u>Der Wucher auf</u>
<u>dem Lande</u> (Leipzig, 1887), pp. 303-24; Tomasz Skorupka, <u>Kto przy</u>
<u>Obrze, temu dobrze</u> (Poznań, 1967), p. 53.

13. A cottager or deputant-laborer cost an estate owner
609 marks yearly in 1873, 800-900 marks in 1910. The wages of
agricultural day-laborers rose from roughly 1.2 marks daily in
1870 to 2.5-3.0 marks in 1910. Otto Münsterberg, Die wirtschaftlichen Verhältnisse des Ostens (Berlin, 1912), p. 11. See also
Vie économique, pp. 54-55, and Juljusz Trzciński, Kwestya robotników rolnych (Poznań, 1907), passim.
14. In 1911 Poznania provided the western provinces with
28,500 Sachsengänger; 21,400 foreign seasonal workers entered
the province in the same year. Deutsche Ostmark, p. 305;
Vie économique, p. 182.
15. Borowski, Rozwarstwienie, pp. 268-69. In 1907, two-
thirds of these holdings were smaller than one hectare. Altogether, they comprised only 6.7 percent of the province's arable
land.
16. See Appendix, tables A2 and A3.
17. On urban development generally, cf. Ludwig Bernhard,
ed., Preussische Städte im Gebiete des polnischen Nationalitäten-
kampfes; Jaffé, Stadt Posen, chap. 6; Wegener, Wirtschaftlicher
Kampf, pp. 141ff.; Łuczak, Życie gospodarczo-społeczne w
Poznaniu; Trzeciakowski, Walka o polskość miast poznańskiego,
chap. 1.
18. Borowski, Rozwarstwienie, p. 75.
19. Calculation based on figures in Borowski, ibid., Annex
76. On urban population, cf. also General Demography of Poland,
p. 170; Łuczak, Życie, p. 47.
20. Łuczak, Przemysł, p. 28. In 1904, the province
counted 130 limited-liability and joint-stock companies, capitalized at 84.4 million marks. Large landowners owned a "decided
majority" of the capital invested in these firms. The province's
industrial development was so closely tied to agriculture that in
1914 "about half the entire industrial wealth of the Duchy was
gathered in the estate owners' hands." Ibid., pp. 46, 51.
21. Łuczak, Położenie ekonomiczne rzemiosła wielkopolskiego,
chaps. 2-4.
22. Łuczak, Przemysł, p. 28.
23. Mitscherlich, Die Ausbreitung der Polen in Preussen,
p. 89; Łuczak, Położenie, pp. 30, 47; "Die Bevölkerung Preussens
nach Haupt-und Nebenberuf (Provinzen)." Statistik des Deutschen
Reichs 204 (1909): 668-84.
24. Vie économique, p. 83.
25. Łuczak, Przemysł, chap. 6; Marchlewski, Stosunki
społeczno-ekonomiczne, part IV. See chap. 7, below, on trade
unionism and working-class politics.
26. Farm census figures in Borowski, Rozwarstwienie,
Annex 74.
27. Vie économique, p. 193.
28. Ibid., p. 198; Mitscherlich, Ausbreitung, p. 23.
29. On these and following population statistics, cf.
Appendix, tables A1, A2, and A3 except where otherwise noted.
30. In the years 1903/1906, the Royal Commission purchased
annually an average of 30,000 hectares; the average for the
period 1907/1912 was 15,000. Similarly, in 1907 the Commission
actually settled 24,000 hectares, but in 1912 only 10,500. Erich
Zechlin, "Die Tätigkeit der Ansiedlungskommission," Ostland
(1914), p. 200.
31. On the partial absorption of the local surplus Polish
village population by Upper Silesian industry, see Lawrence
Schofer, The Formation of a Modern Labor Force. Upper Silesia,
1865-1914 (Berkeley, 1975), chaps. 1-5. On Polish migration to
the Rhenish-Westphalian industrial districts Hans-Ulrich Wehler,
"Die Polen im Ruhrgebiet bis 1918," in Wehler, Sozialgeschichte,
pp. 437-55; Hans Linde, "Die soziale Problematik der masurischen
Agrargesellschaft und die masurische Einwanderung in das

Emscherrevier," ibid., pp. 456-70; and above all Christoph
Klessmann, Polnische Bergarbeiter im Ruhrgebiet 1870-1945
(Göttingen, 1978), chaps. 1-3.
    32. Thus, the rural Protestant population of the
Regierungsbezirk of Poznań was numerically no larger in 1910 than
in 1870. Friedrich Zitzlaff, "Die kleinen Städte," in Bernhard,
Preussische Städte, pp. 12-16; Fritz Vosberg, "Die Mittel- und
Kleinstädte der Provinz Posen," Ostland (1913), pp. 63ff.;
Statistisches Jahrbuch für den preussischen Staat (1913), pp. 21,
25.
    33. In towns with populations smaller than 5,000, Polish
gains after 1895 were moderate, Jewish losses very heavy. In
the larger towns, the Poles' advance was very rapid, the Jews'
losses heavy except in the provincial capital and Bromberg, where
they were light. In the smallest towns, the German Catholic
and Protestant population declined absolutely; in towns of 5,000
and more, its growth was sluggish. Language census figures in
Zitzlaff, "Die kleinen Städte," and Vosberg, "Mittel- und
Kleinstädte." In the city of Poznań, the Polish population rose
between 1890 and 1905 from 50.8 percent to 57.1 percent. Jaffé,
Stadt Posen, p. 371.
    34. The average size of the farms established by the
Colonization Commission was ten hectares, that of farms created
through private parcellation five. Vie économique, p. 16.
    35. Zitzlaff, "Die kleinen Städte," p. 23; Bernhard,
Polenfrage, pp. 519ff.
    36. Władysław Rusiński. "The Role of the Peasantry of
Poznań (Wielkopolska) in the Formation of the Non-Agricultural
Labor Market," East European Quarterly 3, no. 4, pp. 509-24.
    37. Łuczak, Położenie, pp. 62-63.
    38. Łuczak, Przemysł, p. 58; Max Broesike, "Deutsche und
Polen der Provinz Posen im Lichte der Statistik," pp. 386-88;
Geheimes Staatsarchiv, Berlin-Dahlem. Rep. 30, no. 683,
report dated 19 February 1908.
    39. Jaffé, Stadt Posen, p. 411; Bernhard, Preussische
Städte, p. xx; Rzepecki, Ubytek żydów, p. 14.
    40. WAPP, Polizeipräsidium. Syg. 8732, Report dated 18
December 1912.
    41. Geheimes Staatsarchiv. Berlin-Dahlem. Rep. 30, no. 683,
18 February 1908. In RB Bromberg, where in 1910 the Poles
comprised 51 percent of the population, Germans outnumbered Poles
in the professions in these proportions: medical doctors--3:1,
veterinarians--8:1, apothecaries--3:1, lawyers and notaries--4:1.
Ibid. By 1909, Waldow had reduced the number of Poles among the
province's 12,300 railway and postal officials to 667. Waldow,
"Erfolge der Ostmarkenpolitik."
    42. Among the nonagricultural occupations, from 44 percent
in 1882 to 54 percent in 1907.
    43. Geheimes Staatsarchiv, Berlin-Dahlem, Rep. 30, no. 683,
Posen RB president's report of 7 April 1913. These figures do not
include taxes paid in the city of Poznań, whose Polish business
community flourished after 1890. Comparable figures for the
whole province, again excluding the capital city: 1895--18 percent;
1910--25 percent.
    44. Ibid. For the province as a whole (excluding the
capital city), the increases in Polish income and estate taxes
were smaller because of the Germans' greater economic strength in
the Bromberg District. Cf. Trzeciakowski, Walka, p. 143.

Chapter Seven
    1. On official boycotting of Polish business and commercial
firms, see Buzek, Historya, p. 266; Trzeciakowski, Walka, pp. 120
ff. From 1903 all Prussian state officials and from 1908 most
Reich officials in Poznania received Ostmarkenzulagen, or bonuses
of up to 10 percent of their salaries, for fulfilling their "national obligations"--above all, for voting for German nationalist

candidates and joining German nationalist organizations. Few
German officials failed to qualify. Buzek, Historya, pp. 287,
399ff.
    2. Quotation in Blanke, "The Development of Loyalism in
Prussian Poland 1886-1890," The Slavonic and East European
Review 52 (1974): 562.
    3. Reichstag speech of 30 November 1891 and Kościelski's
memorial to the Crown of 6 November 1891, quoted in Trzeciakowski,
Polityka klas posiadających, pp. 116-17, 80.
    4. On the populists' revolt against loyalism, see ibid.,
pp. 115ff., and Harry K. Rosenthal, "Rivalry between 'Notables'
and 'Townspeople' in Prussian Poland: the First Round," The
Slavonic and East European Review 69 (1971), no. 114, pp. 68-79.
The words "compromise" (ugoda) and "compromisers" (ugodowcy),
hurled in these years at the loyalists by the populists, henceforth conveyed a highly polemical sense implying "collaboration"
with the "national enemy" and even "treason."
    5. Trzeciakowski, Polityka, p. 128.
    6. Ibid., pp. 117ff., and Trzeciakowski, "Roman Szymański
1840-1908," Jakóbczyk, Wielkopolanie 2: 355ff.
    7. The Polish agrarians channeled their opposition to the
loyalists' support of Caprivi's commercial polity through the
influential Central Economic Society (CTG). Trzeciakowski,
Polityka, pp. 125ff.
    8. On Polish political ideas and movement from the 1880s
to 1914, see Kieniewicz, Historia Polski 1795-1918, chaps. 19,20,
22-26, and Feldman, Geschichte der politischen Ideen in Polen,
chaps. 8-10. On the origins and early years of the National
Democratic movement, cf. Andrzej Micewski, Roman Dmowski
(Warszawa, 1971), chaps. 1-3. The two most authoritative statements of ND ideology before the Russian revolution of 1905 were
Dmowski's Myśli nowoczesnego polaka, first published in 1903 (3d
edition: Lwów, 1907), and Zygmunt Balicki, Egoizm narodowy wobec
etyki, first published in 1902 (Lwów, 1914).
    9. Jerzy Marczewski, Narodowa Demokracja w Poznańskiem 1900-
1914 (Warszawa, 1967), chap. 2. This is the fullest study of the
ND movement in Poznania before 1914, but see also Jakóbczyk,
Studia, 3: 186ff., and "Bernard Chrzanowski 1861-1944,"
Wielkopolanie, 2: 467ff.
    10. The ND movement found numerous adherents among the secret
Polish student organizations at the universities of Breslau and
Berlin which flourished at the turn of the century. The most
important of these joined the Pan-Polish Związek młodzieży
polskiej (Zet), directed by National Democrats from Russian Poland.
Clandestine Polish student clubs at the Poznanian gymnasiums also
recruited many future ND activits. Marczewski, Narodowa Demokracja,
pp. 113ff.
    11. Ibid., pp. 156ff. On Polish parliamentary and provincial
electoral politics after 1894, see Karol Rzepecki, Naprzód czy
wstecz? (Poznań, 1912) and Historya ustawy wyborczej pruskiej oraz
wyniki wyborów do sejmu pruskiego z 1903 i 1908 r. na ziemiach
polskich (Poznań, 1913); Zygmunt Hemmerling, Posłowie polscy w
parlamencie rzeszy niemieckiej i sejmie pruskim 1907-1914
(Warszawa, 1968); Lech Trzeciakowski, "Sprawy wyborcze i
parlamentarne," in Jakóbczyk, Dzieje Wielkopolski, 2: 525ff.
    12. Jakóbczyk, Studia, 3: 165ff.; Straż played an important
role in coordinating and propagating the school strikes. Cf.
Kulczycki, "School Strikes," 136ff. After 1907, it promoted popular educational programs. The Prussian government and police
viewed Straż with great suspicion. In forbidding priests to join
it, Stablewski was probably more interested in shielding the archbishopric from official harrassment than in crippling the ND movement. On police surveillance of Straż, cf. WAPP. Landrat Posen-
West. Syg. 169, passim.

13. The old clerical-conservative <u>Kuryer Poznański</u>
ceased publication in 1904, an indication of the inner consolidation of the agrarian conservatives in opposition to the populists
and National Democrats. Thereafter, the authoritative conservative daily was the <u>Dziennik Poznański</u>. On Szymański's merger
with the ND movement, cf. Marczewski, <u>Narodowa Demokracja</u>, chap. 3. On
Dmowski's and the Russian ND movement's turn to the right after
1905, see Micewski, <u>Dmowski</u>, chap. 4.
14. Kulczycki, "School Strikes," pp. 153ff.
15. Marczewski, <u>Narodowa Demokracja</u>, p. 205.
16. Speeches of Prince Radziwiłł, 30 January 1908, Landtag,
Herrenhaus; Father Ludwik Jażdżewski, 29 November 1907, Landtag,
HdA; Zygmunt Dziembowski, 30 November 1907, Landtag, HdA;
Radziwiłł, Reichstag, vol. 229, 10 December 1907, and vol. 232, 4
April 1908.
17. Marczewski, <u>Narodowa Demokracja</u>, pp. 227ff.; Pirko,
<u>Bülow a sprawa polska</u>, pp. 315ff.
18. Responding to Bethmann's allegations of revolutionary
tendencies among the Prussian Poles, Chrzanowski pointed out
that not a single Pole had been convicted of high treason since
the founding of the Reich. Speech of 11 December 1907,
Reichstag, vol. 229.
19. Paradoxically, the same <u>Reichsvereinsgesetz</u> of 1908
which limited the public use of the Polish language also shielded
the TDN from police harrassment (although the police managed to
plant more than a few Polish agents among the <u>endecy</u>). On the
formation of the TDN, cf. Marczewski, <u>Narodowa Demokracja</u>, pp.
227ff.
20. Ibid., pp. 286ff. Another reason for the TDN's unwillingness to cooperate with the government arose from the
"russophile" position on the international Polish question which
Dmowski and the <u>Liga Narodowa</u> adopted after 1905. Judging socio-
psychological Germanization and German economic and political
imperialism to be the greatest dangers confronting the Poles, ND
agitation and propaganda in all three partition areas, and
especially in Prussia and Russia, systematically cultivated
Polish opposition to Imperial Germany. This policy dovetailed
with Dmowski's efforts to wring concessions for the Russian Poles
from the Tsarist regime and with the National Democrats' hopes
that, in case of war with Germany, the Triple Entente powers
would champion the liberation of Poznania and Galicia from
German rule. See Micewski, <u>Dmowski</u>, chap. 5; Marczewski,
<u>Narodowa Demokracja</u>, pp. 277ff., 397; Roman Dmowski, <u>Niemcy, Rosya
i kwestya polska</u> (Lwów, 1908), esp. chap. 6.
21. In 1909-10, the Poznanian National Democrats lost the
support of prominent members of the "progressive szlachta." The
desertion in Upper Silesia of the influential populist Wojciech
Korfanty badly weakened ND influence there. Like Korfanty, the
West Prussian peasant-populist leader Wiktor Kulerski resigned
from the TDN in protest against its refusal to explore "compromise"
with Bethmann and the Center Party. Kulerski's <u>Gazeta Grudziądzka</u>,
distributed throughout the eastern provinces, was the most widely
read Polish newspaper in Germany. By early 1914 its daily circulation exceeded 128,000--more than ten times the sales of the
biggest Poznanian daily. Kulerski won his readership, especially
heavy among the peasantry and rural workers, through clever marketing, impassioned and unvarnished denunciations of the government's
Germanization policies, and appeals to the common people's religious and agrarian values. Neither Kulerski nor Korfanty shared
the Poznanian ND's Pan-Polish enthusiasms; "Poland" seemed more
remote to the West Prussian and Silesian Poles than to the
Poles of Poznania, where attachment to the traditions of Polish
statehood had been passed on by the Polish nobility to the ND
intelligentsia. In West Prussia, the <u>szlachta</u> had been thinning

out since Frederick's time, leaving political leadership of the
Polish common people, as among the Silesian Poles, to the clergy
and provincially minded petit bourgeois intelligentsia. Thus it
turned out that the ND movement in Germany only flourished in
Poznania. Cf. Tadeusz Cieślak, "'Gazeta Grudziądzka' (1894-1918),
fenomen wydawniczy," Studia i materiały do dziejów Wielkopolski
i Pomorza, 3 (1957), no. 2, pp. 175-88; Kieniewicz, Historia
Polski, 414ff.; Marczewski, Narodowa Demokracja, pp. 322ff.;
Peter Böhning, "Westpreussisches Polentum und polnische Nation,"
Zeitschrift für Ostforschung 20 (1971), no. 1, pp. 76-94.
    22. Jakóbczyk, Studia, 3: 200-208; Marczewski, Narodowa
Demokracja, pp. 305ff.
    23. Altogether the Polish delegation (Koło Polskie) in the
Reichstag of 1912 numbered eighteen: four deputies from Upper
Silesia, three from West Prussia and eleven from Poznania. Four
were National Democrats, all from Poznania; one, Father Stychel,
had earlier joined the League, but was not publicly associated
with the TDN; two other priests sympathized with the ND but enjoyed general support; five were "independent democrats"; six
were conservatives. Rzepecki, Naprżod czy wstecz? p. 12;
Marczewski, Narodowa Demokracja, p. 363.
    24. DzP, 23-29 August 1913; Hemmerling, Posłowie, p. 191;
Kuryer Poznański [hereinafter KP] 28 May 1914.
    25. Trzeciakowski in Jakóbczyk, Dzieje Wielkopolski, 2:
532, concluded that by 1914 the National Democrats wielded
"decisive influence" over Polish politics in Poznania. "On the
eve of the war . . . National Democracy was taking control of the
political representation of the Polish national movement in
Poznania": Marczewski, Narodowa Demokracja, p. 405. Cf. similar
judgments in Jakóbczyk, Studia, 3: 199, and Kieniewicz, Historia
Polski, pp. 457-59, 470-72. The ND partisan Władysław Poboóg-
Malinowski set the TDN in "first place" among Polish political
movements in Poznania, counting half the Polish Reichstag delegates as its spokesmen. Najnowsza historia polityczna Polski
1864-1945 (Paris, 1953), 1: 200. German historians have been
even more willing to magnify ND influence. Cf. Conze, Polnische
Nation und deutsche Politik, p. 44; Hans Roos, A History of Modern
Poland (New York, 1966), p. 13. Piotr Wandycz more cautiously
put the TDN "on the ascendency." Lands of Partitioned Poland,
p. 326.
    26. After 1909, direction of the ND movement in Prussia
lay in the hands of the TDN's executive committee, headed by
Bernard Chrzanowski and also including Karol Rzepecki and Marian
Seyda. Seyda, Prussian Poland's chief representative to the
central councils of the Liga Narodowa, was the TDN's principal
ideologist. The Liga did not attempt to dictate domestic
political strategy or tactics to the TDN. On membership, KP,
16 September 1911, 24 November 1911; on annual assembly, KP,
22 November 1911; on leadership, WAPP. Poliezei-Präsidium. Syg.
4225, folio 31.
    27. Survey of Polish press 1911-14 and Marczewski, Narodowa
Demokracja, passim. Included in this sample are activists of the
TDN, Centrum Obywatelskie, Narodowe Stronnictwo Ludowe, Liga
Narodowa, Obrona Narodowa, and Sokół. Note that only eight persons
in this sample were descendents of the szlachta.
    28. Vie économique, pp. 174-75. Alongside these banks a
system of sixty-one agricultural purchasing and marketing cooperatives (rolniki) had arisen by 1914. They undercut many Jewish
and German private dealers in agricultural goods. Trzeciakowski,
Walka, p. 120.
    29. Jakóbczyk, Studia, 3: 72 and 60ff. In 1914, thirty-
three of the TCL's forty-five local committee chairmen were
prists. Ibid., p. 62.
    30. Orędownik, 1 June 1913. On the TPN after 1890, cf.
Jakóbczyk, Studia, 3: 27ff.

31. Ibid., 3: 136 and 135ff. At the annual exercises of 1913, however, 1,700 persons took part. KP, 17 August 1913.

32. Jakóbczyk, Studia, 3: 90ff. and 114ff. Figures in text are Reich totals, but most of these societies were located in Poznania and West Prussia.

33. Although a Reich-level ZZP executive was formed in 1909, the regional branches maintained considerable independence. On the Poznanian ZZP, see Wydanie jubileuszowe Związku Robotniczo-Rzemieślniczego Z.Z.P. w Poznaniu 1902-1927 (Poznań, 1927), pp. 38ff.; Tadeusz Filipiak, Dzieje związków zawodowych w Wielkopolsce do roku 1919 (Poznań, 1965), pp. 222ff.

34. On ND influence in various clandestine nationalist youth groups before the war, see Marczewski, Narodowa Demokracja, pp. 347ff. None was of any political importance. Members of one such group jeered the aristocratic "castle-goers" of 1913 in the streets of Poznań. WAPP. Polizei-Präsidium. Syg. 2713, folio 146ff.

35. On the Polish press generally, cf. Trzeciakowski, Walka, pp. 178ff.; Jakóbczyk, Studia, 3: 23 and 139; WAPP. Polizei-Präsidium. Syg. 4930, report of 4 May 1911.

36. On the failure of the Związek Narodowy, cf. Przegląd wielkopolski, 1913, no. 1; Stanisław Karowowski, Historya Wielkiego Księstwa Poznańskiego (Poznań, 1931), 3: 259-60. On the Stronnictwo Ludowe, Przegląd wielkopolski, 1911, no. 42; DzP, 22 November 1911; WAPP. Polizei-Präsidium. Syg. 2764, folios 16-21, 46-52, 55-60, 96-250, and syg. 2713, folio 140.

37. On the Kasyno Obywatelskie, cf. DzP, 14 September 1913; KP, 23 December 1911, 5 September 1913. By 1913, the CTG counted 847 members, nearly all large landowners. Ziemianin, 1913, no. 10.

38. On the abortive Centrum Obywatelskie, cf. DzP, 18 December 1912; KP, 2 September and 2 October 1913; Jakóbczyk, Studia, 3: 200.

39. The overseers of the Dziennik Poznański Company were closely connected with both the Kasyno Obywatelskie and the CTG, as were the leaders of the latter organizations with each other.

40. Poradnik Gospodarski, 1914, no. 11. The average circle member's farm in 1914 covered 13 hectares, illustrating that the system recruited mostly the richer Polish peasants. Ibid. In 1905, among 276 local circle presidents, 107 were estate owners, 85 were priests, and 85 were peasants. Jakóbczyk, Studia, 3: 55.

41. Together, the Goniec wielkopolski and Wielkopolanin circulated in a daily edition of about 15,000. Adding the circulation of the Dziennik Poznański, Przegląd wielkopolski, Ziemianin, and Poradnik Gospodarski produces a total of about 35,000 for the conservative press. Many notables in Polish industrial and commercial life, especially among the older generations, sided with the conservatives against the TDN. Cf. DzP, 5 December 1911.

42. Quotation in Kulczycki, "School Strikes," p. 294.

43. Alongside the ZKTRP stood the Katolickie Stowarzyszenia Kobiet Pracujących (Catholic Societies of Working Women), which by 1911 counted nearly 6,000 members. DzP, 2 March 1912. On these organizations generally, cf. Robotnik, 25 February 1912, 3 March 1912, 23 June 1912, 30 June 1912; Michał Chełmikowski, Związki zawodowe robotników polskich w Królestwie pruskim 1889-1918 (Poznań, 1925), pp. 43ff.; Józef Staszewski "Rola kleru katolickiego w ruchu robotniczym na terenie Wielkopolski i Pomorza (1891-1914)," Zeszyty Naukowe (Toruń, 1957).

44. The founding editor of the Przewodnik, Father Józef Kłos, described it after the war as a "fighting political journal," 25 lat przy stoliku redaktorskim (Poznań, 1936), p. 29. In the Przewodnik of 7 January 1912, he wrote that "voting could be called a special form of confessing one's faith." Votes for "Lutherans and Jews," who "breathe hatred for the church and the nation," or for Polish "secessionists" would be violations of "the holy obligations of conscience."

45. Seyda admitted openly the clergy's "particularly strong
influence over the rural common people" in political matters, extending to the point of controlling their votes in cases of
"secessions." KP, 9 January 1912. The gentry would sometimes pack
local nominating meetings with their estate laborers to assure
victory to themselves or their colleagues. Cf. WAPP. Polizei-
Präsidium. Syg. 2777, folio 310.
46. On a ZZP attempt to organize the 1,300 workers in a
Polish tobacco works ("Patria"), see KP, 16 December 1911.
47. In the 1907 census, 67.6 percent of the employed
Catholic population was engaged in agricultural occupations.
48. Radziwiłł's speech of 10 December 1907, Reichstag, vol.
229; KP, 22 November 1911 and 23 November 1912; Przegląd
wielkopolski, 16 November 1912 and 28 June 1913; Książka
jubileuszowa Dziennika Poznańskiego, Introduction. This and the
following discussion of ND and conservative ideology is based,
except where otherwise or more specifically noted, on the Polish
press and on reports of Polish political meetings from the years
1911-14.
49. DzP, 30 August 1913.
50. Program Polskiego Towarzystwa Demokratycznego (Poznań,
1909), section A.
51. DzP, 27 October 1912.
52. DzP, 24 July 1913; Przegląd wielkopolski, 1911, no. 4;
KP, 11 January 1912.
53. The conservatives argued that high food prices did not
hurt the rural workers, who either received part of their pay in
naturalia, supplied themselves with food from their own plots, or
sold produce and livestock on the market. The landed peasantry
shared their interest in tariff-protected grain, fodder, and livestock prices. Przegląd wielkopolski, 1911, no. 9; Ziemianin,
15 March 1914. The endecy acquiesced in these arguments, as well
as in the proposition that a robust Polish agrarian sector fueling
urban economic development outweighed the disadvantages of high
food prices. KP, 16 September 1911. Marian Seyda, Wyrok
(Poznań, 1913), pp. 18-19. The conservatives bridled at the TDN's
muted support for the abolition of the laws of 1810 and 1854
against rural combinations. This was merely a gesture aimed at
winning the villagers' goodwill, since the government and the
German agrarians in the Landtag were determined to uphold those
laws. In its popular agitation, the TDN seldom raised this
prickly issue. Unionization of rural labor would not necessarily
have benefited urban political or economic interests as they were
represented by the TDN. KP, 24 February and 1 March 1912; DzP,
23 February 1912.
54. Insofar as the agricultural protectionism demanded by
the conservatives impeded east Elbian industrialization, this
was a specious argument. On this and on conservative support of
the boycott, see Przegląd wielkopolski, 1911, nos. 11 and 19;
1913, no. 32; DzP, December 1912, passim. Seyda joined the
conservatives in condemning would-be "bourgeois gentry." KP 30
January 1914.
55. Father F. Kujawiński (pseudonym for Father Ignacy
Geppert), Stronnictwo Demokratyczno-Narodowe w świetle nauki
katolickiej (Poznań, 1913); Father W. Hozakowski, O katolickie
podstawy narodowej democracyi (Poznań, 1913). Both works were
fully endorsed in the Przegląd wielkopolski, 1913, nos. 8 and 13.
56. Geppert, Stronnictwo Demokratyczno-Narodowe, p. 104;
Hozakowski, O katolickie podstawy, pp. 23, 65. "Borussia" is
Latin for Prussia.
57. Seyda, Wyrok, pp. 13-14 and passim; M. Seyda, Inkwizycja
(Poznań, 1913), passim.
58. Program PTD, section B; KP, 17 August 1913; TDN speech
of Wł. Mieczkowski in Ostrowo, quoted ibid., 19 September 1913;
Seyda, Wyrok, pp. 21-22; KP, 14 July 1912. On ND exhortations to

the working classes to cultivate thrift, sobriety, patriotism,
and respect for the TDN's leadership, cf. WAPP. Polizei-
Präsidium. Syg. 4225, speech of Nowicki, TDN meeting of 23
June 1912. At the same meeting, TDN leader Fortuniak even re-
proached the ancestors of his working-class audience for their indifference to the Polish risings of 1830 and 1863.
    59. DzP, 11 May 1912.
    60. Przegląd wielkopolski, 1911, no. 16; DzP, 7 October
1913.
    61. DzP, 22 October 1913.
    62. Poradnik Gospodarski, 1912, p. 10; Seyda, Wyrok,
p. 17.
    63. Przegląd wielkopolski, 1914, no. 25.
    64. Ibid., 1913, no. 6; 1914, nos. 24-25; DzP, 7 February
1914.
    65. KP, 29 February 1912; WAPP. Landrat Posen-West.
Syg. 163, reports on ZZP meetings in Starzyny and Dopiewo, folios
164-67, 175-78; ZZP leader Nowicki told a Poznanian working-
class audience on 23 June 1912 that "the ideal of Social Democracy is robbery, but the ideal of the Polish worker is love of
his nationality and his Catholic faith." WAPP. Polizei-Präsidium.
Syg. 4225, folios 112ff. On ND complaints about the szlachta's
"caste spirit," cf. KP, 30 January 1914.
    66. WAPP. Polizei-Präsidium. Syg. 2771, folios 278ff., TDN
meeting of 19 March 1911.
    67. WAPP, Landrat Posen-West. Syg. 163, TDN meeting in
Zabikowo, 13 December 1912.
    68. Ibid., TCL meeting in Stenschew, 30 June 1910.
    69. KP, 12 October 1912; DzP, 20 June 1912.
    70. KP, 3 September 1913.
    71. KP, 24 and 30 August 1913.
    72. KP, 11 July 1912. Cf. also Program PTD, section B,
and speech of Mieczkowski in Kościan, 9 November 1913, WAPP.
Polizei-Präsidium. Syg. 4225, folios 139-48.
    73. KP, 23 February 1913.
    74. The Polish Landtag delegation seconded the Progressives'
motion in 1908 to replace the three-class voting system with the
Reichstag electoral law. For the Poles, Korfanty said that not
only did democratic suffrage accord with Polish tradition but that
"the nationality policies formulated against us are only possible
in a three-class parliament." Landtag, HdA, 1908 (1), 10
January 1908.
    75. KP, 2 August 1912.
    76. KP, 26 April 1912, 18 May 1912, 25 Jul7 1912, 8 November
1912; 18 October 1913; 6 June 1914.
    77. Marczewski, Narodowa Demokracja, pp. 395ff.; Micewski,
Dmowski, pp. 188ff.
    78. KP, 13 October 1912. On the TDN's veiled pro-Russian
orientation, see KP, 2 May 1912; 23 August 1913; 30 May 1914; 15
July 1914.
    79. Przegląd wielkopolski, 1911, no. 16; 1913, no. 24;
speech of R. Komierowski, reported in KP, 23 November 1912; DzP,
5 November 1912; 1 January 1913, 3 January 1913, 23 March 1913;
25 July 1914.
    80. DzP, 16 February 1912. The conservatives disclaimed any
self-interest in their advocacy of meeting the government half way
to deescalate the nationality conflict: the szlachta and educated
classes could defend themselves against Hakatist assaults on their
nationality and economic well-being; if the TDN baited the government into new anti-Polish measures, the more defenseless Polish
common people would suffer most. DzP, 24 September 1911.
    81. Letter of the "castle-goer" Kazimierz Chłapowski to the
KP, 28 August 1913. See also Prince Drucki-Lubecki's letter of 3
September 1913, which appealed to the principle Render unto Caesar
what is Caesar's. Ibid. On the conservatives' relation to the

state, DzP, 11 September 1911. Cf. also DzP, 24 September 1911;
and the Kasyno Obywatelskie's vindication of the banquet affair,
published in Przegląd wielkopolski, 1911, no. 36; and ibid.,
1913, nos. 35–39.
    82. DzP, 11 September 1911.
    83. DzP, 4 January 1912; Orędownik, 25 May 1913; KP, 28 May
1914. In December 1912 the National Democrats won centrist support for the passage of a reform binding the provincial assembly
to nominate the candidate proposed by a majority of nomination
meetings in any given district. This measure further democratized
Polish political life, but the assembly could not be won for
Rzepecki's proposal that all delegates be directly and popularly
elected to the provincial assembly (rather than through the hierarchy of precinct and county committees). Rzepecki would further
have had each county elect delegates in proportion to its share of
votes in Reichstag elections. Adoption of his plan would have
fully democratized the system of electoral authorities. No vote
was reported on this proposal; presumably the centrists swung
to the conservatives' side to defeat it. KP, 20–21 December 1912.
    84. I have identified the Catholic populists and nonpartisan
centrists on the basis of their unanimous support in the provincial
delegates' assembly, ND deputies through their public connection
with the TDN, and conservatives through the formation of ND-led
blocs of opposition to them. Both Marczewski (Narodowa Demokracja,
pp. 363, 348) and Trzeciakowski ("Sprawy wyborcze," 2: 531–32) considerably exaggerate ND strength in the parliamentary delegations,
partly by taking the TDN's own claims at face value.
    The limits of the National Democrats' influence over Polish
politics are also shown in the episode of the National Council
(Rada Narodowa), formed in 1913 in response to the expropriation
crisis. The TDN wished to make this body into a locally elected
representative of the province's (and ultimately the Reich's)
Polish Organic Work institutions which could, through centralization of funds, promote in concert with the electoral authorities
nationally desirable undertakings wherever needed. The conservatives, fearing the TDN would try to dominate this council, succeeded in persuading the centrists to limit its membership to
parliamentary deputies and executive electoral committeemen and
its authority to recommending new national programs and collecting
a voluntarily contributed "national fund." Thus circumscribed,
the Rada proved redundant within the already well-developed system
of political and Organic Work organizations. On ND plans for the
Rada, see WAPP. Polizei-Präsidium. Syg. 2712. Speeches of
Rzepecki in Krotoszyn, 5–6 December 1912, folios 12–18; TDN meetings in Gostyń and Koźmin, December 1912, ibid., folios 1–3. On
the Rada as it acutally emerged, see KP, 23 November 1912, 4 March
1913; DzP, 30 March 1913; Jakóbczyk, Studia, 3: 209ff. Both
Jakóbczyk and Marczewski (pp. 387ff.) fail to appreciate the extent of the TDN's defeat on this issue, which was a major concern
of Polish politics after 1912.
    85. These figures include the sum of activists known by oc-
cupation in social, cultural, and professionally based Organic
Work institutions. They assume 225 of the Cooperative Union's
local branches were located in Poznania, to the sum of whose directors and overseers the same occupational distribution has been applied as emerges from a sample of 84 cooperative leaders identified
in WAPP. Polizei-Präsidium. Syg. 2748–82: Akta betreffend die
polnische Bewegung 1909ff, passim. To an estimated total of 672
district electoral chairmen and county electoral committeemen,
the occupational distribution yielded by a sample of 135 drawn
from the same police files has been applied. County delegates'
occupations are given in Hemmerling (p. 55), those of parliamentary
deputies and political party activists in the press. No doubt,
many persons held several of the positions included in this

estimate at once. On the other hand, no attempt has been made
here to include elected village or county officials or town
councilmen, though, similarly, many persons holding these posts
figure in this estimate in other capacities. Jakóbczyk estimates
a total of three to four thousand national activitists, but does
not attempt an occupational breakdown. Studia, 3: 238.
    86. The membership of the CTG, Peasant Circles, ZKTRP,
Catholic Working Women's Societies, Industrial and Commercial
Societies middleclass women's societies, Sokół, Polish singing
clubs, and the provincial ZZP totalled 81,603 on the eve of the
war.
    87. Rzepecki, Naprzod czy wstecz? pp. 42-44. On the Reich
level, voting frequency in the 1912 elections was 85 percent.
Because of the three-class law and publicity of balloting, voting
frequency in Landtag elections was traditionally low. Since the
Poles' political leaders treated all elections as opportunities
for nationalist agitation and shows of national strength, they attempted to achieve full turnouts for both Landtag and city council
elections despite the unfavorable circumstances in which they were
held. In the 1908 Landtag elections, average frequency of voting
throughout the province was 64 percent, compared with a Prussian
state average of 33 percent. Rzepecki, Historya, pp. 44-45.
Polish participation was unlikely to have been lower than the
Germans' in these elections. Hence it can be assumed that, even
in public ballotings, two of every three Polish voters took part.
Polish public officials faced administrative reprisals if they
failed to vote the German ticket. German landlords threatened to
fire their Polish estate workers for supporting Polish nationalist
candidates. In such heavily German areas as the Bromberg region,
Polish voters feared loss of work or clientele if they made their
adherence to the nationalist movement known in elections which, in
any case, they could not hope to win. On these pressures facing
Polish voters, see Biblioteka Raczyńskich. Akta Prowincjonalnego
Komitetu Wyborczego (Akta PKW). Rkp. 894III, no. 27, Rkp. 882,
correspondence on Landtag elections of 1913 in Bromberg. On the
electoral authorities' efforts to maximize voter turnout, ibid.,
Rkp. 782II, passim.
    88. Not content with success, Polish leaders worried that,
while Polish voting had increased greatly (especially in Upper
Silesia but also in Poznania) between the 1903 and 1907 Reichstag
elections, it appeared that between 1907 and 1912 the Poznanian
Germans were increasing their turnout faster than were the Poles.
Moreover, the Poznanian socialist vote doubled to 13,000 in
these years. Rzepecki, Historya, pp. 120ff.; Naprzód czy wstecz?
pp. 58ff. Nevertheless, the Poles won all the seats they could
hope for, and when an especially close contest occurred, as in a
1914 Reichstag by-election, Polish voters turned out in full
force. Orędownik, 19 March 1914.
    89. Kulczycki, "School Strikes," pp. 150ff., 250ff. Modern
Polish historiography tends to interpret the strikes as spontaneous, proletarian, and, though national and religious in form,
social-revolutionary in essence. See Gomolec, "Strajki," passim;
Marczewski, Narodowa Demokracja, pp. 177ff.; Kieniewicz, Historia
Polski, p. 459; Jakóbczyk, Dzieje Wielkopolski, 2: 495ff.
    90. WAPP. Polizei-Präsidium. Syg. 2767, meeting of 17
September 1911, folios 328-35. On the socialist movement in
Poznania from the 1880s to 1914, see Bolesław Danilczuk,
Działalność SPD i PPS zaboru pruskiego w Poznańskiem w latach
1891-1914 (Toruń, 1961); Stanisław Kubiak, "Ruch robotniczy w
latach 1891-1914," in Jakóbczyk, Dzieje Wielkopolski, 2: 551-79;
and Filipiak, Dzieje związków, passim.
    91. Danilczuk, Działalność, pp. 55f., 92, 102-3, 113ff.;
Filipiak, Dzieje związków, pp. 139, 238.
    92. On SPD-PPS ideological and organizational frictions, cf.
Danilczuk, pp. 48, 66ff., 123ff.; J. P. Nettl, Rosa Luxemburg

(London, 1966), pp. 842-62; Wehler, Sozialdemokratie und Nationalstaat, chap. 3, part 3.
    93. See Gerschenkron, Bread and Democracy, pp. 28-35, and
Posener Tageblatt, 4 and 6 February 1912, for discussions of the
SPD's failure to come to terms with the east Elbian peasants' and
rural workers' attachment to private-property ideals.
    94. Cf., inter alia, Baron Karl Puttkamer, Die Misserfolge
in der Polenpolitik (Berlin, 1913); Wojciechowski, Życiorys, chap.
6; KP, 24 September 1912 and 12 December 1912.
    95. Jaffé, Stadt Posen, p. 407.
    96. Statistische Monatsberichte der Stadt Posen 1: 95; 7:
120.
    97. DzP, 29 May 1912.
    98. DzP, 13 October 1912. On the TDN's social boycott,
KP, 6 and 23 October 1912.
    99. Biblioteka Raczyńskich. Akta PKW. Rkp. 782II, ms. 69b.
On German electoral compromises 1907-14, see below.
    100. Cf. especially speeches at the massive antiexpropriation
meeting in Gniezno, reported in KP, 29 October 1912. In other
protest meetings organized under their auspices, ND speakers
preached "contempt for the Prussian system." See KP, 15 October
1912, 13 March 1913. On the Catholic populists' anti-German
sentiments, cf., in addition to earlier citations, Przewodnik
Katolicki, 1908, no. 4; 1912, no. 51; Robotnik, 1912, nos. 1-2,
42.
    101. Kazimierz Chłapowski, speech in Inowrocław, quoted in
KP, 23 November 1912.
    102. KP, 12 November 1912.
    103. DzP, 13 November 1913. See also DzP, 4 August 1911 and
12 October 1912. On other Polish press reactions to the Beilis
case, KP, 8 November 1913; Przewodnik Katolicki, 1913, no. 46.
    104. KP, 21 September 1912; Postęp, 21 December 1890, 3
January 1912.
    105. WAPP. Polizei-Präsidium. Syg. 2744a, speech in Chojno,
8 March 1914, folios 15-23; see also Marian Seyda's speech in
Poznań, 19 November 1913, ibid., Syg. 4225, folios 152-54.
    106. KP, 23 August 1912. The National Democrats took over
the populists' boycott slogans and, especially after 1908, strove
hard to establish boycotting of all German and Jewish firms and
services (in cases where Polish alternatives existed) as a "national obligation." The economic impact of the boycott, which was
undoubtedly widely if erratically observed, is hard to judge.
Germans complained of its effectiveness, especially when seeking
special economic treatment from the government. See the petition
of German merchants and artisans in the town of Mrotschen, Geheimes
Staatsarchiv. Berlin-Dahlem. Rep. 30, no. 680, Bd. 6 (1911-18),
dated 22 February 1911. Polish nationalists, however, seldom refrained from chiding the masses for buying from Jews and Germans.
Occasionally Polish workers replied that, if the boycott was
sporadic, it was because the Jews contented themselves with
lower profits than did the Poles. Cf. WAPP. Polizei-Präsidium.
Syg. 2768, meeting in Ostrowo, 29 December 1912, folios 211-15;
Syg. 2754, meeting in Gostyń, 18 February 1912, folios 196-204.
A survey by district commissioners of the boycott's impact in
their localities ordered by the provincial administration in
December 1912 revealed, at least in one county, that the Poles
observed the boycott most rigorously where the clergy recommended
it and where alternative Polish services were readily available.
WAPP. Landrat Posen-West. Syg. 163, folios 220-26. In general,
it is likely that political propagation of boycotting reinforced
the Poles' tendencies to patronize Polish firms offering equivalent services. It is unlikely that Polish buyers deliberately
incurred economic losses through boycotting.
    107. Związek Narodowy meeting reported in DzP, 3 December

1912: See also <u>DzP</u>, 4 December 1912, 5 November 1913, 16 December
1913, 8 January 1914; <u>Przegląd wielkopolski</u>, 1913, nos. 24, 32;
<u>Książka jubileuszowa Dziennika Poznańskiego</u>, p. 178.
   108. Kłos, <u>25 lat</u>, p. 35. In 1914, the Prussian authorities
fined Kłos heavily for "threatening the Jews (żydki)" with his boycott injunctions in the <u>Przewodnik</u>. Ibid., p. 56. Cf. <u>Przewodnik
Katolicki</u>, 22 December 1912, for an example of the Polish press's
heavy emphasis on observing the boycott while shopping for the
Christmas holidays.
   109. On the 1910 secession, Biblioteka Raczyńskich. Akta
PKW. Rkp. 854, petition of 28 March 1910, and Rkp. 924, <u>passim</u>.
   110. Biblioteka Raczyńskich. Akta PKW. Rkp. 894III,
report of 5 December 1909.
   111. In their unsuccessful secession attempt during the
1912 Reichstag elections, staged at a distance from the city of
Poznań, the conservatives appealed to the peasants' antiurban
sentiments to discredit the official candidate, a member of the ND
intelligentsia in the provincial capital. Many peasants ignored
their priests' admonitions to legality--or were encouraged by secessionist priests?--to vote for the dissident conservative, a local
estate owner who lost the first round of the election principally
because his opponent carried the towns. In the runoff, the German
candidate distributed Polish leaflets describing himself as the
son of a local farmer who would represent peasant agrarian interests against the "great city." A small number of Polish rural
voters seriously breached the principle of national solidarity
by voting for him, but the great majority of the ND candidate's
Polish opponents observed "national discipline" and gave him
their votes. Thus ND-conservative rivalry forced the landed
peasantry to choose between what they perceived as their political
and socioeconomic interests and blind obedience to the electoral
authorities and priesthood. Cf. Biblioteka Raczyńskich. Akta
PKW. Rkp. 786, <u>passim</u>.

Chapter Eight
   1. <u>Die Ostmark</u>, 1912, no. 1. The word <u>Gemeinburgschaft</u>
was a ponderous neologism in the still uncrystallized vocabulary
of <u>völkisch</u> politics; <u>Kampfprovinzen</u> was a typical OMV term.
   2. Program of 1894, quoted in Tims, <u>Germanizing Prussian
Poland</u>, p. 42.
   3. <u>Die Ostmark</u>, 1896, no. 8, quoted in Galos et al.,
<u>Dzieje Hakaty</u> [hereinafter cited by title alone], pp. 103-4.
   4. Quotation from manifesto of 1894, ibid., p. 53. The
Marcinkowski Scholarship Fund (TPN) particularly impressed the
OMV's founders. Ibid., p. 54.
   5. Thus Wehler, <u>Das Deutsche Kaiserreich</u>, p. 117, and "Von
den 'Reichsfeinden' zur 'Reichskristallnacht': Polenpolitik im
Deutschen Kaiserreich 1871-1918," in <u>Krisenherde des Kaiserreichs
1871-1918. Studien zur deutschen Sozial- und Verfassungsgeschichte</u>
(Göttingen, 1970), pp. 191-99; Broszat, <u>Zweihundert Jahre deutsche
Polenpolitik</u>, pp. 120ff.; Friedrich Meinecke, <u>The German Catas-
trophe</u> (Boston, 1950), p. 22; Hajo Holborn, <u>A History of Modern
Germany</u>, 3: 352-54. Since 1945, the OMV has found no eminent
apologists. Conservative-nationalist west German historians have
contented themselves with emphasizing its "defensive" character in
face of the "Polish threat." This was the HKT Society's own
argument, repeated after 1918 by Manfred Laubert, <u>Die preussische
Polenpolitik von 1772-1914</u> (Berlin, 1920), chap. 8, and presented
subtly in Schieder, <u>Das deutsche Kaiserreich von 1871 als
Nationalstaat</u>, p. 35, and crudely in Horst Jablonski's pamphlet,
<u>Die preussische Polenpolitik von 1815 bis 1914</u> (Würzburg, n.d.
[ca. 1954]), <u>passim</u>. The American historian Tims conceded a
"defensive" mentality to the Hakatists (<u>Germanizing Prussian
Poland</u>, pp. 42, 271), but in general his analysis stresses the
aggressive anti-Polish effect of their political action. In the

DDR, Jürgen Kuczynski argued that the OMV represented German
monopoly capitalism's interest in economic domination of the Polish
market and working class.   In Poland, Galos and his colleagues,
whose work is based on the recently discovered archives of the OMV,
dismiss this argument for lack of evidence of OMV dependence on
German big business.   They revise traditional Polish views that in
Polish questions the Prussian government was merely the "executive
organ" of the OMV, stressing the Prussian state's powerful influence on it.   But they uphold the view that the OMV was primarily
an anti-Polish propaganda agency successfully pressuring the
government towards increasingly radical Germanization policies.
Cf. Dzieje Hakaty, Introduction, pp. 54-55, 130, 300-311.
    6. On the OMV's influence on post-1896 Polenpolitik, cf.
chap. 5, above, whose argument, especially regarding the inter-
connected "exceptional laws" of 1908, derives from new evidence
linking official motivation directly to the colonization crisis
and the political struggle with the Polish nationalists, not at
all to OMV pressure.   In general, the analysis presented here and
in chap. 5 minimizes the Ostmarkenverein's influence on governmental policy decisions to a far greater degree than the study of
Galos et al., to say nothing of the older literature.
    7. Tims, Germanizing Prussian Poland, p. 287.   In addition,
the OMV claimed over 500 corporate members: city councils, business firms, guilds, student associations, and the like.
    8. Ibid., pp. 254ff.
    9. Kruck, Alldeutscher Verband, p. 22.   The Conservative
leader Heydebrand fought the extension of ADV influence in the
eastern provinces until the eve of the war, but in Poznania pan-
German organization could only have distracted German opposition
to the Poles and thus undercut the ADV's own anti-Polish program.
Ibid., pp. 60ff.; Dzieje Hakaty, p. 187.
    10. On Wilhelminian nationalist-imperialist pressure groups
generally, cf. Puhle, "Parlament, Parteien und Interessenverbände
1890-1914," in Stürmer, Das Kaiserliche Deutschland, pp. 340ff.;
Thomas Nipperdey, "Interessenverbände und Parteien in Deutschland
vor dem Ersten Weltkrieg," in Wehler, Moderne deutsche Sozialgeschichte, pp. 369-88.
    11. Dzieje Hakaty, p. 100; Tims, Germanizing Prussian Poland,
pp. 224ff.
    12. Deutscher Ostmarkenverein, Die deutsche Ostmark (Lissa,
1913), p. v. Cf. also William II's speech in Gniezno, 9 August
1905, Reden, 3: 260-63.   In Effi Briest (1895) Theodor Fontane
expressed the cultivated Berlin official's horror at service in
Poznania in the jingle "Schrimm ist schlimm, / Rogasen zum Rasen, /
aber weh dir, nach Samter / Verdammter."   Effi Briest (München,
n.d.), p. 200.
    13. Ernst Hasse, Deutsche Politik (München, 1907), 1: 130.
    14. Posener Tageblatt [hereinafter PT], 14 January 1914.   For
similar pronouncements, cf. Dzieje Hakaty, p. 157, and Hasse,
Deutsche Politik, 1: 57.   For a full-scale exposition of the HKT
Society's interpretation of German-Polish historical relations,
cf. Dietrich Schäfer, "Geschichtliche Einleitung," Die deutsche
Ostmark, pp. 1-62; Otto Hoetzsch, "Nationalitätenkampf aund
Nationalitätenpolitik in der Ostmark," ibid., pp. 567-623; Wegener,
Wirtschaftlicher Kampf, chap. 3; on Hakatist and other German
publicistic literature on the Prussian Poles, see also Harry K.
Rosenthal, German and Pole: National Conflict and Modern Myth
(Gainesville, Fla., 1976), pp. 39ff.   The scholarly sources of
HKT ideology were varied and distinguished; Sybel and Treitschke
were the politically most influential.   A relatively unpolemical
version of the HKT myth as it applied specifically to Poznania
was Erich Schmidt's Geschichte des Deutschtums im Lande Posen
unter polnischer Herrschaft (Bromberg, 1904); the historical introduction by Max Bär to his Westpreussen unter Friedrich dem
Grossen (Berlin, 1909) breathes a more truculent spirit.   Conserva-

tive German scholars perpetuated the OMV's hostile treatment of
Polish history between the world wars: cf. Brackmann, Deutschland
und Polen (1933). Since 1945, Polonophobic myths have been discredited but have not disappeared from German historiography.
On their survivals, cf. Topolski, Stosunki polsko-niemieckie w
historiografii (1974), passim.
     15. "Das Wesen der Nation ist die Abrenzung nach aussen,
die Persönlichkeit eines Volkes, seiner Rasseneigentümlichkeiten
entsprechend." Quoted in Hasse, Deutsche Politik, 1: 29.
     16. Hoetzsch, in Ostland (1912), p. 3.
     17. Quotations from Alfred Hugenberg's report of 1902 on
"Die Lage in den Ostmarken," reproduced in Hasse, Deutsche Politik,
1: 108-24; Hasse, ibid., text, 1: 58; Hoetzsch, Ostland (1912),
p. 8. The Prussian Poles' legal tactics embarrassed the Hakatists,
forcing them to argue for restrictions on Organic Work activities
and Polish political agitation on account of their revolutionary
and centripetal implications rather than their palpably subversive
nature. The most influential single exposition of these implications was the Berlin professor Ludwig Bernhard's Polenfrage (1908),
which bore the suggestive subtitle, "Das polnische Gemeinwesen
im preussischen Staate." In his Jahrbuch, Schmoller wrote (1913),
"There can be absolutely no doubt that the policy of national
consolidation and self-isolation practiced by the Poles represents
nothing less than the preparation for an intended breakaway from
Germany." Quoted in Ostland (1913), p. 230. Cf. also Die deutsche
Ostmark, pp. 54ff.; report on OMV meeting in Poznań, Posener
Neueste Nachrichten [hereinafter PNN], 10 December 1912; Die Ostmark,
1913, no. 10.
     18. Hoetzsch's speech of 14 September 1907 at the Pan-German
League's annual meeting in Wiesbaden. Nachlass Hugenberg, no. 55,
folio 1.
     19. Quotation in Die deutsche Ostmark, p. 62. On the OMV's
analysis of Polish politics and revolutionary tendencies, cf.
Die Ostmark, 1911, no. 11; 1912, no. 8; 1913, nos. 1, 10, 11;
1914, nos. 3, 5.
     20. Justizrat Wagner in the OMV Executive Committee meeting
of 1912, quoted in Die Ostmark, 1912, no. 12. For similar af-
firmations of conflict see Die Deutsche Ostmark, p. vi; speech of
Consistorial President Balan in Poznań, PNN, 3 April 1914.
     21. Memorial of March 10, 1902, quoted in Dzieje Hakaty,
p. 255. See also Hugenberg, "Lage," pp. 112, 123.
     22. Tims, Germanizing Prussian Poland, pp. 80ff.; Hugenberg,
"Lage," pp. 109-10; Pastor Richard Rassek, "Schule und Kirche im
Sprachenkampfe der Ostmark," Ostland (1913), pp. 104-22.
     23. Hugenberg, "Lage," pp. 109-10, 117; draft of speech on
expropriation, Nachlass Hugenberg, no. 54, folio 1, n.d. [1910].
Note that, apart from Hugenberg's stress on leading the Catholic
church into the German camp, his argument on Polish assimilation
follows the same lines as Bethmann Hollweg's in 1907. Cf. chap.
5, above.
     24. WAPP. Landrat Posen-West. Syg. 272, folios 126ff.
     25. Geheimes Staatsarchiv. Berlin-Dahlem. Rep. 30, no. 680,
vol. 6: "Geschäftsbericht der Gewerbe-Auskunftsstelle des deutschen
Ostmarkenvereins für das Jahr 1912," which said the German "counterboycott" was "without lasting effect," partly because Polish small
businessmen and artisans offered better service than their German
rivals. The Posen Regierungspräsident's office reported in 1913
to Schwartzkopff that German small businesses were succumbing to
Polish competition because the more capable sons of German merchants and artisans abandoned the family trade for state employment. Ibid. Rep. 30, no. 688, report of 7 April 1913. Hugenberg
complained that state service or dissatisfaction with private
career opportunities in the Ostmark drew the "ablest elements in
the thousands" westward, leaving the less ambitious and enter-
prising behind to beg for state subsidies rather than brave the

Poles' competition. "They have seen too good days and have too
little energy for that." Cf. "Lage," pp. 111-12. On OMV boycotting, Die Ostmark, 1913, no. 6; PT, 5 November 1912, 15 May
1913. In 1899, Hugenberg resigned his post with the Colonization Commission to assume leadership of one branch of the province's Raiffeisen rural savings and loan cooperative banking
system. Hugenberg's action represented a split in the German
cooperative movement, which had been launched earlier in the
1890s under the Bund der Landwirte's auspices. After 1900,
Hugenberg's cooperative system, which recruited mainly colonists,
stood in rivalry with the Bund's. By 1912, the former counted
12,200 members, the latter 30,300. In 1904, Hugenberg yielded
leadership of his system to the OMV activist Leo Wegener. Thus
this Raiffeisen network may be counted as a mass base for the OMV
among peasant colonists. Hugenberg also inspired the establishment of the Mittelstandskasse and the Danzig-based Ostbank für
Handel und Gewerbe, important frontier financial institutions but
independent of HKT control. On the German cooperative system,
see Leo Wegener, "Das Genossenschaftswesen," Die deutsche Ostmark,
pp. 447ff.
    26. Hugenberg, "Lage," p. 112.
    27. The slogan "industry Polonizes" became routine. See
Wegener, Wirtschaftlicher Kampf, part 2, chap. 3; Hugenberg,
"Lage," p. 113; Fritz Vosberg in Ostland (1913), p. 79. On the
OMV's Städtepolitik, cf. Die Ostmark, 1913, no. 6.
    28. Dr. Wilhelm John, "Industrie und Handel in Posen und
Westpreussen," Die deutsche Ostmark, pp. 330-60, passim.
    29. On subsidization of eastern agriculture, see chaps.
4,5, above.
    30. Hugenberg, "Lage," pp. 110-14.
    31. Wegener, Wirtschaftlicher Kampf, part 2, chaps 1,2, esp.
138ff.; Waldemar Mitscherlich, Der Einfluss der wirtschaftlichen
Entwicklung auf die ostmärkischen Nationalitätenkampf (Leipzig,
1910), pp. 29-43; Bernhard, Preussische Städte, pp. xxxv ff.;
Vosberg, Ostland (1913), pp. 89ff.; Heinrich von Both, "Das
Ansiedlungswerk," Die deutsche Ostmark, pp. 420-46, passim.
To enhance their reputations for scholarly objectivity, neither
Bernhard nor Mitscherlich joined the OMV, which indeed sometimes
criticized their work for painting the Poles in too favorable a
light. Bernhard was a close political associate of Hugenberg
who, after his departure from Poznania in 1903, maintained no
formal ties with the OMV but in fact acted as a major adviser and
political lobbyist for the more radical wing of the OMV, represented by Hugenberg's friends Fritz Vosberg and Leo Wegener, the
OMV's most energetic organizers and agitators in Poznania. Max
Weber's economic, political, and nationalist criticism of the
Junker estates is well known. See "Capitalism and Rural Society
in Germany" and "National Character and the Junkers," in Hans
Gerth and C. Wright Mills, eds., From Max Weber: Essays in
Sociology (New York, 1958) pp. 363-95.
    32. Quoted in Dzieje Hakaty, p. 263.
    33. On the OMV leaders' reactions, cf. Dzieje Hakaty, pp.
261ff. Heinrich Class, Hasse's successor as head of the Pan-
German League, congratulated Hugenberg for his energetic lobbying on behalf of expropriation while attached to the Prussian
Finance Ministry (1903-7). Hugenberg was, Class wrote flatteringly,
"the driving force" advancing eastern German interests in Berlin.
In addition to his OMV connections, Hugenberg since 1894 had been
a powerful member of the ADV's executive council. Gustav Schmoller
also praised Hugenberg for influencing the government and the
conservative parties in favor of expropriation. Alluding to
Hugenberg's resignation from state service, Schmoller wrote to
him, "You still are considered here in Berlin the best expert on
our colonization in Posen." In 1909, Hugenberg's frustrations with
the poor pay, bureaucratic conservatism, and discrimination against

talented but untitled outsiders in Prussian service were amply
compensated by his appointment as director of the Friedrich
Krupp AG. Nachlass Hugenberg, no. 1, folio 1, Class to Hugenberg,
4 March 1908; no. 28, Schmoller to Hugenberg, 21 February 1908.
    34. Bundesarchiv Koblenz. Nachlass Wegener. No. 63,
Wegener to Hugenberg, 23 January 1909; 23 November 1911.
    35. Ibid. Wegener to Hugenberg, 21 June 1912; 23 November
1911; 12 February 1912. Hugenberg to Wegener, 20 November 1911.
For the Royal Commission to concentrate on creating Restgüter
meant putting Junker interests before peasant colonization.
    36. Ibid. Wegener to Hugenberg, 17 June 1912. The Landrat
von Tilly, a Conservative Party organizer, was Wegener's bête
noire. Tilly was transferred to Königsberg, where official circles
had this to say of his wife: "So eine Dame passt nur in Posen."
    37. Dzieje Hakaty, pp. 280ff.; Die Ostmark, 1914, no. 5;
on OMV hostility to Bethmann, cf. Nachlass Wegener. No. 63.
Wegener to Hugenberg, 13 November 1911.
    38. Ibid. No. 63. Wegener to Hugenberg, 12 February 1912.
    39. Speech of NL deputy Schlee, Verhandlungen des Reichstags,
vol. 287, 29 January 1913.
    40. Puhle, Agrarische Interessenpolitik, pp. 38ff. 283ff.;
Peter G. J. Pulzer, The Rise of Political Anti-Semitism in Germany
and Austria (New York, 1964), pp. 118ff.; Alexander Gerschenkron,
Bread and Democracy in Germany, chaps. 1-6; Booms, Deutsch-
Konservative Partei, pp. 102ff.; Eyck, Das persönliche Regiment,
pp. 52ff., 74ff.
    41. Voting returns in Pinson, Modern Germany, Appendix A.
    42. Conservative losses in both the Reichstag and Landtag
would have been far heavier after 1890 had the regime not refused
to redraw the boundaries of electoral districts to take account of
the massive population shifts since 1871. Cf. Rzepecki, Historya,
pp. 27ff.; Naprzód czy wstecz? pp. 11ff.
    43. Puhle, Agrarische Interessenpolitik, pp. 38, 274-78;
Booms, Deutsch-Konservative Partei, pp. 27ff.; Görlitz, Die Junker,
pp. 282ff., 309ff.
    44. PT, 23 November 1913. Over 1,100 Junkers and farmers
joined the Bund in 1912-13; assuming 400 new members per year in
the period after 1893 puts total membership in 1914 at 8,000.
    45. Leo Wegener, "Das Genossenschaftswesen," Die deutsche
Ostmark, pp. 447ff.; Puhle, Agrarische Interessenpolitik, p. 54.
See above, note 25, on Hugenberg's OMV-oriented branch of the
cooperative movement.
    46. On the Landwirtschaftskammer and the Bund's relation to
it, cf. PNN, 14 January 1914 and 18 February 1914; PT, 17 February 1914; Die deutsche Ostmark, pp. 296ff.
    47. The language census of 1910 located 56 percent of
the German population in rural districts. Like the szlachta, the
Junkers pressured their estate laborers, Germans as well as Poles,
to vote according to their masters' wishes. Moreover, the Protestant clergy, taking a cue from the Polish priesthood, organized
after 1903 evagelische Arbeitervereine devoted to self-help purposes and clerical-conservative cultural activities. By 1913,
thirty parish locals each counting 300-600 members had been
established. Although unobtrusive, these organizations encompassing (if even only formally) a sizable part of the province's
46,000 Protestant rural workers undoubtedly reinforced their acquiescence in the Junkers' political leadership in the countryside. Cf. Kramski, "Społeczeństwo niemieckie," p. 232. On
Endell's role in the German electoral compromises, PNN, 22
October 1911 and 11 November 1911; PT, 22 October 1911.
    48. Cf. report of the United Conservatives' 1912 assembly
in PT, 17 June 1912.
    49. Ibid. Data on the social composition of the United
Conservative Party's province-wide membership is available only
for 1907. Among 423 persons with identifiable occupations, 43

percent were large landowners, 25 percent were state and Reich
officials, 21 percent were mayors, clergymen, schoolteachers,
lawyers and judges, physicians and apothecaries; the remaining
11 percent were manufacturers and industrial entrepreneurs, merchants, and artisan masters in equal proportions. Thus nearly 90
percent were either Junkers or persons working in close connection
with the state. Figures in WAPP. Landrat Posen-West. Syg. 200,
folio 24.

50. Local estate owners were the principal stockholders in
the Ostdeutsche Buchdruckerei und Verlagsanstalt, capitalized in
1910 at 1,250,000 marks; Waldow contributed 10,000 marks from his
Dispositionsfonds as a token of official support. This firm took
over the publication of the Posener Tageblatt, the province's old-
established, authoritative Conservative daily, as well as other
provincially oriented conservative-nationalist publications.
Three small-town German conservative dailies circulated in the
province; so too did the big West Prussian, Silesian, and Berlin
conservative newspapers. Cf. WAPP. Landrat Posen-West. Syg. 200,
folios 281, 335. PT, 12-14 May 1912. The United Conservatives'
efforts to establish local branches resulted by 1909 in seventeen
urban voters' clubs throughout the province. The capital city's
association counted in 1913 more than one thousand members, a
quarter of them members of the private middle classes, the rest
Junkers, peasant farmers and colonists, and state employees.
Major Endell was exceedingly jealous of the Bund's monopoly on
conservative organization and agitation in the countryside and
protested irritably against recruitment of farmers into this
bureaucratically dominated association. On conservative locals,
see Handbuch der Provinz Posen. Nachweisung der Behörden,
Anstalten, Institute und Vereine (Posen, 1909). On the Poznań
local, PNN, 22 April 1913 and WAPP. Landrat Posen-West. Syg. 200,
passim; on Endell's opposition, ibid., folios 214 and 180ff. The
Conservatives' biggest and rhetorically most fiery mass meeting
defended the government's handling of the sensational Saverne
case. Cf. PT, 20 January 1914.

51. Speech reported in PT, 4 December 1911.

52. ". . . Ernstes Pflichtbewusstsein und Unterordnung unter
die Authorität." Editor Ginschel in PT, 8 Feb. 1914. Ginschel, in
addition to being a prominent OMV spokesman, was an active and
impassioned ideologist of the conservative cause. Cf. also
retired Landrat Gossler's speech, PT, 17 June 1912, defining Conservative ideology and appealing to Stahl's slogan of the 1840s,
"Authorität, nicht Majorität"; and Klitzing's and Wenckstern's
Saverne speeches, ibid., 20 January 1914. The Conservatives' 1911
preelection manifesto upheld "the undiminished power of the
Kaiser, a strong government, and all authority in our public
life." Ibid., 7 December 1911.

53. See, for example, the Conservatives' electoral proclamation, PT, 7 December 1911, and ibid., 21 November 1911 and 4
December 1911; Reichstag deputy Schulz's speech, PNN, 4 November
1913.

54. Klitzing, quoted in PT, 20 January 1914. On the Reich-
level Hansabund and Bauernbund, cf. Fischer, Krieg der Illusionen,
pp. 56-58; Berghahn, Germany and the Approach of War, pp. 88ff.;
on these organizations' agitation in Poznania, see below, chap. 9.

55. Gossler's speech, PT, 17 June 1912. After 1908,
German conservatives throughout the Reich denounced ever more
anxiously die Demokratie, a term which covered the threat both
of socialism, democratization of the Prussian electoral law, and
the breakthrough of the principle of ministerial responsibility to
the Landtag and Reichstag majorities. See, for example, Landtag
deputy Hammer's speech, PT, 4 December 1911; Count Westarp's
speech, PNN, 4 November 1913; and the Saverne speeches, PT, 20
January 1914.

56. Speech reported in PT, 17 June 1912.

57. ". . . Wenn es seine Pflicht tut und wenn es einen

energischen zielbewussten Führer hat." Speech at the Bund der Landwirte's provincial assembly quoted in PNN, 16 January 1914.
    58. The occupations of the remaining 3 percent were unlisted. The Society's leaders calculated that by the end of 1906 over half the province's German officials and schoolteachers had joined its ranks. Dzieje Hakaty, p. 183.
    59. Ibid., p. 184.
    60. Die Ostmark, 1912, no. 12.
    61. Dzieje Hakaty, pp. 47ff.
    62. German scholars, and above all Puhle, have misunderstood the Poznanian Bund's relation to Prussian Polenpolitik. Endell did not pressure the Bund's national leaders to support radical anti-Polish measures, as Puhle maintains (Agrarische Interessen-politik, pp. 65, 257ff., 337). In particular, Endell strongly opposed the expropriation bill, as Kramski ("społeczeństwo niemieckie," pp. 205-9) and Pirko (Bülow a sprawa polska, pp. 388-401) have proven.
    63. Endell's letter to PT, 12 May 1912. The United Conserva-tives did not criticize Bethmann's expropriation action; indeed, they expressed some hope it would restrain Polish "radicalism." On the other hand, they had not demanded expropriation before 1912 and did not do so thereafter. See Reichstag Deputy Schulz's speech, PNN, 16 November 1912, and PT, 3 June 1913, 23 January 1914, 25 February 1914, and 23 March 1914.
    64. PT, 31 August 1913. Cf. also PT, 4 January 1912 and 11 July 1912.
    65. Ibid., 25 September 1913 and 17 December 1913.
    66. Speech of 29 November 1907, Landtag, HdA.
    67. On the "German Days" and the Bismarck and Sedan celebrations, PT, 4 April 1914; Tims, Germanizing Prussian Poland, chap. 9.
    68. In 1913, Poznania counted 106 OMV locals, the five eastern provinces altogether claimed 332. Dzieje Hakaty, p. 182.
    69. Quoted in Dzieje Hakaty, pp. 193-94.
    70. Quoted from Die Ostmark, 1908, no. 2, in Dzieje Hakaty, p. 194.
    71. Report of OMV leadership in West Prussia for 1912, quoted ibid., p. 194.
    72. Immanuel Geiss, Der polnische Grenzstreifen 1914-1918. Ein Beitrag zur deutschen Kriegszielpolitik im Ersten Weltkrieg (Lübeck, 1960); Conze, Polnische Nation und deutsche Politik, chap. 4ff., and "Nationalstaat und Mitteleuropa? Die Deutschen des Reichs und die Nationalitätenfragen Ostmitteleuropas im ersten Weltkrieg," in Conze, ed., Deutschland und Europa: Fest-schrift für Hans Rothfels (Düsseldorf, 1951), pp. 201-30; Dzieje Hakaty, pp. 312ff.; Tims, Germanizing Prussian Poland, chap. 11; Booms, Deutsch-Konservative Partei, pp. 120ff.; Martin Broszat, Nationalsozialistische Polenpolitik 1939-1945 (Stuttgart, 1961), passim.
    73. Hugenberg to Bernhard, Nachlass Hugenberg. No. 41, 3 October 1914. Earlier, on 21 August 1914, Hugenberg wrote worriedly to Bernhard that "legends" might arise honoring the Prussian Poles for having "loyally served" the German cause, at home as well as in the trenches. In fact, the Prussian Poles dutifully fought and died in large numbers, and revolted against German rule only after the monarchical order broke down in the revolution of 1918. Hugenberg feared that "legends" of Polish loyalty would impede future colonization and "proper peace terms" (i.e., annexations in the east). Ibid. No. 41, 21 August 1914.
    74. Dzieje Hakaty, pp. 319ff.
    75. Bernhard to Hugenberg, Nachlass Hugenberg. No. 41, 15 December 1914.
    76. The phrase is Schieder's. Cf. Das deutsche Kaiser-

reich von 1871 als Nationalstaat, p. 35. Jakóbczyk endorses it;
see Dzieje Hakaty, p. 307.

Chapter Nine
    1. The Reichstag elections of 1881 returned 115 Progressives,
47 National Liberals, 100 Catholic Centrists, and 12 Social Demo-
crats. Returns of 1893 and 1912 (1912 figures in parentheses):
Progressives--48 (42); NLP--53 (45); Center--96 (91); SPD--44
(110). On the Progressive movement, cf. Eyck, Das persönliche
Regiment, passim; Thomas Nipperdey, Die Organisation der deutschen
Parteien vor 1918 (Düsseldorf, 1961), pp. 176ff.; Friedrich Naumann,
Die politischen Parteien (Berlin, 1910); Ludwig Bergsträsser,
Geschichte der politischen Parteien in Deutschland (München, 1952),
pp. 92ff.; Dieter Grosser, Vom monarchischen Konstitutionalismus
zur parlamentarischen Demokratie (Den Haag, 1970), pp. 60ff.
    2. Votes cast for Progressive candidates increased between
the 1907 and 1912 elections from 1.234 to 1.497 million; National
Liberal and Socialist returns were 1.638/1.663 and 3.259/4.250
million, respectively.
    3. Landtag returns in Hemmerling, Posłowie polscy, p. 126.
    4. The confessional census of 1910 counted 615,000 Jews among
the 65 million citizens of the Reich. Figures cited in Peter G.
J. Pulzer, The Rise of Political Anti-Semitism in Germany and
Austria (New York, 1964), p. 9. Before 1914, Jewish identity was
most commonly understood, by Jews and Christians alike, in a
religious-cultural sense. Most Jews were actively faithful to
their religion. Very few abjured it through conversion to Christianity. Thus between 1889 and 1910 only 12,400 Jews joined
Protestant churches. Ibid., p. 6. Similarly, very few declared
themselves in the official censuses as atheists. In 1910, 99.8
percent of the Poznanian population claimed adherence to one or
another religion. Polish Encyclopedia: Territorial Development,
p. 438. In the following pages, only those individuals will be
identified as Jews who defined themselves as such, or who are
known to have participated actively in specifically Jewish religious or secular organizations.
    5. Toury, Die politischen Orientierungen der Juden in
Deutschland, pp. 245, 275.
    6. Max Kollenscher, Erinnerungen (unpublished manuscript,
Leo Baeck Institute, Jerusalem, n.d.), p. 15; cf. also Toury,
Orientierungen, pp. 202ff.
    7. Quotation from electoral proclamation of the Central
Committee of the FVP in PNN, 1 November 1911.
    8. On the Jews' relation to the Progressive Party, cf.
Toury, Orientierungen, pp. 138ff. Percentage of Jewish voters in
the Progressive electorate estimated assuming a total Jewish
electorate of 150,000 in 1912.
    9. Rzepecki, Ubytek żydów, Tables A and B. The rest of the
province's 26,500 Jews were settled in communities of fifty to
several hundred in the numerous small towns.
    10. PNN, 18 March 1913; Kramski, disseration, 180-82; elec-
tion returns in Rzepecki, Historya ustawy wyborczej pruskiej, pp.
vii, xxxii. From mid 1911 to August 1914, the PNN reported
eighteen public meetings of the Poznanian FVP.
    11. See the Zionist leader Max Kollenscher's statements to
this effect in the Progressive meeting reported in PNN, 19
October 1912.
    12. PNN, 8 and 18 March 1913; 9 April 1914.
    13. Gothein's speech, entitled Heer und Volk, was reprinted
in the PNN, 9 January 1914. Cf. also Posener Tageblatt [PT],
9 January 1914. Other denunciations of the "reactionary parties"
appear in the FVP electoral platform, PNN, 1 November 1911.
    14. See the local, Prussian, and Reich-level FVP programs
reported in PNN, 11 January 1912 and 8 October 1912; 22 January
1913, 5 April 1913, 8 June 1913, and 17 December 1913. In the

Landtag session of 1907/8, the Progressives sponsored a bill to
adopt the Reichstag electoral law in Prussia. It was, predictably,
voted down by the Conservatives and National Liberals. See the
debate in Landtag, HdA, 10 January 1908.

15. Quotation from Georg Wagner, Der Polenkoller: Skizze vom
"Kriegsschauplatz" in den Ostmarken (Leipzig, 1899), pp. 13-14.

16. PNN, 12 December 1912. This was also the view of the
eminent historian and publicist Hans Delbrück who, although not a
member of the Progressive Party, formulated a trenchant and
influential liberal critique of Prussian Polish policies to which
the Progressives frequently appealed. See Delbrück's Die Polenfrage (Berlin, 1894), pp. 41-42 and passim. Delbrück restated
his views in his lectures published in 1914 under the title
Regierung and Volkswille, translated as Government and the Will of
the People (New York, 1923).

17. PNN, 18 December 1912. Cf. also speech of FVP deputy
Hugo Kindler from the Poznań city district, Landtag, HdA, 29
November 1907.

18. Delbrück, Polenfrage, pp. 20ff., 38. On the Progressives' explanations of their part of the passage of the anti-
Polish paragraph of the 1908 Reich Associations Law, see chap.
5, above, and PNN, 18 December 1912.

19. Speech of Deputy Kindler, Landtag, HdA, 16 January
1908; Delbrück, Polenfrage, p. 20; PNN, 12 December 1912.

20. Speech of Deputy Wolff (Lissa), Landtag, HdA, 30
November 1907; Kindler's speeches of 29 November 1907, and 16
January 1908, ibid.; Wagner, Polenkoller, pp. 21-23; PNN, 21
September 1911, 11 January 1914; Delbrück, Polenfrage, pp. 6ff.

21. Wagner, Polenkoller, p. 17.

22. Ibid., pp. 14, 64.

23. Quotation from PNN, 10 April 1914. See also 29
September 1911 and 31 May 1914 for similar condemnations of the
Ostmarkenverein.

24. Kindler's speech of 16 January 1908.

25. Wagner, Polenkoller, p. 57.

26. Quotation from PNN, 31 May 1914. Cf. also ibid. 13
January 1914.

27. Quotation from Wagner, Polenkoller, p. 57. Cf. also
ibid., p. 41; Delbrück, Polenfrage, pp. 41ff.; and PNN, 13 June
1914.

28. Cf. table 6, chap. 6, above.

29. Breslauer, Die Auswanderung der Juden aus der Provinz
Posen, passim; Eyck, Das persönliche Regiment, p. 355.

30. Report of 24 December 1912. WAPP. Polizei-Präsidium,
syg. 2782, folio 51. Cf. also PNN, 10 December 1912, on boycott
losses.

31. On the Conservative-Progressive compromise, see PNN,
10 November 1911, 12 December 1912, and 14 February 1914; PT,
22 October 1911. Despite the collapse in 1909 of the Bülow bloc,
both parties to the compromise honored its terms through the
Landtag elections of 1913, since each received rewards in the
1912-13 elections for concessions made in 1907-8. Among the
Progressives, discomfiture with this alliance with the nationalist
camp was acute after 1909.

32. On political anti-Semitism in Imperial Germany, see
Pulzer, Anti-Semitism, passim; Toury, Orientierungen, pp. 170ff.;
Richard Lichtheim, Die Geschichte des deutschen Zionismus
(Jerusalem, 1954), chap. 4; Kampmann, Deutsche und Juden, chaps.
15-19.

33. Cf. Fritz Stern, The Politics of Cultural Despair, parts
1 and 2 and "Die politischen Folgen des unpolitischen Deutschen,"
in Stürmer, Das kaiserliche Deutschland, pp. 168-86; Kruck,
Alldeutscher Verband, pp. 59ff.; Hasse, Deutsche Politik, pp.
4ff., 50ff.

34. Cf. Puhle, Agrarische Interessenpolitik und preussischer

Konservatismus, 80ff., 116ff., 278ff.; Pulzer, Anti-Semitism, pp.
118ff.
    35. Geheimes Staatsarchiv. Berlin-Dahlem. Königlich
preussische Regierung zu Bromberg. Präsidial-Abteilung. Rep. 30,
no. 635. Police reports of anti-Semitic meetings in Schneidemühl
and Zarnikau of 19 and 22 December 1900, 23 March 1901, 27 March
1902. Letter of Jewish communal officials to the Bromberg
Regierungspräsident dated 30 January 1901.
    36. Ibid. Report of Berliner Tageblatt, 23 January 1901.
See Toury, Orientierungen, p. 209, on anti-Semitic electioneering in Poznania.
    37. Geheimes Staatsarchiv. Berlin-Dahlem. Rep. 30. No. 635.
Report of meeting of 22 December 1900.
    38. Westarp quoted in Toury, Orientierungen, p. 263.
Restriction of anti-Semitic meetings to small German towns in the
province's northern counties appears to reflect official appre-
hension of the inflammatory effect of such agitation in Poznań,
Bromberg, or the predominantly Polish districts. The HKT Society's
monthly journal systematically avoided any anti-Semitic tones.
    39. Schwartzkopff's conversation with Austrian Consul
Pitner reported in Pitner's letter of 28 January 1913 to Berchthold.
Staats-, Haus- und Hofarchiv. Politische Abteilung 3. Fasc.
181 (Preussen III). On Jewish protests against the Prussian
government's discriminatory employment practices, see PNN, 15 March
1912 and 22 April 1914; Kollenscher, Erinnerungen, p. 51; Heppner
and Herzberg, Aus Vergangenheit und Gegenwart, p. 865. The Jewish
birthrate in Germany fell below the German Christian or Polish
level. Zionist leaders complained of the Zweikindersystem
prevalent after the turn of the century. See Lichtheim, Zionismus,
p. 183. In the period 1896-1900, the average number of live
births per every 1,000 Poznanian inhabitants was 45.8 among
Catholics, 35.9 among Protestants, and 19.2 among Jews. Polish
Encyclopedia: General Demography, p. 259.
    40. PT, 2 March 1912.
    41. Puhle, Agrarische Interessenpolitik, pp. 129-33.
    42. Levetzow's speech reported in PNN, 18-19 December 1912.
See also Roesicke's speech reported in PT, 2 March 1912.
    43. On the CV, see Toury, Orientierungen, pp. 204ff. and
Parts E and F, passim.
    44. Kollenscher, Erinnerungen, pp. 71ff.; PNN, 15 March
1912 and 22 April 1914.
    45. Quotation from report on meeting of the Verein liberaler
Juden in PNN, 3 April 1914.
    46. Quotation from report on meeting of the Jüdisch-liberaler
Jugendverein, PNN, 11 November 1913. Poznanian Jewish religious
statistics, ibid., 18 February 1912.
    47. Quotation from Kollenscher, Erinnerungen, p. 17. See
also his Jüdisches aus der deutsch-polnischen Übergangszeit. Posen
1918-1920 (Berlin, 1925), p. 13. On Orthodox-liberal religious
controversies, see Toury Orientierungen, pp. 124ff., and PNN,
10 October 1911, 15 October 1912, 4 March 1913.
    48. PNN, 18 February 1912.
    49. Lichtheim, Zionismus, pp. 99ff. and passim. Reports on
proceedings of Reich Zionist Congress in Poznań, PNN, 26-31 May
1912.
    50. Lichtheim, Zionismus, pp. 15ff.
    51. Max Kollenscher, Jüdische Gemeindepolitik (Berlin, 1909),
p. 32.
    52. Handtke quoted in PNN, 31 May 1912. See also Lichtheim,
Zionismus, pp. 175ff.
    53. The following account, except where otherwise noted,
is based on Kollenscher's Erinnerungen, especially pp. 70ff.:
"Mein jüdischer und zionistischer Weg."
    54. Max Kollenscher, Zionismus und Staatsbürgertum (Berlin,
1904), p. 2.

55. Kollenscher, Jüdisches, p. 13.
56. Kollenscher, Zionismus und Staatsbürgertum, p. 2.
57. Ibid., pp. 4-5.
58. Kollenscher, Erinnerungen, p. 77.
59. Lichtheim, Zionismus, pp. 146, 166ff.
60. Kollenscher, Judische Gemeindepolitik, p. 24; Errinerungen, pp. 4ff., 19; PNN, 15 October 1911, 20 March 1912, 19 October 1912, 1 Janauary 1913, and 17 May 1914.
61. Kollenscher became the German Zionist Union's chief authority on Jewish communal politics. In all likelihood, he found his model for Jewish self-organization in the Polish system of electoral authorities and Organic Work institutions. One of his colleagues reported to Handtke in 1906 that the Poznanian Jews desperately needed to organize their interests "as the Protestants and Catholics have succeeded here in doing so impressively." Quoted in Toury, Orientierungen, p. 341. On local Zionist politics in Poznań, see Kollenscher, Erinnerungen, pp. 74-79. On long-range Zionist political policy, see Kollenscher, Jüdische Gemeindepolitik, pp. 8ff., 23, 31-32.
62. Handtke at Poznań Zionist Congress, PNN, 29 May 1912.
63. Report on Poznań communal elections, PNN, 9 January 1914. The city's Jewish voters were divided among seven districts. On liberal-Orthodox hostility to the Zionists in Poznania, see Toury, Orientierungen, Anhang B: letter of Carl Kassel to Arthur Handtke, Posen, 4 December 1906.
64. The first provincial Zionist conference, staged in 1906, passed a resolution declaring that "the Jews of the eastern marches are suffering greatly from the nationality conflict. They are seriously in danger of being crushed between Polish and German anti-Semitism!" Quoted in Vosberg, Die Stadt Gnesen, p. 152. A similar protest of 1912 emphasized the Poznanian Jews' Bodenständigkeit in the east. PNN, 6 November 1912. For Zionist condemnations of the Bund's anti-Semitism, see PNN, 26 February 1913 and 28 December 1913.
65. On the emergence of the NLP in Poznania, its local organizations, propaganda, and political activities, cf. Posener Zeitung, 7 and 26 April 1910; PNN, 24 January 1912, 19 March 1912, 16 April 1912, 5 June 1912, 20 November 1912 and 4 December 1912; 1 July 1913, and 29 November 1913; 14 January 1914 and 23 April 1914; Kramski, dissertation, pp. 174-75.
66. Ibid., pp. 170ff. Before 1914, the Ostmarkenverein's ties with the local National Liberals were oblique and without significance. Waldow must have realized, however, that a strong NLP in the east would inevitably attract the Hakatists to itself and reduce their dependence on the Conservatives and the Prussian administration.

Conclusion
1. Adolf Hitler, Mein Kampf (Boston, 1943), p. 388. See also pp. 3, 390ff., 652ff.
2. Martin Broszat, Nationalsozialistische Polenpolitik 1939-1945 (Stuttgart, 1961).
3. Vie économique, p. 36.
4. Statistisches Jahrbuch für den preussischen Staat (1913), p. 21.
5. The German Catholics in Poznania resented the Protestant bias of official Germanization policy. They denounced the Hakatists, paraded their loyalty to the Polish archdiocese, and voted for Polish or Catholic Centrist candidates in parliamentary elections. In the local nationality conflict they stood aloof. PT 21 January 1912; PNN, 24 January 1912; Kramski, Społeczeństwo niemieckie, pp. 197-200; Galos et al., Dzieje Hakaty, p. 75.

Appendix
     1. On Prussian population, confessional, and language statis-
tics and their interpretation, cf. Eugen von Bergmann, Zur
Geschichte der Entwicklung deutscher, polnischer und jüdischer
Bevölkerung in der Provinz Posen seit 1824 (Tübingen, 1883);
Polish Encyclopedia, vol. 2, no. 2, General Demography of Poland,
and vol. 2, no. 3, Territorial Development of the Polish Nation;
Leo Wegener, Der wirtschaftliche Kampf der Deutschen mit den Polen
um die Provinz Posen (Posen, 1903); Julian Marchlewski, Stosunki
społeczno-ekonomiczne w ziemiach polskich zaboru pruskiego (1903),
in Pisma wybrane, vol. 1 (Warszawa, 1952); Waldemar Mitscherlich,
Die Ausbreitung der Polen in Preussen (Berlin, 1909); Heinz Rogmann,
Die Bevölkerungsentwicklung im preussischen Osten in den letzten
hundert Jahren (Breslau, 1936); Jerzy Marczewki, Narodowa
Demokracja w Poznańskiem 1900-1914 (Warszawa, 1967), pp. 19ff.
     2. Bergmann, Entwicklung, pp. 35ff.; Wegener, Der wirt-
schaftliche Kampf, pp. 19ff.; Statistisches Jahrbuch für den
preussischen Staat (Berlin, 1913), p. 21.
     3. Fritz Zitzlaff, Die kleinen Städte, in Ludwig Bernhard,
ed., Preussische Städte im Gebiete des polnischen Nationalitäten-
kampfes (Leipzig, 1909), p. 12.

I. Archival Collections

   1. Wojewódzie Archiwum Państwowe w Poznaniu
   Provinz Posen. Polizeipräsidium: Police reports on the
   organization, activities and membership of the Polish
   nationalist movement and on the Poznanian nationality
   conflict in general 1900-17 (Syg. 2712-2713, 2726, 2744a,
   2748-2782, 4222, 4225, 4930, 5750, 6154, 8732).
   Provinz Posen. Landrat Posen-West: Reports and official
   correspondence of Landräte and District Commissioners on the
   Polish nationalist movement (polnische Agitation), on Polish
   land parcellation and acquisition, on the Prussian colonization program, and on local German politics 1901-18 (Syg. 162-
   163, 169, 200, 268, 271-272, 302).
   Provinz Posen. Landrat Posen-Ost: Reports on Polish nationalism and nationality statistics 1900-1913 (Syg. 142, 160).

   2. Biblioteka Raczyńskich (Poznań)
   Akta Prowincjonalnego Komitetu Wyborczego na Wielkie
   Księstwo Poznańskie: Papers and correspondence of the Polish
   electoral authorities on the internal affairs of the Polish
   nationalist movement 1890-1918 (Rkp. 786, 854, 894III, 924).

   3. Archiwum Archidecezjalne w Poznaniu
   Akta Konsystorza Jeneralnego Arcybiskupskiego Poznańskiego
   tyczące się małżeństw mieszanych 1889: Survey of interconfessional marriages in the Poznań Archbishopric during
   the 1880s.

   4. Geheimes Staatsarchiv. Berlin-Dahlem
   Königlich preussische Regierung zu Bromberg. Präsidial-
   Abteilung: Official papers and local reports on nationality
   statistics, the Polish nationalist movement, the Prussian
   colonization program, the boycott question, and anti-Semitic
   agitation in the Bromberg Regierungsbezirk, 1904-18 (Rep.
   30: no. 635, 637, 680 Bd. VI, 683, 688 Bd. I; Rep. 32b: no.
   138, 245).

   5. Bundesarchiv Koblenz
   Nachlass Hugenberg: Correspondence, notes, and official
   papers of Alfred Hugenberg on the German nationalist movement in Poznania, the Prussian colonization program, and the
   nationality policies of the Prussian government 1894-1918
   (No. 1, 9-10, 12, 28, 30, 41, 51, 54-55).
   Nachlass Wegener: Correspondence and private papers of Leo
   Wegener on Poznanian politics and official Polenpolitik
   1905-1912 (No. 47, 63-64).

   6. Oesterreichisches Staatsarchiv: Staats-, Haus- und
      Hofarchiv
   Politische Abeilung III. Faszikel 180-181: Preussen III:
   Preussische Polenpolitik. Enteignungsfrage. 1907, 1908-

1914, 1917-1918: Correspondence of Austrian diplomatic officials in Berlin and Vienna on the course of Prussian
Polenpolitik.

7. Leo Baeck Institute, Jerusalem
Max Kollenscher, Erinnerungen (microfilm, undated [ca. 1950]).

8. Deutsches Zentral-Archiv (Copies of the following documents are in the possession of Professor Witold Jakóbczyk,
Uniwersytet im. A. Mickiewicza, Poznań.)

DZA (Potsdam). Ministerium des Innern (Zentral-Büreau):
Oberpräsident Wilamowitz-Möllendorf's memorial on official
Polish policy, 23 November 1895 (Rep. 77, Tit. 871, no. 1,
Jahr 1896); Oberpräsident Bitter's memorial 4 January 1902
(Rep. 77, Tit. 871, no. 1, Jahr 1902).
DZA (Merseburg). Geheimes Zivilkabinet. Das Oberpräsidium
der Provinz Posen: Oberpräsident Waldow's memorial of 1 May
1909 (Rep. 89H II, Bd. II).

II. Published Documents

Bär, Max, ed. Westpreussen unter Friedrich dem Grossen. Vol. 2,
Quellen. Berlin, 1909.
Baske, Siegfried. Praxis und Prinzipien der preussischen Polen-
politik vom Beginn der Reaktionszeit bis zur Gründung des
Deutschen Reiches (Anhang). Berlin, 1963.
Bussenius, Ingeburg, ed. Urkunden und Akten zur Geschichte der
preussischen Verwaltung in Südpreussen und Neuostpreussen
1793-1806. Frankfurt am Main, 1961.
Flottwell, Eduard Heinrich. Denkschrift, die Verwaltung der
Provinz Posen vom Dezember 1830 bis zum Beginn des Jahres
1841 betreffend. Berlin, 1897.
Jakóbczyk, Witold, ed. Wielkopolska (1851-1914): wybór źródeł.
Poznań, 1954.
Laubert, Manfred. Die Verwaltung der Provinz Posen 1815-1847
(Anhang). Breslau, 1923.
Meinecke, Friedrich. "Drei Denkschriften Boyens über Polen und
Südpreussen aus den Jahren 1794 und 1795." Zeitschrift der
Historischen Gesellschaft für die Provinz Posen, vol. 8
(1893).
Prümers, Rodgero, ed. Das Jahr 1793. Urkunden und Aktenstücke zur
Geschichte der Organisation Südpreussens. Posen, 1895.
Schottmüller, Kurt. Der Polenaufstand 1806/7. Urkunden und
Aktenstücke aus der Zeit zwischen Jena und Tilsit. Lissa,
1907.
Stein, Heinrich Karl Friedrich. "Nassauer Denkschrift." In
Walter Hubatsch, ed. Freiherr vom Stein. Briefe und
amtliche Schriften, vol. 2, part 1. Stuttgart, 1959.

III. Parliamentary Records

Deutsches Reich. Stenographische Berichte über die Verhandlungen des
Reichstags: 1885-86, 1907-8, 1913.
Preussen. Landtag. Stenographische Berichte über die Verhand-
lungen des Hauses der Abgeordneten: 1861-63, 1871-74, 1885-86,
1907-8.
Preussen. Landtag. Stenographische Berichte über die Verhand-
lungen des Herrenhauses: 1871-72, 1885-86, 1907-8.
Stenographische Berichte über die Verhandlungen des Reichstages
des Norddeutschen Bundes im Jahre 1867.
Stenographischer Bericht über die Verhandlungen der deutschen
constituierenden Nationalversammlung zu Frankfurt am Main.
Frankfurt am Main, 1848-50.
Żychliński, Ludwik. Historya Sejmów Wielk. Ks. Poznańskiego do
roku 1847. Vols. 1 and 2. Poznań, 1867.

IV. Printed Statistics

Broesicke, Max. "Deutsche und Polen der Provinz Posen im Lichte
     der Statistik." Zeitschriften des Königlich Preussischen
     Statistischen Landesamts, vol. 25 (1912).
Handbuch der Provinz Posen, Nachweisung der Behörden, Anstalten,
     Institute und Vereine. Posen, 1909.
Jahrbuch für die amtliche Statistik des preussischen Staates.
     Vol. 1. Berlin, 1863.
Krug, Leopold. Betrachtungen über den National-Reichthum des
     preussischen Staats und über den Wohlstand seiner Bewohner.
     Vol. 1. Berlin, 1805.
Preussische Statistik. Vol. 76 (1885), Dritter Theil: Die Ergeb-
     nisse der Berufszählung vom. 5. Juni 1882 im preussischen
     Staate: Landwirtschaftsbetriebe sowie Hauptberuf und
     Religionsbekenntnis der Bevölkerung.
Statistik des Deutschen Reichs. Vol. 204 (1909): Die Bevölkerung
     Preussens nach Haupt- und Nebenberuf (Provinzen). Vol. 206
     (1910): Berufs- und Betriebszählung vom 12. Juni 1907.
     Die Bevölkerung der Bundesstaaten nach Alter, Familienstand
     und Religionsbekenntnis. Vol. 208 (1910): Berufsstatistik:
     Gemeinden mit weniger als 2000 Einwohnern.
Statistische Monatsberichte der Stadt Posen. Vol. 1 (1906) and
     vol. 7 (1912).
Statistisches Handbuch für den preussischen Staat. Berlin, 1913.
Tabellen und amtliche Nachrichten über den preussischen Staat für
     das Jahr 1849. 6 vols. Berlin, 1851-55.

V. Newspapers and Periodicals

     Die Ostmark: 1894-1914
     Dziennik Poznański: 1859, 1908, 1911-14.
     Gazeta Robotnicza: 1912.
     Kuryer Poznański: 1908, 1911-14.
     Orędownik: 1913-14.
     Ostland-Jahrbuch für ostdeutsche Interessen: 1912-13.
     Poradnik Gospodarski: 1914.
     Posener Neueste Nachrichten: 1911-14.
     Posener Tageblatt: 1911-14.
     Posener Zeitung: 1910.
     Postęp: 1890, 1908, 1912.
     Provinzial-Blätter für das Grossherzogtum Posen. Vol. 1 (1846).
     Przegląd wielkopolski: 1912-13.
     Przewodnik Katolicki: 1908, 1912.
     Robotnik: 1908, 1912.
     Ziemianin: 1913.

VI. Memoirs and Political Writings

Balicki, Zygmunt. Egoizm narodowy wobec etyki. Lwów, 1914.
Bernhard, Ludwig, ed. Preussische Städte im Gebiete des polnis-
     chen Nationalitätenkampfes. Leipzig, 1909.
Bernhard, Ludwig. Die Polenfrage: das polnische Gemeinwesen im
     preussischen Staat. Leipzig, 1910.
Bismarck, Otto Fürst von. Gedanken und Erinnerungen. Vols. 1-3.
     Stuttgart, 1898-1919.
Breslauer, Bernhard. Die Auswanderung der Juden aus der Provinz
     Posen. Berlin, 1909.
Bülow, Bernhard Fürst von. Denkwürdigkeiten. Vol. 1. Berlin,
     1930.
Delbrück, Hans. Government and the Will of the People. New York,
     1923.
_____. Die Polenfrage. Berlin, 1894.
Deutscher Ostmarkenverein. Die deutsche Ostmark. Lissa, 1913.
Dmowski, Roman. Myśli nowoczesnego polaka. Lwów, 1907.
_____. Niemcy, Rosya i kwestya polska. Lwów, 1908.

Frederick II. "La guerre des Confédérés. Pöeme." Oeuvres de
    Frédéric le Grand, vol. 14. Berlin, 1850.
Goethe, Johann Wolfgang von. "Vorschlag zur Einführung der
    deutschen Sprache in Polen. Um eine höhere Cultur der
    niederen Classen zu bewirken." Goethe-Jahrbuch, 13 (1892).
Hasse, Ernst. Deutsche Politik. Vol. 1. München, 1907.
Herder, Johann Gottfried. Ideen zur Philosophie der Geschichten
    der Menschheit. Sämtliche Werke, vol. 14. Berlin, 1909.
Herzberg, Friedrich. Süd-Preussen und Neu-Ost-Preussen. Berlin,
    1798.
Hitler, Adolf. Mein Kampf. Boston, 1943.
Hozakowski, W. O katolickie podstawy narodowej democracyi.
    Poznań, 1913.
Hutten-Czapski, Graf Bogdan von. Sechzig Jahre Politik und
    Gesellschaft. Vol. 2. Berlin, 1936.
Kant, Immanuel. "Eternal Peace." In Carl J. Friedrich, ed.,
    The Philosophy of Kant. New York, 1949.
Kłos, Józef. 25 lat przy stoliku redaktorskim. Poznań, 1936.
Kollenscher, Max. Jüdische Gemeindepolitik. Berlin, 1909.
_____. Jüdisches aus der deutsch-polnischen Übergangszeit. Posen
    1918-1920. Berlin, 1925.
_____. Zionismus und Staatsbürgertum. Berlin, 1906.
Książka jubileuszowa Dziennika Poznańskiego 1858-1909. Poznań,
    1909.
Kujawiński, F. [Ignacy Geppert] Stronnictwo Demokratyczno-
    Narodowe w świetle nauki katolickiej. Poznań, 1913.
Marchlewski, Julian. Stosunki społeczno-ekonomiczne w ziemiach
    polskich zaboru pruskiego, in Pisma wybrane. Warszawa,
    1952.
_____. Zur Polenpolitik der preussischen Regierung: Auswahl von
    Artikeln aus den Jahren 1897 bis 1923. Berlin, 1958.
Mitscherlich, Waldemar. Die Ausbreitung der Polen in Preussen.
    Berlin, 1909.
_____. Der Einfluss der wirtschaftlichen Entwicklung auf den
    ostmärkischen Nationalitätenkampf. Berlin, 1910.
Münsterberg, Otto. Die wirtschaftlichen Verhältnisse des Ostens.
    Berlin, 1912.
Naumann, Friedrich. Die politischen Parteien. Berlin, 1910.
Program Polskiego Towarzystwa Demokratycznego. Poznań, 1909.
Puttkamer, Karl. Die Misserfolge in der Polenpolitik. Berlin,
    1913.
Rzepecki, Karol. Historya ustawy wyborczej pruskiej oraz wyniki
    wyborów do sejmu pruskiego z 1903 i 1908 r. na ziemiach
    polskich. Poznań, 1913.
_____. Naprzod czy wstecz? Poznań, 1912.
_____. Ubytek żydów w księstwie poznańskiem. Poznań, 1912.
Seyda, Marian. Inkwizycja. Poznań, 1913.
_____. Wyrok. Poznań, 1913.
Skorupka, Tomasz. Kto przy Obrze, temu dobrze. Poznań, 1967.
Treitschke, Heinrich von. Politics. New York, 1963.
Trzciński, Juljusz. Kwestya robotników rolnych. Poznań, 1907.
Wagner, Georg. Der Polenkoller: Skizze vom "Kriegsschauplatz"
    in den Ostmarken. Leipzig, 1899.
Wegener, Leo. Der wirtschaftliche Kampf der Deutschen mit den
    Polen um die Provinz Posen. Posen, 1903.
Wojciechowski, Jakób. Życiorys własny robotnika. Poznań, 1930.

VII. Scholarly Works on Prussian Poland,
German-Polish-Jewish Relations, and Prussian Polenpolitik

Arnold, Robert. Geschichte der deutschen Polenlitteratur von den
    Anfängen bis 1800. Vienna, 1900.
Barraclough, Geoffrey, ed. Eastern and Western Europe in the
    Middle Ages. London, 1970.
Bartyś, Julian. "Grand Duchy of Poznań under Prussian Rule--
    Changes in the Economic Position of the Jewish Population
    1815-1848." Leo Baeck Institute Yearbook 16 (1972).

Baske, Siegfried. Praxis und Prinzipien der preussischen Polen-
    politik vom Beginn der Reaktionszeit bis zur Gründung des
    Deutschen Reiches. Berlin, 1963.
Bergmann, Eugen von. Zur Geschichte der Entwicklung deutscher,
    polnischer und jüdischer Bevölkerung in der Provinz Posen
    seit 1824. Tübingen, 1883.
Blanke, Richard. "Bismarck and the Prussian Polish Policies of
    1886." Journal of Modern History 45 (1973), no. 2.
_____. "The Development of Loyalism in Prussian Poland 1886-
    1890." The Slavonic and East European Review 52 (1974).
Blejwas, Stanislaus A. "The Origins and Practice of 'Organic Work'
    in Poland: 1795-1863." The Polish Review 14 (1970), no. 4.
Böhning, Peter. "Westpreussisches Polentum und polnische Nation."
    Zeitschrift für Ostforschung 20 (1971), no. 1.
Borowski, Stanisław. Rozwarstwienia wsi wielkopolskiej w latach
    1807-1914. Poznań, 1962.
Brackmann, Albert, ed. Deutschland und Polen, Beiträge zu ihren
    geschichtlichen Beziehungen. Munich, 1933.
Breslauer, Walter. "Jews of the City of Posen One Hundred Years
    Ago." Leo Baeck Institute Yearbook 7 (1963).
Breyer, Richard. "Die südpreussischen Beamten und die Polenfrage."
    Zeitschrift für Ostforschung 4 (1955), no. 4.
Broszat, Martin. Nationalsozialistische Polenpolitik 1939-1945.
    Stuttgart, 1961.
_____. Zweihundert Jahre deutsche Polenpolitik. Munich, 1963.
Bussenius, Ingeburg. Die preussische Verwaltung in Süd- und
    Neuostpreussen 1793-1806. Heidelberg, 1960.
Buzek, Józef. Historya polityki narodowościowej rządu pruskiego
    wobec polaków. Od traktatów wiedeńskich do ustaw wyjątkowych
    z r. 1908. Lwów, 1909.
Chełmikowski, Michał. Związki zawodowe robotników polskich w
    Królestwie Pruskim 1889-1918. Poznań, 1925.
Cieślak, Tadeusz. "'Gazeta Grudziądzka' (1894-1918), fenomen
    wydawniczy." Studia i materiały do dziejów Wielkopolski i
    Pomorza 3 (1957), no. 2.
Conze, Werner. "Nationalstaat oder Mitteleuropa? Die Deutschen
    des Reichs und die Nationalitätenfragen Ostmitteleuropas im
    ersten Weltkrieg." In Werner Conze, ed. Deutschland und
    Europa. Düsseldorf, 1951.
_____. Polnische Nation und deutsche Politik im ersten Weltkrieg.
    Köln, 1958.
Dabinnus, Georg. Die ländliche Bevölkerung Pomerellens im Jahre
    1772 mit Einschluss des Danziger Gebiets im Jahre 1793.
    Marburg, 1953.
Danilczuk, Bolesław. Działalność SPD i PPS zaboru pruskiego w
    Poznańskiem w latach 1891-1914. Toruń, 1961.
"Der Wucher auf dem platten Lande in der Provinz Posen."
    Schriften des Vereins für Sozialpolitik, no. 35. Der Wucher
    auf dem Lande. Leipzig, 1887.
Encylopédie Polonaise. Vie économique de la Pologne prussienne.
    Fribourg, 1917.
Feldman, Józef. Bismarck a Polska. Kraków, 1947.
_____. Das deutsch-polnische Problem in der Geschichte.
    Marburg, 1961.
Feldman, Wilhelm. Geschichte der politischen Ideen in Polen seit
    dessen Teilungen 1795-1914. Munich, 1917.
Filipiak, Tadeusz. Dzieje związków zawodowych w Wielkopolsce
    do roku 1914. Poznań, 1965.
Galos, Adam; Gentzen, Felix-Heinrich; and Jakóbczyk, Witold.
    Dzieje Hakaty. Poznań, 1966.
Geiss, Immanuel. Der polnische Grenzstreifen 1914-1918. Ein
    Beitrag zur deutschen Kriegszielpolitik im ersten Weltkrieg.
    Lübeck, 1960.
Gentzen, Felix-Heinrich. Grosspolen im Januaraufstand. Das
    Grossherzogtum Posen 1858-1864. Berlin, 1958.

Goettingen Research Committee. Eastern Germany. Vol. 1, History.
    Wuerzburg, 1963.
Gomolec, Ludwik. "Strajki szkolne w Poznańskiem w latach 1901-
    1907." Studia i materiały do dziejów Wielkopolski i
    Pomorza 3 (1957), no. 1.
Grot, Zdzisław, ed. Polityczna działalność rzemiosła wielkopolskiego
    w okresie zaborów (1793-1918). Poznań, 1963.
_____. Wydarzenia wrzesińskie w roku 1901. Poznań, 1964.
Hagen, William W. "The Impact of Economic Modernization on
    Traditional Nationality Relations in Prussian Poland 1815-
    1914." Journal of Social History (Spring, 1973).
_____. "National Solidarity and Organic Work in Prussian Poland,
    1815-1914." Journal of Modern History, 44 (1972), no. 1.
_____. "The Partitions of Poland and the Crisis of the Old
    Regime in Prussia 1772-1806." Central European History
    9 (1977), no. 2.
Halecki, Oskar Ritter von. Das Nationalitätenproblem im alten
    Polen. Krakau, 1916.
Hallgarten, Georg. F. W. Studien über die deutsche Polenfreund-
    schaft in der Periode der Märzrevolution. Munich, 1928.
Hemmerling, Zygmunt. Posłowie polscy w parlamencie rzeszy
    niemieckiej i sejmie pruskim 1907-1914. Warsaw, 1968.
Heppner, A., and Herzberg, J. Aus Vergangenheit und Gegenwart der
    Juden und der jüdischen Gemeinden in den Posener Landen.
    Koschmin-Bromberg, 1909.
Jablonski, Horst. Die preussische Polenpolitik von 1815 bis 1914.
    Würzburg, n.d.
Jaffé, Moritz. Die Stadt Posen unter preussischer Herrschaft.
    Ein Beitrag zur Geschichte des deutschen Ostens. Leipzig,
    1909.
Jakóbczyk, Witold. "The First Decade of the Prussian Settlement
    Commission's Activities, 1886-1897." The Polish Review 17
    (1972), no. 1.
_____. Pruska komisja osadnicza 1886-1919. Poznań, 1976.
_____. Studia nad dziejami Wielkopolski w XIX wieku. Vols. 1-3.
    Poznań, 1951-67.
Jakóbczyk, Witold, ed. Dzieje Wielkopolski. Vol. 2. Lata 1793-
    1918. Poznań, 1969.
_____. Wielkopolanie XIX wieku. Vol. 2. Poznań, 1969.
Kampmann, Wanda. Deutsche und Juden. Studien zur Geschichte des
    deutschen Judentums. Heidelberg, 1963.
Kaplan, H. H. The First Partition of Poland. New York, 1962.
Karwowski, Stanisław. Historya Wielkiego Księstwa Poznańskiego.
    Vol. 3. Poznań, 1931.
Kieniewicz, Stefan. The Emancipation of the Polish Peasantry.
    Chicago, 1969.
_____. Społeczeństwo polskie w powstaniu poznańskim 1848 roku.
    Warsaw, 1960.
Klessmann, Christoph. Polnische Bergarbeiter im Ruhrgebiet 1870-
    1945. Göttingen, 1978.
Kocój, Henry K. Niemcy a powstanie listopadowe. Warsaw, 1970.
Kohte, Wolfgang. Deutsche Bewegung und preussische Politik im
    Posener Lande 1848-1849. Posen, 1931.
Kolberg, Oskar. Lud. Ser. 9, W. Ks. Poznańskie. Vols. 1-3.
    Kraków, 1875-77.
Konopczyński, Władysław. Fryderyk Wielki a Polska. Poznań, 1947.
Korth, Rudolf. Die preussische Schulpolitik und die polnischen
    Schulstreiks. Ein Beitrag zur preussischen Polenpolitik
    der Ära Bülow. Würzburg, 1963.
Kozłowski, Jerzy. Niemcy w Poznańskiem wobec Wiosny Ludów (1848-
    1850). Ph.D. dissertation, Uniwersytet im. A. Mickiewicza,
    Poznań, 1972.
Kramski, Aleksander. Społeczeństwo niemieckie w Poznańskiem 1903-
    1911. Ph.D. dissertation, Uniwersytet im. A. Mickiewicza,
    Poznań, 1969.

Krasuski, Jerzy, and Topolski, Jerzy. Stosunki polsko-niemieckie
    w historiografii. Poznań, 1974.
Kulczycki, John. Polish Society in Poznania and the School Strikes
    of 1901-1907. Ph.D. dissertation, Columbia University, 1973.
Labuda, Gerard, ed. Wschodnia ekspansja Niemiec w Europie środkowej:
    zbiór studiów nad tzw. niemieckim "Drang nach Osten."
    Poznań, 1963.
Laubert, Manfred. Die preussische Polenpolitik von 1772-1914.
    Berlin, 1920.
_____. Die Verwaltung der Provinz Posen 1815-1847. Breslau, 1923.
Lehmann, Max. "Preussen und Polen." Historische Aufsatze und
    Reden. Leipzig, 1911.
Lewin, Louis. Die Landessynode der grosspolnischen Judenschaft.
    Frankfurt am Main, 1926.
Lord, Robert H. The Second Partition of Poland. Cambridge, Mass.,
    1915.
Lück, Kurt. Der Mythos vom Deutschen in der polnischen Volksüber-
    lieferung und Literatur. Poznań, 1938.
Łuczak, Czesław. Położenie ekonomiczne rzemiosła wielkopolskiego
    w okresie zaborów. Poznań, 1962.
_____. Przemysł wielkopolski w latach 1871-1914. Poznań, 1960.
_____. Życie gospodarczo-społeczne w Poznaniu 1815-1918.
    Poznań, 1965.
Mahler, Raphael. "Anti-semitism in Poland." In Koppel S. Pinson,
    ed. Essays on Anti-semitism. New York, 1946.
Mai, Joachim. Die preussisch-deutsche Polenpolitik 1885-1887.
    Eine Studie zur Herausbildung des Imperialismus in Deutschland.
    Berlin, 1962.
Marczewski, Jerzy. Narodowa Demokracja w Poznańskiem 1900-1914.
    Warsaw, 1967.
Moritz, Erhard. Preussen und der Kościuszko-Aufstand 1794. Zur
    preussischen Polenpolitik in der Zeit der Französischen
    Revolution. Berlin, 1968.
Namier, Louis. 1848: The Revolution of the Intellectuals. New
    York, 1964.
Neubach, Helmut. Die Ausweisungen von Polen und Juden aus Preussen
    1885/86. Wiesbaden, 1967.
Neveux, Jean-B. "Une province polonaise de l'État des Hohenzollern:
    la Wielkopolska et Poznań (1815-1840)." Revue Historique
    130 (1963).
Nowacki, Józef. Archidiecezja poznańska w granicach historycznych
    i jej ustrój. Vol. 2. Poznań, 1964.
Paprocki, Franciszek. Wielkie Księstwo Poznańskie w okresie
    rządów Flotwella (1830-1841). Poznań, 1970.
Peiser, G. "Über Friedrichs des Grossen burleskes Heldengedicht
    'La guerre des Confédérés,'" Zeitschrift der Historischen
    Gesellschaft für die Provinz Posen 18 (1903).
Perles, J. "Geschichte der Juden in Posen." Monatsschrift für
    Geschichte und Wissenschaft des Judenthums 12-13 (1862-63).
Pirko, Michał. Bülow a sprawa polska. Warsaw, 1963.
_____. Niemiecka polityka wywłaszczeniowa na ziemiach polskich w
    latach 1907-1908. Warsaw, 1963.
Polish Encyclopedia. Vol. 2, no. 2. General Demography of Poland.
    Vol. 2, no. 3. Territorial Development of the Polish Nation.
    Geneva, 1921.
Pulzer, Peter G. J. The Rise of Political Anti-Semitism in Germany
    and Austria. New York, 1964.
Ravens, Jürgen-Peter. Staat und katholische Kirche in Preussens
    polnischen Teilungsgebieten (1772-1807). Wiesbaden, 1963.
Rhode, Arthur. Geschichte der evangelischen Kirche im Posener
    Lande. Würzburg, 1956.
Rhode, Gotthold. "Das Bild des Deutschen im polnischen Roman des
    19. und beginnenden 20. Jahrhunderts und das polnische
    Nationalgefühl." Ostdeutsche Wissenschaft 7 (1961).

Rhode, Gotthold, ed. Geschichte der Stadt Posen. Neuendettelsau, 1953.
Rhode, Ilse. Das Nationalitätenverhältnis in Westpreussen und Posen zur Zeit der polnischen Teilungen. Poznań, 1926.
Rogmann, Heinz. Die Bevölkerungsentwicklung im preussischen Osten in den letzten hundert Jahren. Breslau, 1936.
Röhl, J. C. G. "A Document of 1892 on Germany, Prussia and Poland." The Historical Journal 7 (1964), no. 1.
Rosenthal, Harry K. "Rivalry between 'Notables' and 'Towns-people' in Prussian Poland: The First Round." The Slavonic and East European Review 49 (1971).
_____. "The Election of Archbishop Stablewski." The Slavic Review 27 (1969), no. 2.
_____. "The Problem of Caprivi's Polish Policy." European Studies Review 2 (1972), no. 3.
_____. German and Pole: National Conflict and Modern Myth. Gainesville, Fla., 1976.
Rothfels, Hans. Bismarck, der Osten und das Reich. Darmstadt, 1960.
Rusiński, Władysław. "The Role of the Peasantry of Poznań (Wielkopolska) in the Formation of the Non-Agricultural Labor Market." East European Quarterly 3 (1967), no. 4.
Rusiński, Władysław, ed. Dzieje wsi wielkopolskiej. Poznań, 1959.
Schiper, Ignacy, ed. Żydzi w Polsce odrodzonej. Warsaw, n.d.
Schmidt, Erich. Geschichte des Deutschtums im Lande Posen unter polnischer Herrschaft. Bromberg, 1904.
Schmidt, Hans. Die polnische Revolution des Jahres 1848 im Grossherzogtum Posen. Weimar, 1912.
Schumacher, Bruno. Geschichte Ost- und Westpreussens. Würzburg, 1959.
Staszewski, Józef. "Rola kleru katolickiego w ruchu robotniczym na terenie Wielkopolski i Pomorza (1891-1914)." Zeszyty Naukowe, Toruń, 1957.
Tims, R. W. Germanizing Prussian Poland: The H-K-T Society and the Struggle for the Eastern Marches in the German Empire 1894-1919. New York, 1941.
Topolski, Jerzy, ed. Dzieje Wielkopolski. Vol. 1. Do roku 1793. Poznań, 1969.
Trzeciakowski, Lech. Kulturkampf w zaborze pruskim. Poznań, 1970.
_____. Polityka klas posiadających w Wielkopolsce w erze Capriviego (1890-1894). Poznań, 1960.
_____. "The Prussian State and the Catholic Church in Prussian Poland 1871-1914." The Slavic Review 26 (1967), no. 4.
_____. Walka o polskość miast poznańskiego na przełomie xix i xx wieku. Poznań, 1964.
Vahle, Hermann. "Die polnische Verfassung vom 3 Mai 1791 im zeitgenössischen deutschen Urteil." Jahrbücher für Geschichte Osteuropas 19 (1971).
Wąsicki, Jan. Ziemie polskie pod zaborem pruskim. Prusy nowowschodnie (Neuostpreussen) 1795-1806. Poznań, 1963.
_____. Ziemie polskie pod zaborem pruskim. Prusy południowe 1793-1806. Studium historycznoprawne. Wrocław, 1963.
Webster, C. K. "England and the Polish-Saxon Problem at the Congress of Vienna." Transactions of the Royal Historical Society, 3d ser. vol. 7 (1913).
Wehler, Hans-Ulrich. "Von den 'Reichsfeinden' zur 'Reichskristall-nacht': Polenpolitik im Deutschen Kaiserreich 1871-1918." Hans-Ulrich Wehler, Krisenherde des Kaiserreichs 1871-1918. Göttingen, 1970.
_____. Sozialdemokratie und Nationalstaat. Göttingen, 1971.
Will, Arno. Polska i Polacy w niemieckiej prozie literackiej XIX wieku. Łódź, 1970.
Wydanie jubileuszowe Związku Robotniczo-Rzemieślnego Z.Z.P. w Poznaniu 1902-1927. Poznań, 1927.

VIII. Scholarly Works on German, Polish, and Jewish History

Anderson, Eugene. The Social and Political Conflict in Prussia
    1858-1864. Lincoln, Nebr., 1954.
Anderson, Perry. Lineages of the Absolutist State. London,
    1974.
_____. Passages from Antiquity to Feudalism. London, 1974.
Berghahn, Volker. Germany and the Approach of War in 1914.
    London, 1973.
_____. "Der Bericht der Preussischen Oberrechnungskammer.
    'Wehlers' Kaiserreich und seine Kritiker." Geschichte und
    Gesellschaft 2 (1976), no. 1.
Bergsträsser, Ludwig. Geschichte der politischen Parteien in
    Deutschland. Munich, 1952.
Blackbourn, David. "The Mittelstand in German Society and
    Politics 1871-1914." Social History 4 (Jan. 1977).
Blum, Jerome. "The Rise of Serfdom in Eastern Europe." The
    American Historical Review 42 (1957), no. 4.
Booms, Hans. Die Deutsch-Konservative Partei. Düsseldorf, 1954.
Bracher, Karl D. The German Dictatorship. New York, 1970.
Brock, Peter. "Polish Nationalism." In P. F. Sugar and I. J.
    Lederer, eds., Nationalism in Eastern Europe. Seattle,
    Wash., 1969.
Brunschwig, Henri. La crise de l'état prussien et la génèse de la
    mentalité romantique. Paris, 1947.
Carsten, Francis L. The Origins of Prussia. Oxford, 1954.
Clapham, John H. The Economic Development of France and Germany
    1815-1914. Cambridge, 1961.
Craig, Gordon A. The Politics of the Prussian Army. London,
    1955.
Cynarski, Stanisław. "The Shape of Sarmatian Ideology in Poland."
    Acta Poloniae Historica 19 (1968).
Dahrendorf, Rolf. Society and Democracy in Germany. New York,
    1967.
Dehio, Ludwig. The Precarious Balance. New York, 1965.
Dorn, Walter. "The Prussian Bureaucracy in the 18th Century."
    Political Science Quarterly 46 (1931), no. 4; 47 (1932),
    no. 1, 3.
Droz, Jacques. Les révolutions allemandes de 1848. Paris, 1957.
Eley, Geoff. "Defining social imperialism: Use and Abuse of an
    Idea." Social History, vol. 3 (Oct., 1976).
Engels, Friedrich. Germany: Revolution and Counter-Revolution.
    Chicago, 1967.
Ergang, R. R. Herder and the Foundations of German Nationalism.
    New York, 1931.
Eyck, Erich. Bismarck and the German Empire. London, 1958.
_____. Das persönliche Regiment Wilhelms II. Politische
    Geschichte des deutschen Kaiserreiches von 1890 bis 1914.
    Zürich, 1948.
Finckelstein, Louis, ed. The Jews: Their History. New York, 1970.
Fischer, Fritz. Griff nach der Weltmach. Die Kriegszielpolitik
    des kaiserlichen Deutschlands 1914/1918. Düsseldorf, 1964.
_____. Krieg der Illusionen. Die deutsche Politik von 1911 bis
    1914. Düsseldorf, 1969.
Gerschenkron, Alexander. Bread and Democracy in Germany. Berkeley, 1943.
Gieysztor, Aleksander, ed. Polska dzielnicowa i zjednoczona. Warsaw, 1972.
Gillis, John. "Aristocracy and Bureaucracy in Nineteenth-
    Century Prussia." Past and Present 41 (1968).
Görlitz, Walter. Die Junker: Adel und Bauer im deutschen Osten.
    Glücksburg, 1957.
Gollwitzer, Heinz. Europe in the Age of Imperialism, 1880-1914.
    New York, 1969.
Grosser, Dieter. Vom monarchischen Konstitutionalismus zur
    parlamentarischen Demokratie. Den Haag, 1970.
Hamerow, Theodore S. Restoration, Revolution, Reaction: Economics
    and Politics in Germany 1815-1871. Princeton, 1958.

Hamerow, Theodore S. The Social Foundations of German Unification
    1858-1871. 2 vols. Princeton, 1969-72.
Hartung, Fritz. "Der aufgeklärte Absolutismus." Historische
    Zeitschrift 190 (1955).
_____ . Deutsche Verfassungsgeschichte vom 15. Jahrhundert bis
    zur Gegenwart. Stuttgart, 1950.
Heffter, Heinrich. Die deutsche Selbstverwaltung im neunzehnten
    Jahrhundert. Stuttgart, 1950.
Henderson, W. O. Studies in the Economic Policy of Frederick the
    Great. London, 1963.
Herweg, Holger H. The German Naval Officer Corps: A Social and
    Political History 1890-1918. Oxford, 1973.
Hintze, Otto. Die Hohenzollern und Ihr Werk. Berlin, 1916.
_____ . "Der österreichische und der preussische Beamtenstaat im
    17. und 18. Jahrhundert." Historische Zeitschrift 86 (1901).
_____ . "Preussens Entwicklung zum Rechsstaat." Forschungen zur
    brandenburgischen und preussischen Geschichte 32 (1920).
_____ . "Preussische Reformbestrebungen vor 1806." In Otto
    Hintze, Regierung und Verwaltung. Göttingen, 1967.
Hubatsch, Walter. "Der preussische Staat. Hauptprobleme seiner
    Entwicklung vom 16. bis zum beginnenden 19. Jahrhundert."
    Jahrbuch der Albertus-Universität zu Königsberg 12 (1962).
Kieniewicz, Stefan. Historia Polski 1795-1918. Warsaw, 1968.
_____ . "Le développement de la conscience nationale polonaise
    au XIXe siècle." Acta Poloniae Historica 19 (1968).
Kieniewicz, Stefan, and Kula, Witold, eds. Historia Polski. Vols.
    1-2. Warsaw, 1958-62.
Kieniewicz, Stefan et al. History of Poland. Warsaw, 1968.
Konopczyński, Władysław. Dzieje Polski nowożytnej. Vol. 1.
    London, 1958.
Koselleck, Reinhardt. Preussen zwischen Reform und Revolution.
    Allgemeines Landrecht, Verwaltung und soziale Bewegung von
    1791 bis 1848. Stuttgart, 1967.
Koser, Reinhold. Geschichte Friedrichs des Grossen. 4 vols.
    Stuttgart, 1925.
_____ . "Die preussische Politik von 1786 bis 1806." Deutsche
    Monatsschrift fur das gesamte Leben der Gegenwart 11 (1906-7).
Krieger, Leonard. The German Idea of Freedom. Chicago, 1957.
Kruck, Alfred. Geschichte des Alldeutschen Verbandes 1890-1939.
    Wiesbaden, 1954.
Krüger, Horst. Zur Geschichte der Manufakturen und der
    Manufakturarbeiter in Preussen. Die mittleren Provinzen in
    der zweiten Hälfte des 18. Jahrhunderts. Berlin, 1958.
Kukiel, Marian. Czartoryski and European Unity 1770-1861.
    Princeton, 1955.
Kula, Witold. Théorie économique du système féodal. Pour un
    modèle de l'économie polonaise 16e-18e siècles. Paris, 1970.
Lebovics, Herman. Social Conservatism and the German Middle
    Classes 1914-1933. Princeton, 1969.
Leskiewicz, Janina. "Les entraves sociales au développement de la
    'nouvelle agriculture' en Pologne." Second International
    Conference of Economic History, vol. 2. Paris, 1965.
Leslie, R. F. Polish Politics and the Revolution of November,
    1830. London, 1956.
_____ . Reform and Insurrection in Russian Poland 1856-1865.
    London, 1963.
Leśnordorski, Bogusław. Polska w epoce Oświecenia. Warsaw, 1971.
Lichtheim, Richard. Die Geschichte des deutschen Zionismus.
    Jerusalem, 1954.
Łepkowski, Tadeusz. "La formation de la nation polonaise moderne
    dans les conditions d'un pays démembré." Acta Poloniae
    Historica 19 (1968).
_____ . Polska-narodziny nowoczesnego narodu. Warsaw, 1967.
Małowist, M. "The Economic and Social Development of the Baltic
    Countries from the 15th to the 17th Century." Economic
    History Review 12 (1959).

Mączak, Antoni. "The Social Distribution of Landed Property in
    Poland from the 16th to the 18th Century." Third Interna-
    tional Conference of Economic History. Vol. 1. Paris, 1968.
Meinecke, Friedrich. The German Catastrophe. Boston, 1950.
_____. Weltbürgertum und Nationalstaat. Munich, 1962.
_____. Das Zeitalter der deutschen Erhebung 1795-1815. Leipzig,
    1906.
Meyer, Henry C. Mitteleuropa in German Thought and Action 1815-
    1945. The Hague, 1955.
Micewski, Andrzej. Roman Dmowski. Warsaw, 1971.
Miłosz, Czesław. The History of Polish Literature. London, 1969.
Mommsen, Wilhelm, ed. Deutsche Parteiprogramme. Munich, 1952.
Mommsen, Wolfgang J. "Der deutsche Liberalismus zwischen 'klassen-
    loser Bürgergesellschaft' und 'Organisiertem Kapitalismus.'"
    Geschichte und Gesellschaft 4 (1978), no. 1.
_____. "Domestic Factors in German Foreign Policy before 1914."
    Central European History 6 (1973).
_____. Max Weber und die deutsche Politik 1890-1920. Tübingen,
    1959.
Mosse, George L. The Crisis of German Ideology: Intellectual
    Origins of the Third Reich. New York, 1964.
Nettl, J. P. Roxa Luxemburg. London, 1966.
Nichols, J. Alden. Germany after Bismarck: The Caprivi Era 1890-
    1894. Cambridge, Mass., 1958.
Nipperdey, Thomas. Die Organisation der deutschen Parteien vor
    1918. Düsseldorf, 1961.
_____. "Wehlers 'Kaiserreich'. Eine kritische Auseinanderset-
    zung." Geschichte und Gesellschaft 1 (1972), no. 4.
Pobóg-Malinowski, Władysław. Najnowsza historia polityczna Polski
    1864-1945. Vol. 1. Paris, 1953.
Puhle, Hans-Jürgen. Agrarische Interessenpolitik und preussischen
    Konservatismus im wilhelminischen Reich (1893-1914). Ein
    Beitrag zur Analyse des Nationalismus in Deutschland am
    Beispiel des Bundes der Landwirte und der Deutsch-Konservativen
    Partei. Hanover, 1966.
_____. "Zur Legende von der 'Kehrschen Schule.'" Geschichte und
    Gesellschaft 4 (1978), no. 1.
Reddaway, W. F., ed. The Cambridge History of Poland. Vol. 2.
    London, 1941.
Ritter, Gerhard. Das deutsche Problem. Munich, 1962.
_____. Friedrich der Grosse. Heidelberg, 1954.
Röhl, J. C. G. Germany without Bismarck: The Crisis of Government
    in the Second Reich, 1890-1900. Berkeley, 1967.
Roos, Hans. A History of Modern Poland. New York, 1966.
Rosenberg, Hans. Bureaucracy, Aristocracy and Autocracy: The
    Prussian Experience 1660-1815. Boston, 1966.
_____. "The Rise of the Junkers in Brandenburg-Prussia 1410-
    1653." The American Historical Review 49 (1943-44).
Rusiński, Władysław. "Hauptprobleme der Fronwirtschaft im 16. bis
    18. Jhd. in Polen und den Nachbarländern." First Interna-
    tional Conference of Economic History. Paris, 1960.
Rutkowski, Jan. Historia gospodarcza Polski. Vol. 1. Czasy
    przedrozbiorowe. Poznań, 1947.
_____. "Le régime agraire en Pologne au XVIIIe siècle." Revue
    d'histoire économique et sociale 14-15 (1926-27).
Schieder, Theodor. Das Deutsche Kaiserreich von 1871 als National-
    staat. Cologne, 1961.
Schnabel, Franz. Deutsche Geschichte im neunzehnten Jahrhundert.
    Vol. 1. Freiburg im Breisgau, 1947.
Schofer, Lawrence. The Formation of a Modern Labor Force: Upper
    Silesia, 1865-1914. Berkeley, 1975.
Sheehan, James J. "Conflict and Cohesion Among German Elites in
    the Nineteenth Century." In Robert J. Bezucha, ed., Modern
    European Social History. Lexington, Mass., 1972.

Sheehan, James J. "Liberalism and Society in Germany, 1815-1848."
    Journal of Modern History 45 (1973), no. 4.
Simon, Walter M. The Failure of the Prussian Reform Movement,
    1807-1819. Ithaca, N. Y., 1955.
_____. "Variations in Nationalism during the Great Reform
    Movement in Prussia." The American Historical Review 59
    (1954), no. 2.
Snyder, Louis. German Nationalism: The Tragedy of a People.
    New York, 1969.
Sombart, Werner. Die deutsche Volkswirtschaft im neunzehnten
    Jahrhundert. Berlin, 1909.
Stadelmann, Rudolf. Soziale und politische Geschichte der Revolu-
    tion von 1848. Munich, 1948.
Stegmann, Dirk. Die Erben Bismarcks. Cologne, 1970.
Stern, Fritz. The Politics of Cultural Despair: A Study in the
    Rise of the Germanic Ideology. Berkeley, 1961.
Strauss, Raphael. "The Jews in the Economic Evolution of
    Central Europe." Jewish Social Studies 3 (1941).
Stürmer, Michael, ed. Das kaiserliche Deutschland: Politik und
    Gesellschaft 1870-1918. Düsseldorf, 1970.
Szacki, Jerzy. "L'Évolution du concept du 'nation' en Pologne à
    la fin du XVIIIe et au début du XIXe siècle." Cahiers
    d'histoire mondiale 9 (1965), no. 1.
Thomas, W. I., and Znaniecki, Florian. The Polish Peasant in
    Europe and America. Vol. 1. Chicago, 1918.
Topolski, Jerzy. "L'Influence du régime des réserves à corvée en
    Pologne sur le développement du capitalisme (XVIe-XVIIIe
    siècles)." Rivista di Storia Dell'Agricoltura, 1970.
Toury, Jacob. Die politischen Orientierungen der Juden in
    Deutschland. Tübingen, 1966.
Tschirch, Otto. Geschichte der öffentlichen Meinung in Preussen
    vom Baseler Frieden bis zum Zusammenbruch des Staates (1795-
    1806). Weimar, 1933.
Wandycz, Piotr S. The Lands of Partitioned Poland 1795-1918.
    Seattle, Wash., 1974.
Weber, Max. From Max Weber: Essays on Sociology. New York, 1958.
Wehler, Hans-Ulrich. "Bismarck's Imperialism 1862-1890." Past
    and Present 48 (1970).
Weinryb, Bernard D. The Jews of Poland: A Social and Economic
    History of the Jewish Community in Poland from 1100 to 1800.
    Philadelphia, 1973.
_____. Neueste Wirtschaftsgeschichte der Juden in Russland und
    Polen. Hildesheim, 1972.
Wereszycki, Henryk. "Polish Insurrections as a Controversial
    Problem for Polish Historiography." Canadian Slavonic
    Papers 9 (1967), no. 1.
Werthheimer, Mildred S. The Pan-German League. 1890-1914. New
    York, 1924.
Wyczański, Andrzej. Polska-rzeczą pospolitą szlachecką 1454-1764.
    Warsaw, 1965.
Zajączkowski, Andrzej. "Cadres structurels de la noblesse."
    Annales 18 (1963), no. 1.
Ziekursch, Johannes. Hundert Jahre schlesischer Agrargeschichte:
    vom Hubertusberger Frieden bis zum Abschluss der Bauernbefrei-
    ung. Breslau, 1927.
Zmarzlik, Hans-Günther. Bethmann-Hollweg als Reichskanzler 1909-
    1914. Studien zur Möglichkeiten und Grenzen seiner inner-
    politischen Machtstellung. Düsseldorf, 1957.

IX. On the History and Theory of Nationalism

Bloom, Solomon. The World of Nations: A Study of the National
    Implications in the Work of Karl Marx. New York, 1941.
Bracher, Karl Dietrich. "Über das Verhältnis von Nationalbewusst-
    sein und Demokratie." In Gerhard A. Ritter, ed., Entstehung

und Wandel der modernen Gesellschaft. Festschrift für Hans
Rosenberg zum 65. Geburtstag. Berlin, 1970.

Chlebowczyk, Józef. Procesy narodotwórcze we wschodniej Europie w
dobie kapitalizmu. Warsaw, 1975.

Cobban, Alfred. National Self-Determination. Chicago, 1944.

Conze, Werner. "Nation und Gesellschaft: zwei Grundbegriffe der
revolutionärer Epoche." Historische Zeitschrift 198 (1964).

Dalberg-Acton, John E. E. "Nationality." In The History of
Freedom and Other Essays. London, 1907.

Davies, R. W. Nationalism and Socialism: Marxist and Socialist
Theories of Nationalism to 1917. New York, 1967.

Deutsch, Karl. Nationalism and Social Communication: An Inquiry
into the Foundations of Nationality. Cambridge, Mass., 1966.

Doob, Leonard W. Patriotism and Nationalism: Their Psychological
Foundations. New Haven, 1964.

Gollwitzer, Heinz. "Esquisse d'une histoire générale des idées
politiques au XIXe siècle et plus particulièrement du
nationalisme et de l'impérialisme." Cahiers d'histoire
mondiale 9 (1957).

Handelsman, Marceli. Rozwój narodowości nowoczesnej. Warsaw,
1923.

Hays, Carlton, J. H. The Historical Evolution of Modern Nationalism. New York, 1931.

Kamenka, Eugene, ed. Nationalism. Canberra, 1973.

Kedourie, Elie. Nationalism. London, 1960.

Kohn, Hans. The Idea of Nationalism. New York, 1944.

_____. Pan-Slavism. New York, 1960.

_____. Prophets and Peoples: Studies in Nineteenth Century
Nationalism. New York, 1946.

Lemberg, Eugen. Nationalismus. Vol. 1. Psychologie und Geschichte.
Hamburg, 1961.

Lenin, V. I. Questions of National Policy and Proletarian Inter-
nationalism. Moscow, 1970.

Macdonald, H. Malcolm. "Marx, Engels and the Polish National
Movement." Journal of Modern History 13 (1941), no. 3.

Mazzini, Joseph. The Duties of Man. London, 1862.

Namier, Lewis. "Nationality and Liberty." In Vanished Supremacies.
London, 1958.

Renan, Ernest. "What is a Nation?" In Poetry of the Celtic Races
and Other Studies. London, n.d.

Royal Institute of International Affairs. Nationalism. London,
1939.

Smith, Anthony D. Theories of Nationalism. London, 1971.

Stalin, Joseph. Marxism and the National and Colonial Question.
London, 1940.

Sugar, Peter F., and Lederer, Ivo J. Nationalism in Eastern
Europe. Seattle, Wash., 1969.

Talmon, J. L. Political Messianism: The Romantic Phase. New York,
1961.

Znaniecki, Florian. Modern Nationalities: a Sociological Study.
Urbana, Ill., 1952.